GRANDMA FRANKS'
COOKBOOK

10/6/98

to ELI:
to one great
guy — hope you
enjoy this book

Grandma Franks' Cookbook

A Good Cook's Best Recipes

compiled by James A. Franks
edited by Elizabeth McKenzie

Wild Goose Press
Santa Cruz, California

Wild Goose Press
719 Fairmount Avenue
Santa Cruz, California 95062

www.wildgoosepress.com

Library of Congress Catalog Card Number 98-060746

ISBN 0-9657173-1-3

First Edition

10 9 8 7 6 5 4 3 2 1

Printed in the United States of America

BOOK AND COVER DESIGN BY ELIZABETH MCKENZIE
TYPOGRAPHY BY BECKY LUENING
INDEX BY DENA TAYLOR
RECIPE TESTING BY DON RICHARDS
PHOTOS FROM THE FRANKS FAMILY ESTATE

THIS COOKBOOK is dedicated to my family—my wife Marianne, sons James and Joseph, daughters Annemary, Elizabeth, and Emily.

To all my brothers and sisters both living and deceased—Charles, Joseph, John, Stephen, Mary, and Rita. Special thanks to Mary for her encouragement all along.

To my parents William Taylor and Marguerite H. Franks.

To my grandparents Joseph and Mary Gump and Charles and Ida Franks.

To Elizabeth McKenzie for her patience in putting this book together and for her support.

To all my friends for trying these recipes.

Mary Ida Hill Franks
Grand Junction, Colorado

INTRODUCTION

MARY IDA HILL FRANKS loved to cook the way her husband Charles loved to engineer trains; it was a lifetime preoccupation. Planning, cooking and presenting daily meals provided the foundation for each and every day, for special occasions, for trips and outings as well. In this sense my grandmother's ideas about food were nearly spiritual. She was known to say "Well-nourished bodies are largely dependent on healthful eating. It is a challenge to plan meals which are nourishing and at the same time have the variety to quicken the appetite." But try to do both, she did. My father, William T. Franks, often spoke of the practical yet artful way his mother had run the household, and he spoke of her cooking with pleasure. Guests frequently sat around the table at the Franks' home in Grand Junction for some of the delicious meals Ida was known to prepare. As a girl she collected recipes from her family in Virginia, then added to them as a young married woman in Colorado. She continued to plan and prepare great meals every day of her life until she died in California in the 1930s.

My father held onto a trunk full of her recipes for years, but by the time I got my hands on the old trunk I had only an inkling of the extent of my grandmother's passion for food preparation. Thousands of recipes fluttered out, stuck in scrapbooks, envelopes, handwritten, decorated with drawings or pasted cut-outs. Many of Ida's comments on the success of a given recipe were still visible in the margins, and are preserved here. I started trying some of these dishes and discovered how much they reminded me of old times, but how, in fact, a good taste can't be forgotten.

— J.A.F.

GRANDMA FRANKS' COOKBOOK
TABLE OF CONTENTS

1. SECRET RECIPES OF FAMOUS TEA ROOMS 1
2. THE JOLLY THIMBLE CLUB 7
3. A FEW COOKING SUGGESTIONS & HELPFUL HINTS 12
4. BEVERAGES 16
5. CEREALS 30
6. BREADS 32
7. ROLLS, BISCUITS, MUFFINS & COFFEE CAKE 44
8. GRIDDLE CAKES, WAFFLES, FRITTERS & TOAST 65
9. CAKE 72
10. SMALL CAKES & COOKIES 109
11. SAUCES & ICINGS 122
12. PIES 128
13. FRENCH PASTRY 151
14. PUDDINGS 157
15. GELATIN 173
16. SALADS & DRESSINGS 180
17. SOUPS 187
18. FISH, CLAMS, AND SAUCES 194
19. MEATS 205
20. CHEESE DISHES & CROQUETTES 220
21. VEGETABLES 224
22. LUNCHEON DISHES 236
23. COOKING FOR INVALIDS 242
24. PRESERVING & CANNING 246
25. UPDATING GRANDMA'S COOKBOOK 251

INDEX 317

Wouldn't you like to own or manage a cozy Tea Room of your own? What a delightful place is the typical Tea Room. Even the tiny menu card shows the truly feminine touch—and that is why the Tea Room field is such a field of opportunity for women.

Picture the preparation and serving of these appetizing dainties seasoned with a delicious savor that the ordinary restaurant can never attain. Imagine the joy in planning your own delightful tea shop—with its cozy hospitality—its charming, tasteful surroundings.

LaVeta Franks,
Ida's daughter

1

Secret Recipes of Famous Tea Rooms

"THE OLD SAYING that the way to a man's heart is through his stomach may be true, but thousands of women have also proven that unusual financial success in the fascinating Tea Room Profession often depends on the serving of new and tasty dainties. Included here are many secret recipes which have won fame and fortune for the users."

Chicken Alabama

2 to 2-1/2 lbs. spring chickens
2 medium-sized onions
6 fresh mushrooms (or 12 canned or dried)
1/2 pint cream
1 pint milk

Chop onions finely—fry them in butter till golden brown, add cooked chopped mushrooms and let fry for a few minutes longer. Set aside to use later in sauce.

Quarter the chickens, removing necks and backbones. Season with pepper and salt. Fry in half-butter and half-bacon drippings, slowly, until light brown. Take chicken out of pan, measure grease in pan. It should measure about 1/2 cup. Strain it and replace it in pan. When hot, add 2 level tablespoonfuls of flour and whisk until smooth. Add heated milk, and cream. Add chopped onions and mushrooms. Season with pepper and salt. Lay chicken in gravy, cover, and let simmer for 20 minutes. A casserole is ideal for this last cooking. Serves 4–6.

Oyster Puree

"A popular luncheon soup"

1 pint standard oysters
1 pint water
1 tbsp. flour
1 pint cream

Drain oysters, remove shells—saving liquor. Wash oysters in pint of water, drain again. Grind oysters or chop and squeeze through potato ricer (food processor can be used—2 to 3 impulses *only*).

Heat liquor and water and skim. Thicken with flour and butter which have been cooked together.

Add cream and seasoning and let boil. Just before serving, add oysters and bring to a boil. Serve immediately with whipped cream on top—a dash of paprika.

Mushroom Dream

"Our special parties order it frequently"

4 slices bacon
8 large mushrooms
1/2 can tomatoes
1 tbsp. sugar
1 tbsp. Worcestershire sauce
1 tbsp. flour
4 slices toast

Fry bacon, remove from pan. Cut mushrooms in quarters and saute them in the bacon fat. Add tomatoes, sugar, salt, pepper and Worcestershire. Let simmer 20 minutes. Thicken with flour, rubbed smooth in a little cold water. Serve on toast sprinkled with Parmesan cheese. Place a strip of bacon on each serving. Garnish with parsley. Serves 4.

Potato Flour Muffins

4 eggs
Pinch of salt
1 tbsp. sugar
1/2 cup white-potato flour
1 tsp. baking powder
2 tbsp. ice water

Beat whites of eggs very stiff and dry. Add salt and sugar to beaten yolks and fold into whites. Sift flour and baking powder twice and beat thoroughly into egg mixtures. Add ice water last. Bake in a moderate oven from 15 to 20 minutes.

Curried Eggs (for Fifty)

"A favorite Sunday-night supper dish"

4 quarts milk
2 cups butter
2 cups flour
4 teaspoonfuls salt
1/2 teaspoonful pepper
5 or more teaspoonfuls curry
50 hard-cooked eggs cut in slices

Make a white sauce of first 3 ingredients. Mix salt, pepper, and curry together and add to sauce. Pile sliced eggs in center of platter, put border of hot boiled rice on outside edge and pour sauce on eggs. Use triangles of toast instead of rice if so desired.

Chicken Patty

"Very tasty for a luncheon or buffet supper"

2-1/2 cups milk
2 tbsp. flour
1 teaspoonful salt
1/8 teaspoonful paprika
2 tbsp. flour
3 cups cold, cooked chicken, diced
1 pimento, cut into tiny pieces
1 cup small of French peas

Scald milk, moisten flour with cold milk, add seasoning and flour slowly. When thick, add chicken. Cook over slow fire enough to heat chicken, add pimento and peas last, heating more but stirring very carefully, so as to keep particles of chicken and the peas whole. Serve in heated patty shells.

Chicken Mousse

"Very popular in early spring, served as a luncheon, accompanied with creamed carrots and peas in timbale case and coleslaw"

1 tbsp. gelatin
1/4 cup cold water
1/3 cup boiling water or chicken stock
2 cups cooked chicken, ground very fine
1/8 teaspoonful paprika
1/2 teaspoonful salt (if chicken is used)
1/2 tbsp. finely-mixed parsley
1-1/2 cups whipped cream

Soak gelatin in cold water, add boiling water (or chicken stock) to dissolve it. Mix meat, paprika, cayenne, salt and parsley together. Add gelatin mixture. Mix thoroughly and fold in cream. Cut each olive in 3 slices, or rings, and place in bottom of molds. Pour mixture into individual molds and chill until firm. (Turn out on lettuce leaf.) Serves 6.

Sour Cream Crullers

"They receive special mention everywhere"

2 eggs
1 small tsp. soda
1 cup sour cream
1/2 tsp. salt
1/2 cup milk
4-1/2 cups flour
4 tsp. baking powder

Cream eggs and sugar together, dissolve soda in sour cream to sweeten it, then add cream to sugar and eggs, folding together. Add salt and milk. Sift flour and baking powder together, sifting 3 times, then add to the mixture; have the dough as soft as can be handled; roll out to about 1/2 inch in thickness and cut with circular cutter, leaving hole in center. Fry in deep fat until a golden brown, drain on brown paper, roll in powdered sugar.

Mountain View Special

"This dish was greatly liked for luncheons"

Two lettuce leaves, slice-and-a-half of toast, cut in 3-cornered pieces (buttered). Place toast on lettuce, add 1/2 cup minced chicken, fried in butter, 3 slices fresh tomato; then pour over this a dressing made of Premier salad dressing (or any dressing) and tomato catsup (2 parts dressing to 1 of catsup). Season dressing with a speck of sugar, garnish with stuffed olives.

Tomato Club Sandwich

"A general favorite"

Toast bread cut in circles about size of large tomato, toasting one of the slices on one side only. Butter toasted piece, arrange on this a thick slice of fresh tomato, sprinkle with salt, minced parsley and chives, add a layer of crisply cooked bacon. Cover with the toast which has been toasted on one side. Have the untoasted side up. Spread with a generous amount of grated American cheese. Return to broiler until cheese is melted. Sprinkle with paprika and serve at once.

Orange Blossom Biscuits

"Delicious for afternoon tea"

2 cups flour
3/4 teaspoonful salt
4 tsp. baking powder
2 tbsp. shortening
3/4 cup milk
1 tbsp. sugar

Mix and sift dry ingredients. Rub in the shortening with a fork. Add enough milk to make a soft dough. Toss on lightly-floured board and roll and cut out. Put in pan and rub over with milk. Dot with butter, sprinkle with sugar and cinnamon. Place on top of each biscuit a domino of sugar which has been soaked in orange juice. Bake in hot oven (400 degrees) for 15 minutes.

Whipped Cream Gems

"This gem is one of four Red Wing Specials and has been much in demand"

1/2 cup butter
1-1/2 cup granulated sugar
3 eggs
2 level cups bread flour
2 level tsp. baking powder
10 drops almond extract
1/2 cup sweet milk

Cream the butter and sugar. Add the beaten eggs and beat until light; add sifted flour, baking powder, flavoring and milk to make a smooth batter of medium thick consistency. Bake in well-greased gem pans (muffin tins) 25 to 30 minutes. When cool, cut off tops, hollow out center and fill with whipped cream. Put together and place on top a spoonful of red jelly or a maraschino cherry and a nut meat or two. These can be iced on top before cutting and filling, if desired.

Aristocratic Cake

"I sold over 400 loaves of this cake, made in my kitchen, in one year—at $1.00 a small loaf"

2 cups granulated sugar
1 cup shortening, creamed with sugar
1 cup hot, mashed potatoes
1 cup English walnut meats, chopped fine
3 eggs, well beaten
1/2 cup sweet milk
5 teaspoonfuls melted chocolate
2 teaspoonfuls cinnamon
1 teaspoonful each of cloves and nutmeg
2 cups flour, sifted with 2 teaspoonfuls baking powder

Put together in the order listed. Bake in a slow oven. This will make 2 small loves of bread or one large loaf.

Lemon Pie Filling

"Received first prize at Danbury Fair"

2 lemons
3 cups boiling water
3 tbsp. corn starch
2 cups sugar
2 eggs
A little salt

Grate the yellow rind from the lemons, pour the boiling water over, thicken with the corn starch, previously dissolved in a little cold water, add sugar, cook about 2 minutes.
Roll the lemons, use juice and pulp, removing the seeds. Remove cornstarch from fire, add juice and pulp, and lastly the well-beaten eggs.

This makes two pies with two crusts—if meringue is wanted, use four eggs. The yolks for filling, and stiffly-beaten whites for meringue, placing a moment in 425 degree oven to brown.

Oatmeal Macaroons

2 tbsp. butter
1 cup sugar
Yolks of 2 eggs
2-1/2 cups cooked oatmeal
1 tbsp. flour
2-1/2 tsp. baking powder
1/2 teaspoonful salt
1 tsp. vanilla, almond or lemon flavoring

Cream the butter with 1/2 cup sugar. Cream yolks of eggs with 1/2 cup sugar. Cream the two mixtures together. Add oatmeal, flour, baking powder and salt. Add flavoring. Stir in whites of eggs beaten to a froth. Drop with a teaspoon on buttered baking sheets. Bake in a *slow oven.*

Tea Rolls

1 pint milk
1 cake compressed yeast
2 tbsp. sugar
3 pints bread flour
4 tbsp. lard
1 tsp. salt

Scald milk and let cool—add yeast cake and sugar. Let stand in warm place till foamy.

Add flour, lard and salt. Let stand till light. Roll and cut into small rounds. Butter one half of each round, fold over and press edges, butter top. Let stand till light. Bake in moderate oven.

Sour Cream Cookies

1-1/2 cup light brown sugar
1 teaspoonful each salt, cinnamon and nutmeg
1 cup sour cream
2 eggs
1/2 cup melted shortening (chicken fat is good)
3 cups flour
1 teaspoonful soda
1/2 cup chopped nut meats
1 cup raisins, cut fine

Mix together sugar, salt and spices. Stir in the sour cream; add eggs and melted shortening. Beat well for several minutes. Add the two kinds of flour and soda sifted together. Add the nuts and raisins last. Mix well and drop from spoon on well-greased pan. Bake in hot oven.

Frozen Teapot Dainty

7 cups orange juice, sweetened to taste
1 quart cream, whipped stiff and sweetened

Pour orange juice in mold one inch, and fill with the whipped cream. Put lid on tight. Put ice and salt in pan about 8 inches deep. Set in molds and cover with ice and salt—1 part salt to 4 parts ice. Freeze 3/4 of an hour. When dainties are not all needed at once, put in a few at a time so they will not get too hard.

Teapot-shaped molds for dainties may be ordered from any can factory or tinner. 2 inches high, 2 inches in diameter, tight-fitting lid. (Mashed strawberries, peaches and other fresh fruits used in the same way are delicious.)

Chiffon Pie

Crust:
1-1/2 cup flour
1/2 teaspoonful salt
1/2 cup lard (shortening)
3 to 4 tbsp. water

Sift together flour and salt. Work in lard, using enough water to make stiff dough. Roll out, line in pie plate with pastry and bake in very hot oven 12 minutes.

Filling:
1 orange
1 lemon
3 eggs
5 tbsp. water

Place in double boiler, juice and grated rind of orange and lemon. Bring to a boiling point. Beat egg yolks till light. Add sugar and beat thoroughly. Stir into hot liquid. Cook in double boiler until thick. Cool and place in crust and cover with a meringue, and brown in hot oven.

Pineapple Rice Cream (for Forty)

3 cups rice
4 cups grated pineapple
2 packages Knox gelatin
4 cups sugar
1 quart cream

Boil rice in one gallon of water 25 minutes. Remove to sink in china cap and let cold water run 10 minutes, or until chilled. Drain juice from pineapple and soak gelatin. Add sugar to pineapple, set gelatin over slow heat until clear, return to pineapple and mix the two together. Whip one quart of cream and add to this. Serve in glasses and garnish top with sliced Maraschino cherries.

Lemon Bars

1/2 cup butter
1 cup flour
1/4 cup sifted powdered sugar

Cream butter, add flour and powdered sugar. Press into bottom of ungreased eight inch square pan. Bake in 350 degree oven for twenty minutes.

Then:

2 eggs
1 cup flour
1/4 tsp. salt
3 T. lemon juice
1/4 tsp Baking powder
2 T. flour

Double recipe for 9 x 13 pan.

Combine well beaten eggs, sugar, salt and lemon juice. Mix baking powder and flour, add to egg mixture and mix well. Spread on HOT baked layer. Bake at 350 degrees for twenty five to thirty minutes. Cool, cut in bars. Sprinkle with powdered sugar. I like to double this recipe. Makes 24 bars.

- Mrs. Anne Egle

Sister Sarah's Sugar Cookies

1 cup butter
1 cup sugar
1 cup powdered sugar
1 cup oil
2 eggs
1 tsp vanilla
1 tsp salt
1 tsp baking soda
1 tsp cream tartar
4 cups flour

Mix together flour, salt, baking soda and cream tartar. Cream butter and sugar, add eggs. Beat until light and fluffy, add powdered sugar, oil, vanilla and dry ingredients mixed together. After mixed well, refrigerate for a couple hours or put into freezer until stiff enough to handle. Then roll into 1 inch balls about the size of a quarter. Roll into sugar and put on ungreased cookie sheet and flatten with a fork, like peanut butter cookies. Bake at 350 degrees eight to ten minutes or until light brown.

THE JOLLY THIMBLE CLUB

Grand Junction, Colorado

ORGANIZED OCTOBER 25, 1907

Mrs. Carrie Neeb, President
Mrs. Carrie White, Secretary
Mrs. Mae Carr, Treasurer
Mrs. Hattie Pierce
Mrs. Clough Lane
Mrs. Ida Franks
Mrs. Martha Rodgers
Mrs. Sophia Flynn
Mrs. Adda Raden
Mrs. Olive Winterburn
Mrs. Sylvia Green
Mrs. Anna Horsch

2

THE JOLLY THIMBLE CLUB

Macaroni & Oysters

Boil macaroni in salt water, after which drain through a colander. Take a deep earthen dish. Put in alternate layers of macaroni and oysters. Sprinkle layers of macaroni with grated cheese, salt and pepper to taste. Bake until warm.

Lobster a la Newburg

1 lobster
1 egg
1 cup cream

Put lobster through meat grinder. Melt butter (size of a walnut) in chafing dish. Add lobster, salt to taste, dash of red pepper. Add beaten egg, also a cup of cream. When thoroughly heated, serve on toast with a slice of lemon.

—Mrs. J.N. Neeb

To make a perfect salad there should be a spendthrift for oil, a miser for vinegar, a wise man for salt and a madcap to stir the ingredients up and mix them well together.

— Spanish proverb

Potato Salad

6 medium-sized potatoes, cubed
3 stalks of celery, cubed
2 hard-boiled eggs
1 small onion
1/2 cup walnut meats, put in after the dressing is on

Dressing:

6 tablespoonfuls of vinegar
4 tablespoonfuls of water
1 teaspoonful of salt
1 teaspoonful of mustard
3 teaspoonful of sugar
1/2 teaspoonful of pepper
Butter the size of a walnut

Let this boil and add 2 well-beaten eggs. When cold add 1/2 cup cream.

—Mrs. Jos Pierce

Master, I marvel how the fishes live in the sea! Why, as men do on land; the great ones eat up the little ones.

— Pericles

Oyster Salad

1/2 gallon each fresh oysters and celery, diced
1 cup vinegar
2 teaspoons each of salt, pepper and made mustard
Yolks of 4 hard-boiled eggs
1 raw egg, beaten
2 large spoonfuls of melted butter
2 pickled cucumbers, cut fine

Drain liquor from oysters, throw in hot vinegar in the fire. Let stand until plump. Put at once in cold water and drain off. Set in a cool place.

To prepare dressing, rub salt, pepper and mustard with yolks finely mashed. Add water a drop at a time. When smooth, add beaten egg, then vinegar by the spoonful. Set aside.
Mix oysters, celery and pickles, tossing up well with silver fork. Pour dressing over all.

"Quite pleased your honor," quoth the Peasant.

"This sauce dessert is very pleasant."

—Pope

Fruit Salad for Dessert

Dissolve 1 package of bromaugelon in one quart of boiling water. Set away to harden. Slice 6 bananas, 4 oranges, cut in cubes 1 cup English Walnut meats. Mix bananas and oranges with plenty of pulverized sugar. Serve in orange cups. Put bananas and oranges in bottom of cup, sprinkle nutmeats over them, then slice or two of bromaugelon. Pile whipped cream on top.

—Mrs. F.A. White

Aye, to the leavening, but here's yet in the word

hereafter the kneading, the making of the cake,

the heating of the oven, and the baking. Nay,

you must stay the cooling, too, or you may

chance to burn your mouth.

—Shakespeare

Delicious Nut Cake

1 cup powdered sugar
1/2 cup butter
1/2 cup sweet milk
2 scant cups flour
1 heaping tsp. baking powder
White of 4 eggs
1 cup English walnut meats chopped fine
1 tsp. lemon extract

Cream sugar and butter and add milk. Sift together flour and baking powder. Whip whites of eggs and fold everything together. Add walnuts and lemon extract and bake in a moderate oven until toothpick comes out clean.

I would tempt the dying auchorile to eat;

Back to the world he'd turn his fleeting soul.

And plunge his fingers in the salad bowl!

Serenely full, the epicure would say,

Fate cannot harm me, I have dined today.

—Sydney Smith

Pea Salad

2 cans Monarch peas
1/2 lb. cheese, diced
1 small onion, chopped fine
French dressing
1 tsp. flour
Pinch salt
1/4 tsp. ground mustard
2 eggs
1/2 cup sour cream
1/2 cup vinegar

Mix peas, cheese and onion and moisten very moist with French dressing. Cook the rest of ingredients until quite thick. If it becomes too heavy, thin with more cream or milk. Let cool and add to salad.

—Mrs. E.B. Rodgers

Now good digestion waits on appetite, and

health on both.

—Shakespeare

Mahogany Cake

1 cup sugar
1/2 cup butter, creamed
4 eggs, yolks and whites beaten separately
1 cup sweet milk
1/8 cake Baker's chocolate melted in part of above milk
1 scant tsp. baking powder
1 scant tsp. baking soda
1-1/2 cups flour
Vanilla

Mix ingredients together and bake in layers. Put together with caramel icing.

Caramel Icing

2 cups brown sugar
2/3 cup sweet milk
Butter size walnut

Boil until a drop of caramel hardens in water, then beat until cool, before putting on cake.

—Mrs. J.E. Green

Wouldst thou both eat thy cake and have it?

—Shakespeare

Peanut Wafers

1 pint ground peanuts
2 Tbsp. butter
1 heaping cup sugar
3 well beaten eggs
Pinch salt
3 Tbsp. milk
Enough flour to roll thin wafers after putting in pan.

—Mrs. Thomas Carr

There's no want of meats sir,

Portly and curious viands are prepared

To please all kinds of appetites.

—Massenger

Chicken Salad

1 Chicken, cooked and diced
Nearly as much celery, diced
4 hard boiled eggs

Dressing:
3 raw eggs
1 cup vinegar
2 heaping Tbsp. butter
Salt, pepper, mustard & sugar to taste

Cook over boiling water and pour over salad.

Salmon Pudding

1 can salmon, minced
1 cup cracker crumbs
3 eggs
1 cup boiling milk
1 cup cream or butter size of an egg

Bake and serve with white sauce.

White Sauce:
Butter size of walnut
1 Tbsp. flour
1 cup milk
A little sugar
Salt and pepper to taste

—Mrs. F.R. Rade

Only Lyndall can explain

The links between the cake and brain.

Get your husband what he likes

And save a hundred household strikes.

Give him all he wants to eat.

Make his disposition sweet.

—Anonymous

Nut Cake

1 cup sugar
1/2 cup milk
1/2 cup butter
2 cups sifted flour
2 eggs
1 coffee cup chopped raisins
1 coffee cup chopped walnuts
1/2 tsp. cream of tartar
1/2 tsp. baking soda

Beat butter to a cream. Add sugar, beat until light, add milk. Sift cream of tartar and soda with flour and add. Stir in raisins and nuts. Bake in moderate oven.

—Mrs. E. Winterburn

He hath eaten me out of house and home.

—Shakespeare

Dark Cake

2 squares unsweetened Baker's chocolate
4 eggs, yolks and whites beaten separately
1-1/2 cups sugar
1/3 cup butter
1/2 cup water
2 cups flour
1 tsp. baking powder
1 tsp. vanilla

Melt chocolate in 3 tablespoons of hot water. Bake in layers and put together with caramel filling.

—Mrs. H. Hoesch

It is the bounty of nature that we live; but of philosophy that we live well.

—Seneca

Scalloped Salmon

1 can salmon
1 can Monarch peas
Cracker crumbs
Salt & pepper
Butter

Drain the liquid from the salmon and the peas and reserve. Butter a deep baking dish and cover the bottom with cracker crumbs. Alternate with salmon, peas, and crumbs. The top layer must be crumbs. Add salt, pepper and bits of butter to layers. When the dish is three-quarters full, add the liquid drained from the salmon and peas. Add enough milk to cover. Bake 45 minutes.

—Mrs. Matt Flynn

Let onion atoms lurk within the bowl, and half suspected animate the whole.

—Anonymous

Old Fashioned Potato Salad

8 medium sized potatoes, sliced
4 hard-boiled eggs, sliced
2 onions, finely chopped
Salt and pepper to taste
4 Tbsp. good vinegar
1 cup sweet cream
2 Tbsp. butter

Layer potatoes, eggs and onions with salt and pepper. When all is in the dish, sprinkle vinegar over all. Heat cream and butter until hot and pour over salad. Cover and set away to cool. If preferred, one may use mustard.

—Mrs. Eaton

Mary Ida Franks
Charles Edward Franks
LaVeta Virginia Franks
William Taylor Franks

1903

3

A Few Cooking Suggestions & Helpful Hints

STORAGE TIPS

To keep bread fresh, store a celery rib in the package.

Lemons like water. Lemons stored in a sealed jar of water will produce twice the juice.

To keep brown sugar soft, store in the refrigerator in a plastic bag.

Marshmallows won't dry out if kept in a freezer. Cut with scissors when ready to use.

To keep ice cream fresh, press wax paper against the surface and re-seal the carton.

Cake will stay moist and fragrant if half an apple is kept in the cake box.

Lettuce and celery fare better in the crisper if stored in paper bags rather than plastic.

To keep cottage cheese fresh, store carton in the refrigerator upside down.

To keep popcorn fresh and encourage more kernels to pop, store in the freezer.

Store garlic in a bottle of cooking oil. The flavored oil can be used for salad dressing.

Line bottom of crisper with paper towels of put a few sponges in bottom to soak up moisture and extend vegetable life.

If half an onion is needed, save the root half. It will last longer.

LOWFAT SEASONING

Roast, bake, grill, braise or broil meat, poultry and fish.

Use broth or stock instead of butter to baste poultry and meat.

Use marinades of lemon juice, flavored vinegars or fruit juice mixed with herbs before grilling or broiling or to tenderize leaner cuts of meat.

Skim fat from homemade soups by chilling and removing fat layer that rises to the surface.

Use lowfat yogurt in place of mayonnaise or sour cream in sauces, dips, or topping baked potatoes.

COOKING MAGIC

To thicken thin gravy without getting lumps, stir in a few tablespoons of instant mashed potatoes.

To remove skin off chicken easily, hold it firmly with a paper towel.

Fish thawed in milk will have a fresher flavor.

Meat used for stir frying will slice more easily if first put in the freezer for 45 minutes to 1 hour.

When using oil and vinegar dressing on salad, add oil first. Toss and then add vinegar. Your salad will stay crisp.

Meatballs baked on a foil-lined jelly-roll pan instead of fried hold their shape better and save time.

Catsup flows easier by pushing a straw to the bottom of the bottle, then removing it before pouring. Air gets in, and the catsup comes out.

Ripen tomatoes out of direct sunlight, which softens rather than ripens them.

Don't wrap potatoes in foil. Foil traps the moisture and steams potatoes rather than bakes them.

To keep noodles or rice from boiling over, add a tablespoon of oil to the water.

Chopped fruit and nuts disperse easier in cake batter if they are lightly floured before adding.

To keep potato slices from discoloring, soak in water to which lemon juice has been added.

Chop onions without tears by freezing or refrigerating first.

Rub salt over a cracked egg and you can successfully boil it.

To blanch almonds, let shelled nuts stand in boiling water for a few minutes. Skins will slip off when rinsed under cold water.

Correct greasy gravy by adding a bit of baking soda.

A FEW USEFUL SUGGESTIONS

It pays to buy clean food from clean stores.

It is cheaper to buy in quantities as large as can be safely stored.

Food should be kept clean and covered.

Milk and cream should be kept covered in an ice box.

Salad plants should be washed and left in a cheesecloth bag in an ice box before serving.

Meat and fish should be taken out of paper wrappings when put in an ice box.

Cheese should be wrapped in a clean cloth, dampened in vinegar, and kept in a cool, dry place.

Flour should be sifted before measuring.

Mustard and baking powder settle in the can and should be stirred lightly before measuring.

Salt or sugar lumps should be broken before measuring.

One tablespoon cornstarch thickens as one egg.

One egg equals one-half teaspoon of baking powder.

Any of the flaked, ready-to-serve cereals can be used in the preparation of dishes that call for bread crumbs.

Precautions to be Observed in Heating Milk:

Since milk scorches very easily it is advisable to heat it in a double boiler. If heated directly over the fire, the heat should be low or an asbestos mat should be placed under the pan. If a double boiler is not used, the milk requires careful watching and stirring to prevent scorching.

HINTS FOR SIMPLIFYING DEEP FAT FRYING

Use a deep kettle, preferably of iron or heavy-cast aluminum so that there will be no danger of over-turning on the stove.
Use enough fat to completely cover the food to be cooked, but be careful not to have the kettle more than two-thirds full or the hot fat might bubble over the top during the frying process.

Heat the Crisco to the proper temperature, as gauged by a thermometer or by the standard bread test. Special deep frying thermometers can be purchased at a very reasonable price, but the bread test serves very well, if you have no thermometer.

Drop an inch cube of bread into the hot fat. When it browns in a certain length of time, the fat is ready to cook certain types of foods. Foods which have been previously cooked naturally do not need as long a cooking in the fat as do those which are put into the kettle raw. The previously-cooked foods simply need browning, so the fat can be very hot. The following table gives both the thermometer and bread tests.

Kind of Food	Temperature (F)	Time for Bread
Fritters	365–375°	60 seconds
Croquettes, codfish balls, etc.	385–390°	40 seconds
French fried potatoes	400–410°	20 seconds

Potatoes, croquettes, or any food which does not have to be dropped in to the food piece by piece, can be more easily handled by using a frying basket. This is simply a wire basket with a handle, by means of which the food can be lowered gradually into the hot fat and removed all at once when done.

After frying, the food should be drained on paper to remove excess fat.

The Crisco in which the food was fried may be left in the kettle, covered and moved out of the way until ready for the next frying, unless a large quantity of burned food particles has collected in the kettle, in which case the Crisco should be strained before placing away. Some people find it convenient to keep a special can of Crisco for frying purposes; then the warm fat may be strained directly back into the can after each using. The kettle does not have to be washed, simply wiped out carefully with soft paper.
Crisco can be used over and over again for frying. It does not matter whether you fry onions for lunch, you may use the same Crisco for frying fritters for dinner without any trace of the onion flavor being carried over to the fritters.
Frying with Crisco is a pleasant task because of the freedom from smoke and odors which usually accompany frying. Crisco does not smoke until heated far above the highest temperature ever used for frying.

"EARLY" FIRELESS COOKERY

The Fireless Cooker has become an important factor in the home. The principle employed is the preservation of heat by the use of non-conducting materials. The device ordinarily used is a rectangular box lined on all sides with some substance which will prevent escape of heat, with spaces or wells for the insertion of stone or metal discs or radiators and vessels containing food to be cooked.

Among the advantages of this method are: the improvement in flavor by slower cooking with little opportunity for evaporation; improved appearance of food that is subject to shrinkage when cooked by ordinary methods; saving in labor, as the cooking practically takes care of itself. Dinner may be prepared in the morning, placed in the cooker, and without further attention be ready to serve at any time after 3 or 4 hours. While the time required for cooking is longer than in the usual methods, the actual time consumed in preparation of a meal is considerably reduced.

Directions

Prepare food for cooking as usual. Place in special vessel,

designed to fit into wells of Fireless Cooker, and heat on range or over gas flame until ordinary cooking temperature is reached. Put into cooker with one or more radiators which have been heated for 10 or 15 minutes over hot fire.

For roasting, radiator should be hot enough to brown a pinch of flour immediately. Close cover, fasten lightly so that the steam may escape, and allow cooking to proceed for time specified in recipes.

For baking cake, apples, etc., proceed as for roasting. The time required for baking is slightly longer than that specified for regular ovens. For cake ordinarily baked in a moderate oven, heat radiators hot enough to brown a pinch of flour in half a minute.

The Fireless Cooker is especially convenient for the preparation of cereals, meats, vegetables and other dishes that are ordinarily boiled or roasted. Remember that foods should be thoroughly heated before putting into cooker.

Cereals

Prepare cereal for cooking in double boiler as usual. Boil over fire for 5 minutes; place in larger vessel of boiling water in cooker and allow it to remain 4 or 5 hours or longer. If placed in cooker at night it should remain warm enough to serve for breakfast.

Steaming

Prepare and mix ingredients as directed. Put into greased molds and place in shallow pan of boiling water over very hot radiator in cooker. Fasten cover tight and cook for 5 to 6 hours.

Soups

Place ingredients in vessel; cover with cold water; bring to boil over free flame and boil 5 minutes. Fasten cover and transfer to cooker, using one hot radiator in bottom of well. Cook 3 or 4 hours and season when ready to serve.

For ingredients and special directions for preparing soups, see "Soups."

Roast Meats

Prepare and season meat in usual way. Place in large dry vessel; put very hot radiator in bottom of cooker well; place vessel containing roast on radiator, and place another very hot radiator on top. Close cooker and fasten. Allow it to remain about 1/2 hour per pound of meat.

The roast may be browned in a very hot oven before putting into cooker or just before serving.

Boiled or Stewed Meats

Prepare meat or cooking as usual, searing in frying pan if desired brown. Place in large vessel and over or partly cover with boiling water, boiling with cover fastened tight for 10 or 15 minutes over free flame. Transfer to cooker, using one hot radiator underneath. Cook 2 or 3 hours, season and serve.

Vegetables

Prepare vegetables as usual. Place in vessel with small quantity of boiling water. As there is little evaporation in fireless cookers, allowance does not have to be made for loss by evaporation. Boil over free flame for 5 to 10 minutes. Transfer to cooker, using one radiator in bottom of well. Cook 3 or 4 hours, remove from cooker, season and serve.

TABLE OF MEASURES AND WEIGHTS

2 cups butter	=	1 pound
4 cups flour (pastry)	=	1 pound
2 cups granulated sugar	=	1 pound
2-2/3 cups powdered sugar	=	1 pound
3-1/2 cups confectioners' sugar	=	1 pound
2-2/3 cups brown sugar	=	1 pound
1-7/8 cups rice	=	1 pound
4-1/2 cups Graham flour	=	1 pound
3-7/8 cups entire wheat flour	=	1 pound
4-1/3 cups coffee	=	1 pound
2 cups finely chopped meat	=	1 pound
9 large eggs	=	1 pound
1 square cooking chocolate	=	1 ounce
3 teaspoons	=	1 tablespoon
16 tablespoons	=	1 cup
2 tablespoons butter	=	1 ounce
4 tablespoons flour	=	1 ounce

Cupfuls are measured by standard measuring cup.

OVEN TEMPERATURES

Slow—250 to 350 degrees Fahrenheit
Moderate—350 to 400 degrees Fahrenheit
Hot or "quick"—400 to 450 degrees Fahrenheit
Very hot—450 to 550 degrees Fahrenheit

Slow oven requires 1 burner halfway on

Moderate oven requires 2 burners halfway on

Hot oven requires 2 burners on full.

If the oven is equipped with a heat control, follow directions given by the manufacturer.

Hot Toddy

Juice of 1 lemon
2 Tbsp. honey or sugar
3 oz. bourbon or rye whiskey
boiling water

Put juice of 1 lemon in tall glass or mug. Sweeten with honey or sugar. Add whiskey or rye. Fill glass with boiling water. Stir and drink.

4
BEVERAGES

COFFEE & COFFEE DRINKS

No two people quite agree on how strong a good cup of coffee should be—or the one and only way to make it. One thing is sure. It's hard to make a bad cup if you remember these things:

* Start with a coffee maker that is thoroughly clean. Wash after each use with soapy hot water and rinse well with hot water; never scour with an abrasive pad.

* Always use fresh coffee and freshly drawn cold water. Never use hot water.

* Serve steaming hot coffee as soon as possible after brewing. If necessary to let coffee stand any length of time, remove grounds and hold coffee at serving temperature over very low heat. Keep coffee hot but do not boil.

Chart I

Coffee should be purchased for family use in small quantities, freshly roasted and finely ground. Better color and flavor are secured when finely ground coffee is used. Many kitchens are equipped with a coffee mill. This makes it possible to grind the coffee as needed. Ground coffee should be kept in air-tight tins, because it loses its aroma and flavor quickly.

1 level tablespoon coffee to 1 cup water for weak coffee
2 level tablespoons coffee to 1 cup water for medium coffee
3 level tablespoons coffee to 1 cup water for strong coffee

Old Camp Coffee

The best method of making coffee, as determined by the Better Coffee-Making Committee of the National Association of Coffee Roasters, is as follows:

"Fill a kettle with fresh cold water and put it on to boil. Place over an open china teapot, kept just for coffee, a clean, wet, old linen napkin, or a new square of unbleached muslin, letting it sag toward the center. Put into the depression 4 heaping tablespoons (for 4 cups of coffee) of finely pulverized coffee. This fine pulverization is very important. Ordinary ground coffee will not do at all, and gives weak infusions.

"When the water in the kettle is boiling fiercely, pour it through the coffee slowly until 4 cups have gone through, or a trifle more for 4 cups of coffee.

"Cover and take at once to table.

"Wash the cloth immediately and keep it in a jar of cold water, never permitting it to get dry, and freshening the water every day. Keeping the cloth sweet is essential. Every effort should be made to this end. The least souring ruins the coffee.

"Follow these directions strictly, paying especial attention to having the coffee very fine, like flour, and the water boiling, and you will have excellent coffee even though you buy cheap blends."

Methods of Preparation

Drip

Measure cold water into kettle and heat to boiling. Meanwhile, preheat coffeepot by rinsing with very hot water. Measure drip-grind coffee into cone holding filter paper or into filter section of coffeepot, depending on he type of drip pot used. Pour measured fresh boiling water into upper container; cover. When dripping is completed, remove upper container and filter section and simply pour the coffee.

Vacuum

Measure fresh cold water into lower bowl and heat to boiling. Place filter in upper bowl; add fine or drip-grind coffee. Remove boiling water from heat; reduce heat. Insert upper bowl with a slight twist. Return to heat. Let water rise into upper bowl; stir. Remove from heat. Coffee should return to lower bowl within 2 minutes. Remove upper bowl and serve coffee.

Filtered Coffee

Put coffee into filter and pour the freshly boiling water over it gradually. Remove strainer before serving. If strong coffee is desired, use more coffee for each cup water, rather than refiltering.

Boiled Coffee

For 4 cups. Beat half an egg white with 3 tablespoons cold water; add 3/4 cup ground coffee and stir until moistened; put into scalded coffee pot; add 1 quart boiling water and boil 5 minutes. Add 1/4 cup cold water and allow to stand 3 minutes to settle and serve.

Breakfast Coffee

White of 1/2 egg
4 rounded tablespoons finely ground coffee
4 cups cold water

Mix egg white and dry coffee, add the cold water and bring to boiling point. Boil 3 minutes. Remove from fire, let stand 5 minutes and strain from grounds.

NOTE—Keep the inside of the coffee pot scrupulously clean, as coffee absorbs odors and flavors most readily. Always scald the pot before using. Glass or enamel coffee pots are better than metal.

Iced Coffee

Prepare Strong Coffee (see Chart I). Fill tall glass with crushed ice. Pour hot coffee over ice. If desired, serve with sugar and light cream or whipped cream.

Or, prepare Medium Coffee (see Chart I). Cool. Pour into divided freezer trays; freeze. To serve, pour freshly brewed Medium Coffee over coffee cubes in tall glass.

Demitasse

From the French "demi-tasse," meaning half a cup. This strong after-dinner coffee is always, but always, served in small cups. True devotees make it a daily treat.

Prepare coffee as directed (see Chart I), using 2 tablespoons ground coffee for each 1/3 cup water. (Each demitasse serving should be about 1/3 cup.) Demitasse is often served with a twist of lemon peel. Sugar may be offered but cream is usually shunned.

Café au Lait

Serve in gray ceramic mugs for a Gallic plus.

Prepare coffee as directed (see Chart I), using 3/4 cup ground coffee and 3 cups water.

Heat 3 cups milk. Pour equal amount of hot coffee and hot milk simultaneously from separate pots into each cup.
8 servings (3/4 cup each).

Irish Coffee

An extra-rich, extra-special after-dinner beverage

1 cup chilled whipping cream
1/4 cup confectioners' sugar
1 teaspoon vanilla
3/4 cup ground coffee
3 cups water
4 ounces (1/2 cup) Irish whiskey or brandy
4 to 8 teaspoons granulated sugar

In chilled bowl, beat cream, confectioners' sugar and vanilla until stiff. Refrigerate.

Prepare coffee as directed in Chart I, using the 3/4 cup ground coffee and the 3 cups water.

Heat mugs by rinsing with boiling water; drain. Add 1 ounce (2 tablespoons) whiskey and 1 to 2 teaspoons granulated sugar to each mug; stir. Pour hot coffee into each mug. Top with the whipped cream. Serve immediately.
4 servings (3/4 cup each).

Spiced Coffee

2 cups water
1 tablespoon brown sugar
2 three-inch cinnamon sticks
Peel of 1 orange
1/2 teaspoon whole allspice
1 tablespoon instant coffee

Combine all ingredients except coffee in saucepan; heat to boiling. Strain mixture; pour liquid over coffee in heatproof container and stir until coffee is dissolved. If desired, serve with a twist of lemon peel or a cinnamon stick.
6 servings (1/3 cup each).

Mocha Dessert Coffee

For each serving, place 1 to 2 tablespoons of our ready-to-spread chocolate frosting in cup. Fill with hot coffee; stir until blended. If desired, garnish with whipped cream. Serve immediately.

International Coffee

1/3 cup instant cocoa mix
1/4 cup instant coffee
4 cups boiling water
Sweetened whipped cream

Mix cocoa mix and coffee in heatproof container. Pour in boiling water; stir. Serve with whipped cream.
6 servings (about 2/3 cup each).

Special Dinner Coffee

An after-dinner beverage that doubles as a dessert

For each serving, pour 1 ounce (2 tablespoons) brandy into mug. Fill 2/3 full with hot Strong Coffee (see Chart I). Top with 1 scoop (about 1/4 cup) chocolate ice cream. Serve immediately.

TEA

Freshly boiled water should always be used in making tea. This is important because water below the boiling point does not develop the full flavor of this beverage. Scald an earthenware teapot, put tea in, allowing 1 teaspoon of tea to each cup of freshly boiling water; pour over it the boiling water; cover closely; let stand for 3 to 5 minutes without boiling; pour at once. It is advisable to strain tea from grounds. A tea-ball may be used, and allow the same proportion of tea to water. Place tea-ball in cup or pot and pour over it freshly boiling water. Remove tea-ball in 1 minute or more, according to strength desired.

Would it surprise you to know that tea is the world's favorite beverage? It shouldn't. Even in our own United States, iced tea and hot tea have become round-the-year, round-the-clock refreshers. And afternoon tea, once associated with silver tea services and starched maids, has now become a friendly custom.

Types of Tea

As you learned in your schoolbooks, there are literally hundreds of varieties of tea. The quality varies according to the soil, climate and altitude in which it is grown and the age and size of the leaves when they are picked.

The tea you buy is a delicate blend of some 20 to 30 varieties, carefully selected by expert tea-tasters to maintain the high quality of color, flavor, aroma or body of each brand.

Despite all these varieties, tea can be classified into three broad types: black, oolong or green.

Black Tea undergoes a special processing treatment in which the leaves are allowed to oxidize. This turns the leaves black and produces a rich brew. Over 97% of the tea consumed in the United States is the black type.

Oolong Tea is semi-oxidized. Its leaves are partly brown and partly green. It brews light in color, and a growing number of Americans have come to prefer its delicate flavor.

Green Tea is not oxidized, so the leaves remain green. The brew is pale green in color.

Loose or Teabag?

Loose tea is the classic and, to connoisseurs, the preferred form to use in brewing tea. Following package directions, 1 pound makes about 200 cups.

The teabag was "accidentally" invented at the turn of the century when a tea merchant distributed his samples in small silk bags. Today, the "bags" are made of special filter paper, each bag holding about a teaspoonful of tea.

Method of Preparation

Start with a spotlessly clean teapot made of glass, china or earthenware. Add rapidly boiling water; allow to stand a few minutes and pour out.

Heat cold water to a full roiling boil.

Add tea or teabags to the warm pot, allowing 1 teaspoon of loose tea or 1 teabag for each cup of tea desired. Pour boiling water over the tea (3/4 cup for each cup of tea); let steep 3 to 5 minutes to bring out the full flavor. Stir the tea once to ensure uniform strength.

Strain the tea or remove teabags. If desired, serve with sugar and milk or lemon.

Do not judge the strength of tea by its color; you must taste it.

Iced Tea

Follow directions for preparation of tea (above) except—double the amount of tea. Strain tea over ice in pitcher or into ice-filled glasses.

Note: Tea that has been steeped too long or that has been refrigerated will become cloudy. Pour a small amount of boiling water into tea pitcher to make clear again.

Do-Ahead Iced Tea

A speedy way to make your own on-call iced tea. When you need it, it will always be there.

Use 2 teaspoons loose tea or 2 teabags for each cup of cold water. Place tea in glass container; add water. Cover; refrigerate at least 24 hours. To serve, pour over crushed ice.

Spiced Tea

4 cups boiling water
4 teaspoons loose tea
6 whole cloves, broken into pieces
1/2 teaspoon dried orange peel
1/8 teaspoon cinnamon

Pour boiling water over tea, cloves, orange peel and cinnamon in heatproof container. Cover; let steep 3 to 5 minutes. Stir and strain. 6 servings (2/3 cup each).

Does Your Tea Please You? The Art of Reading Tea Leaves

No beverage in the world is as universally popular as tea. It is used in nearly every civilized country and this delightful drink not only refreshes and invigorates the mind and body but also serves as the medium by which people meet on a basis of friendship and understanding the world over. There is a great difference in tea however. The finest tea at present produced in the world comes from Ceylon, India and Java.

To Prepare the Cup

The hostess who knows that guests are to be diverted by the reading of their cups after tea, will select those of her teacups that flare gently towards the top and restrain their decorations to the outside surface. She will not use a tea-ball or strainer, but will infuse and pour the tea with no attempt to hold out the leaves.

A very little of the beverage should be allowed to remain in the cup at the end of the tea drinking; the reader then instructs the subject to "will" that his true destiny shall find expression in the symbols about to be formed, and to lift the cup by the handle and swish the liquid around in it three times by executing a rapid swinging motion from left to right. He should then invert the cup gently over the saucer, with the handle towards himself, and turn it slowly three times, making a silent wish. The cup is turned *towards* the consultant, to assure his luck.

So much for the rites of preparation.

The reader now takes the cup, which has certain fixed points for her. The handle represents the person who is consulting the oracle; it is also significant of time and distance — the nearer the symbols lie to the handle, the more immediate the time implied or the shorter the distance.

The rim of the cup also signifies present time; the sides represent the future, which becomes more and more remote until the bottom of the cup is reached.

After the reading, the consultant will not look again into her cup and she will be careful to express her appreciation in terms other than thanks to the reader.

Studying the Cup

The reader should first make a leisurely examination of the fortune, sizing up the general atmosphere of good or ill omen, before attempting to interpret in detail. The teacup, like life itself, will usually show a certain amount of good or ill — the larger and more powerful symbols, or those that stand out clearly and distinctly, will overshadow those of less importance or of clouded or wavering formation and will give the reading its general character. Practice will develop the ability of the reader to combine the five great points — symbolism, sympathy, observation, the association of ideas and the ability to draw fitting analogies.

The first silent study of the cup will show whether the fortune is clearly apparent or shrouded in doubt and indecision. If the symbols are clear, even though formed by very few leaves, a very well connected fortune may be read from them. If the outlines lack character, are vague and shapeless, they are not worthy of any attention; the earnest seer claims that in such cases, either the consultant did not concentrate his mind when the pictures were being formed, or his whole destiny is still undetermined because he himself has not given it definite shape.

How to Read the Symbols

An often-heard inquiry is, "How have the symbols formed by the tea leaves acquired such definite meanings?"

This has come about gradually; the old time seers saw certain meanings in certain formations, suggested usually by some association of ideas; out of the many interpretations, a set of symbols that seem to have been common to most seers was evolved. They have become traditions, and are rightly so, for amazing revelations have been made from them.

The important symbols or pictures are easy to memorize, because we, today, easily associate the same ideas with them that occurred to the original spae-wives. ("Spae" is from the Scotch Gaelic, meaning to foretell or divine one's fortune. The spae-wives of Scotland are credited with originating the art of foretelling the future from tea leaves.)

Our divinations concern chiefly the promise of good or ill fortune, success or failure in material affairs, the activities and interests of the consultant, the coming of letters, parcels, gifts, friendly or unfriendly influences, affairs of the heart, indications of travel, joy, sorrow, triumph and so forth.

The mainly recurring symbols should be memorized. These give the keys to the story, which should not be merely a disconnected interpretation of the separate symbols, but should be woven together in a more or less connected manner. This is not difficult, because there are often more obvious connections between the symbols; a parcel with good luck omen close beside it, would naturally be interpreted as a package which will give pleasure to the recipient; a bird flying toward the handle (which we have said, represents the consultant) is the bringer of news and if there is, close by, a symbol of sorrow, or the indication of money, it does not take great cleverness to see that the news will be sad or that it will tell of money; or if both these symbols are connected with the news, it is obvious enough that something in the nature of a legacy is foretold.

We shall discuss the most-found indications under separate headings, to aid the student of cup-reading to understand and memorize them; then, we shall add an alphabetical list of commonly occurring symbols that may be easily consulted as a ready reference.

"Does My Wish Come True?"

Many seers, especially amongst the old followers of the cult, leave out the wishing rite; but the making of the wish lies close to the heart of many people and their first interest, when the cup is examined, is expressed in the eager question, "Do I get my wish?"

When the wish has been included, the seer therefore generally first looks for an omen regarding it. The wish is represented by a complete figure such as a circle, square, oblong, or irregular figure formed by the tea-leaves, enclosing a clear section of the teacup's surface. If the outline surrounding this clear space is slightly broken, the wish will not be filled completely.

The closer the wish-figure is placed to the rim and the handle of the cup, the more promptly the wish will be realized. If the figure lies low on the side or on the bottom of the cup but is still complete, the wish will only be filled at the latest possible moment.

In the absence of the wish-figure, no definite hope for the fulfillment of the wish can be held out by the seer and should the omens of ill-fortune predominate in the cup, it is probable that the wish will not "come true."

Symbols of Good or Ill Fortune

There are many omens that cast an atmosphere of good fortune over the cup or attach themselves to certain symbols in the cup and give them a fortunate significance.

The most common of these are an anchor, clover leaf, crown, arch, butterfly, frog, angel, triangle, tree, flower, bouquet or garland, star, fleur-de-lis.

It is at once apparent, when we look at the list of special omens of ill-fortune that, without any knowledge of the lore of cup-reading, many are included which we would say at once were probably "unlucky"; a cross, serpent, hour-glass, arrow, gun or fire arm, sword, wild beasts, clouds.

These two lists should be carefully memorized. They are, to a great extent, the "adjectives" of cup-reading; a symbol which will simply declare an event, will be given its character by these and similar descriptive omens.

Travel is Indicated

Journeys, big and small, are very commonly foretold in the teacup. The figure itself, and the omens that surround and "qualify" it, will indicate whether it is in the nature of a little excursion or week-end trip, or a journey of pretentious proportions.

An *Arch* indicates a long journey, probably by steamship.

A *Bear,* a long journey, extending over a considerable period of time (corresponding to the bear's winter disappearance).

A *Bird,* if not flying, portends travel.

A *Bridge* indicates a trip of a pleasant nature.

A *Kite,* a long trip, probably by sea, and with considerable attendant honor and prestige.

A *Ladder,* travel, usually with some definite motive rather than just a pleasure trip.

Line of Dots denotes a trip, especially if other signs of travel are present; if the line extends right around the cup, a wonderful trip is indicated, possibly around the world; the length of the line suggests the length of the journey. The straighter the line, the more pleasant the prospect. If the line wavers greatly, the journey is troublesome or attended by losses of some kind.

The position of the omen, its nearness to the rim of the cup, indicates the probable time of the journey. Other omens of good or ill may tell of incidents of travel, pleasant or otherwise.

Affairs of the Heart

An *Anchor* denotes constancy in love.

An *Angel,* bearer of good news, may be the special messenger of love.

A *Chain,* if unbroken, denotes an early marriage; if broken, difficulties in emotional affairs.

Flowers, especially when present in quantities or in a bouquet, are a sign of happy marriage.

A *Harp* is a sign of marital happiness.

A *Heart,* if seen with a ring, speaks clearly of marriage — a genuine love match.

A *Horse-shoe,* if in the picture with any other marriage symbol, promises a most happy engagement or marriage.

A *Man,* appearing in a cup with any of the love symbols, is probably the man in the affair; if his figure is very clearly defined, he is dark; if somewhat indistinct, he is of blond type.

A *Palm tree,* with its tall trunk and crown of leaves, to a maiden is a sign of speedy marriage; to a married woman, a sign of children.

A *Peacock* with a spread tail may denote a happy marriage or a notable piece of good fortune, such as the acquisition of property.

A *Pear* in a woman's cup promises a wealthy marriage.

A *Ring* means marriage; an initial near it will be that of the surname of the future betrothed; if the symbol is clear and well defined, the best is promised; if it is cloudy, the prospect is not untroubled. If it is far down the sides, the marriage is somewhat distant and if right on the bottom, will be postponed or perhaps never take place.

Scissors or a *Sword* speak of lovers' quarrels.

Money Matters

Material prosperity or setbacks in financial affairs have various symbols.

An *Airplane* warns of dangerous projects.

An *Anchor* near other symbols with a business significance, is a good sign.

A *Castle* is a sign of fortune, probably unexpected.

Cattle, a *Cow,* or a *Cock* indicates prosperity.

A *Church* signifies prosperous money ventures.

Clouds, if surrounded by dots, indicate successful ventures.

A *Crown and a Cross* close together indicate a legacy on the death of a friend or relative.

A *Heart,* if surrounded by dots, speaks of affairs of the pocket book rather than the affections and means pleasure that will come through wealth.

A *Hen* promises money in increase of expectations.

A *Moon* (crescent) is a sign of prosperous dealings.

A *Star,* if surrounded by dots, indicates much wealth in the future.

A *Triangle,* always lucky, may foretell a surprise in the form of an inheritance.

A *Wheel* indicates a legacy.

Successful or No?

In the various affairs of life — the achieving of one's ambitions, accomplishment in one's work, happy relations with one's fellow men in a social or a business way, in a word — success is the hope of everyone. There are numerous omens which indicate progress toward the desired goal, no matter what its nature — or warn of probable failure.

Flowers in the absence of omens relating to the affections, may signify success, especially in the arts or in some undertaking not of a financial nature.

A *Hat* signifies the crown of success.

A *Horse* promises fulfillment of ambition, probably through a journey.

An *Hour Glass* is a warning of immediate dangers which may be of a financial nature — indicated, perhaps, by other business omens.

A *House* speaks of substantial business interests.

A *Key* foretells an expansion in business, with increasing revenues.

A *Lion,* when unmistakably defined, forecasts great achievements.

A Question Mark speaks of doubt and possible disappointment.

A *Revolver,* especially in connection with another omen in this group, warns of disaster.

A *Windmill* is a splendid indication to the person who is engaged in hazardous undertakings.

As to General Happiness

Apart from those omens which have particularly to do with the happiness that comes through love, success in money matters, and so forth, there are others that give to the fortune a certain aura of contentment or satisfaction. Amongst these:

A *Bush* foretells a pleasant invitation to a social function.

A *Basket or a Chair* foretells an increase in the family.

Clouds are indications of serious trouble (unless surrounded by dots, when they indicate success in money matters).

Clover, always a lucky sign, especially signifies happiness; if placed down the cup, it foretells new happiness to come.

A *Cross* warns of trouble or deferred hope.

A *Crown* is a sign of coming honors or deep satisfaction through achievement.

A *Deer or other Antlered Animal* foretells business strife, and possible failures.

The *Fleur-de-lis* may be taken as the token of health and happiness if near the top of the cup; lying on the bottom, it betokens disputes and anger.

A *Gun or Rifle* is a sign of unhappiness and sometimes of calamity at the hand of former friends.

An *Owl* is very unfortunate as it indicates illness, humiliation, poverty; it may be hooting a warning against new business undertakings, or to the girl or man who is in love.

A *Pitcher* is a sign of good health.

Snakes or Serpents call for caution to avoid misfortune, probably caused by personal enemies.

Squares are a sign of peace and security.

A *Star* is a sign of happiness and pleasant events.

Straight Lines speak of a long and serene life.

Twisted Outlines foretell grievances, especially when numerous.

An *Umbrella* signifies irritations and discouragements.

News, Letters, Gifts, Personal Relationships

An *Angel* signifies good news.

An *Arrow* foretells a disconcerting letter.

Birds, if flying, are harbingers of good news.

A *Car or Carriage* — the approach of friends.

A *Cat* — treacherous opponents.

A *Circle* indicates the coming of money, or a gift.

A *Fish* foretells good news from a distance.

A *Flag* warns of danger from an unfriendly person.

A *Person,* if walking, is the bearer of good news.

A *Knife* warns of disastrous quarrels.

Squares or Oblongs, whether a single leaf or several leaves, represent letters or parcels, or news by other channels. If dots are close by, money is indicated. If unclouded, the news is good but if clouded, bad news or losses may be expected. An initial near a letter is probably that of the sender.

A *Ship* tells of a visit from a friend.

A *Mountain* signifies powerful friends; a mountain range, powerful enemies.

A *Pig* is a sign of envy, possibly on the part of friends.

Handy Index to Common Symbols

Airplane — dangerous project.
Anchor — good luck; constancy in love.
Angel — good news.
Arrow — disconcerting letter.
Basket — addition to family.
Bear — long journey.
Birds — good luck; travel, flying — good news.
Bridge — pleasant trip.
Bush — pleasant invitation.
Car or Carriage — coming of friends.
Castle — unexpected fortune.
Cat — treacherous enemies.
Cattle — prosperity.
Church — success in finance.
Circle — gift or money.
Clouds — success.
Clover — luck.
Crown — honors.
Crown and Cross — legacy.
Deer — business failure.
Dots — travel, if in lines, money, etc.
Flag — danger from unfriendly influences.
Fleur-de-lis — health and happiness, near rim; anger, if on bottom.
Fish — good news from afar.
Flowers — success and good luck; happy marriage.
Gun — calamity.
Harp — marital happiness.
Hat — crown of success.
Heart — with ring, happy love match; surrounded by dots,

money.

Hen — money beyond expectations.

Horse — fulfillment of ambitions.

Horseshoe — luck; a fortunate trip or near love symbol, happy marriage.

Hour-glass — immediate financial changes.

House — substantial business interests.

Key — increase in business and revenues.

Kite — travel, probably by sea; honors.

Ladder — travel, with definite object.

Lion — achievement.

Man — love affair.

Moon — (crescent) prosperous dealings.

Mountain — powerful friends.

Numbers — read in conjunction with other symbols.

Owl — illness, poverty, humiliation.

Palm tree — speedy marriage or addition to family.

Peacock — happy marriage.

Pear — wealth, success, wealthy husband.

Person walking — good news.

Pitcher — good news.

Pig — good and bad luck.

Question mark — doubt, disappointment.

Revolver — disaster.

Ring — marriage.

Scissors — lovers' quarrel.

Ship — visit from friends.

Snakes — warning against misfortune.

Squares — peace and security.

Star — wealth.

Straight Lines — long serene life.

Sword — lovers' quarrel.

Triangle — luck; unexpected inheritance.

Twisted Outlines — grievances, worries.

Umbrella — irritation or discouragement.

CHOCOLATE DRINKS

Cocoa

The general rule for cocoa is 2 teaspoons cocoa, 1/4 cup cold water, 1 teaspoon sugar and 3/4 cup milk for each cup cocoa desired. Cook the water and cocoa together until thick; add the sugar; stir until dissolved; add milk and boil 1 minute.

Cocoa with Vanilla

3 tbsp. cocoa (for children, 2 tbsp. cocoa)
2 tbsp. sugar
1/2 cup hot water
1-1/2 cups milk
1-1/2 cups water
1/4 tsp. vanilla
Few grains salt

Mix cocoa, sugar and salt and add the hot water; cook over a low fire about 10 minutes. Add the milk which has been scalded with the hot water; cook mixture in a double boiler for 10 minutes; add the vanilla. Whisk with a Dover egg beater just before serving. Place a marshmallow in the cup and pour over it the hot cocoa. Serves 4.

Cocoa Syrup

1/2 cup cocoa
1 cup water
1 cup sugar
1/4 teaspoon salt
1 tablespoon butter
1 teaspoon vanilla

Cook cocoa and water together until it is smooth and thick. Add sugar and salt and cook a few minutes longer. Add butter and vanilla. The sauce may be kept in jars and used for pudding or ice cream sauce or the basis of iced cocoa.

Chocolate

Use 1/2 square of chocolate, 1 tablespoon sugar, 2 tablespoons hot water for each cup of chocolate desired. Break chocolate into pieces, add hot water, cook together until smooth; add sugar; stir until dissolved; add 1 cup scalded milk. Flavor with vanilla. Let cook about 5 minutes in a double boiler. May be served with whipped cream.

or:

2 cups milk
2 cups water
1/3 cup sugar
Few grains salt
2 squares bitter chocolate
1/2 cup water

Scald the milk and water and add it to the sugar and salt. Shave chocolate fine; add the 1/2 cup of water and heat over fire until smooth. Combine chocolate mixture and scalded milk. Continue cooking in a double boiler for 10 minutes. Serves 5.

Hot Chocolate

2 ounces unsweetened chocolate
1 cup water
Pinch salt
1/4 cup sugar
3 cups milk

In large saucepan, heat chocolate and water, stirring until chocolate is melted and mixture is smooth. Stir in salt and sugar. Heat to boiling; reduce heat and simmer 4 minutes, stirring mixture constantly.

Stir in milk; cover and heat through but do not boil. Just before serving, beat with rotary beater until foamy.
6 servings (2/3 cup each).

French Chocolate

Prepare the chocolate mixture ahead of time. And serve in your best china cups for a note of elegance on a special day.

1/3 cup semisweet chocolate pieces
1/4 cup light corn syrup
3 tablespoons water
1/2 teaspoon vanilla
1 cup chilled whipping cream
4 cups milk

Heat chocolate pieces, corn syrup and water over low heat, stirring until chocolate is melted and mixture is smooth. Stir in vanilla. Chill.

In chilled bowl, beat cream until stiff, adding chilled chocolate gradually. Continue beating until mixture mounds when dropped from a spoon. Refrigerate.

Just before serving, heat milk through but do not boil. Fill cups 1/2 full with whipped cream mixture. Fill cups with milk; blend. Makes 8 servings.

Mexican Chocolate

3 ounces unsweetened chocolate
1/2 cup sugar
3 tablespoons instant coffee
1 teaspoon cinnamon
1/2 teaspoon nutmeg
1/4 teaspoon salt
1-1/2 cups water
4 cups milk
Whipped cream

In large saucepan, heat chocolate, sugar, coffee, spices, salt and water over low heat, stirring until mixture is smooth. Heat to boiling; reduce heat and simmer 4 minutes, stirring constantly.

Stir in milk; heat. Beat with rotary beater until foamy. Top with whipped cream. Makes 8 servings (about 2/3 cup each).

Colombian Chocolate

1 package (6 ounces) semisweet chocolate pieces
1 cup Strong Coffee
1 teaspoon cinnamon
Pinch salt
6 cups milk
1/2 teaspoon vanilla

In large saucepan, heat chocolate pieces, coffee, cinnamon and salt over medium heat, stirring until chocolate is melted and mixture is smooth.

Add milk; heat through, stirring occasionally, but do not boil. Stir in vanilla. Just before serving, beat with rotary beater until foamy. Makes 10 servings (about 2/3 cup each).

Hot Cocoa

1/2 cup sugar
1/3 cup cocoa
1/4 teaspoon salt
1-1/2 cups water
4-1/2 cups milk

Mix sugar, cocoa and salt in large saucepan. Add water. Heat to boiling, stirring constantly. Boil and stir 2 minutes. Stir in milk; heat through but do not boil. If desired, add 1/4 teaspoon vanilla. Just before serving, beat with rotary beater until foamy or stir until smooth. Makes 9 servings (2/3 cup each).

Chocolate Malted Milk

1-1/2 tbsp. malted milk
1-1/2 tsp. cocoa
1 tsp. sugar
Few grains salt
1/2 cup water
1/2 cup milk
Few drops of vanilla

Mix the malted milk powder, cocoa, sugar, salt, and water, stirring well. Cook for 3 minutes. Add milk and vanilla. Serve very hot or ice cold. Makes 1 glass of malted milk.

DAIRY DRINKS

Flavored Milks

For each serving, add one of the following to an 8-ounce glass of milk and stir thoroughly. Serve immediately.

Cactus Juice: 2 drops red or yellow food color

Creamy Caramel: 2 tablespoons caramel syrup

Cheery Cherry: 1 maraschino cherry and 2 tablespoons maraschino cherry juice

Choc-O-Nut: 1 tablespoon chocolate syrup and 1 tablespoon chunky peanut butter

Fudgy Chocolate: 1 to 2 tablespoons chocolate syrup, cocoa mix or ice-cream topping

Honeysuckle Nectar: 1 tablespoon honey and 1 tablespoon grape juice, orange juice, lemonade or limeade concentrate

Monkey Juice: 1/2 banana, mashed

Woodsman's Special: 2 tablespoons maple syrup; sprinkle with cinnamon

Milk Shakes

For each serving, measure 3/4 cup milk and ingredients for any Flavored Milk (above) into blender; add 1 scoop of your favorite ice cream. Blend until smooth. (Or, beat all ingredients with rotary beater.)

Ice-Cream Sodas

For each soda, place 2 to 3 tablespoons any flavor syrup (or ice-cream topping) or 1/4 cup crushed fruit with 1 teaspoon sugar in tall glass. Fill glass 1/2 full with chilled sparkling water. Add 1 scoop of your favorite ice cream; stir vigorously, scraping syrup from side and bottom of glass. Fill glass with sparkling water.

Orange-Buttermilk Shake

1 cup buttermilk
1 scoop vanilla ice cream (about 1/2 cup)
1/2 cup orange juice
2 tablespoons brown sugar

Measure all ingredients into blender; mix on high speed until smooth. (Or, beat all ingredients with rotary beater.)
2 servings (about 3/4 cup each).

Mocha Cooler

1 cup Strong Coffee (see Chart I), chilled
1 pint chocolate ice cream
1 teaspoon vanilla
1/2 teaspoon cinnamon
1/4 teaspoon salt

Pour coffee into blender. Spoon in ice cream, vanilla, cinnamon and salt. Blend 10 to 15 seconds. (Or, beat all ingredients with rotary beater.) Serve immediately over ice cubes in tall glasses.
3 or 4 servings.

Hot Chocolate Milk

Heat 1 quart chocolate-flavored milk over medium-low heat until small bubbles form around edge of pan. Beat with rotary beater until foamy. Serve immediately.
6 servings (3/4 cup each).

Spoon-Up Eggnog

Can eggnog be elegant?
Just try this one and see.

4 eggs, separated
1/2 cup sugar
1/8 teaspoon salt
1/2 cup golden or, if desired, 1 to 2 tablespoons rum flavoring
2 cups whipping cream, whipped

Beat egg whites until stiff. Beat egg yolk sugar and salt until very thick and lemon colored; stir in rum.

Fold egg yolk mixture into whipped cream. Fold egg whites into egg yolk-cream mixture. Chill thoroughly.

Serve in cups, with spoons. If desired, sprinkle with nutmeg.

Egg Nog

Few grains salt
1 egg
2 tbsp. fruit juice
1 tbsp. sugar
2/3 cup ice-cold milk
2/3 cup ice-cold water
Few gratings of nutmeg

Add salt to egg white and beat until stiff. Beat yolk until thick and lemon colored; add the fruit juice and sugar. Dilute milk with the water and combine with yolk mixture. Pour into a tall glass, add nutmeg gratings and put egg white on top. Sprinkle top with chopped nuts and serve at once.
Serves 2.

PUNCHES & FRUIT DRINKS

Cranberry-Apple Punch

3 quarts water
2 cups sugar
2 cups strong tea
2 cans (6 ounces each) frozen lemonade concentrate, thawed
2 quarts cranberry cocktail
1 quart apple juice
2 cups orange juice

Heat water and sugar to boiling, stirring constantly until sugar is dissolved. Cool. Prepare tea as directed under "Teas," using 3 teaspoons loose tea or 3 teabags and 2 cups boiling water. Cool. Chill all ingredients. Just before serving, stir together in large punch bowl. 60 servings (about 1/2 cup each).

Rosé Punch

2 bottles (4/5 quart each) rosé, chilled
1/2 cup grenadine syrup
1/2 cup lemon juice
1 quart ginger ale, chilled

In large punch bowl, combine wine, grenadine syrup and lemon juice. Stir in ginger ale. Serve immediately.

22 servings (about 1/2 cup each).

Variation: Creamy Rosé Punch: Spoon 1 pint raspberry sherbet into punch. Do not use ice.

Tahitian Punch

1 can (46 ounces) pineapple juice, chilled
1 can (46 ounces) orange-grapefruit juice, chilled
2 quarts carbonated lemon-lime beverage, chilled
1 pint lemon or lime sherbet

In large punch bowl, stir together juices and carbonated beverage. Spoon sherbet into bowl. Serve immediately.
38 servings (about 1/2 cup each).

Sparkling Cranberry Punch

2 quarts cranberry cocktail, chilled
1 can (6 ounces) frozen pink lemonade concentrate, thawed
1 quart sparkling water, chilled

In large punch bowl, combine cranberry cocktail and lemonade concentrate. Stir in sparkling water. Serve immediately. 25 servings (about 1/2 cup each).

Fruit Glow Punch

1 can (6 ounces) frozen orange juice concentrate, thawed
1 can (6 ounces) frozen lemonade concentrate, thawed
1 quart apple juice, chilled
2 quarts ginger ale, chilled
1 pint lemon or orange sherbet

In large punch bowl, combine concentrates and apple juice. Stir in ginger ale. Spoon sherbet into bowl. Serve immediately.

28 servings (about 1/2 cup each).

Daiquiri Punch

1 bottle (4/5 quart) white rum
2 cans (6 ounces each) frozen daiquiri mix, thawed
2 quarts carbonated lemon-lime beverage, chilled

In large punch bowl, combine rum and daiquiri mix. Stir in carbonated lemon-lime beverage. Serve immediately.
25 servings (about 1/2 cup each).

Hot Apple Cider Punch

1 gallon apple cider
2 teaspoons whole cloves
2 teaspoons whole allspice
2 three-inch cinnamon sticks
2/3 cup sugar
2 oranges, studded with cloves

Heat cider, cloves, allspice, cinnamon and sugar to boiling; cover and simmer 20 minutes. Strain punch and pour into punch bowl. Float oranges in bowl. 32 servings (about 1/2 cup each).

Ice Ring for Punch Bowl

In 6- to 6-1/2-cup ring mold, arrange thin citrus slices and maraschino cherries or strawberries in an attractive design. Pour water into mold to partially cover fruit. Freeze.
When frozen, add water to fill mold 3/4 full; freeze. At serving time, unmold and float fruit side up in punch bowl.
If you prefer, freeze ring without decoration. Or, instead of freezing water, freeze part of a non-sparkling punch recipe itself, this will keep punch cold without diluting it.

Holiday Eggnog

6 eggs
1 cup sugar
1/2 teaspoon salt
1 cup golden rum or, if desired, 1 to 2 tablespoons rum flavoring
1 quart light cream (20%)
Nutmeg

In large bowl, beat eggs until light and foamy. Add sugar and salt, beating until thick and lemon colored. Stir in rum and cream. Chill at least 3 hours. Just before serving, sprinkle with nutmeg. 12 servings (about 1/2 cup each).

Sparkling Orange Eggnog

2 quarts orange juice, chilled
1/2 cup lemon juice
6 eggs
1/4 cup sugar
1/4 teaspoon cinnamon
1/4 teaspoon ginger
1/4 teaspoon cloves
1 quart vanilla ice cream
1 quart ginger ale, chilled
Nutmeg

Into large bowl, measure 3 cups of the orange juice, the lemon juice, eggs, sugar, cinnamon, ginger and cloves. Blend with rotary beater. Stir in remaining orange juice; cover and refrigerate. Just before serving, pour eggnog mixture into large punch bowl. Spoon ice cream into bowl; add ginger ale. Blend with rotary beater. Sprinkle with nutmeg. 30 servings (about 1/2 cup each).

Lemonade

Stir together 3 cups water, 1 cup lemon juice (about 4 lemons) and 1/2 cup sugar. Pour over ice.
5 servings (about 3/4 cup each).

Minted Lemonade: Place bruised mint leaves in glasses before pouring Lemonade. Garnish each serving with a sprig of mint.

Pink Lemonade: Add 2 tablespoons grenadine syrup and 2 to 3 drops red food color. Or, add only the red food color.

Limeade

Stir together 3 cups water, 1 cup lime juice (about 10 limes) and 3/4 cup sugar. Pour over ice. 5 servings (about 3/4 cup each).

Raspberry Shrub

40 ounces frozen raspberries, thawed
6 ounces frozen lemonade
2 quarts ginger ale, chilled

Cook raspberries 10 minutes. Rub through strainer with wooden spoon; cool. Add concentrate; stir in ginger ale. Serve immediately in tall glasses with ice cubes or crushed ice. 12 servings (1 cup each).

Orange Swizzle

1 can (12 ounce) frozen orange juice concentrate
1 quart ginger ale, chilled
Orange half-slices
Maraschino cherries

Reconstitute orange juice with ginger ale. Pour over crushed ice. Serve with an orange slice and cherry on each swizzle stick. 6 servings (about 1 cup each).

Mulled Tomato Juice

2 cans (46 ounces each) tomato juice
1 tablespoon Worcestershire sauce
1 teaspoon salt
1 teaspoon celery salt
1/2 teaspoon oregano
5 drops Tabasco
1/2 cup soft butter

Combine all ingredients in Dutch oven or large kettle. Cover and heat to boiling. Reduce heat; simmer 10 to 15 minutes, stirring occasionally. Serve in small mugs.
15 servings (about 3/4 cup each).

Note: A 15-cup automatic percolator (with basket removed) can be used. Measure ingredients into percolator and let it perk one cycle.

Spiced Cranberry Cider

2 quarts apple cider
1-1/2 quarts cranberry cocktail
1/4 cup brown sugar (packed)
4 three-inch cinnamon sticks
1-1/2 teaspoons whole cloves
1 lemon, thinly sliced

Combine all ingredients in large kettle. Heat to boiling; reduce heat and simmer 15 to 20 minutes. With slotted spoon, remove cinnamon, cloves and lemon slices. If desired, float a fresh lemon slice in each cup. 25 servings (about 1/2 cup each).

Charles and Ida Franks

5

CEREALS

Cereals are valuable and inexpensive food as they furnish energy at a low cost.

Cereal mush or other cereal dishes with milk for breakfast furnishes a meal of excellent food value. It is a good plan to have several different kinds of cereals on hand so that there may be a change from day to day. Corn and oat preparations furnish particularly good winter foods. Corn meal, oatmeal, rice and hominy grits are cheaper than the ready-to-eat breakfast foods. Cereals are rich in starches and should be thoroughly cooked.

Cereal with Fruit. For variety, cereal may be cooked with well-washed dates, raisins or dried apricots or peaches. Slices or sections of fresh apples, peaches and pears may be added during the last 30 minutes of cooking. Cereal molded in cups may be used for dessert.

Cereal may be served with any fruit previously stewed, or fresh fruits, or the cereal may be cooked in strained fruit juice or milk instead of water.

Cereal as a Vegetable. Leftover cereal may be sliced when cold and fried for luncheon or supper. Cereal cooked in soup stock or with meat and seasoned with salt and pepper and butter may be used as a potato substitute.

GENERAL DIRECTIONS FOR COOKING CEREALS

Use a double boiler or 2 saucepans, one a trifle larger than the other. Fill the larger saucepan or lower part of double boiler 1/3 full of water and put the water needed for the cereal in the other vessel. When the water boils, add the salt and cereal slowly so that the water does not stop boiling, and let boil for 10 minutes. Place the pot with cereal into the double boiler and cover and let steam. If the cereal seems to be too thick, add boiling water. The oatmeal, hominy and other coarse-grain cereals are improved by soaking overnight in water. They should be cooked in the water in which they have been soaked.

TIME TABLE AND DIRECTIONS FOR COOKING CEREALS

	Water	Cereal	Salt	Time
Oatmeal	4 cups	1 cup	1-1/2 tsp.	3 hours
Rolled Oats	2-1/2 cups	1 cup	1 tsp.	1/2–1 hour
Rice (boiled)	8 cups	1 cup	1 tsp.	25–30 minutes
Rice (steamed)	3 cups	1 cup	1 tsp.	1 hour
Wheat (rolled)	1-1/2 cups	1 cup	1 tsp.	1 hour
Wheat (granular)	4 cups	1 cup	1 tsp.	1–3 hours
Cornmeal	6 cups	1 cup	1 tsp.	3–6 hours
Cracked Wheat	6 cups	1 cup	1 tsp.	3–6 hours
Hominy	4 cups	1 cup	1 tsp.	1 hour

Note: By using the fireless cooker, the cereal can be boiled 10 minutes over the fire in the evening, and then cooked overnight in the fireless cooker.

Steamed Rice

1 cup rice
1 teaspoon salt
3 to 4 cups boiling water or milk

Cook as other cereal, stirring occasionally with fork to prevent sticking. Let it steam in a double boiler 45 minutes. Put in colander and pour cold water over the rice to wash off the sticky substance. Put colander over the lower part of the boiler again and allow the steam to thoroughly dry the rice.

Browned Hominy

Fry cooked hominy to a golden brown in just enough fat to prevent sticking. Bacon fat or other drippings are preferable to lard because of their flavor.

6

BREADS

GENERAL DIRECTIONS FOR MAKING BREAD

While the liquid used in the making of bread may be all of water where desired, we especially recommend the use of part milk. Not only does it produce a whiter loaf and a more attractive crust, but it is considerably more nourishing, and is well worth the trifling additional expense.

As sugar assists in the fermentation of the yeast, a portion of that used should be added to the yeast and water to hasten its action. Too much sugar, however, makes a sticky dough.

As salt retards fermentation, it should, when bread is set in the morning, be added in the last sifter of flour. When set at night, it should be added with the yeast so the bread will not rise before one is ready to take care of it.

When milk is used, it should be brought to the scalding point, but not boiled, and allowed to cool until it is lukewarm before adding to the yeast. The shortening should be melted in the hot milk.

Great care should be taken that the bread, at no time during its making, gets chilled. When setting bread at night, put it in a warm place, well wrapped. As paper excludes the air more effectually than cloth, cover first with paper, and then wrap in a heavy cloth. Bread made with dry yeast requires greater warmth than that made with compressed.

When setting bread to rise in the morning, an excellent way to insure even rising is to place the bowl or pan containing the bread into a large one containing warm water, and throw a cover over all. Be sure the water is not too hot, but just very warm. Keep it at an even temperature by adding more warm water to it every half hour or so. After kneading, and putting into pans, this same method may be used. Fill a large roasting or baking pan with hot water and set the pans in this. Cover and let rise.

The bowl or pan in which the bread is set to rise should always be well greased, and the bread also well greased by rubbing over with melted butter or lard, to safeguard against a crust being formed. Proper covering is a reasonably safe method, but the greasing makes the protection doubly sure. If you have been careless and a crust has formed over the dough, remove it carefully before kneading into loaves, or an ugly streak or lumps will be found in the bread when baked.

Enough flour should be kneaded into the bread during the first kneading so that no part of it will stick—even ever so slightly—to either the hands or the board. Lack of sufficient flour will cause a heavy streak around the bread, which gives it the appearance of being under-done.

Kneading should always be very quick and light. By heavy, hard kneading, too much flour is used to prevent sticking, making a loaf which is stiff and very compact instead of light and fluffy. A very soft dough can be handled without sticking if the kneading be done lightly and quickly.

Bread may be kneaded in a few moments, if two or three times during the kneading the dough is cut through with a sharp knife and turned inside out. By doing this, it enables one to reach the center of the mass more quickly.

No matter what bread recipe is used, sift a part of the flour in at a time, and when it is of the consistency of griddle cake batter, beat it hard with an egg beater, to fill it with air bubbles. The more the batter is beaten, the less kneading required.

Keep the doors and windows shut while mixing or kneading the bread.

Do not try to mix it stiff in a bowl or pan; it is easier to do so on a floured board.

Knead until the dough has a silky smoothness, is full of blisters and does not stick to the hands or board. Work fast, but lightly. The time will vary with the manner of working.

In using compressed yeast, be sure it is fresh. If it breaks off easily without appearing soft and "soggy" it is fresh; if too soft to handle, it is stale and should not be used.

Many recipes and directions for bread making say that the dough should "double in bulk." This is not quite enough, especially during its first rising and before putting it into the pans. Let it double its bulk, and then half again its original bulk. The bread in the pans is ready for the oven when it has doubled its bulk and when the finger, pressed slightly on it, leaves an impression. If the impression disappears, it should rise longer.

BAKING BREAD

The oven, when bread is first put in, should be quite hot, and the heat should reach its highest point in about ten minutes; it should then gradually be reduced and the bread allowed to bake slowly.

The bread is done when the steam escaping from the bottom of the loaf is not hot enough to be painful. A small loaf should bake from fifty minutes to an hour; a larger one a little longer.

When removing from the oven, never set it where it will rest flat upon any surface or it will be soggy. It should be free from draft, but set in such a way that air can circulate all around it. The best thing for this purpose is a bread or cake rest, or a new small extension screen, kept especially for baking purposes, is excellent.

Bread during the cooling should not be covered, but should be kept free from draft. If the crust is too hard, however, it is a good plan to throw over it for a moment a cloth wrung out of hot water, then cover with a dry cloth, and remove both in a moment.

SHORTENING

Regarding shortening, different opinions exist. Lard makes a whiter loaf, but butter gives a delightful flavor. Some Domestic Science Schools teach the use of no shortening whatever; others use a rounding tablespoon to three loaves of bread. Personally, for the flavor and additional moisture it gives, I prefer the use of two slightly rounding tablespoons of butter. This is much a matter of personal taste, however, so I would suggest your experimenting at different times until you find which method best suits your taste.

To get uniform results, always, in cooking, use pure granulated sugar and pure unadulterated cooking salt. The fine salts which will not cake are excellent for table use, but for cooking purposes the recipes given here have been tested with the unadulterated cooking salt.

WEIGHTS AND MEASURES

4 saltspoons	=	1 teaspoon
3 teaspoons	=	1 tablespoon
4 tablespoons	=	1/2 gill or 1/4 cup
16 tablespoons	=	1 cup
2 cups	=	1 pint
2 pints (4 cups)	=	1 quart
2 cups butter, packed solidly	=	1 pound
1/2 cup butter, packed solidly	=	1/4 pound
2 cups granulated sugar	=	1 pound
2-1/2 cups pulverized sugar	=	1 pound
2 cups milk or water	=	1 pound
4 tablespoons granulated sugar	=	2 ounces, or 1/4 cup
2 tablespoons granulated sugar	=	1 ounce
4 tablespoons flour	=	1 ounce
4 level cups flour	=	1 pound (approx.)
1/4 cup powdered chocolate or cocoa	=	1 ounce (equivalent to 1 sq. unsweetened cake chocolate)

A Dozen Extra Tips for Bakers:

1. Measure ingredients accurately and follow instructions carefully. Baking offers less leeway for interpretation than other forms of cooking.
2. Use a good thermometer to check the oven temperature (Taylor is a reliable brand). Ovens are often inaccurately calibrated, which accounts for many baking problems.
3. Use the pan size called for unless you are an experienced baker and know how to make the necessary adjustments.
4. Use large eggs unless otherwise specified.
5. Buy freshly ground nuts, or briefly pulse-grind whole ones in a food processor with a little granulated sugar to prevent them from becoming pasty.
6. Separate egg whites and yolks carefully, since a speck of fatty yolk in the whites will prevent them from whipping to maximum volume. Eggs separate best when chilled, but whip best at room temperature.
7. To bring cold whole eggs to room temperature, place them in a bowl of warm water for 10 minutes.
8. Line deep loaf pans or large shallow pans with a sheet of parchment or wax paper so that the cakes can be easily turned out of the pan.
9. Measure flour by spooning it into a dry-measuring cup and leveling off with a knife; don't tamp it down.
10. Check the date on your yeast packet before purchasing or using, discard if the expiration date has passed. Store yeast in the refrigerator.
11. Use your microwave oven for melting chocolate or for softening butter.
12. Use a sharp stainless steel paring knife for preparing fruit.

All measurements are absolutely level unless otherwise specified. The measuring cup used is the standard cup, divided off into quarters, halves and thirds, and which when full and leveled off with a knife, holds one-half pint.

Teaspoons and tablespoons are leveled off with a knife. For halves, they are divided by running the knife through the middle lengthwise, then through the middle crosswise.

Where careful measures are taken and the heat properly regulated, results should be perfect.

MEASURING, MIXING AND COMBINING

All dry ingredients should be sifted before measuring.

Flour and sugar should be placed lightly in a cup, a spoon at a time, and leveled off with a knife; they should never be packed solid.

Butter and lard, or other shortening, should be packed solidly and leveled off with a knife.

There are three methods of combining ingredients: stirring, beating and folding. By stirring, the ingredients are thoroughly mixed. By beating, a large amount of air is incorporated, and by cutting and folding, this air which has been previously introduced is not allowed to escape.

In cakes, sugar and butter should be creamed, unless the quantity of sugar is more than double that of butter, in which case half of the sugar should be creamed with the butter and the balanced mixed in the yolks of eggs, after they have been well beaten.

The yolks of eggs should be beaten until thick and lemon colored for a fine cake; also when used in thickening. A well beaten yolk has double the thickening power of one only half beaten.

The whites of the eggs should be beaten until very stiff, and should be folded in at the last. No stirring or beating should be done after the whites have been folded in, or the work already accomplished of incorporating air, will be undone.

Also refer to special articles under Cakes, Pastry and Bread.

Bread Sponge

This bread sponge makes an excellent foundation for any bread, or for various rolls. When making rolls, additional sugar, shortening and salt should be used according to the various recipes given. When making bread by a sponge method, use this sponge, and for rolls remove a cupful or more when light and follow recipes given.

1 cake yeast
1 cup lukewarm water
3 cups lukewarm water additional
1 level tablespoon salt
3 level tablespoons sugar
2 level tablespoons shortening
5 level cups sifted flour (1 lb. 2 oz.)

Dissolve the yeast in the 1 cup of water. Add balance of ingredients and beat hard. Set in a warm place to rise until light, or full of bubbles. It is ready when the bubbles begin to break and it sinks slightly in the center.

White Bread (Quick Method, with Compressed Yeast)

To be set either at night or in the morning. Read carefully Directions on Bread Making for full instructions—especially regarding lightness and baking.

1 cake compressed yeast
3 cups lukewarm liquid (2 water, 1 milk)
2 level tablespoons sugar
1 or 2 tablespoons shortening
1 level tablespoon salt
About 9 cups (2-1/4 quarts) of flour

Dissolve the yeast in 1 cup of the lukewarm water, to which add 1 teaspoon of sugar.

Scald the milk (do not boil) and add the shortening. When lukewarm, add with the other cup of lukewarm water to the yeast and mix well. Sift in gradually the flour, into which has been mixed the salt and balance of sugar, and beat well. When too stiff to mix further with a spoon, use the hands. When well mixed, knead for 3 or 4 minutes. During the kneading cut through the middle and turn inside out to insure reaching the center.

Put in a well greased bowl or enameled or granite pan, grease the top of the dough, cover, first with paper and then with a heavy cloth, and set out of a draft until light.

If set in the morning it should be ready in about 4 hours. If set at night, it will probably be ready for the second kneading about 8 in the morning, although sometimes it is necessary to allow it to rise a little longer. The different in time required is partly due to the difference in temperature and partly to the difference in the time at which the salt is added. (See General Directions.)

When light (see Directions), knead again, put into well greased pan, rub the tops of the loaves with melted butter, and set in a warm place, well covered, to rise until light. This generally requires about an hour.

Bake according to full directions given.

This same method may be used with the bread mixer, putting the dough into the mixer after working in the different ingredients.

(This recipe makes 3 medium sized loaves.)

White Bread (Quick Method, with Potato)

1, 1-1/2 or 2 yeast cakes
1 cup water lukewarm
3 cups water additional
3 tablespoons sugar
1-1/3 tablespoons salt

2 tablespoons fat
1-1/2 cups mashed potatoes
About 15-1/2 cups flour

If 1 cake be used, the bread should be finished and out of the oven in about 6 hours. If 1-1/2 cakes, it should be completed in about 5 to 5-1/2 hours. If 2 cakes, in about 5 hours or less. Personally, I prefer 1 or 1-1/2 cakes. Dissolve the yeast in 1 cup of water. Add balance of lukewarm water, sugar and salt. Add shortening to hot mashed potatoes to melt, and when potatoes are lukewarm, add about 5 cups of the flour, and beat hard, then add balance gradually and knead until smooth and elastic and it does not stick to the hands or board. Follow directions under Recipe 1, for White Bread Quick Method.

White Bread (or Whole Wheat or Graham, with Compressed Yeast)

Set your bread to rise in the morning and follow these rules closely:

To 1 quart of lukewarm (not hot) liquid, composed of equal portions of water and sweet milk (scalded) or water alone, add 2 half-ounce cakes of compressed yeast and stir until completely dissolved, then add 1 tablespoon of salt and 2 heaping tablespoons of sugar.

When salt and sugar are thoroughly dissolved, stir in well sifted flour, preferably with a wooden spoon, to make a stiff batter and beat thoroughly, then add 2 tablespoons of lard and flour enough to make dough sufficiently stiff to turn from mixing bowl to moulding board in a mass.

Knead this dough until it becomes smooth and elastic and ceases to stick to the hands or board.

Put into a well greased earthen bowl, brush lightly with melted butter or drippings, cover well and allow to rise in a warm place about 2 hours, until light. As soon as light, knead well and again place in earthen bowl, covering as before, and set for another rising of about an hour or until light. As soon as light, form into loaves or rolls and place in greased bread or roll pans, brush with melted butter or drippings, cover again with towel and allow to rise about 1-1/4 hours, then bake.

The above recipe has the advantage of being quick, and good bread is sure to result if closely followed.

The above recipe is also excellent for whole wheat or graham bread by simply using whole wheat or graham instead of white flour.

White Bread (Quick Method, with Dry Yeast)

Read carefully General Directions for Bread Making.

1 cake dry yeast
3 cups warm water
3 tablespoons sugar
1 cup warm milk
1 or 2 tablespoons shortening
2 tablespoons salt
About 13 cups Flour

Crumble the yeast and soak in about 2 cups of the warm water, to which has been added 1 tablespoon of the sugar, for about an hour. Scald the milk and dissolve into it the balance of the sugar and the shortening. Let stand until lukewarm, then add, with the other cup of lukewarm water, to the yeast. Measure the flour and add to it the salt. Sift this gradually into the liquid, and when about of the consistency of griddle cake batter, beat with an egg beater until full of bubbles and smooth. Add the balance of the flour. Knead until smooth and elastic and it does not stick to the hands or the board.

Set in a warm place to rise over night. In the morning, when it has doubled its bulk or a little more (see General Directions), knead again. Put into well greased pans, grease the tops of the loaves with melted butter or lard, and let rise until double its bulk. Bake according to full directions given. This recipe makes 4 small or 3 large loaves.

White Bread (with Dry Yeast)

At noon mash fine 3 medium sized potatoes, pour over them a cup of boiling water (do not use water potatoes are boiled in, as it gives bread a dark color), and stir in 1 tablespoon of flour.

Also set 1/2 cake of yeast to soak in 1/2 cup of cold water. When potato mixture is cool, stir in yeast (yeast should soak about 1 hour). Set this mixture in warm place to ferment until evening. In the evening about 8 or 9 o'clock add 3 cups of warm (not hot) water (95 to 100 degrees F.), and enough flour to make a fairly stiff batter. Beat well and cover this sponge, and let rise in fairly warm place overnight.

In the morning, 7 a.m., add 1 level tablespoon of salt, 2 heaping tablespoons of sugar, 2 tablespoons of lard and mix stiff. Knead about 15 minutes until dough becomes smooth and silky and does not stick.

Let rise 1 to 1-1/2 hours and knead about 2 minutes, then let rise about 1 hour and knead about 2 minutes. Let rise again for 45 minutes to 1 hour and mould into loaves. Let rise in pan until loaves double in size and then bake.

Bread made with potatoes retains its moisture longer.

White Bread (Sponge Method, with Compressed Yeast)

2 cakes compressed yeast
2 cups lukewarm liquid
1 tablespoon salt
2 tablespoons sugar
Flour (about 3 cups)

Dissolve the yeast in the warm water, stirring until every particle is thoroughly dissolved; then add the salt, sugar and about 3 cups of flour and beat thoroughly. Set aside in a warm place, free from draft and well covered, to rise until full of air bubbles and they begin to break. It will require about 1-1/2 hours.

Then add to this sponge:

1 tablespoon shortening
2 cups scalded milk (cooled to lukewarm)
2 cups lukewarm water
About 5 quarts Flour

Dissolve the shortening and the salt in the scalded milk and when lukewarm add, with the lukewarm liquid, to the sponge. Beat thoroughly; then sift in the flour gradually, and beat until too stiff to handle with a spoon. Mix in the balance of the flour, turn out on the floured bread board and knead until light and elastic and it does not stick to the hands or the board. Put into a well greased bowl, rub melted fat over the top, and set aside in a warm place, free from draft and well covered, to rise until a little over double its bulk (see General Directions). When light, knead again, put into well greased pans, set aside to rise again and when light, bake.
This recipes makes about 5 loaves.

Whole Wheat Bread (Quick Method, with Compressed Yeast)

Read carefully General Directions for Bread Making.
To be set either at night or in the morning.

1 cake compressed yeast
3 cups lukewarm liquid (2 water, 1 milk)
3 level tablespoons brown sugar
1 or 2 tablespoons shortening
1 level tablespoon salt
About 6 cups (1-1/2 quarts) whole wheat flour

Dissolve the yeast in 1 cup of the lukewarm water, to which has been added a tablespoon of the brown sugar. Scald the milk and add the shortening and the balance of the sugar. When lukewarm, add, with the other cup of lukewarm water, to the yeast. Mix the salt with the flour and sift in gradually. Beat thoroughly with an egg beater when about 1/2 of the flour has been added, until smooth and full of bubbles. Mix in the balance of the flour and knead until smooth and elastic and it does not stick to the hands or the board. Follow directions given for White Bread (Quick Method, With Compressed Yeast). This recipe makes 2 loaves.

Whole Wheat Bread (Quick Method, with Dry Yeast)

Read carefully General Directions for Bread Making.
To be set either in the morning or at night.

1 cake dry yeast
3 cups lukewarm water
3 tablespoons sugar
1 cup lukewarm milk
2 tablespoons salt
1 or 2 tablespoons shortening
About 13 cups Flour

Crumble the yeast and soak in 2 cups of lukewarm water, to which has been added 1 tablespoon of the sugar, for 1 hour. Follow directions given with recipe for White Bread (Quick Method,with Dry Yeast).

(This recipes makes 4 small or 3 large loaves.)

Whole Wheat "Health" Bread

1 cake yeast
1 cup lukewarm water
1-1/2 cups water additional
1/2 tablespoon salt
4 tablespoons molasses
2 tablespoons fat
2-1/2 cups Flour
3-1/4 cups whole wheat flour

Dissolve the yeast in 1 cup of water. Add balance of water, salt, molasses and fat and the white flour. Beat hard and set to rise in a warm place until full of bubbles and they begin to break and settle in the center. Then add the whole wheat flour, knead quickly and lightly, until smooth and elastic and it does not stick to the hands or board. Set in a greased bowl, rub over the top with melted shortening or milk to prevent a crust forming, cover lightly and set in a warm place until light, or until a slight pressure of the finger leaves a dent. Knead again, into 2 loaves and rub over the top with melted shortening or milk, and place in a greased pan in a warm place to rise until light. Bake according to General Directions for Bread Making.

Steamed Brown Bread

3 cups graham flour
1 cup Flour
1 teaspoon salt
1 cup seedless raisins
1-1/2 cups sour milk
1 cup molasses
2 teaspoons soda

Mix together the flours, salt and raisins. Add the sour milk to the molasses and beat in the soda, then add to the dry ingredients. Steam 3 hours. Three-pound lard pails, well greased, or greased baking powder cans are excellent to steam this in. If the small baking powder cans are used, 2-1/2 hours will answer for the steaming.

This recipe will fill about two 3-pound lard pails.

Graham Bread (with Baking Powder)

1 cup Flour
1 teaspoon salt
5 level teaspoons baking powder
2 cups graham flour
1/2 cup sugar
1-2/3 cups sweet milk

Mix and sift the Blend Flour, salt and baking powder, then add the graham flour, sugar and milk. Let stand in a loaf for about 10 minutes before baking, then put in a hot oven. After 15 minutes' baking, reduce the heat somewhat. Bake 1 hour.

(This recipe makes 1 loaf.)

Nut Bread (with Yeast)

1/2 cake yeast
1 cup lukewarm water
1 cup lukewarm milk (scalded first)
2 teaspoons salt
1/3 cup sugar
1 beaten egg
1 tablespoon shortening
1 teaspoon vanilla
5-1/4 cups Flour
1 cup walnut meats, broken

Dissolve yeast in the warm water, then add warm milk and balance of ingredients excepting nuts, beating well until too stiff to beat, then knead lightly. Let rise in a warm place, covered, until light, then knead lightly, working in the nuts. Put in 2 buttered loaf pans (pound loaf pans) and brush over with melted shortening and let rise until light. Bake in an oven regulated as for bread, increase heat first 15 minutes, then decreasing. Rub over with butter when taking from the oven.

Orange Bread

Delicious for Luncheon or Afternoon Tea, or made into sandwiches with orange marmalade between

3/4 cake yeast
1/2 cup lukewarm water
1 cup orange juice
Grated rind of 2 large oranges
1-1/4 teaspoon salt
1/3 cup sugar
1 beaten egg
3 tablespoons melted shortening
5-1/2 cups Flour

Dissolve yeast in the lukewarm water. Add lukewarm orange juice, grated rind,salt and sugar, then beaten egg and shortening. Fold in the flour, then turn out onto a floured board and stretch out, and fold over several times according to "Walker's Easy Bread Making" booklet which will be sent free upon request, or knead lightly. Place in greased bowl, cover with cloth and let rise in a warm place until light, or from 1-1/4 to 1-1/2 hours. It is light when a gentle touch leaves no permanent imprint. When light knead, or fold according to the Walker method, and let rise again for about an hour, or until light. Then knead or fold again and form into a loaf, place in greased loaf pan and let rise until light, which will require about an hour. Brush over the top with melted fat and bake in a moderate oven. It will require about an hour. While still warm but not hot, spread top and sides with Orange Icing.

Orange Icing

Add 2 tablespoons hot orange juice to a cup of sifted powdered sugar, adding a little more sugar if necessary to spread smoothly, and spread on at once, while warm.

Nut Bread

3 cups Blend Flour
5 teaspoons baking powder
1/2 cup sugar
1 teaspoon salt
1 cup broken walnut meats
1 beaten egg
1 cup milk

Mix and sift the dry ingredients. Stir in the nuts. Beat the egg and add to the milk and mix in well. Place in a well greased pan, and bake in a moderately slow oven. It will require about 40 minutes.

Date Bread (with Baking Powder)

3-1/2 cups Blend Flour
4 teaspoons baking powder
1/3 cup sugar
1 teaspoon salt
1/2 teaspoon mace (or omit)
1 cup seeded and cut dates
1/2 cup nuts if desired
1 beaten egg
1 cup milk

Mix and sift flour, baking powder, sugar, salt and mace. Add the dates cut in quarters, and if desired, add also 1/2 cup of nuts. Beat egg slightly, add to milk, and stir in. Pack in a well greased bread pan and place in a slow oven (300 degrees). When fully risen, heat may be increased slightly (350 degrees) and continue baking for 50 minutes to an hour altogether. The time will vary according to the shape and size of pan, which regulates the depth and width of a loaf.

Peanut Butter Bread

2 cups flour
4 teaspoons baking powder
1 teaspoon salt
1/2 cup sugar
1 cup milk
2/3 cup peanut butter

Sift flour, baking powder, salt and sugar together. Add milk to peanut butter, blend well and add to dry ingredients; beat thoroughly. Bake in greased loaf pan in slow oven 45 to 50 minutes. This is best when a day old. It makes delicious sandwiches cut in thin slices and filled with either cream cheese or lettuce and mayonnaise.

Prune or Date Bread

1 cup prunes or dates
2-1/2 cups graham flour or 1 cup flour and 1-1/2 cups graham flour
1/4 cup sugar
1 teaspoon salt
5 teaspoons baking powder
1 cup milk
1 tablespoon melted shortening

Stone and chop fruit (prunes must be soaked several hours and drained). Mix flour, sugar, salt and baking powder; add milk and beat well; add fruit and shortening. Put into greased bread pan; allow to stand 20 to 25 minutes in warm place. Bake in moderate oven 1 hour.

Graham Bread #1

1/4 cup molasses
1 tablespoon salt
2 cups hot liquid (milk or milk and water)
1/4 yeast cake
1/4 cup lukewarm water
3 cups flour
3 cups graham flour
Oil

Add molasses and salt to liquid; cool and when lukewarm add yeast which has been softened in 1/4 cup lukewarm water. Add flours and beat well. Cover and allow to rise overnight or until double in bulk. Beat again and turn into bread pans brushed with oil, having pans 1/2 full; allow to rise but not quite double its bulk. Brush with oil and bake about 1 hour in hot oven (425 ° F.). Reduce the heat the last part of baking and brush again with oil just before taking from the oven. Makes 2 loaves.

Graham Bread #2

1-1/2 cups flour
1-1/2 cups graham flour
4 teaspoons baking powder
1 teaspoon salt
1 egg
1 tablespoon melted shortening
2 tablespoons sugar or molasses
1-1/2 cups liquid (1/2 water and 1/2 milk)

Mix flour, graham flour, baking powder and salt together; add beaten egg, shortening and sugar or molasses to liquid; stir into dry mixture and beat well; add more milk if necessary to make a drop batter. Put into greased loaf pan, smooth with knife dipped in cold water. Bake about 1 hour in moderate oven.

Corn Bread #1

1 cup corn meal
1-1/4 cups flour
4 teaspoons baking powder
3 tablespoons sugar

2 teaspoons salt
1 to 1-1/2 cups milk, depending on the corn meal
2-1/2 tablespoons oil
1 egg

Sift dry ingredients into bowl; add milk to oil and beaten egg; beat well and pour into shallow pan brushed with oil. Bake in hot oven (425 to 450 degrees F.) about 25 minutes.

Makes eight 2-1/2-inch squares.

Corn Bread #2

1 cup corn meal
1 cup flour
4 teaspoons baking powder
3 tablespoons sugar
1 teaspoon salt
1-1/2 cups milk
2 tablespoons melted shortening
1 egg

Mix and sift dry ingredients; add milk, shortening and beaten egg; beat well and pour into greased shallow pan. Bake in hot oven about 25 minutes.

Plantation Corn Bread

An easy-to-make corn bread, given that old-fashioned sour cream goodness and extra corn flavor by Sperry Pancake and Waffle Flour

1 cup Sperry Pancake and Waffle Flour
1 cup corn meal
2 tablespoons sugar
1/2 teaspoon salt
2 eggs
2/3 cup milk
1/3 cup melted butter

Mix flour, corn meal, sugar and salt together thoroughly. Beat eggs until light, add milk, and add to dry ingredients, mixing until smooth. Blend in melted butter. Pour into well greased 8-inch square pan, and bake 30 minutes in a moderately hot oven, 375 degrees.

Baking Powder Bread

4 cups flour
1 teaspoon salt
1 tablespoon sugar
7 teaspoons baking powder
1 medium-sized, cold boiled potato
Milk (water may be used)

Sift together flour, salt, sugar and baking powder, rub in potato; add sufficient milk to mix smoothly into stiff batter. Turn at once into greased loaf pan, smooth top with knifed dipped in melted butter, and allow to stand in warm place about 30 minutes. Bake in moderate oven about 1 hour. When done take from pan, moisten top with few drops cold water and allow to cool before putting away in bread box.

Corn and Rice Pone

2 cups corn meal
5 teaspoons baking powder
1 teaspoon salt
2-1/4 cups milk
4 tablespoons melted shortening
3 eggs
1 cup boiled rice

Mix and sift dry ingredients; add milk and shortening to beaten eggs; stir into dry mixture; mix in rice and pour into shallow greased pans. Bake in hot oven about 30 minutes.

Boston Brown Bread

1 cup entire wheat or graham flour
1 cup corn meal
1 cup rye meal or ground rolled oats
5 teaspoons baking powder
1 teaspoon salt
3/4 cup molasses
1-1/3 cups milk

Mix thoroughly dry ingredients; add molasses to milk, and add to dry ingredients; beat thoroughly and put into greased moulds 2/3 full. Steam 3-1/2 hours; remove covers and bake until top is dry.

Spider Corn Bread

1 egg
1-3/4 cups milk
1 cup corn meal
1/3 cup flour
2 tablespoons sugar
1 teaspoon salt
2 teaspoons baking powder
1 tablespoon shortening

Beat egg and add one cup milk; stir in corn meal, flour, sugar, salt and baking powder which have been sifted together; turn

into frying pan in which shortening has been melted; pour on remainder of milk but do not stir. Bake about 25 minutes in hot oven. There should be a line of creamy custard through the bread.
Cut into triangles and serve.

Nut and Raisin Bread

1-1/2 cups flour
2 cups graham flour
1/2 cup corn meal
1/2 cup brown sugar
1 teaspoon salt
4 teaspoons baking powder
3/4 cup chopped nuts
1 cup ground raisins
2 cups milk
1/2 cup molasses
1/4 teaspoon soda

Sift dry ingredients together. Add nuts and raisins; add milk and mix well, then add molasses and soda which have been mixed together. Bake in 2 small greased loaf pans in moderate oven about 45 minutes.

Health Bread

4 cups whole-wheat flour
1 teaspoon salt
2 tablespoons baking powder
2 eggs
2 tablespoons honey
1 tablespoon oil
1 pint milk

Sift flour, salt and baking powder together; add beaten eggs, honey and oil to milk and add to dry ingredients, mixing thoroughly. Bake in loaf pan brushed with oil in moderate oven (375 degrees F.) for about 1 hour. If desired, 1 cup raisins can be added to dry ingredients.
Makes 1 large or 2 small loaves.

Quick Bread

2 cups boiling water
1 tablespoon sugar
1-1/2 tablespoons salt
1/2 yeast cake
1/4 cup lukewarm water
6 cups sifted flour
2 tablespoons cooking oil

To 2 cups boiling water add the sugar and salt. When lukewarm add the yeast which has been softened in 1/4 cup lukewarm water. Add to this 3 cups sifted flour and beat until light and full of bubbles. Cover and set in a warm place for about 1-1/2 hours. Add oil to this sponge, then remaining flour to make soft dough. Turn out on floured board and knead for about 10 minutes in order to distribute the yeast well. Cover and allow to rise in a warm place overnight or until double in bulk. Mold lightly into 2 loaves; brush top of each with oil; put into loaf pans brushed well with oil and allow to rise until twice the size. Brush with oil. Bake in hot oven (425° F.) for about 1 hour, reducing the heat the latter part of the baking.

Makes 2 loaves.

Boston Brown Bread #2

1 cup corn meal
1 cup graham meal
1 cup rye meal
2 cups sour milk
1 cup dark molasses
2 teaspoons salt
2 tablespoons cooking oil
2 teaspoons soda
Oil

Stir well together all ingredients but the soda and allow to stand for about 15 or 20 minutes for meal to swell. Add soda and beat well to remove all lumps. Brush mold with oil and fill about 2/3 full. Cover closely and steam 2-1/2 hours. Remove covers and put into oven to bake about 1/2 hour.
Makes 4 small loaves.

Nut Bread #2

2 eggs
1 cup sugar
1 cup milk
2 cups flour
1 teaspoon salt
4 teaspoons baking powder
2 tablespoons butter

2 teaspoons soda
Oil

Stir well together all ingredients but the soda and allow to stand for about 15 or 20 minutes for meal to swell. Add soda and beat well to remove all lumps. Brush mold with oil and fill about 2/3 full. Cover closely and steam 2-1/2 hours. Remove covers and put into oven to bake about 1/2 hour.
Makes 4 small loaves.

Nut Bread #3

2 eggs
1 cup sugar
1 cup milk
2 cups flour
1 teaspoon salt
4 teaspoons baking powder
2 tablespoons butter
1 cup nuts

Beat eggs with sugar. Stir in milk alternately with flour, salt and baking powder sifted together. Add melted butter and chopped nut meats dredged with flour.

Pour onto greased pan. Allow to stand 15 minutes before putting in oven. Bake in moderate oven about 40 minutes.

Soft Corn Spoon Bread

2 cups white cornmeal
1-1/2 teaspoons salt
1 cup boiling water
2 tablespoons melted butter
2 eggs
1 cup cold boiled rice
3 teaspoons baking powder
2 cups milk

Sift meal with salt. Pour over boiling water and beat until lumps disappear. Stir in melted butter. Add eggs, beaten until light, and rice. Stir baking powder into milk and add quickly to mixture.

Pour into well-greased earthen dish or enamel pan and bake 3/4 hour in a hot oven. After the first 15 minutes, cover to keep crust from getting too hard.

Gingerbread

2 cups molasses
3/4 cup butter
2 teaspoons baking soda
1 teaspoon powdered sugar
1/2 teaspoon cinnamon
1/2 grated nutmeg
3 cups flour
1 cup buttermilk or sour milk
1 egg
4 teaspoons baking powder

Bring molasses and butter just to boiling point. Stir in baking soda and spices. Remove from fire and add sifted flour and buttermilk alternately. Add egg, beaten until very light, and baking powder. Put in buttered and warmed small tins or on baking sheet. Bake in quick oven (350° F.) 15 minutes.

Soft Gingerbread

1/2 cup shortening
1/3 cup sugar
1 egg
1/2 cup molasses
1/2 teaspoon soda
1 cup boiling water
2-1/2 cups Flour
3 teaspoons baking powder
1/4 teaspoon salt
1 tablespoon ginger
1 teaspoon cinnamon

Cream the shortening and sugar; add the beaten egg, then the molasses, into which has been dissolved the soda, then the boiling water. Mix and sift the flour, baking powder, salt and spices, and sift into this mixture. Beat, spread in a shallow pan and bake in a moderate oven about 20 minutes.

Soft Gingerbread II

1/2 cup shortening
1/2 cup sugar
2 well-beaten eggs
1 cup molasses
2 cups Flour
2-1/2 teaspoons baking powder
1 tablespoon ginger
1 teaspoon cinnamon
1/2 teaspoon allspice
1/4 teaspoon salt
1/2 cup milk

Cream the shortening and sugar; add the beaten eggs, then the molasses. Sift together the dry ingredients and add, alternately with the milk, to the first mixture. Bake in a shallow pan in a moderate oven.

Coconut Gingerbread

3 cups Blend Flour
1/2 teaspoon soda
1/2 teaspoon salt
3-1/2 teaspoons baking powder
1/2 teaspoon grated nutmeg
1/2 teaspoon allspice
1 teaspoon cinnamon
1 teaspoon ginger
1-1/2 cups shredded coconut
1/2 cup shortening
1/2 cup brown sugar
1/2 cup milk
1 cup molasses
2 eggs

Sift together the flour, soda, salt and spices. Mix in the cocoanut. Melt the shortening and mix with sugar, milk and molasses. Add to the dry ingredients. Beat the yolks of the eggs until thick and lemon colored and add next. Beat thoroughly, then fold in Cream the shortening and sugar; add the beaten eggs, then the molasses. Sift together the dry ingredients and add, alternately with the milk, to the first mixture. Bake in a shallow pan in a moderate oven.

Hasty Gingerbread

No more doubts about gingerbread...this is a recipe for a more delicately flavored gingerbread ...it captures a certain delicious flavor that can't be beat.

1/2 cup sugar
2 eggs
1/16 teaspoon soda
1/4 cup molasses
1-1/2 cups Sperry Pancake and Waffle Flour
1 teaspoon ginger
1 teaspoon cinnamon
1/4 teaspoon cloves
1/2 cup water
1/3 cup melted butter

Beat sugar and eggs until fluffy. Dissolve soda in molasses and blend into egg mixture. Sift pancake and waffle flour, measure and sift twice with spices. Add to first mixture, alternately with water. Add melted butter last. Pour into greased and floured deep 9-inch square pan. Bake in moderately hot oven, 400 degrees, for 35 minutes.
9 servings

Baking Powder Biscuits

2 cups flour
1 teaspoon salt
2 Tablespoons baking powder
2 Tablespoons shortening
1/2 cup milk, or enough to make a stiff dough

Sift flour, salt, sugar and baking powder into a bowl. Cut in shortening. Add milk, a little at a time, to make a stiff dough. Turn out on a floured board. Sprinkle flour over the top if sticky and pat into a circle about 1 inch thick. Cut into rounds with a biscuit cutter dipped in flour. Place in a greased pan; bake in a 400° oven for 15 to 20 minutes. Serve hot with butter and honey. *Note:* For shortcake, bake recipe in a 9-inch pie tin and split into wedges. Top with crushed berries and whipped cream.

7
ROLLS, BISCUITS, MUFFINS & COFFEE CAKES

SWEET ROLLS & BATTERS
RULES FOR MAKING QUICK BREADS

Have all necessary utensils ready and ingredients together before starting work.

Keep ingredients as cold as possible, especially the liquid, and it is advisable to keep the shortening cold for biscuits and pie crust.

Sift flour before measuring. After combining dry ingredients, sift again to distribute the baking powder and seasoning evenly throughout the flour.

All measurements should be level.

For batters, such as muffins, beat the eggs in a bowl and add the liquid, then add gradually to the dry ingredients. Add the melted shortening last. Batters should be beaten only enough to thoroughly mix the ingredients.

In making biscuits, the shortening is cut into the dry ingredients or worked in with the fingers.

Handle dough mixtures as little as possible. Too much rolling and mixing develops gluten and tends to toughen the finished product.

Quick breads are baked at a temperature ranging from 350 to 450° F. They are sufficiently baked when golden brown in color, shrink slightly from the sides of the pan and when no batter clings to a toothpick that has been inserted in the center of the product.

Fine granulated sugar makes a finer-textured crust than coarse granulated sugar. If coarse sugar is used it should be sifted and only the finger particles put in the mixture.

Pastry flour made from the winter wheat makes a lighter, whiter and more tender cake than bread flour made from the spring wheat. If bread flour is substituted, about 2 tablespoons less to a cup should be used, or the cake mixture will be too stiff.

Sift flour before measuring. After combining dry materials, flour, baking powder and spices, sift again.

All baking powders contain soda, acid and cornstarch or flour. They fall into three classes depending on the kind of acid which they contain. They are Tartrate powders, Phosphate powders and Combination powders. The general rule for them is: 2 teaspoons Tartrate or Phosphate baking powders to 2 cup flour, 1 teaspoon Combination baking powders to 1 cup flour. Directions for use are usually given on the can. The proportions in these recipes are for Tartrate or Phosphate baking powders.

Break the eggs carefully and in separating see that no particles of the yolks are dropped in the whites. When yolks and whites of eggs are added separately, beat yolks until thick and lemon colored; fold in last the stiffly beaten whites. Long beating is the only way to make a cake fine-grained.

When fruits and nuts are used, they should be lightly dredged with flour.

Grease the pan in which you are baking with melted shortening and sift a layer of flour over this, then shake off surplus.

ROLLS AND BUNS

Butterhorns

1-1/2 cups sponge
1/2 cup mashed potato
1 cup scalded milk, cooled to lukewarm
1/4 cup melted shortening
1 teaspoon salt
1/4 cup sugar
2 egg yolks
1 egg white
Grated rind of 1/2 lemon
6-1/2 cups Blend Flour
Butter or other shortening additional as directed

Beat the eggs together. Add all ingredients to the sponge, mixing in the flour gradually and beating until too stiff to handle with spoon. Knead quickly and lightly until it no longer sticks to the hands or board. Roll out as thin as possible and spread liberally with softened butter. Fold over 3 or 4 times and roll again to about 1/3 inch thick. Cut off strips about 3/4 inch thick and 6 inch long. Roll up in a long flat roll. Brush over with milk and let rise in a warm place in a well-greased shallow pan until light, or when a slight pressure with the finger leaves an impression. Rub over each with a little beaten egg mixed with a teaspoon of water and bake in a hot oven. While warm, spread over each Powdered Sugar Roll Frosting and sprinkle quickly, before it sets, with nuts run through the fine cutter of a food chopper or minced very fine. Walnuts or peanuts may be used, or a mixture.

Cheese Rolls

1-1/2 cups bread sponge
1 beaten egg
3 tablespoons sugar
1 tablespoon shortening, melted
1 cup milk, scalded and cooled to lukewarm
About 5-1/2 cups Blend Flour
1 cup rich grated cheese (preferably rather dry)

Follow directions exactly as given for Egg Rolls, only when the dough has risen until light, cut down instead of kneading, roll out as thin as possible and sprinkle thickly with the grated cheese. Fold over both ends toward the middle, making 3 folds. Roll out to about 1/3" thick, cut in strips as for Egg Rolls and proceed as for Egg Rolls.

Meat Turnovers

One of the most delicious and economical ways to use small amounts of leftover meat, chicken or fish is by serving them in turnovers. Turnovers are made of a rich baking powder biscuit or unsweetened shortcake dough, rolled thinner than for biscuits, cut in squares, with a spoonful of well-seasoned meat or chicken moistened with thickened gravy, or fish with cream sauce just sufficient to hold it together, placed on one half, with the other half fold over to form a triangle. Pinch edges together, rub over with milk and bake in a hot oven for about 15 to 18 minutes. Made with Blend Flour, these are good either hot or cold, and especially satisfying to take on picnics, or to pack in the lunch box.

Baking Powder Biscuits (Crescents)

Follow this exceptionally good recipe.

1/2 cake yeast
1/2 cup lukewarm water
1 cup milk, scalded and cooled to lukewarm
1 teaspoon salt
1/4 cup sugar
1 beaten egg
1/4 teaspoon vanilla or almond
5 cups Blend Flour
2 tablespoons melted shortening
Melted butter
Milk

Dissolve yeast in lukewarm water, add lukewarm milk and balance of ingredients, adding flour gradually and beating well. Knead quickly and lightly and rub over with melted shortening. Set in warm place, covered, to rise until light. Knead again lightly, then roll as thin as possible and brush all over with melted butter. Fold in 3 folds, roll again and cut in strips about 1/2" wide by 5" long. Fold both ends up to lap at the middle for extra thickness at middle, then pull out a little longer and twist. Form into crescents, brush over with melted shortening and place in greased pans. Let rise until light. Then rub over with milk and bake in a hot oven. Another method of forming the rolls into crescents is to cut, after rolling the second time, into 4" squares and dividing each square diagonally through the center, forming 2 triangles, each triangle to make a roll. Begin rolling at the two ends, keeping the point of the triangle in the center to form extra thickness, then form into crescent.

Hot Cross Buns

3-1/2 cups bread sponge
2 teaspoons salt additional
1/2 cup sugar
1/3 cup melted shortening
1 cup scalded milk, cooled to lukewarm
9 cups Blend Flour
Softened shortening, milk or water
Melted butter
Powdered sugar, sifted
Hot water
Vanilla

Into the light bread sponge mix the additional salt, sugar, melted shortening and milk. Add gradually the flour, beating until too stiff to beat, then knead quickly and lightly until it does not stick to the hands or board. Set to rise in a greased bowl. Rub softened shortening over the top or brush over with milk or water to prevent a crust forming. Cover, set in a warm place to rise until light. It is ready when it feels light and delicate when touched, and a pressure made with the finger remains. Place on a floured board, cut down or knead lightly, then roll. Cut off small pieces of the dough, form into round rolls. Brush over with melted shortening, arrange in a well-greased shallow pan and set in a warm place, covered lightly, to rise until a slight pressure made with the finger remains. When ready to bake, cut a cross in the top of each, brush all over with milk and bake in a rather hot oven. Brush over with butter just before removing from the fire. Have ready a mixture of sifted powdered sugar mixed with enough hot water to spread and flavored with vanilla. Brush over the warm rolls through the cross with this frosting.

Hot Cross Buns with Mashed Potato

Use foregoing recipe, only add 1 cup of warm mashed potato and add a trifle more flour and 1/4 teaspoon more of salt unless the potatoes have been salted.

Currant Buns (with or without Potato)

1 cup bread sponge (see Sponge recipe)
1 beaten egg
3 tablespoons sugar
2 tablespoons melted shortening
1 cup mashed potato if desired
1 cup scalded milk, cooled to lukewarm
1 teaspoon salt, if no potato; or 1-1/4 with potato
4-1/2 cups flour (without potato); about 5 cups if potato be used
1 cup currants or seedless raisins
Powdered sugar, sifted
Hot water
Vanilla

Mix together first 8 ingredients, adding flour gradually and beating it until too stiff, then knead lightly and quickly until it no longer sticks. Set in a greased bowl in a warm place, covered, to rise until light (see General Directions under Breads). Then knead lightly or cut down. Work into the dough a cup of currants or seedless raisins. Form into buns, rub over with melted shortening, place in greased pans to rise in a warm place until light, or when a slight pressure made with the finger leaves an impression. Bake in a rather hot oven. When done, rub over with frosting made of powdered sugar mixed with just enough hot water to spread, and flavored with vanilla.

Egg Rolls

1 cup bread sponge
1 teaspoon salt additional
2 beaten eggs
3 tablespoons sugar
2 tablespoons melted shortening
1 cup milk, scalded and cooled to lukewarm
5-1/4 cups Blend Flour (this includes amount necessary for kneading)
Melted shortening or evaporated milk
Butter

Mix first 7 ingredients together, adding the flour gradually, beating it until too stiff, then kneading it quickly and lightly until it does not stick. (See Directions for Kneading under Breads.) Put in a well-greased bowl and set in a warm place, covered, to rise until light, then knead lightly again, roll out to about 1/3" thick. Cut into strips about 3/4" wide by 3" long, form into finger rolls, rub over with melted shortening or evaporated milk and place in greased shallow pans about 1/2" apart. Let rise until a slight pressure of the finger leaves a dent. Bake in a hot oven. It will require about 15 minutes. Brush over with butter before removing from the oven.

Fancy Tea Rings

1 cup bread sponge
1 teaspoon salt
1/4 cup sugar
1 beaten egg
3 tablespoons shortening
1 cup milk, scalded and cooled to lukewarm
1/2 teaspoon vanilla
1/2 teaspoon almond extract
5-1/4 cups Blend Flour
Milk
1/2 cup or more of chopped peanuts or, if preferred, use currants
1/4 cup sugar additional
1/2 teaspoon cinnamon
Butter
Yolk of 1 egg
1 teaspoon water
Additional sugar and cinnamon

Add salt, sugar, egg, shortening, milk, flavoring and flour to the sponge, and knead lightly and quickly. Brush over with milk to prevent crust forming and let rise until light. Then knead lightly and roll as thin as possible. Spread over with currants or nuts mixed with sugar and cinnamon and form into a long roll similar to jelly roll. Cut into 3 pieces for 3 rolls about the size of a dinner plate, or cut into 2 dozen individual rolls. From each end of every roll, cut off a small triangular slice, leaving slanting edges. Form each roll into a twist, then bring the two ends together to form a ring and fasten the shorter ends together. This leaves an open triangle. With the scissors, cut at intervals of every 2" from the outside of the roll, almost through to the inner edge but not quite. With the fingers, form these sections into twisted points. Rub over all with butter and place in buttered greased pans and let rise until light, then brush all over with the yolk of an egg beaten with a teaspoon of water and sprinkle with sugar and cinnamon. Bake in a moderately hot oven. If preferred, this may be decorated with Frosting for Rolls when partly cooled.

Parker House Rolls (from Bread Dough)

Reserve a part of the dough from the regular baking. After the final kneading, cut out to about 1/2 inch thick. Cut with a small biscuit cutter. Across the center of each make an impression with the back of a knife dipped in flour. Brush over one half with melted butter, fold over the other half (like a pocket-book), brush over the top with butter, place in a shallow greased tin about 2 inches apart, cover, set in a warm place and let rise until light. Bake in a quick oven for about 25 minutes.

Parker House Rolls II

4 cups Blend Flour
1 tablespoon sugar
1 teaspoon salt
2 tablespoons butter
1 pint boiling milk
1 cake compressed yeast
1/4 cup warm water

Put flour in bread bowl, make a well in the middle, into which put salt, sugar, butter and hot milk. Let stand without stirring until lukewarm, then add the yeast dissolved in 1/4 cup of warm water; stir all together to make a soft batter, still leaving a little flour around edges; cover closely and set to rise. When very light, mix in the rest of the flour in the bowl, together with enough more to make a soft dough; knead well and set to rise again. If there is time after the second rising to cut down with a knife a few times, the rolls will be much more delicate.

Refrigerator Rolls

1 cup milk, scalded
1/4 cup sugar
1 teaspoon salt
1/3 cup shortening or vegetable oil
2 packages dry yeast
1/2 cup lukewarm water
2 eggs, beaten
5 cups sifted flour (about)

Scald milk. Add sugar, salt, shortening or oil. Stir until dissolved. Cool to lukewarm. Dissolve yeast in lukewarm water; add to milk mixture. Add eggs. Gradually add flour; mix to a smooth, soft dough. Knead on a lightly floured board until smooth and satiny. Shape into a ball and place in a greased bowl; cover with a cloth. Let rise in a warm place until doubled in bulk. (If it is not to be used immediately, dough can be set in refrigerator until needed; then let it rise until doubled in bulk.) Shape into rounds or crescents. Cover. Let rise until doubled in bulk. Bake in a 425° oven for 15 to 20 minutes. Makes 2-1/2 dozen.

Pineapple Rolls

Especially appropriate for afternoon tea or luncheons, but delicious for any time.

1 cake yeast
1/2 cup lukewarm water
1 cup milk, scalded and cooled to lukewarm
1-1/4 teaspoon salt
1/3 cup sugar
3 tablespoons melted shortening
1 beaten egg
5-1/4 cups Blend Flour
Melted fat
Drained, sliced pineapple

Dissolve yeast in the warm water, add lukewarm milk, salt, sugar, melted shortening and beaten egg. Mix well, then fold in the Blend Flour. Turn out on a floured board, and either knead quickly and lightly, or follow method for bread and rolls in "Walker's Easy Bread Making Booklet," which will be sent upon request. Place in greased bowl, rub over top with melted fat, cover with cloth and let rise until light, or until a rather firm pressure with the finger leaves an impression (about double in size). Turn out on floured board and knead again, or fold according to Walker directions. Place back in bowl to rise again until double in size. Then turn out, knead quickly and lightly and form into Parker House rolls with a piece of pineapple folded in each roll. Arrange in greased pans 1/2 inch apart, brush over tops with melted fat and let rise until light, or until a pressure with the finger leaves an imprint. Bake in a hot oven (500°F.) 12 or 15 minutes.

Old Fashioned Sausage Biscuit

1/2 pound well-seasoned pork sausage meat
2 cups Blend Flour
4 teaspoons baking powder
1/2 teaspoon salt
1 tablespoon shortening
2/3 cup milk
Additional milk

Form the sausage meat into thin cakes and brown on both sides in a hot skillet until almost done. Drain off the fat. Prepare biscuits by sifting together the flour, baking powder and salt; cut in shortening, and mix in lightly the milk. Roll on floured board thinner than for ordinary biscuits, about 1/4 inch to 1/3 inch thick. Put piece of sausage between two biscuits, press lightly together and rub over tops with milk. Bake in a hot oven for about 12 to 15 minutes.

Orange Tea Biscuit

2 cups Blend Flour
4 teaspoons baking powder
1/3 teaspoon salt
1/4 cup sugar
Grated rind of 1 orange

1/3 cup shortening
2/3 cups milk
Melted butter
Orange marmalade
Sugar

Mix and sift flour, baking powder, salt and sugar. Add grated rind. Work in shortening lightly between hands, then add milk. Roll on a floured board to 1/4 inch thick. Spread lightly with melted butter. Over one half of dough spread orange marmalade. Fold over the other half and cut with very small biscuit cutter. Sprinkle tops with sugar and place in greased shallow pan. Bake in a hot oven or preheat oven to 550°F for 10 minutes and bake from 8 to 10 minutes according to size. These are delicious served hot or cold for afternoon tea or luncheon, with any salad; or with creamed chicken, creamed fish, etc. Serve without butter.

Tea Biscuits and Variations

2 cups Special Cake Flour
1 teaspoon salt
3 teaspoons baking powder
4 tablespoons shortening
2/3 cup milk

Sift the flour once before measuring. Sift the flour, salt and baking powder together. Cut in shortening with pastry blender or 2 knives. Add the milk to make a soft dough. Roll out, cut with biscuit cutter, and bake 8 minutes in a 475-degree hot oven.
Makes 15 biscuits.

Biscuit Variations:

Cheese Biscuits

To the dry ingredients add 1/4 cup grated cheese and bake mixture as directed.

Butterscotch Biscuits

Make the above recipe and roll out to 1/4 inch thickness. Spread the surface with 2 tablespoons melted butter and 1/4 cup brown sugar. Roll up like a jelly roll and cut into 1/2 inch pieces. Place cut side down in a pan which has been spread with 2 tablespoons butter and sprinkled with 1/2 cup brown sugar, and bake.

Sour Milk or Buttermilk Biscuits

Substitute sour milk or buttermilk for sweet milk in the above recipe. Add 1/4 teaspoon soda and reduce the baking powder to 2 teaspoons, and bake as directed.

Traditional Sweet Roll Dough

2 packages active dry yeast
1/2 cup warm water (105 to 115°)
1/2 cup milk, scalded then cooled to lukewarm
1/2 cup sugar
1 teaspoon salt
2 eggs
1/2 cup shortening or butter or margarine, softened
4-1/2 to 5 cups flour (if using self-rising flour, omit salt)

Dissolve yeast in warm water. Stir in milk, sugar, salt, eggs, shortening and 2-1/2 cups of the flour. Beat until smooth. Mix in enough remaining flour to make dough easy to handle.

Turn dough onto lightly floured board; knead until smooth and elastic, about 5 minutes. Place in greased bowl; turn greased side up. (At this point, dough can be refrigerated 3 to 4 days.) Cover; let rise in warm place until double, about 1-1/2 hours. (Dough is ready if impression remains when touched.)

Punch down dough. Shape dough into desired rolls and coffee cakes (at right and through page 77). Cover; let rise until double, about 30 minutes.

Heat oven to 375°F. Bake as directed.

Quick Buttermilk Sweet Dough

2 packages active dry yeast
1/2 cup warm water (105 to 115°)
1-1/4 cups buttermilk
2 eggs
5-1/2 to 6 cups flour
1/2 cup butter or margarine, softened
1/2 cup sugar
2 teaspoons baking powder
2 teaspoons salt

In large mixer bowl, dissolve yeast in warm water. Add buttermilk, eggs, 2-1/2 cups of the flour, the butter, sugar, baking powder and salt. Blend 1/2 minute on low speed, scraping bowl constantly. Beat 2 minutes medium speed, scraping bowl occasionally. Stir in enough remaining flour to make dough easy to handle. (Dough should remain soft and slightly sticky.)

Turn dough onto well-floured board; knead 5 minutes or about 200 turns. Shape dough immediately (no need to let rise) into desired rolls and coffee cakes (below and through page 77). Cover; let rise in warm place until double, about 1 hour. (Dough is ready if impression remains when touched.)
Heat oven to 375°F. Bake as directed.

Frosted Orange Rolls

3 tablespoons butter or margarine, softened
1 tablespoon grated orange peel
2 tablespoons orange juice
1-1/2 cups confectioners' sugar
1/2 recipe Traditional Sweet Roll Dough (above) or 1/2 recipe Quick Buttermilk Sweet Dough (above)

Beat butter, orange peel, juice and confectioners' sugar until creamy and smooth.

Roll dough into rectangle, 12x7 inches; spread with half the orange filling. Roll up, beginning at wide side. Pinch edge of dough into roll to seal well. Stretch roll to make even.

Cut roll into 12 slices. Place slightly apart in greased round layer pan, 9x1-1/2 inches. Let rise until double. Bake 25 to 30 minutes. While warm, frost with remaining filling.
12 rolls.

Rusks

2-1/4 cups flour
1/2 teaspoon salt
2 tablespoons maple or brown sugar
4 teaspoons baking powder
1/4 teaspoon nutmeg
3/4 teaspoon cinnamon
1 egg
2 tablespoons shortening
1/3 to 2/3 cup water
Milk
Maple or brown sugar

Sift together flour, salt, sugar, baking powder, nutmeg and cinnamon; add beaten egg and melted shortening to water and add. Mix well and turn out on floured board. Divide into small pieces; with floured hands shape into rolls; place on greased shallow pan close together; allow to stand 10 to 15 minutes before baking; brush with milk and sprinkle with a little maple or brown sugar. Bake in moderate oven 20 to 30 minutes.

For hot cross buns, with sharp knife make deep cross cuts on top each; brush with butter, sprinkle with sugar and bake.

Philadelphia Cinnamon Buns

1 cup sugar
4-1/2 cups flour
2 teaspoons salt
8 teaspoons baking powder
4 tablespoons shortening
2 eggs
1 cup water
Melted butter
4 teaspoons cinnamon
8 tablespoons seeded raisins
4 teaspoons shortening
4 tablespoons brown sugar

Sift 4 tablespoons of measured sugar with flour, salt and baking powder; rub shortening in very lightly. Add beaten eggs to water and add slowly to dry ingredients to make soft dough. Roll out 1/4 inch thick on floured board; brush with melted butter, sprinkle with sugar, cinnamon and raisins. Roll as for jelly roll. Have prepared 4 tablespoons shortening creamed well with 4 tablespoons brown sugar. Spread this mixture on the bottom and sides of iron baking pan, or if this cannot be obtained, an iron skillet will do. Cut dough into 2-inch pieces and place with cut edges up on pan. Allow to stand 15 minutes and bake in hot oven 25 minutes. Remove from pan at once, turning upside down to serve.

Luncheon or Sandwich Rolls

4 cups flour
1 teaspoon salt
6 teaspoons baking powder
1 tablespoon shortening
1-1/2 cups milk
Milk
Melted butter

Sift together flour, salt and baking powder; rub in shortening; add milk, and mix with spoon to smooth dough easy to handle on floured board. Turn out dough; knead quickly a few times to impart smoothness; divide into small pieces; form each by hand into short, rather thick tapering rolls; place on greased pans and allow to stand in warm place 15 to 20 minutes; brush with milk. Bake in very hot oven. When almost baked, brush again with melted butter. Bake 10 minutes longer and serve hot. If a glazed finish is desired, before taking from oven brush with yolk of egg which has been mixed with a little water. These rolls make excellent sandwiches, using for fillings either lettuce and mayonnaise, sliced or chopped ham, chopped seasoned cucumbers, egg and mayonnaise with very little chopped onion and parsley, or other filling desired.

Rye Rolls

1 cup flour
3 cups rye flour
1 teaspoon salt
6 teaspoons baking powder
1-1/2 cups milk
1 tablespoon shortening

Sift together dry ingredients; add milk and melted shortening. Knead on floured board; shape into rolls. Put into greased pans and allow to stand in warm place 20 minutes. Bake in hot oven 25 to 30 minutes.

Potato Rolls

4 cups flour
1 teaspoon salt
1 tablespoon sugar
7 tablespoons baking powder
2 medium-sized cold, boiled potatoes
Water or milk
Melted shortening

Sift thoroughly together flour, salt, sugar and baking powder; rub in potatoes or add after putting through ricer; add sufficient liquid to mix smoothly into soft dough. This will require about 1-1/2 cups. Divide into small pieces; knead each and shape into small rolls; place on greased pan and brush with melted shortening and allow to stand in warm place 15 to 20 minutes. Bake in hot oven and when nearly done, brush again with melted shortening.

Nut and Raisin Rolls

2-1/2 cups flour
4 teaspoons baking powder
1/2 teaspoon salt
1 tablespoon sugar
5 tablespoons shortening
1 egg
2/3 cup milk
Butter
Raisins
Chopped nuts
1/2 cup sugar
Egg yolk
Cold water

Sift flour, baking powder, salt and sugar together. Add melted shortening and beaten egg to milk and add to dry ingredients, mixing well. Turn out on floured board and knead lightly. Roll out very thin. Spread with butter and sprinkle with raisins, chopped nuts and small amount of granulated sugar. Cut into about 4-inch squares. Roll up each as for jelly roll. Press edges together. Brush over with yolk of egg mixed with a little cold water and sprinkle with nuts and sugar, and allow to stand in greased pan about 15 minutes. Bake in moderate oven from 20 to 25 minutes.

Butterfly Rolls

1/2 recipe Traditional Sweet Roll Dough or 1/2 recipe Quick Buttermilk Sweet Dough
Butter or margarine, melted
1/2 cup sugar
1 teaspoon cinnamon
1/3 cup flour
2 tablespoons sugar
2 tablespoons butter or margarine
1-1/2 teaspoons cinnamon
Sweet Icing (below)

Roll dough into rectangle, 18x9 inches. Brush with melted butter. Mix 1/2 cup sugar and 1 teaspoon cinnamon; sprinkle evenly over rectangle. Roll up, beginning at wide side. Pinch edge of dough into roll to seal well. Stretch roll to make even. Cut into 1-inch slices. Place pencil in center of each slice parallel to cut sides; press almost through dough. Invert and turn cut surfaces up. Place on greased baking sheet.

Rub together flour, 2 tablespoons sugar, 2 tablespoons butter and cinnamon until crumbly; sprinkle over rolls. Let rise until double.

Bake about 12 minutes. Drizzle rolls with icing.

1-1/2 dozen rolls.

Sweet Icing

Mix 1 cup confectioners' sugar, 1 tablespoon milk and 1/2 teaspoon vanilla until smooth.

Cheese Diamonds

1 package (8 ounces) cream cheese, softened
1/4 cup sugar
3 tablespoons flour
1 egg yolk
1/2 teaspoon grated lemon peel
1 tablespoon lemon juice
1/2 recipe Traditional Sweet Roll Dough or 1/2 recipe Quick Buttermilk Sweet Dough
1/2 cup jam
Chopped nuts

Beat cream cheese and sugar until light and fluffy. Stir in flour, egg yolk, lemon peel and juice.
Roll dough into 15-inch square. Cut into 25-3-inch squares. Place on greased baking sheets. Place 1 tablespoon cheese mixture in center of each square. Bring two diagonally opposite corners to center of each square, overlapping slightly; pinch to seal. Let rise until double.
Bake 12 to 15 minutes. Heat jam until melted; brush lightly over hot rolls and sprinkle with chopped nuts.
25 rolls.

Graham Gems

1 cup flour
1 teaspoon salt
4 teaspoons baking powder
2 tablespoons sugar
1 cup graham flour
1 cup milk
1 egg
3 tablespoons cooking oil

Sift flour, salt, baking powder and sugar together. Mix with graham flour; add milk, beaten egg and oil. Bake in gem pans brushed with oil in hot oven (400 ° F.) about 25 minutes. Makes 12 gems.

Cinnamon Rolls

1/2 recipe Traditional Sweet Roll Dough (above) or 1/2 recipe Quick Buttermilk Sweet Dough
2 tablespoons butter or margarine, softened
1/4 cup sugar
2 teaspoons cinnamon
Sweet Icing

Roll dough into rectangle, 15x9 inches; spread with butter. Mix sugar and cinnamon; sprinkle over rectangle. Roll up, beginning at wide side. Pinch edge of dough into roll to seal well. Stretch roll to make even.

Cut roll into 15 slices. Place slightly apart in greaseed baking pan, 13x9x2 inches, or in greased muffin cups. Let rise until double. Bake 25 to 30 minutes. While warm, frost rolls with icing. Makes 15 rolls.

Variation:

Butterscotch-Pecan Rolls

Before rolling dough into rectangle, melt 1/2 cup butter or margarine in baking pan; sprinkle 1/2 cup brown sugar (packed) and 1/2 cup pecan halves over butter. Roll, slice and bake as directed. Immediately turn pan upside down on large tray. Let pan remain a minute so butterscotch drizzles down over rolls.

Chocolate Cinnamon Rolls

Traditional Sweet Roll Dough or Quick Buttermilk Sweet Dough
2/3 cup cocoa
4 tablespoons butter or margarine, softened
1/2 cup sugar
1 tablespoon cinnamon
Icing (below)

Prepare dough as directed except—mix in cocoa with the first addition of flour.

Divide dough in half. Roll each half into rectangle, 15x9 inches. Spread each with 2 tablespoons butter. Mix sugar and cinnamon; sprinkle half the mixture over each rectangle. Roll up, beginning at wide side. Pinch edge of dough into roll to seal well. Stretch roll to make even.

Cut each roll into 15 slices. Place slightly apart in 2 greased baking pans, 13x9x2 inches, or in greased muffin cups. Let rise until double.

Bake 25 to 30 minutes. While warm, frost rolls with Icing.
2-1/2 dozen rolls.

Icing:

Mix 1-1/2 cups confectioners' sugar, 1 tablespoon milk and 1/2 teaspoon vanilla until smooth.

Caramel Muffins

Nearly every member of the family likes muffins . . . but these caramel muffins really melt in your mouth and leave a flavor that's completely satisfying . . . so delicious!

2 cups Sperry Pancake and Waffle Flour
1/4 teaspoon ginger or nutmeg
3 tablespoons shortening
1 cup milk
1/4 cup brown sugar
2 tablespoons butter, melted

Stir flour in package before measuring. Measure flour, sift with ginger or nutmeg, and cut in shortening. Add milk and stir until well blended. Place in greased muffin tins; sprinkle tops with brown sugar and butter. Bake in very hot oven, 450°F, for 15 minutes. Makes 16 small muffins.

Cinnamon Buns

1-1/4 cups milk
1 yeast cake
1/4 cup sugar
2 teaspoons salt
Flour—about 5 cups
1 egg
1/4 cup cooking oil
1/2 cup brown sugar
4 teaspoons cinnamon
6 tablespoons seedless raisins

Scald the milk. Allow yeast cake to stand in 1/4 cup of milk which has been allowed to cool to lukewarm temperature. Add the sugar and salt to remainder of milk and when lukewarm, add the yeast mixture. Add 1-1/4 cups sifted flour. Beat well; cover and allow to rise until light and full of bubbles. Add beaten egg, oil and sufficient more flour to knead. Knead well on floured board. Then put into bowl; cover and allow to rise until double in bulk.

Roll out dough 1/2 inch thick; brush with oil; sprinkle with brown sugar, cinnamon and raisins. Roll up as for jelly roll and cut into 1-inch pieces. Have prepared 5 tablespoons butter creamed well with 5 tablespoons brown sugar. Spread this thickly over bottom and sides of iron baking pan or iron skillet. Place pieces rather close together with cut sides down on pan. Cover and allow to rise until double in size. Bake in a hot oven (400 to 425° F.) for about 25 minutes. Remove from pan at once; invert and serve.

Makes 12 or 18 small buns.

Parker House Rolls III

1 yeast cake
1-1/4 cups milk, scalded and cooled
3-3/4 cups flour
2 teaspoons salt
1 tablespoon sugar
1/4 cup cooking oil
1 egg
Oil

Soften the yeast in 1/4 cup milk after it has been cooled to lukewarm temperature; then add remainder of milk to 2 cups flour; when cool add the yeast mixture and beat until smooth; cover and allow to rise until very light and bubbles appear—about 40 minutes to 1 hour. Then add all at once salt, sugar, oil and unbeaten egg and mix until smooth batter. Add the remaining 1-3/4 cups flour and turn out on floured board; knead well; return to bowl and cover and allow to rise in warm place.

When double in bulk turn out on slightly floured board; roll out to 1/2 inch in thickness; cut with biscuit cutter; crease across top of each a little less than half; brush small side with oil; fold large side well over the small. Put into pan brushed with oil; allow to rise in a warm place until double in size and bake in hot oven (400 to 425° F.) for about 20 minutes. These rolls twill take from 5 to 6 hours and the recipe makes 14 large or 24 small rolls.

Quick Luncheon Rolls

4 cups flour
2 teaspoons salt
6 teaspoons baking powder
2 tablespoons cooking oil
1-1/2 cups milk
Oil

Sift together flour, salt and baking powder; float oil on milk and add, mixing with spoon to smooth dough easy to handle on floured board. Knead quickly a few times to impart smoothness; divide into small pieces; form each into short, rather thick tapering rolls; place on pans brushed with oil and allow to stand in warm place 15 to 20 minutes; brush with oil. Bake in hot oven (450 to 475° F.). When almost baked brush again with oil. Bake 10 minutes longer and serve hot. Makes 18 rolls.

Biscuits

2 cups flour
4 teaspoons baking powder
1 teaspoon salt
3 tablespoons cooking oil
3/4 cup milk or half milk and half water
Oil

Sift together flour, baking powder and salt; add oil and mix in lightly with steel fork; add liquid slowly; roll or pat out on floured board to about 1/2 inch in thickness, handling as little as possible. Cut with biscuit cutter and bake on pan brushed with oil in hot oven (475° F.) 10 to 15 minutes. Makes 12 biscuits.

Muffins

2 cups flour
3 teaspoons baking powder
1 tablespoon sugar
1 teaspoon salt
1 cup milk
2 eggs
2 tablespoons cooking oil
Oil

Sift together flour, baking powder, sugar and salt; add milk, well-beaten eggs and oil; mix well. Half fill muffin tins brushed well with oil and bake in hot oven (400° F.) 20 to 25 minutes. Makes 12 muffins.

Popovers

2 cups flour
1/2 teaspoon baking powder
1 teaspoon salt
2 eggs
2 cups milk
2 tablespoons cooking oil
Oil

Sift together flour, baking powder and salt. Make a well in flour, break eggs into well; add milk and oil and stir until smooth. Pour into gem pans brushed with oil and put into slow oven (350° F.) for 20 minutes; increase heat to 450° for 10 minutes; reduce heat and allow to dry out for about 10 minutes. Makes 12 popovers.

Molasses Gems from Grandma Broman

2-1/4 cups flour
1 cup sugar
1/2 cup molasses
1 cup sour milk
1 teaspoon soda
2 tablespoons drippings (lard)
Oil

Mix well and bake in gem pans brushed with oil and put into slow oven (350° F.) for 20 minutes; increase heat to 450° for 10 minutes.

5-Minute Coffee Cake

An easier way to making an old favorite . . . this is coffee cake at its best . . . it's quickly made with Sperry Pancake and Waffle Flour . . . only 5 minutes from package to oven.

1 cup Sperry Pancake and Waffle Flour
1/3 cup sugar
1 egg
1/3 cup milk
1/4 cup melted butter

Stir flour in package before measuring. Mix all ingredients together thoroughly, adding melted butter last. Sprinkle with the following topping and bake in a moderately hot oven, 375°, for 20 minutes. Serve warm.
8 servings.

Coffee Cake Topping

1/4 cup brown sugar
1/4 cup flour
1/4 teaspoon cinnamon
2 tablespoons soft butter

Mix all together. The topping should be crumbly in appearance. If a richer topping is desired, 1/4 cup chopped nuts may be added.

Doughnuts

3 tablespoons Crisco
1 cup sugar
2 eggs
1 cup milk
5 to 6 cups flour
4 teaspoons baking powder
1 teaspoon salt
1/4 teaspoon cinnamon
1/4 teaspoon nutmeg

Cream Crisco with half the sugar. Beat the egg with the other half. Combine the two mixtures and stir in the milk and the sifted dry ingredients. Roll out a portion at a time on a well-floured board. Shape with a doughnut cutter and drop into deep Crisco. Turn doughnut as soon as it rises to the surface. Fry until nicely browned on both sides. Drain on paper and sugar when cool.

Doughnut Drops

2 cups sifted flour
1/3 cup sugar
3 teaspoons baking powder
1/2 teaspoon salt
1 teaspoon nutmeg
1 egg, slightly beaten
3/4 cup milk
3 Tablespoons vegetable oil
Oil for frying
Confectioners' sugar or cinnamon and sugar mixture

Sift together dry ingredients. Add egg, milk and oil; stir until smooth. Heat 1 inch oil to 365°. Drop dough by teaspoons into hot oil. Turn after a few seconds and fry until browned on both sides, turning once more. Remove with slotted spoon. Drain on paper towels over a pan. Roll in sugar and serve warm. Makes about 3 dozen.

Cornmeal Muffins

3/4 cup cornmeal
1 cup flour
2 teaspoons baking powder
1 tablespoon sugar
1/2 teaspoon salt
1 egg
3/4 cup milk
1 tablespoon melted Crisco

Combine dry ingredients. Stir in beaten egg, milk and melted Crisco. Drop into well-greased muffin tins. Bake in a hot oven (370 to 400° F.) until brown.

Cream Puffs

3/4 cup water
1/3 cup butter or margarine
3/4 cup flour
1/8 teaspoon salt
3 eggs

In a small saucepan combine water and butter and bring to a boil over medium heat. Remove from heat and beat in flour and salt, all at once. Over low heat, stir until mixture forms a ball and leaves the sides of the pan. Remove from heat. Add eggs all at once. Beat until smooth and satiny looking. Place dough by large spoonfuls on an ungreased cookie sheet. Bake in a 400° oven for 40 minutes without opening door. Remove from oven and cool in a draft-free place. To serve, cut tops from puffs and take out doughy substance in the middle of each puff and discard. Fill puff with cold vanilla pudding or ice cream. Place tops back on. Can be frosted with chocolate frosting.

A. HOT BISCUITS, MUFFINS, GEMS & COFFEE CAKES

Bake hot biscuits, muffins, gems and coffee cakes in a hot oven, placing on a rack above the center of the oven. Use shallow pans for biscuits and fill gem or muffin tins two-thirds full. If gas is used, preheat the oven with full flame for 5 minutes and if a heat regulator is used, adjust to 450°F.

Cooking oil can be used most satisfactorily in breads, biscuits, rolls, muffins and other quick breads. When using it in biscuits and rolls, add to the dry ingredients and mix it in like any solid fat, either mashing in with a fork or cutting in with a knife. Both methods are satisfactory. Cooking oil is a great time saver, as it is all ready for us, while solid fat have to be creamed or melted before adding. It is also more economical than solid fats, for it is a liquid and thus avoids the waste in melting and measuring.

Cooking oil contains no salt, so if used instead of salted shortening increase the salt in proportion of one teaspoon salt to each cup of oil used.

Following are a few delicious recipes but you can take any of these, as well as your old favorites, and use the same amount of oil as butter, lard or other shortening called for.

Biscuits

Of all foods for breakfast, nothing is so appetizing and satisfying as light, flaky, hot Baking Powder Biscuits, with a crisp, brown crust, just from the oven, broken apart and spread with butter, honey, jam or marmalade.

2 cups flour
4 teaspoons baking powder
1/2 teaspoon salt
2 tablespoons shortening
3/4 cup milk, or half milk and half water

Sift together flour, baking powder and salt, add shortening and rub in very lightly; add liquid slowly; roll or part out with hands on floured board to about 1 inch in thickness (handle as little as possible); cut with biscuit cutter. Bake in hot oven 15 to 20 minutes.

Emergency or Drop Biscuits

Same as recipe for Biscuits, with the addition of more milk to make stiff batter. Drop by spoonfuls on greased pan or in muffin tins and bake in hot oven.

Soda Biscuits

1 teaspoon salt
1/2 teaspoon soda
2 cups flour
3 tablespoons shortening
1 cup thick sour milk or buttermilk

Sift together salt, soda and flour. Work in shortening. Add milk gradually, mixing to a stiff dough. It may not be necessary to use all the milk. Place on a floured board. Knead until smooth. Roll to 1/2 inch in thickness. Cut with a small round cutter and bake in a hot oven 12 to 15 minutes.

Whole Wheat or Health Biscuits

2 cups whole wheat flour
3/4 teaspoon salt
4 teaspoons baking powder
2 teaspoons shortening
4 tablespoons cut raisins
1 cup milk

Mix flour, salt and baking powder well or sift through coarse strainer; rub shortening in lightly; add raisins and milk and mix to soft dough. Drop with tablespoon quite far apart on greased baking tin or in muffin tins. Bake in moderate oven about 25 minutes.

Bran Biscuits

1/2 cup bran
1-1/2 cups flour
5 teaspoons baking powder
3/4 teaspoon salt
3 tablespoons sugar
1/2 cup water
2 tablespoons melted shortening

Mix thoroughly bran, flour, baking powder, salt, sugar; add sufficient water to make soft dough; add shortening; roll on floured board to about 1/4 inch thick; cut with biscuit cutter. Bake in hot oven 12 to 15 minutes.

Cheese Biscuits

1-1/2 cups flour
2 teaspoons baking powder
1/4 teaspoon salt
6 tablespoons grated cheese
2/3 cup milk

Sift together flour, baking powder and salt; add cheese, mix in lightly; add milk slowly, just enough to hold dough together. Roll out on floured board about 1/2 inch thick; cut with biscuit cutter. Bake in hot oven 12 to 15 minutes.

20-Minute Cheese Biscuits

1 cup flour
2 teaspoons baking powder
1/2 teaspoon salt
1 tablespoon Crisco
1/2 cup milk*
1/2 cup grated cheese

Sift dry ingredients. Work in Crisco. Add liquid gradually and lastly the cheese, working in with a fork. Roll out to 1/2 inch thick. Cut with small round cutter. Bake in groups of 3 (like a clover leaf) in a hot oven (375° F.) until well browned on top.

* You may substitute 1/2 cup thick sour milk beaten smooth with 1/4 teaspoon soda. It is preferable.

Baking Powder Biscuits

2 cups flour
1 teaspoon salt
4 teaspoons baking powder
5 tablespoons Crisco
1 cup milk or water

Sift together the dry ingredients. Work in Crisco. Stir in liquid gradually. Roll out on floured board to 1 inch thick. Cut into shapes. Place close together on a greased pan and bake in a hot oven (400 to 450° F.) until browned on top.

Salad Rolls

Use about 1/2 cup less milk and add 1 egg to Baking Powder Biscuit dough. Roll as usual, but cut into oblong pieces. Make a deep crease down the center of each. Brush top with beaten egg, sprinkle with sugar and bake as usual.

Tea Biscuits

2 cups flour
3 teaspoons baking powder
1/2 teaspoon salt
1 tablespoon sugar
1 egg
2 tablespoons shortening
1/2 cup water

Sift together flour, baking powder, salt and sugar; add well-beaten egg and shortening to water and add to dry ingredients to make soft dough. Roll out on floured board to about 1/2 inch thick; cut with biscuit cutter. Bake in moderate oven about 25 minutes.

Muffins (Sweet Milk)

2 cups Blend Flour
4 teaspoons baking powder
1/4 teaspoon salt
1 tablespoon sugar
1 egg
1 cup milk
1 tablespoon melted butter

Mix and sift the dry ingredients; beat the egg; mix with the milk and add this to the flour. Then add the melted butter. Beat to a smooth batter; pour into buttered gem pans and bake in a moderate oven.
(Makes about one dozen.)

Bran Muffins

1 cup whole bran
1 cup sour milk
1 cup flour
1 teaspoon baking powder
1/2 teaspoon salt
1/2 teaspoon baking soda
1/2 teaspoon cinnamon
1/4 cup sugar
2 Tablespoons shortening
1 egg, well beaten

Pour milk over bran and set aside. Sift together flour, baking powder, salt, soda, cinnamon and sugar. Set aside. In a large bowl, beat shortening and egg; add bran mixture, mixing thoroughly. Add dry ingredients, stirring only until moistened. Fill muffin cups two-thirds full. Bake in a 400° oven for 20 to 25 minutes.

Cornmeal Muffins

3/4 cup cornmeal
1 cup flour
2 teaspoons baking powder
1 tablespoon sugar
1/2 teaspoon salt
1 egg
3/4 cup milk
1 tablespoon melted Crisco

Combine dry ingredients. Stir in beaten egg, milk and melted Crisco. Drop into well-greased muffin tins. Bake in a hot oven (370 to 400° F.) until brown.

Rice Muffins

1/2 cup boiled rice
1 egg
1 tablespoon melted butter
2 cups Blend Flour
4 teaspoons baking powder
1/2 teaspoon salt
1 tablespoon sugar
1 cup milk

Mash the rice and add to it the beaten egg and butter. Sift together the flour, baking powder, salt and sugar, and add alternately with the milk to the first mixture. Pour into well-greased muffin tins and bake in a hot oven.

(This recipes makes 12 to 14.)

Date Muffins

1/4 cup Crisco
1/4 cup sugar
1 egg
3/4 cup milk
2 cups flour
4 teaspoons baking powder
1 teaspoon salt
1/4 cup chopped dates

Cream Crisco with sugar. Add beaten egg. Stir in milk alternately with sifted dry ingredients. Add dates last. Bake in well-greased muffin tins in a hot oven, 20 to 35 minutes.

Prune Filled Muffins

Delicious for breakfast or luncheon

1 cup cooked, drained prunes
3 tablespoons sugar
2 cups Blend Flour
4 teaspoons baking powder
1/4 teaspoon salt
3 tablespoons sugar
1 beaten egg
1 cup milk
3 tablespoons melted fat

Cook prunes very slowly, adding sugar when nearly done, and drain off the juice. Sift together the flour, baking powder, salt and sugar. Add beaten egg to milk and mix gradually into flour mixture, adding butter. Beat until light and place a spoonful into each greased muffin tin. On top put a tablespoon of the prunes and cover with more batter. Bake in a hot oven (400 to 450° F.) for about 15 to 20 minutes.

Popovers

1/2 teaspoon salt
1 cup flour
7/8 cup milk
1 egg
1/2 teaspoon melted butter

Mix the salt and flour; add the milk gradually. Then add the egg beaten light, and the butter. Use the Dover egg beater and beat 2 or 3 minutes. Turn into very hot buttered gem pans and bake from 30 to 35 minutes in a hot oven. The batter should be as thin as cream.

Iron gem pans are preferable, but not necessary.

(This makes 12.)

Popovers #2

4 beaten eggs
1 cup milk
1 cup flour
1/2 teaspoon salt

Beat the eggs and add the milk. Sift together the flour and salt and add, gradually, while beating constantly, the beaten eggs and milk. Strain through a sieve. Pour into hot gem pans (about half full) and bake in a moderately hot oven for 35 to 40 minutes. Serve at once with fruit sauce, or can be eaten hot with butter. When done they should be crisp shells and hollow inside.

Popovers #3

2 cups flour
1/2 teaspoon salt
2 eggs
2 cups milk

Sift together flour and salt. Make a well in flour, break eggs into well, add milk and stir until smooth. Pour into hot greased gem pans and bake 25 to 35 minutes in very hot oven. If taken out of oven too soon they will fall.

Apple Roll

Baking powder biscuit dough
2 medium-sized tart cooking apples
3/4 cup sugar
1 cup water

Make a rich baking powder biscuit dough. Roll out about 1/2 inch thick. Spread over it the sliced apples, and sprinkle with a very little sugar. Roll up, as you would for cinnamon rolls. Cut off slices about 1-1/2 inch thick.

Make a syrup of the 3/4 cup of sugar and 1 cup of water, by dissolving and boiling 2 or 3 minutes. Pour it into the bottom of a shallow baking pan. Lay the apple rolls in it, sprinkle a little cinnamon and sugar over all, and dot with bits of butter. Bake in a moderate oven until the apples are done, and the crust a golden brown. Turn out on a platter and pour the thick syrup around them. Serve with cream.

Cinnamon Rolls

Make dough as for bread—by any preferred method. After the final kneading, roll out to about 3/4 inch thick, spread melted butter over the top with the back of a spoon. Sprinkle thickly with cinnamon and sugar (in the proportion of 1 teaspoon of cinnamon to 1/2 cup sugar), roll up; then cut off pieces about 1 inch thick across the roll. Lay flat side down on a shallow greased pan, cover and let rise until light. Bake in a quick oven for 20 to 25 minutes.

Sweet Tea Rolls (Finger Rolls)

2 cups Flour
4 teaspoons baking powder
1/4 teaspoon salt
1/4 cup sugar
1/4 cup shortening
1/2 cup raisins (or omit)
1 beaten egg
1/2 cup milk
Milk additional

Mix and sift the dry ingredients, work in the shortening, add beaten egg and milk. If raisins are used, add them to the dry ingredients, after working in shortening. Take a small piece of the dough in the hands (about 1 inch) and roll between the hands into finger lengths—about as thick as the finger. Rub over with milk and place close together in a greased baking pan. Bake in a hot oven.

Swedish Crumpets

2 eggs
1 cup milk
4 cups flour
1/2 teaspoon salt
1 tablespoon Crisco

Beat egg slightly. Add milk. Stir liquid into flour and salt sifted together. Add melted Crisco. Roll out on a floured board a portion at a time to as thin a sheet as possible. Cut into squares about 2 to 3 inches square. Stretch each piece, especially at the edges, before dropping into hot deep Crisco. Fry until delicately brown. Drain and sprinkle generously with powdered sugar when cool.

Cream Scones

2 cups Flour
2 teaspoons baking powder
1/4 teaspoon salt
2 egg yolks
1/3 cup cream
4 tablespoons melted butter

Sift together 3 times the flour, baking powder and salt. Add the yolks of the eggs well beaten, then the cream and melted butter. Work together, roll to about 3/4 inch thick and cut in rounds or diamonds. Bake in a hot oven, as biscuits. Split and spread with butter and jam.

Exposition Scones

2-1/2 cups Flour
1 tablespoon baking powder
2-1/2 tablespoons sugar
1/2 teaspoon salt
1 tablespoon butter
1 tablespoon lard
1/2 cup raisins
1 cup milk

Mix and sift the dry ingredients, work in the butter and lard with the fingers, add raisins and mix thoroughly, then add the milk. Divide into two pieces. Turn out on a floured board and roll to the thickness of a biscuit. Cut into wedge-shaped pieces like a piece of pie and bake in a hot oven. To serve: Split open but do not cut clear through. Fill with jam and close.

Snowballs

2 eggs

1/2 cup sugar
1 tablespoon shortening
1 cup sweet milk
1 teaspoon vanilla
2-1/2 cups flour
2 teaspoons baking powder
Pinch of salt
Powdered sugar

Beat eggs until light. Add sugar, shortening, milk and vanilla. Sift flour, baking powder and salt together. Drop by teaspoonfuls into hot oil (350-360° F.).

Fry like doughnuts. When cool, dust with powdered sugar.

Almond Coffee Cake

3/4 cup shortening (butter and lard mixed)
1 cup sugar
2 eggs
1/2 cup molasses
1/2 cup strong coffee
2 cups Flour
1/2 teaspoon soda
1 teaspoon baking powder
1 teaspoon cloves
1 teaspoon cinnamon
1 teaspoon nutmeg
3/4 cup seedless raisins
Melted butter

Cream the shortening and sugar; add the well-beaten eggs. Beat, and add the molasses; then the coffee.

Sift together the flour, soda, baking powder and spices, and add gradually to the first mixture, reserving enough flour to flour the raisins. Add the raisins last. Beat till smooth. Spread in a shallow pan. Rub melted butter over the top and sprinkle thickly with minced almonds, cinnamon and sugar which have been well mixed together. Bake in rather a hot oven.

(Sufficient for six persons.)

Cinnamon Breakfast Cake

1/4 cup shortening
1 cup sugar
1 beaten egg
2 cups Flour
1 teaspoon cinnamon
4 teaspoons baking powder
1/4 teaspoon ginger
1/4 teaspoon salt
1/2 cup seeded raisins (or omit if preferred)
3/4 cup strong coffee or milk
Sugar
Cinnamon
Butter

Cream the shortening and sugar. Add the well-beaten egg. Mix and sift the dry ingredients and add alternately with the coffee. Beat well, spread in a shallow greased baking pan, sprinkle the top well with sugar and cinnamon and dot with butter. Bake in a moderate oven for about 20 to 30 minutes.

Quick Coffee Cake

2 cups Flour
3 teaspoons baking powder
1/2 teaspoon salt
1/2 cup sugar
1/2 teaspoon cinnamon
3/4 cup milk
1 egg
4 tablespoons melted butter
Cinnamon
Sugar
Butter

Sift together the dry ingredients. Add the milk to the well-beaten egg and beat this gradually into the first mixture. Add the melted butter. Spread on a shallow buttered pan; sprinkle with mixed cinnamon and sugar; add a few dots of butter and bake in a moderate oven. If heat regulator be used, pre-heat oven 3 minutes and bake at 400° F.
(Sufficient for four or five.)

Apple Cake

2 cups Blend Flour
1/2 teaspoon salt
1/2 teaspoon soda
1 teaspoon cream of tartar
3 tablespoons sugar
1/4 cup butter
1 egg
1 cup milk
4 or 5 sour apples
Cinnamon
Sugar
Butter

Mix and sift twice all the dry ingredients. Rub in the butter lightly. Beat the egg and add to the milk and stir this into the dry mixture. Spread this 1 inch thick on a shallow baking pan. Core, pare and cut the apples into eighths and place them, sharp edge down, in parallel rows on top of the dough; press them slightly so that they will penetrate the batter.

Mix 2 teaspoons of cinnamon with 1/4 cup of sugar and sprinkle over the top. Dot with a few small bits of butter and bake in a hot oven for 20 to 30 minutes. Eat hot with butter.
(Sufficient for five or six.)

Peach Cake

2 cups Flour
3 teaspoons baking powder
1/2 teaspoon salt
1/2 cup sugar
1 egg
1/2 cup milk
2 tablespoons butter (or half lard)
Peaches
Sugar
Cinnamon
Butter

Sift together the dry ingredients. Beat the egg and add it to the milk and then stir this well into the first mixture. Add the shortening which has been previously melted. Spread in a shallow pan about 1/2 inch deep. Cover with sliced peaches, pressing them down slightly into the batter. Sprinkle generously with sugar and cinnamon and dot with bits of butter. Bake in a hot oven for about 1/2 hour.
(Sufficient for five or six.)

Sally Lunn

3 cups Blend Flour
5 level teaspoons baking powder
1/2 teaspoon salt
2 tablespoons sugar
2 eggs
1 cup milk

Sift together the dry ingredients. Beat the eggs and add them to the milk and then add gradually the liquid to the dry ingredients. Beat to a smooth batter; spread on a shallow buttered tin, and bake in a moderate oven for about 40 minutes, or until when a straw is inserted it will come out clean. Serve hot with butter.

(Sufficient for five people.)

Nut Frosted Coffee Cake

1 cup blanched almonds, peanuts or walnuts
2 tablespoons butter
1/2 cup brown sugar
2 cups Blend Flour
4 teaspoons baking powder
1/2 cup sugar (additional)
1/2 teaspoon salt
1 teaspoon cinnamon
1 beaten egg
7/8 cup milk or cold coffee
1/4 cup melted butter

Blanch and chop almonds, or remove brown skin and chop peanuts. In the bottom of a baking pan melt the 2 tablespoons of butter, turning it around to coat bottom and sides. Sprinkle the brown sugar and nuts mixed together all over the bottom of pan. Sift together the flour, baking powder, salt and cinnamon. Beat egg and add to milk or coffee and mix with dry ingredients, adding the 1/3 cup melted butter. Spread batter over the nuts and sugar and place on center grate or a little above center in a moderate oven and bake about 20 to 30 minutes. When turned out, the bottom will be covered with a frosting of brown sugar and nuts.

Coffee Cake

2 cups flour
1/2 teaspoon salt
3 tablespoons sugar
4 teaspoons baking powder
2 tablespoons shortening
1 cup milk

Mix and sift dry ingredients; add melted shortening and enough milk to make very stiff batter. Spread 1/2 inch thick in greased pan; add top mixture. Bake about 30 minutes in moderate oven.

Top Mixture

2 tablespoons flour
1 tablespoon cinnamon
3 tablespoons sugar
3 tablespoons shortening

Mix dry ingredients; rub in shortening and spread thickly over top of dough before baking.

Individual Coffee Cakes

2 cups flour
3/4 teaspoon salt
4 tablespoons sugar
3 teaspoons baking powder
4 tablespoons shortening
1 egg
1/2 cup milk
Chopped nuts

Sift dry ingredients together; mix in shortening; add beaten egg to milk and add to dry ingredients to make soft dough; divide dough into 6 long, narrow pieces; with hands roll out on board each piece very long and thin; spread with butter; cut each in two and beginning in center, twist 2 pieces together and bring ends around to form crescent. Put into greased pan; sprinkle with chopped nuts. Bake in hot oven 15 to 20 minutes. While hot, brush over with thin icing made with 1/2 cup confectioner's sugar moistened with 1 tablespoon hot water.

Raisin Tea Ring

3 cups flour
5 tablespoons sugar
4 teaspoons baking powder
1 teaspoon salt
1 cup raisins, washed, drained and floured
1/2 to 3/4 cup milk
3 tablespoons shortening
1 egg
Sugar additional
1/2 cup chopped nuts

Sift dry ingredients together; add raisins; to milk add melted shortening and beaten egg, and add to dry ingredients to make a soft dough; roll out lightly about 1/2 inch thick; divide into 2 long strips and twist together to form a ring; put into greased pan and sprinkle with sugar and nuts; allow to stand about 20 minutes. Bake in moderate oven 20 to 25 minutes.

Muffins

2 cups flour
3 teaspoons baking powder
1 tablespoon sugar
1/2 teaspoon salt
1 cup milk
2 eggs
2 tablespoons shortening

Sift together flour, baking powder, sugar and salt; add milk, well-beaten eggs and melted shortening; mix well. Half fill greased muffin tins and bake in hot oven 20 to 25 minutes.

Blueberry or Huckleberry Muffins

2 cups flour
3 teaspoons baking powder
1 teaspoon salt
1 tablespoon sugar
3/4 cup milk
2 eggs
1 tablespoon shortening
1 cup berries

Sift together flour, baking powder, salt and sugar; add milk slowly, well-beaten eggs and melted shortening; mix well and add berries, which have been carefully picked over and floured. Grease muffin tins; drop one spoonful into each. Bake about 30 minutes in moderate oven.

Cereal Muffins

3/4 cup cooked hominy, oatmeal or other cereal
1/2 teaspoon salt
1-1/2 tablespoons shortening
1 egg
1/2 cup milk
1 cup flour
1/2 cup corn meal
4 teaspoons baking powder

Mix together cereal, salt, melted shortening, beaten egg and milk. Add flour and corn meal which have been sifted with baking powder; beat well. Bake in greased muffin tins or shallow pan in hot oven 25 to 30 minutes.

Crumb Muffins

2 cups stale bread crumbs
1-1/4 cups milk
1 cup flour
2 teaspoons baking powder
1/2 teaspoon salt
2 eggs
1 tablespoon shortening

Soak bread crumbs in cold milk 10 minutes; add flour, baking powder and salt which have been sifted together; add well-beaten eggs and melted shortening; mix well. Heat muffin tins, grease and drop 1 tablespoon of batter into each. Bake 20 to 25 minutes in hot oven.

Rice Muffins

1 cup flour
3 teaspoons baking powder
1/2 teaspoon salt
1 tablespoon sugar
2/3 cup milk
1 egg
1 tablespoon shortening
1 cup cold boiled rice

Sift together flour, baking powder, salt and sugar; add milk slowly; then well-beaten egg and melted shortening; add rice and mix well. Grease muffin tins; drop 1 spoonful of mixture into each. Bake 20 to 30 minutes in hot oven.

Date Muffins

1/3 cup butter
1 egg
2 cups flour
2 teaspoons baking powder
1/2 teaspoon salt
3/4 cup milk
1/2 pound dates

Cream butter, add beaten egg, flour in which baking powder and salt have been sifted, and milk. Stir in dates which have been pitted and cut into small pieces. Bake about 25 minutes in greased gem pans in hot oven.

For sweet muffins sift 1/4 cup sugar with dry ingredients.

Scones

2 cups flour
3 teaspoons baking powder
1 teaspoon salt
2 tablespoons sugar
2 tablespoons shortening
2 eggs
1/3 cup milk
Milk
Sugar additional

Sift together flour, baking powder, salt and sugar; add shortening and mix in very lightly. Beat eggs until light; add milk to eggs and add slowly to mixture. Roll out 1/2 inch thick on floured board; cut into pieces 3 inches square and fold over, making them 3-cornered; brush with milk; dust with sugar. Bake about 25 minutes in hot oven.

Currant Tea Cakes

2 cups flour
3 teaspoons baking powder
1/2 cup sugar
3/4 teaspoon salt
1 egg
1 cup milk
12 tablespoons shortening
1/2 cup currants

Sift together flour, baking powder, sugar and salt; add beaten egg and melted shortening to milk and add to dry ingredients; add currants which have been washed, dried and floured; mix well. The batter should be stiff. Grease hot muffin tins and fill half full. Bake about 20 minutes in hot oven.

Breakfast Gems

3-1/2 cups Blend Flour
5 level teaspoons baking powder
1 teaspoon salt
2 eggs
2 cups sweet milk

Sift together the dry ingredients; beat the eggs until very light and add to the milk. Pour this into the dry ingredients and beat hard to a smooth batter. Bake in a very hot oven for about 15 minutes, or until brown and cooked through.

(This recipe makes about 20 gems.)

Graham Gems

1 cup graham flour
1 cup flour
3/4 teaspoon salt
4 teaspoons baking powder
1 cup milk
1 egg
2 tablespoons molasses or sugar
3 tablespoons shortening

Mix together dry ingredients; add milk, beaten egg, molasses and melted shortening. Bake in greased gem pans in hot oven about 25 minutes.

Green Corn Gems

2 cups green corn put through food chopper
1/4 cup milk, or 1/2 cup if corn is dry
2 eggs

2 cups flour
3 teaspoons baking powder
1 teaspoon salt
1/8 teaspoon pepper

To the corn add milk and well-beaten eggs; add flour, baking powder, salt and pepper which have been sifted together; mix well. Drop into hot greased gem pans. Bake in hot oven 20 to 25 minutes.

Fig Envelopes

2 cups flour
3 teaspoons baking powder
1/2 teaspoon salt
2 tablespoons sugar
1 tablespoon shortening
2/3 cup milk
1 cup chopped figs
Cold milk
1 egg
Sugar

Sift together flour, baking powder, salt and sugar; add shortening and mix in very lightly; add slowly enough milk to form soft dough. Dust board with flour and roll out dough 1/4 inch thick, cut into squares and on each piece put 1 tablespoon of fig; brush edges with cold milk; fold like an envelope, and press edges together. Brush tops with egg beaten with 1 tablespoon milk and 1 teaspoon sugar. Bake about 20 minutes in hot oven.

Coffee Cake

1-1/2 cups flour
2 teaspoons baking powder
1/2 teaspoon salt
1 cup sugar
1 egg
1 cup milk
2 tablespoons butter
Sugar
Cinnamon
Nuts

Sift together flour, baking powder, salt and sugar. Combine beaten egg, milk and melted butter. Stir the liquid into the dry ingredients. Pour out into a shallow pan. Sprinkle surface with sugar, cinnamon and nuts in the proportion of 1 teaspoon cinnamon to 1/4 cup sugar. Dot occasionally with bits of butter. Bake in a hot oven 25 to 30 minutes.

Quick Cinnamon Rolls

2 cups flour
3 teaspoons baking powder
1 teaspoon salt
2 tablespoons Crisco
Milk

Sift dry ingredients. Work in Crisco with fingertips. Stir in just enough milk to moisten mixture. Roll out on a floured board to 1/4 inch thick. Spread with filling mixture (below) and roll up and cut into slices 1/2 inch thick. Bake in a moderate oven about 15 minutes. Serve warm.

Filling:
1/2 cup Crisco
1 cup sugar
1 teaspoon cinnamon
1 egg yolk

Cream Crisco with sugar and cinnamon; add egg yolk.

LANE
TINNING & HEATING

8

GRIDDLE CAKES, WAFFLES, FRITTERS & TOAST

Griddle cakes, as made today with baking powder, have become most popular. Properly made they are delicious, healthful, appetizing and nutritious.

The batter must be thin. The cakes should be small and not too thick—about 1/8 inch thick when baked.

An iron frying pan may be used instead of griddle. In any case, grease only enough to keep the cakes from sticking. Turn only once.

A. GRIDDLE CAKES

Use frying pan or griddle. Grease griddle if necessary (soapstone, aluminum or electric griddles must never be greased). Let fat begin to smoke before cooking the cakes. If large bubbles form at once on top of the cakes, the griddle is too hot.

If the top of the cake stiffens before the underside is cooked, the griddle is not hot enough. Never turn a cake twice. Serve griddle cakes as soon as cooked.

Basic Griddle Cakes

1-3/4 cups flour
3/4 teaspoon salt
3 teaspoons baking powder
2 eggs
1-1/2 to 2 cups milk
1 tablespoon cooking oil

Sift dry ingredients into bowl; add beaten eggs, milk and oil and mix well. Bake on hot griddle slightly brushed with oil. Turn cakes only once; brown other side and serve immediately on hot plate with butter and syrup.
Makes 24 griddle cakes.

Sweet Milk Griddle Cakes

4 cups flour
3/4 teaspoon salt
2 tablespoons baking powder
1 tablespoon sugar
2 eggs
1-1/2 to 2 cups milk
2 tablespoons melted fat

Combine all dry materials and sift. Beat eggs, milk and melted fat together. Add sifted dry materials and beat thoroughly. Place batter in a pitcher. Pour on a hot, greased griddle.

Sour Milk Griddle Cakes

2-1/2 cups flour
3/4 teaspoon salt
1 egg
2 cups sour milk
1-1/4 teaspoons soda
1 tablespoon fat

Follow directions given under Sweet Milk Griddle Cakes.

Corn Cakes

1 cup cornmeal
1-1/2 cups boiling water
1/4 cup milk
1-1/2 cups flour
4 teaspoons baking powder
1-1/2 teaspoons salt
1/4 cup sugar
1 egg
2 tablespoons melted fat

Add meal to boiling water and boil 5 minutes; turn into bowl, add milk and remaining dry ingredients mixed and sifted, then the egg well beaten, and fat. Cook same as other griddle cakes.

Corn Meal Griddle Cakes

1-1/3 cups corn meal
1-1/2 cups boiling water
1 tablespoon shortening
3/4 cup milk
1 tablespoon molasses
2/3 cup flour
1 teaspoon salt
4 teaspoons baking powder

Scald corn meal with boiling water; add shortening, milk and molasses; add flour, salt and baking powder which have been sifted together; mix well. Bake on hot, slightly greased griddle, turning once.

Rice Griddle Cakes

1 cup boiled rice
1 cup milk
1 tablespoon shortening
1 teaspoon salt
1 egg
1 cup flour
2 teaspoons baking powder

Mix rice, milk, melted shortening, salt and well-beaten egg; stir in flour and baking powder which have been sifted together; mix well. Bake on hot, slightly greased griddle, turning only once.

French Pancakes

1 cup flour
2 teaspoons baking powder
1/2 teaspoon salt
2 eggs
1 tablespoon sugar
2 cups milk
1/2 cup cream
Jam
Powdered sugar

Sift together flour, baking powder and salt. Add eggs which have been beaten with the sugar, milk and cream. Beat until smooth. Heat small frying pan in which a little butter has been melted. Pour in just sufficient batter to cover bottom of pan. Cook over hot fire. Turn and brown other side. Spread with jam and roll up. Sprinkle with powdered sugar and serve hot.

Whole Wheat Hot Cakes

2 cups whole wheat flour
4 teaspoons baking powder
1/2 teaspoon salt
1-3/4 cups milk
1 teaspoon molasses
1 tablespoon melted shortening
2 eggs

Sift together flour, baking powder and salt; add milk, molasses and shortening to beaten eggs and add to dry ingredients; mix well. Bake on hot, slightly greased griddle, turning only once.

Hot Griddle Cakes #2

2 cups flour
1/2 teaspoon salt
5 teaspoons baking powder
1-1/2 cups milk
2 tablespoons shortening

Mix and sift dry ingredients; add milk and melted shortening; beat well. Bake on slightly greased hot griddle.

Griddle Cakes with Eggs

1-3/4 cups flour
1/2 teaspoon salt
3 teaspoons baking powder
2 eggs
1-1/2 cups milk
1 tablespoon shortening

Mix and sift dry ingredients; add beaten eggs, milk and melted shortening; mix well. Bake on slightly greased hot griddle, turning only once.

Buckwheat Cakes

2 cups buckwheat flour
1 cup flour
6 teaspoons baking powder
1-1/2 teaspoons salt
1 tablespoon molasses
1 tablespoon melted shortening
2-1/2 cups milk or milk and water

Sift together flours, baking powder and salt; add molasses and shortening to liquid; beat well. Bake on hot, slightly greased griddle, turning only once.

Araby Pancakes

A spicy pancake with a dual personality—equally good as a main dish or a dessert. So easily made with Sperry Pancake and Waffle Flour.

2 cups pancake and waffle flour
1/4 teaspoon mace
1/4 teaspoon cinnamon
1/4 teaspoon nutmeg
1 teaspoon sugar
1 egg, slightly beaten
1-2/3 cups milk

Stir flour in package before measuring. Add spices and sugar, mixed together. Add egg to milk and mix lightly into flour until smooth. Cook on a moderately hot griddle. Serve with melted butter and brown sugar.

15 medium-size cakes

NOTE: These pancakes may be used as dessert cakes when spread with apricot marmalade and topped with whipped cream.

Mexican Pancakes

Different, and exceedingly popular with women who want to serve something new and tasty in pancakes . . . a favorite with gourmets.

1/2 cup yellow corn meal, uncooked
1 teaspoon sugar
1 teaspoon salt
2 tablespoons melted butter
1 cup boiling water
3/4 cup cold milk
1 cup flour
2 eggs, separated

Relishes for serving:
Chopped green onion
Chopped hard-cooked egg
Chopped green pepper
Chopped parsley
Chopped crisp bacon
Snappy Cheese Sauce (below)

Combine corn meal, sugar, salt and butter. Add boiling water and stir until smooth. When lukewarm, add milk, stirring well. Add corn meal mixture to flour, add well-beaten egg yolks, fold in stiffly-beaten egg whites. Bake on moderately hot greased pancake griddle, allowing a longer time than for wheat cakes.

16 medium cakes

To serve: Sprinkle each pancake with any or all of the suggested relishes, serving 2 cakes to each person, and cover with Snappy Cheese Sauce.

Snappy Cheese Sauce

3 tablespoons butter
3 tablespoons flour
1-1/2 cups milk
1/4 teaspoon salt
1/2 cup grated American cheese
1 teaspoon Worcestershire sauce
Few grains cayenne
Few grains paprika

Melt butter, blend in flour and add milk slowly. Cook until thick and smooth. Add remaining ingredients, stirring only until well mixed. Keep warm over hot water.
1-1/2 cups sauce

Crumb Pancakes

2 cups, or more, scalded milk
1-1/2 cups dry, grated bread crumbs
2 eggs
1/2 cup Flour
3-1/2 teaspoons baking powder
1/2 teaspoon salt
1 tablespoon sugar
2 tablespoons melted butter

Scald the milk; add the crumbs; let stand while beating the eggs. Then add the eggs. Mix and sift the dry ingredients twice and add to the mixture. Bake on a hot greased griddle and serve immediately.

This recipe is sufficient for 4 persons

Griddle Cakes (Sour Milk)

Excellent

1 teaspoon soda
2 cups thick sour milk
2 cups flour
1 teaspoon salt
1 tablespoon sugar
2 eggs (1 will do when expensive)
1 tablespoon melted butter

Beat the soda into the milk. Sift together the flour, salt and sugar. Add the beaten eggs and melted butter to the milk and stir all into the dry ingredients. Beat to a smooth batter and bake on a hot griddle.

Sufficient for 4

B. WAFFLES

Gold Medal Waffles

2 eggs
2 cups sour milk
1 teaspoon soda
2-1/4 cups cake flour
2 teaspoons baking powder
1/2 teaspoon salt
6 tablespoons melted shortening

Beat eggs until light and add sour milk and soda. Sift flour once before measuring. Sift flour, baking powder and salt. Beat flour mixture into egg and milk mixture. Add melted shortening, beating until smooth with rotary egg beater. Bake on hot waffle iron.

Makes 8 to 10 waffles.

Time: If gas iron is used it will take 20 seconds to brown the side next to the fire. With an electric iron the time depends upon the size of the iron and the strength of the current. To get a crisp waffle, the iron must be very hot. Do not stir batter after it has stood for a few minutes.

Waffles #1

1-1/2 cups flour
3 teaspoons baking powder
1/2 teaspoon salt
2 tablespoons sugar
1 cup milk
2 egg yolks
2 tablespoons melted fat
2 egg whites

Measure, mix and sift the first 4 ingredients; add the milk gradually, then egg yolks and melted fat, and mix thoroughly. Lastly, fold in the stiffly beaten egg whites. Cook in a well-greased waffle iron.

Waffles #2

2 cups flour
3 teaspoons baking powder
1/2 teaspoon salt
1-1/2 cups milk
2 eggs
2 tablespoons Crisco

Sift flour, baking powder and salt together. Add milk to beaten egg yolks and stir into dry ingredients. Add melted Crisco and fold in stiffly beaten egg whites.

Waffles #3

2 cups flour
4 teaspoon baking powder
3/4 teaspoon salt
1-3/4 cups milk
2 eggs
4 tablespoons melted shortening

Sift flour, baking powder and salt together; add milk to egg yolks, and add to dry ingredients; add shortening; mix in beaten egg whites. Bake in well-greased hot waffle iron until brown; turn once. Serve hot with butter and maple syrup.

Waffles #4

1-1/2 cups flour
2 teaspoons baking powder
1 tablespoon sugar
1/2 teaspoon salt
1 cup milk
3 eggs, beaten separately
1 tablespoon melted butter

Mix and sift dry ingredients, gradually add milk, then well-beaten yolks. Beat thoroughly, adding butter, then fold in the stiffly-beaten egg whites and bake at once on a hot well-greased waffle iron. If waffle iron is not hot enough, waffles will stick. Will fill waffle iron about 4 times

C. FRITTERS

Fritters are served for luncheon, dinner or supper, as an entree, a vegetable or a sweet, according to the ingredients used. The foundation batter is much the same for all fritters, and with some additions the first recipe given can be used for many varieties. By the use of baking powder, a fine fritter batter may be stirred up in a few minutes.

Fritters should be fried in deep fat, hot enough to brown a piece of bread in 60 secs.

Plain Fritter Batter

1 cup flour
1-1/2 teaspoons baking powder
1/4 teaspoon salt
1 egg
2/3 cup milk

Sift dry ingredients together; add beaten egg and milk; beat until smooth.

Corn Fritters #1

3/4 teaspoon soda
1-1/3 cups sour milk
2 eggs
2 cups flour
1/2 teaspoon salt
1/4 teaspoon pepper
1 cup corn (either canned or fresh)
1 teaspoon melted butter

Beat the soda into the sour milk and add the beaten eggs. Sift in the flour and seasoning, and add the corn and butter. Beat well. Fry in hot fat and drain on brown paper. Serve at once. Sufficient for 4 or 5

Corn Fritters #2

1/2 cup milk
2 cups cooked corn
1-1/2 cups flour
1 teaspoon salt
1/3 teaspoon pepper
2 teaspoons baking powder
1 tablespoon melted shortening
2 eggs

Add milk to corn; add flour sifted with salt, pepper and baking powder; add shortening and beaten eggs; beat well. Fry by spoonfuls on hot greased griddle or frying pan.

If fried in deep fat, make batter stiffer by adding 1/2 cup flour and 1 teaspoon baking powder.

Corn Fritters with Sweet Milk

This fritter batter may be used for clams, oysters, oysters plant, etc.

2 cups flour
1/2 teaspoon salt
1 teaspoon sugar
1/4 teaspoon pepper
3-1/2 teaspoons baking powder
2 beaten eggs
1-1/4 cup milk
1 tablespoon melted butter
1 cup cooked corn

Mix and sift the dry ingredients. Add beaten eggs to milk and stir in, beating until smooth. Add melted butter and corn and fry in deep hot fat or sauté in a little hot fat in a skillet. Drain on brown paper.

Clam Fritters

1-1/2 cups flour
2 teaspoons baking powder
1/2 teaspoon salt
1/8 teaspoon pepper
1/8 teaspoon paprika
1/2 cup milk or clam juice
2 eggs
1-1/2 teaspoons grated onion
1 teaspoon melted shortening
10 clams

Sift together dry ingredients; add liquid, beaten eggs, onion, and shortening; rinse clams, put through meat chopper and add to the batter. Take one spoonful batter for each fritter and fry on hot greased griddle or in deep fat.

FRUIT FRITTERS

Fruits other than apples may be used in fritters by following the directions for Apple Fritters (below). Canned whole fruits drained from syrup may also be used. Chop fruit (not too fine) and stir into plain fritter batter. Drop by spoonfuls into deep hot fat, turning until brown. Drain and sprinkle with powdered sugar.

Apple Fritters #1

4 large apples
2 tablespoons powdered sugar
1 tablespoon lemon juice
Plain Fritter Batter (above)

Peel and core apples and cut into slices; add sugar and lemon juice. Dip each slice into Plain Fritter Batter. Fry light brown in deep fat. Drain and sprinkle with powdered sugar.

Apple Fritters #2

1 cup flour
1 teaspoon baking powder
2 tablespoons sugar
1/4 teaspoon salt
1 egg
1 tablespoon Crisco
1/3 cup milk

2 medium-sized cooking apples

Sift dry ingredients. Stir in egg and melted Crisco beaten with milk. Pare and core apples and cut into eighths. Stir slices in batter and drop by spoonfuls into hot Crisco. Fry until well browned. Sprinkle with powdered sugar. Serve with maple syrup.

Banana Fritters

1 cup flour
2 teaspoons baking powder
1 tablespoon powdered sugar
1/4 teaspoon salt
1 egg
1/4 cup milk
1 tablespoon lemon juice
3 bananas

Mix and sift dry ingredients. Add others in order. Force bananas through sieve before adding. Beat thoroughly. Drop by spoonfuls into hot fat. Drain and sprinkle with powdered sugar.

Quick Banana Fritters

Nothing could be more delicious . . . and these fritters are made in a jiffy . . . an ideal emergency dessert.

4 large bananas
Lemon juice
1 cup pancake and waffle flour
1/2 cup milk
1 egg, slightly beaten

Peel bananas, cut in thirds crosswise, and sprinkle with lemon juice and let stand while preparing fritter batter. To pancake and waffle flour add milk and egg, and beat well. Dip each piece of fruit in batter, and fry in deep fat, 360 degrees (or when an inch cube of bread browns in 60 seconds) until a golden brown. Keep warm until serving time. Serve with sweetened whipped cream, sprinkled with nutmeg. Makes 6 servings.

D. TOAST

Buttered Toast

Cut bread a day old into 1/4 inch slices, put slices in a wire toaster or on a grate and place it some distance from the fire that it may dry gradually, and then brown as desired, and butter. Toast, if piled compactly and allowed to stand, soon becomes moist. It should be served as soon after toasting as possible.

Cream Toast

Dip slices of toast into White Sauce (see page 30). Pour remaining sauce on the pieces of toast and serve hot.

French Toast

1/4 teaspoon salt
2 tablespoons sugar
1 cup sweet milk
1 egg, slightly beaten
5 slices of bread
Fat to grease the griddle

Add the salt, sugar and milk to the slightly beaten egg, dip the pieces of bread into the egg mixture. Cook the soaked slices of bread on a well-oiled griddle; brown on one side, turn and brown on the other. Serve with maple syrup or jelly. Served with stewed fruit, makes a good dessert.

Cinnamon Toast

1 teaspoon ground cinnamon
1 cup granulated sugar
Slightly stale bread
Butter

Mix together the cinnamon and sugar and transfer to a shaker. Cut the bread 1/4 inch thick, trim off crusts, and toast quickly so that it will be soft in the middle. Butter generously, shake the cinnamon mixture over, put together in pairs and cut in triangles. Place in a hot oven for a minute or two and serve on a folded napkin on a hot plate.

9

CAKES

GENERAL INSTRUCTIONS FOR SUCCESSFUL CAKE BAKING

Professional cake bakers all agree that the time of the baking of cakes should be divided into quarters. During the first quarter, the batter should become heated and begin to rise. During the second period it should continue to rise and begin to brown. During the third period it should continue browning, and during the fourth it should finish baking and shrink from the pan.

Cakes containing no butter, such as Angel Food and Sponge Cakes, as well as the loaf cakes, require a slower oven than those made with butter or baked in layers.

If heat regulator be used, cake may be put in cool oven and regulator be adjusted at 400° for layer cake or 350° for loaves, reducing heat after cake begins to brown.

In a layer cake, the heat should be moderate to begin with and the batter allowed to rise to its full capacity before the heat is increased. Care should be taken that the oven is not too hot, or a crust will be formed before the batter has fully risen and the cake will be heavy; also in its effort to rise, it will split open across the top and part of the batter will show through, making an ugly loaf. On the other hand, if the oven is too cool, the cake will rise too much and be of coarse texture and too dry.

If the oven be too hot, set a small pan of water inside and the temperature will be quickly reduced.

One other cause of a split across a cake is from too much flour. All recipes in this book have been very accurately measured, the measuring cup being the standard measuring cup, marked off into 1/4, 1/3, 1/2, 3/4 and containing when full, and leveled off with a knife, exactly half a pint. Teaspoons and tablespoons have been filled and leveled with a knife, and for halves divided lengthwise through the middle of the spoon, and for quarters divided again crosswise.

ATTENTION TO PANS

Sponge Cake without baking powder, or Angel Food should be baked in ungreased spout pans, and when done should be inverted and allowed to stand without jarring until cool. If an attempt is made to remove them from the pans while hot, the cells will burst and the cakes be heavy.

Pans for other cakes should be buttered carefully, then either have a light dusting of flour or the bottoms be partly covered with wax paper, which should also be lightly buttered. Loaf pans should be buttered, then the bottom covered with heavy paper, buttered, and fruit cakes or other cakes which require long baking, should have two thicknesses of paper, and buttered paper on the sides. Paper should always be removed as soon as cakes are taken from the oven, or they will be soggy.

Butter substitutes, such as margarines, etc., are satisfactory in cakes, but those made with coconut oil will cause a cake to stick to the pan if used for greasing, so it is best to use butter for greasing the pans.

Cakes should always be stirred or beaten in the same direction. If beaten in one direction, then in another, part of the air is forced out.

Rhubarb Cake

2 cups flour
2 teaspoons baking powder
1/2 teaspoon salt
1/2 cup sugar
1 Tablespoon butter
1 egg
1/2 cup milk
2 cups rhubarb, finely sliced
2 cups sugar
1 Tablespoon butter
3 Tablespoons flour
1 egg
1/2 teaspoon nutmeg

Sift flour with baking powder, salt and 1/2 cup sugar. Stir in butter, egg and milk until dry ingredients are moistened. Spread in a buttered and floured 13x9x2-inch pan. Mix rhubarb, sugar, butter, flour, egg and nutmeg. Spread on top of the batter. Bake in a 350° oven for 45 minutes. Cool and serve.

Special Sponge Cake

The cake that was always special to me was a "Sponge Cake." The recipe was lost when my mother died, but was found in some old papers of my grandmother's. I hope you will enjoy it was much as I did over the years.

—Margrite Coke

6 eggs, separated
1 cup sugar
1 cup flour
1 teaspoon Cream of Tartar
1 teaspoon vanilla

Beat eggs well. Add half the sugar to the beaten yolk and half to the beaten whites, a little at a time. When both have been beaten well, add the whites and yolks together. Then stir in the flour and Cream of Tartar which have been sifted together, then add vanilla. Make sure the flour is sifted, and the sugar, before measuring. Beat the yolks of the eggs until thick and lemon colored, then add the sugar. Sift together the flour and baking powder and beat it thoroughly. Beat the whites to stiff, adding to them the vanilla, and fold in last. Fold very gently over and over until mixed, but do not stir again. Bake in a well-greased tin in a moderate oven.

Angel Food

Before giving the recipe for "Angel Food," please remember that the baking of the cake is just as important as the mixing, if not more so. The oven should be just warm enough when cake is put in. It should be kept this cool until the batter has risen to the top of the pan. Then increase the heat gradually until the cake is well browned over. If the oven is too hot when the cake is put in, it will rise too fast and fall during the baking. This cake should bake in from 35 to 45 minutes. If heat regulator be used, bake at 350°. It is done when, upon pressing the top of the cake lightly with the finger, the cake will spring back, leaving no "finger print." When done, remove fromthe oven, invert the pan and allow it to stand until perfectly cold before removing from the pan.

1 cup Flour
1-1/4 cups granulated sugar
1/4 teaspoon salt
1 cup white of eggs
1/2 teaspoon cream of tartar
1/2 teaspoon almond extract

Sift both the flour and sugar before measuring. Then measure and sift the flour 4 times. Add the salt to the eggs and begin beating. When about half beaten, add the cream of tartar, and continue beating until very stiff and dry. Fold in the sugar, and then the flour. Do not heat or stir, but just gently fold over and over until well mixed. Add the extract. Pour into an ungreased Angel Food pan and bake as directed above.

If these directions are followed carefully, you will undoubtedly have success. The making of an Angel Food is a very simple task after the directions are understood.

Mock Angel Food

1 cup granulated sugar
1-1/3 cups cake flour
3 teaspoons baking powder
1/3 teaspoon salt
2/3 cup scalding milk
1/2 teaspoon almond extract
3 egg whites

Sift together 4 times the flour, baking powder and sugar. Beat in gradually the hot milk, then the vanilla. Add the salt to the whites of eggs and beat until very stiff. Fold in lightly (do not stir) until well mixed. Bake, either in a small Angel Food pan or in a shallow greased pan, and when cool spread with icing. Chocolate is especially good.

The Dark Angel

Chocolate frosted chocolate angel food—studded with walnuts—need more be said?

1/2 teaspoon salt
1-1/2 cups egg whites
1 teaspoon cream of tartar
1-1/2 cups sugar
1 cup sifted flour
4 tablespoons cocoa
1 teaspoon vanilla
1/3 cup walnuts
Walnut halves

Add salt to egg whites and beat with flat whip until foamy. Add cream of tartar and beat until stiff, but not too dry. Sift sugar, measure and fold 1 cupful into egg whites. Sift flour, measure, and sift 5 times with cocoa and remaining sugar. Fold carefully into egg white mixture. Add vanilla and nuts last. Pile in ungreased tube pan, 10 inches in diameter, and bake in slow oven, 325°, for 1 hour and 15 minutes. Take from oven and invert on cake rack until thoroughly cold. Remove from pan and frost with Chocolate Butter Frosting (below) and decorate with walnut halves.
12 servings

Chocolate Butter Frosting

4 tablespoons butter

2 cups powdered sugar
1/4 cup cream or evaporated milk
2 squares unsweetened chocolate, melted (2 ounces)
1 teaspoon vanilla

Cream butter, add sugar gradually, alternating with cream and beating until smooth. Blend in melted chocolate and vanilla. If necessary, thin with cream until frosting is smooth and glossy and easy to spread.

Angel's Ginger Cake

Ginger gives this angel piquance

1/2 teaspoon salt
1-1/3 cups egg whites
1 teaspoon cream of tartar
1-1/2 cups sugar
1 cup sifted flour
1/4 cup chopped preserved ginger
1 teaspoon vanilla

Add salt to egg whites and beat with flat whip until foamy. Add cream of tartar and beat until stiff, but not dry. Sift sugar, measure and fold one-half into egg whites. Sift flour and measure. Sift again 5 times with remaining sugar and carefully fold into egg white mixture. Fold in ginger and vanilla last. Pile into ungreased tube pan (10 inches in diameter) and bake in slow oven, 300°, for 40 minutes, then increase heat to 325° for 35 minutes. Take from oven and invert on cake rack until thoroughly cold. Remove from pan and frost with Lemon Ginger Frosting (below).
12 servings

Lemon Ginger Frosting

1/3 cup heavy cream
3 cups powdered sugar
1 tablespoon preserved ginger syrup
1 tablespoon lemon juice
Thin slices of preserved ginger

Whip cream until slightly thickened. Add powdered sugar gradually, along with ginger syrup and lemon juice, until frosting is stiff enough to spread. Cover cake with frosting and decorate top and sides with thin slices of preserved ginger.

Simple Angel Food

A reliable angel food—always appropriate, always safe . . . easy to make

1 tablespoon cold water
1/2 teaspoon salt
1-1/3 cups egg whites
1 teaspoon cream of tartar
1-1/3 cups sugar
1 cup sifted flour
1 teaspoon vanilla

Add water and salt to egg whites and beat with flat whip until foamy. Add cream of tartar and beat until stiff, but not dry. Stir sugar, measure and fold one-half into egg whites. Sift flour, measure and sift again 5 times with remaining sugar. Carefully fold flour and sugar into egg white mixture and add vanilla last. Pile into ungreased tube pan (10 inches in diameter) and bake in slow oven, 325°, for 1 hour. Take from oven and invert on cake rack until thoroughly cold before removing from pan.
12 servings

Angel Fruit Cake

A heavenly fruited angel cake, featuring that zestful fruit, apricots

1/2 teaspoon salt
1-1/3 cups egg whites
1 teaspoon cream of tartar
1-1/2 cups sugar
1 cup sifted flour
1/4 cup dried apricot puree
2 tablespoons thinly sliced citron
2 tablespoon chopped cherries
1 tablespoon flour
1 teaspoon vanilla

Add salt to egg whites and beat with flat whip until foamy. Add cream of tartar and beat until stiff, but not dry. Sift sugar, measure and fold one-half into egg whites. Sift flour and measure. Sift again 5 times with remaining sugar and carefully fold into egg white mixture, alternating with apricot puree. Dredge citron and cherries with 1 tablespoon flour and fold carefully into mixture. Add vanilla last. Pile into ungreased tube pan (10 inches in diameter), and bake in a slow oven, 325°, for 1 hour. Take from oven and invert on cake rack until thoroughly cold. Remove and frost with 7-Minute Apricot Frosting (below).
12 servings

7-Minute Apricot Frosting

1-1/2 cups granulated sugar
2 egg whites
1/4 teaspoon salt
1/4 cup apricot puree (below)
2 tablespoons cold water

Mix all ingredients together in the top of a double boiler. Place over boiling water and heat continuously with a rotary egg beater for 7 minutes. Remove from heat and continue beating with a flat whip or spoon until partially cool before spreading over cake.

Apricot Puree

2 cups dried apricots
2 cups cold water

Wash apricots, add water and boil gently in covered pan for 30 minutes; while still warm press through a coarse wire sieve. There should be about 3/4 cup puree.

The Peppermint and Chocolate Angel

A man's angel food—chocolate and peppermint, always friends to man

1/2 teaspoon salt
1-1/2 cups egg whites
1 teaspoon cream of tartar
1-1/2 cups sugar
1 cup sifted flour
3 tablespoons cocoa
1 teaspoon vanilla
4 drops peppermint extract

Add salt to egg whites and beat with flat whip until foamy. Add cream of tartar and beat until stiff, but not dry. Sift sugar, measure and fold one-half into egg whites. Sift flour, measure and sift again 5 times with remaining sugar. Carefully fold flour and sugar into egg white mixture. Divide cake batter equally. To one half, gently fold in cocoa and vanilla. Add peppermint to remaining half. Place by spoonfuls in ungreased tube pan (10 inches in diameter), alternating chocolate and peppermint batters. Bake in slow oven, 325°, for 1 hour and 15 minutes. Take from oven and invert on cake rack until thoroughly cold. Remove from pan, cover with Chocolate Peppermint Frosting (below).
12 servings

Chocolate Peppermint Frosting

2 cups sugar
2/3 cup water
1/16 teaspoon salt
1 egg white
1/2 teaspoon lemon juice
1 teaspoon vanilla
2 drops peppermint extract
2 squares unsweetened chocolate, melted (2 ounces)

Combine sugar, water and salt. Place over low heat, stirring only until sugar begins to dissolve. Boil gently until syrup spins a 2-inch thread when dropped from a fork, 240°. Pour syrup slowly over stiffly-beaten egg white, add lemon juice, beating constantly with a rotary egg beater until too heavy to turn. Continue beating with wire whip until cool and creamy and it holds its shape. Add vanilla and spread over top and sides of cake. Blend peppermint with melted chocolate and spread over top of frosting, allowing chocolate to run down sides of cake. Keep in a cool place until chocolate hardens.

Caramel Angel Food

A delicate caramel flavor in this truly new angel food

1-1/3 cups egg whites
1/2 teaspoon salt
1 teaspoon cream of tartar
1 cup granulated sugar
1/4 cup brown sugar
1 cup sifted flour
1 teaspoon vanilla
3 tablespoons caramel syrup (below)

Add salt to egg whites and beat with flat whip until foamy. Add cream of tartar and beat until stiff, but not dry. Sift granulated sugar, measure and fold into egg whites. Sift flour, measure and sift again 5 times with brown sugar. Carefully fold in flour and brown sugar, alternating with caramel syrup. Add vanilla last. Pile into ungreased tube pan (10 inches in diameter) and bake in slow oven, 325°, for 1 hour and 10 minutes. Take from oven and invert on cake rack until thoroughly cold. Remove from pan and cover with Caramel Nut Frosting (below).
12 servings

Caramel Nut Frosting

2 egg yolks
1/4 cup caramel syrup (below)
2-1/4 cups powdered sugar
1/8 teaspoon salt
2 tablespoons heavy cream
1/2 cup chopped nuts
1 teaspoon vanilla

Beat egg yolks slightly, add syrup, 1/4 cup powdered sugar, salt and cream. Blend well and cook over hot water until thick, stirring constantly, 5 minutes. Cool and beat in remaining powdered sugar, nuts and vanilla. Spread over top and sides of cake.

Caramel Syrup

1 cup sugar
1/2 cup water

Melt sugar, and when boiling vigorously, add water all at once. Remove from heat. Any extra syrup may be put in a container and kept in a cool place.

Apple Sauce Cake #1

1 cup sugar
1/2 cup Crisco
1 egg, beaten
1-1/2 cups thick cold apple sauce
4 tablespoons hot water
1 cup raisins (or dates)
1/2 cup nuts
2-1/2 cups pastry flour
1/2 teaspoon salt
1 teaspoon soda
1/2 teaspoon each of cloves and nutmeg
1 teaspoon cinnamon

Cream the sugar and Crisco, add egg, beat well. Stir in apple sauce and hot water. Add raisins and nuts, then dry ingredients sifted together twice. Bake in a moderate oven (360° F.) about 1 hour.
Makes 2 small loaves

Apple Sauce Cake #2

1/2 cup butter
1-1/4 cups sugar
1 beaten egg
1 teaspoon soda
3 tablespoons hot water
1 cup unsweetened apple sauce
2 cups Flour
1 teaspoon baking powder
1 teaspoon cinnamon
1/2 teaspoon cloves
1/2 teaspoon nutmeg
(If preferred, omit spices and flavor with vanilla)

Cream the butter and sugar, add beaten egg. Dissolve soda in hot water and add to apple sauce. Mix and sift dry ingredients and add. Beat well. Bake in a loaf in a rather slow oven or in layers in a moderate oven. Serve plain or with boiled frosting or with apple filling.

Bride's Cake #1

3-3/4 cups sifted cake flour
1-1/2 teaspoons baking powder
1-3/4 cups butter
2 cups sugar
1-1/4 cups egg whites, unbeaten
1/2 teaspoon vanilla
1/4 teaspoon almond extract

Sift flour once, measure, add baking powder, and sift together 3 times. Cream butter thoroughly, add sugar gradually, and cream together until light and fluffy. Add egg whites, 1/4 cup at a time, beating about 3 minutes after each addition. Add flour, a small amount at a time, beating well after each addition. Add flavoring and beat vigorously. Turn into 10-inch tube pan which has been greased, lined on bottom, sides, and around tube with heavy paper,and again greased. Bake in slow oven (275° F.) 1 hour; then increase heat slightly to 300° F. and bake 50 minutes longer, or until done. Insert favors, if desired, wrapping each in waxed paper, and pressing into small slits cut in cake. Spread Ornamental Butter Frosting, and trim with silver dragées. Serve on silver try or platter surrounded with delicate sprays of fern, cosmos, or bridal wreath. Place special bridal favor on top of cake; or tie small wedding bells or other favors to white ribbons and intertwine through sprays.

Bride's Cake #2

1-1/2 pounds butter
2 pounds sugar
2 pounds flour
1/4 teaspoon salt
Whites of 22 eggs
1 tablespoon almond or vanilla extract

Cream the butter; then cream the sugar in with it. The sugar should first have been thoroughly sifted before measuring. Sift in the flour gradually, mixing thoroughly. Beat the salt in with the eggs and when the eggs have been beaten until very stiff, add the extract and fold lightly into the first mixture. Be careful not to stir them in, but fold over and over until blended. Bake in a moderate oven.
(This will serve 90 to 100)

Bachelor Bait

Walnut-spangled chocolate layer, covered with sweet chocolate walnut frosting

1/2 cup butter
1-1/2 cups sugar

3 eggs, separated
3 squares unsweetened chocolate (3 ounces)
1/2 cup strong coffee
2/3 cup milk
2-1/2 cups sifted flour
3 teaspoons baking powder
1/8 teaspoon salt
1 teaspoon vanilla
1/2 cup chopped walnuts

Cream butter, add sugar gradually, and cream until fluffy. Add beaten egg yolks. Melt chocolate over hot water; add 1/4 cup coffee and stir until smooth. Cool and add to creamed mixture. Sift flour, measure, and sift twice with dry ingredients. Add alternately with remaining milk and coffee to first mixture. Add vanilla and chopped nuts. Fold in beaten egg whites. Bake in 2 greased and floured 8-inch layer pans in moderate oven, 350°, for 30 minutes.
12 servings

Chocolate Nut Frosting

2 squares chocolate
1/3 cup heavy cream
2 cups powdered sugar
1 tablespoon cold coffee
1/16 teaspoon salt
1/2 teaspoon vanilla
1/4 cup chopped walnuts

Place chocolate in bowl over boiling water. When melted blend in cream. Remove from heat and gradually stir in powdered sugar, thinning with cold coffee, to right consistency to spread. Add salt, vanilla, and chopped walnuts. Spread between layers and on top of cake.

Brown-Eyed Susan Cake

1/2 cup shortening
1-1/2 cups sugar
3 eggs
2-1/4 cups flour
1/2 teaspoon salt
2-1/2 teaspoon baking powder
1 cup milk
1 tablespoon milk
2 squares chocolate
1/8 teaspoon soda
1-1/2 teaspoons grated orange rind (about 1 orange)
Yellow coloring

Cream shortening, add sugar gradually and cream well. Add the well-beaten egg yolks and beat well. Sift flour once before measuring. Sift flour, salt and baking powder together. Add to the creamed mixture alternately with the milk. Fold in stiffly-beaten egg whites. Divide the batter into two parts. To one part add the tablespoon of milk and the melted chocolate to which the soda has been added. To the other add the grated orange rind and enough yellow coloring to make the batter yellow. Drop by spoonfuls on 2 greased and floured 8-inch tins, alternating the light and dark batter as for marble cake. Bake 30 minutes in a moderate oven (350° F.).
Note: After dividing, batter should be stirred as little as possible.

Special Icing

4 tablespoons butter
3 cups confectioners' sugar
3 tablespoons cream
Grated rind of 1 orange (2 tablespoons)
1 tbs orange juice
2 squares chocolate
Cream
Shaved chocolate

Melt the butter in double boiler. Stir in confectioners' sugar and 3 tablespoons cream. Leave over hot water for 15 minutes to eliminate raw taste. Divide icing in two, allowing greater share for chocolate icing. To smaller amount add 1 tbs orange rind, and orange juice, just enough to make it easy to spread. To the other add the melted chocolate, and just enough cream to make it smooth and glossy. Spread chocolate icing between layers and around sides of cake. Spread orange icing on top of cake. While still moist, sprinkle bits of shaved chocolate and grated orange rind in hit-or-miss fashion over top to give yellow and brown effect.

Birthday Cake

1/2 cup shortening
2 cups sugar
3-1/2 cups cake flour
3/4 teaspoon salt
5 teaspoons baking powder
1-1/2 cups milk
5 egg whits
1-1/2 teaspoons flavoring

Cream the shortening and add the sugar gradually. Sift the flour once before measuring. Mix and sift the flour, salt and baking powder, and add alternately with the milk. Add the flavoring—vanilla and almond together are good. Fold in the stiffly-beaten egg whites. Pour into well-greased and floured pans (either 2 9-inch layer pans or 3 8-inch layer pans), and bake 30 minutes in

a moderate oven (350° F.).
16 servings

Comfort Icing

2-1/2 cups sugar
1/4 cup white corn syrup
3/4 cup water
2 egg whites
1-1/2 teaspoons vanilla

Mix together sugar, corn syrup, and water. Boil without stirring. Remove crystals from around pan during boiling process by means of a wet cloth. Cook until mixture threads, 238° F. Pour hot syrup slowly over stiffly-beaten egg whites, beating with egg beater during the addition. Add vanilla and continue beating with a spoon until the mixture will hold its shape. If this mixture does not set so that it will stay on cake, add 2 or 3 tablespoons of powdered sugar, a tablespoon at a time, until mixture is stiff enough.
Note: Part of icing may be colored pink with vegetable coloring matter and used on sides of cake with white icing on top and between layers. Pink candles to match sides can be placed on top of cake for birthday party.

Caramel or Burnt Sugar Cake

1/2 cup shortening
1-1/2 cups sugar
3 eggs
2-1/4 cups cake flour
1 teaspoon salt
3 teaspoons baking powder
3/4 cup cold water
4 tablespoons caramel syrup

Cream the shortening, add the sugar gradually and cream well. Add the well-beaten egg yolks. Sift flour once before measuring. Sift flour, salt and baking powder together. Add alternately with the water and caramel syrup mixed together. Fold in the stiffly-beaten egg whites and mix well. Pour into 2 well-greased and floured 8-inch layer cake pans, and bake for 30 minutes in a moderate oven (350° F.).

Caramel Syrup

2 cups sugar
3/4 cup hot water

Melt (caramelize) the sugar in a heavy pan, stirring over a low fire, until it becomes a brown syrup. (Not too brown or it will have a disagreeable burnt taste.) Add the hot water and cook until the lumps are dissolved and it is consistency of a heavy syrup. Cool.

Caramel Icing

6 tablespoons caramel syrup
4 tablespoons butter
3 cups confectioners' sugar
1 egg white
1 teaspoon vanilla

Heat caramel syrup and butter together and mix in the confectioners' sugar, leaving over hot water 10 minutes to eliminate uncooked taste. Beat in stiffly-beaten egg white and add vanilla. When cool, spread between layers and on top and sides of cake.

Banana Cake #1

1/2 cup shortening
1-1/2 cups sugar
2 eggs
2-1/4 cups cake flour
1/2 teaspoon baking powder
3/4 teaspoon soda
1/2 teaspoon salt
1/4 cup sour milk
1 cup mashed bananas (2 or 3 bananas)
1 teaspoon vanilla
1 cup cream, whipped and sweetened
2 bananas sliced

Cream shortening and add sugar gradually. Add the well-beaten eggs. Sift flour once before measuring. Sift flour, baking powder, soda and salt together and add alternately with the sour milk and bananas which have been mashed through a sieve. Add flavoring. Pour into greased and floured layer cake pans and bake. When layers are cold, put together with whipped cream and bananas for filling and spread whipped cream over top of cake. Lay slices of banana over top of cream. Bake 30 minutes in a moderate oven (350° F.).
Note: Part of cake can be prepared as directed with whipped cream for immediate use, and the remainder may be iced with white icing, cocoanut or chocolate icing for later use.

Banana Cake #2

1/2 cup shortening
1-1/2 cups sugar
2 eggs

2-1/4 cups sifted flour
1/2 teaspoon baking powder
3/4 teaspoon soda
1/2 teaspoon salt
1/4 cup sour milk
1 cup mashed bananas (2 or 3 bananas)
1 teaspoon vanilla
1 cup cream (whipped and sweetened)
2 bananas, sliced

Cream shortening and add sugar gradually. (This "creaming" is very important.) Add well-beaten eggs and mix thoroughly. Sift flour, measure and sift again 3 times with baking powder, soda and salt to blend evenly. Add alternately with the sour milk and bananas, which have been mashed through a sieve or chopped with a pastry blender. Add vanilla. Pour into 2 greased and floured layer tins and bake for 35 to 45 minutes in a moderate oven, 350°. When layers are cold, put together with whipped cream and sliced bananas for filling, and spread whipped cream over the top of cake. Decorate with thin slices of bananas. Do not spread with whipped cream until just before serving.
12 servings

All-Around Chocolate Frosting

4 tablespoons butter
3 cups sifted confectioners' sugar
3/4 teaspoon vanilla
1/4 teaspoon salt
3 squares unsweetened chocolate, melted
4 tablespoons hot milk (about)

Cream butter; add part of sugar gradually, blending after each addition. Add vanilla, salt, and chocolate, and mix well. Add remaining sugar, alternately with milk, until of right consistency to spread, beating after each addition until smooth. Makes enough frosting to cover tops and sides of 2 9-inch layers, or top and sides of an 8x8x2-inch cake (generously), or about 3 dozen cupcakes.

Hungarian Chocolate Frosting

3 squares unsweetened chocolate
1-1/2 cup confectioners' sugar
2-1/2 tablespoons hot water
3 egg yolks
4 tablespoons butter

Melt chocolate in double boiler. Remove from boiling water, add sugar and water, and blend. Add egg yolks, one at a time, beating well after each. Add butter, a tablespoon at a time, beating thoroughly after each amount. Makes enough frosting to cover tops and sides of 2 9-inch layers.

Brown Stone Front Cake

Mrs. L. G. DeDay

1 cup sugar
1/2 cup butter
2 eggs
1/2 cup sour milk
2-1/2 cups flour
1 teaspoon soda
1 cup grated chocolate
1 egg
1/2 cup sweet milk
1/2 cup brown sugar

Mix first 6 ingredients; set aside. Stir together remaining ingredients and cook until thick, then add to first mixture. Bake in moderate oven.

Caramel Cake #1

1/2 cup butter
1/2 cup sugar
3 eggs, beaten separately
1/2 cup sugar, caramelized
1/4 cup hot water
2-1/2 cups sifted flour
3 teaspoons baking powder
1/2 cup milk

Cream the butter and sugar. Add the egg yolks, beaten until thick and lemon colored. To caramelize the 1/2 cup of sugar, melt in a skillet, stirring constantly until entirely melted and very dark brown. Add hot water to caramel, stirring until thoroughly mixed. Add syrup to first mixture. Then add the sifted flour and baking powder alternately with the milk. Beat until very smooth and fold in the stiffly-beaten egg whites. Turn into buttered and floured layer cake pans and bake in a moderate oven until it shrinks from the sides of the pan. When cool, cover with plain boiled frosting or Caramel Frosting.

Caramel Cake #2

Caramel Part:
1 cup sugar
1/3 cup cold water
1/2 cup boiling water

Dissolve sugar in the cold water; add boiling water and cook without stirring until it turns straw color, then stir constantly until dark brown. Then add 1/2 cup of boiling water and continue cooking about 5 additional minutes.

Cake Part:
1-1/2 cups sugar
1/2 cup butter
2 egg yolks, well beaten
2 cups sifted flour
1 cup lukewarm water
1/2 cup sifted flour
4 teaspoons baking powder
1/2 teaspoon salt
3 tablespoons caramel syrup (above)
1 teaspoon vanilla
4 egg whites, beaten stiff

Cream butter and sugar, add beaten yolks, then add alternately the 2 cups flour and water and beat 5 minutes. Sift together 3 times the 1/2 cup flour, baking powder and salt, and add to beaten mixture, with the syrup and flavoring, then fold in gently the stiffly-beaten whites. Bake in 3 layers in buttered cake pans in a moderate oven and when cool put together with Caramel Frosting or Butter Scotch Frosting.

Chocolate Cake #1

1/3 cup butter
1-1/2 cups sugar
3 eggs, beaten separately
3 squares unsweetened cake or 3/4 cup unsweetened powdered chocolate
1 cup milk
2-1/2 cups Flour
3 teaspoons baking powder
1/2 teaspoon vanilla or almond extract

Cream the butter and sugar. Add the yolks of the eggs, beaten until thick and lemon color. Melt the chocolate and add, or add powdered chocolate sifted with flour. Mix and sift the flour and baking powder 3 times and add alternately with the milk and flavoring. Beat until very smooth and velvety, then fold in the stiffly-beaten whites. Pour into a greased cake pan, lined with waxed paper or slightly floured, and bake in a moderate oven. When cool, spread with chocolate frosting. If baked in layers, it is especially good with Chocolate Jelly Filling between and plain Chocolate or Boiled Frosting on top.

Chocolate Cake #2

1/4 cup Crisco
3/4 cup sugar
2 squares chocolate
2 eggs
1/2 cup milk
1-1/2 cups flour
2 teaspoons baking powder
1/2 teaspoon salt

Cream Crisco with sugar; add melted chocolate, beaten eggs, milk, and flour sifted with baking powder and salt. Bake in 2 layers or 1 large flat pan in a moderate oven, for about half an hour.
Frost with bittersweet icing. Make boiled icing as usual. Over surface, spread melted bitter chocolate in a thin layer.

Chocolate Ribbon Cake

1/3 cup butter
1 cup sugar
3 eggs, beaten separately
2 cups sifted flour
3 teaspoons baking powder
1/2 cup milk
1/2 teaspoon almond or vanilla extract
2 squares unsweetened chocolate, melted, or
1/2 cup unsweetened powdered cocoa

Cream the butter and sugar until very soft, then add the egg yolks beaten until thick and lemon colored. Mix and sift the flour and baking powder, and add alternately with the milk and vanilla. Beat until very light, then fold in the well-beaten egg whites. Divide the batter into 2 parts. Into one, stir the melted chocolate. Have ready 2 buttered layer cake pans. Into them first put a spoonful of one of the mixtures, then a spoonful of the other, alternating until all is used. Bake in a moderate oven until the cake shrinks from sides of the pans. When cool, cover with Chocolate Frosting.

Chocolate Cream Cake

A soft-filling cake similar to Washington Cream Pie

Cake Part:
1-1/2 cups Flour
1-12 teaspoons baking powder
Few grains salt
2 egg yolks
1-1/4 cup sugar
2/3 cup water
1 teaspoon vanilla
2 egg whites

Mix and sift flour, baking powder and salt. Beat egg yolks, add sugar, and add alternately the water and flour mixture. Beat until smooth, then fold in stiffly-beaten whites. Bake in 3 buttered and floured round cake tins in a moderate oven until a gentle pressure leaves no imprint. While baking, prepare the following:

Chocolate Cream Part:
2 tablespoons Flour
1 tablespoon cornstarch
2 tablespoons sugar
1/4 teaspoon salt
1/4 cup powdered unsweetened chocolate or cocoa
1 cup milk
1 beaten egg yolk
1/4 cup butter
1 cup sifted powdered sugar
1 teaspoon vanilla

Into top of double boiler put the flour, cornstarch, sugar, salt and chocolate. Mix, add milk and cook, stirring constantly, until thick and smooth. Mix a small amount with the beaten egg yolk and return this to the double boiler and continue cooking a moment longer. While cooling, cream butter with powdered sugar and vanilla, beat until thick and light, and fold in Chocolate Cream mixture and spread on cake.

Chocolate Nut Cake

1/2 cup butter
2 cups sugar
4 egg yolks
3 squares, or 3/4 cup powdered unsweetened chocolate
2-1/2 cups sifted flour
4 level teaspoons baking powder
1 cup milk
3/4 cup broken nut meats
4 egg whites
1 teaspoon vanilla

Cream butter and sugar, add well-beaten egg yolks, then chocolate grated or melted, or powdered chocolate, and alternately the flour sifted with baking powder and milk, adding nuts with last of flour. Beat until smooth and fold in stiffly-beaten egg whites. Bake in layers or in a deeper cake pan, buttered and floured, according to general directions. When cool cover with chocolate frosting and nuts.

Chocolate Potato Cake

1/2 cup butter
1-1/2 cups sugar
1 cup mashed potato
3 eggs, beaten separately
3 ounces grated or powdered unsweetened chocolate
2-1/2 cups Flour
3 teaspoons baking powder
1/4 teaspoon salt
1/4 cup milk
1 teaspoon vanilla

Cream butter and sugar thoroughly. Add mashed potato, then the well-beaten egg yolks and either powdered or melted cake chocolate. Beat well. Mix and sift the flour, baking powder and salt and add alternately with the milk and vanilla. Beat until light and smooth, then fold in the stiffly-beaten whites. Bake in a buttered and floured pan, preferably one about 2 inches deep. It is done when it shrinks from the sides of the pan and a slight pressure made with the finger leaves no permanent indentation. When cool, cover with a white or chocolate frosting.

Chocolate Cake Moderne

This is a new kind of an old favorite . . . made with Sperry Pancake and Waffle Flour, this cake has lightness and flavor that's unsurpassed

1/3 cup butter
3/4 cup sugar
3 eggs, well beaten
2 squares unsweetened chocolate, melted (2 ounces)
2 cups Sperry Pancake and Waffle Flour
3/4 cup milk
1-1/2 teaspoons vanilla
1/2 cup chopped walnut meats

Cream butter and sugar. Add eggs and beat until smooth. Blend in melted chocolate. Sift flour, measure, and add to creamed mixture alternately with milk to which vanilla has been added. Add chopped nuts last. Pour into 2 greased and floured 8-inch cake pans and bake in moderately hot oven, 375°, for 25 minutes. When cool, ice with any desired frosting. 12 servings.

Chocolate Tier Cake

6 tablespoons sifted cake flour
1/2 teaspoon baking powder
1/4 teaspoon salt
3/4 cup sifted sugar
4 egg whites, stiffly beaten
4 egg yolks, beaten until thick and lemon colored
1 teaspoon vanilla
2 squares unsweetened chocolate, melted
3/4 cup cream, whipped

Sift flour once, measure, add baking powder and salt, and sift together 3 times. Fold sugar gradually into egg whites. Fold in egg yolks and vanilla. Fold in flour gradually. Then beat in chocolate, gently but thoroughly. Turn into 15x10-inch pan which has been greased, line with paper to within 1/2 inch of edge, and again greased. Bake in hot oven (400° F.) 13 minutes,

or until done. Quickly cut off crisp edges of cake and turn out on damp cloth on rack; remove paper. When cold, cut in half lengthwise, then crosswise. Spread 3 of quarters evenly with whipped cream, sweetened and flavored with vanilla; put together as a 4-layer cake, matching edges and placing plain layer on top. Spread top and sides with All-Around Chocolate Frosting. Cut in 3/4-inch slices and serve as a dessert cake.
Serves 8

Chocolate Angel Food

1 cup egg whites
1 level teaspoon cream of tartar
1 teaspoon vanilla or almond extract
Few grains salt
Sugar
1 cup sifted flour
1/3 cup unsweetened powdered chocolate or cocoa

Beat egg whites on a large platter with a wire whisk or fork. Do not use the rotary beater for eggs used in angel food. When half beaten, add the cream of tartar, vanilla and salt and continue beating until very stiff but not dry. Fold in the sifted sugar. Sift together the flour and cocoa and fold in carefully without beating. Turn into an ungreased angel food pan and bake in a slow oven for about an hour, or until a very gentle touch leaves no imprint. Where temperature is used, bake at 325°, but the length of time depends entirely upon the size and shape of pan, and therefore, the depth of cake. The imprint test is the best to go by. When done, invert the pan and let cake remain until cold without disturbing. Then carefully loosen with knife or spatula. If angel or sponge cake are loosened or jarred before cold, the air cells break, the cake falls or shrinks, and is tough. That is why an ungreased pan is used—so the cake will be held in the pan at its full height until cold, when the cake will have become firm enough to handle.

White Top Chocolateer

Here's a cake with very thin batter, as easy to make as gingerbread, and with much the same texture when finished

2 ounces unsweetened chocolate (2 squares)
1-3/4 cups brown sugar
1 cup hot coffee
1/2 cup shortening
2 eggs, separated
2 cups flour
1 teaspoon soda, dissolved in
1/2 cup buttermilk
1 teaspoon vanilla

Melt chocolate in top of double boiler. Add 3/4 cup brown sugar and coffee, stirring until smooth. Cream remaining brown sugar and shortening. Add well-beaten egg yolks and chocolate mixture. Sift flour, measure and add alternately with buttermilk. Add vanilla. Fold in stiffly-beaten egg whites. Pour into 2 8-inch greased and floured cake pans and bake in moderate oven, 350°, for 30 minutes. When cold, put layers together with Boiled Frosting.
12 servings
Note: This batter is very thin. More flour is not necessary.

Boiled Frosting

1 cup sugar
2 tablespoons white corn syrup
1/2 cup water
2 egg whites
1/2 teaspoon vanilla
1/2 cup chopped nuts

Boil sugar, syrup and water to 238°, or when it will spin an inch to two-inch thread when dropped from a spoon. Pour slowly over stiffly-beaten egg whites, beating constantly. Add vanilla and beat until cool and of a consistency to spread. Spread frosting between layers and over top and sides of cake. Sprinkle with chopped nuts.

Mint Chocolate Log

Less than 12 minutes puts this roll in the oven. When cool, old-fashioned peppermint sticks, ground, form the base of the filling and topping.

3/4 cup sugar
5 eggs, separated
1 teaspoon vanilla
1/3 flour
1 teaspoon baking powder
1/4 teaspoon salt
1 cup ground chocolate

Fold sugar gradually into stiffly-beaten egg whites. Beat egg yolks and vanilla until stiff and lemon colored and fold into egg white meringue. Sift flour, measure and sift again 3 times with baking powder, salt and chocolate. Fold gently into egg mixture. Pour into a shallow pan 13x9 inches, lined with greased paper, and bake in hot oven, 400°, for 15 minutes. Turn out on damp

cloth, roll and let stand until cool. Unroll, spread with Peppermint Whipped Cream Filling, re-roll and ice with Peppermint Glaze.
8 servings

Peppermint Whipped Cream Filling

3/4 cup whipping cream
1/4 cup crushed peppermint sticks

Whip cream, adding peppermint sticks just before stiff enough to spread, and continue beating until of the right consistency.

Peppermint Glaze Icing

1 tablespoon crushed peppermint sticks
1 tablespoon cream
3/4 cup powdered sugar

Melt peppermint sticks with cream in top of double boiler. Add powdered sugar, beating until smooth. While still warm spread a thin layer over top of roll.

4-Egg Yolk Cake

How to make use of leftover yolks? Here's the answer . . . and a mighty tasty one, say men folks.

1/2 cup shortening
1 cup sugar
4 egg yolks
1/2 cup ground chocolate
1/2 cup water
2 cups flour
3 teaspoons baking powder
1 teaspoon salt
1/2 cup milk
1 teaspoon vanilla

Cream shortening and sugar thoroughly. Add egg yolks, one at a time, beating well after each addition. Add chocolate mixed to a paste with water. Sift flour, measure and sift again twice with baking powder and salt. Add alternately to creamed mixture with milk to which vanilla has been added. Pour into 2 greased and floured 8-inch layer cake pans and bake in moderate oven, 350°, for 30- minutes. When cool, put layers together and frost with Pineapple Frosting.
12 servings

Pineapple Frosting

1/2 cup butter
3-1/2 cups powdered sugar
1/2 cup grated pineapple, well drained
1/2 teaspoon vanilla

Cream butter, adding sugar gradually along with pineapple and vanilla. Beat until smooth and frosting is of proper consistency to spread.

Southern Cocoanut Cake

1/2 cup Formay
1-1/2 cup sugar
3 egg yolks
1 cup cocoanut
Grated rind 1 orange
3 cups cake flour
1/2 teaspoon baking soda
2 teaspoon baking powder
1 teaspoon salt
1 cup orange juice
3 egg whites

Cream Formay and sugar. Add well-beaten egg yolks, cocoanut and orange rind. Sift and measure flour. Add soda, baking powder and salt. Sift again. Add to first mixture alternately with orange juice. Fold in stiffly-beaten egg whites. Bake in 2 layers 30 to 40 minutes at 350° F. Frost with boiled icing. Then sprinkle generously with shredded cocoanut.

Chocolate Prune Cake

A long-keeping cake with a spicy, rich molasses-like flavor. The cream cheese frosting is the ideal complement to this fruited cake.

1/2 cup shortening
1-1/3 cups brown sugar, free from lumps
2 eggs
2 squares unsweetened chocolate, melted (2 ounces)
2 cups flour
1 teaspoon baking powder
1/8 teaspoon salt
1/2 teaspoon each nutmeg, allspice, cinnamon
1 cup and 2 tablespoons buttermilk
1 teaspoon soda
1 cup cooked prunes, stoned and chopped

Cream shortening and sugar well. Add well-beaten eggs and cream until fluffy. Add chocolate, beating until smooth. Sift flour, measure, and sift again 3 times with baking powder, salt,

and spices. Add alternately to creamed mixture with buttermilk in which soda has been dissolved. Add prunes last. Pour into 2 greased and floured 8-inch layer cake pans and bake in moderate oven, 350°, for 30 minutes. When cool put layers together with Cream Cheese Frosting.
12 servings

Cream Cheese Frosting

1 package cream cheese (3 ounces)
1 egg
1/4 teaspoon lemon rind
1 teaspoon vanilla
4-1/2 cups sifted powdered sugar

Cream cheese and egg until smooth. Blend in lemon rind and vanilla. Add powdered sugar gradually, beating until creamy and stiff enough to spread.

Brownie Cake

A cross between a devil's food and fudge-type cake, with almost a brownie texture. An elusive almond flavor adds piquance to the frosting.

1/2 cup shortening
1 cup sugar
2 eggs
4 squares unsweetened chocolate, melted (4 ounces)
1/4 cup water
2 cups flour
1/2 teaspoon salt
1 cup buttermilk
1-1/2 teaspoons soda
1 teaspoon vanilla

Cream shortening and sugar thoroughly. Add eggs and beat until smooth and creamy. Blend chocolate and sugar to form paste and add to egg mixture. Sift flour, measure and sift again with salt. Add alternately to creamed mixture with buttermilk in which soda has been dissolved. Add vanilla. Pour into 2 8-inch greased and floured layer cake pans and bake in moderate oven, 325°, for 30 minutes. When cool put layers together with Brownie Frosting (below).
12 servings

Brownie Frosting

3 squares unsweetened chocolate (3 ounces)
1/2 cup whipping cream
1 egg
3-1/2 cups sifted powdered sugar
1 teaspoon almond flavoring

Melt chocolate with cream in double boiler. Add slightly-beaten egg and cook until thick and smooth. Remove from stove and add powdered sugar, gradually beating until smooth. Add flavoring last and spread between layers and over top of cake.

Old-Fashioned Chocolate Layer

What's this moist white layer cake doing here? Why, it's Grandmother's version of chocolate cake . . . simplified but just as tempting.

1/2 cup butter
1/1-3 cups sugar
2 cups flour
2 teaspoons baking powder
1/2 teaspoon salt
3/4 cup milk
1 teaspoon vanilla
4 egg whites

Cream butter and sugar well. Sift flour, measure and sift again twice with baking powder and salt. Add to creamed mixture alternately with milk to which vanilla has been added. Fold in stiffly-beaten egg whites. Pour into 3 greased and floured 8-inch layer cake pans and bake in moderate oven, 350°, for 30 minutes. When cool, put layers together with Cooked Chocolate Filling. Frost top and sides with Sweet Chocolate Frosting.
12 servings

Deep South Devil's Food

A rich devil's food loaf, topped with cocoanut-sprinkled boiled frosting.

1/2 cup brown sugar
2 squares unsweetened chocolate (2 ounces)
1/2 cup milk
1/2 cup butter
1 cup granulated sugar
2 eggs, separated
2 cups flour
2 teaspoons baking powder
1/2 teaspoon salt
1/4 teaspoon soda
2/3 cup milk
1/2 teaspoon vanilla

Cook brown sugar, shaved chocolate, and 1/2 cup milk together only until thick and smooth. Cool. Cream butter, add granulated sugar, and cream thoroughly; add egg yolks one at a time, beating after each addition. Sift flour and measure; sift again 3

times with baking powder and salt. Add 1/3 of flour to creamed mixture and mix well. Dissolve soda in chocolate paste, and blend into cake mixture. Add remaining flour alternately with milk to which vanilla has been added. Fold in stiffly-beaten egg whites. Bake in greased and floured deep 10-inch square loaf pan, in a moderate oven, 350°, for 45 minutes. Cool and frost with Boiled Icing.
12 servings

Boiled Icing

1 cup sugar
2 tablespoons white corn syrup
1/4 cup water
2 egg whites
1 teaspoon vanilla
1 cup shredded cocoanut

Boil sugar, syrup and water to 240°, or until it will spin a 2-inch thread when dropped from a spoon. Pour slowly over stiffly-beaten egg whites, beating constantly. Beat until of a consistency to spread; add vanilla, and spread over top and sides of cake. Sprinkle heavily with cocoanut.

Sour-Cream Sweet

Soft chocolate frosting over a fine-textured chocolate layer cake.

1/4 cup hot milk
1/2 cup ground chocolate
1/2 teaspoon soda
1 cup sour cream
1 cup sugar
2 eggs, separated
1 teaspoon vanilla
1-1/2 cups flour
1 teaspoon baking powder
1/2 teaspoon salt

Pour hot milk on chocolate, return to fire for about one minute, or until chocolate and milk form a smooth paste. Let cool. Add soda to sour cream, stirring until dissolved; add sugar, and beat with a rotary beater until cream holds its shape. Beat egg whites until stiff, fold in slightly-beaten egg yolks, then fold this into cream mixture. Fold in chocolate paste and add vanilla. Sift flour and measure; sift again 3 times with baking powder and salt, and fold into cake batter. Bake in 2 greased and floured 8-inch layer pans in a moderate oven, 350°, for 30 minutes.
12 servings

Creamy Chocolate Frosting

3 squares unsweetened chocolate (3 ounces)
1 tablespoons butter
1 cup sifted powdered sugar
1/8 teaspoon salt
1 egg
1/4 cup milk
1 teaspoon vanilla

Melt chocolate over hot water, cool slightly, and blend in butter. Add remaining ingredients. Beat with rotary beater until well mixed. Set in pan of cold or ice water and beat constantly for about 10 minutes, until thick enough to spread.

Spiced Cococake

Delicately spiced chocolate cake, frosted with a penuche-type icing

1/2 cup shortening
1-1/2 cups sugar
2 eggs
1/3 cup cocoa
1/3 cup hot water
3/4 teaspoon soda
1 cup sour milk or buttermilk
2-1/4 cups Drifted Snow "Home-Perfected" Flour
1 teaspoon baking powder
1/2 teaspoon salt
1/2 teaspoon cinnamon
1/4 teaspoon nutmeg
1/4 teaspoon cloves

Cream shortening, add sugar gradually, creaming between each addition. Add eggs one at a time, and beat well. Mix cocoa with hot water and add to creamed mixture. Add soda to sour milk. Sift flour and measure, sift again with remaining dry ingredients and add to cake mixture alternately with sour milk. Pour into 2 greased and floured 9-inch layer pans and bake in a moderate oven, 350°, for 30 minutes.
12 servings

Caramel Frosting

2 cups brown sugar
1/2 cup cream, or undiluted evaporated milk
1/8 teaspoon salt
1 teaspoon vanilla

Blend all ingredients, except vanilla, until smooth. Bring slowly to a boil, stirring occasionally, and cook until syrup forms soft ball in cold water, 234°. Remove from heat and beat constantly until creamy and cool. Add vanilla. If frosting becomes too stiff to spread easily before it is cool, add extra cream or evaporated milk, one drop at a time, and continue beating until cool. Spread between layers and on top of cake.

House of Orange Glacé

Fluffy rich chocolate cake, spread with tart orange filling, topped with meringue

1/2 cup butter
1-1/2 cups sugar
2 eggs
2 squares unsweetened chocolate (2 ounces)
1/2 cup water
2 cups Drifted Snow "Home-Perfected" Flour
1-1/2 teaspoons baking powder
1/4 teaspoon salt
2/3 cup buttermilk, or sour milk
1 teaspoon soda

Cream butter and sugar until fluffy; add eggs separately, creaming between each addition. Melt chocolate in water in top of double boiler, stirring to a smooth paste. Add to creamed mixture, blending thoroughly. Sift flour, measure, and sift again with baking powder and salt. Add to cake mixture alternately with buttermilk to which soda has been added. Bake in 2 greased and floured 8-inch layer pans, in a moderate oven, 360°, for 30 minutes. Cool and fill with Orange Filling (below) and frost with Meringue (below). Return to a slow oven, 300°, for 20 minutes to cook and brown meringue. Cool before serving.
12 servings

Orange Filling

1 cup sugar
1/3 cup Drifted Snow "Home-Perfected" Flour
3/4 cup orange juice
1/4 cup lemon juice
Grated rind of one orange
4 egg yolks, slightly beaten
1 tablespoon butter

Mix sugar and flour thoroughly. Add remaining ingredients in order given. Cook in double boiler 10 to 15 minutes, or until thick and smooth. Cool and spread 3/4 of filling between layers of cake and remaining 1/4 on top.

Meringue

4 egg whites
1/2 cup sugar

Beat egg whites until stiff and slowly fold in sugar. Completely cover top and sides of cake with meringue.

Black and White Fruit Cake

Three-layer fruit-filled chocolate cake, with fruit-decorated white frosting

1/2 cup shortening
2 cups brown sugar
2 egg yolks
1 whole egg
3 squares unsweetened chocolate (3 ounces)
1 cup hot coffee
1/2 teaspoon soda
2 cups Drifted Snow "Home-Perfected" Flour
1 teaspoon baking powder
1/8 teaspoon salt
1 tablespoon vanilla

Cream shortening and sugar; add egg yolks and egg, and beat until light and fluffy. Shave chocolate into hot coffee. Cool and blend in soda. Sift flour, measure, and sift again with baking powder and salt. Add alternately to creamed mixture with coffee-chocolate paste, beating until smooth. Add vanilla and pour into 3 greased and floured 8-inch layer pans. Bake in a moderately hot oven, 375°, for 20 minutes. Cool and frost with White Fruit Frosting.
12 servings

Delicious Chocolate Cakes

1 cup sugar
1/2 cup cooking oil
2 eggs
1 teaspoon vanilla extract
2 squares (2 ounces) unsweetened chocolate
1-3/4 cups flour
1/2 teaspoon salt
2-1/2 teaspoons baking powder
1/2 cup milk

Add sugar to oil slowly. Add well-beaten eggs, flavoring and chocolate which has been melted. Sift together flour, salt and baking powder; add alternately with the milk. Mix thoroughly and put small amount of batter into slightly oiled individual cake tins. Bake in moderate oven (380° F.) for about 18 minutes. Spread cakes thickly with frosting. If cocoa is used instead of chocolate, sift 1/2 cup cocoa with dry ingredients.

Chocolate Frosting

2-1/2 cups confectioners' sugar
4 tablespoons boiling water
1 teaspoon vanilla extract
1/4 teaspoon salt
2 teaspoons cooking oil
1-1/2 squares (1-1/2 ounces) unsweetened chocolate
1 tablespoon cream

To sugar add boiling water slowly to make smooth paste; add vanilla, salt, oil and melted chocolate. Add cream until right consistency to spread.
If cocoa is used here instead of chocolate, mix 5 tablespoons cocoa with sufficient water to make a paste and add after flavoring.
Makes 18 cakes

Cream Layer Cake

1/3 cup cooking oil
1 cup sugar
2 eggs
1 teaspoon vanilla extract
1/2 cup milk
1-3/4 cups flour
1/2 teaspoon salt
3 teaspoons baking powder

Cream oil and sugar together until light; add beaten egg yolks, flavoring and milk slowly; sift flour and salt. Add half, then half-beaten egg whites; add the rest of the flour sifted with baking powder; stir after each addition; fold in remaining egg whites. Bake in 2 oiled layer tins in moderate oven (400° F.) about 20 minutes; cool and put together with Cream Filling (below) and cover top and sides with White Icing (below).

Cream Filling

1/4 cup sugar
2 tablespoons corn starch
2 egg yolks
1 cup scalded milk
1 teaspoon vanilla extract
Rind of 1 orange
1/8 teaspoon salt
2 teaspoons cooking oil
1 teaspoon lemon juice

Mix well together sugar, corn starch and egg yolks. Add slowly to scalded milk. Cook in top of double boiler until smooth and thick. Remove from fire. Add vanilla, orange rind, salt, oil and lemon juice. Cool and spread thickly between layers of cake.

White Icing

2-1/2 cups confectioners' sugar
2 egg whites
2 teaspoons oil
1/2 teaspoon vanilla extract

Add sugar slowly to unbeaten egg whites, mixing until smooth and stiff enough to spread. Add oil and flavoring and spread on top and sides of cake. If icing is too thick, thin by adding a little cream or boiling water.

Chocolate Layer Cake

2 eggs
1 cup sugar
1/3 cup cooking oil
1 teaspoon vanilla extract
1/2 cup milk
1-3/4 cups flour
1/2 teaspoon salt
3 teaspoons baking powder

Separate eggs; save one white for icing. Beat egg yolks well; add sugar slowly, the oil a little at a time, and the vanilla; mix thoroughly and add half the milk and half the flour which has been sifted with salt and baking powder, then add remainder of milk and remainder of flour, mixing well after each addition; fold in beaten egg white. Bake in 3 oiled layer tins hot oven (425 to 450° F.) about 15 minutes. Cool.

Chocolate Filling

3 squares (3 ounces) unsweetened chocolate
3 tablespoons milk
1 tablespoon cooking oil
1 egg yolk
3/4 cup powdered or confectioners' sugar
1 tablespoon corn starch
1/8 teaspoon salt
1 teaspoon vanilla extract

Melt chocolate in top of double boiler; add milk, oil and egg yolk. Stir in sugar gradually; mix corn starch with a little cold water and add, stirring constantly until smooth and thick. Remove from fire; add salt and vanilla and spread thickly between layers of cake.

Chocolate Icing

1 unbeaten egg white
1-1/2 cups confectioners' sugar
2 squares (2 ounces) melted chocolate
1/2 teaspoon vanilla extract
1/8 teaspoon salt
2 teaspoons cooking oil

Put egg white into shallow dish; add sugar slowly, beating with wire whip until of right consistency to spread; add chocolate, vanilla, salt and oil. Mix well and spread on cake.

Country Pork Cake

This is delicious and will keep a long time.

1 pound salt pork (chopped very fine)
1 pint boiling water
1/2 cup molasses
2 cups sugar
9 cups sifted flour
2 teaspoons soda
2 teaspoons cream of tartar
1 teaspoon cinnamon
1 teaspoon cloves
1 teaspoon mace
1 teaspoon allspice
1 teaspoon grated nutmeg
2 pounds raisins (seedless)
1/2 pound citron
1 pound currants
1 pound chopped seeded raisins

Pour the boiling water over the chopped pork and let stand until cool. Add the molasses to the pork and water, then the sugar. Sift together all the dry ingredients (reserving a part of the flour to dredge the fruit) and beat well into the mixture. Bake in large loaves.

Kate Smith's Favorite Coconut Layer Cake

2 cups sifted cake flour
2 teaspoons baking powder
1/2 teaspoon salt
2/3 cup butter or other shortening
1 cup sugar
3 eggs, unbeaten
1/3 cup milk
1 teaspoon vanilla

Sift flour once, measure, add baking powder and salt, and sift together 3 times. Cream butter thoroughly, add sugar gradually, and cream together until light and fluffy. Add eggs, one at a time, beating thoroughly after each. Add flour, alternately with milk, a small amount at a time, beating after each addition until smooth. Add vanilla. Bake in 2 greased 9-inch layer pans in moderate oven (375° F.) 25 to 30 minutes. Spread Coconut Seven Minute Frosting (below) between layers and on top and sides of cake. Double recipe to make 3 10-inch layers.

Coconut Seven Minute Frosting

2 egg whites, unbeaten
1-1/2 cups sugar
5 tablespoons water
1-1/2 teaspoons light corn syrup
1 teaspoon vanilla
1 can Baker's Southern Style Coconut

Combine egg whites, sugar, water and corn syrup in top of double boiler, beating with rotary egg beater until thoroughly mixed. Place over rapidly boiling water, beat constantly with rotary egg beater, and cook 7 minutes, or until frosting will stand in peaks. Remove from boiling water; add vanilla and beat until thick enough to spread. Spread on cake, sprinkling with coconut while frosting is still soft. Makes enough frosting to cover top and sides of Coconut Layer Cake, or top and sides of 8x8x2-inch cake (generously) or about 2 dozen cup cakes.

Ornamental Butter Frosting

4 tablespoons butter
5 cups sifted confectioners' sugar
2 egg whites, unbeaten
2 tablespoons cream (about)
1-1/2 teaspoons vanilla
1/4 teaspoon salt

Cream butter; add part of sugar gradually, blending after each addition. Add remaining sugar, alternately with egg whites, then with cream, until of right consistency to spread. Beat after each addition until smooth. Add vanilla and salt. Makes enough frosting to cover Bride's Cake and use for decorating.

Devil's Food

1 cup unsweetened powdered chocolate, or 4 squares unsweetened cake chocolate
1/2 cup milk
1 egg yolk
1 cup brown sugar
2/3 cup butter
1 cup brown sugar

2 well-beaten egg yolks
2 cups sifted flour
2 teaspoons baking powder
1/2 cup milk (sweet)
1/2 teaspoon soda, dissolved in 1 tablespoon hot water
1 teaspoon vanilla
2 beaten egg whites

If cake chocolate be used, slice thin and melt it. Mix the milk, egg yolk and 1 cup brown sugar and cook in the double boiler until thick, stirring constantly.
Cream together the butter and brown sugar until very soft, then add well-beaten yolks. Mix and sift flour and baking powder and add alternately with milk and dissolved soda. Add vanilla and fold in beaten whites. Use extra egg white for frosting. Bake in a moderate oven.

New Devil's Food Cake

2-1/2 cups sifted cake flour
2-1/4 teaspoons baking powder
3/4 teaspoon salt
1/2 teaspoon soda
2/3 cup butter or other shortening
1-1/4 cups sugar
1 egg, unbeaten
2 egg yolks, unbeaten
3 squares unsweetened chocolate, melted
3/4 cup milk
1 teaspoon vanilla
1/3 cup boiling water
Chopped nuts

Sift flour once, measure, add baking powder, salt and soda, and sift together 3 times. Cream butter thoroughly, add sugar gradually, and cream together until light and fluffy. Add egg and egg yolks, one at a time, beating well after each. Add chocolate and blend. Add flour, alternately with milk, a small amount at a time, beating after each addition until smooth. Add vanilla, then add boiling water, beating quickly and thoroughly. Bake in 2 greased 9-inch layer pans in moderate oven (350° F.) 30 to 35 minutes, or until done. Spread Morocco Frosting (below) between layers and on top and sides of cake. Sprinkle with chopped nuts.

Morocco Frosting

2 egg whites, unbeaten
1-3/4 cups granulated sugar
1/4 cup brown sugar, firmly packed
5 tablespoons water
1 square Baker's Unsweetened Chocolate, melted

Combine all ingredients except chocolate in top of double boiler. Beat with rotary egg beater until well mixed. Place over rapidly boiling water, beat constantly with rotary egg beater, and cook 7 minutes, or until frosting stands in peaks. Remove from boiling water and fold in chocolate carefully but thoroughly.

Chocolate Sauce

2 squares unsweetened chocolate
6 tablespoons water
1/2 cup sugar
Dash of salt
3 tablespoons butter
1/4 teaspoon vanilla

Add chocolate to water and place over low flame, stirring until blended. Add sugar and salt and cook until sugar is dissolved and mixture very slightly thickened, stirring constantly. Remove from fire; add butter and vanilla.
Makes about 1 cup sauce

Fluffy Chocolate Sauce

This sauce may be used as filling for cream puffs; fill just before serving

4 tablespoons Regal Chocolate Sauce
1/2 cup cream, whipped

Fold ingredients together.

Chocolate Mint Sauce

1/2 teaspoon peppermint extract
Regal Chocolate Sauce

Combine ingredients. Serve hot or cold, as desired.

Chocolate Candy Sauce

Crushed peppermint candy
Regal Chocolate sauce

Mix ingredients, varying the amount as desired for flavor.

Devil's Food Cake

2-1/2 cups sifted flour
2-1/4 teaspoons baking powder

3/4 teaspoon salt
1/2 teaspoon soda
3/4 cup butter or other shortening
1-1/4 cups sugar
1 egg, unbeaten
2 egg yolks, unbeaten
3 squares Baker's Unsweetened Chocolate, melted
3/4 cup milk
1 teaspoon vanilla
1/3 cup boiling water

Sift flour once, measure, add baking powder, salt and soda, and sift together 3 times. Cream butter thoroughly, add sugar gradually, and cream together until light and fluffy. Add egg and egg yolks, one at a time, beating well after each. Add chocolate and blend. Add flour, alternately with milk, a small amount at a time, beating after each addition until smooth. Add vanilla, then add boiling water, beating quickly and thoroughly.

Coconut Devil's Food

2 cups sifted cake flour
2-3/4 teaspoons baking powder
1/4 teaspoon salt
3/4 cup butter or other shortening
1-1/2 cups sugar
3 eggs, well beaten
3 squares unsweetened chocolate, melted
3/4 cup milk
1 teaspoon vanilla

Sift flour once, measure, add baking powder and salt, and sift together 3 times. Cream butter thoroughly, add sugar gradually, and cream together until light and fluffy. Add eggs and beat well; then chocolate and blend. Add flour, alternately with milk, a small amount at a time, beating after each addition until smooth. Add vanilla. Bake in 2 greased 9-inch layer pans in moderate oven (350° F.) 30 minutes, or until done. Spread Chocolate Seven Minute Frosting (below) over cake. Sprinkle with Baker's Coconut, Southern Style. Double recipe for 3 10-inch layers.

Chocolate 7-Minute Frosting

3 squares Baker's Unsweetened Chocolate, melted and cooled
Seven Minute Frosting

Stir chocolate, gently but thoroughly, into frosting.

Cheese Cake

1-1/2 cups cottage cheese
1/2 cup sugar
3 tablespoons cream
Grated lemon rind
3 eggs

Combine thoroughly cheese, sugar, cream and lemon rind, then add well-beaten eggs. Line muffin tins or individual pie tins with plain paste. Fill them almost to the top with cheese mixture. Bake in a moderate oven about 15 minutes.

Delicate Cake

1-1/2 cups sifted powdered sugar
1/2 cup butter
1/2 cup cornstarch
1-1/2 cups Blend Flour
1/2 cup milk
Whites of 6 eggs
1/2 teaspoon bitter almond

Sift the sugar before measuring. Cream the butter and sugar. Sift the cornstarch and flour together twice, and add alternately with the milk to the butter and sugar. Beat the whites to a stiff froth and fold in lightly. Flavor with bitter almond. Bake either in a loaf pan or layers in a moderate oven.

Date Cake

Mrs. O.H. Payne

1 cup sugar
1 large tablespoon butter
1 egg, beaten
1/2 tablespoon dates, stoned, cut up, and covered with hot water
2 cups flour
1 teaspoon baking powder
1/2 cup walnuts
Flavoring

Mix sugar and butter and egg, then add date mixture and remaining ingredients. Fold over and over until mixed, but do not stir again. Bake in a well-greased tin in a moderate oven.

Easily-Made Cake #1

1-1/2 cups sugar
1/2 cup butter

3 eggs
3 cups cake flour
3 teaspoons baking powder
2/3 cup water
1 teaspoon vanilla

Put sugar, butter and eggs in a bowl. Cream together, then beat with egg beater until smooth. Add alternately the flour sifted with baking powder, and water, beating thoroughly. Add extract and bake in two layers in a moderate oven.

Easily-Made Cake #2

1/3 cup melted butter
1 unbeaten egg
Milk enough to fill the cup (see directions)
1-1/2 cups cake flour
1 cup sugar
2 teaspoons baking powder
1/2 teaspoon vanilla

Melt butter enough to fill 1/3 cup. Drop in unbeaten egg and fill cup with milk. Mix and sift flour, sugar and baking powder. Add cup containing the butter, egg and milk. Add vanilla and beat thoroughly. Bake in 2 rather small layers.

Emergency Cake

1-3/4 cups cake flour
1 cup sugar
1/4 teaspoon salt
2-1/2 teaspoons baking powder
1/3 cup shortening
2/3 cup milk (not too cold)
1 egg
1 teaspoon flavoring

Stir flour once before measuring. Sift flour, sugar, salt and baking powder together. Measure softened shortening into cup and fill cup with the milk. Add these, with the unbeaten egg, to the flour mixture. Beat well for 2 or 3 minutes. Pour into greased and floured cake pans, one 8-inch square pan or 2 small 8-inch layer pans. Bake 25 to 35 minutes in a moderate oven (350° F.).

Broiled Icing

3 tablespoons melted butter
5 tablespoons brown sugar
2 tablespoons cream or top of milk
1/2 cup shredded coconut

Mix all ingredients together and spread on cake, while it is still warm. Place very low under the broiler, with the flame turned low. Broil until it bubbles all over the surface becomes brown but does not burn.
This will top an 8-inch square cake.

East India Spice Cake

A stir-up spice cake, with a 7-minute coffee-panooka.

2 cups pancake and waffle flour
1/3 cup butter
1 cup brown sugar
1/2 teaspoon cinnamon
1/4 teaspoon cloves
1/4 teaspoon nutmeg
2/3 cup milk
2 eggs

Sift flour and measure. Work flour and shortening together until no lumps of fat remain, and texture is granular like fine corn meal. Have brown sugar free from lumps, mix with spices, and mix thoroughly with flour. Add half the milk, and stir thoroughly. Add unbeaten eggs and mix in. Add rest of the liquid and stir until smooth. Pour batter into 2 greased and floured 8-inch layer pans, and bake in a moderate oven, 350°, for 30 minutes. Frost with Creole 7-Minute Frosting (below).
12 servings

Creole 7-Minute Frosting

1 egg white, unbeaten
1 cup brown sugar
1/4 teaspoon salt
2 tablespoons coffee

Put all ingredients in top of double boiler, place over boiling water, and beat with rotary egg beater for 7 minutes, or until stiff enough to stand in peaks. Spread between layers and on top of cake.

Featherweight White Cake

1/2 cup shortening
1 cup sugar
2/3 cup water
2 cups flour
2 teaspoons baking powder
1/2 teaspoon salt
3 egg whites
1 teaspoon vanilla

Cream shortening with sugar. Stir in alternately water and sifted dry ingredients. Fold in thoroughly stiffly-beaten egg whites. Add vanilla and turn batter into 2 greased layer pans. Bake in a moderate oven (350° F.).
Ice with cocoanut or maple icing.

Foundation Cake

This is a simple, inexpensive cake for everyday use. It may be varied by adding spices, dates and nuts, or by adding chocolate.

1/3 cup butter or part other shortening
1 cup sugar
2 eggs, beaten separately
2 cups cake flour
3 teaspoons baking powder
1/2 cup milk
1 teaspoon vanilla

Cream butter and sugar. Add egg yolks well beaten. Mix and sift flour and baking powder and add alternately with the milk. Beat well, fold in stiffly-beaten egg whites and vanilla and bake in layers in a moderate oven.

Form Cake (with Yeast)

1 cup butter
1 cup sugar
5 eggs
1 cup raisins
Grated rind of 1 lemon
1 cake compressed yeast
1 cup milk
3-7/8 cups cake flour

Cream the butter and sugar and beat in 1 egg at a time; then the raisins and lemon rind. Dissolve the yeast in half of the milk (lukewarm) and add this next; then add the balance of the milk alternately with the flour. Put in a good-sized loaf bread pan and let rise over night. In the morning bake in a moderate oven until when a straw is inserted and withdrawn, it will come out clean and dry.
This makes 1 large loaf

Ribbon Fig Cake

White Part:
1/2 cup butter (scant)
1-1/4 cups sugar
1/2 cup milk
2 cups Blend Flour
2 teaspoons baking powder
Whites of 5 eggs
1 teaspoon vanilla

Cream the butter and sugar. Add alternately the milk and the flour, into which has been sifted the baking powder. Beat the whites of the eggs to a stiff froth and fold in last. Flavor with the vanilla, spread in two layers and bake in a moderate oven.

Gold Part:
1/3 cup butter
1/3 cup sugar
Yolks of 5 eggs, well beaten
1/3 cup milk
1 scant cup cake flour
1 teaspoon baking powder
Figs, halved
Flour

Cream the butter and sugar; add the yolks of eggs, then add alternately the milk and flour, into which has been sifted the baking powder. Put half into a pan, cover closely with halved figs, dust with a little flour, then cover with the rest of the batter and bake. Put this gold layer between.

Star-of-England Fruit Cake

The star of all dark fruit cakes . . . rich and long keeping, it is the deluxe gift cake.

1 cup butter
1-1/2 cups brown sugar
6 eggs, well beaten
1/2 cup light molasses
1/2 teaspoon soda, dissolved in
1 tablespoon water
1 cup strawberry preserves or jam
3 cups flour
1/2 teaspoon salt
2 teaspoons allspice
2 teaspoons cinnamon
1-1/2 teaspoons nutmeg
1-1/2 teaspoons mace
1/2 teaspoon ginger
2 cups currants
1-1/2 cups seedless raisins
1-1/2 cups seeded raisins
1-1/2 cups pitted dates, cut in strips
1-1/4 cups pitted dried prunes, coarsely chopped
3/4 cup candied lemon peel, coarsely chopped
3/4 cup candied orange peel, coarsely chopped
3/4 cup candied grapefruit peel, coarsely chopped
1/2 cup candied pineapple, cut in pieces (2 slices)
3/4 cup candied cherries, cut in two

3/4 cup citron, cut in strips
1-1/2 cups almonds, coarsely chopped
1 cup pecan halves

Cream butter and sugar until fluffy; add eggs and mix thoroughly. Add molasses, soda and strawberry preserves. Sift flour and measure. Sift 2 cupfuls with salt and spices and add to creamed mixture. Dredge mixed fruit and nuts with remaining 1 cupful of flour. Fold into batter and mix well. Line a deep 10-inch tube or spring form pan with heavy paper and grease thoroughly. Pack batter into pan carefully so that there are no holes. Decorate top with slices of pineapple, cherries, and nuts. Bake in a slow oven, 275°, for 3-1/2 hours.
Makes a 10-pound cake

Fruit Cake

1 cup shortening (half butter, half lard)
1 cup sugar
8 eggs
1 teaspoon cream of tartar
2-1/2 cups cake flour
1 teaspoon grated nutmeg
2 teaspoons cinnamon
1/4 teaspoon ground cloves
1/2 teaspoon salt
2-1/2 pounds seedless raisins
1/2 pound chopped citron
1/4 pound candied lemon peel
1 glass grape, loganberry or cherry juice
1/2 pound chopped almonds
2 teaspoons vanilla

Cream the shortening and sugar. Beat the yolks of the eggs until thick and lemon colored and add them to the butter and sugar. Beat the whites of the eggs to a stiff froth, adding to them the cream of tartar; then fold the whites in the first mixture. Brown half of the flour in the oven. Sift the spices and salt with the balance, reserving enough to flour the fruit. Mix all together, then add the juice and fruit, nuts and vanilla last. Bake in a slow oven for about 2 hours, or when a straw inserted in the cake will come out clean and dry. Line the pan with 2 thicknesses of well-buttered paper.

Christmas Fruit Cake

1 pound butter
1 pound brown sugar
1 teaspoon soda
1 pound molasses
1 tablespoon each, cloves, allspice and cinnamon
2 grated nutmegs
4 cups cake flour
12 eggs
2/3 cup grape, loganberry or cherry juice
4 pounds seedless raisins, chopped
2 pounds seeded raisins
1 pound chopped citron

Cream the butter and sugar. Beat the soda into the molasses. Sift all the other dry ingredients with the flour, reserving enough flour to dredge the fruit. Add the molasses to the creamed butter and sugar; then the yolks beaten until thick and lemon colored. Beat in the dry ingredients; then the fruit. Mix very thoroughly and add to the whites, which have been beaten to a stiff froth, last. Bake in one large or several small loaves, in a rather slow oven for about 3 hours, lining the pan with 2 thicknesses of well-buttered paper.

Economy Fruit Cake

1/2 cup butter
1 cup sugar
1 egg
1 teaspoon soda
1 cup sour milk
2 cups cake flour
1 teaspoon cinnamon
1/2 teaspoon cloves
1/2 teaspoon allspice
1 cup raisins and citron if desired

Cream together the butter and sugar and add the well-beaten egg. Beat the soda into the milk and add. Sift together the flour and spices (reserving a tablespoon of the flour to dredge the raisins) and fold in. Bake in a moderate oven until, when a straw is inserted and withdrawn, it will come out clean and dry.

Fig Cake

1/2 cup shortening
1 cup sugar
2 eggs
2 cups cake flour
1 teaspoon baking powder
1/2 teaspoon soda
1 teaspoon salt
1/2 teaspoon cinnamon
1/4 teaspoon cloves
1/2 cup sour milk or buttermilk
2 cups stewed or canned figs
1/2 cup fig juice
1 cup walnuts
1 teaspoon lemon extract
1 teaspoon vanilla

Cream shortening, add sugar gradually and cream together thoroughly. Add the well-beaten eggs. Sift flour once before measuring. Sift flour, baking powder, soda, salt and spices together. Add to the creamed mixture alternately with the sour milk. Cut up figs in 1/2-inch pieces and pack into cup to measure. Add figs and juice, nutmeats and flavoring. Pour into well-greased and floured 9-inch pan and bake 50 minutes in a moderate oven (350° F.).

Fruit Gingerbread with Whipped Cream

1/2 cup shortening
1 cup sugar
1 beaten egg
1/2 cup mild flavored molasses
2-1/3 cups cake flour
1/2 teaspoon salt
2 teaspoon cinnamon
2 teaspoon ginger
1/2 teaspoon allspice
1/2 teaspoon cloves
1 teaspoon soda
1-1/2 teaspoon baking powder
1/4 cup milk or water
1 cup raisins
Grated rind of 1/2 orange
Whipping cream

Cream shortening and sugar, add beaten egg and molasses. Sift together dry ingredients and add alternately with liquid, adding raisins with part of flour. Turn into greased shallow baking pan and bake in a moderate oven, on the lower shelf, for about 1/2 hour or until it shrinks from sides of pan and a gentle touch leaves no imprint. Serve hot or cold with sweetened and flavored whipped cream, or plain. If preferred, bake in gem pans and top with whipped cream.

Frying Pan Cake

1/2 of 1/4 pound butter
1 cup brown sugar
1/2 cup pineapple, cut into cubes, or peaches
2 heaping tablespoons ground nut meats
A plain cheap cake

Slice the butter on the bottom of a skillet or frying pan. Then sprinkle the sugar over butter, add pineapple and nuts sprinkled over the sugar. Now add the cake dough, put it right on top of the ingredients. Bake in a rather slow oven. When done turn out, and when cool serve with whip cream.

Gentlemen's Favorite Cake

1/2 cup butter
2 cups sugar
7 eggs, beaten separately
5 teaspoons water or milk
2 cups cake flour
4 level teaspoons baking powder
Vanilla

Cream the butter and sugar. Add the well-beaten yolks, then the water or milk. Sift together twice the flour and baking powder and add this gradually. Beat thoroughly and then add the whites of the eggs, which have been whipped to a stiff froth, folding them in lightly. Flavor with vanilla. Bake in layers and when cool spread with the following jelly:

Filling:
3 grated sour apples (medium size)
1 cup sugar
1 egg
Grated rind and juice of 1 lemon

Let come to a boil. Remove from the stove, and when it cools, spread.
This will serve about 16

Gingerbread

1/2 cup sugar
1 cup molasses
1/2 cup butter
1 cup boiling water
1 teaspoon ginger
1 teaspoon cloves
1 teaspoon cinnamon
2 teaspoons soda
1 teaspoon baking powder
2-1/2 cups flour
2 well-beaten eggs

Stir first 4 ingredients together and mix well. Sift together dry ingredients and add to this mixture. Then add eggs. Bake in a slow oven about 1/2 hour.
Note: Shortening may be used instead of butter, but a little salt must be added in that case.

Harvest Cake (2 Egg Yolks)

2 cups sifted flour
2 teaspoons baking powder
1/4 teaspoon salt

1/3 cup butter or other shortening
3/4 cup brown sugar, firmly packed
2 egg yolks, unbeaten
2/3 cup milk
1 teaspoon vanilla

Sift flour once, measure, add baking powder and salt, and sift together 3 times. Cream butter thoroughly, add sugar gradually, and cream together until light and fluffy. Add egg yolks and beat well. Add flour, alternately with milk, a small amount at a time, beating after each addition until smooth. Add vanilla. Bake in greased pan, 8x8x2 inches, in moderate oven (350° F.) 45 minutes, or until done. Spread Raisin Butterscotch Frosting (below) on top and sides of cake.

Raisin Butterscotch Frosting

4 tablespoons butter
1/2 cup brown sugar, firmly packed
2 tablespoons water
2-1/4 cups sifted confectioners' sugar
1 egg white, unbeaten
1/2 cup raisins, finely cut

Melt butter and brown sugar together over low flame; then cook and stir until entire mixture bubbles. Add water, bring to a boil, and boil 1 minute, stirring constantly. Cool slightly. Add 1 cup confectioners' sugar gradually, mixing well; then add egg white and beat thoroughly. Add remaining sugar and raisins and beat well. Makes enough frosting to cover tops of 2 8-inch layers, or top and sides of 8x8x2-inch cake.
Note: If egg white is very large, 2 or 3 tablespoons additional confectioners' sugar may be needed.

Jelly Roll

2 cups cake flour
4 tablespoons baking powder
1 teaspoon salt
3 eggs
2 cups sugar
Grated rind of 1 lemon (or 1/2 teaspoon lemon extract)
3/4 cup hot water
1 glass jelly

Sift together three times the flour, baking powder and salt. Beat the eggs until very light and mix the sugar and lemon rind. Sift in alternately the flour and hot water. Bake in a well-buttered and -floured shallow pan in a moderate oven. Turn out onto a damp cloth; trim off the edges, spread with jelly which has been beaten with a fork until of the consistency to spread, and roll up very quickly. Sprinkle the top with powdered sugar.
The roll should be handled very quickly, so it will not crack.

Little Molasses Cakes

3/4 cup shortening
1 cup brown sugar
1 egg
3-1/4 cups cake flour
1/4 teaspoon salt
1 teaspoon soda
1 teaspoon cinnamon
1/2 teaspoon ginger
1 cup hot water
1 cup molasses

Cream the shortening and add the sugar gradually. Add the well-beaten egg. Sift the flour once before measuring. Sift the flour, salt, soda and spices together. Add the hot water to the molasses and add the liquid alternately with the flour mixture. Bake in greased muffin or cup cake pans for 15 minutes in a moderately hot oven (375° F.).
Makes 18 cup cakes

Layer Cake

1 cup butter
2 cups sugar
4 eggs, the whites beaten stiff and added last
2 teaspoons baking powder
3 cups cake flour
1 cup milk
1 teaspoon vanilla

Cream the butter and sugar. Add the yolks of the eggs, which have been beaten thick and lemon colored. Sift together the baking powder and flour twice, then add alternately with the milk to the first mixture. Beat the whites to a stiff froth and fold in last, and flavor with 1 teaspoon of vanilla. Bake in layers in a quick oven.

Lady Baltimore Cake

3 cups sifted cake flour
3 teaspoons baking powder
1/4 teaspoon salt
1/2 cup butter or other shortening
1-1/2 cups sugar
1/2 cup milk
1/2 cup water
1 teaspoon vanilla
1/4 teaspoon almond flavoring
3 egg whites, beaten stiff

Prepare pan. Sift flour once, measure, add baking powder and salt, and sift together 3 times. Cream shortening until light and fluffy, then add sugar gradually, and cream together thoroughly. Add sifted dry ingredients to creamed mixture alternately with milk, a small amount at a time. Beat after each addition until smooth. Add flavorings; fold in egg whites. Bake in layers in moderate oven, 350° F.

Lady Baltimore Filling and Icing

1/4 pound figs
1/2 pound raisins
1/2 pound pecans or English walnuts
2 cups sugar
3/4 cup water
2 egg whites, beaten stiff
1 teaspoon vanilla

Grind fruits and nuts together. Dates and candied or Maraschino cherries may be used. Cook sugar and water to soft ball stage, 238° F. Pour syrup slowly on egg whites. Beat until mixture will stand alone. Add vanilla. Stir fruits and nuts into 2/3 of icing. Spread between layers and on top of cake. Cover entire cake with remaining plain icing.

Lemon Jelly Cake

1/2 cup butter, scant
1-1/3 cup sugar
3 eggs, beaten separately
2 cups cake flour
4 teaspoons baking powder
1/2 cup milk
1/2 teaspoon lemon extract

Cream butter and sugar until very soft, then add well-beaten yolks. Sift together flour and baking powder and add alternately with the milk and extract and beat until very smooth, then fold in stiffly-beaten egg whites. Bake in buttered layer cake tins in a moderate oven until it shrinks from sides of pan and feels firm to a very gentle touch of the finger. When cool, spread with the following filling and sprinkle powdered sugar on top.

Filling:
1 cup sugar
1-1/2 tablespoons cake flour
Grated rind and juice or 1 lemon
1 well-beaten egg
1 tablespoon water

Mix together and boil until thick, stirring constantly. Then beat until creamy and of consistency to spread or until nearly cold.

Mahogany Cake

1/2 cup cocoa dissolved in
1/2 cup hot strong coffee
1/2 cup butter
1-1/2 cups sugar
3 whole eggs beaten light
1 teaspoon soda dissolved in
Milk
1/2 cup milk or water
2 cups cake flour
2 teaspoons baking powder

Dissolve cocoa in hot coffee and cool. Cream butter and sugar, add beaten eggs, then soda and milk alternately with flour previously sifted with baking powder. Add dissolved cocoa and hot coffee. Beat until smooth. Turn into 2 buttered layer cake pans and bake according to directions for layer cakes.
When combined with a center layer of either sponge or angel food, this makes a beautiful cake. Use chocolate or white frosting.

Mocha Layer Cake

1-1/2 cups granulated sugar
2 cups flour
1/2 cup corn starch
3 teaspoons baking powder
1/2 teaspoon salt
1/2 cup cooking oil
1 cup milk
1 teaspoon vanilla extract
Whites of 3 eggs

Sift all dry ingredients together 3 times; add oil to milk and add to dry ingredients. Mix but do not beat hard. Add flavoring; fold in beaten egg whites. Bake in 3 oiled layer tins in hot oven (450° F.) about 15 minutes. Spread the following filling between layers and on top and sides of cake.

Mocha Filling and Icing

3 tablespoons butter
3 cups confectioners' sugar
1-1/2 tablespoons cocoa
1 teaspoon vanilla extract
1 tablespoon oil
3-1/2 tablespoons strong coffee

Cream butter until light; add sugar very slowly; add cocoa and beat until light and smooth; add vanilla, oil and coffee slowly, making the icing soft enough to spread.

Cocoanut Marshmallow Layer Cake

2 eggs
1 cup sugar
1 teaspoon vanilla extract
1/3 cup oil
2/3 cup milk
1-3/4 cups flour
1/2 teaspoon salt
3 teaspoons baking powder

Separate eggs and save the whites for icing and filling. Beat egg yolks until thick and lemon colored; add sugar very slowly; add the vanilla then the oil a little at a time, mixing thoroughly. Add half the milk and half the flour which has been sifted with the salt and baking powder; then add remainder of milk and remainder of flour, mixing well after each addition. Bake in 3 oiled layer tins in hot oven (425° F.) about 20 minutes. Put following filling between layers and on top of cake.

Cocoanut Filling and Icing

1-1/2 cups granulated sugar
1/2 cup water
2 egg whites
1/2 teaspoon vanilla extract
Few drops lemon juice
1 cup fresh grated cocoanut

Cook sugar and water without stirring until syrup spins a thread (240° F.); pour very slowly over stiffly-beaten egg whites. Beat until thick; add flavoring and spread on cake. While icing is soft sprinkle thickly with the grated cocoanut.

Mocha Cake

1/3 cup butter
1/2 cup granulated sugar
1/2 cup brown sugar
2 eggs, beaten separately
2 cups cake flour
3 teaspoons baking powder
1/2 cup very strong coffee
1/2 teaspoon vanilla

Cream butter and sugar until very soft. Add egg yolks which have been beaten until thick and lemon colored. Mix and sift the flour and baking powder and add alternately with the cold coffee. Beat until very smooth, then fold in stiffly-beaten egg whites and vanilla. Bake in layers in a moderate oven or in a deeper pan with little lower heat. When cool, spread with Mocha Frosting.

Nougat Dream Cake

3 eggs, beaten together
1 cup sugar
1 teaspoon vanilla
3 tablespoons melted butter
1 cup cake flour
1 teaspoon baking powder
Few grains salt
2-1/2 tablespoons powdered unsweetened chocolate or cocoa

Beat eggs until light. Add sugar, vanilla and melted butter and beat until light. Sift together the flour, baking powder, salt and cocoa and folding carefully without further beating. Turn into buttered and floured layer cake pans and bake in a moderate oven until a gentle touch leaves no imprint. Spread following filling between layers and serve with sweetened and flavored whipped cream on top.
Note: No liquid is required

Filling for Nougat Cake

1 cup sugar
1 tablespoon cocoa
2 tablespoons corn syrup
1/2 cup milk
1 egg white
1/2 teaspoon vanilla
1/2 cup broken nut meats

Stir sugar, cocoa, corn syrup and milk until it begins to boil but not afterward. Cook until it will form a firm ball when dropped in cold water. Pour slowly over stiffly-beaten white, add flavoring and beat until it can be spread without running off. Add nuts.

Spice Nut Cake

Delicious

1/2 cup butter
1 cup light brown sugar
4 egg yolks
1/2 cup molasses
1 teaspoon soda
1 cup rich sour milk (or half sour cream)
2-1/2 cups cake flour

1-1/2 teaspoons baking powder
1 teaspoon cinnamon
1/2 teaspoon cloves
1/2 teaspoon grated nutmeg
1/2 teaspoon salt
3/4 cup chopped walnuts (not too fine)
1 cup seedless raisins
1/2 cup finely chopped citron

Cream the butter and sugar. Add the yolks of the eggs beaten until thick and lemon colored; then the molasses. Whip the soda into the sour milk or cream. Sift together all of the dry ingredients (reserving enough flour to flour the fruit), and add alternately with the milk to the first mixture. Add the nuts and floured fruit last. Bake in loaves in a moderate oven until when a straw is inserted and withdrawn it will come out clean and dry. The oven should be a little slower than for layer cakes, but not as cool as for sponge cake.
This makes one loaf

Old-Fashioned Marble Cake

Very Fine

White Part:
1/2 cup butter
1-1/2 cups white sugar
2 teaspoons baking powder
2 cups cake flour
1/2 cup milk
Whites of 4 eggs
1/2 teaspoon vanilla

Cream together the butter and sugar. Sift the baking powder with the flour, and add this, with the milk alternately. Beat the eggs until stiff and fold in. Add the vanilla.

Black Part:
1/2 cup butter
1 cup brown sugar
Yolks of 4 eggs
1/2 cup molasses
1/2 teaspoon black pepper
2-1/2 cups Blend Flour
2 teaspoons baking powder
1 teaspoon cinnamon
1/2 teaspoon cloves
1/2 teaspoon allspice
1/2 teaspoon nutmeg
1/2 cup milk

Cream the butter and sugar; add the well-beaten yolks. Sift together all the dry ingredients and add, alternately with the milk, to this mixture.
With a tablespoon drop into a well-greased pan a tablespoon of the White Part, then one of the Black Part, and so on, alternating until it is all in the pan. Bake in a moderate oven.

One Egg Cake

1/4 cup butter
2/3 cup sugar
1 egg
2/3 cup milk
1/4 teaspoon vanilla
2 cups cake flour
3 teaspoons baking powder

Cream the butter and sugar. Add egg well beaten. Add alternately the milk with flavoring and the sifted flour and baking powder. Beat until smooth, turn into 2 buttered and floured layer cake pans and bake in a moderate oven until it shrinks from the sides of the pan. When cool, cover with any preferred frosting, or spread jelly between the layers, and sprinkle the top with powdered sugar.

Orange Cake

1/3 cup butter
1-1/4 cups sugar
3 egg yolks
2 cups cake flour
3 teaspoons baking powder
1/4 cup orange juice and half a grated rind
1/2 cup milk
2 egg whites

Cream the butter and sugar until very soft. Add the egg yolks, beaten until thick and lemon colored, mix and sift the flour and baking powder twice, then add a little, stirring in well, then add the orange juice and rind and mix, then add alternately the balance of the flour and the milk. Beat until very smooth, then fold in the stiffly-beaten egg whites. Turn into buttered layer cake pans and bake in a moderate oven until it shrinks from the sides of the pan. When cool, spread with filling.

Orange Ice-Box Cake

For a Fourth-of-July party, no dessert could be more delicious than an ice-box cake such as this one

12 marshmallows, cut in eighths
1/2 cupful orange pieces
1/4 cupful orange juice
2 tablespoons gelatine (1 envelope)
1/2 cupful sugar dissolved in
1/2 cupful boiling water and

1/2 cupful orange juice
1 cupful whipping cream, beaten stiff
24 lady fingers

Mix marshmallows and orange pieces and let stand. Meanwhile soak for 5 minutes orange juice and gelatine, liquefy over hot water. Add sugar dissolved in water and orange juice. Cool. When beginning to stiffen, beat until fluffy. Fold in marshmallows and orange pieces and lastly whipping cream. Line bottom of spring form with halves of lady fingers. Cut 1 round end from enough halves of lady fingers to stand up around edge of form. The cut ends touch the bottom of the pan. Pour in half the filling. Lay on any pieces or extra lady fingers and cover with rest of filling. Leave in ice box overnight or until thoroughly chilled. Remove sides of spring form when ready to serve. Decorate if desired, with additional whipped cream and orange segments.

Orange Cream Cake (4 egg whites)

3 cups sifted flour
3 teaspoons baking powder
1/2 cup butter or other shortening
1-1/2 cups sugar
1 cup milk
1/2 teaspoon lemon extract
4 egg whites, stiffly beaten

Sift flour once, measure, add baking powder, and sift together 3 times. Cream butter thoroughly, add sugar gradually, and cream together until light and fluffy. Add flour, alternately with milk, a small amount at a time, beating after each addition until smooth. Add lemon extract. Fold in egg whites quickly and thoroughly. Bake in 2 greased 9-inch layer pans in moderate oven (375° F.) 25 to 30 minutes. Spread Orange Filling (below) between layers and Boiled Frosting (below) on top and sides of cake. Decorate top with orange sections, free from all white membrane.
For Silver Cake, bake as directed. Spread Boiled Frosting (below) between layers and on top of cake. Decorate with silver.

Orange Filling

1 cup sugar
5 tablespoons cake flour
Dash of salt
1/2 cup orange juice
3 tablespoons lemon juice
1/4 cup water
1 egg, well beaten
1 tablespoons grated orange rind
2 teaspoons butter

Combine sugar, flour, and salt in top of double boiler; add fruit juice, water and egg, mixing thoroughly. Place over boiling water and cook 10 minutes, stirring constantly. Add orange rind and butter. Cool. Makes enough filling to spread between 2 9-inch layers. May also be used for sponge rolls.

Boiled Frosting

1-1/2 cups sugar
1/2 teaspoon light corn syrup
2/3 cup boiling water
2 egg whites, stiffly beaten
1 teaspoon vanilla, or
1/4 teaspoon orange extract

Combine sugar, corn syrup and water. Bring quickly to a boil, stirring only until sugar is dissolved. Boil rapidly, without stirring, until a small amount of syrup forms a soft ball in cold water, or spins a long thread when dropped from tip of spoon (240° F.). Pour syrup in fine stream over egg whites, beating constantly. Add flavoring. Continue beating with rotary egg beater 10 to 15 minutes, or until frosting is cool and of consistency to spread. Use wooden spoon when too stiff for beater. Makes enough to cover top and sides of 2 9-inch layers.

Orange Layer Cake

2 eggs, separated (save egg whites for icing)
1 cup sugar
1/3 cup cooking oil
1-3/4 cups flour
3 teaspoons baking powder
1/2 teaspoon salt
2/3 cup milk
1 teaspoon vanilla extract

Beat egg yolks well; add sugar slowly, then add oil and half the flour which has been sifted with the baking powder and salt. Add the milk and flavoring and remainder of flour and mix well. Bake in 2 oiled layer cake tins in hot oven (425° F.) about 20 minutes. Put the following filling and icing between layers and on top of cake.

Orange Filling and Icing

Whites of 2 eggs
3 cups confectioners' sugar
Grated rind and soft pulp of 1 orange

Whip eggs to stiff froth; add sugar, a little at a time, until stiff enough to spread. Whip in pulp and rind of orange. Orange coloring may be added if desired.

Spice Cup Cakes with Orange Icing

1/2 cup cooking oil
1/2 cup brown sugar
1 egg
1/2 cup molasses
2 cups flour
3 teaspoons baking powder
1/2 teaspoon salt
1/4 teaspoon soda
1/2 teaspoon allspice
1 teaspoon cinnamon
1/2 cup milk

Cream oil and sugar together thoroughly. Add beaten egg and molasses; add half of dry ingredients which have been sifted together. Add milk and remainder of dry ingredients. Mix well and bake in moderate oven (375° F.) in slightly oiled and floured muffin tins. Frost tops with orange icing.

Prune Cake

1 cup white sugar
2 eggs
1 cup cooked prunes, seeded and washed
2-3 cups prune juice with
1 teaspoon soda stirred in
1/2 teaspoon each cinnamon and nutmeg
1/2 cup nut-meats or raisins
2 cups flour

Sift flour, measure, then sift again. Mix all ingredients. Bake in a loaf or layers.

Frosting:
2 cups powdered sugar
1 teaspoon vanilla
Enough cream or canned milk to make it spread nicely

Frosting for Prune Cake:
1 cup sugar
1/2 cup milk

Boil until it thickens, remove from the fire, beat in a piece of butter the size of a walnut. Spread quickly.

Prune Confection

Soak prunes 10 minutes after pouring boiling water upon them. Take from the water and allow to dry thoroughly. Remove the pits carefully. Use these pitted prunes the same as you would walnuts: chopped or halves dipped in fondant (candy) or fill the cavity left by removing the pit with a mixture of fondant and rolled nuts, then roll the stuffed prunes in powdered sugar. Prunes prepared this way are most delicious and take the place of candy, and are also much healthier. Children should eat prunes as a confection.

Prune Up-Side-Down Cake

Prunes
1 egg
1/2 cup sugar
1 cup sifted flour
1 teaspoon baking powder
1/4 cup milk or water
2 tablespoons melted shortening
1 teaspoon vanilla
2 tablespoons butter
1/2 cup brown sugar
1/4 cup chopped walnuts

Wash and soak prunes in warm water to cover for several hours. Drain and remove pits. Beat egg until light; gradually add sugar and beat till creamy. Measure sifted flour, sift with baking powder. Add to egg mixture alternately with milk or water and beat well; add shortening and vanilla. Melt butter in a small iron frying pan. Spread brown sugar evenly over the pan, then the nuts. Cover with prunes, then pour on cake batter. Bake in moderate oven about 25 minutes.
This cake will serve 5 persons

Prune, Cup or Loaf, Cake

2 cups uncooked prunes (cut fine)
2 cups water
1-1/2 cups sugar
2 tablespoons lard
3 cups flour
1 cup nut meats
1 teaspoon soda
1/2 teaspoon baking powder
1/2 teaspoon cloves
1 teaspoon cinnamon
1/2 teaspoon nutmeg

Boil prunes, water, sugar and lard together for a few minutes. When this mixture is cool, add remaining ingredients. Bake in moderate oven.

Prune Cake (Layer or Loaf)

3 eggs
Vanilla
1-1/2 cup flour
1-1/3 cups sugar
1 cup cooked dried prunes
1 large tablespoonful butter
1 teaspoon baking powder
1/2 cup prune juice
1/2 teaspoon nutmeg
1 teaspoon cinnamon
1 teaspoon soda (level)

This may be used either as a layer or loaf cake. If used as a loaf cake, a cup of nuts may be added. Bake about 45 minutes. For a large cake double the recipe.

Filling for Layer Cake:
2 cups powdered sugar
1 tablespoon butter
Hot water
Vanilla

Add enough water to make it the thickness of whipped cream or so it will spread. Flavor with vanilla.

Prune Cream Cake

1 cup prunes
2 cups flour
1/2 teaspoon allspice
1/2 teaspoon nutmeg
1 teaspoon cinnamon
1/2 teaspoon soda
1 teaspoon baking powder
Pinch of salt
1/2 cup butter
1-1/4 cup sugar
3 eggs
1 cup sour cream
1 teaspoon vanilla

Pour boiling water over the prunes. Let stand 15 minutes, then let dry in the oven, after which pit and chop.
Sift together the dry ingredients, cream the butter, sugar and eggs together (beaten eggs). Mix all, and bake in 3 layers.

Peppermint Candy Cake

1/2 cup shortening
1 cup sugar
2 eggs
1-3/4 cake flour
1/4 teaspoon soda
2 teaspoon baking powder
1/4 teaspoon salt
2/3 cup sour milk or buttermilk
1/3 cup crushed peppermint candy

Cream shortening, add sugar gradually and cream well. Add the egg yolks and beat well. Sift flour once before measuring. Sift flour, soda, baking powder and salt together. Add to the creamed mixture alternately with the sour milk. Fold in stiffly-beaten egg whites. Pour into 2 unusually well-greased and floured layer pans, sprinkle each layer with candy, crushed so no pieces are larger than 1/4 inch. (The candy will probably go to the bottom and melt, so cake should be removed from pans immediately on taking from oven.) When cool, cover with white icing, being careful to put bottoms of two layers together. Sprinkle another 1/3 cup crushed peppermint candy over the top of icing. Bake in 2 8-inch layer pans for 25 to 30 minutes in a moderately hot oven (375° F.).
Note: The old-fashioned red and white peppermint sticks should be used—those that crumble and melt most easily-not the brittle, shiny kind. (7 to 10 sticks for both cake and icing.) If you want to be sure that the candy stays up in the cake, do not add it to the cake before putting it in the oven. Wait until the cake has been in the oven exactly 7 minutes. Then open the oven door and sprinkle the crushed candy evenly over each layer. The bottom of the cake batter will have set sufficiently after 7 minutes at 375° to keep candy from sinking way through. It will be in creamy lumps through the cake.

Ice Cream Icing

1-1/2 cups sugar
3/4 cup water
1/8 teaspoon cream of tartar
2 egg whites
1 teaspoon vanilla

Mix the sugar, water and cream of tartar together. Boil this mixture slowly without stirring until it spins as 8-inch thread, 240 to 244° F., keeping the pan covered for the first 3 minutes of cooking to prevent crystals forming on sides of pan. Pour hot syrup slowly over stiffly-beaten egg whites, and beat with an egg beater constantly. Add vanilla and continue beating with a wire whip until mixture is fluffy and will hold its shape. If icing does not stiffen enough to hold its shape after 25 to 30 minutes beating, let stand a while to dry out before spreading on the cake, or add a little confectioners' sugar to it. Spread between layers, and on top and sides of cake.
Icing for 1 2-layer cake

Potato Cake

2 cups flour
2 cups sugar
1 cup butter
4 eggs
2 teaspoons baking powder
1 cup cold mashed potatoes
1/2 cup milk
3/4 cup melted chocolate
1 cup walnuts
1 tablespoon cinnamon
1 tablespoon cloves
1/2 teaspoon nutmeg
1 teaspoon vanilla
1/2 package seeded raisins
1/2 teaspoon salt

Sift the flour and the sugar before measuring. Beat butter with sugar to a cream. Beat the yolks of the eggs until thick and lemon colored, then add them to the sugar. Sift together the flour and baking powder and beat it thoroughly. Beat the whites to stiff froth, adding to them the vanilla, and fold in last. Fold over and over until mixed, but do not stir again. Bake in a well-greased tin in a moderate oven.

Pound Cake

1 cup Crisco
1 cup sugar (fine granulated or powdered)
4 eggs
1 teaspoon vanilla
1 teaspoon lemon
2 cups flour
1 teaspoon salt

Cream Crisco well. Stir in sugar gradually. Separate eggs, beating whites until stiff and yolks until thick and lemon colored. Add beaten yolks and flavoring to sugar. Cream all thoroughly. Fold in whites alternately with flour sifted with salt. Bake in a loaf pan lined with white paper, in a moderate oven about 1 hour.

Prune Cake

3 eggs
1-1/2 cups sugar
1 cup Crisco (melted)
1 cup sour milk
1 teaspoon cinnamon
1 teaspoon nutmeg
1 teaspoon allspice
1 teaspoon baking powder
2 cups flour
1 teaspoon soda
1 cup chopped prunes (stewed and stoned)

Beat eggs and sugar together. Add melted Crisco, sour milk, and dry ingredients sifted together. Stir in chopped prunes. Bake in 3 layers in a moderate oven and frost when cool with the following:

Filling:
1/4 cup Crisco
1 egg yolk
1-1/2 cups powdered sugar
1 tablespoon cocoa
2 tablespoons coffee infusion

Cream Crisco, stir in egg. Sift powdered sugar and cocoa; add alternately with coffee to Crisco mixture.

Quick Spice Cake

2 cups sifted cake flour
2 teaspoons baking powder
1/4 teaspoon salt
1/2 teaspoon cinnamon
1/2 teaspoon nutmeg
1/4 teaspoon cloves
2/3 cup sugar
5 tablespoons softened butter or other shortening
1/4 cup molasses
2 eggs, well beaten
1/2 cup milk

Sift flour once, measure, add baking powder, salt, spices and sugar, and sift together 3 times. Add butter and molasses. Combine eggs and milk; add to flour mixture, stirring until all flour is dampened; then beaten vigorously 1 minute. Bake in 2 greased 8-inch layer pans in moderate oven (375° F.) 25 minutes, or until well done. Spread Raisin Butterscotch Frosting between layers and on top and sides of cake.

Raisin and Currant Cake

1/2 cup butter
1 cup sugar
3 egg yolks
2-1/4 cups flour
1/4 teaspoon nutmeg
3-1/2 teaspoons baking powder
2/3 cup milk
1/2 cup seedless raisins

1/2 cup currants
Grated rind of 1/2 lemon
2 egg whites

Cream butter and sugar. Add beaten egg yolks, then alternately the sifted dry ingredients and milk, mixing in the fruit with the last of the flour. Add egg whites well beaten and bake in a buttered tube pan in a rather slow oven for 3/4 of an hour, or until done.

Spanish Chocolate Cake

3 ounces chocolate
1 cup sugar
Yolk of 1 egg
1 cup milk
Vanilla
1 cup sugar
1/2 cup butter
1/2 cup sweet milk
2-1/2 cups flour
2 eggs
1 teaspoon soda, dissolved in hot water

Melt chocolate over hot water, then stir into it sugar, yolk and 1 cup milk. Stir until thick. Cool and flavor with vanilla. While this is cooling, beat together the 1 cup sugar, butter, sweet milk, flour, eggs and soda, then add in the cooled chocolate mixture. Bake in layers. Ice on top and between layers with icing.

Orange Sponge Cake

3 eggs
1/2 teaspoon cream of tartar
1 cup granulated sugar
2 tablespoons grated orange rind
1/3 cup orange juice
1-1/2 cups flour
1-1/2 baking powder
1/4 teaspoon salt

Beat the whites of the eggs and cream of tartar until stiff. Add yolks one at a time, beating well after each yolk. Then add sugar gradually, still beating with egg beater. Add orange rind and juice. Fold in flour, baking powder and salt. Bake 18 minutes. Beat the yolks until thick and lemon colored, mix in sugar gradually. Add rind and water and beat with egg-beater. Cut and fold in half the stiffly-beaten whites and gradually cut and fold in the flour sifted with the salt. Fold in balance of egg whites. Turn into an ungreased deep spout cake pan and bake in a slow oven for about an hour. Let stand until cool, inverted, before removing from pan.
The success of this cake depends upon sufficient beating of the yolks, the beating of the whites until stiff and dry, the careful folding in of the flour, and baking in a slow oven in an ungreased tin.

Filling:
1/4 cup sugar
1-1/4 tablespoons flour
1/4 teaspoon salt
2 tablespoons grated orange rind
1/2 cup orange juice
2 tablespoons butter
1 egg yolk

Cook on top of double boiler until smooth.

Sponge Cake

6 eggs, beaten separately
1 cup sugar
Grated rind of 1/2 lemon
1 tablespoon water
1 cup flour
1/8 teaspoon salt

Beat the yolks until thick and lemon colored, mix in sugar gradually. Add rind and water and beat with egg-beater. Cut and fold in half the stiffly-beaten whites and gradually cut and fold in the flour sifted with the salt. Fold in balance of egg whites. Turn into an ungreased deep spout cake pan and bake in a slow oven for about an hour. Let stand until cool, inverted, before removing from pan. The success of this cake depends upon sufficient beating of the yolks, the beating of the whites until stiff and dry, the careful folding in of the flour, and baking in a slow oven in an ungreased tin.

Sponge Cake
Excellent

1 cup cake flour
1 cup sifted super-fine granulated sugar
4 eggs, beaten separately
2 teaspoons baking powder
1/2 teaspoon vanilla

Sift the flour and the sugar before measuring. Beat the yolks of the eggs until thick and lemon colored, then add them to the sugar. Sift together the flour and baking powder and beat it thoroughly. Beat the whites to stiff froth, adding to them the vanilla, and fold in last. Fold over and over until mixed, but do not stir again. Bake in a well-greased tin in a moderate oven. This will serve 8 or 10 slices

A "Sunny" Layer Cake

1 scant cup butter
2 cups sugar
4 eggs
2-1/2 teaspoons baking powder
2-7/8 cups Blend Flour
1 cup milk
1 teaspoon vanilla

Cream the butter and sugar. Add the yolks of the eggs, which have been beaten thick and lemon colored. Sift together the baking powder and flour twice, then add alternately with the milk to the first mixture. Beat the whites to a stiff froth and fold in last, and flavor with vanilla. Bake in layers in a quick oven. This will serve about 16

Sunshine Cake

1 cup Blend Flour
1 cup fine granulated sugar
1/8 teaspoon salt
1/2 teaspoon cream of tartar
6 large egg whites, or 8 small
5 egg yolks
1/2 teaspoon orange, lemon or vanilla extract

Sift flour and sugar separately before measuring, then sift flour 4 times. Add salt and cream of tartar to egg whites when partly beaten, then continue beating until stiff. Carefully fold the sugar into the beaten whites, then fold in the yolks (which should be beaten until thick and lemon colored), and flavoring, and then fold in the flour very lightly. Turn into a deep angel food or sponge cake tube pan and bake in a moderately slow oven until it shrinks from the sides of the pan and slight pressure of the finger leaves no imprint. When done, invert the pan and let stand until cool, then remove. If removed before cooled, the air cells will collapse and the cake will not be so beautifully delicate.

Inexpensive Sponge Cake & Variations

2 eggs
1/4 teaspoon salt
1 cup sugar
1 teaspoon flavoring
1/2 cup milk
1 teaspoon butter
1 cup cake flour
1 teaspoon baking powder

Beat the eggs until very light with a rotary egg beater. Beat in the salt, sugar and flavoring. Beat in the milk which is boiling hot and which has been heated with the butter. Sift the flour once before measuring. Beat in the flour and baking powder which have been sifted together. Pour very quickly into a greased and floured 8x8-inch cake pan. Put immediately in 350-degree oven and bake 25 to 30 minutes.

Variation I: Bake cake in Mary Ann cake pan, fill center with apricot, whip and decorate with whipped cream forced through pastry tube.

Variation II: Bake in Mary Ann cake pan, fill center with sweetened fresh fruit or berries and serve with whipped cream.

Variation III: Bake in cup cake pans and ice with any desired icing or top with whipped cream mixed with ground peanut brittle.

Short Cake

2 cups cake flour
4 teaspoons baking powder
3/4 teaspoon salt
1/2 cup shortening
1/2 cup milk
Berries

Mix and sift the dry ingredients; cut in the shortening and mix lightly with the fingers. Add the milk. Mix, and roll out, handling as little as possible. Either bake in a shallow tin in one piece, and when done split open, butter and lay the berries inside and spread over the top; or, cut with a large biscuit cutter into individual shortcakes, allowing 2 to each person. When done, butter each, cover one with berries, lay the other on top, pour berries over the whole, and decorate the top with whipped cream.
Sufficient for 4 large or 6 medium-size pieces

UPSIDE-DOWN CAKES

Cherry Topsy-Turvies

Individual upside-down cakes, topped with a pineapple cherry surprise

1 cup brown sugar
1/2 cup pineapple juice
1 cup drained pineapple (#2 can)
12 maraschino cherries, sliced
1/4 cup butter
3/4 cup sugar

1 egg
1-1/2 cups flour
3 teaspoons baking powder
1/4 teaspoon salt
1 teaspoon vanilla
2/3 cup milk

Place brown sugar and pineapple juice in saucepan. Boil 5 minutes, remove from heat, and add pineapple. Place cherry rings in bottom of muffin tins; place over this pineapple mixture, and put in oven for 10 minutes.
Cream butter, add sugar gradually, creaming well. Blend in egg. Sift flour, measure, and sift again 3 times with baking powder and salt. Add vanilla to milk, and add alternately with dry ingredients to creamed mixture. Place in muffin tins on top of filling, and bake in a moderate oven, 350°, for 25 minutes. Remove from muffin tins and turn upside down on cake plate, as 1 large cake, dotting with whipped cream between cakes.
12 small cakes

Polka Dot Prune Cake

Prune-flavored sponge, decorated with shiny prune topping and blanched almonds

1/4 cup butter
3/4 cup brown sugar
1/4 cup almonds, blanched
1 cup prunes, steamed and pitted
3 eggs, separated
3/4 cup granulated sugar
1/2 cup prune juice
1 cup flour
1 teaspoon baking powder

Melt butter, add sugar, stir until thoroughly blended; spread evenly over bottom of a deep 9-inch upside down cake pan, or heavy iron skillet. Place whole almonds in sugar in fancy design, and place prunes over these in an even layer. Beat egg yolks until thick, add sugar and prune juice, and beat thoroughly. Sift flour and measure; sift again with baking powder and fold into first mixture. Fold in stiffly-beaten egg whites, pour over fruit, and bake for 50 to 60 minutes in a moderate oven, 350°. Remove from oven, let stand a minute and turn out upside down on cake rack until cool.
8 servings

Apple Upside-Down Cake

A really delightful dessert for any occasion . . . the big difference is in the lightness and unusually appetizing taste obtained by using pancake and waffle flour.

1-1/2 cups pancake and waffle flour
1/3 cup granulated sugar
2 eggs, separated
3/4 cup milk
2 apples
1/2 cup brown sugar
3 tablespoons butter

Sift flour, measure and mix thoroughly with sugar. Add beaten egg yolks to milk and blend with dry ingredients. Beat egg whites stiff and fold in. Peel, core, and slice apples thin and place in frying pan with brown sugar and butter and cook 15 minutes over direct heat. Pour batter over apples and bake in moderately hot oven, 375°, for 25 minutes. Serve upside down.
One 8-inch square

Ginger-Apple Cake

Gingerbread, topped with apples, cooked in lemon candy syrup

3 medium apples
1/2 cup sugar
1/2 cup water
1/2 pound candy lemon drops
1-2/3 cups flour
1 teaspoon baking powder
1/3 cup sugar
1 teaspoon soda
1/2 teaspoon ginger
1/2 teaspoon nutmeg
1/2 teaspoon cinnamon
1/2 teaspoon cloves
1/4 teaspoon salt
1 egg
1/2 cup molasses
1/2 cup hot water
1/2 cup butter, melted

Core and pare apples and cut into eighths. Boil sugar, water and lemon drops for 10 minutes. Add apples a few at a time, and cook until half done. Place on bottom of upside down cake pan (9 inches in diameter, and 2 inches deep), and cover with syrup. Heat in oven 10 minutes, and cover with gingerbread, made as follows:
Sift flour, measure, and sift again with dry ingredients. Beat egg, add molasses, and hot water, and stir into dry ingredients. Add melted butter last. Bake in moderate oven, 350°, for 30 to 40 minutes. Remove from oven, let stand a minute and turn upside down on cake rack until cool.
8 servings

Spiced Humpty-Dumpty

Pineapple, walnuts and dates crown a deliciously fluffy spice cake

1 cup brown sugar
1/4 cup orange juice
4 slices pineapple
4 walnut halves
4 dates, pitted
4 walnut quarters
1/2 cup shortening
1 cup brown sugar
2 eggs
1-1/3 flour
1/4 teaspoon cloves
1/2 teaspoon cinnamon
1 teaspoon baking powder
1/4 teaspoon salt
1/2 teaspoon soda
1/2 cup buttermilk

Boil sugar and orange juice for 5 minutes. Arrange pineapple in upside down cake pan (9 inches in diameter, and 2 inches deep), and place walnut half in the center of each pineapple slice. Stuff dates with walnut quarters, and place between pineapple slices. Pour syrup over, and place in oven for 10 minutes. Cover, while hot, with spice cake batter, made as follows:
Cream shortening and sugar thoroughly, add eggs, beating between each addition. Sift flour, measure, and sift again with spices, baking powder and salt. Dissolve soda in buttermilk, and add to first mixture, alternately with dry ingredients. Bake in moderate oven, 350°, for 30 to 40 minutes. Remove from oven, let stand a minute and turn upside down on cake rack until cool.
8 servings

Apricot Cobbler-Cake

Apricots, almonds and a garnishing of cocoanut decorate this "hot water" sponge cake

4 tablespoons butter
3/4 cup brown sugar
1 tablespoon apricot juice
1/4 cup blanched almonds
12 apricot halves
3 eggs
1 cup granulated sugar
1 cup flour
1 teaspoon baking powder
1/4 teaspoon salt
1/3 cup hot water
1/4 cup shredded cocoanut

Melt butter in bottom of a deep 9-inch upside down cake pan, add sugar and apricot juice, and stir until melted, but do not cook. Place an almond in each apricot half, and arrange cut side down, in a circle around the edge, and one in the center of the pan. Place an almond between apricot halves.
Separate eggs, beat whites stiff, and fold in sugar gradually. Add well-beaten yolks. Sift flour and measure; sift again 3 times with baking powder and salt. Fold carefully into egg mixture. Add hot water slowly, blending well. Pour batter over fruit, and bake in a moderate oven, 350°, for 45 minutes or until cake is done. Remove from oven and turn upside down on cake rack. When cool, place on serving plate and garnish with a ring of cocoanut around the center apricot, taking care not to cover those on the outside.
8 servings

Peach Toffee

Genoese pastry, topped with peach flowers in a butterscotch sauce

1/4 cup butter
6 tablespoons flour
1/16 teaspoon mace
1/2 cup syrup from peaches
1-1/2 cups brown sugar
4 teaspoons lemon juice
4 peach halves
1/4 cup raisins
3/4 cup flour
3/4 teaspoon baking powder
1/4 teaspoon salt
4 eggs
3/4 cup sugar
1 teaspoon vanilla

Rub butter and flour together, add mace, syrup, sugar and lemon juice, and cook, stirring constantly, until thick and smooth. Slice peaches and arrange in bottom of a deep 9-inch upside down cake pan, to resemble a flower. Fill center with raisins, and pour butterscotch mixture over slices. Place in oven for 10 minutes.
Sift flour and measure. Combine baking powder, salt and eggs in a deep bowl. Place bowl over a small bowl of hot (not boiling) water, being sure that upper bowl is not touching water. Add sugar a little at a time, beating constantly until thick (about 5 minutes). Remove from heat, fold in flour, add vanilla, and pour over hot peach butterscotch mixture. Bake in a moderate oven, 350° for 30 minutes. Remove from oven, let stand a minute, and turn upside down on a cake rack until cool.
8 servings

Velvet Lunch Cake

1/2 cup butter
1 cup sugar
1 egg
1 cup sour milk
2 cups flour
1 teaspoon soda
2 tablespoons molasses
1 teaspoon cinnamon
1/2 teaspoon cloves
1/2 teaspoon nutmeg

Cream butter and sugar. Add beaten egg yolk, then alternately the sifted dry ingredients, and bake in a buttered pan in a rather slow oven for 3/4 of an hour, or until done.

Variety Cake

1/2 cup butter
1-1/2 cups sugar
Yolks of 3 eggs
3/4 cup milk
2 cups cake flour
2 teaspoons baking powder
White of 1 egg
1/2 teaspoon cloves
1/2 teaspoon cinnamon
1/2 teaspoon nutmeg

Cream the butter and sugar. Add the well-beaten yolks. Then stir in gradually and alternately the milk and flour, into which has been sifted the baking powder. Then fold in the white of the egg, which has been beaten into a stiff froth. Have ready 3 buttered cake pans. Take two-thirds of this mixture and pour into 2 of the pans. Into the balance of the mixture stir the spices, and pour into the remaining buttered pan and bake in a moderate oven. Put together with boiled icing, using the 2 whites of the egg left.

White Layer Cake

1/3 cup butter
1 cup sugar
1-1/2 cups cake flour
3 teaspoons baking powder
1/2 cup milk
1/2 teaspoon vanilla
3 egg whites

Cream the butter and sugar until very soft. Mix and sift the flour and baking powder 3 times, then add alternately with milk and vanilla. Beat until very smooth, then fold in the stiffly-beaten egg whites. Turn into buttered layer cake pans, and bake in a moderate oven.

White Loaf Cake or Tutti Fruiti Cake

May be made into plain white loaf or white loaf nut cake or Tutti Fruiti as described in the following recipe.

1/2 cup butter
1-1/2 cups sugar
2-2/3 cups cake flour
2 teaspoons baking powder
1/2 teaspoon cream of tartar
1/2 teaspoon salt
1 cup water
1 teaspoon almond extract
1/2 slice candied pineapple (diced)
1/4 cup candied cherries cut in quarters
1 tablespoon sliced citron
1/2 cup broken walnut meats
4 egg whites
Reserve enough flour to flour the fruit and nuts

Cream butter and sugar until very soft. Sift together flour, baking powder, cream of tartar and salt and then sift twice and add alternately with water to creamed butter and sugar, reserving enough flour to flour fruit and nuts. Add flavoring and beat until smooth, then fold in floured fruit and nuts, and then carefully fold in the stiffly-beaten egg whites, without beating again. Turn into buttered pan with bottom either lightly floured or lined with wax paper which should also be slightly buttered. May be baked in a deep loaf, or in baking pan less deep for a 2-inch deep cake. Cover with boiled frosting, decorate with nuts and candied cherries. Follow general directions for cake baking. It is done when a slight pressure made with the finger leaves no imprint.

White Pound Cake

Excellent

3/4 pound butter
1 pound sugar
1 pound cake flour
Whites of 16 eggs
Bitter almond

Cream the butter and sugar (which has been sifted before weighing), then sift in gradually the flour. Beat the whites of the eggs very stiff and fold in lightly. Flavor with bitter almond. Bake in a moderate oven. This makes 2 large loaves and recipe may be easily divided.

Washboard Cookies

1 cup sugar
1 cup brown sugar, firmly packed
1 cup shortening
2 eggs, well beaten
3-1/2 cup flour, sifted
2 teaspoons baking soda
2 teaspoons cream of tartar
1 teaspoon vanilla
1 teaspoon lemon extract
1 cup coconut
1 cup raisins
1/2 cup chopped nuts

Cream together sugars and shortening until smooth. Add eggs and mix well. Sift together flour, soda and cream of tartar. Set aside a small part in which to dredge the raisins, nuts and coconut. Add dry ingredients to batter and mix. Add flavorings, raisins, nuts and coconut. Mix well. Shape dough into small balls. Place on a greased cookie sheet and press flat with a fork. Bake in a 350° oven about 12 minutes.

10

SMALL CAKES & COOKIES

For crisp cookies, chill the dough, or allow it to stand half an hour or longer, roll thin and bake in a hot oven. For soft cookies, do not chill the dough, roll thicker than for crisp cookies, and bake in a more moderate oven.

Cookies with too much flour, or cookies baked very slowly, will be hard, but not crisp. A soft dough, if chilled or allowed to stand, then rolled thin and baked in a hot oven will make splendid crisp cookies and is much more satisfactory than a stiff dough. They require very little flour for rolling when chilled, and are much more easily handled.

Almond Christmas Cookies

3/4 cup shortening
1-1/2 cups sugar
2 beaten eggs
1 teaspoon almond or vanilla extract
2 tablespoons milk
3 cups flour
1-1/2 teaspoons baking powder
1/2 teaspoon salt
1/2 cup finely chopped almonds (walnut or peanuts may be used)

Cream shortening and sugar. Add beaten eggs, flavoring and milk. Mix and sift flour, baking powder and salt and add, mixing in the nuts with some of the flour. Work together thoroughly, then chill. Roll very thin on a floured board and cut with a cookie cutter. Sprinkle the tops with sugar and bake in a rather hot oven. These are much improved after standing several hours, and keep well.

Anise Seed Cookies

1/3 cup shortening
1 cup sugar
2 beaten eggs
1/2 cup finely chopped almonds (or peanuts)
2 cups flour
1/2 teaspoon baking powder
1/4 teaspoon salt
2 teaspoons anise seed
Sugar

Cream shortening and sugar, add beaten eggs and stir in the chopped nuts. Mix and sift the flour, baking powder and salt, and add. Chill thoroughly. Roll thin, cut with cookie cutter or into oblong strips, brush over with milk and sprinkle with anise seed and sugar. Bake in a hot oven.

Australian Date Cookies

1/2 cup butter
3/4 cup sugar
1 egg
1/4 cup milk
1-1/2 cups flour
1/2 teaspoon cream of tartar
1/4 teaspoon soda
1/2 teaspoon salt
1/4 teaspoon nutmeg

Cream the butter and sugar; add the beaten egg and the milk. Sift together the flour, cream of tartar, soda, salt and nutmeg. Roll out; cut with a biscuit cutter. Fold a date in each, pressing the edges together (to resemble Parker House Rolls). Bake in a moderate oven to a light brown. These are better after standing several days. Will keep a long time.

California Nut Cookies

1 cup shortening
1-1/2 cups sugar
2 eggs
1 cup milk
1 teaspoon cream of tartar
1/2 teaspoon soda
1/2 teaspoon salt
3 cups flour
English walnut meats

Cream the shortening and sugar. Add the beaten eggs, then the milk. Sift together the dry ingredients and beat in gradually to a smooth batter. Drop from a teaspoon on a well-greased pan at least 3 inches apart. Into the center of each press half an English walnut. Bake in a quick oven.

Cream Puffs #1

1 cup boiling water
1/2 cup cooking oil
1 cup flour
1/2 teaspoon salt
3 eggs
1 teaspoon baking powder

Heat water and oil in saucepan until it boils up well. Add flour sifted with salt all at once and stir vigorously. As soon as thoroughly mixed, remove from the fire, cool and mix in unbeaten eggs one at a time. Add baking powder; mix again and drop by spoonfuls about 2 inches apart on oiled tin. Shape into circular form. Bake from 35 to 45 minutes in hot oven (400 F.). Cut with sharp knife near the bottom to admit the filling.

Cream Filling:
1/4 cup corn starch
3/4 cup sugar
1/4 teaspoon salt
2 eggs
2 cups scalded milk
1/2 teaspoon vanilla extract

Mix corn starch, sugar and salt together; add slowly beaten eggs and stir into this gradually the scalded milk. Cook about 15 minutes in double boiler, stirring constantly until thickened. Cool slowly and flavor.
For Chocolate Cream Filling add 1-1/2 squares (1-1/2 oz.) unsweetened chocolate to scalded milk.
Makes 18 small puffs

Cream Puffs #2

2/3 cup butter
1 cup boiling water
1-1/2 cups flour
5 eggs
Soda the size of pea
1 teaspoon vanilla

Boil the butter and water together until butter is melted, and stir in the flour while boiling. Remove from the fire and beat till smooth. Let cool and then add the well-beaten eggs and the soda and flavoring. Drop on buttered tins (about 1 tablespoon to a puff), allowing at least 3 inches between each for spreading, and bake half an hour in a quick oven. When cold, split part way open and fill with the following. Puffs which are not baked long enough will fall.

Custard Filling

1 cup sugar
2/3 cup flour
2 eggs
2 cups milk
1/4 teaspoon salt
1 teaspoon (or more) vanilla

Mix together thoroughly the sugar and flour and stir in the well-beaten eggs. Heat the milk to the boiling point and then stir into it the first mixture. Boil until very thick, stirring constantly. When almost cool, flavor to taste with vanilla.
This makes about 18

Whipped Cream Filling

1/2 pint whipping cream
3 tablespoons granulated sugar
1/2 teaspoon vanilla
Powdered sugar

Whip cream, adding granulated sugar and vanilla. Use for filling puffs when puffs are cold and sprinkle tops with powdered sugar.

Strawberry Filling:
Box of strawberries
Sugar
1/2 pint cream

Mash strawberries, sprinkle with sugar and let stand while whipping cream, then mix with cream and fill puffs, or cut berries in halves without mashing, sprinkle with sugar and mix with whipped cream.

Economical Cream Puffs

1/4 cup butter
1 cup hot water
1-1/4 cups flour
1/4 teaspoon salt
3 eggs, unbeaten

Boil butter and water. When butter is melted, add flour and salt quickly and remove from the fire. When cool drop in the unbeaten eggs and beat hard for about 5 minutes, or until smooth. Drop on greased pan allowing about 4 inches between each for spreading. Bake in a moderate oven for about 1/2 hour.
Makes 1 dozen

Filling for Economical Cream Puffs

1/2 cup sugar
1/2 cup flour
1 beaten egg
1-1/2 cups milk
1/8 teaspoon salt
1 teaspoon vanilla

Follow directions above in Custard Filling.

The Children's Cookies

1/2 cup shortening (half butter)
1 cup sugar
1 egg
1/2 cup milk
3 cups flour
1-1/2 teaspoons baking powder
1/2 teaspoon salt
Jelly
Milk

Cream the butter and sugar. Add beaten egg and milk, then the sifted flour, baking powder and salt. Chill and roll thin. Cut half with a cookie cutter and half with doughnut cutter of the same size. On those cut with cookie cutter put a little jelly in the center of each (first beating the jelly slightly with a fork), put a cookie cut with the doughnut cutter on top and press the edges together slightly. Rub over with milk and bake in a quick oven.

Currant Cookies

1/2 cup shortening
1 cup sugar
2 eggs (1 will do, making the cookies less rich)
1/3 cup milk
2-3/4 cups flour
1 teaspoon baking powder
1/4 teaspoon salt
1/4 teaspoon nutmeg
Grated rind of 1 lemon
1/2 cup currants

Cream the shortening and sugar. Add the beaten eggs and milk. Mix and sift dry ingredients. Add lemon rind and stir in, adding currants with last of flour. Roll, cut in squares, brush over with milk and bake in a hot oven.

Chocolate Cream Cookies

1/2 cup shortening
1-1/2 cups sugar
2 squares unsweetened chocolate, melted, or 2 oz. powdered unsweetened or 2-1/2 powdered sweetened chocolate
2 slightly beaten eggs
2 tablespoons milk
1 teaspoon vanilla
3 cups Blend Flour
2 teaspoons baking powder
1/4 teaspoon salt

Cream shortening and sugar. Add melted chocolate or powdered chocolate, and mix in well, then add slightly beaten eggs, milk and vanilla. Mix and sift the flour, baking powder and salt, and add gradually. Roll on a floured board, cut with round cookie cutter and bake in a rather quick oven. When cool, spread between 2 cookies some Uncooked Powdered Sugar Frosting (below).

Uncooked Powdered Sugar Frosting

1 tablespoon butter
1/2 cup powdered sugar
2 teaspoons hot water
1/2 teaspoon vanilla

Mix butter and sugar, and add remaining ingredients.

Chocolate and Cocoanut Dream Cookies

1/2 cup shortening
2 cups sugar
3 squares or 3 oz. powdered unsweetened chocolate
1/2 teaspoon almond extract or vanilla
2 slightly beaten eggs
3 tablespoons milk
3-1/3 cups flour
1/4 teaspoon salt
2 teaspoons baking powder
1 unbeaten egg white
2 tablespoons sugar (preferably powdered)
Cocoanut

Cream shortening and sugar, add powdered or melted cake chocolate, flavoring, eggs and milk. Mix well and add flour sifted with salt and baking powder. Mix, chill, roll and cut with cookie cutter. Spread between 2 cookies a mixture of the egg white, sugar and cocoanut, using sufficient shredded cocoanut to make rather stiff. Press cookies together slightly and bake in a rather hot oven.

Cookies

1 egg
3/4 cup white or brown sugar
5 tablespoons cooking oil
1/4 cup milk
1 teaspoon vanilla or grated rind of lemon
1-3/4 cups flour
2 teaspoons baking powder
1/4 teaspoon salt
1/4 teaspoon grated nutmeg
Raisins or nuts

Beat egg until light. Add sugar slowly, then oil, milk and vanilla. Beat well and add, a little at a time, the flour which has been sifted with the baking powder, salt and nutmeg. Add only sufficient more flour to roll easily. Chill and roll out very thin on floured board. Cut with cookie cutter. Sprinkle with sugar. Put a raisin or piece of nut in the center of each. Bake on oiled tin about 12 minutes in hot oven (400 F.).
Makes 3 dozen cookies

Brownies

2 eggs
1 cup light brown sugar
2 squares chocolate
1/2 teaspoon vanilla
1/2 cup flour
1/4 cup walnut meats

Beat eggs. Stir in sugar, melted chocolate, vanilla, flour and nutmeats. Spread out in a layer 1/2 inch thick on a greased pan and bake in a moderate oven 20 minutes. Cut into oblong strips when partially cool.

Macaroons #1

2 eggs
3/4 cup rolled oats
2 tablespoons Crisco
1/2 cup sugar
2/3 cup cocoanut
2 cups corn flakes
1/2 teaspoon baking powder
1/2 teaspoon salt

Beat eggs well and mix with oatmeal. Let stand while creaming Crisco with sugar. Combine these two mixtures and add cocoanut, corn flakes, baking powder and salt. Drop by spoonfuls on Crisco'ed baking sheet. Bake 15 minutes in moderate oven.

Macaroons #2

Mrs. W.T. Franks

Whites of 2 eggs
1 cup sugar
2 cups corn flakes
1 cup coconut
1/2 cup walnuts
1 tablespoon flour

Beat the whites of the eggs stiff, add sugar and mix well, then add remaining ingredients. Bake in a moderate oven.

Caramel or Butterscotch Cookies

1 cup melted Crisco
4 cups dark brown sugar
4 beaten eggs
1 teaspoon salt
7 cups flour
3 teaspoons baking powder

Cream Crisco with sugar. Add eggs slowly, mixing thoroughly. Then add dry ingredients sifted together twice. Shape into roll about 2-1/2 to 3 inches in diameter. Put in Crisco'ed pan in ice box over night. When ready to bake, slice and bake in quick oven (425 degrees F.).
Makes about 125 cookies

Cocoanut Filling and Icing

1-1/2 cups granulated sugar
1/2 cup water
2 egg whites
1/2 teaspoon vanilla extract
Few drops of lemon juice
1 cup fresh grated cocoanut

Cook sugar and water without stirring until syrup spins a thread (240 degrees F.); pour very slowly over stiffly-beaten egg whites. Beat until thick; add flavoring and spread on cake. While icing is soft sprinkle thickly with the grated cocoanut.

Chocolate Filling

3 squares (3 oz.) unsweetened chocolate
3 tablespoons milk
1 tablespoon cooking oil
1 egg yolk
3/4 cup powdered or confectioners' sugar
1 tablespoon corn starch

1/8 teaspoon salt
1 teaspoon vanilla extract

Melt chocolate in top of double boiler; add milk, oil and egg yolk. Stir in sugar gradually; mix corn starch with a little cold water and add, stirring constantly until smooth and thick. Remove from fire; add salt and vanilla and spread thickly between layers of cake.

Filled Date Bars

1 cup Crisco
1 cup sugar
2 eggs
1/2 cup sour milk
4 cups flour (bread)
1 teaspoon baking powder
1/2 teaspoon soda

Cream Crisco; add sugar and cream again. Add unbeaten eggs one at a time, beating thoroughly after each addition. Add sour milk, then fold in flour which has been sifted with baking powder and soda. Roll out to a sheet as large as the baking pan. Spread with date filling. Cover with a layer of cookie dough. Bake in a hot oven (375 degrees F.). Cut into strips while warm.

Date Filling

2 cups chopped dates
1/2 cup sugar
1/2 cup water
1/2 cup nuts

To dates which have been stoned and chopped, add sugar and water and simmer for 5 minutes. Remove from fire; add chopped nuts and cool.

Date Cookies

1 cup shortening
2 cups sugar
3 beaten eggs
1 teaspoon vanilla
2 tablespoons milk
5 cups flour
4 teaspoons baking powder
1 teaspoon salt
1/2 teaspoon nutmeg
1 cup stoned and cut dates
1/4 cup sugar
1/4 cup water
Milk
Sugar

Cream shortening and sugar. Add beaten eggs, flavoring and milk. Mix and sift flour, baking powder, salt and nutmeg. Mix together and let stand an hour or more before rolling, if convenient. Roll on a floured board. Have ready a paste made by cooking together until thick the dates, 1/4 cup of sugar and 1/4 cup water. Spread the cooled paste on top of one cookie and press another on top, pressing down the edges. Brush over with milk and sprinkle with sugar. Bake in a rather hot oven.

Date Bars

1/2 cup sugar
1/2 cup flour
1/4 teaspoon salt
1/2 teaspoon baking powder
1/2 cup brown sugar
2 eggs, beaten together
1 tablespoon water
1 cup stoned dates, halved
1 cup broken walnut meats
Powdered sugar for rolling

Mix and sift the first 4 ingredients, add brown sugar, then beaten eggs and water. Then add the dates and nuts, floured with a tablespoon of flour. Spread in a buttered and floured shallow pan about 1/2 inch thick. Bake in a moderate oven. When done and slightly cooled, cut into oblongs an inch wide and 3 inches long. When cool, roll in powdered sugar.

Cream Filling

1/4 cup sugar
2 tablespoons corn starch
2 egg yolks
1 cup scalded milk
1 teaspoon vanilla extract
Rind of 1 orange
1/8 teaspoon salt
2 teaspoons cooking oil
1 teaspoon lemon juice

Mix well together sugar, corn starch and egg yolks. Add slowly to scalded milk. Cook in top of double boiler until smooth and thick. Remove from fire. Add vanilla, orange rind, salt, oil and lemon juice. Cool and spread thickly between layers of cake.

Date Tea Cakes

1/3 cup shortening
3/4 cup sugar
1/4 cup milk
1/2 teaspoon vanilla
1 slightly beaten egg
2-1/2 cups flour
3 teaspoons baking powder
1/2 teaspoon salt
Dates

Cream shortening and sugar; add milk and vanilla and slightly-beaten egg. Mix and sift flour, baking powder and salt and add gradually, mixing well. Roll on a slightly floured board and cut with a large, round cookie cutter. On each cookie spread a stoned date, and fold over like Parker House Roll. Bake in a moderate oven.

Doughnuts

1/2 cup sour cream
1/2 teaspoon soda
1 egg
1 cup sweet milk
1 cup sugar
4-1/4 cups flour
1/2 teaspoon salt
4-1/2 teaspoons baking powder
1-1/2 teaspoons nutmeg

Put the sour cream and soda into the mixing bowl and beat with an egg-beater until smooth. Then add the egg and beat. Stir in the milk and sugar. Sift together the flour, salt, baking powder and nutmeg and add, stirring until smooth. Toss on a board well dredged with flour and pat out to about 1/4 inch thick. Cut with doughnut cutter, and fry in hot fat. Drain on brown paper and roll in powdered sugar or cinnamon and sugar.
This recipe makes about 3 dozen medium size

Fruit Nut Bars

1/3 cup butter
1/2 cup light brown sugar
1/2 cup granulated sugar
2 beaten eggs
1/2 teaspoon almond or vanilla extract
1-2/3 cups flour
1-3/4 teaspoons baking powder
1/8 teaspoon salt
1 cup chopped figs
1/2 cup stoned dates
1/2 cup chopped nuts

Cream shortening and sugar, add slightly-beaten eggs and beat until well mixed, then add flour sifted with baking powder and salt, adding fruit and nuts with part of flour. Turn into a buttered and floured shallow pan or pans, spreading to a depth of about 1/2 inch. Bake in moderate oven until a very gentle pressure leaves no imprint. When cool, cut into bars and inch wide by 3 inches long and roll in powdered sugar; or cut into 3-inch squares and serve with whipped cream on top.

Doughnuts (Sour Milk)

4 cups flour
1-1/2 teaspoons salt
1-3/4 teaspoons soda
1-3/4 teaspoons cream of tartar
1-1/2 teaspoons grated nutmeg
1 cup sugar
1/2 tablespoon butter
1 cup sour milk
1 egg well beaten

Mix and sift the dry ingredients. Work in the butter with the tips of the fingers. Add the sour milk and the beaten egg. Mix thoroughly; toss on board dredged with flour and knead slightly. Roll to 1/4 inch in thickness, cut with doughnut cutter and fry in hot fat. Drain on brown paper, dust with powdered sugar and cinnamon.
This makes 24 large or 30 medium

Drop Cakes

1 cup shortening (half butter, half lard)
2 cups light brown sugar
2 eggs
1 cup raisins (or more)
3 cups flour
1 teaspoon cinnamon
1/2 teaspoon cloves
1-1/4 teaspoons soda
1/2 teaspoon salt
1/2 teaspoon vanilla
3/4 cup sweet milk

Cream the butter and sugar; add the beaten egg. Sift together all the dry ingredients and add alternately with the milk. Drop from a teaspoon onto buttered tins, allowing room for spreading, and bake in a quick oven. The degree of heat in the oven affects the amount of spreading. If you prefer rather firm little cakes, have the oven quite hot when they are first put in; if you prefer them flatter, more like cookies, and not so dry, have the oven more moderate and they will spread, be thinner, and therefore bake more quickly.
This makes about 70 small drop cakes

Fig Bars

1/2 cup shortening
1 cup sugar
1 slightly-beaten egg
1/4 cup milk
1 teaspoon vanilla
2-1/2 cups flour
3 teaspoons baking powder
1/2 teaspoon salt
1/2 pound layer figs

Cream shortening and sugar. Add beaten egg, milk and vanilla. Mix and sift flour, baking powder and salt, and add. Let stand an hour or more, then roll rather thin and cut into oblong cookies of uniform size. Put a layer of figs between 2 cookies and bake on greased pans in a moderately hot oven.

French Cocoanut Cakes

1/2 cup butter
1/2 cup sugar
2 eggs, beaten separately
1 cup cake flour
2 teaspoons baking powder
1/4 cup milk
1-1/2 cups shredded cocoanut
1 teaspoon vanilla

Cream the butter and sugar. Add the yolks of eggs well beaten; then the flour, into which has been sifted the baking powder. Then the milk and cocoanut. Beat till smooth and fold in the whites of the eggs, beaten to a stiff froth. Pour into 12 buttered gem pans and bake in a moderate oven for 20 minutes. When cool, ice, if desired.

Ginger Drops

1-3/4 cups flour
1/2 teaspoon salt
1 cup sugar
2 teaspoons baking powder
1 teaspoon ginger
1/2 cup milk
1 beaten egg
1/4 cup melted shortening

Mix and sift the dry ingredients. Add milk and beaten egg, then melted butter or other shortening. Beat, drop from a teaspoon onto buttered pans and bake in a hot oven. When cool, spread with Powdered Sugar Frosting used for Rolls.

Ginger Snaps #1

1 cup shortening
1 cup molasses
2 cups brown sugar
1 tablespoon ginger
1 teaspoon cinnamon
1 scant teaspoon soda
1/4 teaspoon salt
2 beaten eggs
4 cups flour (or enough to roll easily)

Heat first 7 ingredients to the boiling point; remove from the stove and beat. Then add eggs and flour. Toss on well-floured board; then cut with a cookie cutter. Bake in a quick oven.

Ginger Snaps #2

1/2 cup molasses
1/3 cup brown sugar
1 teaspoon salt
1 teaspoon soda
1 teaspoon baking powder
1 teaspoon ginger
1 tablespoon vinegar
1/2 cup cooking oil
1/4 cup hot water
2-3/4 cups flour

Mix molasses and brown sugar together; add salt, soda, baking powder and ginger and mix thoroughly. Add liquids, mixing after each addition. Lastly add flour. Mix and chill. Roll out very thin on floured board; cut with cookie butter. Bake on oiled tin in hot oven (450 degrees F.) for about 7 minutes.
Makes 4 dozen snaps

Less Expensive Ginger Snaps, or Molasses Cookies

1 cup molasses
1/2 cup shortening
3-1/2 cups flour
1/2 teaspoon salt
3/4 tablespoon ginger
1/4 teaspoon cinnamon

Bring molasses and shortening to a boil. Mix and sift the dry ingredients and when shortening is melted, add them to the mixture. Chill thoroughly, then roll as thin as possible, rolling but part of the dough at a time. Keep cool while rolling and working or cookies will need more flour, which will make them hard instead of crisp.

Inexpensive Molasses Cookies

Wonderful Ginger Snaps if dough is chilled

1/3 cup shortening
3/4 cup molasses
1 teaspoon soda
1/4 cup warm milk
2-1/2 teaspoons ginger
1/2 cup sugar
1/2 teaspoon salt
2 teaspoons baking powder
2-3/4 cups flour

Add shortening to molasses and bring to a boil. Remove from fire and when melted, add the soda dissolved in the milk, then the balance of the sifted dry ingredients. Chill thoroughly, then roll and bake in a moderate oven. For soft cookies, roll to about 1/4 inch thick. For crisp cookies, roll as thin as possible.

Nut Sticks

2 eggs
1-1/2 cups sugar
1/2 cup oil
4 tablespoons milk
1 teaspoon lemon or almond extract
4 cups flour
3 teaspoons baking powder
1/2 teaspoon salt
1/2 cup chopped blanched almonds

Beat one egg yolk; add sugar and oil; add beaten whites of 2 eggs and 3 tablespoons milk and flavoring; mix well. Sift together flour, baking powder and salt and add, mixing well. Roll half of dough at a time less than 1/4 inch thick on floured board, cut into strips, 1 by 3 inches. Brush with remaining yolk of egg mixed with 1 tablespoon milk and sprinkle with chopped nuts. Bake in moderate oven (400 degrees F.) about 10 minutes.

Our Hermits

1/2 cup shortening
1-1/2 cups brown sugar
2 eggs
2 tablespoons sweet milk
1 teaspoon soda
3 cups flour
1 teaspoon grated nutmeg
1/2 teaspoon cinnamon
1/4 teaspoon cloves
Grated rind of lemon
1/2 cup chopped citron
2 cups raisins
1 cup chopped nuts

Cream the butter and sugar. Add the beaten eggs, then the milk. Sift together the soda, flour and spices, reserving enough flour to flour the fruit. Beat into a smooth batter. Add the fruit and nuts. Drop from a teaspoon on a well-greased tin and bake in a moderate oven. These will keep a long time.

Nut Cookies

1/3 cup butter
1-1/2 cups sugar
1 egg
1/2 teaspoon soda
1/2 cup thick sour cream
2-1/2 cups flour
1/4 teaspoon baking powder
1/2 teaspoon salt
1 cup chopped nuts
1/2 teaspoon vanilla

Cream the butter and sugar. Add the well-beaten egg. Beat the soda into the cream and add to the first mixture. Sift together the flour, baking powder and salt; beat in gradually, adding the nuts and vanilla last. Roll thin. Sprinkle the tops generously with finely minced nuts and sugar, which have been mixed together. Cut with a cookie cutter and bake in a quick oven.

Oatmeal Cookies

1 cup shortening
1 cup sugar
1 egg beaten
2/3 teaspoon soda
1 cup milk
2 cups flour
1 teaspoon salt
1 teaspoon cinnamon
1/2 teaspoon cloves
1/2 teaspoon nutmeg
2 cups oatmeal
1 cup raisins
1 cup chopped nuts

Cream the butter and sugar and add the beaten egg. Dissolve the soda in the milk and add to the first mixture. Sift in the flour, salt and spices (reserving enough flour to flour the raisins). Add the raisins and nuts and drop from a teaspoon on a buttered tin, allowing plenty of room for them to spread.

Oatmeal Fruit Filled Cookies

1 cup shortening
1 cup sugar
1 teaspoon soda
1/2 cup hot water
2 cups flour
3 cups oatmeal

Cream the shortening and sugar. Dissolve the soda in the hot water, and add, alternately with the sifted flour and oatmeal. Roll thin, cut with a cookie cutter and bake in a hot oven. When done, spread the following filling between 2 cookies (like sandwiches).

Filling:
1 pound seeded and chopped dates
1 cup sugar
1/3 cup water

Let boil until thick, stirring constantly to prevent burning, and when cool, spread.

Oatmeal Cookies

1/2 cup shortening
1 cup sugar
1 egg
1-1/2 cups flour
1/2 teaspoon salt
1 teaspoon cinnamon
1/2 teaspoon soda
2 cups rolled oats (uncooked)
1/2 cup raisins or dates
1/2 cup milk

Cream the shortening and sugar; add beaten egg. Mix and sift the flour, salt, cinnamon and soda and add to first mixture. Then add oats and raisins, and last, the milk. Drop from teaspoon onto greased baking tins and bake in moderate hot oven. Nuts may be added if desired.

Orange Cup Cakes

2 eggs
1-1/2 cups sugar
2/3 cup milk
5 tablespoons cooking oil
1-3/4 cups flour
3 teaspoons baking powder
1/3 teaspoon salt
1 teaspoon orange extract
Grated rind of 1 orange

Beat eggs until light and add sugar slowly; then add about a tablespoon of milk then oil a little at a time, beating well between each addition. Sift flour, baking powder and salt together and add alternately with remainder of milk to first mixture. Add flavoring and orange rind and mix well. Bake in small oiled cake tins in moderate oven (400 degrees F.) about 12 minutes. When cool, spread with following orange icing.

Orange Icing

2 tablespoons cooking oil
2-1/2 cups confectioners' sugar
1 teaspoon orange juice
Grated rind and pulp of 1/2 orange
1 egg white

Put oil, sugar and orange juice into bowl; add rind and pulp from which the skin and seeds have been removed; beat all together until smooth. Fold in beaten egg white and spread on top of cakes.
Makes 12 cakes

Patty Cakes

1/4 cup butter
1 cup sugar
2 eggs
1-1/2 cups flour
2-1/2 teaspoons baking powder
1/2 cup milk
1/2 teaspoon vanilla

Cream the butter and sugar until very soft. Add the well-beaten egg yolks. Mix and sift the flour and baking powder and add alternately with the milk. Flavor and beat until very light, then fold in the stiffly-beaten egg whites. Bake in buttered gem pans in a moderate oven, until they shrink from the sides of the pan. Serve plain or frosted. Are especially good if split and Chocolate Jelly Filling is spread between.

Peanut Cookies

1/4 cup shortening
1/2 cup sugar
1 beaten egg
1-1/2 cups flour
2 teaspoons baking powder
1/4 teaspoon nutmeg

1/2 teaspoon salt
2 tablespoons milk
1/2 teaspoon vanilla
2/3 cup chopped peanuts

Cream the shortening and sugar, add beaten egg. Mix and sift dry ingredients and add alternately with milk and vanilla, stirring in the peanuts with part of the flour mixture. Roll thin, cut with cookie cutter or into squares and bake in a moderate oven.

Peanut Butter Cookies

1 cup peanut butter
1/4 cup shortening
1-1/2 cups sugar
1 beaten egg
1/2 cup milk
~1/2 teaspoon vanilla
2-1/2 cups flour
1/2 teaspoon salt
2 teaspoons baking powder
1/4 teaspoon nutmeg

Cream the peanut butter and shortening, work in the sugar. Add the egg and milk, then the sifted dry ingredients. Roll thin, cut with cookie cutter and bake in a moderate oven.

Rich Christmas Cookies

1 cup shortening (half butter)
2 cups sugar
3 egg yolks
2 egg whites
1/4 cup milk
1 teaspoon vanilla
4-1/2 cups flour
2 teaspoons baking powder
1 teaspoon salt

Cream butter, shortening and sugar. Add 2 whole eggs and 1 extra yolk beaten together, then add milk and flavoring. Sift together the flour, salt and baking powder and add gradually. Chill thoroughly or let stand over night. Then roll very thin and cut with fancy cutters. Brush over some of them with the slightly-beaten egg white mixed with a tablespoon of powdered sugar, and sprinkle with minced nuts. Into part, work caraway seeds. Brush over others with milk, sprinkle with sugar and press a raisin the center.

Spice Cakes #1

1/4 teaspoon soda
1 cup thick sour cream
1 cup sugar
2 eggs
1/4 teaspoon salt
1-3/4 cups flour
1-1/2 teaspoons baking powder
1 teaspoon cinnamon
1/2 teaspoon cloves
1 teaspoon nutmeg

Beat the soda into the cream. Add the sugar, then the well-beaten yolks. Sift together the other dry ingredients and beat in gradually; mix to a smooth batter, then fold in the stiffly-beaten whites. Bake in buttered gem pans in a moderate oven.
This makes 12 or 14

Small Spice Cakes #2

1/2 cup butter (or half shortening and butter)
1/2 cup sugar
2 eggs
1/2 cup molasses
1/4 teaspoon soda
3/4 teaspoon baking powder
1 teaspoon cinnamon
1 teaspoon nutmeg
1/4 teaspoon allspice
2-1/4 cups flour
3 tablespoons milk

Cream the butter and sugar, add the yolks of the eggs beaten until thick and lemon colored; then the molasses. Sift together all the dry ingredients and add alternately with the milk. And last, folding them in lightly, the well-beaten whites of the eggs. Bake in gem pans in a moderate oven.
This makes 16 or 18

Sour Cream Drop Cakes

3/4 cup shortening (half butter and half lard)
2-1/4 cups sugar
1 egg
1 teaspoon soda
1 cup sour cream
3-3/4 cups flour
1/2 teaspoon baking powder
3/4 teaspoon salt
1 cup chopped nuts
1 cup seedless raisins

1/2 teaspoon vanilla

Cream the shortening and sugar and add the beaten egg. Whip the soda into the cream and add to the fist mixture. Sift together the flour, baking powder and salt (reserving enough flour to flour the raisins). Beat in thoroughly, adding the nuts, raisins and vanilla last. Drop from a teaspoon on greased tins and bake in a quick oven.

Sweet Milk Drop Cakes

1 cup shortening
1-1/2 cups sugar
2 eggs
1/2 cup milk
2-1/2 cups flour
2 teaspoons baking powder
1/2 teaspoon salt
1 cup (or less) chopped nuts
1 teaspoon almond extract

Cream the shortening and sugar. Add the well-beaten yolks of the eggs; then the milk. Sift together the flour, baking powder and salt, and stir in the first mixture. Add the nuts and extract. Beat smooth. Drop from a teaspoon and bake in a moderate oven. Allow plenty of room for spreading.

Sugar Cookies

1 cup shortening (butter and fat)
1-1/2 cups sugar
3 eggs
1 teaspoon vanilla
1/2 cup milk
3 cups flour
2-1/2 teaspoons baking powder
1 teaspoon salt
1 teaspoon grated nutmeg

Cream the butter and sugar; add the beaten eggs, vanilla and the milk. Sift together the flour and baking powder, salt and nutmeg and beat gradually into the first mixture. Roll thin; cut with a cookie cutter and sprinkle the top with sugar. Bake in a quick oven.

Sponge Drops

1-1/2 cups flour
1 cup sugar
1-1/2 teaspoons baking powder
2 eggs, beaten separately
1/2 cup milk
1/2 teaspoon vanilla
Grated rind of 1/2 a lemon (or omit)
Nut meats

Mix and sift the flour, sugar, baking powder, add beaten egg yolks to milk and vanilla and add. Fold in whites. Drop from tip of spoon onto buttered pans, making rounds about the size of a quarter, allowing room for spreading. Press a nut meat in the center of each and bake in a moderate oven.

Chocolate Turtle Cookies

1/2 cup all-purpose flour
1/2 teaspoon baking powder
1/4 teaspoon salt
1-1/2 tablespoons instant espresso powder
2 teaspoons vanilla extract
12 ounces semisweet chocolate, coarsely chopped
1/4 cup (1/2 stick) unsalted butter, cut into 4 pieces
1-1/2 cups granulated sugar, divided
4 large eggs, lightly beaten (at room temperature)
2 cups coarsely chopped walnuts or pecans
12 ounces (about 2 cups) semisweet chocolate chips
2 cups pecan halves, for decoration

Preheat the oven to 350 degrees F. Line 2 baking sheets with baking parchment or aluminum foil. In a medium bowl, stir together the flour, baking powder, and salt. In a small cup, dissolve the espresso powder in the vanilla extract. In the top of a double boiler over hot, not simmering, water, melt the coarsely chopped chocolates with the butter, stirring frequently until smooth. Transfer the chocolate mixture to a large bowl. Using a wire whisk, stir in 1/2 cup of the sugar. Gradually stir in the eggs. Mix in the remaining 1 cup of sugar and the espresso-vanilla mixture. Stir in the flour mixture. Stir in the chopped nuts and the chocolate chips. Using a 1/4-cup measuring cup, drop the dough onto the prepared baking sheets, leaving about 2 inches between cookies. Insert 5 pecan halves around the bottom of each cookie to represent the turtle's 4 legs and head. Bake the cookies, 1 baking sheet at a time, for 10 to 12 minutes, or until the cookies' tops start to crack. Do not over-bake; the cookies should be soft and fudgy. Cool the cookies on the sheets, set on a wire rack. Store in an airtight container for up to 5 days. These cookies freeze well.
Makes about 24 cookies

Vanilla Wafers

1/2 cup shortening (part butter)
1 cup sugar
1 beaten egg
1/3 cup milk
1-1/2 teaspoons vanilla
2-1/4 cups flour

2-1/4 teaspoons baking powder
1/2 teaspoon salt

Cream the shortening and sugar. Add egg well beaten, then milk and vanilla. Mix and sift the flour, baking powder and salt and add. Chill thoroughly. Keep cool while rolling and cutting. Roll as thin as possible, taking but a portion of the dough at a time. Cut with small cookie cutter, or cut into squares and bake in a moderate oven.

Fudge

12 ounces semisweet chips or coarsely chopped chocolate squares
1 cup marshmallow cream
2 cups granulated sugar
3/4 cup evaporated milk
2 tablespoons butter
1 teaspoon vanilla extract
1/8 teaspoon salt
1 cup chopped nuts

Lightly butter a 9-inch-square pan. In a large heat-resistant bowl, stir together the chocolate and marshmallow cream; set aside. In a 3-quart heavy sauce pot, mix the sugar, milk, and butter, stirring to combine well. Over low heat, gradually bring the mixture to a boil, stirring until the sugar dissolves. Dip a pastry brush in cold water and wash down the sides of the pot. Continue to boil for 5 minutes, stirring constantly without touching the sides of the pot. Pour the hot mixture over the chocolate mixture in the bowl. Add the vanilla and salt. Stir until the chocolate melts and the mixture is smooth. Stir in the nuts.Spread the mixture into the prepared pan, smoothing the surface. Refrigerate 4 hours or until firm. Cut into squares to serve.
Makes about 2 pounds of fudge.

SUNFLOWER

11

SAUCES & ICINGS

Apricot and Peach Sauce

1 tablespoon flour
2 tablespoons sugar
1/4 teaspoon salt
1 cup cream (if milk is substituted add 1 tablespoon butter)
2 whole fresh peaches or 4 halves canned peaches or apricots
Whites of 3 eggs

Mix together the flour, sugar and salt. Heat the cream in the double-boiler and when hot add the dry ingredients and stir until thick. Then beat in the peaches, which have been mashed through a colander. Cook 2 minutes. Remove from the fire and add the whites of the eggs, which have been beaten to a stiff froth. Serve cold.

Butterscotch Sauce

For puddings, custards and ice cream

1 cup brown sugar
2 tablespoons flour
1/8 teaspoon salt
1 tablespoon butter
1 cup top milk or cream
2 tablespoons butter (additional, see directions)
1/2 teaspoon vanilla

Mix together the sugar, flour, salt, tablespoon butter and cream. Cook, stirring constantly, until it begins to thicken. Then add balance of butter and vanilla. Stir a moment longer until butter is melted and serve hot.

Caramel Sauce

1 tablespoon flour
1 cup light brown sugar
1 rounding tablespoon butter
1/2 cup cream

Mix the flour well into the sugar, then work in the butter and when smooth, add the cream. Cook in a double-boiler for about 10 minutes.

Chocolate Sauce #1

2 ounces unsweetened chocolate, powdered or cake
4 tablespoons water
1 cup sugar
2 tablespoons flour
1/8 teaspoon salt
2 cups milk
~1 teaspoon vanilla

Put chocolate and water in skillet and stir until chocolate is dissolved. Add the sugar mixed thoroughly with the flour and salt, then pour in gradually the milk and cook, stirring constantly, until it begins to thicken. Serve hot or cold.

Chocolate Sauce #2

Follow directions above, only add one beaten egg to the milk before mixing. When done, chill, and fold in when cold half a pint of whipping cream beaten stiff.

Cream Sauce

1 egg
1 cup powdered sugar
1 teaspoon vanilla
1 cup whipped cream

Beat the egg until very light and stir into it gradually the powdered sugar. Add the flavoring and just before serving fold in the whipped cream.

Cream Filling

1/4 cup cornstarch
3/4 cup sugar
1/4 teaspoon salt
2 eggs
2 cups scalded milk
1/2 teaspoon vanilla extract

1/2 teaspoon vanilla extract

Mix corn starch, sugar and salt together; add slowly beaten eggs and stir into this gradually the scalded milk. Cook about 15 minutes in double boiler stirring constantly until thickened. Cool slowly and flavor.
For Chocolate Cream Filling add 1-1/2 squares (1-1/2 ounces) unsweetened chocolate to scalded milk.
Makes 18 small puffs

Maple Sauce

1 tablespoon flour
Pinch of salt
1 tablespoon butter, melted
2 egg yolks
1/2 cup hot maple syrup
2/3 cup whipped cream

Mix the flour and salt, and blend with the butter. Add the yolks of the eggs beaten until very light and then add very slowly, beating constantly, the hot maple syrup. Cook in double-boiler 5 minutes. remove from the stove, strain through a sieve and beat into it quickly the cream, which has been previously whipped. Serve cold.

Maple Flavor Sauce

1/2 cup brown sugar
1/2 cup white sugar
2 tablespoons flour
1/8 teaspoon salt
1 cup water
1 tablespoon butter
1/2 teaspoon maple flavoring.

Following directions for Plain Pudding Sauce

Mocha Sauce #1

2 tablespoons flour
1 cup sugar
1 cup cold strong coffee
1/8 teaspoon salt
1 tablespoon butter

Mix the flour thoroughly with the sugar, add gradually the coffee, salt and butter and cook, stirring constantly until it begins to thicken. Serve hot or cold.

Mocha Sauce #2

1 cup sugar
1 tablespoon flour
1/8 teaspoon salt
1 cup cold strong coffee
1 tablespoon butter
1/2 pint whipping cream
1/2 teaspoon vanilla

Mix together the sugar, flour and salt, add coffee gradually and butter. Cook, stirring constantly until it thickens. Chill, fold in whipped cream and flavoring.

Nut Sauce

For Nut Sauce, add 1 cup of nuts to either the recipe for Caramel or Maple Sauce.

Boiled Frosting

1 cup sugar
1/4 teaspoon cream of tartar
1/3 cup water
White of 1 egg
Flavoring

Mix together the sugar, cream of tartar and water and boil without stirring until, when dropped from a fork, it spins a long thread. Remove from the fire and let stand while beating the white of the egg to a stiff froth; then pour the syrup very slowly into the egg, beating constantly with a fork, until thick enough to spread without running off the cake. Add the flavoring and spread while warm.
(For a large cake of a thick frosting, double this recipe.)

Banana Filling

1 tablespoon soft butter
1 cup powdered sugar
1 unbeaten egg white
1/2 teaspoon lemon extract
1-1/2 ripe bananas, mashed

Cream butter and sugar. Add unbeaten egg white and flavoring and beat until light, then beat in the mashed bananas. Spread on cake when cake is cool.

Banana Whip Filling

2 bananas, mashed
1/2 pint whipping cream
Few drops lemon extract
1/4 cup powdered sugar

Mash the bananas after whipping the cream until nearly stiff, then stir bananas, extract and sugar in and whip again with rotary egg-beater until very light. Spread on a colored cake.

Custard Sauce

2 tablespoons sugar
1 tablespoon flour
1/8 teaspoon salt
3 egg yolks
2 cups milk
1/2 teaspoon flavoring

Mix together the sugar, flour and salt and add the yolks of the eggs well beaten. Heat the milk in the double-boiler and when hot add the above and cook until it thickens. When cold, flavor with vanilla or almond extract.

Foamy Sauce

2 tablespoons butter
1 cup powdered sugar
1 egg
Pinch of salt
Few drops vanilla
1 cup whipped cream

Cream the butter and sugar. Add the well-beaten egg. When smooth add the salt and vanilla and just before serving, beat into it very smooth 1 cup of whipped cream.

Hard Sauce

2 cups pulverized sugar
1/2 cup butter
1 unbeaten egg white
1 teaspoon vanilla

Cream together the well-sifted sugar and butter. Drop in the egg white unbeaten and the vanilla and beat with a rotary egg beater until very smooth and light. Chill thoroughly before serving.

Fruit Sauce

1/2 cup sugar
2 tablespoons flour
1 cup water
2 tablespoons butter
1/2 cup any fruit juice

Sift together the sugar and flour, gradually add the water and boil 3 to 5 minutes, stirring constantly. Add the butter and stir in slowly the fruit juice and cook a minute more. Very tart fruit may require more sugar.

Lemon Sauce

2 tablespoons flour
1 cup sugar
1/8 teaspoon salt
1 cup water
Grated rind of 1 lemon
2 tablespoons butter
1/2 teaspoon lemon extract

Mix flour, sugar and salt, add water gradually and lemon rind, and cook, stirring constantly until it thickens; then add butter and flavoring, and when butter is melted serve at once.

Orange Sauce

1 cup sugar
1/4 cup flour
1/4 teaspoon salt
Grated rind of an orange
1/2 cup orange juice
1 cup water

Mix the dry ingredients thoroughly, add the liquid and boil, stirring constantly, until thickened.

Plain Pudding Sauce

2 tablespoons flour
1 cup sugar
1/8 teaspoon salt
1 cup water
2 tablespoons butter
1 teaspoon vanilla or lemon extract

Mix the flour, sugar and salt, and add gradually the water, and cook, stirring constantly, until it thickens; then add butter, and when melted add flavoring and remove from fire.

Lemon Filling

3 eggs
3 tablespoons corn starch
2 tablespoons flour
1 cup sugar
1/3 cup cold water
2 cups boiling water
5-7 tablespoons lemon juice
2 teaspoons grated lemon rind
1/2 teaspoon salt

Separate eggs, saving whites for meringue. Mix corn starch, flour and sugar with cold water until smooth; mix in yolk of eggs, slightly beaten. Add slowly to boiling water. Cook 8 minutes in top of double boiler stirring constantly. Add butter. Remove from fire; add lemon juice, lemon rind and salt. Pour into baked crust.

Meringue

3 egg whites
3 tablespoons sugar
1 teaspoon baking powder

Beat egg whites until very light; add sugar, a little at a time beating constantly, and baking powder; beat until thick. Spread thickly on top of pie; bake in moderate oven (325 degrees F.) about 10 minutes or until light brown.

Butterscotch Filling

2 tablespoons butter
1/2 cup brown sugar
1 egg yolk
3 tablespoons flour
1 cup boiling milk
2 tablespoons caramel syrup
1/8 teaspoon salt

Cream the butter and sugar, add egg yolk, then flour, mixing well. Then add gradually the milk and caramel syrup, dissolved in the boiling milk. Cook in double-boiler until thick. When cool spread between layers, and use white frosting flavored with a tablespoon of caramel syrup for the top and sides.

Caramel Icing

1 cup light brown sugar
1/2 cup cream
1/4 teaspoon cream of tartar
1 level tablespoon butter

Boil until it spins a thread when dropped from a fork. Remove from the stove and beat until it begins to get creamy; then spread.
For a large cake, this recipe should be doubled, and half milk and half cream may be used instead of all cream, if preferred.

Chocolate Frosting

1 cup sugar
1/3 cup water
1/8 teaspoon cream of tartar
1-1/2 squares chocolate, melted, or
1/4 cup powdered unsweetened cocoa or chocolate
1 egg white, beaten stiff

Mix sugar, water and cream of tartar and stir until it comes to a boil, then cook without stirring until it will spin a long thread when dropped from the tip of a fork. Have ready the cake chocolate, either melted or grated, or powdered chocolate, unmelted, and have egg white beaten stiff. Slowly pour the syrup over the egg white, beating constantly and adding chocolate as soon as all syrup is added to egg white, and continue beating until stiff enough to spread without running off, or until an impression is left in the frosting by the whisk, fork or spoon, which does not instantly close.

"My Favorite" Uncooked Chocolate Frosting

1/4 cup butter
2 cups powdered sugar, first sifted
1/3 cup powdered cocoa
1 unbeaten egg white
3 tablespoons evaporated milk or cream

Cream together the butter and powdered sugar sifted with the cocoa. Drop in unbeaten egg white and beat with rotary beater, adding cream and beating until light and fluffy. This will keep soft and fluffy for days.

Chocolate Jelly Filling

1 egg well beaten
1 cup sugar
1/2 cup grated chocolate or powdered cocoa
1/4 cup milk
1/2 teaspoon vanilla

Add the beaten egg to the sugar and stir in the chocolate and milk. Let boil until thick, stirring constantly. When partially cool, add the vanilla and when cold spread between and on top of the cake.

Fluffy Uncooked Frosting

1/3 cup butter
1-3/4 cups powdered sugar
1/2 teaspoon vanilla or almond
1 unbeaten egg white

Cream the butter and sugar. Add vanilla and the unbeaten egg white. Beat all with a rotary egg-beater until very fluffy and light. Use plain or with nuts or cocoanut.

Maple Frosting

1/2 pound maple sugar
5 tablespoons water

Break the sugar into small pieces and dissolve in the water. Boil 5 minutes. Remove from the fire and pour into a deep bowl and beat quickly until it begins to get thick and creamy; then spread; if it becomes rough, smooth with a knife dipped in hot water.

Marshmallow Filling

2 cups sugar
1/2 cup water
Whites of 2 eggs

Boil together the sugar and water until it spins a thread. Beat the whites of 2 eggs until very stiff and pour over them the hot icing, beating constantly. Have ready the marshmallows, which have been melted over hot water, and pour the icing over the marshmallows.

Mocha Frosting

1/3 cup soft butter (not melted)
2 cups powdered sugar
1 tablespoon powdered unsweetened chocolate, or 1/2 square unsweetened chocolate, or 2-1/2 tablespoons sweetened
1 tablespoon very strong coffee or 1 teaspoon coffee extract

Cream the butter and sugar and work in the chocolate and coffee. Beat until light.

Fluffy Mocha Frosting

1/4 cup butter
2 cups powdered sugar
1 tablespoon very strong coffee, or 1 teaspoon coffee extract
1 unbeaten egg white
1/2 ounce unsweetened chocolate (either powdered or melted cake chocolate)

Cream the butter and sugar, add the balance and beat all with an egg-beater until very fluffy. Then spread on the cooled cake.

Orange Cream Filling #1

4 tablespoons flour
1 cup sugar
Juice of 1 orange and enough water to make 1 cup
1 egg yolk
Pinch of salt
Grated rind of 1 orange
1 tablespoon butter

Mix the flour and sugar very thoroughly. Mix a part of the liquid with the lightly-beaten egg yolk, and add to sugar and flour. Add orange rind and balance of liquid. Cook, stirring constantly until very thick, add butter, cook a few seconds longer and when almost cool, spread on the cake layers.

Orange Filling and Icing #2

Whites of 2 eggs
3 cups confectioners' sugar
Grated rind and soft pulp of 1 orange

Whip eggs to stiff froth; add sugar, a little at a time, until stiff enough to spread. Whip in pulp and rind of orange. Orange coloring may be added if desired.

Strawberry Filling

1/2 pint whipping cream
1/2 cup powdered sugar
1 egg white
1 box strawberries, crushed

Beat together thoroughly the cream, powdered sugar and egg white, then fold in the crushed berries. Serve as a "frosting" poured over sponge or plain cake.

Molasses Pecan Pie

3 eggs, slightly beaten
3/4 cup unsulphured molasses
3/4 cup light corn syrup
2 tablespoons melted butter or margarine
1/8 teaspoon salt
1 teaspoon vanilla
1 tablespoon flour
1 cup pecans
1 unbaked 8-inch pastry shell

Combine the eggs, molasses, corn syrup, butter, salt and vanilla; mix well. Mix the flour with a small amount of egg mixture. Stir into remaining egg mixture. Add pecans. Turn into pastry shell. Bake in a 325° oven for 60 minutes or until done. Serve cold.

12

PIES

If those who have difficulty in making first-class flaky pie crust will study these explicit directions, they should find it a very simple matter from now on to have a pie of which they may be justly proud.

First: The ingredients should be very cold. In summer if the lard is soft and there is no ice at hand, set it in a pan of cold water for a while, or until it is firm. Also let the water run until it is very cold.

Second: Sift the slat and flour together into the mixing bowl; then put in the lard. Chop the lard into the flour, just as you would chop hash with an old-fashioned chopper or knife. Keep chopping it until the mixture looks much like cornmeal, then take up a little lightly between the two hands and rub together (every so lightly), just tossing and rubbing until it is pretty well mixed. Then add the water. The majority of people use too much water in their pie crust; the less used the better. Too much water always makes a tough crust. Cut and stir in the water with a knife, not using the hands at all. If it is pressed together compactly with the hands, the crust will be tough.

Third: Roll it out. With one rolling, roll as thin as possible and then fold it over and over, as you would fold up a paper into a small space (each fold makes a flake); do not press it together, but just fold it lightly. Then roll it again to fit a pie tin.

It is not at all necessary to have a good pie crust as thin as paper, as some people seem to think, but roll it about one-eighth inch thick.

For a one-crust pie, invert a pie tin, grease the bottom of it and fit the pie crust over the bottom, baking it "upside down." Turn under the edges to make a double, smooth edge, and press down edges with the fingers or a fork, dipped in cold water. Perforate the bottom with a fork.

For a double-crust pie moisten the rim of the under crust and always press the edges together and make several incisions in the top. If the pie is a very juicy one, take a strip of muslin about an inch wide and sufficiently long to encircle the edge of the pie. Wring out of cold water. Fasten it securely around and there will be no juice running over in the oven.

Fourth: Baking. The baking of pie is perhaps the most important part. It is here that even the best of pie crust may be spoiled. The oven should be very hot when a pie is put in, so hot that the crust will begin to brown before the lard has any chance to melt. Then, the heat may be reduced for a double pie crust, although with just a pie shell it is well to maintain this heat throughout the baking.

In a single-crust pie, bake the pie shell first and cook the filling separately. Let both get perfectly cold before putting together. If they are put together when either one or the other is warm, there will be the possibility of a soggy crust.

In a double-crust pie or berry pie, the whole trick is in having the oven hot enough when it is first put in, so that a brown crust forms on the bottom before the juice has a chance to sink in. After about ten minutes, the temperature may be reduced to allow the contents to cook thoroughly. In some pies, where the filling needs almost no cooking, the heat may be continued.

Where heat regulator is used, preheat oven ten minutes with full flame. Place on high rack of bake oven, adjusting at 475 degrees. When browning begins, reduce heat to 350 degrees.

How to Measure Shortening: Here is the easiest and most accurate way to measure your shortening. For the standard recipe calling for 1/3 cup of shortening, fill the measuring cup with 2/3 cup cold water and add shortening until the water reaches the 1 cup line; drain the water, and the shortening is accurately measured. If the quantity is doubled, fill the cup with 1/3 cup of cold water and add shortening until the water reaches the top.

Mixing Shortening With Flour: The shortening may be cut into the flour with two knives, a fork or finger tips; use whichever seems easier, for each will give excellent results. Avoid handling the dough too much.

To make a tender crust the flour particles must be surrounded by shortening, which means mixing the shortening quite thoroughly with the flour before adding the liquid. To make a pastry both tender and flaky, cut the shortening in thoroughly, leaving a few pieces of the shortening in sizes of a pea or a little larger.

Adding the Water: Add the water slowly, using just enough to hold the mixture together; too much makes a tough crust, and too little makes it very crumbly and difficult to handle.

If an error is made, and too much water is added, making the dough sticky, rather than adding simply more flour, which would make a tough crust, add flour *to which more shortening has been added,* using the same proportions as in the original crust, or 1/3 as much shortening as flour. This will make more pastry, but will make good crust, whereas just flour would make a poor product. An extra shell or a few tarts could be made from the remaining pastry.

Rolling: In rolling out the dough, touch it almost as lightly as you'd touch the tulle bow on your best Sunday bonnet. Roll lightly, and lift rolling-pin between each rolling. Dust the pin with as little flour as needed.

While rolling the pastry, always lift the rolling-pin when reaching the edge; in other words, never press hard to make the outside edges stick to the board.

Baking: Bake single shells in a hot oven (450 degrees) for about 10-15 minutes.

Custard pies should go into a piping hot oven (400 degrees) for 15 minutes to set the crust, and then reduce temperature to 300 and finish baking, about 30 minutes.

Two-crust pies, where the filling is cooked before as in mince, about 30-40 minutes in a hot oven (450 degrees).

Two-crust pies with uncooked filing such as apple, bake in a hot oven (450 degrees) for 15 minutes, reduce temperature to 350 and bake 20-30 minutes longer, depending upon the size of the pie.
And Just a Final Hint: Remember the fluffy meringue for your fruit tart pies. And don't neglect the deep-dish, one-crust model of pie. It can be fruit, or a meat and vegetable mixture.

How to Make Shortening Pastry

1 cup flour
1/2 teaspoon salt
1/3 cup shortening
2 to 3 tablespoons cold water

Sift flour, measure and mix with the salt. Cut the shortening into the flour until the particles are the size of peas. Using a fork, add the water, sprinkling a very small portion over the pastry at a time. Use just enough to hold the mixture together. Roll out and line pie pan. If possible, chill thoroughly in refrigerator before baking. This is sufficient to make a one-crust, 9-inch pie. Double the recipe for a two-crust pie.

Pastry

Either bread or pastry flour can be used for pastry. To make your own pastry flour, substitute 1 tablespoon corn starch for 2 tablespoons flour in each cup of flour used.

Mix cooking oil with dry ingredients just as you would any solid fat.

Have all materials as cold as possible.

Handle paste as little and as lightly as possible.

For best results roll out paste; fold; chill in ice box and allow to stand for about 1/2 hour; roll out again as above, then bake in very hot oven.

Before filling berry pies, brush paste over with white of egg or sprinkle lightly with a little flour. This keeps the juice from soaking into the paste.

Always cool fillings before adding to pie as the hot filling is apt to soak into the crust and make it soggy.

2 cups flour
1/2 teaspoon salt
1 teaspoon baking powder
1/3 cup cooking oil
1/4 cup cold water

Sift together flour, salt and baking powder; add oil and rub in very lightly with tips of fingers or cut in with knife. Add cold water slowly, just enough to hold dough together. Handle paste as little and as lightly as possible. Divide into halves; roll out one part very thin on floured board and use for bottom crust. Prick in several places with fork. Fill pie and roll out other half of paste for top. Cover pie loosely, bringing edges of paste well over pan; press edges together; trim off paste; prick top with fork and bake in hot oven (450 degrees F.), reducing temperature after 15 minutes. Time required depends upon filling.

This recipe is sufficient for one double-crust medium sized pie with 2 to 4 small tarts.

Pie Crust

1-1/2 cups Blend Flour
1 teaspoon salt
2/3 cup lard, or other shortening
1/4 cup cold water

Ingredients should be very cold, and General Directions for Pie Crust explicitly followed.

Pastry for Two-Crust Pie

1-1/2 cup flour
1/2 cup shortening
1/2 teaspoon salt
1/4 cup water

Combine flour and salt. Cut in shortening until mixture resembles grains of rice. Add water, a little at a time, mixing to a workable dough. Use more water if needed. Divide dough in half; roll out top and bottom half of crust on a floured board.

Graham Cracker Crust

1-1/2 cups graham cracker crumbs
2 tablespoons sugar
1/4 cup melted butter

Mix all ingredients and press in bottom and sides of a 9-inch pie pan. Can be baked 10 minutes in a 350° oven or placed in refrigerator for 1/2 hour to set.

Fried Apple Pie

1 teaspoon baking powder
1 teaspoon salt
2 cups flour
2 tablespoons butter
1 egg yolk
4 tablespoons sugar
1/2 cup milk
Apple sauce
Cinnamon
Nutmeg

Sift baking powder and salt with flour. Work in butter with finger tips. Combine egg, sugar and milk, and stir into flour mixture. Roll out on a well-floured board to 1/4 inch thick. Cut into rounds about 4 to 5 inches in diameter. Spread half the circle with thick apple sauce, well seasoned with cinnamon and nutmeg. Fold over the other half of crust, fastening the edges well with a fork.
Fry in deep oil heated to 360° F. or until an inch square of bread browns in 60 seconds. Drain on paper. Sprinkle with powdered sugar.

Apple Pie #1

1-1/2 cups flour
1-1/2 teaspoons baking powder
3/4 teaspoon salt
1/3 cup cooking oil
Cold water
4 cups or 1 quart sliced apples
6 tablespoons sugar
1 tablespoon butter
Cinnamon or nutmeg

Sift together flour, baking powder and salt; add oil and mix in very lightly; add just enough water to hold dough together. Roll out half on floured board. Line bottom of pie plate allowing paste to come over edge. Add apples which have been washed, pared and cut into small pieces; sprinkle with sugar and small pieces of butter; flavor with cinnamon or nutmeg. Roll out remainder of pastry and cover pie; fold lower paste over edge of top crust, pressing edges tightly together. Prick top and bake in moderate oven (400 degrees F.) about 30 minutes.
Makes 1 large pie

Apple Pie #2

1-1/2 cups flour
1-1/2 teaspoons baking powder
1/2 teaspoon salt
1/3 cup shortening
4 apples, or 1 quart sliced apples
4 tablespoons sugar
1 tablespoon butter
Cinnamon or nutmeg
Cold Water

Sift flour, baking powder and salt; add shortening and rub in very lightly; add just enough water to hold dough together. Roll half out on floured board, line bottom of pie plate; fill in apples, which have been washed, pared and cut into thin slices; sprinkle with sugar and small pieces of butter; flavor with cinnamon or nutmeg; wet edges of crust with cold water; roll out remainder of pastry; cover pie, pressing edges tightly together, trim off extra pastry; prick top, and bake in moderate oven 30 minutes.

Old-Fashioned Apple Pie

Shortening pastry
4 or 6 tart apples
1/2 to 3/4 cup sugar
1/2 teaspoon cinnamon
1/4 teaspoon salt
2 tablespoons butter

Line pie pan with shortening pastry. Pare, core, and cut the apples into eighths. Put a row around the plate 1/2 inch from the edge, and work toward the center until the plate is covered. Mix the sugar, cinnamon and salt together and sprinkle over the apples. Then pile on the remaining apples and dot with butter. Wet the edges of the under crust, cover with upper crust which has been slit or pricked with a fork to allow steam to escape. Press the edges together, trim, and bake in a hot oven (450 degrees F.) for 15 minutes, then reduce temperature to 350 degrees and bake until apples are tender, about 20-30 minutes.
Note: For pleasant variety, 1/2 glass currant or crabapple jelly can be placed in spoonfuls over the apples just before adding the top crust.

Apple Cream Pie

3 or 4 tart apples
1/4 teaspoon salt
1/2 cup sugar (more if preferred)
1/4 cup flour
3 eggs
2 tablespoons water
1 tablespoon lemon juice
Grated rind of 1 lemon
1/4 cup butter
1/2 pint cream
3 dessert spoons sugar
Few drops lemon juice

Core, but do not pare, the apples. Cut into rather small pieces. Mix together thoroughly the salt, sugar and flour. Mix into the flour and sugar the yolks of the eggs, which have been beaten very light; then add the water, the lemon juice and rind and the apples. Cook in a double-boiler until thick. Remove and stir in rapidly the whites of the eggs, which have been beaten into a stiff froth. Set aside to cool. When ready to serve, spread in pie shells which have been previously baked and cooled, and on top spread cream, which has been beaten stiff with sugar and a few drops of lemon juice.
Sufficient for 1 large or 2 small pies.

Berry Pie #1

3 cups blueberries, huckleberries or blackberries
1 teaspoon flour
1/4 teaspoon salt
2/3 cup sugar

Line pie plate with pastry, allowing sufficient to come well over edge. Fill heaping full with berries; sprinkle with flour, salt and sugar; dot with small pieces of butter. Cover with top crust or strips of pastry across top. Fold lower paste over edge of top crust. Press edges together with fork. This keeps in the juice. Bake about 45 minutes in hot oven (425 degrees F.).

Berry Pie #2

3 cups blueberries, huckleberries, blackberries or olalliberries
1 teaspoon flour
1/4 teaspoon salt
2/3 cup sugar
1 teaspoon butter

Line a pie plate with plain paste; fill heaping with berries; dredge with flour, salt and sugar; dot with small pieces of butter; cover with top crust or strips of pastry across top. Bake about 45 minutes in moderate oven.
Other fruit pies can be made in the same way.

Fruit Turnovers

1 cup flour
1 teaspoon baking powder
1/2 teaspoon salt
1/4 cup cooking oil
Cold water

Sift together flour, baking powder and salt; add oil and rub in very lightly with finger tips. Add cold water slowly, using jut enough to hold the dough together; roll out on slightly floured board about 1/8 inch thick. Cut into 4-inch squares. Put tablespoon jam, stewed fruit, such as apricots, peaches or rhubarb drained, in center. Moisten slightly edges of paste. Fold paste over to form triangular tart or as desired. Press edges together with fork; prick tops. Bake in hot oven (500 degrees F.) about 10 minutes.
Makes 6 turnovers.

Berry or Cherry Pie

Berries should be carefully washed and picked over, or cherries should be stoned. The amount of sweetening depends upon the sourness of the fruit. For sour cherries, gooseberries, currants, etc. a cup of sugar and 4 level tablespoons of Blend Flour, well mixed with the sugar, should be used. For sweeter fruit, such as raspberries, sweet cherries, strawberries, etc. 1/2 cup of sugar and 4 level tablespoons of Blend Flour is about the right proportion. Dot with a few bits of butter. Cinnamon may be added (1/2 teaspoon to a pie) to the sugar if desired. Put fruit, sugar and flour between 2 pie crusts and bake in a quick oven. If the fruit is very juicy, butter a strip of muslin about an inch wide and long enough to encircle the pie, and wrap around the edge, fastening securely. This will prevent the juice running out in the oven.

Banana Cream Pie

1/4 cup flour
2 tablespoons cornstarch
1/2 cup sugar
1/4 teaspoon salt
3 eggs beaten separately
1 pint milk
Grated rind of half a lemon
1/2 teaspoon lemon extract
1 cup sliced bananas (more may be used)

1/2 pint whipping cream
Few drops lemon extract
1 tablespoon sugar

Mix and sift the dry ingredients. Add beaten eggs to milk and stir in gradually until very smooth. Add grated lemon rind. If not perfectly smooth, beat with rotary egg-beater. Cook in double-boiler, stirring constantly, until very thick. Then add flavoring. when partially cool, stir in the freshly sliced bananas. Chill. When fold in half of the stiffly-beaten cream, flavored with a few drops of lemon extract and a tablespoon of sugar and spread in a baked and cooled pie crust. Arrange across the top, pressed into the balance of the cream so they will not discolor, a few slices of bananas.

New Banana Cream Pie

1 recipe plain pastry
1/2 cup sugar
4 tablespoons flour or 3 tablespoons cornstarch
1/2 teaspoon salt
2 cups milk, scalded
2 eggs
1 teaspoon vanilla
2 bananas

Prepare a baked pie shell. Mix sugar, flour or cornstarch and salt. Add milk gradually, and cook until thick and smooth in the top of a double boiler. Stir constantly. Moisten egg yolks with a little filling. Stir a little of the hot mixture above into the egg yolks. Beat well, and add vanilla. Cover bottom of pie shell with sliced bananas over the top. Spread with meringue made from the egg whites. Bake in a moderate oven (350 degrees F.) about 15 minutes.

Butterscotch Pie #1

3 egg yolks
9 tablespoons brown sugar
4 tablespoons corn starch
3 cups milk
3/8 teaspoon salt
4 tablespoons butter
1-1/2 teaspoons vanilla extract

Beat egg yolks with sugar; mix corn starch with a little water to make smooth paste; add to first mixture, then add milk and salt. Cook in double boiler until thick. Remove from fire; add butter and vanilla. Cool; add beaten whites of eggs, or use them for meringue on top. Pour into a baked crust. If meringue is used, spread on top and return to oven to brown. Otherwise spread sweetened whipped cream on top. Fills one 8-inch pie shell.

Butterscotch Pie #2

1-1/2 cups brown sugar
1/2 cup flour
1/2 teaspoon salt
1-3/4 cups condensed milk
7/8 cup water
3 eggs
3 tablespoons butter

Mix sugar, flour, and salt thoroughly; scald milk and water together; add milk to dry mixture, stirring until well blended. Return to the double boiler and cook for 25 minutes, stirring occasionally; add to well-beaten egg yolks and continue cooking for 2 minutes; add butter. Pour filling into baked pastry shell. Cover with meringue made by folding 4 tablespoons sugar and 1/4 teaspoon baking powder into 3 stiffly-beaten egg whites. Brown in a slow oven (300 degrees F.). Makes 1 large pie.
To make Raisin Butterscotch Pie use the same recipe, adding 1 cup of raisins to the filling.

Butterscotch Pie #3

1-1/2 cups brown sugar
1-1/2 cups water
2 tablespoons flour
3 tablespoons cornstarch
2 egg yolks
3 tablespoons Crisco
Pinch of salt
1 teaspoon vanilla
2 egg whites
4 tablespoons sugar
1/4 teaspoon baking powder

Heat brown sugar and water to boiling point. Pour over sifted flour and cornstarch and cook until thick. Add egg yolks slightly beaten, and cook for 1 minute longer. Remove from fire; add Crisco, salt and flavoring, and let cool. Pour into baked crust, cover with meringue made by beating egg whites until frothy, adding sugar and baking powder and beating until stiff. Put in oven to brown.

Butterscotch Pie #4

1/2 cup brown sugar
1/4 cup flour
1/4 teaspoon salt
1 pint milk
1 tablespoon cornstarch
2 eggs beaten separately
2 tablespoons butter

1/2 teaspoon vanilla
4 tablespoons sugar

Mix together thoroughly the brown sugar, flour and salt. Add a little of the cold milk to the cornstarch and mix to a smooth paste. Beat the egg yolks until thick, stir in the cornstarch mixture, and mix this with the sugar and flour and add gradually the milk. Cook in a double boiler, stirring almost constantly, until very thick. Chill. Turn into a pie crust which has been previously baked and cooled. Pile on top in irregular piles, a meringue made of the stiffly-beaten whites to which has been added 4 tablespoons sugar, and brown lightly in a slow oven.

Banana Custard Pie

1/4 cup flour
1/2 cup sugar
1 level tablespoon cornstarch
1/4 teaspoon salt
3 eggs beaten separately (2 will answer)
2 cups milk
1/2 teaspoon lemon extract
1 cup sliced bananas
1 tablespoon sugar
Few drops lemon juice

Mix the dry ingredients, add beaten egg yolks and gradually the milk and flavoring. Cook in double-boiler until very thick. Then add bananas. Chill. Then spread in pie shell previously baked and cooled and on the top place a meringue made by beating the egg whites with a tablespoon of sugar and lemon juice and browning delicately in a moderate oven.

"Bridge Pies"

1/4 cup butter
1 cup white sugar
2 eggs
4 tablespoons milk
1/2 cup walnut meats (cut)
1 cup seedless raisins

Cream the butter and sugar; add the eggs well beaten, then the milk, nuts and raisins. Make pastry and cover gem pans with it. Fill with the above and bake in a quick oven until the crust is done. There should be no upper crust. Serve cold with or without a spoonful of whipped cream on top.
This makes 12.

Chocolate Cream Pie #1

1 recipe plain pastry
3 squares unsweetened chocolate
2-1/2 cups milk
4 tablespoons flour
1 cup sugar
1/4 teaspoon salt
2 tablespoons butter
2 eggs
2 teaspoons vanilla

Prepare a baked shell with shortening pastry. Melt chocolate. Scald 2 cups milk. Combine flour with sugar and salt and moisten with 1/2 cup cold milk. Stir into hot milk and continue stirring until mixture is thick and smooth. Add chocolate, butter, and egg yolks and mix well. Remove from fire, add vanilla and pour into pastry shell. Cover with meringue and bake 15 minutes in a moderate oven (350 degrees F.).

Chocolate Cream Pie #2

2-1/2 cups milk
3 squares unsweetened cake, or 3/4 cup unsweetened powdered chocolate
1/2 teaspoon salt
3/4 cup flour
3/4 cup sugar
4 eggs
1 teaspoon vanilla
1/2 pint whipping cream
2 tablespoons sugar
1/2 teaspoon vanilla

Put 1-1/2 cups of the milk, together with the chocolate and salt, in the double-boiler and stir frequently until chocolate is melted and smooth. Mix together thoroughly the flour and sugar, then add to them the beaten egg yolks and stir until smooth, adding gradually the balance of the milk. When entirely free from lumps, stir this into the hot mixture in double-boiler and cook, stirring vigorously until very thick and smooth, if necessary, using an egg-beater. When done, let stand while beating the egg whites until stiff and dry, then slowly pour the hot mixture over them, adding the flavoring. If added quickly, the whites will cook in lumps. Chill thoroughly. Have ready a pie shell baked and chilled and just before ready to serve, spread the cold mixture in to the cold cooked crust and on top pile in irregular mounds the cream beaten stiff with 2 tablespoons of sugar and vanilla.
Sufficient for 2 medium size pies.

Chocolate Cream Pie #3

2 cups milk
2/3 cup sugar
2 squares (2 ounces) unsweetened chocolate

2-1/2 tablespoons corn starch
1 egg
1/2 teaspoon vanilla extract
1/4 teaspoon salt
Whipped cream

Scald milk, sugar and chocolate together in top of double boiler. When thoroughly mixed and dissolved add corn starch which has been mixed with a little cold milk, stirring until smooth. Add beaten egg and cook until smooth and thick. Add vanilla and salt; cool and bake in one crust in moderate oven (375 degrees F.) about 20 minutes. Cool and before serving spread thickly with sweetened whipped cream.
Makes 1 pie.

Chocolate Cream Pie #4

1 square chocolate, chipped
1-1/2 cups milk, scalded
4 tablespoons cornstarch
3/4 cup sugar
1/8 teaspoons salt
Cold water
2 egg yolks
1 teaspoon vanilla
1 baked pie shell

Heat chipped chocolate with milk as it is scalding. Combine paste made of cornstarch, sugar, salt and a little cold water with hot milk, stirring constantly. Cook 15 minutes in double boiler, stirring constantly, until thickened and well flavored and spoon leaves marks in mixture. Stir into beaten egg yolks. Add flavoring and cool. Fill crust, cover with meringue, and brown in oven, 325 degrees F.

Coconut Custard Pie

1 recipe plain pastry
3 eggs
1/8 teaspoon salt
1/4 cup sugar
1 teaspoon vanilla
1/8 teaspoon nutmeg
2 cups milk, scalded
1/4 cup shredded coconut

Line pie plate with shortening pastry. Beat eggs slightly, add salt, sugar, vanilla and nutmeg, and gradually add the hot milk. Add coconut, mix well and pour into pie plate. Bake in a hot oven (400 degrees F.) 15 minutes, then decrease temperature to 350 and bake 30 minutes longer.
Makes one 9-inch pie.

Carrot Pie (Mock Pumpkin)

4 tablespoons flour
1/4 cup sugar
1 tablespoon cornstarch
1 teaspoon cinnamon
1 teaspoon salt
1/4 teaspoon ginger
1 cup mashed carrots
1 egg
1/3 cup molasses
1-1/4 cups milk

Mix together thoroughly all the dry ingredients. Cut the carrot into thin slices and boil until very soft; then mash until absolutely free from lumps. Beat the egg and add to the carrot; then the molasses and milk. Beat together thoroughly and then sift in the dry ingredients. Boil all together until very thick (a double-boiler is preferable, as it scorches easily) and when done set away to cool. When perfectly cold, fill a pie shell, which has been previously baked and cooled, and serve.
Sufficient for 2 medium pie shells.

Caramel Pie

2 cups milk
1/3 cup white sugar, caramelized
1/2 cup brown sugar
1/4 teaspoon salt
1/2 cup flour
2 eggs beaten separately
1 tablespoon butter
1/2 teaspoon vanilla

Put milk in double-boiler and while heating, place white sugar in sauce pan and stir until free from lumps, melted, and a rich dark brown. Then put this in the hot milk. Mix together the brown sugar, salt and flour. Add the egg yolks beaten thick. Into this pour slowly a little of the hot mixture and when blended, turn this mixture back into the double-boiler. Cook, stirring constantly until very thick. Add the butter before removing from the fire, and when cooked, add vanilla. Chill. Spread in a pie shell previously baked and cooled and on top spread a meringue made by beating the egg whites until stiff with a tablespoon of granulated sugar. Pile the meringue on in irregular piles and brown delicately in a moderate oven.

Cheese Rings

2 cups flour
1 teaspoon baking powder
1 teaspoon salt
Pinch cayenne pepper

1 tablespoon butter
1 tablespoon lard
2/3 cup grated cheese
2/3 cup water (very cold)

Sift together the flour, baking powder, salt and pepper and chop into it the butter and lard until like cornmeal. Then mix into it with a knife the grated cheese, then the water. Roll out very thin, cut with a very small doughnut cutter into rings, and bake in a moderate oven until light brown.

Chocolate Pie

1 cup milk
1/4 teaspoon salt
1-1/2 squares or 1/3 cup powdered unsweetened chocolate
3 tablespoons flour
1/3 cup sugar
2 eggs, beaten separately
1 teaspoon vanilla
2 tablespoons sugar

Put milk, salt and chocolate into the double-boiler. Mix together thoroughly the flour and sugar, then add gradually the beaten egg yolks, stirring until very smooth. Pour a little of the milk from the double-boiler into this, stirring smooth, and then return all to the double-boiler. Cook stirring constantly until very thick. Chill. Have ready a baked chilled pie crust and when ready to serve, spread the filling in and on top pile in irregular mounds a meringue made of the stiffly-beaten egg whites and 2 tablespoons sugar. Set in a slow oven or under a low flame to brown delicately, watching very closely.
Sufficient for one medium size pie.

Clam or Oyster Pie #1

Shortcake Dough (below)
1 quart oysters or clams
1 tablespoon celery seed
Salt
Pepper
Butter
Blend Flour
1 quart sliced potatoes

Line a baking dish with shortcake dough rolled about 1/3 inch thick. Cover the bottom with a layer of the oysters or clams. Sprinkle with celery seed and with salt and pepper to taste, pour over a little melted butter and dredge thoroughly with Blend Flour. Cover this with a layer of sliced boiled potatoes, seasoned with salt and pepper, melted butter and dredged with flour. Over this add part of the shortcake dough cut up into small pieces, then another layer of oysters or clams, seasoned with salt, pepper, butter and dredged with flour, then potatoes until all is used. Pour over all the liquid, or if not sufficient to moisten add a little milk. Cover with the balance of the crust, pres the edges together, make incisions in the top and bake in a moderate oven for about 35 minutes, or until the crust is perfectly done. Half this recipe will be ample for four.

Clam or Oyster Pie #2

This recipe permits of much variation: Clams or oysters may be used, or a mixture of half clams and half celery, or oysters and celery, or oysters and mushrooms, etc.

Clams or oysters in liquor
3 tablespoons butter
4 tablespoons Blend Flour
1 cup rich milk or part cream
1/8 teaspoon pepper
1/2 teaspoon salt (or more)
1/8 teaspoon dry mustard
Dash celery salt (if no celery used)
Milk

Have ready in a baking dish either a rich baking powder biscuit dough or shortcake dough according to recipes in this book. Drain juice from clams or oysters for sauce. Melt butter, add flour and stir until smooth. Then add milk and the oyster or clam liquor, with enough milk or cream additional to fill the cup. Cook, stirring constantly until thickened, adding while cooking pepper, salt, mustard and celery salt, if used. A little onion salt or onion juice may be used if desired. Chill. Then pour into the cold uncooked crust, cover with a crust, perforate the top, rub over with milk and bake in a hot oven.

Short Cake

2 cups Blend Flour
4 teaspoons baking powder
3/4 teaspoon salt
1/2 cup shortening
1/2 cup milk

Mix and sift the dry ingredients; cut in the shortening and mix lightly with the fingers. Add the milk. Mix, and roll out, handling as little as possible. Either bake in a shallow tin in one piece, and when done split open, butter and lay the berries inside and spread over the top; or, cut with a large biscuit cutter into individual shortcakes, allowing 2 to each person. When done, butter each, cover one with berries, lay the other on top, pour berries over the whole, and decorate the top with whipped cream.
Sufficient for 4 large or 6 medium size pieces.

Cocoanut Cream Pie

1/2 cup Blend Flour
1 cup sugar
1/4 teaspoon salt
3 eggs, beaten separately
2 cups milk
1 cup shredded cocoanut
1 teaspoon vanilla
1/2 pint whipping cream
3 tablespoons sugar
1/2 teaspoon almond extract or vanilla
Shredded cocoanut

Stir together the flour, sugar and salt until well mixed. Add the yolks of the eggs, which have been previously beaten until very thick and lemon colored. Gradually add milk. Cook until very thick. Remove from the stove, stir in the cocoanut and then add the stiffly-beaten whites of the eggs. When almost cool add the flavoring. Have ready a pie shell which has been previously baked, and when both the shell and filling are cold, put in the filling and just before serving cover the top with 1/2 pint of cream, which has been whipped very stiff and to which has been added 3 tablespoons sugar, 1/2 teaspoon almond extract or vanilla, and sprinkle the top with a little shredded cocoanut. Sufficient for 1 one large or 2 small pies.

Cream Pie

1/4 cup Blend Flour
1/2 cup sugar
1/4 teaspoon salt
2 eggs
1 pint milk
1/2 teaspoon flavoring extract
Sugar

Mix and sift the dry ingredients; add the yolks of the eggs, which have been beaten until thick and lemon colored, then add gradually, stirring constantly, the milk. Put on the stove in the double boiler, and boil until thick, as for a stiff custard. Remove and when partially cool, add the flavoring. When perfectly cold spread into pie shell which has been previously baked and cooled, and on the top spread the whites of the eggs beaten to a stiff froth with 2 dessert spoons of sugar, and set in the oven a moment to brown.

Chocolate Pie

2 squares chocolate
1 cup boiling water
1 cup milk
4 tablespoons flour
7/8 cup sugar
1/4 teaspoon salt
3 eggs
1 tablespoon butter
1/2 teaspoon vanilla
4 tablespoons sugar
1/4 teaspoon baking powder

Melt the chocolate, add the boiling water and milk and continue heating until the mixture is smooth. Mix flour, sugar and salt and d the hot chocolate mixture gradually, stirring so as to prevent lumping. Return to double boiler and cook 25 minutes, stirring occasionally. Pour over the well-beaten egg yolks, beating constantly. Return to double boiler and cook 2 minutes longer. Add flavoring and pour into baked pastry shell. Cover with meringue made by folding 4 tablespoons sugar and 1/4 teaspoon baking powder into stiffly-beaten egg whites. Brown in a slow (300 degrees F.) oven.
Makes 1 pie

Custard Pie

3 eggs
3/4 cup sugar
1 teaspoon salt
2 cups milk
1 teaspoon vanilla extract

Beat eggs; add sugar, salt and scalded milk slowly. Line pie plate with paste, page 26; pour in custard. Bake in moderate oven 25 to 30 minutes. The custard is baked when a knife put in center comes out dry.

Coconut Pie

Coconut Pie is made the same way as Custard Pie, adding 1 cup fresh grated coconut, and using only 2 eggs. Bake as above.

Cranberry Pie

2 recipes Plain Pastry
1 cup cranberries
1 cup seedless raisins
1/2 cup dried figs
1/2 cup walnut kernels
1 cup sugar
1 tablespoon flour
1/4 teaspoon salt
1/4 cup water

Line pie pan with shortening pastry. Chop cranberries, raisins, figs and walnuts; add sugar, flour, salt and water. Mix well and pour into pastry-lined pie pan. Cover with a top crust and bake in a hot oven (450 degrees F.) for 10 minutes, then reduce temperature to 350 degrees and bake 20-30 minutes longer.

Mock Cherry Pie

Mrs. George Lucas

1 cup raisins
1 large tablespoon flour
1 cup cranberries, cut in halves
1 cup sugar
Butter the size of a walnut

Cook raisins until tender, then add flour. When done add cranberries, sugar and butter. Bake in a moderate oven.

Grape Pie

Grapes
2 cups sugar
1/2 cup butter
2 tablespoons flour
4 eggs

Remove skins from grapes and save. Cook pulp and rub through a sieve. Use 2 cups of the skins and pulp. Bake in one crust and put beaten whites over the top. I cooked my skins and pulp some after I took seeds out of pulp.

Lemon Cream Pie #1

1-1/2 cups sugar
6 level tablespoons Blend Flour
1 level tablespoon cornstarch
1/2 teaspoon salt
2 lemons
3 eggs
2 cups water
1/2 tablespoon butter
2 tablespoons sugar

Mix together thoroughly the sugar, flour, cornstarch and salt; add lemon rind grated and beaten egg yolks. Mix smooth and add gradually the water and cook in a double-boiler, stirring frequently until very thick. When about half done, add the juice of the lemons. Chill thoroughly and spread in baked and cooled crusts. Pile on top a meringue made by beating the whites of the eggs stiff with 2 tablespoons of sugar and browning delicately in the oven or under a low flame, watching constantly to prevent scorching.
Sufficient for 2 medium pies.

Lemon Cream Pie #2

1-1/2 cups sugar
4-1/2 tablespoons flour
Few grains salt
3/4 cup milk
3/4 cup water
2 eggs
1 tablespoon butter
5 tablespoons lemon juice
1 teaspoon grated lemon rind
2 tablespoons powdered sugar or granulated sugar
1/8 teaspoon baking powder

Mix sugar, flour and salt thoroughly; scald milk with the water; add milk to dry mixture, stirring until well blended. Return to the double boiler and cook for 25 minutes, stirring occasionally; add to well-beaten egg yolks and continue cooking for 2 minutes; add butter, lemon juice and rind. Pour filling into baked pastry shell. Cover with meringue made by folding 2 tablespoons powdered sugar or granulated sugar and 1/8 teaspoon baking powder into 2 stiffly-beaten egg whites. Brown in a slow (300 degrees F.) oven.
Makes 1 pie

Lemon Cream Pie #3

1 recipe Plain Pastry
1/4 cup flour
1/4 cup cornstarch
1 cup sugar
2 cups boiling water
1 teaspoon grated lemon rind
1/4 cup lemon juice
1/2 teaspoon salt
2 eggs
1 tablespoon butter

Prepare a baked pie shell. Mix flour, cornstarch and sugar and combine with boiling water. Cook on top of double boiler until thick and smooth, stirring constantly. Add lemon rind, juice, salt, egg yolks and butter. Mix thoroughly. Pour into baked pastry shell and cover with meringue. Bake in moderate oven (350 degrees F.) for 15 minutes.

Lemon Chiffon Pie #1

1 recipe Plain Pastry
4 eggs
1 teaspoon grated lemon rind
3 tablespoons lemon juice
1 cup sugar

Prepare a baked pastry shell. Beat egg yolks slightly in top of double boiler, add lemon juice and 1/2 cup sugar and mix well. Cook until thick or custard coats the spoon. Stir constantly. Beat egg whites until stiff and beat in the sugar gradually. Fold lemon mixture into the egg whites. Pour in a baked pastry shell. Bake about 20 minutes in a moderate oven (375 degrees F.).

Lemon Chiffon Pie #2

4 eggs
3 tablespoons lemon juice
1 grated lemon rind
1 cup sugar
1 baked pie shell

Beat yolks until light. Add lemon juice, rind, and 1/2 cup sugar and beat until smooth. Cook over hot water until thick. Beat whites, add remaining sugar, beating constantly. Beat yolk mixture into whites and cook over hot water until mixture leaves sides of pan. Pour into baked pie shell and put under low flame in broiler until it becomes browned.

Lemon Fluff Pie

1 lemon, juice and rind
3/4 cup sugar
1/4 cup Blend Flour
1 tablespoon cornstarch
1/4 teaspoon salt
2 eggs, beaten separately
1 cup water
1 tablespoon butter

Mix together the grated rind, sugar, flour, cornstarch and salt. Add beaten egg yolks mixed with water. Cook in double boiler until it begins to thicken, then add lemon juice and butter and continue cooking until very thick. Remove from fire and pour the hot mixture very slowly into the stiffly-beaten whites. Be careful not to turn the whites into the hot mixture, or they will cook in small lumps. The hot mixture must be added to them very slowly, folding them in carefully until well blended. Then chill. When cold, spread into a pie shell previously cooked and cooled, and sprinkle the top with powdered sugar.

Fluffy Lemon Pie

1/3 cup cooking oil
1/4 cup boiling water
1-1/2 cups flour
1/2 teaspoon salt
1 teaspoon baking powder

Mix oil with boiling water. Sift flour, salt and baking powder together. Stir dry ingredients into liquid. Turn out on floured board and roll out to 1/8 inch in thickness. Line pie plate; bake in hot oven (500 degrees F.) 10 to 12 minutes and fill with the following mixture:

Filling:
3 egg yolks
1/2 cup sugar
1/4 teaspoon salt
Juice and rind of 1 lemon
3 tablespoons boiling water
3 egg whites
1/2 teaspoon baking powder

Cook first 5 ingredients over boiling water until thick, stirring constantly. Beat egg whites stiff, then beat in baking powder and add to thickened mixture; pour into baked pastry shell and return to oven (400 degrees F.) until puffed up and a delicate brown.
Makes 1 pie

Lemon Meringue Pie #1

1 cup flour
2 tablespoons corn starch
1/2 teaspoon baking powder
1/2 teaspoon salt
1/4 cup cooking oil
Cold water

Sift flour, corn starch, baking powder and salt into bowl; add the oil and rub in lightly with the finger tips or mix in with a steel fork; add water, about 3 tablespoons, slowly until of right consistency to roll out. Roll out very thin on slightly floured board. Place very loosely over pie tin, bringing the paste over the edge of plate. Trim off ends and press edge down with a fork. Prick crust and bake in very hot oven (500 degrees F.) until light brown. Fill with the following:

Filling:
3 eggs

3 tablespoons corn starch
2 tablespoons flour
1 cup sugar
1/3 cup cold water
2 cups boiling water
5-7 tablespoons lemon juice
2 teaspoons grated lemon rind
1/2 teaspoon salt

Separate eggs, saving whites for meringue. Mix corn starch, flour and sugar with cold water until smooth; mix in yolk of eggs, slightly beaten. Add slowly to boiling water. Cook 8 minutes in top of double boiler, stirring constantly. Add butter. Remove from fire; add lemon juice, lemon rind and salt. Pour into baked crust.

Meringue

3 egg whites
4 tablespoons sugar
1 teaspoon baking powder

For the meringue beat the 3 remaining egg whites until very light; add sugar a little at a time, beating constantly, and baking powder; beat until thick. Spread thickly on top of pie; bake in moderate oven (325 degrees F.) about 10 minutes or until light brown.

Lemon Meringue Pie #2

2 cups water
3 tablespoons corn starch
2 tablespoons flour
1 cup sugar
1/2 cup cold water
3 eggs
4 tablespoons lemon juice
1 teaspoon grated lemon rind
1 teaspoon salt
3 tablespoons sugar
1 teaspoon baking powder

Line pie plate loosely with pastry and bake quickly until light brown. Put water on to boil. Mix corn starch, flour and sugar with additional 1/2 cup cold water until smooth; mix in egg yolks; add slowly to boiling water. Cook 5 minutes, stirring constantly; add lemon juice, rind and salt. Pour into baked crust. Beat egg whites; add 3 tablespoons sugar and 1 teaspoon baking powder. Spread thickly on top of pie. Bake in hot oven about 5 minutes until light brown.

Lemon 3-Decker

Reading the layers from bottom to top: lemon custard, lemon sponge, whipped cream

1 cup sugar
1/4 cup cornstarch
2 tablespoons flour
1/17 teaspoon salt
2 cups boiling water
2 tablespoons butter
3 eggs
1/2 cup lemon juice
1 tablespoon grated lemon rind
Plain Pastry (see recipe for Lemon Meringue Pie)
1/2 cup whipping cream
1 tablespoon sugar

Sift sugar, cornstarch, flour and salt together; add slowly to boiling water, and stir until thick and smooth. Add butter, place over boiling water, and cook 15 minutes. Beat together 2 egg yolks, and 1 whole egg, and add slowly to hot mixture. Cook, beating constantly, for 5 minutes. Remove from heat, and blend in lemon juice and rind. Pour one-half of mixture into a 9-inch baked pie shell. Beat 2 egg whites until stiff, and fold into remaining hot mixture. Place on first layer in pie shell. When cold and firm, spread top with sweetened whipped cream.
6 servings

Lemon Pie-Cake

A surprise sponge topping over a lemon custard filling

1 cup sugar
3 tablespoons flour
2 tablespoons butter
3 eggs, separated
1/3 cup lemon juice
1 tablespoon grated lemon rind
1 cup milk
Flaky Pastry (see recipe for Tennessee Angel Pie)

Mix sugar, flour, and butter, until of the consistency of corn meal. Blend in slightly-beaten egg yolks, lemon juice, and rind, and add milk. Fold in stiffly-beaten egg whites. Brush inside of a 9-inch baked pie shell lightly with 1 teaspoon unbeaten egg white, and place in oven 2 minutes, to cook egg white. Pour mixture into glazed shell, and bake in moderate oven, 350 degrees, for 35 minutes, or until firm in the center.
6 servings.

Black Bottom Lemonaire

Fluffy gelatine filling, topped with whipped cream, and set in chocolate pastry

3/4 cup sugar
3 tablespoons flour
1/4 teaspoon salt
3/4 cup milk, scalded
3 eggs, separated
1/4 cup butter
1 tablespoon gelatine, dissolved in
3 tablespoons cold milk
1/2 cup lemon juice
1 tablespoon grated lemon rind
1/2 cup whipping cream
1 tablespoon sugar

Mix sugar, flour and salt, and add slowly to hot milk, beating until smooth. Cook 15 minutes, over hot water, stirring occasionally. Add beaten egg yolks slowly, beating briskly, and cook 5 minutes. Remove from heat and blend in butter and gelatine, stirring until gelatine is dissolved. Add lemon juice and rind. Cool, fold in stiffly-beaten egg whites, and turn into a 9-inch baked chocolate pastry shell. Cover with sweetened whipped cream, and let stand in refrigerator until firm (about 30 minutes).
6 servings

Chocolate Pastry

3/4 cup flour
1/4 cup ground chocolate
1/2 teaspoon salt
1/4 cup shortening
3 tablespoons ice water
2 tablespoons butter

Sift flour and measure; sift again 3 times with chocolate and salt. Cut in shortening coarsely, and add barely enough ice water to make a stiff dough. Turn out on slightly floured board, and roll to 1/4 inch thickness. Spread with half of butter, fold over, and roll out. Spread with remaining butter, fold over, and roll out again. Fold in quarters and chill .Fit over back of a 9-inch pie tin, and prick liberally with a fork. Bake in a hot oven, 425 degrees, for 10 minutes. Remove shell to inside of pan and finish baking.
One 9-inch pie shell

Mince Meat Pie #1

8 pounds lean neck beef
2 handsful salt
2 pounds kidney suet
2 pounds seedless raisins
2 pounds currants, washed and drained
1 quart boiled cider
1 pint vinegar
10 cups sugar
3 tablespoons cinnamon
2 tablespoons cloves
2 whole nutmegs, grated
2 gallons chopped apples

Cover beef with cold water. Add salt, and let boil till done. Drain. When cool chop fine with suet. Boil together in water to cover for half an hour. Then add raisins and currants. Add cider, vinegar, sugar, and spices. Boil 1/2 hour in beef broth and water in which the raisins and currants were cooked. Now add apples and cook 15 minutes longer.
Makes 12 quarts

To make 12 pints:
4 pounds meat
1 pound suet
1 handful salt
1 package seedless raisins
2 packages currants
1 pint cider
1/2 pint vinegar
6 or 8 cups sugar
1-1/2 tablespoons cinnamon
1 tablespoon cloves
1 tablespoon nutmeg
1 gallon apples

Prepare same as large recipe.

Mince Meat #2

2 quarts chopped cooked lean beef
5 quarts chopped raw apples
1 quart chopped suet
1 quart boiled cider
1 quart New Orleans molasses
6 pounds granulated sugar (if expensive, part corn syrup may be used)
2 pounds or more seeded raisins
1 pound seedless raisins
1 pound currants
1/2 pound finely sliced citron
Grated rind of 2 lemons
Juice of 4 lemons
2 tablespoons cinnamon
2 tablespoons cloves
1 tablespoon allspice
1/4 cup salt
1 teaspoon nutmeg
1/2 pint grape, loganberry or other berry juice

Cook the meat until tender and mince. Apples should be cored, but if skins are not very thick and apples are chopped fine, they need not be peeled. Mix all together and simmer 1 hour, then seal as you would canned fruit. With alcoholic liquor previous cooking is not necessary, but it is apt to spoil without it. When ready to make into pies, moisten the amount required with sweet cider, add bits of butter and bake in a double crust in a hot oven.

Mince Pie #3

Mince Pie should always be made with two crusts. Line pie plate with paste and fill with mince meat, cover with paste and bake in hot oven 25 minutes.

2 pounds fresh lean beef, boiled and chopped fine when cold
1 pound suet, chopped very fine
5 pounds chopped apples
1 pound seeded raisins
2 pounds currants
3/4 pound sliced citron
1-1/2 teaspoons cinnamon
1 grated nutmeg
2 tablespoons ground mace
1 tablespoon ground cloves
1 tablespoon allspice
1 tablespoon fine salt
2-1/2 pounds brown sugar
1 quart sherry or 1 quart boiled cider
1 pint brandy

Mix all ingredients thoroughly. Pack in jars. Store in cold, dry place. Allow to stand 24 hours before using.

Mock Mince Pie

1 cup chopped apples
1 cup seeded raisins
1/2 cup seedless raisins
1/2 cup currants (omit if desired)
1/4 cup finely sliced citron
1 cup fine dry bread crumbs
1/2 cup molasses
1 cup sugar
1/2 cup finely chopped suet
1/2 cup sweet cider or grape juice or berry juice
1/2 teaspoon cinnamon
1/4 teaspoon cloves
1/4 teaspoon allspice
1 teaspoon salt

Mix all well together and use as a filling for double crust pies. Sufficient for 4 small or 3 large pies. May easily be made in smaller or larger quantities.

Fruited Minced Pie

2 recipes Plain Paste
2 or 3 bananas, sliced or diced
2 cups mince meat

Line pie pan with shortening pastry. Cover with a layer of sliced bananas. Spread with 1 cup of mince meat, another layer of bananas, and the remaining mince meat. Cover with shortening pastry. Bake in a hot oven (450 degrees F.) 30 minutes.

Old-Fashioned Meringue

A recipe from Revolutionary Days, adjusted to the tastes of 1935

1/2 flour
1 cup sugar
1-1/2 cups water
2 tablespoons butter
3 egg yolks, slightly beaten
1 teaspoon grated lemon rind
1/3 cup lemon juice
3 egg whites
6 tablespoons sugar

Mix flour and sugar. Add water and butter, and bring to a boil in top section of a double boiler. Place over hot water, and cook 20 minutes, stirring occasionally. Add 1/2 cup of thickened filling slowly to egg yolks, stir into remaining filling, and cook 5 minutes longer. Remove from heat. When lukewarm, add rind and lemon juice, and pour into a 9-inch baked pie shell. Cover with meringue, made by adding sugar slowly to stiffly-beaten egg whites. Bake 20 minutes in a slow oven, 300 degrees.
6 servings

Plain Pastry

1 cup flour
1/3 teaspoon salt
1/3 cup shortening
3-4 tablespoons ice water

Sift flour and measure; sift again with salt. Cut in shortening coarsely. Add barely enough ice water to hold together. Roll out on lightly floured board, and fit over the back of a 9-inch pie tin. Prick liberally with a fork, and bake in a very hot oven, 500 degrees, until it begins to brown, about 10 minutes. Change shell to inside of pan, reduce heat to 450 degrees, and finish baking.
One 9-inch pie shell.

Meat Pie

5 medium potatoes
4 carrots
3 stalks celery (all diced)
2 cups water
2 medium onions
2 tablespoons fat
3-1/2 cups cubed cold beef
2 tablespoons flour
2 tablespoons water
Baking Powder Biscuit dough

Parboil together potatoes, carrots and celery in 2 cups water. Chop onions and brown in fat. Add beef; brown. Thicken 2 cups of stock from the vegetables with flour mixed with water. Salt and pepper to taste. Add to this all the diced vegetables, the meat and onion. Place in a casserole. Cover with baking powder biscuit dough. Bake at 400 degrees for 45 minutes.

Orange Pie

2 tablespoons gelatine
2 tablespoons cold water
4 eggs
1/2 cup sugar
1 cup orange juice
3 tablespoons lemon juice
Grated rind of 1 lemon
Few grains salt
Whipped cream
Candied orange peel

Soak gelatine in 2 tablespoons cold water for 5 minutes. Beat egg yolks until light; add sugar, orange juice, lemon juice, rind and salt. Cook over hot water until slightly thickened, stirring frequently. Add gelatine and stir until dissolved. Cool. As it begins to thicken fold in stiffly-beaten whites of eggs. Pour into a baked pie shell and chill. Before serving top with whipped cream and sprinkle with candied orange peel.

Frosted Orange Juice

Heaping tablespoon or small dipper of vanilla ice cream
Chilled orange juice

Place ice cream in a tall glass. Fill glass with juice and stir until the cream is partially dissolved, then serve.

O-So-Good Pie

1 cup sugar
1/2 cup seedless raisins
1/2 cup pecans, chopped medium fine
1 tablespoon butter
2 tablespoons vinegar
1 tablespoon water
1/4 teaspoon cloves
1/2 teaspoon cinnamon
2 eggs, beaten separately

Mix all ingredients, adding the well-beaten whites of eggs last.

Orange Meringue Pie

1 recipe Plain Pastry
3 tablespoons flour
2 tablespoons cornstarch
1/8 teaspoon salt
1/4 cup sugar
1 cup boiling water
1 teaspoon grated orange rind
3/4 cup orange juice
1 tablespoon lemon juice
2 eggs
2 teaspoons shortening

Invert a pie pan and cover the outside with shortening pastry. Prick well with a fork and bake in a hot oven (450 degrees F.) for 12 minutes. Slip pastry shell into another pan.
Mix flour, cornstarch, salt and sugar together and blend with the boiling water. Cook until mixture is thick and smooth, stirring constantly. Add grated rind and fruit juices and blend well. Mix egg yolks with a little filing and stir into the hot mixture, add shortening and beat well. Pour into baked pie shell and cover with meringue. Bake in moderate oven (350 degrees F.) 15 minutes.

Prune Whip Pie

Pie shell
1 pound prunes
3/4 cup sugar
3/4 cup chopped nut meats
2 egg whites
1 cup whipped cream
2 tablespoons powdered sugar
1/2 teaspoon vanilla

Line pan and bake pastry.
Soak prunes overnight and simmer till soft. Remove stones, cut in pieces and add sugar and nut meats. Fold in egg whites,

beaten stiffly.
Pour into baked shell. Bake at 375 degrees F. for 20 minutes. When cool, decorate with whipped cream to which has been added powdered sugar and vanilla.

Prune Pie #1

1 recipe Plain pastry
2 cups cooked prunes
1 cup prune juice
1/4 cup orange marmalade or candied orange peel
1 tablespoon flour
1/2 cup sugar

Pit prunes, cut into pieces. Mix sugar and flour together and combine with prune juice. Cook until thick and smooth. Add prunes, marmalade, flour and blend well. Pour into shell.

Prune Pie #2

1/2 pound prunes
Water to cover
2 tablespoons flour
1 tablespoon butter
1 teaspoon lemon juice
3 tablespoons prune juice
1/3 to 1/2 cup sugar (see directions)

Amount of sugar depends upon tartness of prunes. Soak prunes in enough water to cover for several hours, then simmer until soft, letting cook until juice is reduced to 3 tablespoons. Cool and remove the stones and cut prunes in quarters. Mix together the flour and butter until well blended, and stir in the lemon juice and prune juice gradually. Turn the prunes into a pie shell and pour over them the mixture, with sugar. Put on a top crust and press down the edge. Make several incisions in the top. Bake in a hot oven.

Pineapple Cream Pie

1/2 cup sugar
5 level tablespoons flour
1/4 teaspoon salt
2 eggs
1 cup hot water
1 cup grated pineapple
1 tablespoon butter
1/2 pint cream
3 tablespoons sugar
Few drops lemon extract

Mix thoroughly the dry ingredients. Add well-beaten egg yolks, then gradually add the water. Cook in double-boiler and when it begins to thicken, add the pineapple and butter and cook, stirring frequently, until very thick. Remove from fire and let stand while beating the egg whites until stiff and dry, then slowly pour over them the cooked mixture, folding in until blended. Chill thoroughly. When ready to serve, spread into previously cooked and chilled pie crust and on top pile irregularly the cream whipped stiff with sugar and lemon extract.
Sufficient for 1 large or 2 small pies.

Pumpkin Pie #1

1/4 cup Flour
1/4 teaspoon ginger
1 teaspoon cinnamon
1/4 teaspoon cloves
1/2 teaspoon salt
1/4 cup sugar
1 egg
1-1/3 cups milk
1 cup canned pumpkin or mashed pumpkin
1/3 cup molasses

Mix and sift the dry ingredients. Beat the egg and add, then mix in the milk, then add to the pumpkin. Stir in the molasses. Boil in the double-boiler for about 20 minutes. When perfectly cold, spread into pie shells, which have been previously baked and which also are cold.
If you wish a glazed top, rub over with beaten egg or evaporated milk, set in the oven again for a couple of minutes.
Filling for 2 medium sized pies.

Pumpkin Pie #2

1 recipe Plain Pastry
3 eggs
1-1/2 cups milk
1 cup pumpkin
3/4 cup sugar
3/4 teaspoon ginger
1-1/2 teaspoons cinnamon
1/4 teaspoon salt

Line a pie pan with shortening pastry. Beat eggs slightly; add milk. Mix pumpkin with sugar, spices and salt, add to milk and blend thoroughly. Pour into pie pan and bake 15 minutes in hot oven (400 degrees F.), reduce temperature to 300 and bake about 20-30 minutes.

Pumpkin Pie #3

1-1/4 cups steamed pumpkin
7/8 cup brown sugar
1 teaspoon cinnamon
1 teaspoon ginger
2 tablespoons orange juice
1/2 teaspoon salt
2 eggs
1 cup condensed milk
1/4 cup water

Mix materials in order given and pour into an unbaked pastry shell. Place in a hot (450 degrees F.) oven to set the crust. After 10 minutes reduce the temperature to 250 degrees F. for the rest of the period. Bake about 1 hour.
Makes 1 pie

Pumpkin Pie #4

2 cups stewed and strained pumpkin
2 cups rich milk or cream
1 cup brown or granulated sugar
2 eggs
1 teaspoon salt
1/2 teaspoon ginger
2 teaspoons cinnamon
1/2 teaspoon allspice

Mix pumpkin with milk, sugar, beaten eggs, salt and spices, and beat 2 minutes. Pour into pie tin which has been lined with pastry. Place in hot oven for 15 minutes, then reduce heat and bake 45 minutes in moderate oven.

Pumpkin Pie #5

1 cup steamed strained pumpkin
1/2 teaspoon salt
1/2 teaspoon ginger
1/2 teaspoon cloves
2 teaspoons cinnamon
3 eggs
1 cup sweetened condensed milk
1 cup water
Unbaked pie crust

Mix ingredients in the order given; pour into pan lined with unbaked pie crust. Bake in a hot oven (450 degrees F.) for about 10 minutes, then reduce the temperature to moderate (350 degrees F.) and bake for about 35 additional minutes, or until the filling has set.

Thanksgiving Pumpkin Parfait

Red applesauce layer on spiced pumpkin custard, topped with candy-decorated whipped cream

Part 1:
2 tablespoons flour
1/4 cup sugar
1/4 teaspoon ginger
1/4 teaspoon nutmeg
1/8 teaspoon salt
1 cup milk, scalded
1 egg, slightly beaten
1/4 cup pumpkin
1 tablespoon honey
1-1/2 teaspoons gelatine, soaked in
2 tablespoons water
Flaky Pastry (see recipe for Tennessee Angel Pie)

Combine dry ingredients, add scalded milk slowly, stirring constantly, and cook 15 minutes over hot water. Mix egg, pumpkin, and honey, and add slowly to hot mixture. Cook 5 minutes longer. Add gelatine, cool and pour into a 9-inch baked pastry shell. Let stand while preparing Part 2.

Part 2:
1 tablespoon gelatine, soaked in
2 tablespoons cold water
1-1/2 cups Red Applesauce (below)
1/2 cup whipping cream
1 tablespoon sugar
Cinnamon "red hot" candies

Dissolve gelatine in hot red applesauce. Let stand until firm (about 1 hour). When cool, pour over pumpkin custard. Before serving, cover with sweetened whipped cream, and decorate with "red hots" to produce polka dot effect.
6 servings

Red Applesauce

4 cups sliced apples
1/2 cup water
1/2 cup cinnamon "red hot" candies
1 slice lemon
1/2 cup sugar

Cook all ingredients together until apples are soft. Strain and measure.

Cinderella Coach-and-Six

Pecan pumpkin filling, garnished with mounds of whipped cream and pecan halves

1 cup pumpkin
3/4 cup brown sugar
1/2 teaspoon cinnamon
1/2 teaspoon ginger
1/4 teaspoon nutmeg
1/2 teaspoon salt
2 eggs, slightly beaten
1 cup top milk
Flaky Pastry (see recipe for Tennessee Angel Pie)
1/2 cup chopped pecans

Mash pumpkin to remove lumps, and add dry ingredients, mixed together. Add eggs to milk, and stir into pumpkin mixture. Pour into 9-inch baked pastry shell, sprinkle with pecans, and bake in a moderately hot oven, 375 degrees, for 55 minutes, or until firm in the center. Cool and top with whipped cream. 6 servings

Peter Pumpkin

Orange-tanged pumpkin custard filling, crowned with a delicate sponge topping

3/4 cup sugar
3 tablespoons flour
2 tablespoons butter
1/4 cup orange juice
1 tablespoon grated orange rind
1/4 teaspoon cinnamon
1/4 teaspoon ginger
1/4 teaspoon nutmeg
1/2 teaspoon salt
1/2 cup pumpkin
1/2 cup milk
3 eggs, separated
Flaky Pastry (see recipe for Tennessee Angel Pie)

Cream sugar, flour and butter together, until of the consistency of corn meal. Add orange juice and rind. Mix spices and salt with pumpkin, add milk, and well-beaten egg yolks. Blend pumpkin and orange mixtures, and fold in stiffly-beaten egg whites. Pour into a 9-inch baked pastry shell, and bake in a moderately hot oven, 375 degrees, for 50-55 minutes, or until firm in the center.
6 servings

Pumpkin Pudding Pie

Fluffy pudding-type pumpkin filling, topped with delicious unbaked honey meringue

1-1/2 cups pumpkin
3/4 cup sugar
1/4 teaspoon cinnamon
1/4 teaspoon cloves
1/2 teaspoon ginger
1/4 teaspoon salt
2 egg, separated, and
2 egg yolks
1-1/2 cups milk
Flaky Pastry (see recipe for Tennessee Angel Pie)

Mash pumpkin to remove lumps, and add dry ingredients mixed together. Beat egg yolks slightly, add to milk, and stir into pumpkin mixture. Beat whites stiff, but not dry, and fold in. Pour into 9-inch baked pastry shell, and bake in a moderately hot oven, 375 degrees, for 55 minutes, or until firm in the center. Cool, and top with Unbaked Honey Meringue, before serving.
6 servings

Unbaked Honey Meringue

2 egg whites
1/4 cup honey
1/4 teaspoon cream of tartar
1/8 teaspoon salt
2 teaspoons butter

Place egg whites, honey, cream of tartar, and salt in the top of a small double boiler over briskly boiling water, and beat rapidly with a rotary egg beater for 3 minutes, or until it stands in stiff peaks. Remove from heat and very carefully fold in butter until well blended.

Pumpkin Mince Meringue

Two popular fall pies—mince and pumpkin—combined and topped with brown sugar meringue

1-1/2 cups pumpkin
3/4 cup brown sugar
1/4 teaspoon cinnamon
1/4 teaspoon ginger
1/2 teaspoon salt
1 cup milk
3 egg yolks
1/2 cup mincemeat (condensed)
1/2 cup apples, chopped
Plain Pastry (see recipe for Lemon Meringue Pie)
6 tablespoons brown sugar
3 egg whites

Mash pumpkin to remove lumps; add dry ingredients mixed together, and milk blended with slightly-beaten egg yolks. Mix

mincemeat with apples, and place in bottom of 9-inch glazed baked pastry shell (see recipe for Lemon Sponge Pie for glazing directions). Pour pumpkin mixture on top. Bake in a moderately hot oven, 375 degrees, for 55 minutes, or until firm in the center. Remove from oven, top with meringue made by adding sugar slowly to stiffly-beaten egg whites, and return to a slow oven, 300 degrees, for 20 minutes to brown and cook meringue.
6 servings

Pilgrim Pumpkin Pie

A heavenly spiced old-fashioned pumpkin pie, made with molasses and a dash of genius

1-1/2 cups pumpkin
3/4 cup brown sugar
1 teaspoon cinnamon
1/8 teaspoon cloves
1/2 teaspoon ginger
1/2 teaspoon nutmeg
1/2 teaspoon salt
2 eggs, slightly beaten
2 cups evaporated milk, undiluted
2 tablespoons molasses
2 tablespoons butter, melted
Plain pastry (see recipe for Lemon Meringue Pie)

Mash pumpkin to remove lumps, and add dry ingredients, mixed together. ~recipe ends here

BAKE @ 450° for 10 min & @ 350° for 45 min

Pineapple Pie

4 tablespoons flour
2/3 cup sugar
1/8 teaspoon salt
1-1/3 cups crushed pineapple
1 cup condensed milk
1 cup water
2/3 teaspoon vanilla
3 eggs
4 tablespoons sugar
1/4 teaspoon baking powder
3 egg whites

Follow method given for lemon pie, adding vanilla and well-drained pineapple in place of the lemon. Use 4 tablespoons sugar, 1/4 teaspoon baking powder and 3 egg whites for the meringue.
Makes 1 large pie

Pineapple Icebox Pie

1/2 cup condensed milk
1 cup pineapple juice
1 package lemon-flavored gelatin
6 cups corn flakes
6 tablespoons soft butter
1 cup powdered sugar
2 egg yolks
1-1/4 cups canned, crushed pineapple, drained
1/4 teaspoon salt
1 tablespoon lemon juice

Chill milk until icy cold. Meanwhile, heat pineapple juice. Add gelatin and stir until dissolved. Chill until mixture begins to thicken. While gelatin mixture is chilling roll corn flakes into fine crumbs. There should be 1-1/2 cups. Put 1 cup crumbs in bottom of buttered 9-inch pie pan. Cream butter and sugar together until light and fluffy. Beat in egg yolks vigorously. Spread mixture over crumbs in pan. Cover with 1/4 cup crumbs. Chill. Stir crushed pineapple and salt into thickened lemon gelatin mixture. Whip chilled milk with rotary beater until light and fluffy. Add lemon juice and continue whipping until stiff. Fold into pineapple gelatin mixture. Pour over second layer of crumbs and top with remaining 1/4 cup crumbs. Chill at least 3 hours, or overnight.
Serves 6

Note: A No. 2 can will yield 1-1/4 cups crushed pineapple and 1 cup juice. One and one-half cups ginger snap or vanilla wafer crumbs may be substituted for the corn flakes.

Pineapple Cream Pie

1/2 cup sugar
5 level tablespoons flour
1/4 teaspoon salt
2 eggs
1 cup hot water
1 cup grated pineapple
1 tablespoon butter
1/2 pint cream
3 tablespoons sugar
Few drops lemon extract

Mix thoroughly the dry ingredients. Add well-beaten egg yolks, then gradually add the water. Cook in double-boiler and when it begins to thicken, add the pineapple and butter and cook, stirring frequently, until very thick. Remove from fire and let stand while beating the egg whites until stiff and dry, then slowly pour over them the cooked mixture, folding in until blended. Chill thoroughly. When ready to serve, spread into previously cooked and chilled pie crusts and on top pile

irregularly the cream whipped stiff with sugar and lemon extract.
Sufficient for 1 large or 2 small pies.

Deep Dish Peach Pie

2 recipes Plain Paste
8 to 10 peaches
1/2 cup sugar
1/2 teaspoon grated orange rind
1/4 cup orange juice
Powdered sugar

Line the sides of a deep pan (about 2 inches deep) with pastry. Slice peaches and mix with the sugar and place in the pan; sprinkle orange rind over the top, and add orange juice. The addition of several peach pits, 6 to 8, will add more flavor to pie. Cover with a top crust, and bake about 40 minutes in a hot oven (450 degrees F.), reducing temperature to 300 for last 10 minutes. Just before taking from the oven, sprinkle with powdered sugar and return to oven for browning. Serve with plenty of cream if you wish.

Raisin Pie #1

1/2 cup flour
1/2 teaspoon salt
1 cup sugar
1 egg yolk
2 cups water
1 cup seedless raisins
Grated rind and juice of 1 lemon

Mix together thoroughly the flour, salt and sugar. Beat the egg yolk and add to it a part of the water. Mix everything together and boil slowly until very thick and the raisins are soft. It will require about 4 or 5 minutes. Stir constantly. When perfectly cold, put between 2 pie crusts and bake in a hot oven until the crust is done.
Sufficient for 1 pie

Raisin Pie #2

2 tablespoons cornstarch
1/2 cup sugar
1/4 teaspoon salt
3/4 cup water
1 tablespoon Crisco
1 tablespoon lemon juice
1 cup raisins (seedless)
Grated rind of lemon

Mix cornstarch, sugar and salt; stir in water. Cook until thick. Add Crisco, lemon juice and raisins. Cool before pouring into pie tin lined with a pie shell.

Rhubarb Pie #1

2 cups rhubarb
1 tablespoon corn starch or flour
1/4 teaspoon salt
1 cup sugar

Cut off root, stem ends and peel; cut into small pieces; put into deep pie plate which has been lined with paste. Sprinkle with cornstarch, salt and sugar. Cover with paste and bake in hot oven about 1/2 hour.

Rhubarb Pie #2

2 cups cut rhubarb
4 level tablespoons flour
1/4 teaspoon salt
1 cup sugar
1 egg yolk
1 level tablespoon butter

Have ready a good pie crust.
Cook the rhubarb with about a tablespoon of water (just enough to keep from burning), and when it begins to get soft and the juice runs, remove and set aside to get cold. Sift together the flour, salt and sugar and add the beaten egg and butter. Mix this in with the rhubarb and when perfectly cold fill the pie crust, put on a top crust, pinch the edges well together, make incisions in the top and bake in a very hot oven until the crust is done.

Rhubarb and Raisin Pie

4 level tablespoons flour
1 cup sugar
1/2 teaspoon salt
1 egg yolk
3/4 cup water
1 cup rhubarb
1 cup raisins
Juice and grated rind of 1 lemon

Mix together thoroughly the flour, sugar and salt. Beat the egg yolk and add to the water. Put everything on the stove and boil gently, stirring constantly, until thick. Remove from the fire and when perfectly cold put between 2 pie crusts and bake in a hot oven until the crusts are done.
Filling for 1 large or 2 small pies

Strawberry Pie

1 cup flour
1/2 teaspoon salt
2 teaspoons baking powder
4 tablespoons shortening
1/4 cup cold water
1 quart strawberries
1/2 cup sugar
1/2 cup strawberries
2 cups boiling water
1 tablespoon corn starch

Sift flour, salt and baking powder together; rub in shortening very lightly with finger tips; add water slowly to make a stiff dough. Roll out on floured board and use for bottom crust of pie, being careful to fold the paste well over the edge of pie plate. Bake in hot oven 12 to 15 minutes.
If glazed crust is desired, brush edges after baking with boiling hot syrup (2 tablespoons syrup and 1 tablespoon water) and return to oven for 1 or 2 minutes until syrup hardens. Fill the baked crust with fresh selected hulled strawberries and cover with syrup made as follows:
Add 1/2 cup sugar and 1/2 cup strawberries to 2 cups boiling water; bring to a boil and strain; add 1 tablespoon corn starch which has been mixed with little cold water. Cook over hot fire for a minute or two, stirring constantly; remove from fire and beat hard; return to slow fire, cook very gently until thick. Pour while hot over strawberries. Serve either hot or cold.

Sour Cream Pie

2 tablespoons flour
1 cup sugar
1/4 teaspoon salt
1 cup thick sour cream
3 eggs, beaten together
1/4 cup seedless raisins

Sift together the flour, sugar and salt. Whip the cream until thick (like whipped cream) and beat the eggs, and add these to the dry ingredients. Flour the raisins and add last. Bake in either a single or double crust pie, in a hot oven. The oven should be very hot when the pie is first put in, to avoid the filling sinking into the crust.
Filling for 1 pie

Squash Pie

2 slightly-beaten eggs
1-1/2 cups steamed squash, drained of all juice and mashed
1/4 cup sugar
2 tablespoons Blend Flour
1 tablespoon cornstarch
1 teaspoon salt
1 teaspoon cinnamon
1/2 teaspoon ginger
1/4 teaspoon cloves
1-1/4 cup rich milk or part cream
1/4 cup molasses

Mix beaten eggs into the mashed squash. Mix and sift the dry ingredients, and add alternately with the milk and molasses. Mix thoroughly. Either cook in a double-boiler until very thick, stirring frequently, then chill and when cold put into a previously baked and cooled crust, brush with a little beaten egg or evaporated milk and glaze by placing for a moment in a moderate oven; or bake in a single crust, first brushing over the bottom of crust with egg white.

Cream Cheese Pastry

1/2 cup cream cheese (1 package)
1/4 cup shortening
1 cup flour
2 teaspoons sugar
1/4 teaspoon salt

Cream together cheese and shortening; sift flour, measure, and sift again ~ recipe ends here

Tennessee Angel Pie

A delicate, fluffy lemon pie of the chiffon-type, enhanced by flaky pastry

3 eggs, separated
1 cup sugar
3 tablespoons cold water
4 tablespoons lemon juice
1 tablespoon grated lemon rind

Beat egg yolks with 1/2 cup sugar, water, lemon juice, and rind. Set over boiling water, and stir briskly until it begins to thicken. Cook 10 minutes longer, stirring occasionally. Beat egg whites stiff, add remaining sugar slowly, beating well. Fold hot lemon mixture into egg whites, and turn into a 9-inch baked pie shell. Bake in a moderately hot oven, 375 degrees, for 15 minutes.
6 servings

Flaky Pastry

1 cup flour
1/4 teaspoon salt
1/3 cup shortening
3-4 tablespoons ice water
1 tablespoon butter

Sift flour, measure, and sift again with salt. Cut in shortening coarsely. Add just enough ice water to hold together. Turn out on lightly floured board, roll in oblong shape; spread with butter and fold in half, then in thirds, making 6 layers. Roll out, fit loosely over back of 9-inch pie tin, and prick liberally with a fork. Chill thoroughly. Bake in very hot oven, 500 degrees, until it begins to brown, about 10 minutes. Change shell to inside of pan, reduce heat to 450 degrees, and finish baking.
One 9-inch pie shell

Vinegar Pie

1 cup sugar
1 tablespoon lemon extract
2 tablespoons flour
3 eggs
Butter the size of an egg
1 cup water
4 tablespoons vinegar

Mix sugar and flour together, then add extract, flour, egg yolks, butter, water and vinegar and cook until thick. Pour in baked crust and put egg whites on top and brown.

Whip Cream Pie

2 cups thick cream
Sugar to taste
Flavoring
Jelly
Cherries

Line pie pan with crust and bake until brown. Beat cream, put on ice when cool, add sugar to taste and flavoring. Spread jelly on crust, on top of that put whip cream; garnish daintily with cherries.

13

FRENCH PASTRY

French pastry, with puff paste as the foundation, has always been considered as something very difficult to make, and to be attempted only by one with many years of cooking experience. The real fact of the matter is, it is one of the easiest of all forms of cookery if the principles be once understood. As for pie crust, all ingredients should be very cold. The mixing bowl should be chilled and the water used should be ice water if possible; if not, let the water run until cold. Every fold makes a flake and intense heat is necessary before the Paste is put in the oven. The heat should be reduced later. The recipe given will make a large quantity. It may be made when convenient and then freshened the day it is to be used. For Patties (Patés) it should be served hot. If for Cones, Tarts, etc., serve cold.

PASTRY MAKING

To obtain the best results in any type of pastry, a few general rules should be observed.

Do not mix the fat too thoroughly with the flour—the coarser the mixture, the flakier the crust will be.

Crisco is particularly desirable for pastry making because it mixes so easily with the flour, forming a mixture of just the right consistency. The Crisco crust is convenient to handle, and always tender and flaky, when properly made.

Add only enough water to hold the dry ingredients together in a lump, so that the mixture may be rolled out to a sheet. Excess water causes the crust to be tough besides involving difficulty in rolling.

Do not use too much flour on the board for rolling. A piece of canvas or a heavy towel spread out and well floured is more satisfactory for rolling the dough than a board or enamelled surface. The meshes of the cloth hold just the right amount of flour to keep the dough from sticking. The cloth may be shaken out after each using and folded up for the next time—it does not have to be washed after every pie.

Roll only one crust at a time, using a gentle pressure and rolling from the center out. Lift up the edges of the crust occasionally to see whether it is sticking to the board. If necessary, sprinkle a little flour under the crust. Fit the crust carefully into the curves of the pan, leaving no air spaces to bulge the crust up during baking. If the crust is to be baked before adding the filling, prick it generously with a fork—this will also help to eliminate "bubbles" in the crust.

Fasten two-crust pies well at the edges by brushing the lower edge with water and pressing the upper edge down with a fork or by folding in to scallops with the finger tips. The juice may be further prevented from escaping, particularly in berry pies, by adding flour to the sugar used for sweetening.

The upper crust should always be pricked or slashed occasionally to allow the escape of steam.

To prevent soaking of the lower crust, the surface may be sprinkled with flour or brushed with egg white before adding the filling.

Bake all pastry in as hot an oven as possible, taking into consideration the kind of filling, size of pie, etc.

Custard pies should be started in a hot oven (375° F.) to set the crust, then the heat quickly reduced to 300 or even less to bake the custard slowly.

Apple pies should be baked at 400° until browning starts, the temperature reduced to cook the apples thoroughly. When a fork pierces the center easily, the apples are cooked.

Pie crust, either plain or flaky, needs a hot oven (about 400° F.).

Puff paste also bakes best at high temperatures, though for patty shells it is well to reduce the heat after raising to cook the center thoroughly.

PASTRY

Plain Paste

1/2 teaspoon salt
1-1/2 cups flour
1/3 cup Crisco
Water

Sift salt with flour. Cut Crisco in with knives or work in coarsely with finger tips. Stir in gradually just enough water to hold dry ingredients together. Divide into 2 parts and roll out separately to form lower and upper crusts for pie, or 2 pie shells.

Puff Paste

4 cups flour
1 egg yolk
1 teaspoon salt
Juice of 1/2 lemon
1 cup cold water
3 cups butter

Put the flour onto a pastry board, marble slab or in a china or earthenware mixing bowl. Make a hole in the center and drop in the unbeaten egg yolk, salt and lemon juice. Stir in the flour a little at a time, adding very cold water gradually, as is necessary to mix it. It will require about 1 cup. The paste should be soft and flexible (softer than pie crust), but not sticky. Put in a very cold place for 15 minutes. In hot weather, if there be no ice, set the bowl containing the paste in a larger bowl of very cold water. Then roll out a little larger than a large pie tin.
Put the butter in a cloth and squeeze out all the water. Then lay the butter—all of it—in the center of the paste. Fold over the edges so as to conceal the butter, and roll again very thin. Then fold it up, making 3 or 4 folds. Set aside again to chill for 15 or 20 minutes (longer will do no harm). Roll again very thin and fold up as before. Repeat this process 3 times, chilling after each. Then roll again and it is ready for use.

Apple Butter Patties

3 medium-sized apples
2 tablespoons water
2 egg yolks
1 tablespoon flour
1/2 cup sugar (more if required)
1 rounded tablespoon butter
Juice of 1/2 lemon and little grated rind

Make Puff Paste. Cut as for chicken patties.
Peel, core and cut the apples into small pieces and boil in the 2 tablespoons of water until very soft, stirring frequently to avoid scorching. Beat until smooth, then add the slightly beaten egg yolks. Mix flour and sugar thoroughly and melt the butter. Mix all together and put a spoonful into each patty and bake. Serve either hot or cold.

Apricot-Pineapple Tartlets

Puff Paste
A little beaten egg or evaporated milk

Prepare Puff Paste. Roll out about 1/4 inch thick. Cut with large round cookie cutter first dipped in water to insure a smooth edge. Cut for each tartlet one round with the cookie cutter and one with a doughnut cutter of the same size. Put the 2 cookie rounds on top of each other and the round cut with the doughnut cutter on top of that. Bake in a hot oven (first brushing over with a little beaten egg or evaporated milk). When cold put in the center of each a spoonful of the following filling:

Apricot-Pineapple Filling

1 cup apricot pulp (from either fresh, canned or stewed dried apricots pressed through a colander)
1/2 cup grated canned pineapple or 1-1/2 slices pineapple cut in small pieces
1/2 cup sugar (or sugar to taste)

Mix together and boil, stirring constantly, until very thick (about 5 minutes). When cold use with the Tartlets.

Banbury Tarts

Puff Paste
A little beaten egg

Prepare Puff Paste and roll very thin, and cut into circles with large biscuit cutter; into the center of each put in a spoonful of the following filling. Fold over each side to meet the middle. Rub over the top with a little beaten egg and bake in a hot oven about 20 minutes.

Banbury Tart Filling

1 cup seeded raisins, chopped
1/2 cup seedless raisins
1/2 cup chopped nuts (not too fine)
1/4 cup cracker crumbs
1 cup sugar
1 egg
Juice and grated rind of 1 lemon
Grated rind of 1/2 orange (this may be omitted if not convenient)

Supreme Chicken Patties

Prepare patty shells form Puff Paste recipe by rolling thin, cutting one circle with biscuit cutter and one with doughnut cutter for each patty, reserving the small circle removed by doughnut cutter for top. Pile on top of each other, the doughnut circle on top. Brush all over with a little beaten egg. Bake in a hot oven. Serve very hot, filled with hot Supreme Chicken.

Supreme Chicken Filling

1 cup rich cream
1 cup milk
1 cup chicken stock
1/3 cup flour
1/4 cup butter
2 cups diced chicken (preferably white meat)
1/2 cup chopped mushrooms
2 tablespoons cooked peas (without liquid)
Dash nutmeg
1/2 teaspoon celery salt
Salt, pepper and paprika to taste

Mix together the cream, milk and chicken stock and bring to a boil. Work together the flour and butter until perfectly smooth, then stir into the boiling liquid. Cook, stirring constantly, until thick. Add chicken mushrooms, peas and seasonings, and cook, stirring constantly, for about 5 minutes more. Pour at once into hot patty shells, sprinkle with a very little minced parsley, and set the small piece of Puff Paste removed by the center of the doughnut cutter on top.

Lemon Butter Tarts

Puff Paste
A little beaten egg

Roll Puff Paste very thin and cut in fancy shapes with cookie cutter. Brush over with beaten egg and bake in a hot oven. When cold put on each a spoonful of Lemon Butter.

Lemon Butter Filling

2 level tablespoons flour
1-1/2 cups sugar
4 eggs, beaten together
Juice and grated rind of 3 large lemons
1/3 cup butter

Mix together the flour and sugar and add the eggs, well beaten. Mix thoroughly, add the balance of ingredients and cook, stirring constantly, until thick.

Macaroon Patties

Make Puff Paste. Roll thin and cut as for Chicken Patties. When cold fill with the following Macaroon Filling:

Macaroon Filling

1 dozen macaroons
1/2 pint whipping cream
Sugar to taste
Few drops almond extract
3 tablespoons sweet chocolate (melted)
Ground nuts

Use dry almond macaroons and crush with rolling pin. Whip the cream, sweeten to taste, add almond extract and melted sweet chocolate. Then add the macaroon crumbs. Fill the patties and sprinkle some ground nuts on top.

Marshmallow Divinity Tarts

Make Puff Paste. Roll thin and cut into fancy shapes. Bake, and when cold fill with Marshmallow Divinity.

Marshmallow Divinity Filling

1/2 pint whipping cream
1 dozen marshmallows
1/2 cup chopped nut meats
Few drops almond extract
2 tablespoons powdered sugar

Cut the marshmallows into small pieces and place in top of double-boiler. Let stand until very soft, then add 1 tablespoon of the cream and beat smooth. Remove from fire and let stand while whipping balance of cream, adding to the cream the sugar and flavoring. Then pour in the marshmallows and nuts and mix with a fork. Put a spoonful on each tart when cold. Good served with hot chocolate.

Marseilles Circlets

Prepare Puff Paste. Roll thin and cut into circles with cookie and doughnut cutter of the same size, allowing one of each for each Circlet. Put the circle cut with the doughnut cutter on top. Brush over with beaten egg and fill with the following filling:

Marseilles Filling

1 cup sugar
1/3 cup water
1 cup grated cocoanut (fresh cocoanut, if possible)
1/3 cup butter
3 egg yolks

Boil the sugar and water together to a thick syrup (about 12 minutes). Then add the cocoanut and boil 10 minutes longer. Remove from fire and add the butter. Let stand while beating the egg yolks very thick, then stir in and put a spoonful onto each pattie Circlet and bake in a hot oven until the crust is done (about 10 to 15 minutes).

Orange Tarts

Make Puff Paste and roll very thin. Cut into diamonds and brush with beaten egg. Bake in a hot oven. Have ready the following filling and when perfectly cold put a spoonful on top of each diamond and decorate with a section of orange:

Orange Tart Filling

3 tablespoons Blend Flour
Pinch of salt
1/2 cup sugar
3 eggs (well beaten)
Grated rind of 2 oranges
1/2 cup orange juice
Juice of 1/2 lemon
1 heaping tablespoon butter

Mix together the flour, salt and sugar, and add the beaten eggs. Mix everything together and boil, stirring constantly, until very thick.

Sun Fruit on Cheese

Cream cheese pastry sets off cocoanut-tanged lemon filling and cocoanut meringue

2 cups water
1/2 cup shredded cocoanut
1/3 cup cornstarch
1/2 cup sugar
2 tablespoons butter
3 egg yolks
1/3 cup lemon juice
1 tablespoon grated lemon rind
3 tablespoons sugar
1 egg whites
1/4 cup cocoanut

Bring water and cocoanut to a boil in top of double boiler. Mix cornstarch and sugar, and add slowly to boiling water, beating constantly until thick. Place over boiling water, add butter, and cook 15 minutes, stirring occasionally. Add beaten egg yolks slowly, beating briskly. Add lemon juice and rind, cook 5 minutes and remove from heat. Cool and turn into a 9-inch baked pie shell. Cover with meringue, made by adding 6 tablespoons sugar slowly to 3 beaten egg whites. Sprinkle top with cocoanut, and bake in moderately slow oven, 325 degrees, for 20 minutes.
6 servings

Queen Patties (Paté)

Prepare Puff Paste. Roll about 1/4 inch thick and cut to fit pattie pans or muffin tins. Prick the bottom and sides with a fork. Take fresh or canned sliced peaches and fill the patties with the slices (sharp edge down) arranged closely together. Over each put a spoonful of the following previously prepared custard. Sprinkle the top with a little cinnamon and sugar, rub the edge with a little beaten egg or evaporated milk, and bake in a hot oven about 15 minutes.

Custard for Queen Patties

2 eggs
2 tablespoons sugar
Pinch of salt
1 cup milk

Beat the eggs slightly and stir in the sugar and salt, then add slowly the hot milk. Pour into a small pudding dish and set in the oven in another pan containing boiling water. Bake until it begins to set; then remove and put a spoonful into each pattie, return to the stove and finish baking.

Reception Hearts

Puff Paste
A little beaten egg
Powdered sugar

Make Puff Paste. Roll thin. Cut with a heart-shaped cookie cutter first dipped in water to insure a smooth edge. Put 2 together (on top of each other) and rub the top and sides with a little beaten egg. Sprinkle with sifted powdered sugar and bake in a hot oven for about 15 minutes. Cut a hole through the top and when cold fill the cavity with the following Chocolate Almond Filling, and if desired put a little whipped cream on top of each:

Chocolate Almond Filling

1 cup milk
1-1/2 squares unsweetened chocolate, or 1/3 cup unsweetened powdered chocolate
Pinch of salt

2 tablespoons flour
1 tablespoon cornstarch
1/2 cup sugar
3 eggs
1/2 cup chopped almonds
Few drops almond extract

Put the milk, chocolate and salt in a double-boiler and cook, stirring occasionally, until the chocolate is melted. Mix together the flour, cornstarch and sugar and add the eggs well beaten, then stir into the milk, and cook, stirring occasionally, until very thick. Remove from the fire, add the almonds and extract, and when cold fill the Reception Hearts.

Supreme Tart Filling

Patty Shells
1 egg white
1/4 cup powdered sugar
1 cup shredded cocoanut
1/4 teaspoon almond extract or vanilla

Mix all together without beating the egg white, working it into a paste. Fill the shells and bake in an oven first very hot for 5 minutes, then reduce the heat. They should be delicately browned on top and taste similar to cocoanut macaroons. Prepare patty shells as for Supreme Chicken Patties. Before baking fill with the above mixture, then bake and serve cold, with or without a spoonful of sweetened and flavored whipped cream on top.

Cheese Straws

Roll out flaky pastry to 1/4 inch thick. Sprinkle generously with rated cheese. Fold over the four edges to the center. Roll out gcarefully. Fold in half and roll out again. Repeat twice. Cut into strips about 1/2 inch wide. Bake in a hot oven until slightly browned.

Patty Shells

Roll part of puff paste to 1 inch in thickness, part to 1/2 inch. With cookie cutter, cut rounds of thin paste for bottoms of shells. Place on white paper on a pan. Cut rounds of thick paste with a doughnut cutter. Place the layer with the whole on the thin layer, fastening the two together by brushing between with water. Place in a hot oven (400 to 450° F.) and bake for 20 to 30 minutes or until risen and browned on the surface.

14

PUDDINGS

In all pudding recipes where raisins, figs, currants or nuts are specified, any one or a combination of these may be used interchangeably.

In all recipes where milk is specified, evaporated milk may be used in the proportion of half water and half milk, and where cream is used, evaporated milk may be used undiluted or diluted with one-fourth water.

Apple Dumplings #1

2 cups flour
4 teaspoons baking powder
3/4 teaspoon salt
1/3 cup shortening
1/3 cup milk

Sift together the dry ingredients; work in the shortening; then add the milk. Mix, handling as little as possible; roll out, cut into squares large enough to cover the apple. Core and pare the apples. Set one in the center of each square; fill the hole with sugar. Add about a teaspoon of water to the sugar in each apple and a small bit of butter. Sprinkle with sugar and cinnamon. Fold the pastry over the apple, pressing the ends together at the top. Bake in a moderately hot oven for about 25 or 30 minutes.

Apple Dumplings #2

1 cup sugar
1/4 cup butter
2-1/2 cups sliced apples
2 cups hot water

Mix together and let come to a boil. Prepare dumplings as follows and drop into the apple syrup by spoonfuls (it will make eight).

Dumplings #1

1 cup flour
2 teaspoon baking powder
3/4 cup cream

Sift the flour and baking powder and add the cream. Drop, as directed above, into the hot syrup. Cover closely, and let boil slowly for 20 minutes without lifting the cover. Serve hot with butter and sugar.

Dumplings #2

Especially delicious with stewed chicken.

7/8 cup milk
1 tablespoon butter
Few grains salt
1 cup flour
1 egg

Put milk, butter and salt in stew pan and when hot and butter is melted, stir into it briskly the flour. Cook, stirring constantly until it leaves the sides of the pan (about 1 minute). Cool slightly, then add the beaten egg and beat hard until smooth. Drop by dessert-spoonfuls into stew and cook, tightly covered, for 12 minutes without lifting cover. Serve immediately.

Apple Flop

2 cup flour
2 teaspoons baking powder
1/2 teaspoon salt
1/4 cup sugar
1/2 cup milk
1/4 cup melted butter
5 or 6 medium size apples

Into the mixing bowl sift the first 4 ingredients. Add gradually the milk, then the melted butter. Have ready a shallow baking pan lined to a depth of an inch with thinly-sliced apples. Sprinkle them with sugar, a little cinnamon, dot with butter and pour over 1/4 to 1/3 cup of water. Spread the batter over them and bake in a moderate oven for about 20 to 30 minutes, or until apples are soft and crust is done. Turn out onto a serving dish, upside down, so apples will be on top. Sprinkle them well with sugar and serve with cream while hot.

Apple Fritters

1 cup flour
1-1/2 teaspoon baking powder
1/8 teaspoon salt
2 tablespoons powdered sugar
1 beaten egg
1/2 cup milk
2 rather tart apples
Powdered sugar to roll them in

Mix and sift the dry ingredients. Add beaten egg to milk and add this gradually. Pare, core and cut apples into eighths or smaller pieces, or may be cut into rings 1/4 inch thick. Roll into powdered sugar, then stir into batter and fry by spoonfuls in deep hot fat. Drain on brown paper, and roll in powdered sugar. Serve hot. If desired, may be served with syrup.

Soft Custard

2 tablespoons corn starch
1 quart milk
3 eggs
1/2 cup sugar
1/4 teaspoon salt
1 teaspoon vanilla extract

Mix corn starch with 1 cup of the measured milk. Scald remaining milk in top of double boiler. Beat eggs slightly and add sugar and salt. Stir scalded milk slowly into eggs and return to double boiler. Add corn starch, stirring constantly until thick and smooth and cook 20 minutes. Remove from fire; add flavoring. Serve with stewed or fresh fruit or use for Floating Island.
If fewer eggs are used, add 1 tablespoon corn starch for each egg omitted.

Blanc Mange

5 tablespoons corn starch
1 quart milk
1/2 cup sugar
1/2 teaspoon salt
1 teaspoon vanilla extract

Mix corn starch to a smooth paste with 1 cup of the measured milk. Scald rest of milk; add sugar, salt and corn starch, stirring constantly. Cook in top of double boiler for 20 minutes until thick and smooth. Remove from fire; add flavoring and pour into mould, dipped in cold water. Chill, serve cold with chocolate or fruit sauce or fresh fruit and whipped cream.

Favorite Apple Pudding

2 cups sliced and peeled apples
1/4 cup sugar
1/4 cup flour
1/2 teaspoon cinnamon
2 tablespoons butter

Prepare the apples. Mix sugar, flour and cinnamon. Arrange apples in layers in baking dish (small bread pan greased is satisfactory), covering each layer with the mixture, and dot with butter. Cover with the following dough, making several incisions in the top for steam to escape:

Apple Pudding Dough:
1 cup Blend Flour
2 teaspoons baking powder
1/4 cup sugar
1/4 teaspoon salt
1/4 cup shortening
1/3 cup milk

Mix and sift the dry ingredients, work in the shortening as for biscuit dough, and add milk. Spread over the apples and bake in a moderate oven until apples and crust are done; time depends upon variety of apples; about 25 to 30 minutes.

Apricot or Peach Gems

2-1/2 cups flour
3/4 teaspoon salt
3 teaspoons baking powder
2 eggs
1 pint milk
1 teaspoon melted butter
1 teaspoon sugar

Sift together the dry ingredients. Beat the eggs and add to the milk. Mix into the dry ingredients and add the melted butter. Beat to a smooth batter. Have ready greased muffin pans, put a spoonful in each and lay a peach or apricot on top, hollow side up. Sprinkle with a little sugar and nutmeg and bake. Serve with cream and sugar.
This makes about 12 or 14.

Banana Puffs

2 eggs (beaten separately)
3 medium or 2 large ripe bananas
1 tablespoon melted butter
1 tablespoon sugar

1/2 cup milk
1-1/2 cups flour
2 teaspoons baking powder
1/2 teaspoon salt
1/2 teaspoon cinnamon

Beat the yolks of the eggs until thick and lemon colored; then beat in the bananas, which should be cut and mashed. Add the butter and sugar, and then add alternately the milk and the flour, into which should be sifted the baking powder, salt and spice. Drop from a spoon into hot fat and fry as you would doughnuts. Drain on brown paper and roll in powdered sugar. Serve at once. Will serve 5

Steamed Berry Pudding

2 cups Blend Flour
2 teaspoons baking powder
1/2 teaspoon salt
1/2 cup sugar
2 eggs, beaten separately
1 cup milk
2 tablespoons melted butter
2 cups berries, floured

Mix and sift the dry ingredients, beat yolks, add to milk, and gradually stir into dry mixture. Add butter and beat well, then stir in the floured berries. Fold in the stiffly-beaten whites, turn into greased pudding molds, filling not more than 2/3 full, and steam 2 hours. Serve hot with Plain or Fruit Pudding Sauce.

Baked Carrot (or Mock Plum) Pudding

1 teaspoon soda, dissolved in
1 tablespoon hot water
1 cup molasses
1 teaspoon salt
1-1/2 cups Blend Flour
1 teaspoon cinnamon
1 teaspoon grated nutmeg
1 teaspoon cloves
1/2 teaspoon allspice
1 cup brown sugar
1 cup grated raw carrots
1 cup grated raw potatoes
1 cup chopped suet
2 cups seedless raisins

Dissolve the soda in the hot water, then add to the molasses. Sift all the dry ingredients (excepting the sugar) with the flour, then mix everything in the order given. Bake 3 hours in a moderate oven. Serve hot with sauce.Will make 2 loaves

Baked Custard

4 eggs
1/2 cup sugar
1/4 teaspoon salt
1 teaspoon vanilla extract
1 quart milk

Beat eggs, sugar, salt and vanilla together; scald milk and add very slowly, stirring constantly. Put into greased baking dish or small molds; place in pan of water in slow oven and bake 30 to 40 minutes. Test with knife which will come out clean when custard is baked.
For Caramel Custard add to eggs 4 tablespoons Caramel Sauce.

Cherry Cobbler

1-1/2 cups flour
3 teaspoons baking powder
1/2 teaspoon salt
1/2 cup shortening
1/4 cup milk
Cherries
Sugar
Butter

Mix and sift the dry ingredients; cut in the shortening, then mix lightly with the fingers. Add the milk, mixing it in with the knife. Roll out, fold 2 or 3 times, then roll again to fit a large pie tin. Spread one-half thickly with cherries; sprinkle the cherries with plenty of sugar, dot with butter. Fold over the other half of the pastry, pressing the edges together. Make a few incisions in the top as you would in pie, and bake in a hot oven. Serve with cream or sauce. Will serve 5 or 6

Cherry Pudding

1 cup flour
2 teaspoons baking powder
1 tablespoon sugar
1/2 teaspoon salt
1/3 cup butter (or lard and butter)
1/2 cup milk
1 cup cherries without the juice

Sift together the dry ingredients, work in the butter; then add the milk and then the cherries. Bake about 1/2 hour in a hot oven. Serve with the following sauce:

Sauce:
2 tablespoons flour
1/2 cup sugar

1 cup cherry juice
1 cup hot water
2 tablespoons butter

Sift together the flour and sugar. Add gradually the cherry juice, beating until smooth, then the hot water. If there is not enough cherry juice, use enough additional water to make 2 cups of liquid altogether. Cook until it thickens. Then add butter and serve hot.
Will serve 4 or 5

Cherry Puffs

3/4 cup flour
1-1/2 teaspoon baking powder
1/4 teaspoon salt
1/3 cup sugar
2 beaten eggs
1/2 cup milk
1 pint canned cherries and juice (preferably pie cherries), or 1 pint fresh pitted pie cherries

Mix and sift the first 4 ingredients. Beat eggs, add to milk and stir in, mixing well. Drain the juice from the cherries and save for the sauce.
Butter individual pudding molds (cups or jelly glasses will do). In each put 2 tablespoons cherries and pour over enough butter to fill the cups 2/3 full. Steam 35 minutes. Turn out onto individual small plates, with cherries on top. Top with Sauce used for Cherry Pudding.

Steamed Chocolate Pudding

1-1/2 cups flour
3 teaspoons baking powder
1/2 teaspoon salt
1 cup sugar
1/4 cup shortening
1/2 cup powdered unsweetened or 3 squares cake chocolate
1 beaten egg
1 cup milk
1 teaspoon vanilla

Mix and sift the first 4 ingredients. Work in the shortening. Add chocolate. Beat the egg and add to the milk, then mix all together. Turn into a buttered mold and steam for one hour. Serve hot with cream, whipped cream or hard sauce.

Chocolate Bread Pudding

2 cups bread crumbs
2 cups milk
2 cups water
1/2 cup sugar
2 eggs
2 squares unsweetened chocolate or 1/2 cup powdered unsweetened chocolate
Pinch of salt
1 teaspoon vanilla

Soak the crumbs in the liquid, add the sugar, beaten eggs, grated chocolate, salt and flavoring, and bake in a buttered pudding dish in a moderate oven for one hour. Serve with Hard Sauce. Where strict economy is necessary, all water may be substituted in place of part milk, although the pudding, of course, will not contain so much nourishment. Also, instead of using 2 whole eggs, use the yolks of 2 and white of 1, reserving the other white for use in the recipe for Hard Sauce.
Will serve 6

Chocolate Pudding

5 tablespoons corn starch
1 quart milk
2-1/2 ounces unsweetened chocolate or 1/2 cup cocoa (mixed with sugar)
3/4 cup sugar
1/4 teaspoon salt
1 teaspoon vanilla extract
Sweetened whipped cream

Mix corn starch with 1/4 cup of the cold milk until smooth. Melt chocolate in double boiler. Add sugar and salt gradually. Add milk slowly, stirring constantly until scalded. Stir corn starch into mixture and cook until thick and smooth, about 20 minutes. Add flavoring and pour into mould dipped in cold water. Chill. Serve cold with sweetened whipped cream. If cocoa is used, mix with sugar and add as above.

Chocolate Pudding (Cheap)

2 cups flour
3 tablespoons baking powder
1/2 teaspoon salt
1/2 cup sugar
1 beaten egg
1 cup milk
2 squares melted chocolate or 1/2 cup unsweetened powdered chocolate

Sift together the flour, baking powder and salt, add the sugar, then the beaten egg and milk, and last the melted chocolate. Steam 1-1/2 hours and serve hot with Hard or Foamy Sauce.
Will serve 5 or 6

Chocolate Nut Pudding

1/2 cup flour
1/2 cup grated chocolate or powdered
1/2 teaspoon salt
1/2 cup milk
2 tablespoons butter
5 eggs yolks well beaten
3/4 cup sugar
1 cup sliced almonds (or broken walnuts)
5 egg whites beaten stiff

Mix together thoroughly the flour, chocolate, salt, milk and butter and cook in a double-boiler until thick like custard. Turn out to cool and when cool add, in the order given, the beaten yolks, sugar, nuts and beaten whites. Pour into buttered molds and steam one hour. Serve with whipped cream or Hard Sauce.
Will serve 6

Cottage Pudding

1 cup flour
1/2 cup sugar
1/8 teaspoon salt
2 teaspoons baking powder
1/2 cup milk
1 egg
2 tablespoons melted shortening

Sift together flour, sugar, salt and baking powder; add milk, beaten egg and shortening; beat well and bake in greased shallow pan in hot oven about 20 minutes. Serve with lemon, chocolate or other sauce.

Cottage Pudding (Sweet Milk)

2 tablespoons butter
1 cup sugar
1 egg
2 cups flour
4 teaspoons baking powder
1/2 teaspoon salt
1 cup milk

Cream the butter and sugar; add the well-beaten egg. Sift together the flour, baking powder and salt, and add, alternately with the milk, to the first mixture. Bake in a shallow pan in a moderate oven. Serve hot with sauce.

Cottage Pudding Sauce

1 tablespoon flour
1 cup sugar
1 egg
1 level tablespoon butter
1 cup boiling water
1/2 teaspoon vanilla (or lemon)

Mix the flour and sugar and stir in the beaten egg till smooth. Add the balance of the ingredients (excepting the flavoring) and let come to a boil. Remove from the stove, flavor and serve with Cottage Pudding.
Will serve 6

Cottage Pudding (Sour Milk)

2 tablespoons butter
1 cup sugar
2 eggs
1/2 teaspoon salt
1 teaspoon soda
1 cup sour milk
2-1/4 cups flour

Cream the butter and sugar; add the well-beaten eggs. Beat the soda into the sour milk and add, alternately with the flour, to the first mixture. Bake in shallow pan in a moderate oven and serve with Cottage Pudding Sauce.
Will serve 6

Yorkshire Pudding

To be served with roasts

2 cups flour
1/2 teaspoon salt
1 pint milk
3 eggs
Fat from roasting meat

Measure flour after first sifting. Mix in the salt, add milk gradually, beating to a smooth paste, then add the eggs beaten until very light. Heat a shallow baking pan or layer cake pans and pour over them enough fat taken from the pan in which meat is roasting to thoroughly grease, with a little superfluous fat (an extra teaspoon to a pan). Pour in the pudding mixture from 1/3 to 1/2 inch deep. Bake in a hot oven (450 to 500) for 18 to 20 minutes, basting with some of the fat in the pan when well risen. Cut in squares and serve hot with the roast. If preferred, bake in hot, well-greased muffin pans, basting as directed. Sufficient for 6 to 8 persons

Date Pudding

3 cups flour
1 teaspoon salt
1 teaspoon cinnamon
1 teaspoon cloves
1 teaspoon nutmeg
1/2 cup sugar
1 teaspoon soda
1 cup sour milk
1-1/2 cups chopped suet
2 eggs, well beaten
1 cup molasses or corn syrup
Grated rind and juice of 1 lemon
1 pound stoned, chopped and floured dates

Mix and sift the dry ingredients (excepting the soda, which should be beaten into the milk). Add the suet, then the well-beaten eggs, molasses and balance of ingredients. Steam 5 hours.

Fig Blanc Mange

5 tablespoons flour
1/2 teaspoon salt
1/2 cup sugar
1 quart milk
1 cup chopped figs
1/2 cup chopped nuts
1/2 cup shredded cocoanut
Grated rind of a lemon

Mix together thoroughly the flour, salt and sugar. Heat the milk in the double-boiler to the boiling point and stir in the above. Stir till perfectly smooth, then add the figs, nuts, cocoanut and lemon. Remove from the stove. Serve cold with whipped cream or any sauce.
Will serve about 8 or more.

Fig Pudding

3 tablespoons flour
1 teaspoon baking powder
1 cup sugar
1/4 teaspoon salt
1 cup chopped walnuts
1 cup chopped figs
2 eggs, beaten separately
1/2 teaspoon vanilla

Mix and sift the dry ingredients and stir in the nuts and figs. Add the beaten yolks of the eggs, then fold in the whites. Bake 1/2 hour in a moderate oven. Serve with Hard Sauce.
This serves 6

Steamed Fig Pudding

1/2 cup flour
1 cup graham flour
1 teaspoon soda
1-1/2 cups chopped figs
1-1/2 cups bread crumbs
1 cup molasses
1/2 cup sugar
1 egg
1 cup chopped beef suet
2 cups milk
1/4 teaspoon salt

Mix in the order given and steam 2-1/2 hours. Serve hot with cream and sugar.

Fruit Bread Pudding

2 cups bread crumbs
2 cups milk
2 cups water
2 beaten eggs
1/2 cup sugar
2 cups of any fruit
1 tablespoon melted butter
1/4 teaspoon salt
1/2 teaspoon grated nutmeg

Mix in the order given and bake in a buttered pudding dish in a moderate oven for 1 hour. Serve with cream and sugar or any sauce. Will serve 6

Graham Pudding

1-1/2 cups graham flour
1 teaspoon salt
1 teaspoon cinnamon
1 teaspoon nutmeg
1/4 teaspoon cloves
1/2 teaspoon soda
1/2 cup molasses
1 egg
1 cup milk
1 cup seedless raisins
1/4 cup butter

Mix together the flour, salt and spices. Beat the soda in the molasses. Beat the egg and add to the milk. Flour the raisins. Melt the butter. Beat all together and steam for 2 hours. This will serve about 8 or more.

Graham Delight Pudding

2 eggs
3/4 cup sugar
4 cups milk (or half water)
1 cup chopped nuts
1 cup seedless raisins or dates
1 2/3 cups graham flour
1 teaspoon salt
1/4 teaspoon nutmeg

Beat the eggs until very light and mix in the sugar; then add the liquid, nuts and raisins. Let come to a boil. Then add the flour, into which has been mixed the salt and nutmeg, and boil all 10 minutes. Stir frequently to avoid scorching. Pour into a shallow buttered pan and when cool cut into squares to resemble caramels. Arrange attractively on individual plates and serve with whipped cream.

Huckleberry Pudding

3/4 teaspoon soda
1 cup mild flavored molasses
3-1/4 cups flour
2 teaspoons baking powder
1/2 teaspoon salt
2 cups huckleberries
2/3 cup water

Beat the soda into the molasses, then add alternately the flour sifted with baking powder and salt and the huckleberries, beating well. Add the water, beat and turn into a buttered mold. Steam 2 hours. Serve hot with plain pudding sauce or with hard sauce.

Delicious Lemon Bread Pudding

1/4 cup melted butter
2 tablespoons flour
Grated rind of 1 lemon
1/8 teaspoon salt
1/4 cup sugar
2 eggs and 1 extra yolk
1 cup milk
2 cups bread crumbs, not very dry
1 cup warm water
1 tablespoon sugar
Few drops lemon extract

Mix the melted butter gradually with the flour, add lemon rind, salt and 1/4 cup sugar. Beat the 2 eggs and extra yolk, mix with the milk and stir into first mixture. Pour this over the crumbs which have been standing with the water poured over them. Bake in a moderate oven until set (about 40 minutes). Then beat the white of egg remaining with 1 tablespoon sugar and the lemon extract, spread on top, and return to the oven to brown delicately.

Nut and Raisin Bread Pudding

2 cups bread crumbs
2 cups milk
2 cups water
2 beaten eggs
1/2 cup sugar
2 tablespoons melted butter
1/4 teaspoon salt
1/2 teaspoon cinnamon
1/4 teaspoon nutmeg
1 cup raisins
1/2 cup nuts

Mix in the order given and bake in a buttered pudding dish in a moderate oven for an hour. Serve with Hard Sauce or cream and sugar.
Where strict economy is necessary, all water may be substituted instead of part milk, although the pudding will not, of course, contain so much nourishment. Also instead of using 2 whole eggs, use the yolks of 2 and the white of 1, reserving the other white for use in the Hard Sauce recipe.
Will serve 6

Individual Orange Pudding

1/4 cup butter
1/2 cup sugar
1 beaten egg
1/4 cup orange juice
1/4 cup water
Grated rind of 1/2 orange
1-1/2 cups flour
2-1/2 teaspoons baking powder

Cream the butter and sugar, add beaten egg, mix juice and water and add with rind. Mix and sift the flour and baking powder and add. Bake in buttered muffin pans in a moderate oven and serve hot with Orange Sauce.
Serves 8

Orange Sauce

1 cup sugar
1/4 cup flour
Grated rind of an orange
1/4 teaspoon salt
1/2 cup orange juice
1 cup water

Mix the dry ingredients thoroughly, add the liquid and boil, stirring constantly, until thickened.

Pineapple Meringue Pudding

3 tablespoons corn starch
1/3 cup cold milk
2-2/3 cups scalded milk
2 egg yolks
1/3 cup sugar
1/2 teaspoon salt
1-1/2 cups grated pineapple
1 tablespoon lemon juice

Mix corn starch with cold milk to make a smooth paste. Add slowly to scalded milk in double boiler, stirring constantly until mixture thickens. Cook 15 minutes. Beat egg yolks slightly; add sugar and salt. Stir slowly into first mixture and cook 5 minutes. Cool slightly; add pineapple and lemon juice and pour into mould dipped in cold water, or in serving dishes. Top with meringue and serve very cold.

Spiced Prune Pudding

1/2 pound prunes
3 cups cold water
1 cup sugar
1/4 teaspoon salt
3/4 teaspoon cinnamon
1/4 cup corn starch
1 tablespoon lemon juice
Sweetened cream

Wash prunes, soak in cold water 1/2 to 1 hour and cook in same water until soft; then cut in half and remove pits. Measure the liquid, adding boiling water to make 3 cups. Place in double boiler. Add prunes, sugar, salt and cinnamon. Cook 10 minutes. Mix corn starch with enough cold water to make smooth paste and stir slowly into prune mixture. Cook stirring constantly until it thickens, then cook 15 minutes longer. Add lemon juice, pour into mould dipped in cold water or glasses and chill. Serve with sweetened cream.

Peach Dumplings

2 cups fresh or sliced canned peaches
1 cup water
1/4 cup sugar
2 tablespoons butter
2 cups flour
3 teaspoons baking powder
1/4 teaspoon salt
1/4 cup sugar
1 cup milk

Bring 1 cup of the peaches and the water, sugar and butter to a boil slowly. Mix and sift the dry ingredients, add the milk and the remaining peaches. When liquid mixture is boiling, drop in the dumplings by spoonfuls, cover closely and cook 20 minutes without lifting cover. Serve with sugar and a piece of butter on each.

Peach Puffs

2 eggs, beaten separately
1 scant cup sliced ripe peaches
1/3 cup milk
1-1/2 cups flour
2 teaspoons baking powder
1/2 teaspoon salt
1/4 teaspoon vanilla
1 tablespoon melted butter
1 tablespoon sugar
Powdered sugar

Beat the yolks of the eggs until very thick and add the fruit. Beat thoroughly and then add alternately the milk, together with the flour, into which has been sifted the baking powder and salt. Beat the whites of the eggs to a stiff froth and add the vanilla. Fold this into the mixture until blended. Drop from a tablespoon into hot lard and fry as you would doughnuts. Drain on brown paper and roll in powdered sugar. Serve immediately.
Sufficient for 6

Peach Sandwich Pudding

1/4 cup shortening
1/3 cup sugar
1 beaten egg
1-1/2 cups flour
1-1/2 teaspoon baking powder
1/4 teaspoon salt
1/2 cup milk
Canned or fresh sliced peaches

Cream the shortening and sugar, add the egg, mix and sift the dry ingredients and add alternately with the milk. Beat well. Put a spoonful of the batter in a buttered muffin tin, add sliced peaches sprinkled with a little sugar (if fresh peaches be used), add another spoonful of batter and bake in a moderate oven for about 25 to 30 minutes. Serve hot with following sauce:

Sauce:
2 tablespoons flour
4 tablespoons sugar
Grated rind of a lemon or orange
1/8 teaspoon salt
1 cup liquid (using peach juice, juice of an orange or lemon and water to fill cup)
1 tablespoon butter

Mix dry ingredients thoroughly, add liquid and cook, stirring constantly until thick. Add butter and serve hot.

Puzzle Pudding

1-1/2 cups sugar
2 tablespoons flour
1 cup prunes, figs or dates, chopped fine
1 cup walnut meats, chopped
Whites of 4 eggs

Mix together the sugar and flour and add to the mixed fruit and nut meats. Beat the whites of the eggs to a stiff froth and fold in. Bake in a slow oven for 35 to 40 minutes. Serve either hot or cold with cream.

Poor Man's Pudding

1/2 cup chopped suet
1/2 cup seeded raisins
1/2 cup currants
1-1/2 cups grated bread
1 cup flour
2 teaspoons baking powder
1/2 cup brown sugar
2 cups milk

Mix ingredients in order given; beat well. Put into greased mold; place in covered saucepan with boiling water half way up sides of mold. Steam 2 hours. Turn out carefully. Serve with hard or other sauce.

Hard Sauce

1/3 cup butter
1 cup powdered sugar
1/2 teaspoon flavoring extract

Cream butter until very light; add sugar very slowly, beating until light and creamy. Add flavoring and beat again.

Christmas Plum Pudding #1

2-1/4 cups flour
1 teaspoon cinnamon
1 teaspoon cloves
1 teaspoon nutmeg
1 cup currants or seedless raisins
1 cup seeded raisins, split
1 cup suet, chopped fine
1 cup molasses
1 teaspoon soda, dissolved in
1/4 cup boiling water

Mix and sift the flour and spices. Flour the fruit. Mix together in the order given. Steam 3-1/2 hours and bake 1/2 hour.

Christmas Plum Pudding #2

1/2 pound shortening
1/2 pound sugar
6 eggs, beaten separately
1 cup milk
1/2 cup grape, loganberry or cherry juice
5 cups flour
1/2 tablespoon cloves
1/4 teaspoon mace
2 teaspoons grated nutmeg
1/4 pound chopped citron
1 pound seedless raisins
1 pound seeded raisins
1/2 pound suet, chopped fine

Cream the butter and sugar; add the yolks of the eggs well beaten; then the milk and juice alternately with the flour, into which has been sifted the spices. Dredge the fruit and add, then fold in the whites of the eggs.
This can be either steamed for 2-1/2 hours or put into a closed can or bag and boiled 2-1/2 hours. Serve hot with sauce.

Mock Plum Pudding

1/2 cup shortening
1 cup sugar
1 cup flour
1 teaspoon soda
1 teaspoon cinnamon
1 teaspoon nutmeg

1 teaspoon salt
1/2 teaspoon cloves
1 cup grated carrots
1 cup grated potatoes
1 cup seedless raisins
1/2 cup seeded raisins

Cream the shortening and sugar, mix and sift all the dry ingredients. Stir everything together and steam 4 hours. Serve with lemon or Hard Sauce.

Snowballs

1-1/4 cups flour
1/4 teaspoon salt
1/2 teaspoon grated nutmeg
1 teaspoon baking powder
1 cup sugar
Grated rind of a lemon
2 eggs
4 tablespoons milk
Pulverized sugar
Fruit sauce

Sift together the dry ingredients. Beat the yolks of the eggs until light and add to the milk. Beat into the first mixture, and lastly fold in the stiffly-beaten whites. Fill well-buttered cups half full and steam for 30 minutes. Roll in pulverized sugar and serve with fruit sauce.
This will serve about 6

Tapioca Pudding

1/2 cup pearl tapioca or 3 tablespoons minute tapioca
1 quart milk
1 teaspoon melted butter
6 tablespoons sugar
1/4 teaspoon salt
2 eggs
1 teaspoon vanilla or lemon extract

Soak tapioca in cold water one hour; drain; add milk and butter, and cook in double boiler until tapioca is transparent. Add sugar and salt to beaten eggs and combine by pouring hot mixture slowly on eggs. Return to double boiler and cook until thick. Add flavoring and serve hot or cold with cream.

PUDDING SAUCES:

Hard Sauce

1/3 cup butter
1 cup powdered sugar
1/2 teaspoon flavoring extract

Cream butter until very light; add sugar very slowly, beating until light and creamy. Add flavoring and beat again.

Foamy Sauce

6 tablespoons butter
1 cup powdered sugar
3 eggs
1 teaspoon vanilla extract
2 tablespoons boiling water

Cream butter; add sugar slowly, beating continually; beat egg yolks until thick and add gradually; beat well; add stiffly-beaten egg whites, flavoring and water. Before serving heat over boiling water 5 minutes, stirring constantly.

Chocolate Sauce

1 ounce unsweetened chocolate
2 tablespoons butter
1/2 cup boiling water
1/2 cup sugar
1/2 teaspoon vanilla extract
Few grains salt

Melt chocolate in top of double boiler. Add butter and when mixed pour water on slowly, stirring constantly, then add sugar. Bring to boiling point and boil 5 minutes without stirring; add vanilla and salt and serve hot.

Maple Sauce

1 cup sugar
1 cup water
1 teaspoon corn starch
1 tablespoon lemon juice
1 tablespoon maple flavoring

Heat half the sugar in frying pan; stir continually; when brown add water and boil; add remainder of sugar, corn starch mixed with a little cold water, lemon juice and maple flavoring; boil 3 minutes. Serve hot.

Lemon or Orange Sauce

1 cup water
2 tablespoons sugar
1 teaspoon corn starch

2 tablespoons lemon or orange juice

Boil water, sugar and corn starch mixed with little cold water. Boil 5 minutes and add fruit juice and 1 tablespoon caramel if dark color is desired.

Fruit Sauce

1/3 cup butter
1 cup powdered sugar
White of 1 egg
1 cup fresh strawberries or raspberries

Cream butter; add sugar gradually; add egg beaten until stiff and beat well; add slowly fruit which has been carefully prepared and mashed. Beat until creamy.

Caramel Sauce

2 cups granulated sugar
5 cups boiling water

Melt sugar in saucepan and heat, stirring constantly until golden brown; add boiling water. Cook 3 minutes.

Baked Custard

1/2 cup sugar
6 tablespoons flour
6 eggs
1 quart milk (scalded)
Pinch of salt
1 teaspoon flavoring
1 tablespoon butter

Mix the sugar and flour. Beat the eggs slightly and stir them into the flour and sugar. When smooth, stir into the hot milk; add salt. As soon as the sugar is dissolved, pour into custard cups or into a baking dish, and set in a pan of hot water. Bake in a moderate oven until a silver knife may be inserted and withdrawn clean. Do not allow the water in the pan to boil or the custard will separate.

Boiled Custard

1 pint scalded milk
4 eggs (beaten separately)
4 tablespoons flour
6 tablespoons sugar
1/8 teaspoon salt
1/2 teaspoon vanilla

Heat the milk. Beat the egg yolks until thick. Mix the flour, sugar and salt and stir into the egg yolks, beating smooth. Then pour this slowly, stirring constantly, into the hot milk and cook until thick. Have ready the egg whites eaten very stiff and pour the cooked custard slowly over them. Flavor and chill.

Caramel Custard

1/2 cup sugar, caramelized
1 pint hot milk
3 tablespoons flour
1/4 cup cold milk
2 eggs
Pinch of salt

To caramelize the sugar, put in skillet and stir briskly over the fire until entirely melted and golden brown. It will first lump before melting. Turn this into the hot milk in the double-boiler. Blend the flour with the cold milk and stir into the hot mixture, stirring until it begins to thicken and the caramel is well blended with the milk. Beat the eggs and gradually pour the hot mixture over them, pouring very slowly so they will not cook in lumps. Butter a baking dish and pour in the custard. Set in a pan containing hot water and place in oven to bake slowly until set, or until a knife inserted may be withdrawn clean. It will require from 25 to 40 minutes. Serve hot or cold with cream and sugar, or cold with sweetened and flavored whipped cream.

Apple Trifle

Apples (enough to make 2 cups after cooked and strained)
1/4 cup water
1 lemon, juice and grated rind
2 tablespoons butter
1/2 teaspoon vanilla
Sugar to taste

Pare, core and cut the apples and stew until soft with the water, lemon juice and rind. Mash through a colander and measure 2 cups. Add the butter and vanilla, and sweeten to taste. Let stand while preparing the custard.

Custard:
1 pint milk
1/4 cup flour (unsifted)
1/2 cup sugar
4 egg yolks
4 egg whites
2 tablespoons sugar

Heat the milk. Mix together the flour and sugar, and stir in the egg yolks beaten thick. Pour this slowly into the hot milk and

stir briskly. Cook until it thickens. Beat the egg whites very stiff and divide into 2 parts. Pour the custard mixture slowly over half of them, stirring briskly; then stir in the apple mixture. Sweeten the remaining egg whites with 2 tablespoons sugar and spread on top. Set in the oven to brown slightly.
This is excellent served hot with Custard Pudding Sauce or cold with whipped cream.

Almond Custard

3 cups milk
1 cup cream (all milk will answer)
1/3 cup flour (unsifted)
1-1/4 cups sugar
5 eggs, beaten separately
3/4 teaspoon salt
Grated rind of 1 lemon
1/4 pound macaroons (these may be omitted if preferred)
1 cup minced almonds
1 teaspoon almond extract

Heat the milk and cream. Mix the flour and sugar and add the egg yolks beaten thick. Stir till smooth, then pour gradually into the hot liquid, stirring constantly. Add salt and lemon rind. Cook over hot water stirring constantly until thick. Arrange the macaroons in a glass dish and when the custard is cool, pour over them. Pile whipped cream on top.

Blanc Mange

Excellent for a sick person

1 pint milk
1/3 cup flour (unsifted)
1/3 cup sugar
Pinch salt
1 teaspoon vanilla
2 egg whites

Heat the milk. Mix thoroughly the flour, sugar and salt and stir into the hot milk. Cook, stirring constantly, until very thick. Remove from fire and partially cool, then add vanilla. Beat egg whites stiff and dry and gradually pour the mixture over them, stirring briskly. Serve cold. It is attractively served with a spoonful of jelly, marmalade, or a maraschino cherry on top.

Chocolate Blanc Mange

Blanc Mange
1/2 square unsweetened chocolate
4 tablespoons hot water

Follow the recipe for Blanc Mange. When done, divide into 2 parts. Melt chocolate and add hot water. Stir constantly until thick and glossy, then pour this into half of the Blanc Mange. Serve in individual glasses. Put a spoonful of the white mixture in the bottom and a spoonful of the chocolate on top. Decorate with blanched almonds, and if desired put a small spoonful of whipped cream in the center.

Butterscotch Custard

1/2 cup brown sugar
1/4 cup flour
1 tablespoon cornstarch
1/4 teaspoon salt
3 eggs, beaten together
1 pint milk
2 tablespoons granulated sugar
2 tablespoons butter

Mix together thoroughly the brown sugar, flour, cornstarch and salt. Beat the eggs and mix in them half of the milk. Mix the other half of the milk with first mixture, and carefully combine. Heat in double-boiler. Put granulated sugar in an iron skillet and melt, stirring constantly. It will first lump, then melt. When very brown, add this to the hot mixture. Cook, stirring constantly, until thick, adding the butter shortly before removing from the fire. Use no vanilla or other flavoring or you will detract from the "butterscotch" flavor. Chill and serve, plain or with whipped cream.

Dainty Chocolate Dessert

1/4 cup flour
2 tablespoons cornstarch
1/2 cup sugar (more if desired very sweet)
2 eggs, beaten separately
2 cups milk
2 ounces unsweetened or 2-1/2 ounces sweetened chocolate
1 teaspoon vanilla

Mix together thoroughly the flour, cornstarch and sugar, then the beaten egg yolks and gradually the milk. If powdered chocolate be used, add. If cake chocolate, first shave fine or melt and then add. Cook in double-boiler, stirring almost constantly, until thick. Then add vanilla and cool slightly. Beat the egg whites until stiff and pour slowly over them the slightly cooled mixture. Chill. Serve with cream and sugar or with 1/4 pint of cream whipped and sweetened with 1 tablespoon sugar and 1/2 teaspoon vanilla.

Charlotte Russe

Serve with Sponge Cake

2 level tablespoons granulated gelatine
1/4 cup water
1/3 cup powdered sugar
1 pint whipping cream
1 teaspoon vanilla
2 egg whites (or omit; see directions)

Soak the gelatine in the water 5 minutes and dissolve by holding over hot water. Stir in the sugar and cream beaten stiff with flavoring. When it begins to set fold in the stiffly-beaten egg whites and turn into mold first rinsed in cold water. Serve on slices of sponge cake. If desired, 1 egg white may be used, or eggs may be omitted, but they increase the quantity, do not alter the flavor and when eggs are expensive, are an economy.

Custard Charlotte with Sponge Cake

1 cup sugar
1/3 cup flour
1/8 teaspoon salt
2 tablespoons cornstarch
2 eggs, slightly beaten
2 cups milk
1 teaspoon vanilla
1/2 pint whipping cream (1 pint may be used)

Mix together the first 4 ingredients thoroughly, then add the beaten eggs, milk and vanilla and cook in a double-boiler until thick. Chill. When cold, beat with an egg beater, and fold in the cream whipped stiff. Serve on slices of sponge cake or hollow out a sponge cake, filling the shell with the mixture.

Cocoanut Cream Souffle

5 tablespoons flour (unsifted), dissolved in
4 tablespoons milk
1 cup milk
Pinch salt
3 tablespoons butter
4 eggs, beaten separately
1/4 cup sugar
1/2 square unsweetened chocolate or 2 tablespoons powdered cocoa or chocolate
1/4 cup boiling water
1 cup shredded cocoanut
1 teaspoon vanilla

Put the flour and the 4 tablespoons of milk in a cup and stir until very smooth, then pour into the balance of the milk. Add salt and cook, stirring constantly until very thick. Add butter. Beat egg yolks thick and add them to the sugar, then pour the hot mixture slowly over them, beating vigorously. Let cool. Melt the chocolate and add to it 1/4 cup of boiling water and cook, stirring constantly, until smooth and glossy. Pour into the mixture, add cocoanut and vanilla and then fold in the stiffly-beaten whites. Turn into a buttered pudding dish and bake in a moderate oven until firm. It will require about 35 minutes. It should be served immediately upon taking from the oven or it will fall. It is also necessary to avoid draughts with all souffles when taking from the oven.

Coffee Custard

1 cup milk
2 cups strong coffee
1/4 cup flour (unsifted)
3/4 cup brown sugar
4 eggs, beaten separately
Pinch of salt
2 tablespoons sugar

Heat the milk and coffee. Mix together the flour and sugar and add to them the egg yolks beaten thick and the salt. Pour this into the hot liquid, stirring briskly. Beat the egg whites stiff and divide in 2 parts. Remove the hot custard from the fire and pour slowly, beating constantly, into half the egg whites. Turn into a buttered pudding mold, set in a pan of warm water and bake in a moderate oven until, when a knife is inserted it can be drawn out clean. Add 2 tablespoons sugar to the remaining egg whites, spread on top of the custard and brown slightly. Serve either hot or cold with cream and sugar.

Fruit Whip

Any fruit pulp will answer; prunes, peaches, apricots or apples are especially good.

1 cup fruit pulp sweetened to taste
4 tablespoons flour (unsifted)
3 tablespoons sugar (additional)
1/2 teaspoon salt
2 eggs, beaten separately
1 cup milk
1-1/2 teaspoons lemon juice

Canned, fresh or dried fruit may be used. If dried fruit, it should first be soaked several hours with sugar and enough cold water to cover, then cook slowly (using the water in which it was soaked) until very soft. Press the fruit through a colander. There should be 1 cup of pulp. Sweeten to taste. Mix flour, sugar and salt. Beat the egg yolks and add. Add milk slowly and stir till very smooth, then cook, stirring constantly, until thick and creamy. Have ready the egg whites beaten stiff and dry, and pour this hot mixture slowly over them, stirring briskly. Stir in the fruit pulp and lemon juice and cool. Serve very cold either with whipped cream or with Custard Sauce.

Orange Cream

2 egg yolks
1/3 cup flour (unsifted)
1 cup sugar
1/2 cup orange juice
1/2 pint heavy cream

Beat the egg yolks until thick. Mix flour and sugar and add to the yolks, stirring until smooth. Add the orange juice and let cook until thick. Cool. Whip the cream and divide into 2 parts. Pour the custard mixture into half, beating until well mixed. Sweeten the other half of the cream. Pour the custard mixture into a glass dish and heap the balance of the whipped cream on top. Decorate with orange sections.

Sliced Oranges with Orange Cream

2 egg yolks
1/2 cup orange juice
3 tablespoons flour (unsifted)
1 cup sugar
1 rounding tablespoon butter
2 egg whites
Sliced oranges
Sugar

Beat the egg yolks until thick, add orange juice. Mix flour and sugar and add to the yolks, stirring until smooth. Add the butter and cook until slightly thickened. Have ready the egg whites beaten stiff and pour the hot mixture slowly onto them, stirring until smooth. Cool, and serve in individual dishes poured over sliced oranges which have been sprinkled with sugar.

Peach Souffle

Sliced peaches (fresh, canned or stewed)
Sugar
1 cup scalded milk
3 tablespoons butter
1/4 cup flour (unsifted)
1/2 cup sugar (additional)
2 eggs, beaten separately

Into the bottom of an earthenware pudding dish put a layer of sliced peaches about an inch deep. Sprinkle with sugar.
Heat the milk and put in the butter. Mix the flour and sugar. Beat the egg yolks until thick and add, stirring until smooth and pour slowly into the hot milk, stirring briskly. Remove from the fire, and pour slowly, while constantly folding, over the stiffly-beaten egg whites. Pour over the peaches and bake in a moderate oven 35 to 40 minutes. Avoid draughts when taking from the oven and serve immediately or it will fall. Excellent served with Foamy Sauce #2.

Pineapple and Banana Dainty

4 ripe bananas
1/2 cup pineapple, cut in small pieces
2 egg whites beaten stiff
2 cups hot milk
1/3 cup flour (unsifted)
1/2 cup sugar
Pinch salt
4 egg yolks
1/2 teaspoon vanilla

Mash the bananas, mix in the pineapple. Beat the 2 egg whites very stiff and fold in. Heat the milk. Mix together the flour, sugar and salt. Beat the egg yolks very thick and stir in the flour and sugar mixture. Pour this gradually, stirring briskly, into the hot milk and cook, stirring constantly, until it thickens. Serve in a glass dish or individual glass dishes. Put a spoonful of the fruit mixture in, cover with a little of the custard and put another spoonful of the fruit on top. Decorate with a maraschino cherry or with a bit of pineapple. Serve very cold.

Cheese Souffle

3 tablespoons melted butter
1/4 cup flour (scant)
1/3 cup milk
1/2 teaspoon salt
1/8 teaspoon cayenne
Pinch of grated nutmeg
1/3 cup grated cheese
3 eggs

Melt the butter and stir in the flour until well blended, then add the milk gradually and stir and cook until smooth and thick (about 2 minutes). Add the salt, pepper and cheese. Remove from the stove and add the yolks of the eggs, which have been beaten until thick and lemon colored. Cool and then fold in the whites beaten to a stiff froth. Pour into a well-buttered baking dish and cook for 20 to 25 minutes in a rather slow oven. Serve immediately and be careful to avoid draughts in taking it to the table, lest it fall.
This will serve 4 or 5

Cherry Surprises

Can be made with fresh or canned pie cherries

1-1/2 cups cooked cherries, sweetened to taste
1-1/2 cups flour
2 level teaspoons baking powder
1/8 teaspoon salt
2 tablespoons sugar
1/4 cup shortening
5 tablespoons cold water

If fresh cherries are to be used, stone, cover with water and add sufficient sugar to sweeten to taste, amount depending entirely upon sourness of cherries. Mix and sift the flour, baking powder, salt and sugar. Work in the shortening as for biscuits. Add the cold water and roll very thin on a well floured board. Cut into 4-inch squares. Have the sweetened cherries drained and cold. Put a spoonful on each square and fold over to form a triangle, or 3-cornered turnover. Press the edges together and drop into deep, hot fat and fry as you would doughnuts. Drain on heavy unglazed paper and roll in powdered sugar. If preferred, they may be baked as ordinary turnovers and served with Cherry Sauce.

15

GELATIN

For years, Gelatin has been esteemed for deliciousness, sparkling beauty, economy and ease of preparation. But not until recently have its *healthful* qualities been understood.

Scientific experiments have now proved that Gelatin is a body-building, energizing food of real value—*and a food that requires very little digestive effort.* Think how important this is! So many desserts tax digestion severely; but the important nourishment that Gelatin contains is given to the body quickly, easily and completely. A Gelatin dessert is not merely a delicacy. It is a real benefit to health.

For Dissolving Gelatin:
Do not use more than 1 pint of water or fruit juice, or liquid of any kind, for each package of Gelatin used.

For Cooling:
Gelatin may be cooled quickly by dissolving a package in 1/2 pint of boiling water and then adding 1/2 pint of ice water and setting it in cracked ice.

If Too Hard:
If Gelatin should harden before you are ready to mold it, soften by setting the pan or bowl containing it in hot water.

For Layered Gelatin:
In making Gelatin in layers, let each layer harden before adding another, and be sure the Gelatin poured upon any hardened layer is so cool it will not soften the layer.

To Remove Gelatin From the Mold:
To remove Gelatin from the mold, fill with warm water in a pan large enough to admit the whole mold and dip the mold to the edge. Place a plate over the mold and turn them over together, with a little shake added. If this does not loosen the Gelatin dip a second time.

To Whip Gelatin:
To whip Gelatin successfully, use a Ladd or Dover egg-beater and a dish rather deep but not large. When Gelatin has become cold and is still liquid set the dish in a pan of ice water or very cold water and whip until Gelatin is of consistency of whipped cream or until it will drop from a spoon in a lump-like mass.

To Add Fruit to Gelatin:
To place fruit in layers in Gelatin, pour a little Gelatin in the bottom of the mold and let it harden. On this arrange fruit as desired and add carefully enough cold liquid Gelatin to hold the fruit in place but not to cover it. When this Gelatin has hardened add more cold liquid Gelatin. This process can be repeated until the mold is full. Do not fold fruit or nutmeats into Gelatin until it has congealed sufficiently to hold them in place and prevent their rising to the top. In mixing whipped cream or eggs with Gelatin do not fold it in until the jelly has begun to thicken and is like a heavy syrup in consistency.

Strawberry Gelatin

Dissolve a Gelatin in a pint of boiling water. Pour into mold and pack in ice or stand in a cold place. When set, turn out on a plate and serve plain or garnished with fruits or whipped cream.

Strawberry Loaf

Dissolve a package of Strawberry Gelatin in a pint of boiling water. When cool whip the Gelatin and fold in one cup of whipped cream, one pint of fresh strawberries halved, and a dozen diced marshmallows. Mold. Serve in slices.

Cherry Gelatin

Dissolve a package of Cherry Gelatin in a pint of boiling water. Pour into mold and pack in ice or stand in a cold place. Unmold and serve plain or garnished with fruits or whipped cream.

Gelatin Fruit Cocktail

Cut baskets out of oranges. Save the pulp and juice. Add 1/2 cup canned pineapple cut in cubes, 1/2 cup white grapes cut in half and seeded, 1/2 cup maraschino cherries and 1/2 cup sugar. Dissolve a package of Lemon or Orange Gelatin in a half pint of boiling water, and add the juice from the fruit in the baskets, pour the Gelatin over it, and set in a cold place to harden. Serve with a fruit salad dressing. Gelatin fruit cocktails and salads can be made of any fruit except uncooked pineapple and may be served beautifully in sherbet glasses.

Cocoanut Orange Gelatin

Dissolve a package of Orange Gelatin in 1/2 pint of boiling water. Add the grated rind of an orange and 1/2 cup sugar. Cut the pulp of the orange in small pieces and cover with sugar. Drain, add enough cold water to the juice to make 1/2 pint and stir into the dissolved Gelatin. Strain the liquid into individual molds, add a few pieces of orange pulp, sprinkle with cocoanut and let cool. When set add more Gelatin, orange pulp and cocoanut, continuing the process until the molds are full. Serve on flat glass dishes with sweetened whipped cream.

Neapolitan Gelatin

Dissolve a package of Lemon Gelatin in a pint of boiling water. Pour 2/3 of it into a properly shaped mold and when it has set whip the rest, pour it on and let it harden. Dissolve a package of Strawberry or Raspberry Gelatin in a pint of boiling water and when it is cold put 2/3 of it, a spoonful at a time, on the Lemon Gelatin. For the fourth layer whip the rest of the Strawberry or Raspberry Gelatin and pour it on the hardened plain layer. For a three-layer piece whip half the Gelatin from a package, any flavor except Chocolate, making two layers of it, with a layer of the unwhipped Gelatin between them.

Cherry Salad

Dissolve a package of Cherry Gelatin in a pint of boiling water. As it begins to thicken add 2 tablespoons candied ginger cut fine, 1 cup white cherries and 1 cup cooked pineapple cut small. Set to harden. Serve with fruit salad dressing.

Macaroni Salad

Dissolve a package of Lemon Gelatin in a pint of boiling water. When it begins to thicken add 1 cup macaroni cooked and cut fine, 1/2 cup shredded cabbage, 1/2 green pepper shredded, 1/2 cup celery and 1/4 teaspoon salt. Mold and serve as a salad with mayonnaise. If convenient, garnish with rings of stuffed olives.

Gelatin Charlotte Russe

Make a custard of 3 egg yolks beaten slightly, 2 cups of milk, and 1/3 cup of sugar. Cook until thickened. Dissolve 1/2 package of Lemon Gelatin in 1/2 cup of boiling water and add to the custard. Whip and fold in 1/2 pint of whipped cream. Serve with lady-fingers.

Apple Sauce Molded in Gelatin

Cook 6 tart apples until very tender in 1 pint of boiling water. Add 1/2 cup of sugar and while still boiling hot, stir in 1 package of Raspberry or other fruit flavor of Gelatin. Beat thoroughly to remove all lumps, or put through a strainer. Set in a cold place to congeal and serve with sweetened cream either plain or whipped. Very nice for children.

Pineapple Bavarian Cream

Dissolve a package of Lemon Gelatin in 1/2 point of boiling water. Cool slightly and add 1/2 pint of juice from a can of pineapple. When cold and beginning to thicken whip until it will drop from a spoon in a lump-like mass and quickly fold in 1 cup of crushed pineapple. Add 2 cups whipped and sweetened cream. Pour into mold and set in a cold place to harden. Turn from the mold and garnish with sliced pineapple and cherries or grapes, or pile lightly in stem glasses and garnish with cherry rings or pineapple.

Cream Fig Pudding

Dissolve a package of Lemon Gelatin in a pint of boiling water. When cold and beginning to thicken whip to the consistency of whipped cream. Then add 1 cup of whipped cream and 1 cup of chopped figs cooked to a jam. Serve in sherbet glasses or turn from a mold.

Health Salad

Dissolve a package of Lemon Gelatin in 1 cup of boiling water and add 1 cup of juice from a can of crushed pineapple. Cook and add 1 cup of the crushed pineapple, one cup raw carrot, 1/4 cup sugar, 1 teaspoon salt. Serve on lettuce with salad dressing.

Lemon Gelatin

Dissolve a package of Lemon Gelatin in a pint of boiling water. Pour into mold and pack in ice or stand in a cold place. When set turn out on a plate and serve plain or garnished with fruits and whipped cream.

Imperial Salad

Drain juice from 1/2 can pineapple, add 1 tablespoon of vinegar and enough water to make a pint. Heat to boiling point and dissolve in it 1 package of Lemon Gelatin. Just as Gelatin begins to set add 3 slices of canned pineapple diced, 1/2 can

Spanish pimentos shredded, and 1 medium-sized cucumber salted and cut fine. Mold in individual molds or in one large mold and slice. Serve with cream salad dressing.

Coffee Gelatin

Dissolve a package of Lemon Gelatin in a pint of strong coffee while it is still at boiling point. While still hot add 4 tablespoons sugar. Set away to harden. As it begins to thicken fold in 1 cup of cream that has been whipped. Serve garnished with sweetened whipped cream.

Raspberry Gelatin

Dissolve a package of Raspberry Gelatin in a pint of boiling water. Pour into mold and pack in ice or stand in a cold place. When set turn out on a plate and serve plain or garnished with fruits or whipped cream. Plain desserts of Strawberry, Cherry, Orange, and Lemon Gelatin are made and served in the same way. Plain Chocolate Gelatin should be made with hot milk.

Cottage Cheese Salad

Drain the juice from a 1-quart can of crushed pineapple, add enough water to the juice to make 1 quart, heat to boiling point and dissolve 2 packages of Lemon Gelatin in it. When it begins to thicken fold in the crushed pineapple and 2 cups of fresh cottage cheese. Mix thoroughly and mold. Fresh pineapple should not be used.
This will make 16 generous portions.

Raspberry Bavarian Cream

Sprinkle 1/2 cup sugar over a pint of fresh raspberries and let stand a few minutes. Dissolve a package of Raspberry Gelatin in a little less than a pint of boiling water, then add juice from raspberries to make 1 pint liquid. When cold and beginning to thicken whip until it will drop from a spoon in a lump-like mass. Fold in 1 cup of cream, whipped and sweetened, and the berries. Canned raspberries may be used by draining the juice from them and adding water to make 1 pint of liquid.

Gelatin Horseradish Relish

Dissolve a package of Lemon Gelatin in a scant pint of boiling water and 2 tablespoons vinegar. Add 1 pimento, 1/2 green pepper cut fine, and 1/2 cup grated horseradish. As it begins to thicken mold in sweet green peppers, and when set cut in slices. Serve with meat or fish.

Spanish Gelatin Salad

Dissolve a package of Lemon Gelatin in a pint of boiling water and 1 tablespoon of vinegar. Mix lightly 1 cup of finely shredded cabbage, 1 cup chopped celery, 1/2 cup chopped pickle and about 1/3 of a small can of pimentos. Season with salt. Mold in teacups or individual Gelatin molds. Serve on crisp lettuce leaves with mayonnaise dressing.

Paradise Pudding

Take 1/4 pound blanched almonds, 1 dozen marshmallows, 1 dozen maraschino cherries, 1/2 dozen macaroons. Cut these fine and set aside in a cool place. Dissolve a package of Lemon Gelatin in a pint of boiling water and when cold set the dish in cold (or ice) water and whip to consistency of whipped cream. Then fold in 1 cup of whipped cream, the cut fruit, nutmeats, etc., and 1/2 cup of sugar. Turn into an oblong cake tin and set in a cold place to harden. Serve in slices. Dip the knife in hot water before slicing.

Orange Gelatin

Dissolve a package of Orange Gelatin in a pint of boiling water. Pour a little of the Gelatin into the mold. When it has cooled lay in sliced oranges, add a little cool Gelatin and let it harden. Then add another layer of oranges and more Gelatin until the mold is full. Serve plain or with whipped cream.

Mint Gelatin

To 1-3/4 cups water add 1/4 cup weak vinegar and 2 tablespoons sugar. Let come to boiling point; add 1/4 cup finely chopped fresh mint leaves and boil 1 minute. Add a little Burnett's green for deeper color. Strain through a fine cloth and dissolve one package of Lemon Gelatin in the hot liquid. Delicious with lamb.

Gelatin Fruit Cup

Cut up any fruit in season, place in glasses and pour over it any flavor of Gelatin just as it begins to thicken. When hard, top with whipped cream and garnish; or, serve as a fruit salad with fruit salad dressing instead of whipped cream.

Cardinal Salad

Dissolve a package of Lemon Gelatin in one pint, less 1/2 cup, of boiling water and add 1/2 cup of juice of canned beets. When cool add 1 cup celery shredded, 1 cup beets diced, 1/2 cup Spanish onion chopped fine, 1 green pepper shredded, 1/4 teaspoon salt. Mold in individual molds, turn out on lettuce and serve with mayonnaise dressing. The onion may be omitted.

Nut Frappe

Dissolve a package of Gelatin, any flavor, in a pint of boiling water. Set aside to harden. Stir 4 tablespoons of sugar into 1/2 pint of whipped cream. When Gelatin is cold and beginning to thicken mix Gelatin and whipped cream by beating with a fork, and add 1 cup chopped nuts. Serve in sherbet glasses with fresh or preserved fruit, saving some of the nuts to use as a garnish.

Gelatin Macedoine

Dissolve a package of Gelatin, any flavor except Chocolate, in a pint of boiling water. While it is cooling chop fine such candied fruit—cherries, a pear, peach, apricot—as may be chosen for the purpose. As the jelly begins to thicken stir the candied fruit into it, mixing thoroughly. Top with whipped cream, a cherry and half a dozen nutmeats.

Peach Whip

Dissolve a package of Lemon Gelatin or Orange Gelatin in 1/2 pint of boiling water. When cold and still liquid add a 1/2 pint of peach juice and whip. Then fold in 1 cup of whipped cream and 1 cup of crushed and sweetened peaches from which the juice has been drained, and mold. Canned peaches are preferred for this fine dessert.

Gelatin with Fruit Juices

Dissolve a package of Strawberry, Raspberry or Cherry Gelatin in 1/2 pint of boiling water and add 1/2 pint of strawberry, raspberry or cherry juice, cold. Serve plain or garnished with whipped cream or custard sauce.

New Prune Dessert

Soak 1 pound of dried prunes (overnight if possible) in water to cover. Simmer over low heat until tender, adding 1 cup of sugar before removing from fire. Remove the pits from 1 cup of the prunes and drain off all juice from the pulp. Crack the pits and save the nutmeats. Over these pour boiling water to remove the rough husks, as in blanching almonds. Dissolve a package of Orange Gelatin in a pint of boiling water. When cool add the prune pulp and meats. Mold and serve with plain or whipped cream.

Spiced Jellied Peaches

Dissolve a package of Orange Gelatin in 1 cup of boiling water. Add 1 cup of juice from spiced peaches, or canned peach juice that has been spiced, and line the bottom of large or small molds. When firm arrange on this a cup of spiced or canned peaches cut fine, and add the remaining Gelatin, which should be cold and partly congealed. Set in a cold place to harden. Serve as a relish.

Cranberry Mold

Measure 1 pint of boiling water, remove 1/2 cup to allow for other liquids to be added, and dissolve a package of Lemon Gelatin in it. When it is cold and beginning to thicken add the juice of 1/2 of a lemon, 1/2 cup finely celery, 1/2 cup shredded pineapple, 1 cup thick cranberry sauce sweetened, and mold. Serve as a salad with cooked salad dressing. Garnish with a bit of whipped cream.

Plum Pudding

Dissolve a package of Lemon Gelatin in a pint of boiling water and while it is still hot stir in 3/4 cup Grape-Nuts, 3/4 cup seeded raisins, 3/4 cup English walnut meats, 3/4 cup cooked prunes and 1/4 cup citron—all cut fine; 1/2 teaspoon cinnamon, 1/4 teaspoon cloves. Salt to taste. Mix and let harden. Serve with whipped cream or pudding sauce.

Berry Frappe

Dissolve a package of Raspberry or Strawberry Gelatin in a pint of boiling water. Whip and pile in frappe glasses partly filled with crushed fresh raspberries or strawberries. A cup of whipped cream may be folded into the whipped Gelatin if desired. Use canned berries when the fresh fruit is out of season.

Salmon Salad

Measure 1 pint of boiling water, remove 2 tablespoons of it and use 2 tablespoons of lemon juice instead. Add 1/4 teaspoon of salt and dissolve a package of Lemon Gelatin in the hot liquid. Pour a little Gelatin in bottom of mold and pack in ice. When it begins to thicken press in 1 cup of red salmon and let this layer harden. Then add another layer of Gelatin and 1 cup of green peas. When again firm add the last layer of Gelatin and 1 cup of carrots, diced. Set away to harden for at least 2 hours. Serve garnished with greens, carrots and salad dressing.

Snow Pudding

Dissolve a package of Lemon Gelatin in a pint of boiling water. When cold and still liquid whip with an egg-beater to consistency of whipped cream. Let stand until firm and then pile by spoonfuls into sherbet glasses and serve with a custard flavored with the grated rind of fresh lemon or with the banana sauce described next.

Banana Sauce

Mash 1 banana, add 1/4 cup sugar and the juice of 1/2 lemon. Beat 1 egg, yolk and white, very stiff and add to it the banana mixture. This is particularly good with Snow Pudding, the golden sauce contrasting beautifully with the white dessert.

Cherry Almond Gelatin

Dissolve a package of Cherry Gelatin in a pint of boiling water. Pour half into a bowl or mold. Just as it begins to harden, drop in a row of blanched almonds or walnut meats. When hard pour in rest of Gelatin, add another row of almonds, and set away to harden. Gelatin of any of the other fruit flavors may be made up in the same way with other nutmeats.

Apple Snow Gelatin

Dissolve a package of Raspberry Gelatin in a pint of boiling water. When cool turn into sherbet glasses, filling them 3/4 full. When firm pile Apple Snow on top. For an Apple Snow that is particularly good with Gelatin if served immediately after being made, grate 1 large apple and fold in the beaten whites of 2 eggs and 4 tablespoons sugar.

Baked Apple De Luxe

Core 6 nice round apples (do not pare them); fill with sugar and small bits of butter, sprinkle cinnamon and nutmeg over them and bake until tender in a pan containing just enough to form a syrup with the juice from the apples as they bake. Whip Gelatin from 1 package, any flavor except Chocolate. Place apples in individual dishes and pour some of the syrup from the apples around each one. When slightly cool top each apple with the whipped Gelatin, piling it high.

Gelatin in Quartered Oranges

Dissolve a package of Gelatin, any flavor except Chocolate, in a pint of boiling water. Cut oranges in halves and scoop out all the pulp. Fill them with cool Gelatin. When hard, with a thin sharp knife that has been dipped in hot water, cut the halves in two, making quarters.

Chocolate Charlotte

1-1/2 teaspoons gelatine
2 tablespoons cold water
1 square bitter chocolate
1/2 cup sugar
1/2 cup water
1-1/2 cups condensed milk
1/2 teaspoon vanilla
6 lady fingers

Soak granulated gelatine in 2 tablespoons cold water for 5 minutes. Melt shaved chocolate in double boiler, add sugar, 1/2 cup water, and 1/2 cup condensed milk. Let cook 5 minutes or until smooth; pour over gelatine and stir until dissolved. When cool, add the vanilla. Whip 1 cup of condensed milk which has been chilled for a couple of hours, gradually add the chocolate and gelatine mixture and stir until it begins to thicken. When well thickened pour carefully into a mold which has been lined with lady fingers. Let stand in a cold place for an hour or more. When ready to serve turn out on a flat dish, cover with whipped cream, and garnish with maraschino cherries or nuts.
Serves 5

Macaroon Dessert

1-1/4 tablespoons gelatine
3/4 cup water
1-3/4 cup condensed milk
2 egg yolks, slightly beaten
1/4 cup sugar
1 teaspoon vanilla
9 macaroons, crumbled

Soak gelatine for 5 minutes in 1/4 cup water mixed with 1/4 cup of condensed milk. Scald 1/4 cup of condensed milk diluted with 1/2 cup water; pour over slightly-beaten egg yolks to which the sugar has been added; cook in a double boiler until the mixture thickens slightly (about 3 minute); pour over the gelatine and stir until dissolved. When cool, add the vanilla. Whip 1 cup of condensed milk which has been chilled for a couple of hours, gradually add the gelatine mixture and stir until it begins to thicken. Add the crumbled macaroons and

pour into a mold. Let stand in a cold place for an hour or more. When ready to serve turn out on a flat dish and garnish as desired.
Serves 5

Pineapple Bavarian Cream

1-1/4 teaspoons gelatine
1/4 cup cold water
1 cup grated pineapple and juice
1/2 cup sugar
1/8 teaspoon salt
3 tablespoons lemon juice
1 cup condensed milk

Soak gelatine in cold water for 5 minutes. Heat pineapple, sugar and salt; add the soaked gelatine and lemon juice. Set in a pan of cold water to cool. Whip the condensed milk which has been chilled for a couple of hours; as soon as the pineapple mixture begins to thicken add it to the whipped milk. Pour into a mold and chill.
Serves 5

Prune Cream

3/4 cup condensed milk
1-1/2 teaspoons lemon juice
3/4 cup powdered sugar
Few grains salt
1 cup chopped cooked prunes
1/4 teaspoon gelatine

Whip condensed milk. Add lemon juice, sugar, and few grains of salt to chopped cooked prunes. Fold the prune mixture into the whipped condensed milk.
Serves 5

Star-Spangled Snacks

1 package (4-serving size) Berry Flavor Gelatin
1 package (4-serving size) Gelatin, any red flavor
2 cups boiling water
1 cup cold water
2 cups whipped cream

Dissolve each package of gelatin completely in 1 cup boiling water in separate bowls. Stir 1/2 cup cold water into each bowl of gelatin.
Pour each mixture into separate 8-inch square pans. Refrigerate until firm, at least 3 hours.

Cut each pan into 1/2-inch cubes. Spoon the blue cubes evenly into 8 dessert dishes; cover with whipped topping. Top with red cubes.
Makes 8 servings

German Potato Salad

1/4 cup sugar
1 tablespoon flour
2 teaspoons salt
1/4 teaspoon pepper
1/4 cup vinegar
2/3 cup water
4 slices bacon, diced and browned
1/4 cup bacon drippings
4 cups cold, cooked, cubed potatoes
1 hard-boiled egg
2 tablespoons chopped onion
Sprig parsley

Combine sugar, flour, salt and pepper in the top of a double boiler. Stir in vinegar, water, bacon and bacon drippings. Cook, stirring constantly, about 5 minutes, or until thick. Place potatoes, onions, egg and parsley in a greased casserole or baking pan. Pour dressing over and mix to coat all. Heat in a 350° oven for 30 minutes. Serves 6 to 8.

16

SALADS & SALAD DRESSINGS

Salads are usually are made from either vegetables or fruits or combinations of both should be more commonly used. They should be cold, crisp, well mixed and attractively served with oil dressing, mayonnaise, or a boiled dressing. Salad plants include lettuce, romaine, endive, chicory, escarole, sorrel and water-cress, and vegetables such as onion, cabbage, celery, cucumber and tomatoes.

Potato Salad #1

2 cups freshly boiled potatoes
1 teaspoon salt
1/8 teaspoon pepper
Few drops onion juice
1 tablespoon finely minced parsley
About 3 tablespoons olive oil
1 tablespoon vinegar

Cut potatoes in 3/4 inch cubes. Add seasoning, then olive oil, only what the potatoes will absorb, then add vinegar and mix carefully until it is absorbed. Mound on a bed of lettuce in a shallow dish. Egg yolks make an attractive garnish if put through a ricer. Tomatoes cut in eighths added to potato salad make a pleasant variation.

Potato Salad #2

1 quart cold boiled potatoes
1 onion finely sliced
1/2 teaspoon salt
Chopped parsley
1/2 cup French dressing
Lettuce

Cut potatoes into slices or cubs; add onion; mix with salt, parsley and French dressing. Serve on lettuce leaves with boiled dressing.

Egg Salad

1. Cut the whites of hard-boiled eggs into eighths lengthwise, arrange on lettuce to simulate the petals of a flower. Put yolks through ricer and arrange in the center of whites. Serve with boiled dressing.
2. Cut eggs lengthwise in quarters and serve on lettuce with boiled dressing.
3. Chop whites finely and arrange on lettuce. Put yolk through ricer and mound in the center. Serve with boiled dressing.
4. Diced hard-boiled eggs and sliced cucumbers may be added to potatoes. Egg and fish combine very well with water-cress or escarole.

Deviled Eggs

Cut hard-cooked eggs crosswise or lengthwise, remove yolks, mix with vinegar and seasoning, or with boiled dressing. Refill yolks in the whites. Cold minced ham or chicken may be added to the yolks. French dressing may be used instead of vinegar.

Chicken Salad #1

Remove bones and gristle, fat and skin, from cold, cooked meat. Cut meat into 1/2 inch cubes and mix it with an equal amount of celery which has been scraped, chilled and cut in small pieces. Moisten with French dressing. Add mayonnaise dressing or boiled dressing to taste. Arrange on lettuce leaves; garnish with curled celery.
Veal, flaked fish, such as salmon, tuna, etc., may be mixed and used in the same way.

Chicken Salad #2

3 cups cold chicken, cut into pieces
1 cup celery, cut into small pieces
1 teaspoon salt
1/4 teaspoon pepper
1-1/2 cups mayonnaise
Lettuce
2 hard boiled eggs
Olives

Mix well chicken, celery, seasoning and 1/2 cup mayonnaise. Serve cold on lettuce; garnish with sliced egg and olives. Cover with mayonnaise, to which capers have been added if desired.

Cheese and Nut Salad

1 cup cheese
1/2 cup sweet cream
1 tablespoon melted butter
Salt
Cayenne
1/3 cup chopped nuts
1/3 cup chopped pimento
1/3 cup chopped olives

Mash the cheese, moisten with cream and melted butter, season with salt and cayenne, add chopped nuts, pimento and olives, press into a mold and let stand 2 hours. Cut in slices and serve on lettuce with mayonnaise dressing. Combine mild cream cheese with pimento, shape into small balls and serve on head lettuce with French dressing.

Other Cheese Combinations

Grate raw carrots and combine them with cottage cheese in the proportion of half carrot and half cheese. Season with mayonnaise, form into balls and serve on lettuce with French dressing. Dates are good stuffed with cream cheese. Slices of orange may be added. Tomatoes also may be stuffed with cheese.

Macedoine Salad

Shredded lettuce
1 cup cooked carrot, strips
1 cup cooked potatoes cubes
1 cup cooked string beans
2 tablespoons finely chopped parsley
French dressing

Arrange shredded lettuce on salad plates. Mix vegetables with French dressing. Put a spoonful on each plate. Serve.

Cole Slaw

Finely shred cabbage, soak 1 hour in cold water and drain. Mix shredded cabbage with salad dressing. Serve on lettuce leaves. Finely chopped green pepper, onion and pimento may be added.

Waldorf Salad

2-3 apples (see directions below)
1 cup celery
1 cup nut meats
Salad dressing to moisten

Cut slice from tops of green or red apples; scoop out the inside pulp, leaving just enough to hold the skin in place. Measure 1 cup of cubed apple. Fill the shells with salad mixture and serve on lettuce leaves. A little salad dressing may be put on top of each. The apple, cut in cubes, celery, and nut mixture may be served on lettuce with salad dressing.

Fruit Salad #1

2 oranges
3 bananas
1/2 pound malaga grapes
4 slices pineapple, cubed
12 walnuts

Mix fruit and serve salad dressing on top, or add fruit salad dressing to moisten. Mix with whipped cream or fruit salad dressing, or salad dressing only. May be served in orange cups.

Fruit Salad Dressing

2 eggs
1/4 cup sugar
1/4 cup pineapple
1/4 cup lemon juice
1 cup whipped cream

Beat eggs, add sugar, pineapple and lemon juice. Cook in double boiler, stirring constantly until thickened, then set aside to cool. Whip the cream and fold into the mixture just before serving. Very delicious for all fruit salads.

Fruit Salad #2

1/2 pound Malaga grapes
2 pears
1 grapefruit
1 orange
1 head lettuce
French dressing

Wash, peel; remove seeds from all fruit; cut grapes into halves, pears in lengthwise pieces, grapefruit and orange into sections; allow to stand on ice. Serve on lettuce leaves with French dressing. Alligator pears, cassaba melon or other fruit may be substituted for above.

Peach Salad

6 peaches
Lemon juice
Lettuce leaves
1/2 cup cream cheese
2 tablespoons condensed milk
1/2 cup mayonnaise

Peel and cut peaches in half (or use halves of canned peaches). Sprinkle with lemon juice to prevent discoloring. Place 2 halves on lettuce leaf on each salad plate. Soften cheese with the condensed milk and combine with the mayonnaise. Put mixture into a pastry bag and fill the hollows of peaches leaving a rose on top, or simply fill carefully with a spoon.
Serves 6

Mayonnaise #1

4 tablespoons flour
1 tablespoon sugar
1 tablespoon mustard
1 teaspoon salt
Paprika
1 cup salad oil
1/4 cup cider vinegar
3/4 cup water
1 egg
2/3 cup condensed milk

Mix dry ingredients and add to this gradually 1/4 cup of salad oil, 1/4 cup of cider vinegar, and 3/4 cup of water. Stir until smooth. Cook over a slow fire until thick and the flour is well cooked, stirring constantly. Remove from fire and beat into the mixture the egg (which has been slightly beaten), 2/3 cup of condensed milk, and 3/4 cup of salad oil. Add the milk and oil slowly and beat very smooth. It will keep indefinitely.
This makes 3 cups of mayonnaise.

Mayonnaise #2

1 egg yolk
1 teaspoon salt
1/16 teaspoon cayenne pepper
2 tablespoons vinegar or lemon juice
1 cup salad oil

Have utensils and ingredients cold. Put egg yolk, seasonings and vinegar or lemon juice into shallow dish or bowl if egg beater is used; add oil 1 teaspoon at a time until 1/4 cup is added, beating after each addition. Continue adding oil in larger quantities until all is added.
To make a larger quantity of mayonnaise simply beat in 1/4 teaspoon salt, a dash of cayenne, 1/2 tablespoon vinegar or lemon juice to each additional 1/2 cup oil.
This dressing can be kept covered in a cold place for several days and if it is too stiff can be thinned out with a little lemon juice or vinegar just before serving.

Mayonnaise #3

1 whole egg
1 teaspoon powdered sugar
1-1/4 teaspoons salt
1/16 teaspoon cayenne pepper
2 tablespoons vinegar or lemon juice
1-1/2 cups oil

Have utensils and ingredients cold. Put egg, powdered sugar, seasonings and vinegar or lemon juice into shallow dish or bowl if egg beater is used; add oil 1 teaspoon at a time until 1/4 is added, beating after each addition. Continue adding oil in larger quantities until all is added. This dressing using 1 whole egg will not begin to thicken as quickly as when egg yolk only is used but will be just as stiff when all the oil is added.
To make a larger quantity of mayonnaise simply beat in 1/4 teaspoon salt, a dash of cayenne, 1/2 tablespoon vinegar or lemon juice to each additional 1/2 cup salad oil. If dressing is not all used at once, cover and keep in a cold place.

No Egg Mayonnaise

1/2 teaspoon salt
Few grains pepper
1/2 teaspoon mustard
1/2 teaspoon sugar
1/4 teaspoon paprika
2 tablespoons condensed milk
1/2 cup salad oil
1 tablespoon lemon juice or vinegar

Mix dry ingredients with condensed milk. Add oil gradually, beating constantly. Add lemon juice or vinegar and beat until smooth.
This makes 2/3 cup of dressing.

Cooked Salad Dressing #1

1 teaspoon mustard
1 teaspoon salt
Dash cayenne
2 tablespoons sugar
1-1/2 tablespoons flour
2 egg yolks, beaten

2 tablespoons melted butter
1/2 cup condensed milk
1/2 cup water
1/4 cup vinegar

Mix dry ingredients in top of double boiler. Gradually add egg yolks and butter; then add the milk diluted with the water; stir constantly to keep smooth. Cook over hot water for 10 minutes. Remove from fire, cool, and add vinegar.

Cooked Salad Dressing #2

1 teaspoon dry mustard
1 tablespoon corn starch
2 teaspoons salt
1-1/2 tablespoons sugar
Few grains cayenne
Yolks of 2 eggs
1/3 cup hot vinegar
1 cup milk
2 tablespoons salad oil
Whites of 2 eggs

Mix the dry ingredients. Add egg yolks, hot vinegar and milk a little at a time stirring continually. Put into double boiler and stir cooking until thick. Take from fire and add oil. Mix in beaten egg whites; cool and serve.
If mixture starts to curdle set top of double boiler in pan of cold water and beat with rotary egg beater until smooth.

Boiled Salad Dressing #3

1/2 tablespoon salt
1-1/2 tablespoons sugar
1 teaspoon mustard
1/2 tablespoon flour
Few grains cayenne
1/2 cup vinegar
2 eggs
3/4 cup milk
1 tablespoon butter or other shortening

Mix dry ingredients in top of double boiler; add vinegar and beaten egg yolks and mix; add milk and butter. Cook.

Tomato Salad

6 tomatoes
1 head of lettuce
Mayonnaise
Paprika

Select tomatoes of good shape and color. Peel and cut 3 thin slices off the top of each tomato and arrange on lettuce on salad plates. Cover slices and top of tomato with mayonnaise; sprinkle with paprika.
If desired, the inside of the tomato may be scooped out and the cup sprinkled with salt. Then invert and chill; when ready to serve add a chicken filling made by combining 1 cup chopped chicken, 1/2 cup diced celery, and 1/3 cup nuts with mayonnaise. Or a vegetable filling may be made by combining diced tomato, 3/4 cup of diced celery, 1/3 cup nuts, and 1/2 cup chopped olives or sweet pickles with mayonnaise.
Serves 6

Stuffed Celery

6 stalks celery
2 tablespoons condensed milk
1/4 teaspoon salt
1 teaspoon onion juice
Paprika
Mayonnaise
1 teaspoon chopped green pepper
2/3 cup cream cheese
Lettuce leaves

Select crisp stalks of celery having deep grooves. Add milk and seasoning to the cream cheese. Pile mixture securely into the grooves of celery, leaving a fluffy, rough surface. Cut into 4-inch lengths. Select a small crisp celery tip and place into one end. Sprinkle with paprika and lay 2 or 3 stalks on a lettuce leaf.

Chicken Salad

1 quart cold boiled chicken, cut into small cubes
1 pint finely cut celery
1 teaspoon salt
1/8 teaspoon pepper
2 hard boiled eggs
French dressing
Lettuce leaves
2 cups mayonnaise dressing
6 olives
Paprika

Mix chicken which should be very tender, with celery, seasoning and 1 egg cut into small pieces; marinate with little French dressing, and let stand in cold place 1 hour. Serve on lettuce leaves and spread mayonnaise over top. Garnish with olives and remaining egg cut into slices. Dust with paprika.

Vegetable Salad #1

1 cup finely cut red cabbage
1 cup cold boiled red beets
1 cup cold boiled carrots
1 cup cold boiled potatoes
1 cup finely cut celery
Salt
Pepper
1 head lettuce
1/2 cup pimentos
1 cup French dressing

Soak cabbage in cold water 1 hour; drain and add beets, carrots potatoes and celery. Mix well together, season with salt and pepper and serve on lettuce leaves. On top put strips of pimento and serve with French dressing, to which may be added 1 teaspoon onion juice.

Vegetable Salad #2

Use fresh boiled vegetables in season. Serve cold on lettuce leaves or other salad green and cover with mayonnaise.
Any combination of vegetables, such as beets, beans, peas, asparagus tips and carrots, is excellent.

Marquise Salad

3 firm tomatoes
1/2 cup chopped onion
1/2 cup chopped parsley
2 tablespoons salad oil
Lettuce
French dressing

Peel tomatoes and cut in half. Mix onion and parsley, add oil; let stand 2 hours before using. When ready to serve line salad bowl with lettuce, place tomatoes in it and on each half put 1 tablespoon onion and parsley mixture. Pour on French dressing. Everything should be ice cold.

Lobster Salad #1

Boiled lobster
French dressing
Lettuce
Mayonnaise
Olives
Hard-boiled eggs
Capers

Cut cold boiled lobster into small pieces. Marinate with French dressing; put on lettuce leaves; cover with mayonnaise and garnish with lobster claws, olives, hard-boiled eggs and capers.

Lobster Salad #2

Put live lobster in large kettle of boiling water with 1 tablespoon salt to each quart of water. Boil rapidly for 20 minutes. When cold remove from shell; remove intestinal vein and cut lobster into small pieces for serving.
Marinate slightly with French dressing, and serve very cold on lettuce leaves. Cover with mayonnaise, and garnish with hard boiled eggs, olives and capers if desired.

Fish Salad

2 cups shredded lettuce
1 can tuna fish or 1-1/2 pounds any cold boiled fish
1/2 cup French dressing
1 teaspoon onion juice
1 cup finely cut celery
1/2 cup mayonnaise
1 teaspoon chopped parsley

Line dish with lettuce; place fish in center; pour over French dressing to which onion juice has been added and cover with celery; put mayonnaise on top. Sprinkle with chopped parsley.

Avocado (Alligator Pear) Salad

Pare avocadoes. Cut into slices. Arrange on lettuce leaves or romaine and serve very cold with Roquefort or French dressing. Or if desired the avocadoes can be simply cut in half, stone removed and half filled with French dressing.

Avocado and Grape Fruit Salad

Pare avocadoes and grape fruit, removing all white skin and seeds from the latter. Slice the avocadoes and arrange with pieces of grape fruit on lettuce or romaine. Serve with French dressing.

Bartlett Pear and Cream Cheese Salad

Bartlett pears
Lettuce or other salad greens
Cream cheese
Seasoning
Pimento or green pepper
Paprika

French dressing or mayonnaise

Use fresh ripe pears. Pare; cut into halves; remove cores and stems. Place on lettuce leaves or other salad greens. Fill hollows with seasoned cream cheese balls. Garnish with small strips of pimento or green pepper and paprika. Serve cold with either French dressing or mayonnaise.
Canned pears from which the syrup is drained can be used if desired.

French Dressing #1

1/2 teaspoon salt
1/8 teaspoon white pepper
1/8 teaspoon paprika
1/2 teaspoon powdered sugar
Pinch of mustard
4 tablespoons olive oil
1 tablespoon vinegar
1 tablespoon lemon juice

Mix dry ingredients, add oil and stir until thoroughly mixed; then add vinegar and lemon juice, a few drops at a time and beat until an emulsion is formed. Or, ingredients may all be placed in a bottle and shaken vigorously together to form an emulsion. A dressing for fruit salad can be made by adding 1/4 cup of cream whipped to the above quantity of French dressing.

French Dressing #2

1 tablespoon lemon juice or vinegar
1/2 teaspoon salt
1/8 teaspoon pepper or few grains cayenne pepper
3 tablespoons oil

Put first 3 ingredients into a bowl. Add oil, beating constantly. Serve very cold.

Roquefort Dressing

To French Dressing, add 3 tablespoons Roquefort cheese which has been crumbled with fork. Add the cheese just before serving.

Thousand Island Dressing

To each cup of mayonnaise take the following:
2 tablespoons chopped green pepper
2-1/2 tablespoons chopped pimentos
1 teaspoon onion juice
1 hard cooked egg, chopped fine
1 teaspoon Worcestershire sauce
1 tablespoon tomato catsup
2 tablespoons chili sauce
1/2 cup whipped cream

Mix first 7 ingredients; add salt if necessary; mix thoroughly with mayonnaise and fold in whipped cream. Serve ice cold on lettuce or other greens or use as cocktail sauce.

Russian Dressing

1 cup mayonnaise
2 teaspoons chili sauce
1 can pimentos chopped fine

Mix ingredients, adding a dash of grated cheese if desired.

Ida's son, William Taylor Franks

17

SOUPS

Soup stock is the liquid in which bones, cooked or uncooked meat and vegetables have been boiled.

Gravies and browned pieces of meat are often added to the soup kettle for color and flavoring.

The stock should be strained, quickly cooled and all fat removed.

A great variety of soups may be made by adding to any soup stock, previously cooked macaroni, spaghetti, vermicelli, noodles or vegetables.

Cream soup, puree, bisque or chowder are heavy soups and contain sufficient nourishment to be the chief articles of food at a meal. Cream soups are made with thickened milk, combined with meat stock, fish stock or vegetables stock and pulp.

Clear soups, such as bouillon and consomme are used as appetizers at the beginning of a heavy meal.

To clarify soup, use 1 egg white to each quart of cold stock. Beat egg slightly, and add to stock. Heat gradually till near the boiling point, stirring all the time. Cook gently for 15 minutes. Remove to back of range and add 1/4 cup cold water. Let stand a few minutes, then strain through cheesecloth placed over strainer. Heat and add any further seasoning desired.

Water in which vegetables are cooked should be saved. Any left-over vegetables heated in this stock and put through a sieve can be made into a vegetable soup by following the directions given for Cream of Potato Soup.

Soup Stock

1 pound meat
1 pound bone
1 quart cold water
1 teaspoon salt
1/2 cup minced onion
1/2 cup carrot
1/2 cup turnip
6 peppercorns
1 teaspoon sweet herbs
1 small bay leaf
1 sprig parsley
1 piece celery root
4 cloves

Cheap cuts of meat, skin, neck or joints and small scraps of meat, such as the flank end of steak or left-overs and bones of roasts, may be used for soup stock. Cut the meat into small pieces. For each pound of meat and bone use about 1 pint of water. Put the meat and bone into cold, salted water. Let soak for 1 hour. Then let simmer gently about 3 hours. During the last hour of cooking add from 1/2 cup to a cup of mixed vegetables for each pound of meat. Mixed herbs and spices may be tied in cheesecloth and added, and left in simmering soup as long as desired. The froth should be skimmed from stock as it rises, if clear soup is desired. When cooking soup stock in a fireless cooker add the vegetables in the beginning.

Scotch Broth

3 pounds mutton from the neck
2 quarts cold water
2 teaspoons salt
1 sliced carrot
2 sliced onions
4 stalks celery
1 tablespoons barley, soaked overnight

Remove the skin and fat from meat that has been wiped with a damp cloth. Cut the meat into small pieces, put into the kettle and add the water. Heat gradually to boiling point, skim and cook about 2 hours, adding vegetables at the end of the first hour. Strain, cool and remove any fat. Reheat to boiling point, add barley and cook until the barley is soft. The meat should not be thrown away, but used in stews, croquettes, or meat cakes. If combined with a little broth, the flavor is restored.

Brown Soup Stock

6 pounds shin of beef
3 to 6 quarts cold water
1/2 cup carrot
1/2 cup turnip
1/2 cup celery
1/2 cup onion

1/2 cup onion
1 bay leaf
6 cloves
1 tablespoon mixed herbs
2 sprigs parsley

Wipe beef and cut lean meat into inch cubes; brown one-third in hot frying pan; put remaining two-thirds with bone and fat into soup kettle; add water and allow to stand 30 minutes. Place on back of range; add browned meat and heat gradually to boiling point. Cover and cook slowly 6 hours; add vegetables and seasoning one hour before it is finished. Strain and put away to cool. Remove all fat; reheat and serve.

Bean Soup

2 cups beans
6 cups water
2 tablespoons finely cut onion
2 tablespoons finely cut bacon
1 teaspoon salt
1/8 teaspoon pepper
2 tablespoons chopped parsley
1 teaspoon thyme
3 tablespoons flour
Cold water

Soak beans in water over night. Drain and put into saucepan with 6 cups boiling water and boil slowly 2 hours or until soft; add onion and bacon which have been fried light brown; boil 5 minutes; add salt, pepper, parsley and thyme. Mash beans with back of spoon and add flour which has been mixed with a little cold water; boil 5 minutes and serve.

Black Bean Soup

1 pint black beans
2 quarts water
1 onion
1/2 tablespoon salt
1/8 teaspoon pepper
1-1/2 tablespoons butter
1-1/2 tablespoons flour
1 lemon
1 hard-boiled egg

Wash and soak beans overnight in 2 quarts water. In the morning add onion sliced and simmer until beans are soft. Add more water if necessary. Rub through a sieve and reheat; add seasonings and butter and flour rubbed together. Just before serving add thin slices of lemon and egg.

Split Pea Soup

1 cup dried split peas
3 quarts cold water
4-inch cube salt fat pork
1 ham-bone
1/2 onion
2 tablespoon flour
2 tablespoons fat
1/8 teaspoon pepper
1-1/2 teaspoons salt

Pick over peas and soak overnight; drain; add cold water, pork, ham-bone, or water in which ham has been boiled, and onion. Simmer 3 or 4 hours, or until peas are soft. Rub through a sieve. Add the flour mixed with fat to soup. Boil 5 minutes, stirring constantly. Add seasonings. Thin with milk if necessary.

Corn Chowder

Fat salt pork, 1 inch by 3 inches
1 sliced onion
4 potatoes cut in 1/4-inch slices
2 cups boiling water
1 quart milk
1 can corn
Salt and pepper
8 crackers
Cold milk

Cut pork into small pieces and try it out in a pan over a slow fire. Add the sliced onion and cook 5 minutes without burning. Strain fat into a saucepan. Add potatoes and 2 cups boiling water to fat and cook until potatoes are soft. Then add the milk and corn. Heat to boiling point. Season with salt and pepper. Moisten crackers in cold milk. Serve crackers on top of chowder.

Fish Chowder

Salt pork fat, 1 inch by 3 inches
1 sliced onion
6 potatoes, cut into cubes
1 pint boiling water
2 cups flaked cod, or fresh cod
1 quart milk
1 tablespoon salt
1/8 teaspoon pepper
8 soda crackers
Cold milk

Fry out fat, add sliced onion and cook to a light brown, without burning. Strain fat into saucepan, add potatoes and boiling water and cook 10 minutes. Add the fish and simmer 20 minutes. Add the milk and seasonings. Heat to boiling point and serve with crackers, split and previously dipped in cold milk.

Creole Soup

1/4 cup rice
3 cups boiling water
1/2 cup cut onion
2 tablespoons bacon drippings
2 cups tomatoes
2 teaspoons salt
1 teaspoon sugar
1/8 teaspoon paprika
1 tablespoon cut parsley

Wash rice, add boiling water and boil 30 minutes. Cook onions in pan with drippings until tender, but not brown; add tomatoes and boil 10 minutes; rub through strainer into boiled rice and water; add seasoning and sprinkle with parsley. Add a little chopped green pepper if desired.

Onion Soup

2 cups finely chopped onion
2 tablespoons butter or bacon drippings
4 cups rice water or vegetable stock
1 teaspoon salt
1/8 teaspoon white pepper
1/8 teaspoon paprika
2 tablespoons chopped parsley

Cook onions and butter or drippings in covered saucepan, shaking pan often. When onions are tender add rice water or stock; boil 5 minutes; add seasoning and chopped parsley.

Oyster Stew

1 pint oysters
1 teaspoon salt
1/8 teaspoon pepper
1/4 teaspoon celery salt
Paprika
2 tablespoons butter
1 tablespoon chopped parsley
2 cups condensed milk
2 cups water

Carefully clean the oysters, removing any bits of shell. Heat in their own liquor until the edges curl. Season and add with butter and parsley to the condensed milk and water which have been scalded together.

Cream Soups

This is the foundation or sauce for many fish and vegetable cream soups.

1 quart milk
1 tablespoon butter
1 teaspoon salt
1 teaspoon white pepper
2 tablespoons flour
Cold water
1 cup boiling water

Scald milk and add butter and seasoning; thicken with flour, which has been mixed with little cold water. Thin with boiling water and boil 2 minutes.

For pea soup boil and mash 1 pint green peas and add to sauce.

For cream of celery boil 1 pint cut celery until tender; rub through sieve, add to milk, and proceed as above.

For potato soup boil and mash 6 large potatoes, stir into milk, proceed as above, and strain. Just before serving stir in a tablespoon chopped parsley.

For corn soup add to sauce a can of corn or corn cut from 6 ears boiled fresh corn, 1 tablespoon sugar, and boil 15 minutes. Strain and serve.

For cream of fish soup add to milk about 1 pound of boiled fish, which has been put through sieve and proceed as above.

Garnishes for Cream Soups

What a magic effect a little garnishing has and how easily it converts a simple dish of soup into one that is deliciously attractive! The following garnishes are all suitable for cream soups:

Vegetables cut into fancy shapes
Dash of paprika
Bit of chopped parsley
Little grated cheese
Spoonful of whipped cream
Spoonful of puffed rich
Croutons
Toasted cheese sticks
Squares of custard

Cream of Tomato Soup #1

1/2 can or 1 pint tomatoes
2 teaspoons sugar

1/4 teaspoon soda
1 teaspoon salt
Pepper
1 quart milk
1 slice onion
1/4 cup flour
1/4 cup butter

Stew tomato and sugar, strain, add soda and seasoning. Scald milk in double boiler with 1 slice onion. Add flour well blended with butter; cook thoroughly. Remove onion from milk. Combine mixtures, adding tomato to milk slowly, strain, serve at once in a hot dish.

Cream of Tomato Soup #2

1 tall can of condensed milk
1 can of tomato soup

Heat the milk and the tomato soup in different pans but at the same time, watching carefully to prevent scorching. When both are piping hot (not boiling) and you are ready to serve, pour the hot tomato in to the hot milk and serve immediately. To avoid curdling be sure to pour the tomato into the milk and instead of vice versa. Do not combine the tomato and milk until ready to serve, as these should be heated separately. This makes a thick and delicious soup.
Serves 4

Cream of Tomato Soup #3

1 quart tomatoes
4 tablespoons butter
4 tablespoons flour
1 quart milk
1 tablespoon salt
1/2 teaspoon pepper
1/4 teaspoon soda

Stew tomatoes slowly 1/2 hour. In the meantime, melt butter, stir in flour and cook over low flame, adding milk slowly; add seasoning. Strain tomatoes; add soda; stir into sauce and serve immediately.

Cream of Celery Soup #1

3 cups celery, cut in 1-inch pieces
2 cups boiling water
2 cups milk
2 tablespoons fat
2 tablespoons flour
1/2 teaspoon salt
1/8 teaspoon pepper

Wash and scrape celery and cut into 1-inch pieces; add water and cook until very soft and tender; rub through sieve. Heat milk in double boiler, and add milk to celery. Melt fat, add flour and seasoning and mix with soup.

Cream of Celery Soup #2

3 cups celery
1 slice onion
2 tablespoons butter
3 tablespoons flour
1 teaspoon salt
1/8 teaspoon pepper
Paprika
2 cups condensed milk
2 cups celery liquor

Wash, scrape, and cut celery in 1/2-inch pieces; cook with slice of onion in 3 cups boiling water until celery is soft—about 30 minutes. Drain (saving the celery liquor) and rub through a sieve. Make a white sauce of the butter, flour, seasonings, condensed milk, and celery liquor. Combine celery pulp and white sauce and serve while hot.
Serves 6

Avocado Soup

1 medium-sized avocado
1 cup light sour cream
1 teaspoon lemon juice
1/4 teaspoon hot pepper sauce
1 envelope chicken-flavor bouillon
1 cup water

Seed and peel avocado; chop some for garnish. In blender at medium speed or food processor with knife blade attached, blend sour cream, lemon juice, hot pepper sauce, bouillon, water, and remaining avocado. Pour into 4 bowls; garnish with chopped avocado.
Makes 4 servings

Chicken Soup

Grandma appreciated the challenge of preparing a dish that would be equally appropriate for Passover or Easter. Her solution was this versatile soup recipe.

6 cans (13-3/4 ounces each) chicken broth
1 pound chicken backs, wings, and necks

3 carrots, chopped
2 leeks, chopped
2 celery ribs, chopped
1 turnip or parsnip, chopped
1 red onion, chopped
1/4 cup chopped parsley
2 garlic cloves, finely chopped
2 teaspoons dried basil leaves

Passover addition:
12 to 16 matzoh balls

Easter additions:
2 cups freshly cooked orzo
Juice of 1 lemon
1/4 cup chopped fresh dill

Pour all of the chicken broth into a large saucepot. Bring the broth to a boil over high heat. Add the remaining ingredients except the "additions," cover, reduce the heat to low, and cook for 1 hour.
Remove all the chicken bones. Cook the soup over high heat for 10 minutes longer.
Add the "addition" of your choice and serve.
Makes 8 servings.

Cream of Pea Soup

1 can peas
1 slice onion
1-1/2 teaspoons sugar
1-1/2 teaspoon salt
1/8 teaspoon pepper
2 tablespoons butter
2 tablespoons flour
1 cup condensed milk
1 cup water

Drain and measure liquid from peas and add enough water to make 2 cups of liquid. Add peas, onion, sugar, salt and pepper and simmer for 15 minutes. Rub through a sieve. Make a white sauce of butter, flour and condensed milk diluted with water. Add a dash of paprika. Combine pea mixture and white sauce and serve while hot.
Serves 6

Cream of Potato Soup #1

4 medium-sized potatoes
1 quart of milk
1/2 medium-sized onion
2 tablespoons fat
2 tablespoons flour
1 teaspoon salt
1/8 teaspoon pepper

Pare potatoes very thin and cook, in enough water to cover, until soft. Drain off water and save. Rub potatoes through a sieve. Heat milk, onion and potato water (about 1 cup) in double boiler. Remove onion and add liquid to potatoes. Melt fat, mix with flour. Stir into hot soup. Season and serve hot. Two tablespoons of finely chopped parsley added just before serving adds greatly to the attractiveness of the soup.

Cream of Potato Soup #2

3 medium-sized potatoes
2 slices onion
1/2 teaspoon salt
3 cups water
2 tablespoons butter
2 tablespoons flour
1-1/2 teaspoons salt
1/8 teaspoon pepper
1/4 teaspoon celery salt
2 cups condensed milk
2 cups potato water
1 tablespoon chopped parsley

Cut potatoes in small pieces and cook with onion in boiling salted water until tender—use 3 cups of water and 1/2 teaspoon salt. Drain (saving the potato water) and rub the potatoes through sieve. There should be about 2 cups of potato pulp. Make a white sauce of the butter, flour, seasonings, condensed milk, and potato water. Add slowly to the potatoes, stirring to keep smooth. Reheat in the double boiler. Sprinkle with chopped parsley and serve very hot.
Serves 6

Cream of Mushroom Soup

1 can of mushrooms (8 ounces - get can containing stems and broken pieces)
2 tablespoons butter
3 tablespoons flour
1/8 teaspoon pepper
1 teaspoon salt
Paprika
2 cups condensed milk

Drain and measure liquor from mushrooms and add enough water to make 2 cups of liquid. Add chopped mushrooms and simmer for 15 minutes. Make white sauce of the butter, flour, seasonings, and condensed milk. Add mushrooms with their liquid and serve while hot.

Italian Bean Soup

1/4 pound cooked ham, in one piece
2 medium-size celery stalks
2 medium-size carrots
1 medium-size onion
1 medium-size zucchini (about 8 ounces)
2 15- to 19-ounce cans white kidney beans, rinsed and drained
1 tablespoon olive or salad oil
1/2 teaspoon dried basil leaves
1/4 teaspoon pepper
14-1/2- to 16-ounce can stewed tomatoes
1 13-3/4- to 14-1/2-ounce can chicken broth
1/2 medium-size bunch spinach, chopped, with tough steams removed (about 1 cup packed)
2 cups water
Grated Parmesan cheese (optional)

About 45 minutes before serving, cut ham into 1/2-inch pieces; dice celery, thinly slice carrots; chop onion; dice zucchini. Remove 1-1/2 cups white kidney beans to medium bowl; with potato masher or fork, mash beans until smooth.

In 5-quart Dutch oven or saucepot over medium-high heat, in hot olive or salad oil, cook ham, celery, carrots, onion, zucchini, basil, and pepper until vegetables are tender and begin to brown, about 15 minutes.

Stir in stewed tomatoes, chicken broth, chopped spinach, mashed white beans, and 2 cups water, using spoon to break up tomatoes; over high heat, heat to boiling. Reduce heat to low; cover and simmer 15 minutes to blend flavors. Stir in remaining beans; heat through.

To serve, spoon soup in to large soup bowls. Sprinkle each serving with grated Parmesan cheese, if you like.

Makes 5 main-dish servings

Tuna-Potato Chip Casserole

2 cups tuna, flaked
2 tablespoons butter
1 cup sliced fresh mushrooms
1/2 green pepper, diced
1 teaspoon minced onion
1/2 cup sliced stuffed olives
1 3-oz. bag potato chips
2 cups white sauce

Melt butter in skillet. Sauté mushrooms, pepper and onion over low heat for 5 minutes. In a greased casserole, lightly combine all ingredients. Top with crushed potato chips. Bake in a 375° oven for 30 minutes. Serves 4.

White Sauce:
2 tablespoons butter
2 tablespoons flour
2 cups milk

18

Fish, Clams & Sauces

Fish, like meat, is a building food and contains some mineral matter. For variety it can be used in place of meat. At some seasons of the year, fish from local waters can be bought very cheap.
Fish contains the same food value as meat at a much smaller cost, tastes good, and is easily digested.
As white-fleshed fish is considered more easily digested than the red-fleshed, it should be selected for invalids, convalescents or those suffering from weak digestion.
Select a fish that has bright eyes and gills, shiny scales and firm flesh, and is free from a disagreeable odor.

PREPARATION OF FISH FOR COOKERY

Cover board or table with paper before laying fish down. Remove scales by scraping a dull knife from tail to head, snapping scales off. Rinse knife in water occasionally. Wet hands before touching fish, and odor will come off more easily. Dip hands in salt so that fish will not slip, and hold by tail. If inner organs have not been removed in market, make a lengthwise incision in belly and draw or scrape them out carefully, so that membrane which lines cavity is not broken. Remove head if desired. Remove fins with scissors. Wash inside and out in salted water. Sprinkle fish with salt if it is to be kept overnight. Handle fish carefully when cooking, as flesh falls apart easily, and have all utensils well greased, as skin sticks readily when heated.

METHODS OF COOKING FISH

Fish suitable for broiling are: Split mackerel, whitefish, cod, shad, trout, etc.; sliced halibut and salmon, white smelts and small fish. To broil—brush with melted fat, sprinkle with flour, salt and pepper, and cook over a flame.
Fish suitable for baking whole are: Whitefish, cod, haddock, small salmon, shad. Follow directions for baked fish.
Fish suitable for boiling are: Salmon, halibut, cod, haddock, trout, etc. Cook in piece of cheesecloth. Add 1 tablespoon vinegar and 1 tablespoon salt to earth quart of water.
Fish suitable for frying are the white-fleshed ones. Cook in deep fat, or saute in a little fat in a frying pan.

TIME TABLE FOR COOKING FISH

Baking—thick fish, 1 lb.	10–15 mins
Baking—thin fish, 1 lb.	8–10 mins
Boiling—thick fish, halibut, salmon, 1 lb.	15 mins
Boiling—thin fish, such as flounder, 1 lb.	8 mins
Frying—fillets or steak	4–7 mins
Frying—smelts or trout	3–5 mins

When the fish can be easily separated from the bone, the fish is sufficiently cooked.

Fish—Baked, With Stuffing

A fish weighing from 2-1/2 to 4 pounds
1 cup crumbs (bread or crackers, or half and half)
1/4 cup melted fat
1/4 teaspoon salt
1/8 teaspoon celery salt
1/8 teaspoon pepper
Few drops onion juice, if liked
1/4 cup water
Melted fat
Salt and pepper
Flour

Mix ingredients (except fish) in order given. If a dry filling is desired, the water may be omitted. Three tablespoons catsup, chopped parsley, capers, pickles, or oysters may be added. Clean and wipe the fish. Rub the inside with salt. Fill with stuffing and sew together. Cut diagonal gashes 1-1/2 inches apart on both sides of the fish and place a strip of bacon or salt pork fat in each gash. Brush with melted fat, sprinkle with salt and pepper. Dredge with flour, tie in the shape of a letter "S" and bake in a dripping pan. When the flour is browned, baste the fish once in 10 minutes. Cook until the flesh is firm and separates easily from the bone.

Broiled Finnan-Haddie

Wash the fish thoroughly; let soak 1/2 hour in cold water, skin side up; cover with water which is simmering, not boiling. Let stand 15 minutes, then drain carefully and wipe dry, brush over with fat and broil over slow fire about 15 minutes. Remove to hot platter, sprinkle with bits of butter, and with juice of 1/2 lemon. Serve at once.

Creamed Finnan-Haddie

Put Finnan-haddie in a baking pan, cover with cold water. Bring water to boiling point slowly. Cook over low fire 1/2 hour. Drain and rinse, separate fish in flakes. Make white sauce, add flaked fish and 1 or 2 hard-boiled eggs sliced.

Broiled Salt Mackerel

Let soak in cold water 12 hours, skin side up. Drain and wipe dry. Brush over with melted fat. Broil on a well-greased broiler skin side down, basting with butter once or twice. Remove carefully to serving dish and pour over 1/2 cup of hot white sauce. Sprinkle with finely chopped parsley. It may be served with melted butter in place of the white sauce.

Fried Smelts

To clean smelts, spread open outer gills, and with the forefinger take hold of the inner gills and pull gently; the parts unfit for food are all attached to these inner gills, and come away together, leaving the smelt in perfect shape. Rinse thoroughly and wipe dry. If smelts are small, dip in milk and roll in flour, or in egg and bread crumbs. Fry in deep fat.

Codfish Balls #1

1 cup salt codfish
2 cups potatoes
1 tablespoon butter
1/8 teaspoon pepper
1 egg

Wash fish in cold water and pull into small pieces, keeping fish in water while doing so. Wash and pare the potatoes and cut into pieces before measuring. Cook the fish and potatoes together in boiling water until the potatoes are tender, then drain and shake over the fire until dry; mash, and beat thoroughly with a wire potato masher. Add the butter, pepper and salt if needed. Cool slightly, then add beaten egg, and beat until light. Take up mixture in a spoon, molding slightly with a knife, and drop into deep hot fat. Fry until brown, about 1 minute. Drain on absorbent paper. Mixture for codfish balls may be served hot, without frying, or turned into a buttered baking dish and browned in the oven and served as a baked dish, or shaped into flat cakes and sauted in frying pan. To make codfish puff, prepare in same manner, only use 2 well-beaten eggs. Cook like an omelet.

Codfish Balls #2

1 cup salt codfish
2 cups potatoes, cut into cubes or small pieces
1/8 teaspoon pepper
1/2 tablespoon butter
1 egg

Pick over, wash and shred fish into small pieces. Put potatoes into deep saucepan; cover with cold water; add fish and boil until potatoes are soft. Take off fire; drain well; beat up with wire whip or fork until light and all lumps are out of potatoes; add seasoning, butter and slightly-beaten egg. Drop by spoonfuls into deep fat, hot enough to brown a piece of bread in 40 seconds, and fry until golden brown. Drain on brown paper and serve immediately.

Codfish Balls #3

1 cup salt codfish
2 cups potatoes, cut into cubes or small pieces
1/8 teaspoon pepper
1/2 tablespoon cooking oil
1 egg

Pick over, wash and shred fish. Put potatoes into deep saucepan; cover with cold water; add fish and boil until potatoes are soft. Take off fire; drain well; beat up with fork until light and all lumps are out; add seasoning, oil and slightly-beaten egg. Drop by spoonfuls into deep oil hot enough to brown a piece of bread in 40 seconds (385 degrees F.), and fry until golden brown. Drain on paper and serve immediately.
Makes 12 codfish balls

Scalloped Flaked Cod or Other Fish

1 pound flaked cod (or canned salmon or tuna fish)
1-1/2 cups white sauce
1/4 cup buttered crumbs

Arrange fish and sauce in layers in a well-greased baking dish. Cover with bread crumbs. Bake until heated throughout and crumbs are browned on top. Any kind of cooked fish may be flaked and prepared in this way. Layers of boiled onion or green pease may be used in this recipe. This recipe is suitable also for canned salmon or tuna fish.

Salmon Loaf

1 cup flaked cooked salmon or canned salmon
1 cup stale bread crumbs soaked in 1 cup scalded milk
1 teaspoon salt
1 tablespoon butter
1/2 teaspoon onion juice
2 egg yolks, beaten
1 teaspoon lemon juice
2 egg whites, stiffly beaten

Combine ingredients in order given, folding in the stiffly-beaten egg whites last. Place mixture into a well-greased and crumbed pan and bake in a moderately hot oven or steam the mixture. Serve with white sauce, or the following:

Sauce for Fish

2 tablespoons butter
2 tablespoons flour
1-1/2 cups milk, scalded
1/2 cup liquid from fish
2 tablespoons lemon juice
1 egg yolk

Melt butter, add flour, then heated milk gradually. Add liquid from fish and lemon juice just before removing from fire. Just before serving, beat sauce into yolk of egg. Serve hot. One tablespoon catsup may be added, if desired.

Oysters—Fried

Select large oysters, remove pieces of shell, wash and wipe dry. Roll in well-seasoned, dry bread crumbs, which have been sifted. Dip in egg (beaten with 1 tablespoon water or oyster juice), and again in the crumbs. Fry in deep fat.

Scalloped Oysters #1

1 quart oysters
3/4 cup cold water
6 tablespoons butter
2 cups crumbs
1/2 teaspoon salt
Cayenne
3/4 cup liquid

Wash oysters with water in colander and remove pieces of shell. Strain the juice. Melt butter, add crumbs and seasoning. Line the bottom of a greased baking dish with 1/4 of the crumbs, then add 1/2 the oysters. Add 1/4 more crumbs, and remainder of oysters and liquid, which may be liquid from oysters, or milk. Cover with buttered crumbs. Bake in a moderate oven 30 to 40 minutes. A large shallow pan is always preferable to a deep baking pan, as there should be only 2 layers of oysters.

Scalloped Oysters #2

2 cups bread crumbs
25 oysters with liquor
1 teaspoon salt
1/4 teaspoon pepper
1/2 cup milk and cream
2 tablespoons butter

Grease baking dish and cover bottom with bread crumbs, then lay oysters in carefully; season and cover with bread crumbs; pour over milk and oyster liquor and cover top with butter. Bake in hot oven 15 to 20 minutes.

Oyster Stew

1 quart oysters
3/4 cup cold water
1 quart milk
1/4 cup butter
1/2 tablespoon salt
1/8 teaspoon pepper

Clean the oysters by placing in colander and pouring water over them. Pick over carefully, removing any bits of shell that adhere. Reserve liquid, heat to boiling point, strain through double cheesecloth over wire strainer. Add oysters, cook until edges begin to curl. Add oysters and liquor to hot, scalded milk; add butter and seasoning. Serve at once.

Paprika, celery salt, onion juice, parsley or mace may be used as additional seasoning, if desired.

For oyster soup, thicken the milk, using 1/2 tablespoon flour for each cup of milk. Prepare as for white sauce.

Broiled Fish

Clean, wash and split, removing backbone and fins along the edge. Very large fish should be cut into slices. Dry with cheesecloth; season with salt and pepper. Cook on well-greased broiler, from 10 to 20 minutes, turning once. Remove to hot platter; add melted butter and sprinkle with hopped parsley; garnish with slices of lemon and serve.

Baked Fish

Prepare as for Broiled Fish. Brush pan with drippings; place fish, skin side down; dust with salt, pepper and flour; pour over 2 tablespoons melted butter and 1/2 cup milk. Bake in hot oven 20 to 25 minutes or until brown. Remove to hot platter, sprinkle with chopped parsley and serve.

Fried Fish #1

Clean, removing head and tail, unless fish are small; wash with cold water and dry with cheesecloth; dust with salt, pepper and flour on both sides. Heat 1 tablespoon bacon drippings or other fat in heavy pan over the fire. Put in fish; brown quickly on both sides; reduce heat and fry 5 to 10 minutes longer. Serve with chopped parsley and lemon or sauce tartare.

Fried Fish #2

Filet of sole, smelts, oysters and other fish are better and more digestable fried in deep cooking oil. Wash fish; cut large fish into pieces convenient for frying. Smelts and oysters are fried whole. Dip in batter or roll in flour, then egg, and cover with bread crumbs. Fry in deep cooking oil hot enough to brown a piece of bread in 60 seconds (375 degrees F.) until nice golden brown and cooked through. Oysters take but a few minutes and are sufficiently cooked when light brown.

Fritter Batter

1 cup flour
1-1/2 teaspoons baking powder
1/2 teaspoon salt
1 egg
1/2 cup milk
1 tablespoon cooking oil

Sift dry ingredients together; add beaten egg, milk and oil; beat well until smooth.

Planked Fish

Prepare as for Broiled Fish. Heat plank, brush with drippings and dust with salt and pepper. Place fish, skin side down, doubling thin part so that it will not burn. The oven must be hot before putting in plank; cook 20 minutes; reduce to moderate heat and leave in oven 10 to 20 minutes longer. Melt 1 tablespoon butter, add 1 teaspoon salt and 1/8 teaspoon pepper, and pour over fish. Garnish with potato roses, lemon and parsley and serve on the plank.

Fish Chowder

2 or 3 slices salt pork
6 medium-sized potatoes
1 small onion
3 pounds fresh fish
2 teaspoons salt
1/8 teaspoon pepper
2 quarts milk

Cut pork in dice pieces; fry crisp, and turn into chowder kettle. Pare and cut potatoes into pieces. Peel and chop onion fine. Put potatoes into kettle with part of onion. Cut fish into convenient pieces, and lay over potatoes; sprinkle over with rest of onion; add seasoning and enough water to come to top of fish; cover closely and cook until potatoes are soft; add milk and let it scald up again. Pilot bread or crackers, split and soaked, may be added just before last boiling. If milk is not available a smaller quantity of water may be used.

Boiled Lobsters or Crabs

The lobster should be purchased alive and plunged into boiling water in which a good proportion of salt has been mixed. Continue to boil according to size, about 20 minutes. Crabs should be boiled in the same manner, but only a little more than half the time is necessary.

To open a boiled lobster, wipe off shell, break off large claws; separate tail from body; take body from shell, leaving "lady" or stomach, on shell. Save green fat and coral; remove small claws. Remove woolly gills and discard, break body through middle and pick out meat from joints. Cut with sharp scissors through length of underside of tail, draw meat from shell. Draw back flesh on upper end and pull off intestinal cord and discard. Break large claws and remove meat.

Creamed Oysters

To each 30 oysters use 1 cup thin cream sauce. Drain oysters, saving liquor for soup, put into shallow pan over quick fire and cook about 1 minute or until edges curl, stirring constantly, and add to sauce.

Or put on oysters with 1 tablespoon butter; add 1 tablespoon flour which has been mixed with a little cold water; add 1/2 cup milk, 1/2 teaspoon salt and 1/8 teaspoon pepper. Worcestershire sauce may be added if desired. Boil 1 minute and serve on thin squares of toasted bread; garnish with parsley.

Fried Oysters

Wash and drain oysters. Season with salt and pepper, dip in flour, egg and then bread or cracker crumbs. Fry in hot fat until golden brown. Drain well and garnish with lemon and parsley.

Clam Chowder

25 clams
6 potatoes
1 onion
1/8 pound finely cut salt pork
2 teaspoons salt
1/8 teaspoon pepper
1 quart milk

Chop hard parts of clams. Slice potatoes and onion thin. Put pork into kettle and cook a short time; add potatoes, onion, seasoning and juice of clams. Cook 2-1/2 hours; then add clams. Boil 15 minute and just before serving add hot milk.

Shell Fish a la Newburg

2 cups finely cut shrimp, scallops, lobster, or crab meat
2 tablespoons butter
1 tablespoon flour
1 cup milk
2 hard-boiled eggs
1 teaspoon salt
Cayenne pepper to taste
1/4 teaspoon paprika
1/4 cup sherry

If canned fish is used cover with cold water 20 minutes and drain. Melt butter in saucepan; add flour and stir until smooth; add cold milk slowly; boil until thick. Rub egg yolks through strainer and add, stirring until smooth; add seasoning, and finely chopped egg whites; add fish; put all in top of double boiler over fire for 14 minutes; add sherry and serve immediately.

Clam Omelet

1 can minced clams
1 tablespoon butter
3 eggs
1/4 teaspoon salt
1/8 teaspoon pepper
3 tablespoons cream or milk
1 tablespoon cheese
Bacon for garnish

Drain clams. Melt butter in frying pan, add clams and cook 3 minutes. Beat eggs thoroughly, add salt, pepper, and cream or milk and pour into pan with clams. When set and browned on the bottom, sprinkle cheese over top. Fold and serve garnished with strips of bacon. Fresh stewed tomatoes make an excellent sauce poured over this omelet.

Clam Fritters #1

1 can minced clams
1 cup flour
1/2 teaspoon baking powder
1/4 teaspoon salt
1/8 teaspoon pepper
1 egg, well beaten
1/2 tablespoon minced parsley
1 teaspoon lemon juice

Drain claims, reserving liquid. Mix and sift flour, baking powder, salt and pepper. Add 1/3 cup liquid from clams and well-beaten egg. Mix thoroughly and stir in drained clams, parsley and lemon juice. Drop by tablespoonfuls into deep fat heated to 390 degrees F. Fry until golden brown. Drain on paper. This recipe makes 8 to 10 small fritters.

Clam Fritters #2

1-1/2 cups flour
2 teaspoons baking powder
1 teaspoon salt
1/8 teaspoon pepper
1/4 teaspoon paprika
1/2 cup milk or clam juice
1 egg
2 teaspoons grated onion
2 teaspoons cooking oil
10 clams

Sift together the dry ingredients, add liquid, beaten egg, onion and cooking oil. Rinse clams in cold water; put through meat chopper and add to batter. Take 1 spoonful of batter for each fritter and fry in deep oil hot enough to brown a piece of bread in 60 seconds (375 degrees F.). Drain on unglazed paper and serve immediately.
Makes 16 fritters

Clam Patties

2 cans minced clams
1/2 cup milk or cream
2 tablespoons butter
2 tablespoons flour
1/4 teaspoon salt
A sprinkle of cayenne

1/4 teaspoon onion juice
1/4 teaspoon Worcestershire sauce
1 egg well beaten
Puff paste pattie shells

Drain clams, reserving liquid. Heat 1/2 cup of clam liquid and milk or cream. Melt butter in top of double boiler, add drained clams and cook 3 minutes. Add flour, salt, cayenne, onion juice and Worcestershire sauce and when well blended add hot clam liquid and cook for 10 minutes over hot water. Stir in well-beaten egg just before serving and serve in pattie shells of puff paste.

Clam Poulet

1 can minced clams
2 tablespoons butter
3 tablespoons flour
1/2 teaspoon salt
1/8 teaspoon pepper
1/4 teaspoon paprika
1 cup milk
3 sweet pickles
1 hard-cooked egg
2 pimentos finely diced
Buttered toast

Drain clams, reserving liquid. Melt butter in top of chafing dish or double boiler. Add flour, salt, pepper and paprika and stir together. Gradually add liquid drained from clams and milk and stir constantly until thick and smooth. Add clams, pickles, egg and pimentos. Serve very hot on slices of buttered toast.

Savory Clams

1 can whole clams
2 tablespoons butter
3 tablespoons flour
1/2 teaspoon salt
1/8 teaspoon pepper
1 cup milk
1/3 cup finely chopped celery
3/4 cup bread crumbs
Bacon for garnish

Drain clams and cut into pieces. Melt butter in saucepan, add clams and cook 3 minutes. Add flour, salt and pepper and gradually milk. Cook until mixture thickens, stirring constantly. Turn into greased ramekins, sprinkle with celery. Cover with crumbs and place a small piece of bacon on top of each. Bake 20 minutes in a hot oven, 350 degrees F.

Clam Devils

1 can whole clams
2 tablespoons vinegar
1 teaspoon horseradish
1/2 teaspoon Worcestershire sauce
1/3 cup olive oil
1/4 tcaspoon salt
1/4 teaspoon paprika
Bread crumbs
Egg, beaten
Shredded lettuce

Drain clams. Make a sauce of vinegar, horseradish, Worcestershire sauce, olive oil, salt and paprika and mix together. Place clams in this sauce and allow to stand 1 hour. Drain, dip in crumbs, in beaten egg and again in crumbs. Fry in deep hot fat at a temperature of 390 degrees F. Drain on paper and serve at once with lettuce tossed in dressing from clams.

Clam Novelty

1 can whole clams
1 egg
1 cup milk
1 cup cooked rice
1/4 teaspoon salt
1/8 teaspoon paprika
1 teaspoon onion juice
Cheese sauce

Drain clams and cut in pieces. Beat 1 egg and add milk, cooked rice, salt, paprika, onion juice and clams. Turn mixture into buttered ramekins. Place these in a pan of hot water and bake in a moderate oven, 350 to 400 degrees F., until mixture is firm. Turn molds on to a hot platter and serve with cheese sauce.

Clam Saute on Toast

Drain 1 can whole clams and cut in pieces. Dredge with flour, season with salt, pepper and a few drops of Worcestershire sauce and fry in butter about 7 minutes. Serve very hot on toast.

Clam Molds

1 can minced clams
1 tablespoon gelatine
2/3 cup boiled salad dressing
1/3 cup minced celery
1 small green pepper minced

Drain clams and reserve the liquid. Soak gelatine in clam liquid and dissolve over heat. Combine with clams, salad dressing, minced celery and minced green pepper. Mix well and turn into individual molds. Chill and turn out on lettuce leaf. Serve with mayonnaise.

Clam Bisque

1 cup water
1 can minced clams
2 whole cloves
2 allspice berries
2 peppercorns
2 tablespoons butter
2 tablespoons flour
2 pints milk

Add water to clams and liquid from clams, simmer with spices and strain. Melt butter, add flour, stir in gradually 1 pint of the milk and cook until smooth and thick. Then add 1 pint milk and clam mixture. Heat and serve in bouillon cups with whipped cream on top.

Clam Souffle

1 can minced clams
1-1/2 tablespoons butter
2 tablespoons flour
Salt
Pepper
1/2 cup milk
1/2 cup bread crumbs
3 well-beaten egg yolks
3 well-beaten egg whites

Drain clams, reserving liquid. Melt butter and add flour and seasonings. Gradually add 1/2 cup of liquid drained from clams, and milk and cook until mixture thickens. Add clams, bread crumbs, and yolks. Fold in whites. Bake in a well-greased pan in an oven 380 to 400 degrees F. for 30 minutes.

Clam Italienne

1 can whole clams
2 tablespoons butter
1 tablespoon finely minced onion
1/4 cup strained cooked tomatoes
1/4 teaspoon salt
1 tablespoon minced parsley
2 drops tabasco sauce
3 tablespoons grated cheese
Hot toast

Drain clams and cut in pieces. Melt butter and cook 1 finely minced onion in it until brown. Add tomatoes and cook 5 minutes. Add salt, clams, parsley and tabasco sauce and cook until mixture is thoroughly heated. Add grated cheese and serve at once on slices of toast. Garnish with parsley.

Clam Croquettes

1 can whole clams
2 tablespoons butter
4 tablespoons flour
1/4 teaspoon salt
1/4 teaspoon paprika
1 tablespoon chopped parsley
1 teaspoon lemon juice
1 teaspoon onion juice
2 hard-cooked eggs
Egg, beaten
Crumbs

Drain clams, reserving liquid, and cut clams in pieces. Heat liquid. Melt butter, add flour and gradually the heated clam liquid, stirring constantly. Add salt, paprika, parsley, lemon juice, onion juice, eggs chopped fine, and the clams. Mix well, chill and shape. Dip in egg and crumbs and fry in deep hot fat at a temperature of 390 degrees F. until golden brown. Serve with tartar sauce.

Scalloped Clams

1 can minced clams
1 tablespoon butter
2 tablespoons flour
1 cup cream
2 well-beaten egg yolks
Salt
Pepper
1 tablespoon chopped parsley
1 tablespoon lemon juice
Crumbs
Butter

Drain clams. Make a white sauce of butter, flour and cream, remove from the fire and add well-beaten egg yolks, salt, pepper, parsley, lemon juice and the clams. Fill small, well-greased ramekins with the mixture, sprinkle lightly with crumbs, dot with butter, arrange in a baking pan and brown 7 minutes in a hot oven, 400 degrees F.

Clam Scramble

1 can minced clams
2 tablespoons butter
3 eggs
1/4 cup milk
1/4 teaspoon salt
1/4 teaspoon paprika
Hot buttered toast
Bacon for garnish

Drain clams. Melt butter in the top of the double boiler. Beat eggs until light. Add milk, salt and paprika and turn mixture into melted butter. Cook until mixture begins to thicken, and add drained clams. Continue cooking until mixture is thick. Serve at once on strips of hot buttered toast garnished with strips of crisp bacon.

Clams Michele

3 tablespoons butter
1 onion
1 green pepper
3 cups stewed tomatoes
2 cups cooked spaghetti
1 can whole clams
1/2 teaspoon salt
1/8 teaspoon pepper
4 tablespoons grated cheese

Melt butter, add finely chopped onion, chopped green pepper and stewed tomatoes. Add cooked spaghetti and liquid drained from clams, salt and pepper. Cook until spaghetti has absorbed most of the liquid. Add clams cut in quarters. Turn into greased casserole, sprinkle with cheese and brown in a hot oven.

Salmon Croquettes

1-3/4 cup flaked salmon
1 teaspoon lemon juice
1 cpu white sauce
Salt and pepper
Crumbs
1 egg
Parsley

Add flaked salmon and lemon juice to white sauce and season with salt and pepper. Shape, roll in crumbs, then in slightly-beaten egg, and again in the crumbs. Fry in deep fat, heated until hot enough to brown a piece of bread in 40 seconds (375 degrees F.). Drain and garnish with parsley.
Serves 5

White Sauce for Croquettes

3 tablespoons butter
3 tablespoons flour
1/2 teaspoon salt
Few grains pepper
1/2 cup condensed milk
1/2 cup water

Melt fat in top part of double boiler; add flour and seasonings and mix thoroughly. Add the condensed milk diluted with the water and stir constantly until smooth and thick. Place over hot water and continue cooking for 10 minutes, stirring occasionally.

Shrimp Wiggle

2-1/4 tablespoons butter
2-1/4 tablespoons flour
1/2 teaspoon salt
Few grains pepper
Paprika
3/4 cup condensed milk
3/4 cup water
1 cup shrimps
1 cup canned peas
Toast points

Make a white sauce of the butter, flour, seasonings, and condensed milk diluted with the water. Drain the shrimps, remove the dark vein; break the shrimps into pieces and add to white sauce. Also add the drained peas. When the mixture is thoroughly heated serve on toast points. Garnish with parsley or olives.
Serves 5

Tuna Fish a la King

2 tablespoons butter
1/2 green pepper, shredded
1 hard-cooked egg
1/2 cup chopped mushrooms
3 tablespoons flour
1 cup condensed milk
1 cup water
Salt and pepper
1-1/2 cups tuna fish
1/2 cup peas

Saute green peeper and mushrooms in butter until tender (about 10 minutes), keeping covered while cooking. Remove mushrooms and pepper and blend flour with the fat. Add the condensed milk diluted with the water and cook until the mixture is thickened, stirring constantly to prevent lumping.

Place flaked tuna fish, peas, egg, mushrooms, and pepper in top of double boiler. Pour over this the sauce and continue cooking over hot water for 10 minutes. Serve in pattie shells or on toast points. Lobster or shrimp may be used instead of tuna fish.
Serves 6

SAUCES FOR FISH AND VEGETABLES

How tempting a most ordinary food is made by the addition of an attractive sauce—one that is smooth and creamy, with delicate flavors well blended! The generous use of a variety of sauces is, to be sure, one of the secrets of French cookery. Sauces containing liberal amounts of milk not only stimulate the appetite and cause digestive juices to flow more freely but also are very nutritious.

White Sauce

Melt fat in top part of double boiler; add flour and seasonings and mix thoroughly. Add the condensed milk diluted with the water and stir constantly until smooth and thick. Place over hot water and continue cooking for 10 minutes, stirring occasionally.

Cheese Sauce

Add 1/3 cup of grated cheese to 1 cup of White Sauce No. 2 and stir until it is melted. Serve hot with vegetables or fish.

Pimento Sauce

Add 3 tablespoons chopped pimento to 1 cup of White Sauce No. 2. Serve hot with vegetables or fish.

Egg Sauce

Add 1 chopped hard-cooked egg, 1 tablespoon chopped parsley, and 1/4 teaspoon celery salt to 1 cup of White Sauce No. 2. Serve hot with vegetables or fish.

Caper Sauce

1/2 cup condensed milk
1/2 cup water
2 tablespoons butter
1 small onion
2 tablespoons flour
1/2 teaspoon salt
1/8 teaspoon pepper
1/4 cup capers

Scald the condensed milk and water together. Melt the butter, add chopped onion and when brown add the flour and let brown; add the salt, pepper, and scalded milk, stirring constantly. Cook for about 5 minutes and add the drained capers. Serve hot with fish.

Mock Hollandaise Sauce

1 tablespoon butter
2 tablespoons flour
1/2 teaspoon salt
1/8 teaspoon pepper
3/4 cup condensed milk
2 egg yolks
1/4 cup butter
1 tablespoon lemon juice
Few grains cayenne

Follow method given above for White Sauce. Stir in beaten egg yolks after sauce is cooked and then add butter, bit by bit, and finally the lemon juice. Serve hot with vegetables or fish.

Thin Cream Sauce

1 tablespoon butter
1 tablespoon flour
1 cup milk or cream
1/2 teaspoon salt
1/8 teaspoon white pepper

Melt butter in saucepan, add flour and mix well; add cold milk slowly, stirring until smooth and creamy; add salt and pepper and boil about 3 minutes.

Thick Cream Sauce

2 tablespoons butter
2-1/2 tablespoons flour
1 cup milk or cream
1/2 teaspoon salt
1/8 teaspoon white pepper

Make as directed for Thin Cream Sauce.

Tomato Sauce

3 slices bacon cut into small pieces
1 slice onion—chopped
2 tablespoons flour

1-1/2 cups strained tomatoes
1/2 teaspoon salt
Few gratings of nutmeg
Cayenne
1 tablespoon chopped green peppers

Put bacon into saucepan, add onion and brown slightly. Add flour and tomatoes which have been heated, and stir until thick and smooth. Add seasoning and peppers.

Egg Sauce (for Fish)

2 chopped hard-boiled eggs
1 tablespoon chopped parsley
1 teaspoon lemon juice or vinegar
1 cup white sauce

Add eggs, parsley and lemon juice to white sauce after removing from fire.

Sauce Tartare

1 cup mayonnaise
1 tablespoon capers
1 tablespoon olives
1 tablespoon pickles
1 tablespoon parsley

Make mayonnaise. Chop other ingredients very fine, and press in a cloth until quite dry. Blend gradually with the mayonnaise.

Maitre d'Hotel Butter

2 tablespoons butter
1 tablespoon lemon juice
1/2 teaspoon salt
1/8 s white pepper
1 tablespoon chopped parsley

Cream butter; add gradually lemon juice, seasoning and parsley. Keep cold until served.

Hollandaise Sauce

1/2 cup butter
2 beaten egg yolks
1 tablespoon lemon juice
Salt
Cayenne
1/2 cup boiling water

Cream butter; add gradually, stirring well, egg yolks, lemon juice, salt and cayenne; add boiling water slowly. Stir over boiling water until thick as boiled custard. Serve immediately.

Horse-Radish Sauce

2 tablespoons butter
2 tablespoons grated fresh horse-radish
1 tablespoon very thick cream
1/2 teaspoon lemon juice

Cream butter; add horse-radish, cream and lemon juice. Keep very cold.

Prime Rib Au Jus

5 pounds prime ribs
1 cup water
1/4 cup vinegar
2 stalks celery, diced
1 cup water
1/8 cup vegetable oil
2 carrots, diced
1 onion, chopped
2 bay leaves
1/2 teaspoon sage
1/2 teaspoon salt
4 raw potatoes, cut up
1 green pepper, diced
1 clove garlic
1/2 teaspoon thyme
2 cups tomatoes
1/4 teaspoon pepper
1 teaspoon paprika

Place beef in roasting pan with water. Add ingredients in order as above. Bake in a 300° oven for 2-1/2 hours. Baste meat every 30 minutes. Serves 6.

19

MEATS

Good beef is dark, purple in color when first cut, but turns to a bright red. It should be well streaked with a firm fat of yellowish color that crumbles easily. The flesh should be firm and, when pressed with the finger, no mark should remain.

Veal should be pink; it is usually less firm than beef. If used too young, it is watery and flabby.

Mutton should be dullish red, rather firm and streaked with firm white or slightly yellow fat.

Lamb, which is in season between May and November, should be pink, with more red color in the bones than mutton.

Pork should be pale in color. It is less firm than beef and has soft fat.

All meat should be removed from the papers wrappings as soon as it comes from the market. Paper absorbs meat juices, and if meat remains in the paper too long, it will taste of it. Before cooking, meat should be wiped with a clean, damp cloth, but it should never be put in water because water draws out the meat juices. Meat should always be kept in a cool place.

One of the fundamental, underlying principles in the cooking of meat is that heat hardens protein.

High temperature hardens and toughens meat; therefore, it should only be used to form a coating or to sear the meat on the outside. This also is the best means of retaining the juices, and if lower temperature is used to complete the cooking, the finished product will not be tough and indigestible.

Pounding and chopping helps to break the connective tissue. It is, however, likely to open the thread-like meat fibers and release and juices. If flour is pounded into the meat, it will hold and help retain the juices. The natural flavor of tougher meats is developed by long, slow cooking.

TIME TABLE FOR ROASTING (PER POUND)

Beef, round	10–12 minutes
Beef ribs (well done)	12–15 minutes
Beef ribs (rare)	8 to 10 minutes
Mutton, leg (well done)	15 minutes
Mutton, leg (rare)	8 minutes
Mutton, loin (rare)	8 minutes
Mutton, shoulder (stuffed)	15 minutes
Lamb (well done)	20 minutes
Veal (well done)	25 minutes
Pork (well done)	30 minutes
Chicken	15 minutes
Duck	20–25 minutes
Goose	18–20 minutes
Turkey, 8-lbs.	15–20 minutes

BEEF

Roast Beef

Wipe meat; rub with salt; put on rack in dripping pan. Place in a hot oven 450 degrees F. until meat is seared on the outside, then reduce the temperature to moderate 350 degrees F. and roast according to above time schedule. Baste the meat every 10 or 15 minutes with the fat that collects in the pan.

Pan-Broiled Steak

Trim fat from steak, also part of bone, if desired. Wipe with damp cloth. Heat frying pan till very hot, or until blue smoke arises. Rub surface of pan with little fat. Place steak in pan, searing it quickly, first one side, then on the other and turning every 10 seconds. After both sides are seared, reduce heat under the pan and cook steak more slowly. Stand on edge to brown fat. Keep pan free from fat. Steak is done rare when well browned and puffy. If 1 inch thick, this will take about 8 minutes. If desired well done, it will require 12 to 15 minutes or more.

Hamburger Steak

Chop finely 1 pound lean raw beef; season highly with salt, pepper and a few drops of onion juice. Add 1/2 cup milk gradually; mix with a fork and shape into cakes. Heat a frying pan, rub with the fat of meat and pan-broil the steaks. Turn cakes often during the cooking. One cup of dried bread crumbs, or cold cooked rice, may be added to the mixture before it is shaped into balls.

Meat Loaf

Shape hamburger mixture (with bread crumbs) into a loaf; lay slices of bacon across the top. Place in baking pan and bake at 400 degrees F. for 45 minutes. If the oven is being used for something that requires a low temperature, the meat loaf can be baked for 2 hours at 300 degrees F. Serve with gravy made from fat in pan by adding flour. Allow to brown, add boiling water.

Flank or Round Steak, Stuffed & Rolled

1 pound top round, or flank 1/2 inch thick
1 onion, sliced
1/4 cup carrot, cubed
2 or 3 small slices suet
1 cup boiling water or stock

Stuffing:
1 cup crumbs
2 tablespoons butter (melted)
2 tablespoons parsley
1/2 teaspoon onion juice
2 tablespoons chopped celery
1/2 teaspoon salt
1/8 teaspoon paprika

Trim edges of steak, spread stuffing over it, roll and tie it, and lay it on onion and carrot in pan with suet on top. Pour the water or stock into pan, cook, closely covered, for 20 minutes or more in a hot oven, then uncover and cook 30 minutes longer. Serve with brown gravy made from drippings in pan.

Savory Pot Roast

2 tablespoons vegetable oil
3-1/2 to 4 pounds beef round or chuck pot roast
1 can (10-3/4 ounces) Campbell's Cream of Mushroom Soup
1 pouch Campbell's Dry Onion Quality Soup and Recipe Mix
1-1/4 cups water
6 medium potatoes, quartered (about 5-1/2 cups)
6 carrots, cut into 2-inch pieces
2 tablespoons all-purpose flour

Prep time: 5 minutes. Cooking time: 3 hours.
In 6-quart saucepot, in hot oil, brown roast on all sides. Spoon off fat. Stir in mushroom soup, onion soup mix and 1 cup of the water. Reduce heat to low. Cover; cook 2 hours. Add vegetables. Cover; cook 45 minutes or until roast and vegetables are fork-tender. Remove roast and vegetables. Stir together flour and remaining 1/4 cup water until smooth. Gradually stir into soup mixture. Cook until mixture boils and thickens, stirring constantly. Garnish with fresh parsley if desired.
8 servings

Creamed Chipped Beef

1/4 pound chipped beef
2 tablespoons butter
2-1/2 tablespoons flour
Pepper
1/2 teaspoon salt
3/4 cup condensed milk
3/4 cup water

Shred the dried beef, cover with hot water, let stand 10 minutes, then drain. Make a white sauce of the butter, flour, seasonings and condensed milk diluted with water. Add the chipped beef and serve on toast points or with mashed or baked potatoes.
Serves 4

Swiss Steak

Select a slice of round steak cut about 2 inches thick. A steak from the top of the round is preferable. For a small family, half of the slice will suffice for 2 meals. A full slice from heavy beef will weigh 4 or 5 pounds. Pound into the steak, on both sides, as much flour as it will take up (nearly 1 cup).
Brown the meat on both sides in bacon or salt pork fat. Peel an onion for each person to be served; cook 5 minutes with 1 No. can of tomatoes, pour over the meat and bake about 2 hours at a temperature of 350 degrees F.

Pot Roast of Beef—Gravy

Nearly any of the tougher meats may be used. The rump or lower part of the round is preferable. Wipe meat, sear in hot frying pan, or in the kettle for roasting. Lard outer surface if meat is lean, or few slices of salt pork may be cooked with meat. After meat is seared, add 1/2 cup boiling water to 2 pounds meat, and cover tightly. Cook slowly until meat is very tender and well browned, adding only enough water to prevent burning. Season when nearly done. Serve with brown gravy made with liquid left in the pan. Instead of water, strained tomatoes may be used with pot roast. For seasoning, in addition to salt and pepper, a bit of bay leaf, parsley, a few cloves, or slices of carrot may be cooked with the roast.

Gravy

To each cup of liquid add, gradually, 2 tablespoons flour mixed till smooth, with an equal quantity of cold water. Cook as white sauce. Strain.

VEAL

Roast Veal

The leg, cushion (thickest part of leg), and loin are suitable pieces for roasting. When leg is to be used, it should be boned. Wipe meat; sprinkle with salt and pepper; stuff and sew in shape. Place on rack in dripping pan, dredge meat and bottom of pan with flour, and place around meat strips of salt pork. Have oven hot 450 degrees F. until meat is seared over; then reduce. Bake 3 or 4 hours in moderate oven 350 degrees F., basting every 15 minutes with 1/2 cup butter melted in 1/2 cup boiling water, until used; then baste with fat in pan. Serve with brown gravy.

Veal Loaf

2 pounds veal
1/4 pound fat salt pork
1/2 cup dry crumbs
2 teaspoons salt
1/2 teaspoon pepper
1 tablespoon chopped parsley
1 tablespoon lemon juice, if desired
2 tablespoons tomato catsup
1 onion
1 egg
1/4 cup milk
1/4 cup bacon fat

Select lean veal, remove skin and membrane, chop fine with salt pork. Add crumbs, seasoning. Brown minced onion in little fat, before adding. Beat egg slightly, add with milk, mix well. Pack in a bread pan, smooth evenly on top and bake in slow oven 2 hours, basting frequently with bacon fat. Meat may be shaped into loaf in roaster and baked in oven. May be served hot, with brown gravy or tomato sauce, or may be used cold.

Veal Cutlets

2-1/2 pounds veal (from round)
1 egg
1 tablespoon water
Fine bread crumbs
Salt
Pepper
4 tablespoons drippings or butter

Wipe meat and cut into pieces for individual serving, removing bone, skin and tough membranes. Skewer small pieces of meat together with wooden tooth-picks. Beat egg and water, so that white is well broken, but not light. Dip meat in sifted, seasoned bread crumbs; dip in egg, then in crumbs again. Melt fat in frying pan. When hot, brown cutlets quickly on both sides. Pour sauce over cutlets, cover, then cook at low temperature for 1 hour or until tender, turning occasionally.

Veal Birds

1-1/2 pounds veal steak
1/4 cup flour
2 tbsp fat
1-1/2 cups boiling water

Wipe veal and trim off fat; cut into 6 pieces of uniform size; spread each piece with stuffing, roll and fasten with tooth-picks. Roll the birds in part of the flour and brown in melted fat. Remove and add the rest of the flour and boiling water—make a smooth gravy. Place birds in a casserole, pour the gravy over them and bake 1 hour at 375°F. Make stuffing according to recipe for flank steak.

Stew with Dumplings

2 pounds lean beef, mutton or veal
1 quart potatoes
2 cups cut carrots
2 cups cut onions
1 cup tomatoes
1 tablespoon salt
3/4 tsp pepper
1 tbsp flour
2 tbsp chopped parsley

Wipe meat, cut into small pieces, put in kettle, cover with boiling water and boil slowly 1-1/2 hours; add carrots and onions; boil 15 minutes, then add potatoes, salt, pepper, and tomatoes; add boiling water, if needed to cover vegetables; boil 30 minutes. Add dumplings and boil 10 minutes without lifting cover. Put meat and vegetables on platter with dumplings around edge. Add flour which has been mixed with a little cold water; boil 3 minutes; pour over stew and sprinkle with parsley.

Dumplings

1 cup flour
2 tsp baking powder
1/2 tsp salt
1 tsp shortening
cold water

Sift flour, baking powder and salt; rub in shortening lightly with fingers; add enough water to make dough hold together. Drop by spoonfuls into stew.

Liver and Bacon

Have liver cut in thin slices; wash, drain, dry and roll in flour. Put bacon thinly sliced into very hot frying pan; turn until brown and transfer to hot platter. Fry liver quickly in the hot bacon drippings, turning often. When done put on platter with bacon. Pour off all but 1 or 2 tablespoons fat, add 1 to 2 tablespoons flour, and stir until brown. Add hot water gradually to make smooth gravy, season and boil 1 minute.

Easter Roast Leg of Lamb with Scallions and Potatoes

1 leg of lamb (6 to 8 pounds), trimmed of visible fat
12 small garlic cloves
12 small sprigs of rosemary
2 tsp salt
2 tsp coarsely ground black pepper
1/4 cup olive oil
2 pounds small potatoes, well scrubbed
1 pound scallions, root ends trimmed
2 cups dry white wine
1 tbsp prepared mustard

Using the point of a small sharp knife, cut 12 slits in the leg of lamb. Insert a garlic clove and rosemary sprig in each slit. Rub the lamb all over with the salt, pepper, and oil. Cover and refrigerate overnight. Preheat the oven to 400°F. Place the lamb on rack in a roasting pan. Roast for 25 minutes, then add the vegetables. Continue cooking the lamb about 1-1/2 hours longer for medium (meat thermometer reaches 160°F.) or until the lamb is done to your liking. (Remove the vegetables if they are getting overcooked.) Transfer the lamb to a cutting board. Remove and discard excess fat from the pan drippings. Place the roasting pan on the stove top and add the wine. Cook over high heat and boil until the mixture is reduced to about 3/4 cup and is slightly thickened, scraping up the browned bits from the bottom. Stir in the mustard to finish the sauce.
Remove the garlic cloves and rosemary before carving the lamb. Serve the lamb with sauce and vegetables. Makes 12 servings.

Veal and Ham Pie

1-1/2 pounds veal
2 hard-cooked eggs
1/2 pound ham
1 tbsp flour
1 tsp grated lemon rind
1 tsp powdered herbs, salt, pepper, red pepper and mace to taste
1 tbsp chopped parsley
Pastry or biscuit dough
Stock

Cut veal and ham into thin slices. Trimmings from roast may be used. Mix on plate the flour, salt, pepper, red pepper, mace, powdered herbs and lemon rind, roll each piece of veal in this seasoning, and lay in deep casserole, alternately, layers of veal, ham, and eggs cut in slices; pile this in center of the dish, add one cupful of water, and parsley; cover with dough and bake in hot oven for 1-1/4 hours.
When baked, add a little well seasoned stock. Serve hot or cold.

Kidney Stew

1 pound kidney
1 carrot
1/2 medium-sized onion
2 cups water
2 tbsp flour
2 tbsp drippings

Scrape and slice carrot, peel and slice onion, and cook together in 2 cups of water until tender. Soak kidneys in water for 1 hour. Drain, clean and dry. Dredge with flour, slice, and brown in frying pan with drippings. Remove kidneys from frying pan, add flour to the fat, and brown. Add to this the 2 cups of water in which the carrots and onions were cooked. Boil until thickened. Add kidneys, onion and carrots. Season with salt and pepper, cook for 3 minutes and serve.

LIVER

Liver and Bacon

Fry bacon—cut liver in slices 1/2 inch thick, dredge lightly with flour, season with salt and pepper, fry in bacon fat.

Braised Liver

Take a calf's liver and skewer into shape. Place a small piece of fat pork or bacon on the top of it and around it. In the covered baker, place 1/4 cup each of diced carrot, onion and celery. Add 1/4 teaspoon of peppercorns, 2 cloves, a bit of bay leaf and 2 cups of water or of brown stock. Cover closely and bake slowly for 2 hours, removing the cover during the last 20 minutes. Make a brown sauce, using the liquid, and pour it around the liver on serving.

LAMB AND MUTTON

Rules for Roast Beef can be followed for Roast Lamb. The leg, shoulder, or loin are suitable for roasting.

Lamb or Mutton Stew

2 pounds lamb or mutton
1 onion
1/2 cup carrot
1/2 cup celery
1 quart stock or water
6 potatoes
1 tsp salt
1/4 tsp pepper

Cut meat into small pieces. Dredge with flour, brown in fat in a heavy frying pan. Brown the diced onion, carrot and celery. Combine with meat, add water or stock made from the bones and trimmings. Cook slowly about 1 hour. Add potatoes and cook until they are soft. Dumplings should be added about 10 minutes after the potatoes. Thicken gravy, if necessary, before adding dumplings.

Dumplings

2 cups flour
4 tsp baking powder
1/2 tsp salt
1 cup milk or water

Sift dry ingredients together in mixing bowl. Mix to drop batter with liquid. Drop from spoon into boiling stew, being careful that there is plenty of water and no possibility of boiling dry. Cover closely and cook undisturbed, and rapidly, for from 10 to 20 minutes, depending on size.

Braised Leg of Mutton

Have the butcher bone a leg of mutton. Wipe, stuff, sew and place in deep pan. Cook 5 minutes in 1/4 cup butter, a slice each of onion, carrot, and turnip cut in dice, 1/2 bay leaf and a sprig each of thyme and parsley; then add 3 cups hot water, 1-1/2 tsp salt, and 12 peppercorns. Pour over mutton, cover closely and cook in oven slowly 3 hours, uncovering for the last 1/2 hour. Remove from pan to hot platter. Brown 3 tbsp butter, add 4 tbsp flour, then pour on slowly the strained liquor; there should be 1-3/4 cups.

Pan Broiled Chops

Chops may be either loin or rib. Wipe and remove superfluous fat. Put chops in a smoking-hot frying pan. Sear quickly on both sides. Sprinkle with salt and pepper. Reduce the heat and continue cooking, turning frequently. For rare chops, cook about 8 to 10 minutes; for well done, 10 to 15 minutes.

Roast Lamb

Wipe meat with damp cloth. Put one or two thin slices of onion on top; season with salt and pepper. Put into roasting pan in hot oven and roast for about one hour and a quarter. Reduce the heat after lamb has been roasting about 20 minutes. Serve on hot platter with brown gravy or mint sauce.

Roast Stuffed Shoulder of Lamb with Browned Potatoes

3-1/2 or 4 pounds shoulder of lamb

Dressing:
2 cups stale bread crumbs
1 tbsp finely cut onion
1 tbsp drippings
1 tbsp chopped parsley
1 tsp salt
1/8 tsp pepper

Wipe lamb with damp cloth; fill pocket with dressing and sew up. Put into hot oven for 20 minutes. When well browned, season with salt and pepper, add 1 cup cold water and roast 45 minutes; add 1 quart white potatoes, which have been washed, pared and boiled, and roast until potatoes are brown. Remove to platter. Add water to pan to make 2 cups of gravy. Thicken gravy by adding 1 tablespoon flour mixed with a little cold water, season and cook until smooth.

Pot Roast of Beef with Browned Potatoes

Wipe beef with cloth, put into iron kettle or frying pan and brown well on all sides. Add 2 tablespoons cut onion, 1 tablespoon salt, 1/4 teaspoon pepper and 2 cups boiling water; and boil slowly 1-3/4 hours; add water as it boils away, 1 cup at a time. After adding potatoes, boil 30 minutes. Place meat and potatoes on hot platter. Add 1 tablespoon flour mixed with a little cold water to gravy and boil. Pour over meat and sprinkle with chopped parsley. Carrots cut in small pieces may be added with potatoes.

Baked Veal with Tomato Sauce

1 thin veal cutlet
1 tsp drippings
1 tsp chopped onion
1 tsp chopped parsley
1/2 cup bread crumbs
1/2 tsp salt
1/8 tsp pepper

Trim edge of cutlet and spread on board or platter. Fry onion in drippings until tender; add bread crumbs and parsley mixed with enough water to hold them together; spread on cutlet and roll; tie in three or four places. Dust with salt, pepper and flour. Place in pan; add 1/2 cup hot water. Roast in hot oven 35 to 45 minutes, adding water if needed. Remove to hot platter; pour tomato sauce around meat and garnish with parsley.

Veal Cutlet

Cutlet may be cooked whole or cut into pieces for serving. Dust with salt, pepper and flour; dip in 1 egg beaten with 1 tablespoon milk, then in bread crumbs. Brown on both sides in shallow fat in hot frying pan. Add boiling water to cover; season and cook slowly for 1 hour. Thicken gravy with 1 tablespoon flour mixed with a little cold water.

Roast Loin of Pork

Wipe pork with damp cloth. Put into pan in very hot oven for 20 minutes, or until well browned, then add 1 teaspoon salt, 1/8 teaspoon pepper and 1 cup cold water. Roast slowly 3 to 4 hours. Add water as necessary. To gravy, add 1 tablespoon flour mixed with cold water, season and boil until thick.

Apple Sauce

Wipe, pare and quarter sour apples; remove seeds and core; put into saucepan and add cold water to almost cover. Cook slowly until soft. Add about 1/2 cup sugar for each quart of apples. Cook a few minutes longer; remove from fire; add little lemon peel and serve either hot or cold.

Roast Pork with Apricots

1 2-pound boneless pork loin roast
6 to 8 dried apricots and/or prunes, pitted
1 medium onion, chopped
1 celery stalk, chopped
1 carrot, chopped
1 cup homemade meat stock or canned chicken broth

Preheat the oven to 375°F. Make a hole in the center of the roast with a sharp knife. Enlarge the hole using the handle of a wooden spoon. Fill the cavity with the dried fruit.
Place the meat and vegetables in a shallow roasting pan and roast for 1 to 1-1/4 hours or until meat thermometer reaches 160°F. for medium. Occasionally add stock to the pan and, using a wooden spoon, scrape the pan and, using a wooden spoon, scrape the pan to loosen the vegetables. (This is called deglazing the pan.)
Remove the pork roast and let stand for 10 minutes before carving. Meanwhile, continue to deglaze the pan with the stock until a sauce has formed. Reheat if necessary. Slice the pork and serve with the vegetable sauce. Makes 6 servings.

Baked Ham

Wash and scrub ham in warm water; soak overnight. Whether a whole or half ham, put on to boil with cold water enough to cover; boil slowly 4 to 5 hours or until tender, allowing about 30 minutes to the pound. Cool in water in which it was boiled; remove skin carefully; put in pan; cover with 1 cup brown sugar and 1 teaspoon pepper; add 2 cups cold water; bake in very hot oven 45 to 60 minutes; baste often. When brown add 1 cup cider or 1/2 cup vinegar and thicken with 2 tablespoons flour.

Plain Fried Ham

Cut a thin slice from the center of a ham and gash the fat on the edge in several places; put in hot frying pan, brown quickly on one side, then turn and brown lightly on the other side. Then cook very slowly until tender. Apples cored and sliced, but not peeled, may be fried in the ham fat and served with the ham.

Baked Ham

1 slice ham about 2 inches thick
1 tbsp flour
2 tbsp brown sugar
3/4 cup condensed milk
3/4 cup water

Trim off fat, cut into small pieces, and mix with the sugar. Rub the flour into the ham, then put into a baking dish. Sprinkle fat-sugar mixture over the top and pour over it the condensed milk diluted with water. Place in a hot (450°F.) oven. After 15 minutes reduce the temperature to 275°F.—a slow oven. Bake until tender, about 2-1/2 hours. Garnish with hard boiled eggs and parsley. Enough milk should remain for gravy. Large slice of ham serves 8.

Beef Loaf

1/2 lbs. pork
1/2 lbs. veal
1 lb. beef
1/2 cup bread crumbs
1/2 onion, finely chopped
1/3 cup condensed milk
1/3 cup water
1 egg, slightly beaten
1-1/2 tsp salt
Few grains pepper
4 thin slices of fat salt pork or bacon

Put meat through a food chopper, mix, and add ingredients in order given. Shape in a loaf; put in a pan and lay across the top of the loaf the slices of salt pork or bacon. Place in a hot oven (425°F). After 15 minutes reduce the heat to 300°F—a slow oven. Bake 1-1/2 hours, basting frequently. Garnish with parsley. Serves 6.

Pork Chops and Potatoes with Condensed Milk

6 potatoes
1-1/2 tsp. salt
Few grains pepper
1 tbsp butter
3/4 cup condensed milk
1-1/4 cups water
Bread crumbs
2 tbsp flour
6 pork chops
1 egg

Scald condensed milk and water in a double boiler. Pare and slice potatoes in 1/4 inch slices. Place a layer in a buttered baking dish, sprinkle with salt and pepper, dredge with flour, and dot over with bits of butter. Repeat and add the scalded milk until it can be seen through the top layer. Dip pork chops in egg and roll in bread crumbs. Place on top of potatoes and bake in a moderate (350°F) oven until the potatoes are soft. Serves 6.

Creamed Sweet Breads

1 lb. sweetbreads
1 tbsp. vinegar or lemon juice
2/3 cup peas
2-1/4 tbsp. butter
2-1/4 tbsp. flour
Pepper
1/2 tsp. salt
3/4 cup condensed milk
3/4 cup water

Soak the sweet breads in cold water for an hour. Cook until tender (about 20 minutes) in boiling water to which 1/2 tsp. salt and 1 tbsp. vinegar or lemon juice have been added. When tender plunge into cold water to harden. Remove membranes and cut or break into small pieces. Add the peas. Make a white sauce of the butter, flour, seasonings, and condensed milk diluted with 3/4 cup water. Add sweetbreads and peas, reheat and serve in patty cases or on toast points. Diced chicken or mushrooms may be added, if desired. Serves 6.

Veal Birds

1-1/2 lbs. veal steak (1/4 inch thick)
3 slices bacon
1/2 small onion
1 tbsp. butter
1/2 cup bread crumbs
1/2 tsp. salt
1/2 tsp. pepper
1 tsp. summer savory
3 tbsp. bacon drippings
1/2 cup condensed milk

Cut veal steak into strips 4x2-1/2 inches, each strip making a bird. Chop trimmings of veal, bacon, and onion and brown in 1 tbsp. butter. Add bread crumbs, salt, pepper, and savory. Moisten with hot water. Spread each piece of veal with a thin layer of the mixture, being careful not to put it too close to the edge. Roll and fasten with skewers or white cord. Sprinkle with salt and pepper, dredge with flour, and fry in bacon drippings until well browned. Add water to half cover the meat and cook slowly about 40 minutes or until tender. Take birds out of pan and remove skewers or cord. Add condensed milk to the juice in the pan and heat. Pour this gravy over the birds and serve at once. Serves 5.

POULTRY

How to Clean

Singe fowl over free flame. Cut off head just below bill. Untie feet, break bone and loosen sinews just below joint; pull out sinews and cut off feet. Cut out oil sac. Lay breast down, make small slit from backbone toward head; loosen windpipe and crop and pull out. Push back skin from neck and cut off neck close to body. Make slit below end of breastbone, put in fingers, loosen intestines from backbone, take firm grasp of gizzard and draw all out. Cut around vent so that intestines are unbroken. Remove heart, lungs and kidneys, wash inside and out with cold water, then wipe dry with cloth. Cut through thick fleshy part of gizzard and remove inside heavy skin without breaking, then cut away gristly part so that only thick fleshy part is used.

Roast Chicken

After chicken has been dressed and cleaned, fill with stuffing, truss securely in compact shape, and lay on its back in roasting pan. Dredge with flour, salt and pepper, dot with bits of butter, if desired, and place in hot oven. As soon as flour is browned, reduce temperature to 350°F., begin to baste with cup of hot water every 10 minutes. Cook until breast meat is tender, about 1 hour for 4-pound chicken. Longer for larger chicken.

Stuffing for Roast Chicken

4 cups bread crumbs
2 tsp. salt
1/4 tsp. pepper
1 egg, slightly beaten
1/2 tsp. poultry, seasoning or onion
2 tbsp. butter, melted
2 to 3 cups boiling water

Mix in order given, combine thoroughly and use to stuff chicken. Butter may be omitted if chicken is fat, or beef drippings may be substituted. If a dry, crumbly dressing is desired, omit the boiling water.

Chicken Fricassee

3 pounds chicken
1 onion
2 cloves
1/2 bay leaf
1 tsp. salt
1/4 cup chopped salt pork fat or other fat
1/3 cup flour

Singe, draw and disjoint a 3-pound chicken. Wash and rinse carefully. Put into a saucepan with 1 quart of water, 1 sliced onion with 2 cloves pressed into it, bay leaf and salt. Simmer slowly until tender. Remove chicken, dredge the pieces generously with the flour, salt and pepper, and brown in the salt pork fat or other fat in a frying pan. When the pieces of chicken are nicely browned on both sides, add the stock in which the chicken has been cooked. If the gravy is not thick enough, add flour thickening to it. Season to taste. Arrange the browned chicken on a platter. Pour the gravy over it. Surround with a border of boiled rice. This is a good way to utilize fowls which need long, slow cooking to make them tender.

To Fry Chicken

Select young chicken. Cut up. Wash, drain, but do not dry. Dredge well with flour and seasoning. Use drippings for fat—salt pork, bacon, beef or chicken fat will do, or use part butter and part other fat. Cook chicken slowly in fat in frying pan until tender, and well browned. Serve with cream or milk gravy.

Chicken a la King #1

2 tbsp. butter or chicken fat
1/4 green pepper, shredded
3/4 cup mushrooms, chopped
3 tbsp. flour
1/4 pimiento, shredded
1 cup chicken broth
1 cup condensed milk
Salt and pepper
1-1/2 cup cold chicken

Saute the green pepper and mushrooms in the butter until tender (about 10 minutes), keeping them covered while cooking. Remove the mushrooms and pepper and blend the flour and seasonings with the fat left in the pan; then add the broth and condensed milk and cook until thickened, stirring constantly. Place the chicken, cut in 1/2 inch dice, pimiento, green pepper, and mushrooms in top part of double boiler. Pour over this the sauce and continue cooking over hot water for 10 minutes. Serve in patty sheels or on toast points. Serves 6.

Chicken a la King #2

2 tbsp. butter
1/4 pound fresh mushrooms
1 tsp. salt
2 tbsp. flour
2 cups milk or 1 cup milk and 1 cup chicken stock
2 cups cooked chicken cut in pieces
1 pimiento
1/4 tsp. pepper

Melt the butter, add the mushrooms, cover and cook about 5 minutes, dredge with flour, add seasonings and liquid, chicken and pimiento. Allow to cook a few minutes until sauce thickens, serve on toast or in patty shells.

Chicken a la Maryland

Cut up chicken as for fricassee. Dip in egg and bread crumbs. Bake in oven, adding small amount of water and basting frequently. Fifteen minutes before removing from oven, add 2 cups cream or milk, and simmer gently. Remove chicken, and thicken liquid.

Chicken Pie

1 chicken
1/2 onion
1 tbsp. parsley
Bit of bay leaf
Salt
1/8 tsp. pepper
1/4 cup flour
Pie crust or biscuit dough

Dress, clean, and cut up chicken. Put in a stewpan with onion, parsley, and bay leaf, salt and pepper. Cover with boiling water, and cook slowly until tender. Thicken stock with flour diluted with enough cold water to pour easily. Cover the chicken mixture with crust in which several incisions have been made. Wet edge of crust and put around a rim, which is close to edge. Bake in a moderate oven 350°F. until crust is well risen and browned.

Prune and Apple Stuffing

3 cups bread crumbs
1/4 cup melted fat
1 tsp. salt
1 cup apples, pared, cut in eighths, and stewed in a little sugar
Few grains pepper
1/2 cup soaked, stewed and stoned prunes
1/2 cup nut meats, broken into pieces, if liked

Mashed Potato Stuffing

2 cups mashed potatoes, highly seasoned with salt and pepper
1/2 cup chopped, parboiled onions
2 egg yolks
2 tbsp. melted fat
1/4 tsp. sage

Mix ingredients in order given.

Poultry Dressing

2 cups stale bread
1 tbsp. finely cut onion
1 tbsp. drippings
1 tbsp. finely cut parsley
1/2 tbsp. salt
1/8 tsp. pepper
1/4 tsp. paprika
Powdered sage if desired

Soak bread in cold water 5 minutes and press out all water. Put drippings and onion into pan and cook slowly, stirring constantly, until onion is tender but not brown. Add bread, parsley and seasoning and mix well together.

Oyster Dressing

20 oysters
2 tbsp. butter
4 cups bread crumbs
1/2 tbsp. salt
1/4 tsp. pepper
1 tbsp. chopped parsley

Drain and rinse oysters with cold water. Put butter in saucepan with oysters and bring to boiling point; add bread crumbs, seasoning and parsley; mix carefully, so that oysters will not be broken.

Giblet Gravy

Boil neck, gizzard and wing tips together until tender. Pour off excess of fat in pan in which poultry has been roasted; add enough stock from the gizzard and neck to make 3 cups of gravy. Chop gizzard, liver and heart and add; then add 1 teaspoon finely cut onion, 1 teaspoon salt, 1/8 teaspoon pepper, 2 tablespoons flour mixed with a little cold water. Boil 3 minutes.

Fricassee of Chicken

Prepare and cut up as for fried chicken. Put into saucepan with just enough boiling water to cover; add a teaspoon salt, a little pepper and, if desired, a teaspoon of onion juice. Boil slowly 2 hours or until tender; add a little water from time to time, as it boils away. Thicken with a tablespoon flour mixed with a little cold water and add tablespoon of finely chopped parsley. Serve with border of hot boiled rice or dumplings.

Fried Chicken

Singe, wash and clean chicken; cut into pieces as follows: two second joints, two drumsticks, two wings, breast cut into two pieces, backbone cut into four pieces. Wipe with damp cloth; sprinkle with salt and pepper; dredge in flour. Put into frying pan with 2 tablespoons bacon drippings or half drippings and half butter and brown quickly. Add a little water, cover, reduce heat and fry slowly on both sides. Remove chicken; mix 1 tablespoon flour with whatever gravy or fat is in pan; add 1 cup cold milk or water; boil until thick.

Caribbean-Fried Chicken

1 2- to 3-pound frying chicken, cut into eighths
1 lemon, cut in half
3 garlic cloves, finely chopped
3 tbsp. Hungarian paprika
2 tbsp. ground black pepper
2 tsp. salt
2 tbsp. dark soy sauce
2 tbsp. Louisiana hot sauce
2 cups vegetable oil
1 cup all-purpose flour

Arrange the chicken pieces in a single layer on a plate. Squeeze the lemon over the chicken and store the chicken in the refrigerator for 15 to 30 minutes.
Rub the garlic into the chicken and sprinkle the chicken on all sides with the paprika, pepper, and salt. Sprinkle the soy sauce and hot sauce evenly over the chicken.
In a large heavy skillet, heat the oil over medium-high heat until hot. Meanwhile, put the flour in a paper bag. Add the chicken pieces and shake until the chicken is coated on all sides; shake off any excess. Place the chicken in the oil and cook the chicken for 10 to 15 minutes on each side until browned and cooked through. Drain the chicken and several layers of paper towels and serve. Makes 4 servings.

Chicken Pie

Singe, draw and clean a 4-lb. chicken as usual. Disjoint, cut the breast into four pieces, cut the thigh and leg apart. Save the neck, wing tips, heart, gizzard and liver for soup. Put on the rest with enough boiling water to cover; cook 2 hours.

Add 2 quarts washed, pared and diced white potatoes. Cook 20 minutes, or until the potatoes are tender. Add 1 tablespoon salt, 1/4 teaspoon pepper, 1 tablespoon chopped parsley and 2 tablespoons flour mixed with a little cold water. Boil 3 minutes. Pour all into dish, cover with rich pastry. Bake 20 minutes in moderate oven.

Pastry

Sift together 1 cup flour, 2 teaspoons baking powder, 1 teaspoon salt; rub in very lightly 4 tablespoons shortening; add just enough cold water to make a stiff dough. Roll out on floured board and put over top of pie.

Chicken and Broccoli

1/4 cup extra-virgin olive oil
2 garlic cloves, finely chopped
1/2 pound boneless, skinless chicken breasts, cut into 1/2-inch-wide strips
1-1/2 cups small broccoli flowerets
3/4 cup oil-packed sun-dried tomatoes, thoroughly drained and thinly sliced
1 tsp. dried basil leaves
Pinch of crushed red pepper flakes
Salt and pepper to taste
1/4 cup dry white wine
3/4 cup chicken broth
1 tbsp. butter or margarine
1/2 pound bow-tie pasta, cooked according to package directions and drained
Grated Parmesan cheese (optional)

In a large skillet, heat the oil over medium heat. Saute the garlic for about 1 minute, until golden, stirring constantly. Add the chicken strips and saute until white and almost completely cooked. Add the broccoli and saute until crisp-tender, then add the sun-dried tomatoes, dried basil leaves, red pepper flakes, salt, and pepper. Add the wine, then add the broth and butter. Cook for about 3 to 5 minutes, or until heated through, stirring occasionally. Toss the freshly cooked pasta with the chicken mixture. Serve with Parmesan cheese, if desired. Makes 4 servings.

Crispy Chicken with Asparagus Sauce

4 skinless, boneless chicken breast halves or 8 boneless chicken thighs
1 egg or 2 egg whites, beaten
1/2 cup dry bread crumbs
2 tbsp. vegetable oil
1 can (10-3/4 oz.) canned cream of asparagus soup
1/3 cup each milk and water
Hot cooked rice
Chopped parsley

In pie plate, dip chicken into egg; coat with bread crumbs. In skillet over medium-low heat, in hot oil, cook chicken 15 minutes or until browned on both sides and no longer pink. Remove; keep warm. In same skillet over low heat, combine soup, milk and water. Heat through, stirring occasionally. Spoon soup mixture over chicken. Serve with rice. 4 servings.

Roast Goose, Bread and Apple Dressing

Wipe inside with damp cloth, and season with salt and pepper; put in dressing and sew up. Push back skin and cut off neck. In the skin put 2 apples, which have been pared and quartered; tie the skin. Put in pan breastbone up; dust with salt, pepper and flour. Place in hot oven; when browned baste with 2 cups cold water; turn breast side down and roast 2 hours, basting three or four times with cold water. Ten minutes before serving turn breast side up. Remove fat and make gravy as directed for Roast Poultry.

Apple Dressing

1 tbsp. drippings
2 tbsp. chopped onions
1 quart finely chopped apples
4 cups stale bread crumbs
1 egg
1 tsp. salt
1/2 tsp. grated nutmeg
1/8 tsp. pepper
1/8 tsp. paprika
2 tbsp. chopped parsley

Put drippings and onion into frying pan, cook a few minutes and add apples. Cover bread with cold water a few minutes, remove and press out all water. Put into pan; add seasoning and beaten egg and parsley. Mix well until thoroughly cooked.

LEFT-OVER MEATS

General Directions

Almost any left-over meat may be combined with other foods, well seasoned, and be made up into very palatable dishes. Beef, veal, mutton, lamb, chicken, and ham are all desirable and may be combined. Fish may be substituted for meat in many recipes. Trim off carefully all non-edible parts.
Cut or chop meat in fine pieces of uniform size. Do not mash.

Casserole of Rice and Meat

2 cups chopped, cooked meat
1 tsp. salt
1/4 tsp. pepper
1/4 tsp. onion juice
1 tbsp. chopped parsley
1 egg
1/4 cup fine bread crumbs
4 cups cooked rice

Season the meat, mix with crumbs and beaten egg, and add meat stock to make mixture pack easily. Line a greased mold, or baking pan, with 2 or 3 cups rice. Pack rice well and fill with meat, cover with the remainder of the rice, cover tightly and steam or bake about 45 minutes. Remove the mold. Serve with tomato sauce.

Shepherd's Pie or Scalloped Meat

2 cups chopped, cooked meat
2 cups mashed potato
2 cups left-over gravy
1 tsp. salt
1/8 tsp. pepper
1/8 tsp. paprika
1 tsp. onion juice
1 or 2 tbsp. butter

It is unnecessary to follow above proportions. Use available amounts of meat and potato, and gravy, and season to taste. Line bottom of buttered baking dish with well beaten mashed potato (either hot or left-over). Add thick layer of meat and gravy, then layer of potato, until dish is full. Make the top crust of potato. Dot with bits of butter. Or, meat and gravy may be placed in lower part of baking dish with single thick layer of mashed potato for the crust. Stiffly beaten egg white may be folded into mashed potatoes before adding to meat, if desired. Bake in hot oven until potatoes are brown, or if cold potatoes have been used, until thoroughly heated and browned. Crumbs, macaroni or rice may be substituted for potatoes.

Minced Meat on Toast

Use any meat, put through food grinder or chop fine in chopping bowl. Heat in gravy, white sauce, or tomato sauce. Add butter, season well, and serve on hot toast.

Hash

1 to 2 cups chopped meat
2 cups cubed potato
1 tsp. salt
1/4 tsp. pepper
1 tsp. mixed onion or celery
3 to 4 tbsp. butter
Enough milk, water or stock to moisten

Any available left-over meat may be used, taking about equal parts of meat and potato. Chop meat first, then add potato and chop together. Season. Melt fat (1 tbsp. to each cup of hash) in frying pan, spread hash evenly and cook slowly for 20 minutes. Shake the pan occasionally to prevent sticking. The hash may be put in a buttered pan and baked in the oven.

Baked Rice and Meat

2 cups cold, cooked meat (chicken, beef, veal or lamb)
2 cups meat stock
1 cup canned tomatoes, salt and pepper
1/2 cup rice
2 tbsp. butter
1 tbsp. Worcestershire sauce
2 medium-sized onions

Cook the meat, which has been cut in cubes, stock, tomatoes, one of the onions cut fine, Worcestershire Sauce and seasonings together for about 10 minutes. Melt the butter in a frying pan and add the onion and uncooked rice. Allow both to brown slightly and add them to the other mixture. Turn all into a buttered casserole and bake 40 minutes.

Meat Croquettes

2 cups chopped, cooked meat
1-1/4 cups White Sauce
1/2 teaspoon salt
1/8 teaspoon pepper

In general, use equal amounts of white sauce and meat. Less will be needed if meat is freshly cooked than if canned meat is used. Meat should be chopped fine, seasoned rather highly, then moistened with sauce as soft as can be handled. Let chill thoroughly on flat dish, then divide evenly into separate portions, allowing 2 tablespoons for each croquette. Shape into balls, cylinders, cones or any desired shape. Roll and sift dry crumbs, beat egg with 1 tablespoon water. Roll croquettes in crumbs, dip in egg, again roll in crumbs, and fry in deep fat, until light brown in color. Drain on paper. They may be served with sauce. Any meat or combination of meats may be used. Fish, eggs and macaroni may be used in same way. Seasoning may be onion, parsley, celery salt. Lemon juice combines well with fish or chicken.

Meat Stew

Cut any left-over cooked meat into 2-inch cubes. Brown in melted fat together with 1 or 2 onions depending on the amount of meat. Add carrots diced and potatoes—cover with stock and cook slowly until the vegetables are almost soft, thicken the gravy with flour and water. Drop dumplings on top, cover lightly and cook about 15 minutes longer. The stock for the stew can be made from the bones and trimmings or from meat or vegetable extract.

MEAT SUBSTITUTES

Milk, eggs and cheese contain the same tissue building properties as meat and can be used in place of it. Dried peas and beans, some cereals and nuts make satisfactory substitutes for meat, particularly when they are combined with any of the above foods. They can also be used with meat to extend the flavor.

EGGS

Boiled Eggs

Drop into boiling water and boil 3 to 3-1/2 minutes for soft boiled, 12 to 20 minutes for hard boiled; or place eggs in boiling water, cover, and cook over moderate heat without boiling from 8 to 10 minutes for soft, 20 to 40 minutes for hard cooked.

Scrambled Eggs

6 eggs
6 tbsp. milk
3 tbsp. butter
1/8 tsp. pepper
1/2 tsp. salt

The general rule is to use 1 tbsp. milk and 1/2 tbsp. butter for each egg. Beat eggs slightly to mix whites and yolks, add salt, pepper and milk. Pour butter into hot omelet pan. When melted, pour in the mixture. Cook slowly at a low temperature, until creamy consistency, lifting from bottom of pan with spatula, as it thickens. Do not stir, but leave in rather large masses. Serve on hot buttered toast.

Poached Eggs

Break eggs and drop carefully one at a time into boiling water in shallow greased frying pan. Cook slowly until eggs are set. Remove each with skimmer and serve on toast garnished with parsley.

Baked Eggs

Toast Circular pieces of bread from which a little of the centers have been removed. Place pieces on a buttered dish. Break an egg and drop contents in the center of bread. Sprinkle with salt and pepper, dot with butter, pour on a little milk or cream and bake in a moderate oven until eggs are cooked.

Baked Eggs with Cheese

Follow directions for baked eggs, sprinkling slices of toast with cheese before eggs are dropped onto them, or slip eggs into buttered egg shirrers. Cover with white sauce, sprinkle with grated cheese and buttered crumbs. Bake until eggs are set.

Poached Eggs in Cream

Put half cup of cream sauce into shallow baking dish. Open eggs carefully and place on sauce. Cook over boiling water from 10 to 15 minutes or until eggs are set or as firm as desired. Cover with half cup of cream sauce, sprinkle with chopped parsley and dust with paprika and serve.

Scalloped Eggs and Ham

4 hard-cooked eggs
3/4 cup or 1 cup cold chopped ham or meat
1-1/2 cups buttered hard crumbs
1 pint white sauce

Chop the eggs, and follow the rule, alternating the eggs and meat, or add chopped eggs and meat to the sauce.

Plain Omelet

Beat 3 eggs with 3 tablespoons milk; add 1/2 tsp. salt and 1/8 tsp. pepper, and mix. Melt 1 tsp. fat in hot frying pan; pour in eggs; lift edges of omelet, allowing thin portions to run underneath, shaking pan until egg is set; when brown underneath, fold over and serve on hot platter.

Puffy Omelet

4 eggs
1/2 tsp. salt
1/8 tsp. pepper
2 tsp. baking powder
1 tbsp. cornstarch
1/2 cup milk or half milk and half water

Separate eggs; mix salt, pepper, baking powder, cornstarch and milk with yolks of eggs. Beat whites until light though not dry and mix in well with yolks. Put into greased hot frying pan and cook slowly until well puffed up. Dry out in oven, fold over in half and serve immediately on hot platter. If desired serve on hot platter. If desired serve with tomato sauce, added before omelet is folded.

French Omelet

6 eggs
6 tbsp. liquid
1/2 tsp. salt
1/4 tsp. pepper
3 tbsp. butter

The general rule is, for each egg use 1 tbsp. liquid, 1/2 tbsp. butter. Season to taste. Break eggs into bowl, beat slightly to mix, or until they can be taken up on spoon; add seasonings and liquid, which may be cold water, milk, or stock. Have ready a smooth, hot pan (lightweight, small pan is best), in which butter has been melted. Shake the pan so that every part is coated with butter. Pour beaten eggs into pan. As eggs cook, shake pan lightly, and with fork or spatula, gently lift egg. Tip pan, so that some of uncooked portion can run to side. When puffed, creamy, and lightly browned on the bottom, take pan in left hand, tilting pan downward. With knife, loosen edge of omelet from pan. Make slight cut in middle at each side at right angles to the handle of the pan, but not entirely through the omelet. Fold quickly, and turn on to a hot plate, from which it is to be served, at once.

Creamy Omelet

6 eggs
1-1/2 cups White Sauce
1 tsp. salt
1/4 tsp. pepper
3 tbsp. butter

Make either French or puffy omelet, using white sauce instead of water. Pour another 1/2 cup white sauce around it before serving, after it has been placed on a hot platter.

Fancy Omelets

A great variety of omelets can be made by either mixing chopped vegetables, fruits, meats, or shellfish with plain omelet before cooking, or folding them in after cooking.

Eggs Florentine

On a bed of cooked and seasoned spinach place eggs which have been poached. Pour over White Sauce seasoned with grated parmesan cheese.

Stuffed Eggs

5 hard-cooked eggs
3 tbsp. American cheese (grated)
1 tsp. vinegar
1 cup White Sauce
1/4 tsp. mustard
1 tsp. salt
1 tbsp. butter
Few grains of cayenne

Cut the hard-cooked eggs in halves lengthwise; remove yolks, mash, add grated American cheese, vinegar, mustard and salt and a few grains of cayenne. Add melted butter. Shape in balls size of original yolks, refill whites. Place in a baking dish, pour around white sauce. Bake in an oven with buttered crumbs.

Lasagna

1 pound ground beef
1/4 cup butter
1 cup chopped onion
1 garlic bud, minced
3 6-ounce cans tomato paste
2-1/2 teaspoons salt
1 No. 2 can tomatoes
1 pound broad noodles, boiled
1 pound mozzarella cheese, shredded
2 pounds dry cottage cheese
1 cup Parmesan cheese

Brown meat in butter. Add onion and garlic. Stir in tomato paste, water, salt, and tomatoes. Cook over low heat for 45 minutes. Cook noodles, rinse and drain. Butter a 13x9x2-inch baking dish. Line dish with layer of noodles, sauce and cheese, ending with sauce and cheese. Bake in a 375° oven for 30 minutes. Let stand for 10 minutes before cutting. Serves 8 to 10.

20

CHEESE DISHES & CROQUETTES

One pound of cheese contains as much fuel value as 2 pounds of meat. Cheese may be added to white sauce and served with boiled rice or boiled vegetables or plain on toast. Cheese may be combined with left-over cereal mush, and baked as a souffle or shaped into cakes and baked in the oven or browned in a little fat in a pan.

Cheese Fondue

1 cup stale bread crumbs
1 cup or 1/4 lb. cheese (cut fine)
1 cup milk
2 eggs
1 tbsp. butter
1/2 tsp. salt
1/8 tsp. mustard
1/8 tsp. paprika

Mix bread, milk and cheese in a double boiler. When cheese is melted, add eggs, beaten until well mixed, add seasonings. Cook until thick and perfectly smooth.

The same mixture may be prepared by placing bread and cheese in layers, in buttered pudding dish, and pouring over it milk, mixed with egg and seasoning, then baking until firm, in moderate oven 325°F. testing with knife, as for all custard mixtures. Dish should be set in pan of water to bake.

Macaroni, rice, or other cooked cereal may be substituted for bread crumbs. More or less cheese may be used. One egg will often be sufficient, or 3 may be preferred. Whites and yolks may be separated and whites stiffly beaten, folded in last. Then bake in buttered pudding dish.

Cheese Souffle

4 tbsp. granulated tapioca
1-1/3 cups milk
1-1/3 cups grated cheese
4 egg yolks well beaten
4 egg whites beaten stiff with 1 tsp. salt

Cook milk and tapioca in double boiler until tapioca is clear. Add cheese and stir until melted. Add egg yolks and mix well. Fold in egg whites. Bake in greased baking dish set in pan of hot water at 350°F. 50 minutes.

Rarebit

1/2 cup milk or cream
2 cups or 1/2 lbs. cheese
2 tbsp. butter
1 egg
1/2 tsp. salt
Sprinkle cayenne

Put milk and grated cheese in upper part of double boiler, or blazer of chafing dish. When cheese is melted, add butter. Pour this mixture over egg, slightly beaten, then return to double boiler. Add seasoning. Stir constantly, and cook until smooth and thick. Serve at once, over slices of toast, or hot crisp crackers.

Baked Rice and Cheese

3 cups cooked rice
Butter
1-1/2 cups cheese grated
Milk
1/2 tsp. salt
Bread crumbs

Cover bottom of buttered baking dish with rice, sprinkle with cheese, season and dot with butter. Repeat until rice and cheese are used. Add milk to half the depth of rice. Cover with crumbs. Bake at 350°F. about 20 minutes or until cheese melts and crumbs are brown.

Cottage Cheese

Heat sour milk to about 100°F. and turn into a strainer lined with cheesecloth. Pour over 1 quart hot water. Let curd hang in cheesecloth bag until all whey has drained off. Add enough cream and melted butter to moisten. Add salt.

Macaroni and Spaghetti

Macaroni and spaghetti are starchy foods, and dishes made from either are served in place of potatoes, and when combined with cheese, also as a meat substitute. If they are carefully and thoroughly cooked, they are pleasing in appearance and palatable. They should be cooked in rapidly boiling, salted water until tender, then drained and rinsed in cold water. This keeps the pieces from becoming mushy and sticking together. They may be used interchangeably in recipes, for they differ in form, rather than in content.

Spaghetti and Tomatoes

Cook spaghetti in boiling salted water until tender. Drain and rinse. Put a layer of the spaghetti in a buttered baking dish. Cover it with a layer of tomato sauce made like White Sauce II, using strained canned tomatoes instead of milk. Dot with 1/4 inch cubes of bacon and onion, chopped fine. Repeat layers until dish is full. Cover with buttered crumbs and put in an oven and bake until hot throughout. A little grated cheese may be sprinkled on each layer of tomatoes, if desired.

Lasagna Primavera

1 8-ounce package lasagna noodles
3 carrots, cut into 1/4-inch slices
1 cup broccoli flowerets
1 cup 1/4-inch sliced zucchini
2 10-ounce packages frozen chopped spinach, thawed
1 8-ounce container ricotta cheese
1 26-ounce jar marinara sauce with mushrooms
12 ounces mozzarella cheese, shredded
1/2 cup grated Parmesan cheese

Bring 3 quarts of water to boil in a 6-quart saucepot over high heat. Add lasagna noodles and cook 5 minutes. Add carrots; cook 2 more minutes. Add broccoli, zucchini, and crookneck squash and cook the final 2 minutes or until pasta is tender. Drain well.

Squeeze the liquid out of the spinach. Mix spinach with ricotta cheese.

Preheat oven to 400°F. In 13x9 inch baking pan, spread one-third of marinara sauce. Arrange half of noodles on sauce. Put half of each of the vegetables, spinach mixture, and mozzarella cheese on the noddles. Pour half of the remaining sauce over these layers. Repeat layering and top with remaining sauce. Sprinkle with parmesan cheese. Place on a large baking sheet that has been lined with foil. Bake lasagna, uncovered, about 30 minutes or until hot in the center. Let stand 10 minutes before serving.

Lasagna may also be assembled up to 2 days before baking and refrigerated, covered, until one hour before baking. If cold, bake for one hour at 350°F.

Macaroni with Cheese

1 cup macaroni
1-1/3 cups White Sauce
1/4 cup chopped or grated cheese
Buttered crumbs

Break macaroni into pieces 1 inch long, boil, strain and rinse. Stir cheese into hot, well seasoned white sauce and put macaroni and sauce in buttered baking dish in layers; sprinkle buttered crumbs on top and brown well in hot oven.

Croquettes

Salmon Croquettes

1 cup cooked salmon
1 tbsp. butter
1 tbsp. flour
1/4 cup milk
1 tsp. lemon juice
1/2 tsp. salt
1/8 tsp. pepper

Make a cream sauce with the butter, flour and milk. Put salmon into bowl and add the sauce, lemon juice and seasoning; mix with fork until salmon is well broken. Set aside and when cold, mold into desired shapes; roll in bread crumbs, then in egg beaten with 1 tablespoon cold milk, then in bread crumbs. Fry in deep hot fat.

Rice Croquettes

1 cup rice
2 eggs
3 tbsp. milk
1 tsp. salt
1 tbsp. sugar
1 tbsp. butter
1 tsp. chopped parsley

Wash rice several times and boil with 2 quarts boiling water 30 minutes. Drain well and put into top of double boiler. Add 1 egg beaten with 2 tbsp. milk, salt, sugar, butter and parsley; cook until egg thickens. Cool and shape into cones, balls or oval cakes. Dip into egg beaten up with 1 tbsp. milk. Roll in bread crumbs and fry in deep hot fat until brown.

Nut and Potato Croquettes

2 cups hot riced potatoes

1/4 cup cream or milk
1/2 tsp. salt
1/8 tsp. pepper
Few grains cayenne
Yolk of 1 egg
1/3 cup chopped pecan nut meats
1/2 tsp. baking powder

Mix all ingredients with fork until light. Shape as for croquettes. Roll in bread crumbs. Dip in egg which has been mixed with a little cold water. Roll in bread crumbs again and fry in deep hot fat until brown. Drain on unglazed paper and serve.

Chicken Croquettes

2 tbsp. butter
2 tbsp. flour
1 cup milk
2 tsp. salt
1 tsp. Worcestershire sauce
1/8 tsp. paprika
1/8 tsp. pepper
1 tbsp. chopped parsley
2 cups chopped, cooked chicken
2 eggs

Melt butter in saucepan; add flour and cold milk slowly, stirring until smooth and creamy; add seasoning and parsley. Boil 3 minutes. Add chicken; mix well and pour out on platter to cool. When cool enough to handle take a large spoon of the mixture in floured hands; shape into balls, cones or oval cakes and put in fat to brown.

Glazed Parsnips

3 cups parsnips, sliced diagonally in 1/2-inch slices
3/4 cup boiling water
1/2 teaspoons salt
2 tablespoons butter
1/4 cup orange juice
1 teaspoon grated orange rind

Place parsnips in water with salt. Bring to a boil. Simmer, covered, about 20 minutes. Drain. Heat remaining ingredients together in a saucepan. Pour over parsnips in serving dish. Serves 6.

21

VEGETABLES

Vegetables should form a large part of our daily diet. They contain water and mineral matter and also health-promoting vitamins. In addition, they contain woody fibers or cellulose which stimulate the intestines.

General Rules for Cooking Vegetables

Wash thoroughly. Pare, peel or scrape, if skins must be removed. Skins should be left on to keep in all the food value possible. Beets must never be peeled before cooking. Soak in cold water until ready to cook. Cook in freshly boiling salted water until tender.

Allow 1 teaspoon salt to 1 quart of water. Use as little water as is possible without burning, except for strong flavored vegetables like cabbage and turnips. These should be cooked uncovered in a large quantity of water. Greens like spinach and kale need only the water which clings to them from washing. To preserve the color of green vegetables, cook uncovered. Water in which vegetables have been cooked is called vegetable stock and should never be thrown away, but used in soups and sauces.

Winter vegetables should be kept in a cool, dark, dry place. Fresh vegetables may be washed and kept on ice in a clean piece of cloth.

Summer vegetables should be cooked on the same day they are gathered. Look them over and wash well, cutting out all decayed parts. Always cook vegetables in freshly boiled water, using as little as possible—just enough to cover. Keep water boiling until done. When cooking green vegetables add salt during the last few minutes of cooking.

Time for cooking vegetables varies with the age of the vegetables and the hardness of the water. Test them by pricking with a fork. Never add soda to vegetables as it has a tendency to destroy the vitamins.

General Table for Cooking Vegetables

Vegetables	Special Directions	Time for Cooking	Serve
Asparagus	Tough lower ends cut off.	15 to 30 minutes	On toast with drawn butter or other sauce.
Beets (old)	Cook unpeeled.	1 to 4 hours	With butter.
Beets (young)	Cook unpeeled.	20 to 30 minutes	With vinegar.
Green Beans	Remove strings and cut in 1 inch lengths.	20 to 30 minutes	With butter.
Brussel Sprouts	Remove wilted or yellow leaves. Soak in salted cold water for an hour.	15 to 20 minutes	With butter or any sauce.
Cabbage	Cut small head of cabbage into 4 parts. Soak in cold, salted water.	15 to 30 minutes	With butter or cream sauce.
Carrots	Scrape, do not peel. Cut in slices or cubes, if large or old.	20 to 30 minutes	With butter or cream sauce.

Vegetables	Special Directions	Cooking	Serve
Cauliflower	Remove green leaves and thick stalk. Soak head down in cold water containing teaspoonful of salt and teaspoonful of vinegar.	20 to 25 minutes	With butter or cream sauce.
Celery	Remove leaves. Scrape stalk. Cut in 3-inch pieces.	30 minutes	With butter or cream sauce.
Cucumbers	Peel and cut in thick slices.	15 minutes	With butter or flour and butter sauce.
Corn on cob	Remove husks and silk.	15 to 20 minutes	Wrap in napkin.
Onions	Peel and cut off roots.	20 to 40 minutes	With butter or cream sauce.
Parsnips	Wash and boil and then scrape off the skins. Cut in slices.	35 to 40 minutes	With butter or cream sauce.
Peas	Shell and boil slowly. Add salt when nearly done.	15 to 30 minutes	
Potatoes	Scrape when old and cook with skins on when young.	25 to 30 minutes	
Spinach	Wash thoroughly in 5 or 6 waters. Use very little water in cooking.	15 to 20 minutes	Chopped and served with butter and a little vinegar, if desired, or with cream sauce.
Squash (summer)	Peel and cut (if the squash is very old, the seeds should be removed).	15 to 30 minutes	Mashed, with salt, pepper and butter.
Squash (winter)	May be served as summer squash, only always remove seeds and stringy portion.	1 to 1-1/2 hours	Mashed.
Tomatoes	Peel and cut in pieces.	20 to 30 minutes	Add sugar, or salt and pepper.
Turnips	Peel and slice. Mash with wooden masher when done.	40 to 50 minutes	Mashed, with butter, salt and pepper.
Lima Beans	Boil gently and add salt when they are nearly done.	15 to 30	With butter.

Asparagus

Tough lower ends should be cut off. Cook in deep saucepan standing upright. The steam will cook the tender tips while the hard stalks will be cooked in the boiling water. Or break into 1 inch pieces, cooking tip parts first and adding the tender tips the last 15 minutes. Serve on toast with drawn butter or with white or Hollandaise sauce.

Saucy Asparagus

1 can 10-3/4 oz. Cream of Asparagus soup
2 tbsp. milk
1-1/2 lb. fresh asparagus spears (24 to 30), trimmed and cut into 1-inch pieces

In 2-quart saucepan over medium heat, combine soup and milk. Heat to boiling, stirring often. Add asparagus. Cover; cook over low heat 10 minutes or until asparagus is tender, stirring occasionally. Serve with grated Parmesan cheese if desired. 8 servings.

Cheddar Baked Potato Slices

1 can Cream of Mushroom soup
1/2 tsp. paprika
1/2 tsp. pepper
4 medium baking potatoes, cut into 1/4-inch slices (about 4 cups)
1 cup shredded Cheddar cheese

In small bowl, combine soup, paprika and pepper. In greased 2-quart oblong baking dish, arrange potatoes in overlapping rows. Cover with foil; bake at 400°F. 45 minutes. Uncover; bake 10 minutes or until potatoes are fork-tender. 6 servings.

Sweet Potato "Souffle"

3 pounds sweet potatoes or yams, peeled and cut into cubes
2 large eggs
3/4 cup firmly packed brown sugar, divided
1/2 cup (1 stick) butter, melted and divided
1 tsp. salt
1 tsp. ground cinnamon
Up to 1/2 cup orange juice
1 cup pecan halves

Preheat over to 375°F. In a large saucepan over high heat, bring the potatoes and enough water to cover them to a boil. Reduce the heat, cover, and simmer for 15 to 20 minutes, or until the potatoes are soft. Drain. In a large bowl, beat the potatoes with an electric mixer until they are smooth. Beat in the eggs, 1/4 cup of the brown sugar, 1/4 cup of the butter, the salt, and cinnamon. Starting with 1/4 cup, beat in just enough orange juice to make the mixture moist and fluffy. Scrape the sweet potato mixture into a 2- to 3-quart souffle dish and smooth the surface into an even layer. Arrange the pecan halves over the top. Sprinkle the remaining 1/2 cup of brown sugar over the pecans. Drizzle the top with the remaining 1/4 cup of melted butter. Bake for 25 to 30 minutes, or until the top is bubbly all over. Makes 10 servings.

Buttered Vegetables

Most vegetables may be served buttered. After they are boiled and drained, they should be returned to the stove and the butter and seasoning added. The pan should be well shaken so the butter will coat the vegetables.

Scalloped Cabbage

Any vegetable or a combination of vegetables can be prepared this way.

1/2 head cabbage
1-1/2 cups white sauce
1/4 tsp. pepper
1/2 cup bread crumbs
1 tsp. salt

Soak and wash half a head of firm cabbage in salted water. Then boil cabbage. Allow to cook and cut fine. Into a well greased baking dish put a layer of well seasoned cabbage (salt, pepper), a layer of white sauce, and continue making layers until all of the ingredients are used. Put well buttered bread crumbs over top of the mixture. Bake (covered) until the mixture is bubbling hot. Then remove cover and brown.

Stuffed Cabbage

1 medium-sized cabbage
1 pound beef
1 slice bacon or salt pork
1 onion
1/2 cup bread crumbs
1/2 cup milk
1 egg
Seasoning
1 green pepper

Select solid cabbage, not too large, remove outside leaves, cut out stalk end, leaving a hollow shell. Chop uncooked beef, with bacon and onion. Add crumbs soaked in milk, beaten egg, salt and pepper. Shape mixture into balls or cakes, arrange in cabbage. Arrange strips of sweet pepper on top of cabbage, tie in cheesecloth, then steam or boil until tender. Serve with tomato sauce.

Celery, Creole Style

1 cup diced celery
2 tbsp. finely chopped onion
1 tbsp. butter
2 tsps. finely chopped green pepper
1/3 cup canned tomatoes
1/2 cup boiling water
1/3 teaspoon salt

Put celery in saucepan with boiling water and boil 10 minutes or until tender. Melt butter, add onion, salt and pepper, and cook slowly 5 minutes and stir in the tomatoes, add celery and cook the entire mixture 10 to 15 minutes longer.

Succotash

To a pint of cooked corn add a pint of cooked and seasoned shelled lima beans. Serve buttered or in milk.

Corn a la Southern

1 can corn
2 eggs
2 tbsp. melted butter
1 pint scalded milk
1 medium-sized green pepper
1 tsp. salt
1/8 tsp. pepper

Chop pepper, mix ingredients in order given pour into buttered pudding dish, and bake slowly until firm. Fresh corn cut from the cob may be used in the same manner.

Fried Eggplant

Peel an eggplant, cut in thin slices, sprinkle with salt and pile on a plate. Cover with weight to extract the juice and let stand for 1-1/2 hours, or soak in brine for same time. Dredge with flour and fry slowly until crisp and brown, or dip in egg and crumbs, fry.

Stuffed Eggplant

1 eggplant
1 cup crumbs
2 tbsp. butter
1/2 tbsp. onion
1 egg
Seasoning

Cook eggplant 15 minutes in enough boiling salted water to cover. Cut a slice from top and with a spoon remove pulp, taking care not to work too close to skin. Chop pulp, add soft stale bread crumbs. Melt butter, add finely chopped onion, and cook 5 minutes. Add to chopped pulp and bread, season with pepper and salt, and, if necessary, moisten with a little water. Cook 5 minutes, cool slightly, and add 1 beaten egg. Refill shell with mixture and bake 40 minutes at 350°F.
Cooked rice or macaroni may be substituted for crumbs. Chopped meat may be added.

Creamed Mushrooms

Wash and stem mushrooms. Remove the peeling if it seems tough. Melt in a saucepan about 2 tbsp. butter for every 1/2 pound of mushrooms. Add mushrooms, cover tightly and cook over a low fire 10 minutes. Dredge lightly with flour, season with salt and pepper and cover with thin cream. Cook 5 minutes longer and serve on toast.

Boiled Onions in White Sauce

Peel the onions and cut off the roots, dropping into cold water as fast as they are peeled. Drain from the cold water and put in a stewpan with boiling water to cover generously. Add 1 teaspoon of salt for each quart of water. Boil rapidly for 10 minutes, with the cover partly off the saucepan. Drain off water and cover onions with hot, sweet milk (1 quart of onions will require 1 pint of milk). Simmer for 1/2 hour. thicken sauce with 1 tablespoon butter, combined with 1 level tablespoon flour. Add 1 teaspoon of salt and 1/4 teaspoon of white pepper.

Okra, Rice and Tomatoes

1 quart okra pods
1 cup rice
1/2 can tomatoes
2 tbsp. butter
Salt and pepper
Sprinkle of paprika

Broiled Tomatoes

6 good-sized tomatoes

1 cup finely ground cooked chicken
2 tbsp. grated cheese
Milk
Salt
Pepper

Sprinkle flour over cooked chicken and add milk enough to moisten well. Heat in saucepan until thickened. Cut tomatoes in half crosswise, spread with chicken mixture, sprinkle cheese on top. Put under broiler turned on half way. Broil until lightly browned on top.

Fried Tomatoes

Slice firm unpeeled tomatoes. Dip in flour to which salt and pepper have been added. Fry to a light brown on both sides; about 5 or 6 slices at a time, taking care not to break them. Remove from pan, pour into milk and let come to a boil. Pour over tomatoes. Usually enough flour is left in pan to slightly thicken sauce.

Hashed Turnips

Chop cooked and drained turnips into rather large pieces. Return to the stewpan, and for 1-1/2 pints of turnips, add 1 teaspoon of salt, 1/4 teaspoon of pepper, 1 tablespoon of butter and 4 tablespoons of water. Cook over a very hot fire until the turnips have absorbed all the seasonings. Serve at once.

Baked Beans

1 quart beans
1/2 pound salt fat pork
1 teaspoon mustard
3/4 cup molasses
1 teaspoon salt

Pick over and wash beans; cover with cold water and soak overnight. In the morning, drain, cover with fresh water and cook slowly below boiling point until soft, then drain. Put 1/4 inch slices of salt pork in the bottom of an earthen bean pot or covered crock. Put beans in pot and bury the remaining pork (which should be gashed in several places) in the beans. Mix the salt, mustard and molasses in a cup; fill the cup with boiling water and pour the mixture over the beans. Add enough more boiling water to cover beans. Cover bean pot, put in oven, and bake in a slow oven 300°F. 5 to 8 hours. If baked a long time, they become dark and have a rich flavor.

Red Beans

Red beans may be cooked as lima beans. They may be served in white sauce, tomato or meat-stock sauce.

Stuffed Peppers

6 green peppers
1/2 cup English walnuts, chopped
1 large onion
1 tsp. salt
1 tsp. melted fat
1/8 tsp. pepper
1/2 cup bread crumbs
1/2 cup milk

Select broad peppers that will stand on end and are easy to serve. Cut top from each pepper. Remove seeds and parboil 15 minutes. Stuff with filling mixed in the order given above. Bake 20 minutes at 400°F., basting frequently with hot water. Any leftover meat can be substituted for the nuts. Tomatoes and rice make an excellent filling for peppers.

Chili Con Carne

1 pint dried lima beans or kidney beans, soaked overnight
2 cups beef, chopped
1 tsp. salt
1/4 cup suet, forced through food chopper
1 red pepper, cut in strips
1/2 onion, sliced
1/8 tsp. pepper
1/2 tsp. mustard
1 tbsp. vinegar
Tomatoes to cover

Arrange ingredients in layers in a bean pot. Cover with water and bake slowly at a temperature of 300°F. 3 or 4 hours.

Spinach Au Gratin

3 tbsp. butter
3 tbsp. flour
1/2 tsp. salt
1/8 tsp. pepper
1/2 cup condensed milk
1 can spinach
3/4 cup spinach liquid
1/4 cup grated cheese
1/2 cup dried bread crumbs combined with 2 tbsp. melted butter

Melt the butter; add flour and seasonings and mix thoroughly; add condensed milk and the liquid from the can of spinach. Stir constantly until smooth and thick. Add the grated cheese and as soon as this is melted add the spinach. Put the mixture into a casserole, cover with buttered bread crumbs and put in the oven for 10 minutes or until the crumbs are browned. Serves 5.

Scalloped Cabbage

1 medium head of cabbage
3 slices of broiled bacon
1 cup white sauce
1/2 green pepper
1/2 cup bread crumbs stirred in 2 tbsp. melted butter

Cut cabbage in quarters, cook in boiling salted water (using 1 tsp. salt to 1 quart water) until tender—about 15 minutes. Cut the broiled bacon in small squares, dice the green pepper, and add both to the white sauce. Put alternate layers of cabbage and white sauce in a casserole, shaking salt over each layer of cabbage before adding the white sauce. Cover the top layer with buttered crumbs and brown in a moderate oven. Serves 6.

Corn Souffle

3 tbsp. butter
4 tbsp. flour
1 tsp. salt
1/8 tsp. pepper
1/4 tsp. celery salt
1/2 cup condensed milk
1/2 cup water
1 cup canned corn
2 tbsp. chopped pimiento
3 eggs

Make white sauce of the butter, flour, seasonings, and condensed milk diluted with the water. Add the corn, pimiento, and beaten egg yolks. Fold in beaten egg whites and pour into buttered baking dish; bake in a slow oven until firm (about 30 minutes). Serves 5.

Creamed Vegetables

Use 2 cups of vegetable to one cup of white sauce. In making the white sauce use the water in which the vegetables have been cooked, rather than plain water. Pour the white sauce over the vegetables and mix gently with a fork so as to preserve the dices, squares, strips, or slices of vegetable. Variety may be obtained by adding grated cheese, diced pimiento, shredded green pepper, chips of broiled bacon, or celery salt to the white sauce.

Stuffed Baked Potato

6 medium sized potatoes
2 tbsp. butter
1 tsp. salt
1/2 tsp. pepper
2 tbsp. condensed milk
2 tbsp. water
1 egg white
2 tbsp. grated cheese

Bake potatoes in a hot oven for 45 minutes or until soft. Remove from oven and cut off the top third of each; then scoop out insides. Mash potatoes, add seasoning, and then the condensed milk and water heated together; beat well; add egg white well beaten. Refill potato shell; sprinkle top with grated cheese and put into a hot oven to brown. Serve at once. Serves 6.

Baked Cauliflower

1 medium cauliflower
1 cup white sauce
1/3 cup bread crumbs stirred in 1 tbsp. melted butter

Remove leaves and trim off stalk from the cauliflower. Soak in a solution of 1 tbsp. vinegar, 1 tsp. salt, and 1 quart of cold water for 5 minutes to remove dirt and insects. Cook whole, stem up, in boiling salted water until tender (about 10 minutes). Put cauliflower in a buttered baking dish, pour the white sauce over it, and cover with buttered bread crumbs. Brown in a moderate oven. Serves 6.

White Sauce for Creamed Vegetables

1-1/2 tbsp. butter
1-1/2 tbsp. flour
1/2 tsp. salt
few grains pepper
1/2 cup condensed Milk
1/2 cup water

Pickled Beets

Wash and boil six medium sized beets until tender. Remove skins; slice or cut into quarters; cover with 1/2 cup vinegar, 1 teaspoon salt, 1/8 teaspoon pepper and 1 tablespoon sugar.

Creamed Carrots

Wash and scrape carrots; cut into thin slices. Cover with

boiling water and boil until tender. Drain and mix with cream sauce or melted butter. Sprinkle with chopped parsley.

Boiled New Cabbage

Cut cabbage into quarters, removing hard part of core, and place in cold water 30 minutes. Drain, cover with boiling water and boil, without a cover, 30 minutes or until tender. Drain, put into dish and pour over Cream or Béchamel Sauce.

Cole Slaw

Wash cabbage; cut into quarters, and then slice very thin; allow to stand in cold water 30 minutes; drain well and cover with boiled or French dressing.

Spinach

Pick over carefully and wash thoroughly in several waters until every bit of sand is removed. Put into large kettle and add very little boiling water, about 1/2 cup. Young spinach does not need any water. Boil until tender or about 25 minutes. Drain thoroughly, chop fine and drain again. Season with salt and pepper and garnish with slices of hard-boiled eggs.

Cauliflower

Remove leaves and wash cauliflower; place in uncovered saucepan, stem end down; cover with boiling water; boil 35 minutes or until tender and serve with Cream Sauce.

French Fried Potatoes

Pare and cut potatoes into long even pieces. Put into cold water for about an hour. Drain and dry well. Fry in deep fat until brown and cooked through; drain on unglazed paper. Salt just before serving. Sweet potatoes may be prepared in same way.

Potato Cakes

Pare and boil 1 quart potatoes; mash and season with salt, pepper and paprika; add 1 tablespoon melted butter; mix lightly. Take a spoonful into floured hands and roll. Dip in egg beaten with 1 tablespoon cold milk, then in flour. Fry in deep or shallow hot fat.

Brussels Sprouts

Wash and cover with cold water for an hour. Drain; put over fire in saucepan of boiling water; boil 20 to 25 minutes without a cover. Drain and cover with cream sauce; or serve with salt, pepper and melted butter.

Boiled Corn

Husk corn, removing all silk. Put corn into fresh boiling water to cover; boil rapidly for 5 minutes. Remove from water and place on platter on which a napkin has been spread, covering corn with ends of napkin. Serve immediately.

Lima Beans

Shell beans just before using. Rinse in cold water. Put into saucepan; cover with boiling water and boil until tender. Drain and add seasoning and melted butter.

Kohlrabi

Peel turnip-shaped globe; cut into small pieces; boil until tender, 30 to 35 minutes. Add one teaspoon salt to each quart water. Serve plain with melted butter and pepper, or with cream sauce. The leaves may be stemmed and cooked as greens, boiling 40 minutes.

Candied Sweet Potatoes

Boil 1 quart sweet potatoes in salted water until tender; drain and scrape off skins; cut into slices and lay in shallow greased baking dish; brush with melted drippings or butter; sprinkle with 1/2 cup brown sugar; add 2 tablespoons butter. Bake in hot oven until well browned.

Baked Tomatoes

6 tomatoes
2 cups soft bread crumbs
1/2 teaspoon salt
1/8 teaspoon pepper
1 tablespoon butter

Wash tomatoes and cut off stem ends; remove pulp from center and fill with bread crumbs seasoned with salt and pepper; sprinkle with bread crumbs and place small piece of butter on each. Bake in hot over 30 minutes. The pulp may be seasoned to taste, cooked in the pan and served as a sauce.

Browned Parsnips

1 quart parsnips
1 teaspoon salt
2 tablespoons butter or bacon drippings
1/8 teaspoon pepper

Wash, pare and cut parsnips into 1/2-inch slices. Cover with boiling water and boil until tender, 25 to 30 minutes; drain. Brown on greased griddle or frying pan. Season with salt and pepper.

Oyster Plant

Wash and cover with boiling water. Cook 40 to 60 minutes or until soft. Peel, cut in pieces and serve with Cream Sauce.

Stuffed Potatoes

Bake 4 large potatoes. Cut in half lengthwise and, without breaking skins, scoop out insides and mash; add 1/2 teaspoon salt, 1/8 teaspoon pepper, 1 teaspoon chopped parsley, 1 tablespoon melted butter and mix with fork. Return to shells, put a few drops milk on top; rough with fork; sprinkle with paprika. Place in oven until brown.

A. SAUCES

These sauces can also be used for meat or fish.

Hollandaise Sauce

1/2 cup butter
2 eggs yolks
1/4 tsp. salt
Sprinkle of cayenne
1 tbsp. lemon juice

Divide butter into 3 pieces. Put 1 piece in a pan with the egg yolks and lemon juice and cook over hot water, stirring constantly with wire whisk. Don't let water touch pan or egg will cook too quickly. As the sauce thickens, add the second piece of butter, then the third. Remove from fire, add seasoning. One tablespoon of cream added helps to keep the sauce from separating.

Hollandaise Sauce #2

2 egg yolks
2 tbsp. oil
1 tbsp. lemon juice
1/2 teaspoon salt
few grains cayenne pepper
1/2 cup boiling water

Add yolks of eggs one at a time to oil. Beat well; add lemon juice, salt and pepper. About 5 minutes before serving add boiling water slowly and stir rapidly. Cook over water or in double boiler until it thickens. Serve hot on cauliflower, asparagus or fish.

Golden Sauce

3 tbsp. butter
3 tbsp. flour
1-1/2 cups milk
1/4 tsp. salt
1/8 tsp. pepper
2 egg yolks
1 tsp. lemon juice or vinegar

Make sauce of first 3 ingredients, salt and pepper. Beat egg yolks slightly and just before serving, add sauce and heat. Add lemon juice and serve at once.

Mint Sauce

8 stalks mint, or 2 tbsp. dry mint
2 tbsp. sugar
1/2 cup vinegar

Wash mint and pick leaves from stems. Chop fine. Add sugar to vinegar. Pour over mint leaves. Let stand 1 hour.

Cream or White Sauce

I
1 tbsp. butter
1 tbsp. flour
1 cup milk
1/4 tsp. salt

II
2 tbsp. butter
2 tbsp. flour
1 cup milk
1/4 tsp. salt

III
3 tbsp. butter
3 tbsp. flour
1 cup milk
1 tsp. salt

Melt butter in saucepan, then add flour, stirring until mixture becomes foamy, but not brown. Add milk, continue stirring to ensure smoothness, cook until thickened. Season.
White Sauce I is used in preparation of creamed vegetables. II is used in cream soups and scalloped dishes. III is that usually used for croquettes.
The general rule for use of white sauce for creamed scalloped vegetables is to use half as much white sauce as vegetables. For example, for 1 pint of potatoes, use 1 cup of white sauce.
For croquettes, use equal amounts of white sauce and meat. Chill mixture before using.

Cheese Sauce

Add 1/3 cup of grated cheese to 1 cup of White Sauce No. 2 and stir until it is melted. Serve hot with vegetables or fish.

Pimiento Sauce

Add 3 tbsp. chopped pimiento to 1 cup of white sauce No. 2. Serve hot with vegetables or fish.

Egg Sauce #1

Add 1 chopped hard cooked egg, t tbsp. chopped parsley, and 1/4 tsp. celery salt to 1 cup of white sauce No. 2. Serve hot with vegetables or fish.

Caper Sauce

1/2 cup Carnation Milk
1/2 cup water
2 tbsp. butter
2 tbsp. flour
1 small onion
1/2 tsp. salt
1/8 tsp. pepper
1/4 cup capers

Scald the Carnation and water together. Melt the butter, add chopped onion and when brown add the flour and let brown; add the salt, pepper, and scalded milk, stirring constantly. Cook for about five minutes and add the drained capers. Serve hot with fish.

Mock Hollandaise Sauce

1 tbsp. butter
2 tbsp. flour
1/2 tsp. salt
1/8 tsp. pepper
3/4 cup Carnation Milk
2 egg yolks
1/4 cup butter
1 tbsp. lemon juice
Few grains cayenne

Follow method given above for White Sauce. Stir in beaten egg yolks after sauce is cooked and then add butter, bit by bit, and finally the lemon juice. Serve hot with vegetables or fish.

Egg Sauce #2 (For Fish)

1 cup white sauce
2 chopped hard-boiled eggs
1 tbsp. chopped parsley
1 tsp. lemon juice or vinegar

Add eggs, parsley and lemon juice to white sauce after removing from fire.

Cocktail Sauce

To one cup thick mayonnaise add one teaspoon finely chopped parsley, one tablespoon chopped pimientos, one tablespoon finely chopped olives, two tablespoons tomato catsup and a few drops Tabasco.
Serve on cold crabmeat, lobster, shrimp or oysters.

Caramel Sauce

1 cup brown sugar
2 tbsp. cornstarch
1-1/2 cups boiling water
1/2 tsp. salt
1-1/2 tbsp. oil
1 tsp. vanilla extract

Mix sugar and cornstarch; add boiling water; stir until thickened and cook 10 minutes; add salt, oil and vanilla and serve immediately or place over boiling water until ready to serve.

Sauce Tartare

To 1 cup mayonnaise add 1/4 teaspoon mustard, and 1 teaspoon powdered sugar. Just before serving mix in 1 tablespoon each of finely chopped capers, olives, pickles and parsley.

Sauce Tartare

Make 1 cup mayonnaise, chop very fine 1 tablespoon each of capers, olives, pickles and parsley. Press in a cloth till quite dry. Blend gradually with the mayonnaise.

Gravy

4 tbsp. fat from roast
2 cups boiling water
3 tbsp. corn starch
1/2 tsp. salt
1/4 tsp. pepper

Put pan with fat over fire. Add boiling water slowly. Mix corn starch with a little cold water and add to fat stirring well until smooth. Add seasoning and cook until thick.
More boiling water can be added if thinner gravy is desired. Strain and serve.

Brown Sauce or Gravy

1 tbsp. butter or fat in which meat was cooked
1 tbsp. flour
1 cup beef stock or boiling water
salt and pepper

Brown butter in saucepan; add flour and brown; add liquid and stir until smooth and thick. Season to taste and simmer 5 minutes.

Currant Jelly Sauce

1/2 glass currant jelly
1 cup hot brown sauce

Melt jelly over slow fire. Add sauce; stir well and simmer one minute.

Maitre d'hôtel Butter

2 tbsp. butter
1 tbsp. lemon juice
1/2 tsp. salt
1/8 tsp. white pepper
1 tbsp. chopped parsley

Cream butter; add gradually lemon juice, seasoning and parsley. Keep cold until served.

Mint Sauce

1/4 cup chopped mint leaves
1/2 cup vinegar
1/4 cup water
1/4 cup brown or granulated sugar

Cook all ingredients in saucepan over very slow fire for about one-half hour. Do not allow to boil. Serve hot.

Horse-Radish Sauce

2 tbsp. butter
2 tbsp. grated fresh horse-radish
1 tbsp. very thick cream
1/2 tsp. lemon juice

Cream butter; add horse-radish, cream and lemon juice. Keep very cold.

Cranberry Sauce

1 quart cranberries
2 cups sugar
1 cup water

Put all together into saucepan. Cover until it boils. Remove cover and cook about 10 minutes or until berries have all burst. Pour into mold, chill and serve.
For Cranberry Jelly strain and put into mold and chill.

Apple Dressing

1 tbsp. drippings
2 tbsp. chopped onions
1 quart finely chopped apples
4 cups stale bread crumbs
1 egg
1 tsp. salt
1/2 tsp. grated nutmeg
1/8 tsp. pepper
1/8 tsp. paprika
2 tbsp. chopped parsley

Put drippings and onion into frying pan, cook a few minutes and add apples. Cover bread with cold water a few minutes, remove and press out all water. Put into pan; add seasoning and beaten egg and parsley. Mix well until thoroughly cooked.

RELISHES

Chili Sauce

1 peck ripe tomatoes, finely chopped
12 onions (size of egg), finely chopped
6 green peppers (small), finely chopped
1 pint brown sugar
1 pint vinegar
3 tbsp. salt
1/2 tbsp. allspice
1 tbsp. cinnamon
1/4 tbsp. cloves
1/2 tsp. paprika

Mix the first 6 ingredients together and cook until nearly done, before adding the spices.

Mustard Pickle

1 quart small cucumbers
1 quart large cucumbers, sliced or diced
2 quarts small pearl onions
1 quart green tomatoes, sliced
2 quarts small green tomatoes
2 quarts butter beans or celery cut in 2-inch pieces
3 small heads cauliflower, torn apart
6 green peppers, cut in strips

Prepare vegetables overnight and soak in a strong brine made by adding 2 cups of salt to each gallon of water. In the morning bring to the boiling point and let simmer until vegetables are tender. Drain thoroughly in a colander and cover with the following mustard dressing: Mix together 1-1/4 cups sugar, 4 tbsp. each flour and powdered mustard, 1/2 tbsp. turmeric, 1 teaspoon celery salt; add slowly 3 pints of hot vinegar; stir till smooth. Cook in double boiler till it thickens. Pour over hot vegetables; simmer for 5 minutes. Pack in hot, clean jars.

22
LUNCHEON DISHES

Chicken Patties

2 tbsp. butter
2 tbsp. flour
1 cup chicken stock
1/2 tsp. salt
few grains cayenne pepper
1 cup cold diced chicken

Melt butter in saucepan; stir in flour; add chicken stock; season and bring to a boil; add chicken and cook slowly 5 minutes. Fill patty shells and serve at once.

Royal Patty Shells

2 cups flour
2 tsp. Royal Baking Powder
1/2 tsp. salt
4 tbsp. shortening
ice water

Sift flour, baking powder and salt together; add shortening and rub in very lightly with tips of fingers; add very slowly enough water to make stiff dough. Roll out thin; cut into circles and form on the outside of patty or muffin tins. Bake in hot oven, open side down, until light brown; remove carefully from tins and return shells to oven and bake 5 minutes, open side up.

Boston Baked Beans

1 quart beans
1/2 pound salt pork
1 tbsp. salt
1/4 tsp. pepper
1/2 tsp. dry mustard
2 tbsp. molasses

Wash and soak beans overnight. Put half into bean pot; wash salt pork and place in center; add remainder of beans, salt, pepper, mustard, molasses and 4 cups cold water; cover. Put into slow oven and bake 8 hours. Add more water if needed.

Baked Macaroni with Cheese

1 cup macaroni
1 tbsp. butter
1 tbsp. flour
1 cup milk
1/2 cup grated cheese
1 tsp. salt
1/8 tsp. pepper
1/8 tsp. paprika

Boil macaroni in salted water until soft; drain and rinse with cold water.

Sauce

Melt butter in saucepan; add flour, mix well and add cold mild slowly, stirring until smooth; add cheese, salt, pepper and paprika. Boil 2 minutes.

Cheese in Scallop Shells or Ramekins

1 cup milk
2 cups bread crumbs
1/2 tsp. salt
1/8 tsp. pepper
1/4 tsp. Worcestershire sauce
2 cups grated American cheese

Pour milk over bread crumbs, add seasoning, half the cheese and mix well; fill greased scallop shells or ramekins; sprinkle with remainder of cheese and a few fresh bread crumbs and bake in moderate oven 30 minutes.

Cheese Straws

1 cup grated American cheese
1 cup flour
1 tsp. Royal Baking Powder
1/16 tsp. cayenne pepper
1/4 tsp. paprika
1 egg

2 tbsp. milk

Mix together cheese, flour, baking powder, cayenne pepper and paprika; add beaten egg; mix well; add milk enough to make a stiff dough. Roll out 1/4 inch thick, on floured board; cut into strips 5 inches long and 1/4 inch wide. Bake in hot oven 15 minutes.

Kidney Beans with Bacon

Wash and soak 1 pint kidney beans in cold water overnight; drain, cover with boiling water, add 1/4 pound bacon, boil until beans are tender, and drain. Season beans with salt and pepper to taste. Brown thin slices of bacon in frying pan, and serve over beans.

Tomatoes and Eggs

Grease muffin tins; put one thick slice of unpeeled tomato into each tin; season with salt and pepper; break one egg on top of each slice; again season with salt and pepper and put a small piece of butter on top of each egg. Bake in oven until egg is set but not hard. Serve on rounds of toast and garnish with parsley.

Corn Pudding

1 quart fresh corn cut from cob
1 tsp. salt
1/4 tsp. pepper
3 eggs slightly beaten 2 cups milk
3 tbsp. melted butter

Put all ingredients into greased baking dish and bake in moderate oven until firm.

Scotch Potatoes

1 quart potatoes
1 quart onions
1 tsp. salt

Wash, pare and cut potatoes and onions in half-inch rounds. Put into saucepan with boiling water to cover, adding salt. Boil 25 or 30 minutes, or until tender. Drain, put into dish and cover with Thick Cream Sauce. Bake in hot oven about 25 minutes.

French Toast

1/2 cup flour
1 tsp. Royal Baking Powder
1/4 tsp. salt
1/2 cup milk
1 egg
sliced bread

Sift together flour, baking powder and salt; add milk and beaten egg; beat well. Into this dip bread, fry in hot fat, drain, and serve hot with powdered sugar.

Cheese Soufflé

2 tbsp. butter
3 tbsp. flour
1/2 cup milk
1/2 tsp. salt
few grains cayenne
1 cup grated American cheese
yolks of 3 eggs
2 tsp. Royal Baking Powder
whites of 3 eggs

Melt butter, add flour, and when well-mixed add milk slowly. Add salt, cayenne, and cheese. Remove from fire, add yolks of eggs beaten until light. Cool mixture and mix in baking powder and beaten egg whites. Bake in greased dish 25 minutes in slow oven. Serve at once.

A. The Lunch Box

The lunch carried from home requires thought in planning so that it will be satisfying, nutritious and appetizing. The container used plays a large part in keeping the lunch in good condition.

The lunch box should be dust-proof, well ventilated and easily washed. Metal boxes have these advantages, and when collapsible they are easy to carry home. Some are arranged in compartments and are equipped with thermos bottles.

Baskets are not easily cleaned and unless the food is well wrapped, it dries out quickly.

Fibre boxes are cheap, but they are absorbent and therefore hard to keep clean.

Wax paper, paper napkins, paper plates and containers, paper or collapsible metal cups, thermos bottles and sealtight jars all aid in preparing lunches.

The container should be lined with a paper napkin and each article wrapped separately in waxed paper, and placed in the order in which the food will be eaten. Articles should be packed compactly so that the food cannot be shaken about.

The lunch box menu should be planned to include a substantial food, a juicy fruit or vegetable, a simple dessert and a beverage.

Sandwiches, which are usually included, should be made from day-old bread, which may be graham, whole wheat, rye, rolls or white bread.

In cutting the bread, arrange the slices so that they will fit together.

Cream the butter or butter substitute until soft enough to spread easily. The butter tends to prevent a soft filling from making the bread soggy.

Sandwiches

Meat

Minced ham with cream or salad dressing.
Left-over meat, minced, with cream or salad dressing.

Dried beef, plain or frizzled.

Slices of beef, ham, chicken, lamb, sprinkled with salt or spread with a little salad dressing.

Broiled sliced bacon.

Beef or pork liver cooked until tender, put through food grinder, mixed to a paste with melted butter, seasoned with salt, pepper and onion juice.

Half liver and half hard-cooked egg.

Fish

Tuna fish or salmon, plain or mixed with salad dressing.
Sardines, minced, with lemon juice added.

Egg

Hard-cooked, chopped and mixed with salad dressing.
Scrambled, plain or in milk, or with bits of chopped bacon.

Cheese

Cream cheese with chopped nuts, olives or peppers, or a combination of these.
Sliced cheese with salad dressing or mustard on rye bread.
Cottage cheese with onions and cream or salad dressing used with brown bread. Pimiento may also be added.
Add India relish to well-seasoned fresh cottage cheese.
Add chopped English walnuts to cottage cheese. This will make a dark filling but a good flavor.
Chopped parsley, cottage cheese and salad dressing.

Fruit

Date combination.
Chopped dates, 6; butter, 2 teaspoons; orange or lemon juice, few drops (2 sandwiches).
Wash dates and put through chopper. Add a little salt, equal amount or more of peanut butter or cream cheese and a few drops of lemon juice. Mix well.
NOTE: Cooked prune pulp or raisins may replace dates.
Chop dates, add little sweet fruit juice, heat and rub to a smooth paste. Add shredded coconut and a few chopped nuts and orange or lemon juice. (Excellent with brown bread.)
Jams and jellies.
Ripe bananas mixed with chopped peanuts or peanut butter.

Vegetable

Plain lettuce with salad dressing.
Sliced tomato with salad dressing, or lettuce and tomato.
A small amount of diced, pickled cucumber with cottage cheese.
Pickled beets, chopped and mixed with cottage cheese.
Chopped celery, apple, nuts or olives (any proportion preferred), salad dressing.
Mixed pickle, sour or sweet, with chopped egg.
Mashed left-over beans or rubbed through colander, mixed with tomato sauce or salad dressing and chopped sour pickle or green pepper relish.

Additional Lunch Box Suggestions

Vegetable soups made with either meat stock or cream can be kept hot in thermos bottle.

Hard-cooked eggs are frequently used. As a variation, the yolk may be removed, seasoned with salt, pepper, mixed with salad dressing and put back in the white.

Fruit or vegetables, such as apples, apple sauce, baked apples, peaches, oranges, lettuce, tomatoes or celery, make a good combination with sandwiches.

Vegetable salads, such as potato salad, Boston baked beans and potato chips, add variety to the lunch of the adult, but are not suitable for the child's meal away from home.

A bottle of milk should be included in the lunch boxes of school children.

For dessert, one may use nuts and raisins, a few dates or figs.

Custards, with varied flavorings, cereal puddings, and gelatin puddings are also good. These may be made in individual cups and packed in the lunch box.

Plain cookies, date or raisin cookies or sponge cake may be added as a dessert. Pie, pickles, doughnuts or griddle cakes, or rich cakes should not be included in the school lunch box.

Suggested Cold Lunches

For Industrial Workers

1 minced ham sandwich with white bread
1 Swiss cheese sandwich with rye bread

1 whole tomato
1 apple dumpling
1 cup coffee (in thermos)

———

Vegetable soup (in thermos)
2 broiled bacon sandwiches on whole wheat bread
1 doughnut and 1 apple
1 bottle milk

———

2 salmon and lettuce sandwiches on whole wheat bread
Potato chips
1 orange
2 cookies
1 bottle of milk

For School Children

1 cottage cheese sandwich on brown bread
1 jelly sandwich on white bread
1 apple
1/2 pint bottle of milk

———

2 egg sandwiches on whole wheat bread
Celery
Apple sauce
Milk

———

2 tomato sandwiches on whole wheat bread
1 baked apple
Small cake and milk

———

B. SANDWICHES

Deviled Ham Sandwiches

Mince fine 1 medium-sized sour pickle and a few stuffed olives. Add 1 small can of deviled ham and mix to a past with salad dressing. Spread between thin slices of buttered bread and lay a leaf of lettuce between.

Sardine and Egg Sandwiches

Work together to a paste—after removing the bones—an equal quantity of sardines and hard boiled eggs—about three hard boiled eggs to a box of sardines. Add very small bits of lettuce and spread between thin slices of buttered bread.

Tongue Sandwiches

Put cold boiled tongue through the meat chopper and mince very fine. Lay a lettuce leaf on 1 slice of bread, spread with the tongue, cover with a layer of very thinly sliced sweet pickles, spread the other slice of bread with salad dressing and lay on top.

Club Sandwiches

Toast slices of bread and butter lightly. On one slice lay a piece of lettuce and cover with sliced chicken or turkey spread with a little salad dressing. Cover with a slice of toast. On top of this lay strips of hot broiled bacon and cover with another slice of toast.

When making Club Sandwiches, everything should be in readiness before you begin. Have the oven warm—but not hot—and a large pan ready to hold each sandwich as made. Place each in the pan in the oven and cover closely to slightly soften by steam and keep hot until all are done, then serve immediately.

Dream Sandwiches

1 cup raisins
1 cup nuts
1 teaspoon lemon juice
Boiled Salad Dressing

Put the raisins and nuts together through the meat grinder, add the lemon juice and enough salad dressing to make a "paste" which can be easily spread. Butter thin slices of "Fisher's Blend Flour Bread," and spread the filling between. If desired, also add a leaf of lettuce between each sandwich.

Salted Almond Sandwiches

Salted Almonds
Pimento
Lettuce
Salad Dressing

Chop the almonds in the food chopper and moisten with a little salad dressing. Spread 1 slice of the bread with canned pimento; lay a lettuce leaf on top; spread with the salted almonds, and cover with another slice.

Stuffed Olive and Cheese Sandwiches

Mix to a paste with a silver fork, creamed breakfast or Neufchatel cheese and stuffed olives in the proportion of 1/3 olive to 2/3 cheese. Spread thin slices of bread with Mayonnaise Dressing instead of butter, and put the filling between.

Rochester Sandwiches

Either cold chicken, turkey or veal are most appropriate for these sandwiches. Free the meat of every particle of fat and gristle and mince very fine. To 1 cup of minced meat add 1/4 cup of minced nut meats. Mix together thoroughly. Season to taste with salt and pepper and mix to a paste with a little sweet cream. If the weather is so warm there is danger of the cream souring, use salad dressing instead. Spread between thin slices of bread.

23

COOKING FOR INVALIDS

Food for invalids, which should be given as prescribed by a doctor, is classified as:

Liquid diet, including milk, cream soups, broths and fruit beverages.

Soft diet which includes, in addition to the above, cereals, soft cooked eggs, milk toast, custards and ice cream.

Light diet, which includes liquid and soft, and such foods as chicken and baked potatoes.

Full diet, which is the diet of a normal person.

Fruit beverages and beef tea, though not especially nourishing, are useful stimulants to the jaded appetite.

Toast should be cut thin and crisped all through. It may be softened with hot milk or water. Cereals should be thoroughly cooked.

Cream soups add variety to the milk diet.

Gelatins and ices furnish a tempting means of serving liquid foods in solid form.

The tray should be made as attractive as possible, never overcrowded. Cover it with a fresh napkin and use the daintiest china the household affords.

If disease is contagious, before removing the tray from the room, wrap all left-over food in paper and burn as soon as possible.

Put the dishes in a pan large enough so they can be completely covered with cold water. Boil for 15 minutes.

Oatmeal Gruel

1/4 cup rolled oats
1-1/2 cups boiled water
1/4 teaspoon salt

Add oatmeal mixed with salt to boiling water. Boil 2 minutes. Cook in double boiler 1 hour. Strain, bring to boiling point and add milk or cream to thin.

Oatmeal Water

2 tablespoons oatmeal
1 quart cold water
Cook slowly for about 2 hours, boiling down to a pint. Strain while hot and add enough cold boiled water to make 1 quart of fluid. Set aside in covered dish to cool.
Rice Gruel
1 tablespoon rice
1 cup milk

Wash rice, cover with cold water and let stand 2 hours. Drain, add milk and cook 1-1/2 hours in double boiler. Strain and season. Serve hot or cold.

Rice Water

2 tablespoons rice
3 cups cold water
Cream or milk
Salt for seasoning

Wash rice by placing in strainer and allowing cold water to run through. Soak 30 minutes in cold water, heat gradually to boiling point until rice is soft. Strain, reheat rice water, season with salt; and if too thick, dilute with boiling water. Add milk or cream as the case may require.

Barley Water

2 tablespoons barley
1 quart cold water

Wash barley, add water and let soak 4 hours. Cook in same water until water is reduced one-half, if to be used for infant feeding; for adults, reduce liquid to 1 cup. Salt and cream or lemon juice and sugar may be added as the case requires.

Toast Water

Good in case of nausea.

Two slices of bread toasted until thoroughly dextrinized, 1 cup boiling water. Break toast in pieces, add water and allow to stand 1 hour. Strain through cheesecloth, season and serve hot or cold.

Albumen Beverages

White 1 egg
1/3 cup orange or lemon juice
Syrup to taste

Beat egg white to a froth, add fruit juice, strain, sweeten. Serve cold. Syrup for fruit beverages can be made by cooking 1 cup of sugar and 1 cup of water 12 minutes.
Albumen water is made by adding 1/2 cup water to the egg white, omitting the fruit juice and syrup.
Albumenized milk is made by using 1/2 cup milk with the egg white.
Fruit drinks are made by combining sugar syrup, plain or carbonated water, and fruit juice.

Peptonized Milk

1 tube Peptonizing Powder
1/2 cup cold water
1 pint fresh milk

Put powder into a sterilized quart bottle, add water, and shake until powder is dissolved; add milk, shake and place on ice. Use as needed, always keeping remainder covered on ice.

Creamed Chicken

To 1/2 cup cold, cooked chicken, add 1/4 cup White Sauce I. Serve on toast.

Broiled Sweetbread

Soak sweetbread for 1 hour in enough cold water to cover. Cook in boiling water to which salt and 1 tablespoon of vinegar have been added for 20 minutes. Drain, plunge into cold water. Dry and separate meat from tubes and membrane. Split lengthwise. Sprinkle with salt and pepper and place on broiler. When sweetbread is heated, brush both sides with melted butter. Continue to broil.

Eggnog

1 egg
1 to 2 tablespoons sugar
3/4 cup milk

Speck nutmeg and salt
Beat yolk, add sugar, salt and milk, strain, add stiffly beaten white and nutmeg.

Coddled Eggs

Allow 1/4 cup milk for each slightly beaten egg. Cook mixture in a double boiler, stirring constantly until thickened. Season with salt and pepper and serve on buttered toast.

Scrambled Eggs

Allow 1 tablespoon of milk for each egg, slightly beaten. Pour in a buttered pan. Cook until creamy, stirring and scraping from the bottom of the pan as it thickens.

Soft Custard

1 pint milk scalded
1/4 cup sugar
2 egg yolks
Flavoring
Speck of salt

Beat the eggs, add sugar and salt and scalded milk slowly. Cook in a double boiler, stirring constantly until the mixture coats the spoon, add flavoring.

Baked Custard

Instead of cooking the above mixture over hot water, strain into custard cups or mold set in pan of water. Bake in slow oven 325° F. until firm. Custards are done when puffy on top and firm in center, or when a silver knife, inserted in the center, comes out clean.

Junket

2 cups milk
2 tablespoons sugar
1/2 teaspoon vanilla
2 teaspoons rennet, or 1/2 junket tablet
2 teaspoons lukewarm water

Heat the milk to lukewarm (99° F.) in double boiler. Add sugar and flavoring, and stir until sugar is dissolved. Add junket dissolved in water, and pour into dish from which custard is to be served. Let stand until cool and firm. Serve with cream, soft custard, fruit, or fruit syrup. Cinnamon, nutmeg, coconut, chocolate, cocoa, or other flavor may be substituted for vanilla.

Pineapple Juice

Peel a very ripe pineapple, cut into small pieces and put through fruit press or potato ricer to extract all juice. Strain and serve with cracked ice.

Egg and Orange Juice

1 egg white
Juice of 1 orange
Sugar

Add orange juice sweetened to taste to egg white and beat well. Chill on ice and serve cold.

Beef Tea

1 pound lean beef
1 cup cold water

Cut beef up into small pieces or put through meat chopper. Put into fruit jar; add water and allow to stand 15 to 20 minutes to draw out the juice. Place on trivet or rack in pan of cold water; heat very slowly for about 2 hours. The water must not boil. Season, strain, cool and remove fat. Beef tea may be served hot or cold.

Scraped Beef

Scrape meat with sharp knife from lean beef cut from round until nothing but connective tissue is left. Form into small balls and broil slowly for about 2 minutes. Season and serve. For sandwiches do not cook but spread between thin slices of bread and season.

Spanish Cream

2 cups scalded milk
4 egg yolks
1/4 cup sugar
2 tablespoons granulated gelatin
1/4 cup cold water
1 teaspoon vanilla extract
1 pint cream

Pour scalded milk very slowly over egg yolks and sugar which have been mixed together. Cook slowly in double boiler until thick and smooth. Pour over gelatin which has been soaking in 1/4 cup of water. Chill, add vanilla and beat with egg whip until thick. Add the cream which has been whipped and chill in molds.

Gluten Muffins

2 cups gluten flour
3 teaspoons Royal Baking Powder
1 egg
1 tablespoon butter
2 cups milk

Sift together flour and baking powder; add beaten egg and melted butter to milk and add. Mix well and bake in greased muffin tins in moderate oven about 35 minutes.

24

PRESERVING & CANNING

General Directions

Test all jars for leakage before using. To do this, fill with water, put on rubber and cover, seal and invert.

Sterilize all utensils, jars, covers, etc., by covering with cold water, and boil for 10 minutes. Use only new rubbers and dip in boiling water just before using.

Use a wide-mouthed funnel when filling jars to avoid loss of material and keep jar rim clean.

Invert all jars after filling and sealing. Fruit should be sound, firm and not overripe. All fruit should be carefully prepared. Clean fruit, clean hands, clean utensils, and a clean kitchen free from flies, are essential for safety and success.
Keep products in a cool place. Avoid freezing in winter.

Canning

Canning is the operation of preparing sterilized food so that it will keep indefinitely.

The custom of canning fruit in syrup is based on the improvement in flavor and texture which sugar gives to fruit. Sugar is not necessary for its preservation. Success depends upon thorough sterilization—that is, killing the organisms which cause food to spoil, and then sealing carefully to prevent their entrance. Fruit may be canned in water, in fruit juice and in syrup.

Preserving

The only difference between preserving and canning fruit is that sugar is always used in preserving, while in canning it is used in smaller quantity or not at all. In preserving the old rule of equal weights of sugar and fruit may be followed.

Directions for Canning by Open-Kettle Method

By this method which is generally used, for preserves, jams and marmalades, food is completely cooked and poured boiling hot into sterilized jars.

Prepare fruit, which may or may not be peeled, and cut into pieces depending on the variety. Blanch or scald peaches and similar fruits to loosen skin and chill by plunging into cold water. Cook slowly in as little water as possible or in fruit juice or fruit syrup until done. Fill the sterilized jars, seal and invert.

Directions for Canning by Can-Cooked Method

By this method uncooked or partly cooked food is packed in can or jar, covered with liquid and both jar and contents sterilized.

Pare fruit if desired or blanch or scald in boiling water a small quantity of the fruit at a time. (See time table.) Do not blanch cherries, sour cherries excepted, berries or plums.

Chill outside of the blanched fruit by immersing it for a few minutes in a vessel of cold water. Remove skin from such fruits as peaches.

Pack firmly in clean, tested jars to within one-half inch of top.

Fill jars to within 1/4 inch of top with boiling water, fruit juice, or syrup.

Place a new rubber on each jar, adjust cover and partly seal.

Place jars on false bottom of water bath and sterilize for required time. (See time table.) If the hot-water bath method is used, jars should be immersed in sufficient boiling water to cover tops to depth of about 1 inch. Do not begin to time the sterilizing until water boils. Keep water boiling during sterilizing period.

Remove jars from sterilizer. Seal them and invert to cool. Avoid a draft on jars, but cool as rapidly as possible.

Wash and label jars. Wrap in paper or store in dark place to prevent loss of color of red fruit.
Vegetables may also be canned by this method.

Use of Sugar in Canning Fruit

Sugar is used in canning fruit for the purpose of improving flavor and is not necessry for preservation.

Material adapted from U.S. Food Administration and New York State Dept. of Agriculture.

Thin syrup—1 part sugar to 2 parts water for sweet fruits.

Medium Syrup—1 part sugar to 1 part water for berries and medium sweet fruits.

Thick Syrup—2 parts sugar to 1 part water for sour fruits.

To make syrup add sugar to boiling water. Stir until all sugar is dissolved, then boil 2 or 3 minutes.

Canned Peaches

Scald sound, firm freestone peaches, a small number at a time, in boiling water just long enough to loosen skins; dip them quickly into cold water and slip off skins. Cut peaches in halves, and remove stones. Have ready a syrup made by boiling sugar and water together until sugar has dissolved, using 1/2 to 3/4 cup sugar to each cup water. Allow about 1 cup syrup for each quart jar of peaches. Put in 1 cracked peach pit for every quart of syrup.

Can-cooked Method—Pack peaches in overlapping layers with rounded side uppermost and blossom end facing glass. Fill each jar with hot syrup and adjust rubber, cover and upper clamp, thus partly sealing jar. Place jars on a rack in hot water to cover tops to a depth of 1 inch. Bring water to boiling point, and boil pint jars 16 minutes, quart jars 20 minutes. Remove jars, seal and invert to cool.

Open-kettle Method—Cook peaches in syrup until tender; then with sterilized spoon slip them carefully into sterilized jar; fill jar to overflowing with syrup. Adjust rubber, cover, seal immediately, and invert to cool.

Canned Cherries

Wash. Cherries should be pitted before being canned in order to conserve space. Can sweet cherries as berries. Blanch sour cherries 1/2 minute, in boiling water. Dip in cold water; drain and pack closely into hot sterilized jars. Cover with boiling water or boiling medium syrup. Loosely seal. Sterilize 16 minutes in boiling water bath. Remove jars at once, tighten covers, invert to test seal and cool.

Canned Pears

Wash and peel fruit and follow directions for canned peaches.

Canned Berries

Blackberries, blueberries, huckleberries, raspberries, loganberries, gooseberries and strawberries should be canned as soon as possible after picking. Hull or stem; place in strainer and wash by lifting up and down in pan of cold water.

Pack into hot sterilized glass jars, using care not to crush fruit. To insure a close pack, put a 2 or 3 inch layer of berries on the bottom of the jar and press down gently with spoon. Continue in this manner until jar is filled. Boiling water or boiling thin or medium syrup should be poured over the fruit at once. Loosely seal. Sterilize 16 minutes in boiling water. Remove jars, tighten covers, invert to test seal and cool.

Asparagus

Asparagus for canning must be fresh and tender. Select tips of uniform size and maturity and wash. Cut into lengths according to containers to be used. Scrape off scales, tough outer skins and hard ends and tie in bundles large enough for one jar.

Immerse the lower ends in boiling water and leave them immersed for 5 minutes, then the entire stalks, leaving them in 1 to 3 minutes longer.

Cold dip, drain, pack neatly, tips up, in hot sterilized jars. Add salt and cover with boiling water. Loosely seal, sterilize two hours in boiling water bath. Remove as soon as time is up. Tighten covers, invert to test seal and cool.

Beans

Green String Beans and Wax Beans.—The beans should be tender and fresh, and graded according to size and washed. Leave whole or break in uniform pieces. Blanch 5 to 10 minutes until the pod will bend without breaking. Cold dip, drain well and pack into hot jars. Add salt and cover with boiling water. Loosely seal and sterilize two hours in boiling water. Remove when time is up. tighten covers, and invert to test seal.

Corn

Make careful selection of tender, juicy sweet corn, at best stage for table use. Can as soon as possible after gathering. Remove husks and silk; blanch tender ears 5 minutes, older ears 10 minutes. Cold dip and cut from cob but not too close. Pack at once into hot sterilized jars. As corn swells during sterilization, leave space of 1 inch at top. Add salt and cover with boiling water. Be sure that water penetrates through corn to the bottom of jar. Loosely seal and sterilize three hours in boiling water. Remove when time is up, tighten covers, invert to test seal and cool.

JAMS

Jams are usually made with small fruits or with chopped large fruits. Cook slowly with an equal weight of sugar until thick; put into sterilized tumblers or jars and seal.

Raspberry Jam

Pick over berries. Mash a few in bottom of preserving kettle; continue until fruit is used. Heat slowly to boiling point and add equal quantity of heated sugar. Cook slowly 45 minutes. Put into sterilized jars.

Blackberry, gooseberry or other berry jam may be made in this way.

Plum Conserve

4 pounds plums
1 cup seeded raisins
2 oranges
sugar
juice of 1 lemon
1/2 pound walnuts

Wash plums; remove stones; add raisins and oranges which have been sliced very fine. Measure and add 3/4 cup sugar to each cup fruit and juice. Put into kettle, cook slowly about 45 minutes or until thick like jam, stirring to keep from burning. Add lemon juice and chopped nuts. Pour into sterilized jars.

Spiced Currants

3 lbs. white sugar
5 lbs. ripe currants
1 tablespoon cinnamon
1 tablespoon nutmeg
1 tablespoon cloves
1 tablespoon allspice
1/2 pint vinegar

Boil currants one hour, then add sugar, spices and one-half pint vinegar, boil one-half hour longer. Pour into jars and store.

Jellies

Heat and mash fruit until juice runs readily. If fruit is not entirely broken up rub through coarse sieve. Pour into sterilized jelly bags of unbleached muslin or doubled cheesecloth and drain thoroughly but do not squeeze. Take 7/8 cup sugar for each cup of juice. Boil juice 8 to 20 minutes (berries and currants less than other fruits); add sugar which has been heated in oven; stir until sugar is dissolved and boil about 5 minutes. Pour into hot sterilized tumblers. Hard fruits like apples and quinces should be cut up, covered with cold water and cooked until tender before turning into jelly bags.

Pickles

Pickled Peaches
2 pounds brown sugar
2 cups vinegar
1 ounce stick cinnamon
1/2 ounce whole cloves
4 quarts peaches

Boil sugar, vinegar and spices 20 minutes. Dip peaches quickly in hot water; then rub off the fuzz with a cloth. Place a few peaches at a time in syrup and cook until tender. Pack into sterilized jars. Adjust sterilized rubbers, and fill each jar to overflowing with hot strained syrup. Put on sterilized covers and seal jars immediately.

A Time-Table for Canning Fruits by the Can-Cooked Method

	TIME OF COOKING		
FRUIT	Time of Blanching Minutes	If the hot-water bath is used Minutes	If the pressure cooker is used (5 pounds) Minutes
Apricots, Peaches	1-2	16	10
Blackberries		16	6
Cherries, Strawberries, Grapes, Plums		16	10
Fruit Juices		20	10
Huckleberries, Raspberries		16	8
Pears	1-2	20	10
Pineapples		60	40
Quinces	1-2	60	40

Chow Chow

1 quart small white onions
1 quart small cucumbers
2 heads cauliflower
3 green peppers
1 quart vinegar
6 tablespoons mustard
3 tablespoons flour
1 cup sugar
1 tablespoon turmeric

Peel onions and add cucumbers, cauliflower cut into small pieces and sliced peppers. Sprinkle with salt; cover with water and allow to stand over night. Drain and cook in salt water until vegetables are tender, and drain again. Boil vinegar in kettle and add paste made with mustard, flour, sugar, turmeric and a little cold vinegar, stirring until mixture thickens; add vegetables and cook slowly 10 minutes. Seal in sterilized jars.

Sweet Tomato Pickles

1/2 peck green tomatoes
4 onions
4 green peppers
1 cup salt
1/2 cup white mustard seed
2 teaspoons pepper
3 teaspoons cinnamon
3 teaspoons allspice
3 teaspoons cloves
2 quarts vinegar
1 pound brown sugar

Chop tomatoes, onions and peppers; cover with salt and allow to stand over night. Drain; and add to vinegar, spices and sugar which have been heated to boiling. Cook 15 minutes and seal in sterilized jars.

Tomato Catsup

6 quarts tomatoes
1/2 cup brown sugar
3 tablespoons salt
1-1/2 tablespoons black pepper
1/2 tablespoon cloves
2 tablespoons cinnamon
1 tablespoon allspice
1-1/4 cups vinegar

Remove stems from tomatoes; cut into small pieces. Put all ingredients together in kettle and allow to simmer slowly until cooked down to one-half. This will take about four hours. Stir occasionally to keep from burning. Strain and pour into sterilized jars and seal. This is a highly seasoned sauce suitable for serving on meats or baked beans.

Grandma Franks' Family Today

Mother's Old-Fashioned Apple Pie

4 to 5 cups peeled and sliced tart apples
1-1/2 cups sugar
1/3 cup flour
1 teaspoon cinnamon
1/4 cup water
1 tablespoon butter
Pastry for double crust, 9-inch pie

Prepare pastry. Roll out half and line pan. Combine sugar, flour and cinnamon in a bowl; stir in water. Add apples, mixing to coat thoroughly. Pour into pan and dot with butter. Roll out top crust; cut a design in the center to allow steam to escape. Place top crust on pie, pressing around the edge to seal. Brush pastry with milk and sprinkle with sugar. Bake in a 350° oven 45 to 60 minutes or until apples are tender and crust is browned.

25
UPDATING GRANDMA'S COOKBOOK

MEAT DISHES
Filet of Beef

Instead of roast beef, we used a lean filet and poached it gently in beef broth till tender and juicy. Instead of Yorkshire pudding: our light-as-air popovers, made with egg whites only.

Popovers

1/4 teaspoon coarsely ground black pepper
1/4 teaspoon dried thyme leaves
salt
1 3-pound beef tenderloin roast (large end), tied
1 tablespoon olive or salad oil
1 13-3/4- to 14-1/2-ounce can beef broth
1 garlic clove, cut in half
1 bay leaf
1 pound green beans
2 16-ounce bags carrots

1. Prepare Popovers.
2. While Popovers are baking, poach tenderloin: On waxed paper, mix pepper, thyme, and 1 teaspoon salt. Roll beef tenderloin roast in pepper mixture to coat evenly.
3. In 8-quart Dutch oven over medium-high heat, in hot olive or salad oil, cook tenderloin until browned on all sides, about 8 minutes. Stir in beef broth, garlic, and bay leaf; over high heat, heat to boiling. Reduce heat to low; cover and simmer 20 to 25 minutes for rare. (Internal temperature of tenderloin should register 130°F. on meat thermometer when removed from cooking broth.)
4. While beef is cooking, trim ends from green beans; cut each carrot lengthwise in half. Set aside.
5. When tenderloin is done, remove from Dutch oven; keep warm. Add carrots to Dutch oven; over high heat, heat to boiling. Reduce heat to low; cover and simmer 15 to 20 minutes until carrots are tender-crisp.
6. Meanwhile, in 3-quart saucepan, over high heat, in 1 inch boiling water, heat green beans to boiling. Reduce heat to low; cover and simmer 5 to 10 minutes, stirring occasionally, until beans are just tender-crisp. Drain beans; toss with 1/4 teaspoon salt. Place beans on large platter; keep warm.
7. When carrots are done, with slotted spoon, remove carrots to platter with beans, reserving cooking broth. Discard garlic and bay leaf.
8. To serve, discard string from tenderloin. Slice tenderloin into 1/4-inch-thick slices. Arrange tenderloin slices and Popovers on same platter with vegetables. Serve cooking broth in gravy boat to serve over tenderloin and vegetables. Makes 9 main-dish servings.

Popovers: Preheat oven to 375°F. Grease twelve 2-1/2" x 1-1/4" muffin-pan cups; set aside. In large bowl, with mixer at medium speed, beat 6 large egg whites until frothy; beat in 1 cup low-fat milk (1%) and 2 tablespoons olive or salad oil until blended. Beat in 1 cup all-purpose flour, one 1/2-ounce envelope natural butter flavor granules, and 1/4 teaspoon salt until smooth. Fill each muffin-pan cup about one-half full. Bake 50 minutes, then with tip of small knife, quickly make small slit in top of each popover to let steam escape; bake 5 minutes longer. Immediately remove popovers from cups.

Beef Teriyaki and Rice

3 tablespoons soy sauce
1 tablespoon dry sherry
2 teaspoons brown sugar
1-1/2 teaspoons garlic powder
1 teaspoon ground ginger
3/4 pound flank steak strips
1 tablespoon oil
3 cups bite-size vegetables
1 cup beef broth
4 teaspoons cornstarch
1-1/2 cups Original Minute Rice

Mix soy sauce, sherry, brown sugar and seasonings. Add beef; let stand 10 minutes to marinate. Stir-fry beef in hot oil in skillet until browned. Add vegetables; stir-fry until tender-crisp. Mix broth and cornstarch; add to skillet. Bring to boil, boil 1 minute. Prepare rice as directed on package. Serve beef mixture over rice. Serve 4.

Filet Mignon with Mushroom Sauce and Crisp Potato Pancakes

2 large baking potatoes (about 1-1/4 pounds), peeled and shredded
salt

1/4 cup grated Parmesan or Romano cheese
1 large egg white
chopped parsley
4 beef tenderloin steaks (filet Mignon), each 1-1/4 inches thick and about 6 ounces
1/4 teaspoon coarsely ground black pepper
1/4 teaspoon dried thyme leaves
olive or salad oil
1 10-ounce package mushrooms, each cut into quarters
1/4 cup dry red wine
1-1/2 teaspoons cornstarch
1 teaspoon red wine vinegar
parsley sprigs for garnish

1. Preheat oven to 450°F. In medium bowl, mix shredded potatoes with 3/4 teaspoon salt. Place shredded potatoes between several layers of paper towels and press out as much liquid as possible. Return shredded potatoes to bowl; add grated Parmesan cheese, egg white, and 1/4 cup chopped parsley.
2. Spray jelly-roll pan generously with nonstick cooking spray. Shape potato mixture into 8 mounds in jelly-roll pan; press into 3-inch pancakes. Bake the potato pancakes 12 to 15 minutes; turn with pancake turner and bake 12 minutes longer until potato pancakes are golden brown.
3. Meanwhile, sprinkle steaks with pepper, dried thyme leaves, and 3/4 teaspoon salt. In 10-inch skillet over medium-high heat, in 1 tablespoon hot olive or salad oil, cook steaks 5 minutes; turn steaks and cook 4 to 5 minutes longer for rare or until of desired doneness. Remove steaks to 4 warm dinner plates; keep warm.
4. In drippings remaining in skillet and 1 tablespoon additional hot olive or salad oil, over medium-high heat, cook mushrooms and 1/2 teaspoon salt, stirring frequently, until mushrooms are golden and tender.
5. In cup, mix red wine, cornstarch, red wine vinegar, and 3/4 cup cold water until blended; stir into mushrooms in skillet and cook, stirring, until mixture boils and thickens; boil 1 minute. Stir in 1 tablespoon chopped parsley.
6. To serve, spoon mushroom sauce over steaks. Serve with potato pancakes. Garnish with parsley sprigs. Makes 4 servings.

Beef Tortillas

1 large carrot
1/2 small cucumber
1/4 teaspoon salt
1 3-ounce package cream cheese with chives, softened
2 tablespoons prepared white horseradish
1 tablespoon milk
4 8-inch flour tortillas
greenleaf lettuce or romaine leaves
1/2 pound thinly sliced cooked roast beef (from deli)
sliced jalapeno peppers for garnish

1. Into small bowl, coarsely shred carrot and cucumber; stir in salt. In another small bowl, with spoon, mix cream cheese, horseradish, and milk until blended.
2. Spread horseradish mixture along center of tortillas. Top with lettuce leaves, then roast-beef slices. Sprinkle with shredded vegetables. Fold two opposite sides of each tortilla over filling, overlapping slightly.
3. To serve, arrange tortillas on platter; garnish each tortilla with a few jalapeno pepper slices. Makes 4 servings.

Black-Pepper Steak With Herbed Potatoes

1-1/2 pounds medium-size red potatoes, cut into 1/2-inch cubes
1 garlic clove, minced
1/2 teaspoon dried thyme leaves
olive or salad oil
salt
4 beef rib eye steaks, each about 3/4 inch thick
3/4 teaspoon black pepper
1 8-ounce package mushrooms, thinly sliced
1 tablespoon all-purpose flour
1 tablespoon soy sauce
1 tablespoon chopped parsley

1. Preheat oven to 475°F.
2. In medium bowl, mix potatoes, garlic, thyme, 1 tablespoon olive or salad oil, and 1 teaspoon salt. Evenly spread potatoes in 15-1/2" by 10-1/2" jelly-roll pan. Bake 20 to 25 minutes until tender and golden, stirring occasionally.
3. Meanwhile, trim excess fat from rib eye steaks. Sprinkle steaks on both sides with pepper and 3/4 teaspoon salt.
4. In 12-inch skillet over medium-high heat, in 1 tablespoon hot olive or salad oil, cook steaks until browned on both sides, about 8 minutes for rare or until desired doneness. Remove steaks to 4 dinner plates; keep warm.
5. In same skillet over medium-high heat, in 2 teaspoons hot olive or salad oil, cook mushrooms, stirring occasionally, until mushrooms are tender, about 5 minutes.
6. In cup, with fork, mix flour, soy sauce, and 3/4 cup water. To mushrooms in skillet, add flour mixture; over high heat, heat until mixture boils and thickens, stirring often.
7. To serve, stir chopped parsley into potatoes; arrange potatoes on plates with steaks. Spoon mushroom sauce over steaks. Makes 4 main-dish servings.

Creamy Chicken & Vegetables With Savory Biscuits

1-1/2 cups reduced-fat baking and pancake mix with buttermilk

1/2 teaspoon dried thyme leaves
1/2 teaspoon coarsely ground black pepper
low-fat milk (1%)
4 medium-size boneless, skinless chicken-breast halves (about 1-1/2 pounds)
1 large carrot
1 large celery stalk
1 medium-size red pepper
1 small onion
3 tablespoons olive or salad oil
salt
2 tablespoons all-purpose flour
1-1/2 teaspoons chicken-flour instant bouillon
1 8-3/4-ounce can whole-kernel corn, drained
1/2 cup frozen peas
parsley sprigs for garnish

1. Preheat oven to 450°F. In medium bowl, with fork, mix baking and pancake mix, dried thyme leaves, black pepper, and 1/2 cup low-fat milk until blended.
2. Spray small cookie sheet with nonstick cooking spray; spoon biscuit batter into 4 mounds, about 3 inches apart, on cookie sheet, spreading each to about a 3-inch round. Bake biscuits 8 to 10 minutes until golden; remove biscuits to wire rack.
3. Meanwhile, cut chicken-breast hales into 1-inch pieces. Thinly slice carrot and celery stalk. Dice red pepper; chop onion.
4. In 12-inch skillet over medium-high heat, in hot olive or salad oil, cook chicken-breast pieces and 1/2 teaspoon salt until chicken loses its pink color throughout. With slotted spoon, remove chicken pieces to bowl.
5. In oil remaining in skillet over high heat, cook carrot, celery, red pepper, onion, and 1/2 teaspoon salt, stirring frequently, until vegetables are tender.
6. While vegetables are cooking, in 2-cup measuring cup, with wire whisk or fork, mix flour, chicken bouillon, and 2 cups low-fat milk until blended.
7. Return chicken-breast pieces to skillet with vegetable mixture; add corn, frozen peas, and milk mixture. Over high heat, cook, stirring, until mixture boils and thickens; boil 1 minute.
8. To serve, slice each biscuit horizontally in half. Place bottom halves on each of 4 warm dinner plates; spoon chicken and vegetable mixture over biscuit bottoms; top with top of biscuit. Garnish with parsley sprigs. Makes 4 main-dish servings.

Yankee Pot Roast

2 tablespoons salad oil
1 4- to 4-1/2-pound boneless beef chuck cross rib pot roast
2 teaspoons salt
1 teaspoon sugar
1/2 teaspoon pepper
1/2 teaspoon dried thyme leaves
1 bay leaf
8 medium-size potatoes (about 2-1/2 pounds), peeled and halved
8 medium-size carrots (about 1-1/4 pounds), cut into 3-inch pieces
1 pound small white onions
1/4 cup all-purpose flour
parsley sprigs for garnish

1. In 8-quart Dutch oven over medium-high heat, in hot salad oil, cook beef chuck cross rib pot roast until well browned on all sides. Stir in salt, sugar, pepper, thyme leaves, bay leaf, and 3 cups water; over high heat, heat to boiling. Reduce heat to low; cover and simmer 2-1/4 hours.
2. Add potatoes, carrots, and onions; over high heat, heat to boiling. Reduce heat to medium-low; cover and cook 45 minutes or until meat and vegetables are fork-tender.
3. Remove strings, if any, from pot roast. Arrange meat and vegetables on warm large platter and keep warm. Skim off fat from the liquid in the Dutch oven. Discard bay leaf.
4. In small bowl, stir flour and 1/2 cup water until blended; gradually stir into liquid in Dutch oven. Cook over medium heat, stirring, until gravy boils and thickens. Serve gravy in gravy boat. Garnish platter with parsley. Makes 12 main-dish servings.

Beef Stew

3 medium-size carrots
1 large onion
1 large celery stalk
olive or salad oil
1 pound beef for stew, cut into 1-1/2-inch chunks
1 extra large vegetable-flavor bouillon cube
1 teaspoon salt
1/2 teaspoon pepper
3 medium-size potatoes (1 pound)
2 15- to 19-ounce cans garbanzo beans
1 cup frozen peas

1. Cut carrots into 2-inch pieces; dice onion; cut celery into 1/2-inch-thick slices.
2. In nonstick 12-inch skillet over medium-high heat, in 1 tablespoon hot olive or salad oil, cook beef until well browned on all sides. With slotted spoon, remove to bowl; set aside.
3. In any drippings remaining in skillet, and one more tablespoon olive or salad oil, cook carrots, onion, and celery until golden brown. Return meat to skillet; stir in vegetable bouillon cube,

salt, pepper, and 2 cups water. Over high heat, heat to boiling. Reduce heat to low; cover and simmer 15 minutes.
4. Meanwhile, cut potatoes into bite-size chunks.
5. Stir in potatoes; cook 45 minutes longer or until meat and potatoes are tender, stirring occasionally. Drain beans. Stir beans and frozen peas into stew; heat through. Makes 6 main-dish servings.

Steak & Potatoes

6 medium-size baking potatoes
1 garlic clove
1 teaspoon salt
3/4 teaspoon coarsely ground black pepper
1/2 teaspoon dried thyme leaves
1 beef top round steak, 1-1/4 inches thick (about 1-1/2 pounds)
1/3 cup pimento-stuffed olives, coarsely chopped
1 8-ounce container fat-free sour cream alternative
thyme sprigs for garnish

1. Preheat oven to 450°F. Place potatoes in shallow pan; bake 45 minutes or until fork-tender.
2. Meanwhile, into small bowl, press garlic through garlic press. Stir in salt, coarsely ground black pepper, and thyme leaves. Rub garlic mixture on steak. Place steak on rack in broiling pan; set aside.
3. Prepare sour cream topping for potatoes: Reserve 1 tablespoon chopped olives for garnish. In small bowl, mix sour cream with remaining chopped olives. Sprinkle reserved olives on top; cover and refrigerate until serving time.
4. When potatoes are done, remove potatoes from oven and keep warm. Preheat broiler if manufacturer directs. With broiling pan at closest position to source of heat, broil steak 12 to 15 minutes for rare, turning once.
5. To serve, place steak on large platter. Arrange potatoes around steak. Serve with sour cream mixture for each person to spoon over potato. Garnish with fresh thyme. Makes 6 main-dish servings.

Pot Roast

1/2 pound small white onions
1 small rutabaga (about 12 ounces)
1/2 16-ounce bag carrots
1 10-ounce package mushrooms
1 3-1/2-pound broiler-fryer, cut into quarters
3 tablespoons all-purpose flour
1-1/4 teaspoons salt
olive or salad oil
2 14-1/2-to 16-ounce cans stewed tomatoes
1 tablespoon sugar
1 teaspoon Worcestershire
1/2 teaspoon browning and seasoning sauce

1. Peel onions, leaving a little of the root ends to help hold their shape during cooking; cut each lengthwise in half. Peel rutabaga; cut into 1-1/2-inch chunks. Cut carrots into 2" by 1/2" pieces. Cut large mushrooms in half.
2. Remove skin from chicken quarters. In large bowl, combine flour and salt; add chicken; toss to coat.
3. In 8-quart Dutch oven over medium-high heat, in 2 tablespoons hot olive or salad oil, cook chicken quarters until browned on both sides; return chicken to bowl.
4. In same Dutch oven in 1 tablespoon additional olive or salad oil, cook onions until browned. Add stewed tomatoes, sugar, Worcestershire, browning and seasoning sauce, cut-up vegetables, and chicken with any juice in bowl. Over high heat, heat to boiling. Reduce heat to low; cover and simmer 35 minutes or until chicken loses its pink color throughout and vegetables are tender. Makes 4 main-dish servings.

Meat Loaf with Braised Onions

1 tablespoon olive or salad oil
2 medium-size carrots, shredded
1 medium-size celery stalk, chopped
1 medium-size onion, chopped
1 teaspoon salt
1/4 teaspoon pepper
1 medium-size bunch spinach, coarsely chopped (2 cups, packed)
1-1/2 pounds lean ground beef
1/2 cup drained oil-packed dried tomatoes, chopped
3 slices firm white bread, torn into small crumbs
2 tablespoons grated Parmesan cheese
2 large egg whites
Braised onions
parsley sprigs for garnish

1. In nonstick 12-inch skillet over medium-high heat, in hot olive or salad oil, cook carrots, celery, onion, salt, and pepper, stirring occasionally, until vegetables are tender. Stir in spinach and cook, stirring constantly, until spinach wilts.
2. Preheat oven to 350°F. In large bowl, mix ground beef with vegetable mixture, dried tomatoes, bread crumbs, grated Parmesan, and egg whites until well blended.
3. In 13" by 9" roasting pan, shape meat mixture into 8" x 5" loaf, pressing firmly. Bake meat loaf 1 hour. Meanwhile, prepare Braised Onions.
4. Serve meat loaf with Braised Onions. Garnish with parsley sprigs. Makes 8 servings.
BRAISED ONIONS: In nonstick 12-inch skillet over high heat, in 1/2 cup boiling water, heat 4 medium-size onions, each

cut crosswise in half, 1 tablespoon light corn-oil spread, 3/4 teaspoon sugar, and 1/2 teaspoon salt to boiling. Reduce heat to low; cover and simmer 10 minutes. Remove cover and cook, turning occasionally, until all liquid evaporates and onions are tender and golden brown.

Meatballs & Spaghetti

You'll love these new meatballs made with lots of cut-up vegetables, a small amount of meat. Simmer them in a store-bought sauce to cut down on cooking and preparation time.

Olive or salad oil
1 large onion, finely chopped
1 medium-size carrot, shredded
3/4 teaspoon salt
3/4 teaspoon dried basil leaves
1/4 teaspoon pepper
2 medium-size bunches spinach (about 1-1/2 pounds), tough stems removed and coarsely chopped
1/2 pound lean ground beef
1/2 cup dried bread crumbs
1/4 cup grated Parmesan cheese
1 large egg
1 tablespoon all-purpose flour
1 26-ounce jar marinara sauce
3/4 16-ounce package spaghetti

1. In nonstick 12-inch skillet over medium-high heat, in 1 tablespoon hot olive or salad oil, cook onion, carrot, salt, basil, and pepper, stirring frequently, until vegetables are tender. Add chopped spinach and cook, stirring, until spinach wilts. With slotted spoon, remove vegetable mixture to large bowl.
2. Into vegetable mixture in bowl, stir ground beef, bread crumbs, Parmesan, and egg until blended. With hands, shape ground beef mixture into 16 balls. Roll each ball in flour to coat lightly.
3. Wipe skillet clean. In 1 tablespoon hot olive or salad oil over medium-high heat, cook meatballs until browned on all sides, turning them carefully, and removing them to plate as they brown.
4. Into skillet, stir marinara sauce and 1/2 cup water. Return meatballs to skillet; over high heat, heat to boiling. Reduce heat to low; cover and simmer 20 minutes.
5. Meanwhile, prepare spaghetti as label directs; drain. Serve meatballs with spaghetti. Makes 4 main-dish servings.

Surf 'N' Turf Grill

3 medium-size red potatoes (8 ounces)
1 boneless beef rib steak, 1 inch thick (about 1/2 pound)
1/2 cup diavolo sauce
2 teaspoons dark brown sugar
salt
2 large green onions
2 tablespoons margarine or butter (1/4 stick)
3/4 teaspoon fresh thyme leaves, minced or 1/8 teaspoon dried thyme leaves
1 2-pound lobster (have lobster split lengthwise in half at fish market)
3 tablespoons milk
2 tablespoons mayonnaise
1 teaspoon Dijon mustard
1/8 teaspoon coarsely ground black pepper
Boston lettuce leaves
parsley sprigs for garnish

1. In 2-quart saucepan over high heat, heat unpeeled potatoes and enough water to cover to boiling. Reduce heat to low; cover and simmer 15 to 20 minutes until potatoes are fork-tender; drain.
2. Meanwhile, cut steak into 4 cubes. In bowl, mix diavolo sauce, brown sugar, and 1/2 teaspoon salt; stir in steak to coat.
3. Cut green onions into 2-inch-long pieces. On two 8-inch-long skewers, thread steak cubes alternately with green onions, reserving any remaining diavolo sauce mixture in bowl to brush on steak while cooking.
4. Preheat broiler if manufacturer directs. In small saucepan over low heat, heat margarine or butter and thyme until margarine is melted. Remove the sand sac from head part of lobster. Arrange steak kabobs and lobster halves, cut side up, on rack in broiling pan. Place broiling pan 4 to 5 inches from source of heat. Broil steak 5 to 8 minutes for rare, brushing with reserved diavolo sauce mixture. Broil lobster about 15 minutes, brushing occasionally with melted margarine or butter mixture. Cover body of lobster with loose tent of foil to avoid overcooking after 5 minutes of broiling.
5. While steak and lobster are cooking, cut unpeeled potatoes into 1/2-inch cubes. In small bowl, mix milk, mayonnaise, mustard, pepper, and 1/4 teaspoon salt until blended. Stir in potatoes.
6. To serve, on each of 2 large platters, arrange 1 steak kabob, one half lobster, and a mound of potato salad on a Boston lettuce leaf. If you like, serve with additional melted margarine or butter for dipping broiled lobster. Garnish platters with parsley sprigs. Makes 2 servings.

Stuffed Veal with Roasted Potatoes

3/4 pound medium mushrooms
1 medium onion
olive or salad oil
salt
coarsely ground black pepper

1 3-pound rolled boneless veal shoulder roast
1 small bunch spinach (about 1/2 pound)
1 teaspoon dried thyme leaves
8 large potatoes (about 3-1/2 pounds)

1. Finely chop mushrooms and onion. In 12-inch skillet over medium-high heat, in two tablespoons hot olive or salad oil, cook mushrooms, onion, 1/2 teaspoon salt, and 1/4 teaspoon pepper until liquid evaporates and vegetables are lightly browned. Reduce heat to medium; cook until vegetables are tender and golden.
3. Meanwhile, untie veal shoulder roast; place fat side down on work surface. To make veal evenly thick, with meat mallet, pound veal between 2 sheets of plastic wrap into a rectangle about 12" by 10".
3. Remove stems from spinach; discard. Rinse leaves with running cold water; pat dry with paper towels. Arrange spinach leaves over veal; top with mushroom mixture. Starting from a narrow end, carefully roll veal jelly-roll fashion. With string, tie veal roast at about 2-inch intervals.
4. In cup, mix thyme, 3/4 teaspoon salt, and 1/2 teaspoon pepper. Rub mixture over veal roast. Place roast on small rack in large roasting pan. Insert meat thermometer into center of veal roast. Roast veal in 325°F. oven 1-1/4 hours, brushing occasionally with pan drippings.
5. After veal has roasted 1-1/4 hours, cut potatoes into 2-inch chunks. In large bowl, toss potatoes with 1 tablespoon olive or salad oil, 1/2 teaspoon salt, and 1/4 teaspoon pepper. Add potatoes to roasting pan, turning to coat with drippings. Roast veal and potatoes 1 hour longer, turning potatoes occasionally, until potatoes are fork-tender and temperature on meat thermometer reaches 160°F.
6. To serve, slice veal roast. Arrange veal and potatoes on large platter. If not serving right away, cover and refrigerate to serve cold later. Makes 8 servings.

Pork Chop Supper

4 medium-size potatoes (about 1-1/2 pounds)
1/2 cup low-fat milk (1%)
salt
1 large bunch spinach
olive or salad oil
1 medium-size Golden Delicious apple
4 1-1/4-inch thick boneless pork loin chops (American's Cut)
3/4 cup apple cider or apple juice
3/4 teaspoon cornstarch
2 tablespoons cider vinegar

1. Peel potatoes and cut into 1-inch chunks. In 3-quart saucepan over high heat, heat potatoes and enough water to cover to boiling. Reduce heat to low; cover and simmer 10 minutes or until potatoes are fork-tender. Drain potatoes and return to saucepan. Over medium-low heat, add low-fat milk and 3/4 teaspoon salt. With potato masher, mash potatoes until smooth; keep warm.
2. Meanwhile, trim tough stem ends from spinach. In 4-quart saucepan over medium-high heat, in 1 tablespoon hot olive oil, cook spinach and 1/4 teaspoon salt just until spinach wilts; keep warm.
3. Peel and core apple; cut into thin wedges. In 10-inch skillet over medium-high heat, in 1 tablespoon hot olive or salad oil, cook pork chops 5 minutes, sprinkling with 1/2 teaspoon salt. Turn pork chops and cook 3 to 5 minutes longer until pork just loses its pink color throughout, sprinkling with another 1/2 teaspoon salt. Remove pork chops to warm platter; keep warm.
4. In cup, mix apple cider and cornstarch. Stir cider mixture, vinegar, and apple wedges into drippings in skillet; over high heat, heat to boiling. Boil 2 minutes or until apple wedges are tender.
5. Arrange mashed potatoes and spinach on platter with pork chops. Spoon cider sauce and apple wedges over pork. Makes 4 main-dish servings.

Pork-Chop Schnitzel

1 tablespoon milk
1 tablespoon Dijon mustard
1 teaspoon salt
1/2 teaspoon pepper
1/4 cup dried bread crumbs
1 teaspoon dried basil leaves
4 boneless center cut pork loin chops (America's Cut), each 1-1/4 inches thick and about 6 ounces
2 tablespoons olive or salad oil
3 tablespoons lemon juice
parsley sprigs and lemon wedges for garnish

1. In pie plate, mix milk, Dijon mustard, salt, and pepper. On sheet of waxed paper, mix bread crumbs and dried basil. Dip pork chops, one at a time, first in mustard mixture, then in bread-crumb mixture, to coat both sides well.
2. In 10-inch skillet over medium-high heat, in hot olive or salad oil, cook the breaded pork chops until golden brown on both sides, 3 to 4 minutes, turning the chops once.
3. Add lemon juice and 1/4 cup water to pork chops in skillet. Reduce heat to low; cover and simmer 8 to 10 minutes until pork chops are fork-tender and just lose their pink color throughout.
4. To serve, arrange pork chops on 4 dinner plates; spoon sauce over. Garnish with parsley sprigs and lemon wedges. Makes 4 main-dish servings.

Pork Cutlets with Vegetables Italienne

1 pound pork loin sirloin cutlets
1 8-ounce package medium-size mushrooms
1 small onion
1 medium-size zucchini (about 8 ounces)
1 medium-size yellow straightneck squash (about 10 ounces)
2 medium-size plum tomatoes
1 medium-size lemon
1 small bunch basil
3/4 teaspoon salt
1/4 teaspoon pepper
olive or salad oil
2 teaspoons all purpose flour
1 teaspoon beef flavor instant bouillon

1. Trim fat from pork cutlets, if any. With meat mallet or dull edge of French knife, pound pork cutlets to 1/4-inch thickness. If cutlets are large, cut in half.
2. Cut each mushroom in half; dice onion. Slice zucchini and yellow squash lengthwise in half, then cut crosswise into 1/2-inch-thick diagonal slices. Cut plum tomatoes into thin wedges.
3. From lemon, grate 1 teaspoon peel and squeeze 2 teaspoons juice. Slice enough basil leaves to measure 1/4 cup, loosely packed; reserve remaining basil leaves for garnish.
4. Sprinkle pork cutlets with salt and pepper. In nonstick 12-inch skillet over medium-high heat, in 1 tablespoon hot olive or salad oil, cook pork cutlets, half at a time, until golden brown on both sides, about 2 minutes, turning them once, and removing cutlets to large platter as they brown; keep warm.
5. In drippings remaining in skillet and 1 additional tablespoon hot olive or salad oil over medium-high heat, cook mushrooms and onion, stirring frequently, until they are golden. Add zucchini and yellow squash; cook, stirring, until tender-crisp.
6. In cup, mix flour, beef bouillon, and 3/4 cup water until blended. Into vegetable mixture in skillet, stir beef bouillon mixture and lemon peel and juice. Over high heat, heat to boiling; boil 1 minute. Stir in tomato wedges and sliced basil; heat through.
7. To serve, arrange vegetable mixture on same platter with pork cutlets. Garnish with basil sprigs. Makes 5 servings.

Hormel Ham 'n Cheddar Success

2 bags Success Rice
2 cups frozen mixed vegetables (thawed)
1-1/2 cup sliced mushrooms
1/2 cup chopped onion
1 tablespoon butter or margarine
1 (11 ounce) can nacho cheese soup
1/2 cup milk
2 (5 ounce) cans Hormel Chuck Ham, drained and flaked

Prepare rice according to package directions. Prepare mixed vegetables according to package directions, omitting margarine and salt. In large skillet, sauté mushrooms and onion in butter until tender. Stir in soup and milk. Add Hormel Chuck Ham and cooked vegetables. Simmer until thoroughly heated. Serve over warm Success Rice. Serves 6-8.

Spinach Supper Salad

1/2 cup peanut butter
1/4 cup salad oil
2 tablespoons milk
1/4 teaspoon ground red pepper
1/8 teaspoon salt
1 green onion, minced
2 slices bacon
1 small head lettuce
1/2 10-ounce package spinach
1 Red Delicious apple, cut into thin wedges
1 small cucumber, sliced
4 ounces Cheddar cheese, diced

1. In small bowl, with fork, beat peanut butter, salad oil, milk, pepper, salt, and green onion until smooth; set aside.
2. Cut bacon into 1-inch pieces. In small skillet over medium-low heat, cook bacon until browned, stirring. With slotted spoon, remove bacon to paper towel to drain.
3. Tear lettuce and spinach into small pieces. On each of 4 dinner plates, arrange some lettuce, spinach, apple, cucumber, cheese, and bacon. Spoon dressing over salads. Makes 4 main-dish servings.

LAMB

Leg of Lamb with Toasted Coconut Couscous

1 tablespoon dried rosemary leaves, crushed
1 tablespoon olive or salad oil
2 teaspoons salt
1 teaspoon coarsely ground black pepper
1 garlic clove, minced
1 4-1/2-pound lamb leg shank half, butterflied*
1 cup couscous (precooked semolina)
1 cup dried currants or seedless raisins
1/2 cup shredded coconut, toasted
parsley sprigs for garnish
1/2 cup Greek olives or pitted ripe olives

1. Preheat oven to 375°F. In cup, mix crushed rosemary, olive

or salad oil, salt, coarsely ground black pepper, and minced garlic; rub mixture over lamb.
2. Place lamb, fat side up, on rack in large roasting pan. Insert meat thermometer into center of lamb. Roast lamb about 50 minutes or until thermometer reaches 130°F. for rare or until of desired doneness.
3. Meanwhile, in saucepan, prepare couscous as label directs; stir in currants and toasted coconut.
4. To serve, cut lamb into thin slices. Arrange lamb and couscous on large platter. Tuck parsley sprigs in between lamb slices. Top with Greek olives. Makes 8 servings.
TO GRILL OUTDOORS: Prepare outdoor grill for barbecuing. Meanwhile, prepare couscous as in step 3; keep warm. Prepare lamb as in step 1. Place lamb on grill over medium heat. Cook 20 minutes for rare or until of desired doneness, turning lamb occasionally, Slice and serve lamb as in step 4.
*Ask meatman to bone lamb leg shank half and slit the meat lengthwise to spread flat like a thick steak.

SEAFOOD

Spicy Stir-Fried Shrimp

1/4 cup chili sauce
2 tablespoons soy sauce
2 tablespoons dry sherry
4 green onions
2 tablespoons salad oil
1-1/4 pounds shelled and deveined large shrimp
1/4 teaspoon crushed red pepper
1 tablespoon chopped parsley

1. In small bowl, mix chili sauce, soy sauce, and sherry. Cut green onions into 3-inch pieces.
2. In 4-quart saucepan over high heat, in hot salad oil, cook green onions until lightly browned, about 3 minutes, stirring frequently. Stir in shrimp and crushed red pepper. Cook shrimp over high heat, stirring quickly and constantly, 2 minutes. Add chili-sauce mixture and continue cooking 2 minutes longer or until shrimp are tender and opaque throughout. Stir in parsley. Makes 4 main-dish servings.

Scrod With Lemon-Garlic Bread Crumbs

2 slices white bread
2 tablespoons margarine or butter (1/4 stick)
1 garlic clove
4 small scrod or cod fillets (about 6 ounces each)
2 tablespoons lemon juice
3/4 teaspoon salt
parsley sprigs and lemon wedges for garnish

1. Preheat oven to 450°F. In blender at high speed, blend bread until fine crumbs form.
2. In 10-inch skillet over medium heat, heat margarine or butter until hot. With garlic press, press garlic into skillet and cook until lightly browned. Stir in bread crumbs and continue cooking, stirring frequently, until bread crumbs are lightly toasted. Remove skillet from heat.
3. In 13" by 9" glass baking dish, arrange scrod fillets; sprinkle with lemon juice and salt. Press bread-crumb mixture on top. Bake scrod, uncovered, 10 to 15 minutes, until fish flakes easily when tested with a fork.
4. To serve, arrange fish on platter; garnish with parsley sprigs and lemon wedges. Makes 4 main-dish servings.

Broiled Salmon with Corn & Tomato Salsa

4 salmon fillets (about 6 ounces each)
1 tablespoon teriyaki sauce
1/2 teaspoon coarsely ground black pepper
1 tablespoon olive or salad oil
1 small red onion, chopped
3/4 teaspoon salt
1 8-3/4-ounce can whole kernel corn, drained
1 4-ounce can chopped mild green chilies, drained
1 medium-size tomato, seeded and diced
2 tablespoons chopped parsley
2 tablespoons lemon juice
1 teaspoon sugar

1. Preheat broiler if manufacturer directs. Place salmon fillets, skin side down, on rack in broiling pan. Brush tops of fillets with teriyaki sauce; sprinkle with black pepper.
2. With broiling pan at closest position to source of heat, broil salmon fillets 6 to 7 minutes, without turning, until golden brown and fish flakes easily when tested with a fork.
3. Meanwhile, in 1-quart saucepan over medium heat, in hot olive or salad oil, cook red onion and salt until onion is tender. Stir in corn, green chilies, tomato, parsley, lemon juice, and sugar; heat through.
4. To serve, place salmon fillets on 4 warm dinner plates; spoon corn and tomato salsa over. Makes 4 servings.

Linguine With Shrimp

3/4 16-ounce package linguine or spaghetti
salt
1 large onion
1 large tomato

1 cup pitted ripe olives, drained
2 tablespoons capers
1 small bunch basil
olive or salad oil
1 pound shelled and deveined large shrimp
2 tablespoons lemon juice 1-1/2 teaspoons chicken-flavor instant bouillon

1. In saucepot, prepare linguine as label directs, using 2 teaspoons salt in water; drain. Return linguine to saucepot; keep warm.
2. Meanwhile, chop onion; seed and dice tomato; coarsely chop olives; chop capers. Chop enough basil leaves to equal 1/2 cup, loosely packed.
3. In 12-inch skillet over medium-high heat, in 2 tablespoons hot olive or salad oil, cook onion until tender. Add shrimp and 1/2 teaspoon salt; cook, stirring frequently, until shrimp turn opaque throughout, about 5 minutes.
4. In cup, mix lemon juice, chicken bouillon, and 2/3 cup water until blended. Into shrimp mixture in skillet, stir lemon-juice mixture, tomato, olives, capers, chopped basil, and 2 tablespoons olive or salad oil; heat through. To serve, toss shrimp mixture with linguine in saucepot. Spoon onto 4 dinner plates. Makes 4 main-dish servings.

Squid Salad

2 pounds cleaned squid
salt
2 small zucchini (about 6 ounces each)
1 7-ounce jar roasted red peppers
1/2 cup reduced fat, cholesterol free mayonnaise dressing
3 tablespoons chopped parsley
3 tablespoons lemon juice
2 tablespoons Dijon mustard
1/2 teaspoon coarsely ground black pepper
1 15- to 19-ounce can garbanzo beans, drained

1. Rinse squid with running cold water. Cut squid bodies crosswise into 1/2-inch-thick rings; cut tentacles into several pieces if large.
2. In 3-quart saucepan over high heat, heat 1 inch water and 1 teaspoon salt to boiling. Add squid; heat to boiling. Reduce heat to medium; cook 3 to 5 minutes until squid is tender and turns opaque; drain.
3. Cut zucchini into 1/2-inch cubes; slice red peppers. In large bowl, stir mayonnaise dressing, parsley, lemon juice, mustard, pepper, and 1/2 teaspoon salt. Add squid, zucchini, red peppers, and garbanzo beans; toss to coat with dressing. Cover bowl and refrigerate squid salad at least 1 hour or until well chilled. Makes 6 servings.

Chilled Cod with Peppers

2 pounds cod fillets
salt
1 medium-size yellow pepper
1 medium-size red pepper
1 small red onion
1/2 cup pitted ripe olives
1/2 cup pimento-stuffed olives
2 medium-size lemons
3 tablespoons white wine vinegar
2 tablespoons olive or salad oil
1 tablespoon brown sugar
1 tablespoon chopped fresh cilantro or parsley
1 teaspoon coarsely ground black pepper
1 tablespoon pickling spice
2 16-ounce cans Great Northern beans
cilantro sprigs for garnish

Day ahead:
1. Remove any bones from cod. Sprinkle with 1-1/2 teaspoons salt; cover and refrigerate overnight.
About 4 hours before serving or early in day:
2. Cut yellow and red peppers into thin strips. Cut onion lengthwise in half; cut each half crosswise into thin slices. Slice ripe and stuffed olives. Cut half of 1 lemon into paper-thin slices.
3. Into large bowl, squeeze 3 tablespoons juice from remaining 1-1/2 lemons; stir in vinegar, olive or salad oil, brown sugar, cilantro, black pepper, and 1 teaspoon salt. Add peppers, onion, olives, and lemon slices; toss to coat with dressing; set aside.
4. If cod is large, cut into 4" by 4" pieces. In 12-inch skillet over high heat, heat cod, pickling spice, and 1/2 cup water to boiling. Reduce heat to low; cover and simmer 5 minutes or until cod flakes easily when tested with a fork. Drain cod well; place in 13" by 9" glass baking dish. Pour vegetable mixture over cod; cover and refrigerate until chilled, at least 2-1/2 hours.
5. To serve, rinse and drain Great Northern beans. Place beans on large platter; arrange cod and vegetable mixture over beans; pour over any remaining dressing. Garnish with cilantro sprigs. Makes 6 servings.

Grilled Swordfish with Warm Cabbage Slaw

1/4 cup seasoned rice vinegar
1/4 teaspoon crushed red pepper
salt
2 large cucumbers
1 small head red cabbage (about 1 pound)
olive or salad oil
2 tablespoons distilled white vinegar
4 swordfish steaks, each 1 inch thick (about 1-1/4 pounds)
1 teaspoon minced fresh thyme or 1/4 teaspoon dried thyme leaves

1/4 teaspoon coarsely ground black pepper
fresh thyme sprigs for garnish

1. In bowl, mix rice vinegar, crushed red pepper, and 1/2 teaspoon salt. Cut cucumbers into bite-size pieces. Add cucumbers to rice vinegar mixture; toss to coat. Set aside.
2. Thinly slice cabbage. In 12-inch skillet over high heat, in 2 tablespoons hot olive or salad oil, cook cabbage, white vinegar, and 1/2 teaspoon salt, stirring occasionally until cabbage is tender-crisp, 5 to 10 minutes.
3. While cabbage is cooking, preheat broiler if manufacturer directs. Arrange swordfish steaks on rack in broiling pan. In bowl, mix minced thyme, pepper, 1 tablespoon olive or salad oil, and 3/4 teaspoon salt. Brush mixture on swordfish. With broiling pan at closest position to source of heat, broil swordfish 8 to 10 minutes, turning fish once, until it just loses its pink color throughout.
4. To serve, on 4 dinner plates, arrange swordfish steaks with cabbage mixture. With slotted spoon, spoon marinated cucumbers along side; garnish with fresh thyme. Makes 4 servings.

Rolled Fillet of Sole with Rice

Rice Timbales
1 8-ounce package mushrooms
1 medium-size onion
6 sole or flounder fillets (about 6 ounces each)
2 tablespoons olive or salad oil
1 tablespoon all-purpose flour
1 14-1/2-ounce can pasta-style tomatoes
1/2 cup beef broth
1 tablespoon lemon juice
1/2 teaspoon salt
1/2 teaspoon black pepper
parsley sprigs for garnish

1. Prepare Rice Timbales; keep warm.
2. Meanwhile, thinly slice mushrooms and onion. Starting from a wide end, roll each sole fillet jelly-roll fashion.
3. In 12-inch skillet over medium-high heat, in hot olive or salad oil, cook mushrooms and onion until liquid evaporates and vegetables are tender and lightly browned.
4. In cup, mix flour with 1/4 cup water. Add flour mixture, tomatoes, beef broth, lemon juice, salt, and pepper to vegetables in skillet; over high heat, heat to boiling. Boil 1 minute. Add rolled sole fillets seam side down. Reduce heat to low; cover and simmer 15 minutes or until fish flakes easily when tested with a fork, occasionally spooning sauce over rolls.
5. To serve, arrange sole fillets on 6 dinner plates. Spoon sauce over and around fillets. Invert Rice Timbales onto plates with fish. Garnish with parsley sprigs. Makes 6 servings.

RICE TIMBALES: In 2-quart saucepan over medium-high heat, heat 1 tablespoon olive or salad oil, until hot. Stir in 1 medium-size onion, chopped, and 1 medium-size carrot, diced; cook until tender but not browned. Stir in 1 cup regular long grain rice and 3/4 teaspoon salt; cook, stirring frequently, until rice grains are opaque. Add 2 cups water; over high heat, heat to boiling. Reduce heat to low; cover and simmer 20 minutes or until rice is tender and all liquid is absorbed. Remove saucepan from heat; stir in 1 tablespoon chopped parsley. Grease six 4-ounce timbale molds or custard cups. Pack hot rice firmly into molds.

Tilefish with Browned-Butter Sauce

Steamed Potatoes
1 bunch watercress
4 tilefish or scrod fillets (about 6 ounces each)
2 tablespoons all-purpose flour 1-1/2 teaspoons paprika
1/2 teaspoon black pepper 1/2 teaspoon salt
1 tablespoon salad oil
2 tablespoons margarine or butter (1/4 stick)
2 tablespoons capers, chopped
1 tablespoon lemon juice

1. Prepare Steamed-Potato Mushrooms; keep warm.
2. While potatoes are cooking, rinse watercress thoroughly; drain well. Chop enough watercress to equal 1 tablespoon. Reserve remaining watercress to line platter.
3. Remove bones from fish fillets, if any. On waxed paper, mix flour, paprika, pepper, and salt. In nonstick 12-inch skillet over medium-high heat, heat salad oil until hot. Coat tilefish fillets with flour mixture and add to skillet. Cook fillets about 6 minutes until browned on both sides and fish flakes easily when tested with a fork, turning fillets once. Remove fillets to plate; keep warm.
4. To drippings in skillet, add margarine or butter. Cook over medium-high heat until browned but not burned. Stir in capers, lemon juice, chopped watercress, and 1 tablespoon water; heat through.
5. To serve, place watercress and Steamed-Potato Mushrooms on large platter. Arrange tilefish fillets on top of watercress. Spoon browned butter sauce over fish. Makes 4 servings.
STEAMEDPOTATOES: Cut 12 small red potatoes (about 1-1/2 pounds), unpeeled, to resemble mushrooms: Press 3/4-inch round biscuit cutter into one end of a potato. With sharp knife, slice potato all around cutter so that knife edge touches the cutter and does not cut all the way through potato. Carefully remove cutter from potato, leaving "stem" intact. Trim stem end. Reserve potato trimmings for use another day. Repeat with remaining potatoes.
In 4-quart saucepan in 1 inch water, place steamer basket or colander and potatoes; over high heat, heat water to boiling. Reduce heat to medium-low; cover and cook about 20 minutes

or until potatoes are tender.

Fish "Fry"

Much better (and better for you) than deep-fried fish, our lightly breaded cod fillets are baked, then served with a tangy no-fat tartar sauce.

1 egg white
1/3 cup dried bread crumbs
2 tablespoons grated Parmesan cheese
3/4 teaspoon dried basil leaves
1/4 teaspoon pepper
salt
4 6-ounce cod fillets
1/2 cup nonfat mayonnaise dressing
1/4 cup finely chopped dill pickles
1 tablespoon chopped parsley
2 teaspoons lemon juice
1-1/2 teaspoons hot pepper sauce
basil sprigs and lemon wedges for garnish

1. Preheat oven to 450°F. In pie plate, with fork, beat egg white slightly. On waxed paper, mix bread crumbs, Parmesan cheese, dried basil, pepper, and 1/2 teaspoon salt. Dip cod fillets in egg white, then bread-crumb mixture to coat.
2. Place cod fillets on ungreased cookie sheet; bake 10 to 12 minutes, without turning fish, until fish flakes easily when tested with a fork. If you like golden brown bread coating, turn oven control to broil. Broil fish with cookie sheet at closest position to source of heat 2 to 3 minutes.
3. Meanwhile, in small bowl, mix mayonnaise dressing, pickles, parsley, lemon juice, hot pepper sauce, and 1/4 teaspoon salt.
4. To serve, arrange cod fillets on warm platter. Garnish with fresh basil and lemon wedges. Serve with tartar sauce. Makes 4 main-dish servings.

Pan-Sautéed Cajun Catfish

3 tablespoons yellow cornmeal
1 teaspoon chili powder
1 teaspoon dried oregano leaves
1/2 teaspoon paprika
1/2 teaspoon salt
1/4 teaspoon pepper
4 6-ounce catfish fillets
2 tablespoons olive or salad oil

1. On waxed paper, mix cornmeal, chili powder, oregano, paprika, salt, and pepper. Dip fillets into cornmeal mixture to coat both sides evenly.
2. In 12-inch skillet over medium-high heat, in hot olive or salad oil, cook catfish fillets 8 minutes or until fish flakes easily when tested with a fork, carefully turning fillets once with a pancake turner. Makes 4 main-dish servings.

Shrimp Scampi

1-1/4 pounds large shrimp
1 medium-size bunch spinach
2 medium-size tomatoes
1 garlic clove
1 pound small red potatoes
olive or salad oil
salt
1 tablespoon chopped parsley
1 tablespoon lemon juice
1/2 teaspoon lemon-pepper seasoning salt
parsley sprigs for garnish

1. Shell and devein shrimp, leaving tail part of shell on, if you like. Discard tough stems from spinach; coarsely chop spinach. Cut each tomato in half; squeeze halves to remove seeds. Cut tomatoes into 1/2-inch chunks. Mince garlic.
2. Cut each potato in half. In 3-quart saucepan over high heat, heat potatoes and enough water to cover to boiling. Reduce heat to low; cover and simmer 15 minutes or until potatoes are fork-tender. Drain; keep warm.
3. Meanwhile, preheat oven to 450°F. In large bowl, combine spinach, tomatoes, 1 tablespoon olive or salad oil, and 1/2 teaspoon salt. Toss to coat. Place spinach mixture in four 1-1/2-cup shallow casseroles.
4. In same large bowl, combine shrimp, garlic, chopped parsley, lemon juice, lemon-pepper seasoning salt, 1 tablespoon olive or salad oil, and 1/2 teaspoon salt; toss to coat shrimp. Arrange shrimp mixture over spinach mixture. Bake casseroles 12 to 15 minutes until shrimp are cooked through.
5. To serve, arrange each casserole on plate; place some potatoes along side and garnish with parsley. Makes 4 main-dish servings.

Hearty Seafood Stew

2 medium-size carrots
1 large onion
1 medium-size celery stalk
1 garlic clove
2 tablespoons olive or salad oil
1-1/4 teaspoons salt
1/4 teaspoon pepper
2 medium-size zucchini (about 10 ounces each)
3 medium-size red potatoes (1 pound)
1 pound monkfish or cod fillets
1/2 pound large shrimp

1/2 pound sea scallops
1 dozen littleneck clams
1 14-1/2- to 16-ounce can stewed tomatoes
1 8-ounce bottle clam juice
1 tablespoon lemon juice
1 bay leaf
2 tablespoons chopped parsley

1. Cut carrots into 1-inch chunks; dice onion; cut celery into 1/2-inch-thick diagonal slices. Crush garlic with garlic press or finely mince.
2. In 5-quart Dutch oven over medium heat, in hot olive or salad oil, cook carrots, onion, celery, salt, and pepper until vegetables are tender-crisp, about 15 minutes. Stir in garlic; cook 1 minute.
3. Meanwhile, cut zucchini and potatoes into 1-1/2-inch chunks. With sharp knife, remove any dark membrane from monkfish. Cut monkfish into 2-inch chunks. Shell and devein shrimp. Rinse shrimp and scallops with running cold water. With stiff brush, scrub clams with running cold water to remove any sand.
4. Into vegetable mixture in Dutch oven, stir potatoes, stewed tomatoes, clam juice, lemon juice, bay leaf, and clams; over high heat, heat to boiling. Reduce heat to low; cover and simmer 20 minutes.
5. Add zucchini, monkfish, shrimp, and scallops; over high heat, heat to boiling. Reduce heat to low; cover and simmer 10 to 12 minutes longer, gently stirring occasionally, until clams open fully, seafood is opaque throughout, and potatoes and zucchini are tender. Sprinkle with chopped parsley.
6. To serve, discard bay leaf. Serve stew in soup bowls. Makes 6 servings.

Black-Pepper Steak With Herbed Potatoes

1-1/2 pounds medium-size red potatoes, cut into 1/2-inch cubes
1 garlic clove, minced
1/2 teaspoon dried thyme leaves
olive or salad oil
salt
4 beef rib eye steaks, each about 3/4 inch thick
3/4 teaspoon black pepper
1 8-ounce package mushrooms, thinly sliced
1 tablespoon all-purpose flour
1 tablespoon soy sauce
1 tablespoon chopped parsley

1. Preheat oven to 475°F.
2. In medium bowl, mix potatoes, garlic, thyme, 1 tablespoon olive or salad oil, and 1 teaspoon salt. Evenly spread potatoes in 15-1/2" by 10-1/2" jelly-roll pan. Bake 20 to 25 minutes until tender and golden, stirring occasionally.
3. Meanwhile, trim excess fat from rib eye steaks. Sprinkle steaks on both sides with pepper and 3/4 teaspoon salt.
4. In 12-inch skillet over medium-high heat, in 1 tablespoon hot olive or salad oil, cook steaks until browned on both sides, about 8 minutes for rare or until desired doneness. Remove steaks to 4 dinner plates; keep warm.
5. In same skillet over medium-high heat, in 2 teaspoons hot olive or salad oil, cook mushrooms, stirring occasionally, until mushrooms are tender, about 5 minutes.
6. In cup, with fork, mix flour, soy sauce, and 3/4 cup water. To mushrooms in skillet, add flour mixture; over high heat, heat until mixture boils and thickens, stirring often.
7. To serve, stir chopped parsley into potatoes; arrange potatoes on plates with steaks. Spoon mushroom sauce over steaks. Makes 4 main-dish servings.

Creamy Chicken & Vegetables With Savory Biscuits

1-1/2 cups reduced-fat baking and pancake mix with buttermilk
1/2 teaspoon dried thyme leaves
1/2 teaspoon coarsely ground black pepper
low-fat milk (1%)
4 medium-size boneless, skinless chicken-breast halves (about 1-1/2 pounds)
1 large carrot
1 large celery stalk
1 medium-size red pepper
1 small onion
3 tablespoons olive or salad oil
salt
2 tablespoons all-purpose flour
1-1/2 teaspoons chicken-flour instant bouillon
1 8-3/4-ounce can whole-kernel corn, drained
1/2 cup frozen peas
parsley sprigs for garnish

1. Preheat oven to 450°F. In medium bowl, with fork, mix baking and pancake mix, dried thyme leaves, black pepper, and 1/2 cup low-fat milk until blended.
2. Spray small cookie sheet with nonstick cooking spray; spoon biscuit batter into 4 mounds, about 3 inches apart, on cookie sheet, spreading each to about a 3-inch round. Bake biscuits 8 to 10 minutes until golden; remove biscuits to wire rack.
3. Meanwhile, cut chicken-breast halves into 1-inch pieces. Thinly slice carrot and celery stalk. Dice red pepper; chop onion.
4. In 12-inch skillet over medium-high heat, in hot olive or salad oil, cook chicken-breast pieces and 1/2 teaspoon salt until chicken loses its pink color throughout. With slotted spoon, remove chicken pieces to bowl.
5. In oil remaining in skillet over high heat, cook carrot, celery, red pepper, onion, and 1/2 teaspoon salt, stirring frequently,

until vegetables are tender.
6. While vegetables are cooking, in 2-cup measuring cup, with wire whisk or fork, mix flour, chicken bouillon, and 2 cups low-fat milk until blended.
7. Return chicken-breast pieces to skillet with vegetable mixture; add corn, frozen peas, and milk mixture. Over high heat, cook, stirring, until mixture boils and thickens; boil 1 minute.
8. To serve, slice each biscuit horizontally in half. Place bottom halves on each of 4 warm dinner plates; spoon chicken and vegetable mixture over biscuit bottoms; top with top of biscuit. Garnish with parsley sprigs. Makes 4 main-dish servings.

Chicken Salad

2 tablespoons lime juice
1 teaspoon sugar
1/2 teaspoon ground ginger
1/4 teaspoon salt
1/8 teaspoon pepper
2 cups cubed, cooked chicken
2 peaches or nectarines, cubed
1/4 cup sliced green onions
1/4 cup toasted slivered almonds (optional)

Chicken Breasts With Mushrooms & Artichokes

1 12-ounce package mushrooms
olive or salad oil
salt
4 large skinless, boneless chicken-breast halves (about 1-1-/2 pounds)
1/2 teaspoon Italian seasoning
1 teaspoon chicken-flavor instant bouillon
1 teaspoon cornstarch
1 14-ounce can quartered artichoke hearts, drained

1. Cut mushrooms in half if they are large. In 12-inch skillet over medium-high heat, in 1 tablespoon hot olive or salad oil, cook mushrooms and 1/4 teaspoon salt until golden brown, about 10 minutes; remove to small bowl.
2. Sprinkle chicken breasts with Italian seasoning and 1/2 teaspoon salt. In same skillet over medium-high heat, in 1 tablespoon hot olive or salad oil, cook chicken breasts until juices run clear when chicken is pierced with a knife, turning once, about 8 to 10 minutes. Remove chicken to 4 dinner plates; keep warm.
3. In small bowl, stir bouillon, cornstarch, and 3/4 cup water until smooth; stir into skillet. Over high heat, cook, stirring constantly, until sauce boils and thickens slightly. Stir in artichoke hearts and mushrooms; heat through. Spoon mushroom mixture over chicken. Makes 4 main-dish servings.

Chili Broiled Chicken

1 tablespoon olive or salad oil
1 small onion, minced
1/2 medium-size green pepper, minced
1-1/2 teaspoons chili powder
1/4 cup orange juice
1 tablespoon brown sugar
2 tablespoons cayenne pepper sauce
1 tablespoon tomato paste
1/2 teaspoon salt
4 medium-size skinless, boneless chicken-breast halves (about 1-1/4 pounds)

1. In 2-quart saucepan over medium-high heat, in hot olive or salad oil, cook onion and green pepper until browned, stirring occasionally. Add chili powder and cook 1 minute, stirring constantly.
2. Preheat broiler if manufacturer directs. To same saucepan, add orange juice and remaining ingredients except chicken, stirring until well blended; over high heat, heat to boiling. Boil 2 minutes to blend flavors; remove from heat.
3. Add chicken-breast halves to saucepan; turn to coat with sauce. Arrange chicken-breast halves on rack in broiling pan. Place pan in broiler with chicken about 5 inches from source of heat; broil chicken 3 minutes. Turn chicken and spoon on remaining sauce. Broil 5 minutes longer or until juices run clear when chicken is pierced with a knife. Makes 4 main-dish servings.

"Fried" Chicken

For our update of Grandma's Southern Fried Chicken, we baked the chicken instead of frying it and removed all the skin first—reducing fat, not flavor.

2 whole large chicken breasts (about 2-1/2 pounds)
4 large chicken legs (about 2-1/4 pounds)
1 8-ounce container plain nonfat yogurt
1-1/4 teaspoons salt
1 cup dried bread crumbs
1-1/2 teaspoons dried cilantro leaves or dried parsley flakes
3/4 teaspoon coarsely ground black pepper
Chili-Spiced Salsa
cilantro or parsley sprigs for garnish

1 Preheat oven to 425°F. Remove skin and fat from chicken pieces. Cut each breast in half; cut each leg at joint, separating

drumstick from thigh. In pie plate, mix yogurt and salt. On waxed paper, mix bread crumbs, dried cilantro, and black pepper. Coat chicken pieces lightly with yogurt mixture, then dip in bread-crumb mixture to coat.
2. Arrange chicken pieces in single layer in large roasting pan. Bake 40 to 45 minutes, without turning, until chicken is fork-tender and juices run clear when chicken is pierced with a knife.
3. Meanwhile, prepare the Chili-Spiced Salsa.
4. When chicken is done, if you like, turn oven control to broil. Broil chicken in roasting pan 4 to 5 minutes until coating is golden brown.
5. To serve, arrange chicken on warm large platter. Garnish with cilantro or parsley sprigs. Serve with Chili-Spiced Salsa. Makes 6 main-dish servings.
Chili-Spiced Salsa: In large bowl, mix 1 large tomato, chopped, 1 large cucumber, seeded and chopped, 1 medium-size carrot, shredded, one 17-ounce can whole kernel corn, drained, one 4-ounce can chopped mild green chilies, 3 tablespoons white wine vinegar, 1 tablespoon olive or salad oil, 1-1/4 teaspoons chili powder, 1-1/4 teaspoons salt, and 1/2 teaspoon sugar until well blended.
For a tasty change serve chunky vegetable salsa as a light, refreshing accompaniment.

Chicken Pot Pie

olive or salad oil
2 large skinless, boneless chicken breast halves (about 1 pound), cut into 1-inch chunks
1 small onion, finely chopped
2 tablespoons all-purpose flour
3 medium-size red potatoes (about 1/2 pound), cut into 1-inch chunks
2 medium-size carrots, slices
2 medium-size parsnips, cut into 1-inch chunks
1 13-3/4- to 14-1/2-ounce can chicken broth
1 9-ounce package frozen Italian green beans, thawed
4 sheets fresh or frozen (thawed) phyllo (about 17" by 12" each)
olive oil nonstick cooking spray
1/4 cup dried bread crumbs

About 1 hour before serving:
1. In 4-quart saucepan over medium-high heat, in 1 tablespoon hot olive or salad oil, cook chicken until it just loses its pink color throughout. With slotted spoon, remove chicken to bowl.
2. In drippings in saucepan and 1 more tablespoon hot olive or salad oil, over medium heat, cook onion until tender and lightly browned. Stir in flour; cook 1 minute. Stir in potatoes, carrots, parsnips, and chicken broth; over high heat, heat to boiling. Reduce heat to low; cover and simmer until vegetables are tender, about 15 minutes. Stir in frozen Italian green beans; heat through.
3. Stir chicken into mixture in saucepan; spoon into a shallow 1-1/2-quart casserole.
4. Preheat oven to 375°F. Place phyllo on waxed paper; cover loosely with plastic wrap to prevent phyllo from drying out. Place 1 sheet of phyllo on work surface; spray lightly with olive oil cooking spray; sprinkle with 1 tablespoon bread crumbs. Keeping crumb-side up, gather edges of phyllo to fit top of casserole; gently place phyllo on top of chicken mixture so edge is within rim of casserole. Repeat with remaining phyllo to cover chicken mixture completely.

Chicken Salad

6 medium-size red potatoes (about 1 Pound)
3 packages refrigerated roasted chicken-breast halves (about 1-1/2 pounds)
2 medium-size plum tomatoes
1 small zucchini (8 ounces)
1/2 cup pitted ripe olives
1 13-3/4- to 14-ounce can artichoke hearts, drained
1 15- to 16-ounce can wax beans, drained
1/3 cup low-fat milk (1%)
1/4 cup nonfat mayonnaise dressing
2 tablespoons chopped parsley
1 tablespoon lemon juice
1 teaspoon Dijon mustard
1/2 teaspoon salt
1/4 teaspoon pepper

About 30 minutes before serving:
1. Cut each potato into quarters. In 3-quart saucepan over high heat, heat potatoes and enough water to cover to boiling. Reduce heat to low; cover and simmer 10 minutes or until potatoes are fork-tender. Drain.
2. Meanwhile, discard skin and bones from chicken breasts; tear meat into large chunks. Cut each tomato into thin wedges; cut zucchini into small chunks; slice each olive in half. Cut each artichoke heart into quarters.
3. In large bowl, mix cooked potatoes, chicken breast meat, tomato wedges, zucchini, olives, artichoke hearts, and wax beans.
4. In small bowl, with fork, mix milk, mayonnaise dressing, parsley, lemon juice, mustard, salt, and pepper until blended. Add to chicken mixture in bowl, tossing to coat well. Makes 6 main-dish servings.

Turkey Piccata

1 pound turkey cutlets
1/8 teaspoon pepper
all purpose flour
salt
1 medium-size bunch broccoli
olive or salad oil

1 cup chicken broth
1 tablespoon lemon juice
1 tablespoon capers, chopped
parsley sprigs for garnish

1. Cut each turkey cutlet in half if large. On waxed paper, combine pepper, 2 tablespoons flour, and 3/4 teaspoon salt. Dip turkey cutlets into flour mixture to coat.
2. Cut broccoli into 3" by 2" spears; discard tough stem ends. In 4-quart saucepan over high heat, in 1 inch boiling water, heat broccoli and 1/4 teaspoon salt to boiling; reduce heat to low; cover and simmer 5 minutes or until tender-crisp; drain; return to saucepan and keep warm.
3. In 12-inch skillet over medium-high heat, in 2 tablespoons hot olive or salad oil, cook turkey cutlets, half at a time, 2 to 3 minutes until turkey loses its pink color throughout; remove to plate.
4. Into drippings in skillet and 1 tablespoon hot olive or salad oil, stir 1 tablespoon flour; cook until flour begins to brown slightly, about 30 seconds, stirring constantly. Gradually stir in chicken broth and lemon juice. Over high heat, heat until sauce boils and thickens slightly; boil 1 minute.
5. Return turkey cutlets to skillet; heat through.
6. Arrange turkey cutlets and broccoli spears on platter. Stir capers into sauce remaining in skillet; pour sauce over cutlets. Garnish with parsley sprigs. Makes 4 main-dish servings.

Chili with Turkey

1 tablespoon olive or salad oil
3/4 pound ground turkey
2 medium-size celery stalks, thinly sliced
2 medium-size carrots, thinly sliced
1 medium-size onion, chopped
1 small zucchini (6 ounces), diced
3/4 teaspoon salt
1/4 cup all-purpose flour
3 tablespoons chili powder
2 14-1/2- to 16-ounce cans stewed tomatoes
1 13-3/4- to 14-1/2-ounce can beef broth
1 11-ounce can vacuum-packed whole kernel corn
1 4-ounce can chopped mild green chilies
1 tablespoon hot pepper sauce
2 15-1/4- to 19-ounce cans red kidney beans, rinsed and drained

1. In 5-quart Dutch oven or saucepot over medium-high heat, in hot olive or salad oil, cook ground turkey, celery, carrots, onion, zucchini, and salt, stirring frequently, until any liquid evaporates and turkey and vegetables begin to brown, about 15 minutes.
2. Over medium heat, stir in flour and chili powder; cook 1 minute, stirring constantly. Add stewed tomatoes, beef broth, corn with its liquid, chopped green chilies with their liquid, hot pepper sauce, and 1/2 cup water.
3. Over high heat, heat to boiling. Reduce heat to low; cover and simmer 15 minutes to blend flavors. Stir in kidney beans; heat through. Makes 6 main-dish servings.

Turkey Meat Loaf

3 slices light whole-wheat or white bread
1 12-ounce package mushrooms
2 medium-size carrots
1 large onion
1 large celery stalk
1 small red pepper
2 tablespoons salad oil
salt
2 pounds ground turkey
1 8-ounce container nonfat plain yogurt
1/2 cup chili sauce
1/4 cup chopped parsley
1-1/2 teaspoons chili powder

1. Finely chop bread; set aside. Finely chop mushrooms, carrots, onion, celery, and red pepper. In 12-inch skillet over medium-high heat, in hot salad oil, cook vegetables and 1/2 teaspoon salt until vegetables are tender and well browned, about 20 minutes. Remove skillet from heat; cool slightly.
2. Preheat oven to 375°F. In large bowl, mix ground turkey, yogurt, chili sauce, chopped parsley, chili powder, and 1 teaspoon salt until well blended. Stir in vegetable mixture and bread.
3. In jelly-roll pan, pat turkey mixture into 12" by 5" oval loaf. Bake 50 minutes or until meat thermometer inserted into thickest part of meat loaf reads 165°F. Makes 8 main-dish servings.

Fettucine Alfredo

3/4 16-ounce package fettuccine or linguine
salt
1 tablespoon all-purpose flour
1/4 teaspoon coarsely ground black pepper
1/4 teaspoon ground nutmeg
2 cups low-fat milk (1%)
1/2 cup grated Parmesan cheese
1 tablespoon chopped parsley
parsley sprigs for garnish

1. Prepare fettuccine as label directs, using 2 teaspoons salt in water. Drain; keep warm.
2. In 5-quart saucepot, mix flour, pepper, ground nutmeg, and 3/4 teaspoon salt; stir in milk. Cook over medium-high heat, stirring constantly, until mixture boils and thickens slightly; boil 1 minute. Remove saucepot from heat.
3. Stir in fettuccine, grated Parmesan cheese, and chopped parsley. Toss to coat well. Serve immediately, garnished with parsley sprigs. Makes 4 main-dish servings.

Macaroni & Cheese

1 16-ounce package elbow macaroni
2 medium-size tomatoes (about 1 pound)
1 16-ounce package light pasteurized process cheese spread
1-1/2 cups lowfat milk (1%)
2 tablespoons finely chopped parsley
1/4 teaspoon coarsely ground black pepper`

1. In saucepot, prepare elbow macaroni as label directs, but do not use salt in water.
2. Meanwhile, cut tomatoes into 1/2-inch chunks. Cut pasteurized process cheese spread into 1-inch chunks.
3. When pasta is done, drain and return to saucepot. Stir in milk and cheese spread and heat over low heat until cheese melts. Stir in tomatoes, parsley, and pepper, stirring gently until heated through. Makes 4 main-dish servings.

Broccoli Lasagna

1 20-ounce package frozen chopped broccoli
1 26-ounce jar marinara sauce
2 14-1/2- to 16-ounce cans stewed tomatoes
1 tablespoon sugar
2 8-ounce packages no-boil lasagna noodles
2 8-ounce packages shredded low-fat mozzarella cheese (4 cups)

1. Place broccoli in colander under running water to thaw; squeeze out excess water. In large bowl, combine broccoli, marinara sauce, stewed tomatoes, sugar, and 1 cup water, stirring to break up the tomatoes.
2. Preheat oven to 375°F. In 13" by 9" glass or ceramic baking dish, spread 1 cup tomato-sauce mixture.
3. Arrange one-fourth uncooked noodles over sauce, making sure to leave a 1/2-inch space between noodles and sides of baking dish because the uncooked noodles will expand during baking. Top with one-fourth tomato sauce and one-fourth shredded mozzarella.
4. Repeat layering noodles, sauce, and mozzarella as above in step 3, three more times.
5. Cover baking dish with foil; bake lasagna 45 minutes. Uncover and bake 15 minutes longer or until cheese is lightly browned. Makes 10 main-dish servings.

Asparagus Quiche

1/2 pound asparagus
1 15-ounce package refrigerated piecrust (1 9-inch crust)
1 8-ounce container liquid whole eggs (reduced cholesterol)
2 cups low-fat milk (1%)
1-1/4 teaspoons salt
1/4 teaspoon ground nutmeg
1/8 teaspoon black pepper
1/4 pound light Jarlsberg cheese, shredded (1 cup)

1. Discard tough ends from asparagus; trim scales if stalks are gritty. Cut asparagus into 1-inch pieces.
2. In 1-quart saucepan over high heat, in 1-1/2 inches boiling water, heat asparagus to boiling. Reduce heat to medium-low; cook 3 to 5 minutes until asparagus are tender-crisp. Drain; set aside.
3. Let piecrust dough stand at room temperature to soften and place dough round in 9-inch pie plate as label directs. Flute edge.
4. Preheat oven to 375°F. In large bowl, with wire whisk or fork, mix liquid whole eggs, low-fat milk, salt, nutmeg, and pepper; stir in cheese and asparagus.
5. Pour mixture into piecrust. Bake quiche 25 to 30 minutes or until knife inserted in center comes out clean. Makes 6 main-dish servings.

Ravioli with Vegetables

1 13-ounce package frozen jumbo cheese ravioli
1 medium-size carrot
1 small zucchini (about 6 ounces)
1 13-3/4- to 14-1/2-ounce can chicken or beef broth with less salt
2 teaspoons grated, peeled ginger root
1/4 bunch watercress

1. Prepare ravioli as label directs; drain. Keep warm.
2. Meanwhile, cut carrot into matchstick-thin strips; dice zucchini. In 3-quart saucepan over high heat, heat chicken or beef broth and carrot to boiling. Reduce heat to low; cover and simmer 5 minutes. Stir in zucchini and grated ginger. Over high heat, heat to boiling. Reduce heat to low; cover and simmer 5 minutes longer, until vegetables are tender-crisp.
3. To serve, place watercress sprigs in 3 large shallow bowls. Arrange ravioli in bowls with watercress. Spoon broth with

vegetables over ravioli. Serve immediately. Makes 3 main-dish servings.

Lemon-Flavored Potato Salad

6 medium-size potatoes (about 2 pounds)
2 medium-size lemons
3 tablespoons extra-virgin olive oil or olive oil
1 tablespoon Dijon mustard
2 teaspoons sugar
1 teaspoon salt
1/2 teaspoon dried basil leaves
coarsely ground black pepper
2 medium-size cucumbers
2 cups loosely packed spinach leaves

1. In 5-quart Dutch oven or saucepot over high heat, heat unpeeled potatoes and enough water to cover to boiling. Reduce heat to low; cover and simmer 30 minutes or until potatoes are fork-tender. Drain; cool potatoes until easy to handle. Peel and cut potatoes into bite-size chunks.
2. Meanwhile, prepare dressing: From lemons, grate 1 tablespoon peel and squeeze 1/4 cup juice. In large bowl, with wire whisk or fork, mix lemon peel, lemon juice, olive oil, Dijon mustard, sugar, salt, basil, and 1/4 teaspoon coarsely ground black pepper.
3. Cut each cucumber lengthwise in half; slice cucumber halves crosswise into 1/4-inch-thick slices. Slice spinach leaves into thin strips.
4. Add potatoes, cucumbers, and spinach to dressing; toss to coat well. Spoon potato salad onto platter; sprinkle with 1/4 teaspoon coarsely ground black pepper. Cover and refrigerate if not serving right away. Toss to serve. Makes 6 accompaniment servings.

Chinese Pepper Steak

1 16-ounce package firm tofu
2 tablespoons soy sauce
1 tablespoon Oriental sesame oil
2 teaspoons grated, peeled ginger root
1 cup regular long grain rice
1/4 pound medium-size mushrooms
1 medium-size red pepper
1 medium-size yellow pepper
1/4 pound Chinese pea pods
1 green onion
2 tablespoons salad oil
1/8 teaspoon salt

1. Cut tofu lengthwise into 1/2-inch-thick strips, then cut each strip crosswise in half.
2. In medium bowl, with rubber spatula, gently stir tofu, soy sauce, Oriental sesame oil, and grated ginger root until blended. Set aside.
3. Prepare rice as label direct; keep warm.
4. Meanwhile, cut each mushroom into quarters. Cut red and yellow peppers into 1/2-inch-wide strips. Remove stem and strings along both edges of each pea pod. Chop green onion.
5. In 12-inch skillet over medium-high heat, in hot salad oil, cook mushrooms, red and yellow peppers, Chinese pea pods, green onion, and salt until tender-crisp and lightly browned, stirring frequently. Gently stir in tofu mixture; heat through. Serve with hot cooked rice. Makes 4 main-dish servings.

Minestrone Soup

1/2 cup tubetti or elbow macaroni
salt
1 large onion
1 medium-size carrot
1/2 small head Savoy cabbage (about 3/4 pound)
2 tablespoons olive or salad oil
1 14-1/2- to 16-ounce can stewed tomatoes
3 envelopes instant vegetable broth and seasoning
1 15-1/4- to 19-ounce can red kidney beans
1 16- to 19-ounce can white kidney beans (cannellini)
1 10-ounce package frozen chopped spinach
1/2 teaspoon dried thyme leaves
1/4 teaspoon coarsely ground pepper

1. Prepare pasta as label directs, using 2 teaspoons salt in water; drain.
2. Meanwhile, chop onion and carrot. Coarsely slice cabbage and discard any tough ribs. (You should have about 8 cups sliced cabbage.)
3. In 5-quart Dutch oven or saucepot over medium heat, in hot olive or salad oil, cook onion and carrot until tender.
4. Add cabbage, stewed tomatoes, instant broth, and 6 cups water; over high heat, heat to boiling. Reduce heat to low; cover and simmer 30 minutes or until cabbage is very tender.
5. Add cooked pasta, red and white kidney beans with their liquid, frozen spinach, thyme, and pepper; over high heat, cook until spinach is completely thawed and mixture is hot. Makes 8 servings.

Open-Faced Hummus Sandwiches

1 15- to 19-ounce can garbanzo beans
2 tablespoons lemon juice
1 garlic clove

olive or salad oil
salt
2 small tomatoes
1 small cucumber
3 6- to 8-inch pitas, split
1 small eggplant (about 1 pound)
1 tablespoon chopped fresh cilantro or parsley
1/2 teaspoon coarsely ground black pepper

1. Prepare hummus: Drain garbanzo beans, reserving 1/4 cup liquid. In food processor with knife blade attached, blend garbanzo beans with their reserved liquid, lemon juice, garlic, 2 tablespoons olive or salad oil, and 1/4 teaspoon salt until smooth.
2. Preheat broiler if manufacturer directs. Slice tomatoes and unpeeled cucumber into 1/4-inch-thick slices.
3. Place pitas, split-side up, on cookie sheet and brush with 1 tablespoon olive or salad oil. Place cookie sheet in broiler at closest position to source of heat; broil pitas until lightly browned. Remove pitas to wire rack.
4. Slice unpeeled eggplant crosswise into 1/4-inch-thick slices. Place eggplant slices on same cookie sheet; brush both sides of slices with 2 tablespoons olive or salad oil. Sprinkle with 1/2 teaspoon salt. Broil eggplant slices 10 to 12 minutes until browned and tender, turning slices once halfway through broiling time.
5. To serve, spread hummus on toasted pita halves; top with broiled eggplant, tomato slices, and cucumber slices. Drizzle sandwiches with 1 tablespoon olive or salad oil; sprinkle with chopped cilantro and coarsely ground pepper. Makes 3 servings.

Rice & Vegetable Bundles

1-1/2 cups brown rice
salt
2 small carrots
1 medium-size zucchini (10 ounces)
1 bunch green onions
1/2 pound Fontina or mozzarella cheese
2/3 7-ounce jar roasted red peppers, drained (1/2 cup)
1 tablespoon dried basil leaves
1/2 cup frozen peas
8 sheets fresh or frozen (thawed) phyllo, each about 17" by 12" nonstick cooking spray
1 14-1/2-ounce can chunky pasta-style stewed tomatoes
1 small tomato, chopped

1. In 3-quart saucepan, prepare brown rice as label directs, using 1/2 teaspoon salt in water.
2. Meanwhile, shred carrots and zucchini. Reserve 1 large green onion; chop remaining green onions. Shred cheese; chop roasted red peppers.
3. In 10-inch skillet over medium-high heat, in hot olive or salad oil, cook carrots, zucchini, chopped green onions, basil, and 1/2 teaspoon salt until vegetables are tender.
4. While vegetables are cooking, in 2-quart saucepan, heat reserved green onion and enough water to cover to boiling. Boil 1 to 2 minutes until green onion is wilted; drain. Separate green onion into 4 long pieces.
5. When vegetables are done, stir in cooked brown rice, shredded cheese, roasted red peppers, and frozen peas.
6. Preheat oven to 375°F. On work surface, lay 1 sheet phyllo; spray with nonstick cooking spray. Lay a second sheet phyllo crosswise over first sheet; spray with nonstick cooking spray.
7. Spoon one-fourth of brown-rice mixture onto center of phyllo sheets. Gather phyllo together to form bundle; tie with a piece of green onion. Place bundle on ungreased large cookie sheet. Repeat with remaining phyllo, brown-rice mixture, and green-onion pieces to make 4 bundles in all. Spray bundles with nonstick cooking spray. Bake 20 minutes or until phyllo is golden brown.
8. While phyllo bundles are baking, in same 2-quart saucepan over medium heat, heat stewed tomatoes, chopped tomato, and 2 tablespoons water to boiling. Reduce heat to low; cover and simmer 5 minutes.
9. Spoon tomato sauce onto 4 warm dinner plates; top with phyllo bundles. Makes 4 servings.

Bean & Cheese Salad

1 10-ounce package frozen baby lima beans
2 bunches watercress
1 small head radicchio or 1/8 small head red cabbage
1/3 cup Mediterranean or pitted ripe olives
1 garlic clove
1 15-1/4- to 19-ounce can red kidney beans
1 16- to 19-ounce can white kidney beans (cannellini)
1 11-ounce package goat cheese or 1 8-ounce package light cream cheese (Neufchatel)
4 slices white bread
1/2 teaspoon coarsely ground black pepper
2 tablespoons red wine vinegar
1/2 teaspoon sugar
1/4 teaspoon salt
olive or salad oil
1/4 teaspoon dried thyme leaves

1. Preheat oven to 375°F. In 3-quart saucepan, prepare frozen lima beans as label directs.
2. Meanwhile, remove tough stems from watercress. Thinly slice radicchio or red cabbage. If using Mediterranean olives, remove pits; coarsely chop olives. Mince garlic. Rinse and drain red and white kidney beans. Cut goat cheese crosswise into 1-inch-thick rounds (if using cream cheese, cut into 8 chunks).

3. Cut crusts from bread slices (reserve crusts for making bread crumbs another day). Cut each slice into thirds. Arrange bread on small ungreased cookie sheet. Bake 10 minutes or until golden on both sides, burning bread once. Remove toast from cookie sheet.
4. Wipe cookie sheet clean; line it with foil. Place cheese on cookie sheet; sprinkle with pepper. Bake 5 minutes or until cheese is warm.
5. In large bowl, with wire whisk or fork, mix red wine vinegar, sugar, salt, and 1 tablespoon olive or salad oil until blended. Add radicchio and watercress; toss to coat; set watercress salad aside.
6. Drain lima beans. Over low heat, gently stir in garlic, red and white kidney beans, olives, thyme, and 2 tablespoons olive or salad oil; heat through.
7. To serve, arrange watercress salad on 4 dinner plates. Spoon bean mixture onto salad; top with cheese. Serve with toast. Makes 4 servings.

Stuffed Pizza

3 medium-size plum tomatoes (about 1/2 pound)
1 12-ounce jar roasted red peppers, drained
2 16-ounce packages hot-roll mix
1 cup pizza sauce
1 10-ounce package frozen chopped broccoli, thawed and squeezed dry
1 10-ounce package frozen chopped spinach, thawed and squeezed dry
1 8-ounce package shredded part-skim mozzarella cheese (2 cups)
1 tablespoon olive or salad oil fresh rosemary for garnish
1 teaspoon coarse salt (optional)

1. Slice plum tomatoes crosswise into 1/4-inch-thick slices. Chop roasted red peppers.
2. Prepare 1 package of hot-roll mix as label directs for pizza dough; shaped into a ball and let rest. Meanwhile, prepare second package of hot-roll mix for pizza dough.
3. Preheat oven to 400°F. On lightly-greased 14-inch-round pizza pan, press first ball of dough to edge of pan. Spread pizza sauce over dough, leaving 1-inch border; top with chopped broccoli, chopped spinach, roasted red peppers, and sliced tomatoes. Sprinkle with shredded mozzarella cheese.
4. On lightly-floured surface, with floured rolling pin, roll second ball of dough into a 14-inch round. Fold round in half and transfer to top of pizza; unfold, and with fork, press edges of dough together to seal.
5. Brush top of pizza with olive or salad oil. Garnish top with a few fresh rosemary sprigs and sprinkle with coarse salt. Cut a few short slashes on top to allow steam to escape during baking.
6. Bake pizza on bottom rack in oven 25 to 30 minutes until crust is golden brown and filling is hot. Makes 12 servings.

Rice & Mushroom Mold

2 extra large vegetable bouillon cubes or 4 envelopes instant vegetable broth and seasoning
2-1/4 cups regular long-grain rice
1/4 cup grated Parmesan cheese olive or salad oil
1 pound mushrooms, chopped
1/2 16-ounce bag carrots, diced
1 large onion, chopped salt
1 10-ounce package frozen chopped broccoli, thawed
1/4 pound Fontina or Swiss cheese, shredded (1 cup)
2 tablespoons all-purpose flour
2 small tomatoes
parsley sprig for garnish

1. In 4-quart saucepan over high heat, heat 1 bouillon cube (or 2 envelopes) and 4-1/2 cups water to boiling. Stir in rice; heat to boiling. Reduce heat to low; cover and simmer 20 minutes or until rice is tender and all liquid is absorbed. Remove saucepan from heat; stir in Parmesan cheese.
2. Meanwhile, in 12-inch skillet over medium-high heat, in 2 tablespoons hot olive or salad oil, cook mushrooms, carrots, onion, and 1/2 teaspoon salt until any liquid evaporates and vegetables are well browned. Stir in broccoli and shredded Fontina; remove from heat.
3. In 2-quart saucepan over medium heat, in 2 tablespoons hot olive or salad oil, cook flour until bubbly. Stir in 1-1/2 cups water and remaining vegetable bouillon cube (or 2 envelopes). Over high heat, heat sauce to boiling, stirring frequently; boil sauce 1 minute.
4. Preheat oven to 350°F. Grease well deep 2-quart oven-safe bowl. Spoon 1-1/2 cups rice mixture into bowl; smooth rice with back of spoon pressing gently. Pour 1/2 cup sauce over rice. Top rice with half of vegetable mixture, then half of remaining rice and half of remaining sauce, smoothing and gently pressing layers with back of spoon. Repeat layering with remaining vegetables, rice, and sauce.
5. Bake 30 minutes or until hot and top layer of rice is firm to the touch. Meanwhile, dice tomatoes. To unmold cover bowl with platter and invert; remove bowl. Garnish with diced tomatoes and parsley sprig. Makes 6 servings.

Squash Kabobs

2 small yellow straightneck squash (about 6 ounces each)
2 small zucchini (about 6 ounces each)
2 green onions
1 small garlic clove

1 tablespoon cider vinegar
1 tablespoon Dijon mustard
1-1/2 teaspoons salt
1 teaspoon dried oregano leaves
1/2 teaspoon pepper
olive or salad oil
1 12-ounce jar roasted red peppers, drained
1 cup orzo (rice-shaped pasta)
1 10-ounce package frozen peas
1 cup walnuts, toasted and coarsely chopped
2 tablespoons soy sauce

1. Cut yellow squash and zucchini into 1-1/4-inch chunks. Cut green onions into 1-inch pieces. Mince garlic.
2. In medium bowl, mix garlic, cider vinegar, Dijon mustard, salt, oregano, pepper, and 1 tablespoon olive or salad oil. Add yellow squash, zucchini, green onions, and roasted red peppers and toss until well coated. Let stand 15 minutes to blend flavors.
3. Meanwhile, in saucepot, prepare orzo as label directs, adding frozen peas during last 5 minutes of cooking; drain. Return orzo mixture to saucepot; stir in toasted walnuts, soy sauce, and 2 tablespoons olive or salad oil; keep warm.
4. Preheat broiler if manufacturer directs.
5. On four 12-inch-long bamboo or all-metal skewers, alternately thread yellow squash, green onion, roasted red peppers, and zucchini. Place skewers on rack in broiling pan. Place pan in broiler at closest position to source of heat; broil kabobs 10 minutes, turning once, or until vegetables are tender-crisp.
6. To serve, spoon orzo mixture onto large platter; top with kabobs. Makes 4 servings.

French Onion & Cabbage Soup

2 large onions (about 8 ounces each)
1 small head green cabbage (about 1-1/2 pounds)
olive or salad oil
salt
1/2 8-ounce loaf French bread
1/2 teaspoon dried thyme leaves
1/4 teaspoon pepper
1/4 teaspoon garlic powder
2 extra large vegetable bouillon cubes or 4 envelopes instant vegetable broth and seasoning
1/4 pound Gruyere or Swiss cheese, shredded (1 cup)

1. Cut each onion lengthwise in half; cut each half crosswise into 1/4-inch slices. Cut cabbage into 1/4-inch slices; discard any tough ribs.
2. In 5-quart Dutch oven or saucepot over medium heat, in 2 tablespoons hot olive or salad oil, cook onions, cabbage, and 1 teaspoon salt 20 minutes or until tender and browned, stirring occasionally.
3. Meanwhile, preheat oven to 450°F. Cut bread into 1-inch chunks. Into jelly-roll pan, measure 2 tablespoons olive or salad oil; add bread chunks to pan and sprinkle with thyme, pepper, garlic powder, and 1/4 teaspoon salt. With rubber spatula, gently toss bread to coat evenly. Bake 10 minutes or until lightly toasted, stirring once halfway through baking.
4. Turn oven control to broil. Into cabbage mixture in Dutch oven, stir bouillon cubes and 7 cups water; over high heat, heat to boiling.
5. Arrange 5 large (16-ounce) ovensafe soup bowls in jelly-roll pan for easier handling; ladle soup into bowls. Top with toasted bread chunks, then shredded cheese. Place pan in oven on rack about 5 to 7 inches from source of heat; broil 3 minutes or until cheese is melted and browned. Makes 5 servings.

Potato Dumpling Platter

1 medium-size head green cabbage (about 2 pounds)
1 medium-size onion
3 tablespoons salad oil
1 teaspoon salt
1/4 teaspoon coarsely ground black pepper
1 16-ounce package frozen potato pierogies
2 medium-size tomatoes, cut into 1/2-inch pieces

1. Coarsely slice cabbage; discard any tough ribs. Thinly slice onion. In 5-quart Dutch oven over medium heat, in hot salad oil, cook cabbage, onion, salt, and pepper 20 minutes or until vegetables are tender and lightly browned, stirring occasionally.
2. Meanwhile, prepare potato pierogies as label directs for boiled pierogies. Drain.
3. When cabbage is done, stir in tomatoes; heat through. Gently stir pierogies into cabbage mixture. Makes 4 servings.

Artichoke With Cracked-Wheat Salad

2 large artichokes
2 large lemons
1 5.25-ounce box tabouli mix
1/4 cup olive oil
3 small plum tomatoes
1 small cucumber
1/3 cup Kalamata or pitted ripe olives
1/4 cup chopped parsley
Kalamata olives or pitted ripe olives and parsley sprigs for garnish

1. Cut off stems and 1 inch across top of each artichoke. Pull off any small, loose, or discolored leaves from around bottom of artichokes. With kitchen shears, trim thorny tips from leaves. Rinse artichokes well under running cold water.

2. Squeeze 1/4 cup juice from lemons. In 4-quart saucepan over high heat, heat 2 tablespoons lemon juice and 1 inch water to boiling. Place artichokes on their stem ends in boiling water; heat to boiling. Reduce heat to low; cover and simmer 30 to 40 minutes until a leaf can be pulled off easily.
3. Meanwhile, prepare tabouli mix with olive oil and 1 cup water; let sit 30 minutes. Remove seeds from tomatoes; dice tomatoes. Peel cucumber; remove seeds and dice. If using Kalamata olives, remove pits; chop olive.
4. Into bowl with tabouli mix, stir tomatoes, cucumbers, chopped olives, parsley, and remaining 2 tablespoons lemon juice.
5. When artichokes are done, cut each artichoke in half. With spoon, scoop out fuzzy choke from center of each half; discard. Place 1 artichoke half on each dinner plate with some tabouli mixture. Garnish with a few olives and parsley sprigs. If not serving right away, cover and refrigerate to serve cold later. Let each person scoop some tabouli with their artichoke leaves to eat. Makes 4 servings.

Vegetable Gumbo

3/4 cup regular long-grain rice
3 tablespoons olive or salad oil
3 tablespoons all-purpose flour
1 medium-size green pepper, chopped
1 medium-size celery stalk, chopped
1 medium-size onion, chopped
1 14-1/2- 16-ounce can stewed tomatoes
1 extra large vegetable bouillon cube or 2 envelopes instant vegetable broth and seasoning
1 10-ounce package frozen sliced okra
1 cup frozen baby lima beans
1 cup frozen whole-kernel corn
1 tablespoon Worcestershire
3/4 teaspoon salt
1/2 teaspoon hot pepper sauce
1/4 teaspoon dried thyme leaves

1. Prepare rice as label directs, using 1-3/4 cups water; keep warm.
2. Meanwhile, in 5-quart Dutch oven over medium heat, into hot olive or salad oil, stir flour; cook, stirring constantly, until flour is dark brown but not burned, about 10 to 15 minutes.
3. Add green pepper, celery, and onion and cook over medium heat until vegetables are tender-crisp, stirring occasionally. Gradually stir in stewed tomatoes, vegetable bouillon cube, frozen okra, frozen lima beans, frozen corn, Worcestershire, salt, hot pepper sauce, thyme, and 2-1/2 cups water; over high heat, heat to boiling. Reduce heat to low; cover and simmer 15 minutes to blend flavors and until vegetables are tender.
4. To serve, ladle soup into 4 large soup bowls; place a scoop of rice in each bowl. Makes 4 servings.

Tofu Chili

1 medium-size yellow straightneck squash (about 10 ounces)
1 large onion
1 large green pepper
1 16-ounce package firm tofu, drained
2 tablespoons salad oil
3 tablespoons chili powder
2 14-1/2- to 16-ounce cans stewed tomatoes
1 15-1/4- to 19-ounce can red kidney beans
1 15- to 16 ounce can black beans
1 teaspoon sugar
shredded sharp Cheddar cheese (optional)

1. Cut yellow squash lengthwise into quarters; cut each quarter crosswise into 1/2-inch-thick slices. Chop onion, green pepper, and tofu.
2. In 5-quart Dutch oven or sauce-pot over medium-high heat, in hot salad oil, cook onion and green pepper until tender. Stir in chili powder; cook 1 minute.
3. Add tomatoes, kidney and black beans with their liquids, sugar, squash, tofu, and 1-1/2 cups water; over high heat, heat to boiling. Reduce heat to medium-low; simmer, uncovered, 20 minutes.
4. Serve chili in bowls. If you like, top servings with shredded cheese. Makes 6 servings.

Creamy Polenta With Ratatouille

1 8-ounce package mushrooms
2 small zucchini (about 6 ounces each)
1 medium-size onion
1 small eggplant (about 3/4 pound)
olive or salad oil
salt
1 14-1/2- to 16-ounce can stewed tomatoes
2 tablespoons capers, chopped
1-1/4 teaspoons sugar
1/4 teaspoon dried oregano leaves
2-1/2 cups milk
2/3 cup cornmeal
2 tablespoons grated Parmesan cheese
1 tablespoon margarine or butter

1. Cut each mushroom in half or into quarters if large. Cut zucchini into 1-inch chunks. Chop onion. Cut half of eggplant into 3/4-inch pieces; wrap and refrigerate remaining half eggplant for use another day.
2. In 12-inch skillet over medium-high heat, in 2 tablespoons hot olive or salad oil, cook mushrooms, zucchini, and onion, stirring frequently, until vegetables are golden brown. Add

eggplant, 1 tablespoon olive or salad oil, and 1 teaspoon salt, and cook, stirring, until eggplant is well coated and begins to brown.

3. Stir in stewed tomatoes, capers, sugar, oregano, and 2 tablespoons water; over high heat, heat to boiling. Reduce heat to low; cover and simmer 20 minutes or until vegetables are tender, stirring occasionally.

4. About 15 minutes before serving, in 3-quart saucepan over high heat, heat mild and 1/2 teaspoon salt to boiling. Reduce heat to medium; gradually sprinkle in cornmeal, stirring constantly with wire whisk to prevent lumping. Cook over low heat, stirring frequently, until mixture is thick and creamy, about 10 minutes. Stir in grated Parmesan cheese and margarine or butter.

5. To serve, spoon polenta onto 4 warm dinner plates; top with vegetable mixture. Makes 4 servings.

Corn & Cheddar Soufflé

4 tablespoons margarine or butter (1/2 stick)
1 green onion, chopped
1/4 cup all-purpose flour
1/2 teaspoon dry mustard
1/2 teaspoon salt
3/4 cup milk
2 ounces sharp Cheddar cheese, shredded (1/2 cup)
1 8-1/2 to 8-3/4-ounce can cream-style corn
4 large eggs, separated
1 large egg white (optional)
1/2 teaspoon cream of tartar

1. Prepare cheese sauce: In 3-quart saucepan over medium heat, in hot margarine or butter, cook green onion until tender. Stir in flour, mustard, and salt; cook 1 minute. Gradually stir in milk and cook, stirring constantly, until mixture boils and thickens. Stir in cheese and creamed corn until cheese melts. Remove saucepan from heat; cool sauce slightly.

2. Meanwhile, preheat oven to 350°F. Grease 1-1/2-quart soufflé dish or straight-sided casserole.

3. In small bowl, with mixer at high speed, beat egg whites and cream of tartar until stiff peaks form. Stir egg yolks into cheese sauce. With rubber spatula, gently fold beaten egg whites into cheese sauce, one-third at a time, just until blended.

4. Pour mixture into soufflé dish. If you like, make "top hat": With back of spoon, make 1-inch-deep indentation around mixture 1 inch from edge (the center will rise higher than the edge, making a top-hat effect when the soufflé is done).

5. Bake soufflé 40 to 45 minutes, until knife inserted under top hat comes out clean. Serve immediately. Makes 4 servings.

Tomato-Pesto Custard Pie

1 small eggplant (about 3/4 pound)
2 tablespoons olive or salad oil
2 cups all-purpose flour
salt
3/4 cup shortening
1 quart milk
8 large eggs
1 8-ounce package shredded part-skim mozzarella cheese (2 cups)
1/2 cup refrigerated pesto sauce
3 medium-size plum tomatoes, seeded and diced

1. From eggplant, cut ten 1/4-inch-thick slices. Wrap and refrigerate remaining eggplant to use another day. In 12-inch skillet over medium heat, in hot olive or salad oil, cook eggplant slices in 1 layer, until golden brown on both sides, removing them to paper towels to drain as they brown.

2. Meanwhile in medium bowl, mix flour and 1/2 teaspoon salt. With pastry blender or two knives used scissors-fashion, cut in shortening until mixture resembles coarse crumbs. With fork, stir 5 to 6 tablespoons cold water into flour mixture, 1 tablespoon at a time, until dough is just moist enough to hold together. Shape dough into a ball.

3. On floured surface, with floured rolling pin, roll dough into a rectangle 2 inches larger all around than inverted 13" by 9" glass baking dish. Gently ease dough into baking dish; fold overhang under to make a stand-up edge; flute.

4. Prevent oven to 375°F. In large bowl, with wire whisk or fork, beat milk, eggs, and 1/2 teaspoon salt until blended. Stir in shredded mozzarella cheese and pesto sauce. Pour custard mixture into piecrust; sprinkle with diced tomatoes. Arrange eggplant slices over top of pie. Bake pie 40 minutes or until knife inserted in center of pie comes out clean. Makes 12 servings.

Asparagus Risotto

2 pounds asparagus
1 extra large vegetable bouillon cube or 2 envelopes instant vegetable broth and seasoning
olive or salad oil
salt
1 medium-size onion
1-1/2 cups regular long-grain rice
shaved Parmesan cheese for garnish
1/4 teaspoon coarsely ground black pepper

1. Break off tough ends from asparagus and use them for making broth in step 2. Trim scales from asparagus stalks if

stalks are gritty. Slice asparagus into 2-inch pieces.
2. In 3-quart saucepan over high heat, heat asparagus ends, vegetable bouillon cube, and 6 cups water to boiling. Reduce heat to low; cover and simmer 15 minutes. With slotted spoon, remove asparagus ends; discard, reserving vegetable broth. You should have about 5-1/2 cups liquid. Add enough water, if needed, to equal 6 cups.
3. Meanwhile, in 5-quart Dutch oven or saucepot over medium-high heat, in 2 tablespoons hot olive or salad oil, cook asparagus pieces with 1/2 teaspoon salt until asparagus is tender-crisp, stirring frequently; remove to plate.
4. In blender at low speed, blend one-third of cooked asparagus pieces and 1 cup water until pureed. Pour asparagus puree into saucepan with vegetable broth; over high heat, heat to boiling. Reduce heat to low to maintain simmer.
5. Dice onion. In same 5-quart Dutch oven or saucepot over medium-low heat, in 2 tablespoons hot olive or salad oil, cook onion until tender but not browned. Stir in rice and 3/4 teaspoon salt; cook, stirring frequently, until rice grains are coated with oil.
6. Add 1/2 cup simmering vegetable broth to rice and cook, stirring frequently, until liquid is completely absorbed. Continue cooking, adding vegetable broth, 1/2 cup at a time, and stirring after each addition until all liquid is absorbed and rice is creamy-tender but still firm, about 25 minutes.
7. When rice is cooked, stir in asparagus pieces; heat through.
8. Spoon risotto onto 4 warm dinner plates; garnish with shaved Parmesan cheese and black pepper, if you like. Makes 4 servings.

Veggie-Topped Potatoes

4 large baking potatoes (each about 12 ounces)
3 large green onions
1 large red pepper
1 large bunch broccoli
olive or salad oil
1/4 pound light pasteurized process cheese spread, shredded (1 cup)
1 envelop instant vegetable broth and seasoning
1 cup milk
3/4 teaspoon salt
1/4 teaspoon coarsely ground black pepper

1. Preheat oven to 450°F. Place potatoes in shallow pan; bake 45 to 50 minutes until fork-tender.
2. While potatoes are baking, prepare vegetables: Cut green onions into 1-inch pieces; slice red pepper into 1-inch-wide strips. Cut broccoli into 2" by 1" pieces.
3. In 12-inch skillet over medium-high heat, in 1 tablespoon hot olive or salad oil, cook green onions and red pepper until tender-crisp. With slotted spoon, remove vegetables to small bowl.
4. In same skillet over high heat, in 2 tablespoons additional hot olive or salad oil, cook broccoli, stirring quickly and constantly until evenly coated with oil; add 1/4 cup water; reduce heat to medium; cover and cook 2 minutes. Uncover and stir-fry 5 minutes or until broccoli is tender-crisp.
5. Push broccoli to side of skillet; over medium-high heat, stir in shredded pasteurized process cheese spread, instant broth, and 1 cup water until cheese melts. Add red-pepper mixture and cook until vegetables are heated through. Keep warm.
6. When potatoes are tender, remove from oven but do not turn oven off. Cut thin slice from top of each potato. With spoon, scoop out potato, leaving 1/8-inch-thick shell. In large bowl, with potato masher, mash potatoes with milk and slat until potatoes are smooth. Spoon potato mixture back into potato shells. Place stuffed potatoes on cookie sheet or jelly-roll pan and bake 10 to 15 minutes longer until potatoes are heated through and lightly browned.
7. To serve, arrange stuffed potatoes on 4 dinner plates. Sprinkle potatoes with coarsely ground pepper; spoon vegetables onto each serving. Makes 4 servings.

Eggplant & Potato Moussaka

2 small eggplants (about 1-1/4 pounds each)
olive or salad oil
salt
1 large onion
6 medium-size potatoes (about 2 pounds)
1 28-ounce can Italian plum tomatoes
1 teaspoon sugar
1 teaspoon dried oregano leaves
2 tablespoons tomato paste
1/3 cup grated Parmesan cheese
1/4 cup all-purpose flour
3 cups low-fat milk (1%)
1/8 teaspoon ground nutmeg
1 large egg

1. Preheat broiler if manufacturer directs. Cut eggplants crosswise into 1/2-inch-thick slices. In large bowl, toss eggplant slices with 2 tablespoons olive or salad oil and 1 teaspoon salt. Arrange eggplant slices in single layer on rack in broiling pan. With oven rack at closest position to source of heat, broil eggplant 15 minutes or until tender and browned, turning slices once halfway through broiling.
2. While eggplants are cooking, prepare potato layer: Chop onion. In 4-quart saucepan over medium-high heat, in 2 tablespoons hot olive or salad oil, cook onion 10 minutes or until tender and golden. Meanwhile, peel potatoes; cut each potato into 1/4-inch slices.
3. To onion in saucepan, add tomatoes with their liquid, sugar, oregano, and 1-1/4 teaspoon salt, stirring to break up tomatoes. Add potato slices; over high heat, heat to boiling. Reduce heat

to low; cover and simmer 20 to 25 minutes until potatoes are tender.

4. With slotted spoon, remove potatoes to large bowl. Into liquid remaining in saucepan, stir tomato paste; over high heat, heat to boiling. Reduce heat to low; simmer, uncovered, 5 minutes or until liquid thickens slightly. Add tomato mixture and 1/4 cup Parmesan cheese to potatoes in bowl; toss.

5. In 2-quart saucepan over medium heat, in 2 tablespoons hot olive or salad oil, cook flour until bubbly but not browned; stir in milk, nutmeg, and 1/2 teaspoon salt. Over medium heat, cook until sauce boils and thickens, stirring frequently; boil 1 minute. Remove saucepan from heat. In small bowl, beat egg. Stir small amount of hot sauce into beaten egg; stir egg mixture back into sauce in saucepan.

6. When eggplant slices are done, turn oven control to 375°F. In 13" by 9" glass or ceramic baking dish, arrange half of eggplant slices. Top with potato mixture, then remaining eggplant slices. Pour sauce evenly over top; sprinkle with remaining Parmesan cheese.

7. Bake moussaka 30 minutes or until hot and cheese on top is lightly browned. Makes 8 servings.

Curried Beans & Broccoli

2 medium-size onions
1 medium-size red pepper
1 small bunch broccoli
olive or salad oil
2 15- to 19-ounce cans garbanzo beans, drained
2 tablespoons chopped parsley
salt
1 extra large vegetable-bouillon cube or 2 envelopes instant vegetable broth and seasoning
4 teaspoons curry powder
1 teaspoon sugar
1/4 teaspoon pepper
1 tablespoon lemon juice
2 teaspoons cornstarch

1. Cut each onion lengthwise in half, then cut each half crosswise into 1/2-inch-thick slices. Cut red pepper into 1/4-inch-thick slices. Cut broccoli into bite-size pieces.

2. In 12-inch skillet over medium-high heat, in 2 tablespoons hot olive or salad oil, cook onions, stirring occasionally, until tender-crisp. Add red pepper and cook, stirring frequently, until onions and red pepper are tender. Stir in garbanzo beans and chopped parsley.

3. Meanwhile, in 3-quart saucepan over high heat, in 1 inch boiling water, heat broccoli and 1/4 teaspoon salt to boiling. Reduce heat to low; cover and simmer 5 minutes or until tender-crisp; drain.

4. In cup, with fork, mash vegetable bouillon cube with curry powder, sugar, pepper, and 1/4 teaspoon salt until blended. Stir in garbanzo-bean mixture in skillet; cook, stirring constantly, 1 minute.

5. In 2-cup measuring cup, with fork, mix 1-1/2 cups water with lemon juice and cornstarch until blended; stir into garbanzo-bean mixture. Over high heat, heat to boiling; boil 1 minute.

6. Spoon mixture onto warm large platter; top with broccoli. Toss to serve. Makes 4 servings.

Barley-Stuffed Peppers

1 cup barley
1 extra large vegetable bouillon cube or 2 envelopes instant vegetable broth and seasoning
1 large onion
3 medium-size carrots
2 tablespoons olive or salad oil
1/2 teaspoon salt
1 cup frozen peas
2 tablespoons chopped parsley
6 ounce sharp Cheddar cheese, shredded (1-1/2 cups)
2 14-1/2- to 16-ounce cans Italian-style stewed tomatoes
2 medium-size red peppers
2 medium-size green peppers
2 medium-size yellow peppers

1. In 3-quart saucepan over high heat, heat barley, vegetable bouillon cube, and 2-2/3 cups water to boiling. Reduce heat to low; cover and simmer 1 hour or until liquid is absorbed and barley is tender.

2. Meanwhile, chop onion; shred carrots. In 10-inch skillet over medium-high heat, in hot olive or salad oil, cook onion until almost tender. Stir in grated carrots and salt; cook 5 minutes or until vegetables are tender and lightly browned.

3. When barley is done, stir in onion mixture, frozen peas, parsley, and 1 cup shredded cheese. In food processor with knife blade attached or in blender at medium speed, blend stewed tomatoes until almost smooth. Pour stewed tomatoes into shallow 2-1/2-quart casserole.

4. Preheat oven to 350°F. Cut off top from each pepper; reserve tops for garnish. Remove seeds from peppers. Cut thin slice from bottom of each pepper so it will stand level. Fill peppers with barley mixture.

5. Stand peppers in tomato sauce in casserole; sprinkle with remaining shredded cheese. Bake peppers 1 hour or until peppers are tender when pierced with a knife. Loosely cover peppers with foil during last 30 minutes of baking to prevent overbrowning.

6. To serve, arrange pepper tops on stuffed peppers. Serve stuffed peppers in casserole or transfer them to deep platter to serve. Makes 6 servings.

Pepper & Tomato Omelet With Roast Potatoes

1-1/2 pounds medium-size red potatoes
olive or salad oil
salt
coarsely ground black pepper
1 large onion
1 large green pepper
3 medium-size plum tomatoes (about 1/2 pound)
1/2 teaspoon dried thyme leaves
1 tablespoon chopped parsley
6 large eggs
parsley sprigs for garnish

1. Preheat oven to 450°F. Cut each potato into quarters. In medium bowl, mix potatoes, 1 tablespoon olive or salad oil, 1/2 teaspoon salt, and 1/4 teaspoon pepper. Evenly spread potatoes in 15-1/2" by 10-1/2" jelly-roll pan. Bake potatoes until tender and golden, about 30 minuets, stirring occasionally.
2. Meanwhile, thinly slice onion; cut green pepper into 1/8-inch-wide strips, Remove tough area around stem of each tomato. Cut each tomato lengthwise in half; squeeze halves to remove seeds; coarsely chop.
3. In nonstick 12-inch skillet over medium-high heat, in 2 tablespoons hot olive or salad oil, stir onion, green pepper, thyme, 1/2 teaspoon salt, and 1/4 teaspoon pepper until vegetables are coated with oil. Reduce heat to medium-low; cover and cook until vegetables are tender, stirring occasionally, about 15 minutes. Stir in tomatoes and chopped parsley; heat through. Remove vegetable mixture to bowl. Wipe skillet clean.
4. In bowl, with fork, beat eggs, 1/2 teaspoon salt, and 1/3 cup water until blended. In same skillet over medium heat, heat 2 tablespoons olive or salad oil until hot. Pour egg mixture into skillet; cook until set around edge. With rubber spatula, gently lift edge as it sets, tilting skillet to allow uncooked portion to run under omelet. Shake skillet occasionally to keep omelet moving freely in pan.
5. When omelet is set but still moist, spoon vegetable mixture over half the omelet. Tilt skillet and, with spatula, fold omelet in half; slide onto warm platter. Serve with roast potatoes. Garnish with parsley sprigs. Makes 4 servings.

Layered Polenta

1 small bunch spinach (about 1/2 pound)
3 plum tomatoes
1/2 cup oil-packed dried tomatoes, drained*
1/2 7-ounce container refrigerated pesto sauce
2 teaspoons salt
2 cups yellow cornmeal
1/4 pound Jarlsberg cheese, shredded (1 cup)
1/2 teaspoon coarsely ground black pepper

1. Chop 2 cups packed spinach leaves. Dice 2 tomatoes; reserve remaining tomato for garnish. Chop dried tomatoes.
2. In small bowl, mix chopped spinach leaves with pesto. In another bowl, mix diced fresh tomatoes with dried tomatoes.
3. Line 9" by 5" loaf pan with foil. In 4-quart saucepan over high heat, heat salt and 6 cups water to boiling. Reduce heat to medium; gradually sprinkle in cornmeal, stirring constantly with wire whisk to prevent lumping. Cook over low heat, stirring frequently until mixture is very thick and creamy, about 10 minutes. Remove saucepan from heat; stir in shredded Jarlsberg cheese.
4. Preheat oven to 350°F. Working quickly, spread one-third of polenta into loaf pan; top with all of tomato mixture, spreading evenly to cover. Spread with half of remaining polenta, then with all of spinach mixture. Top with remaining polenta, spreading evenly for a smooth top. Cover top loosely with foil. Bake loaf 15 minutes or until heated through.
5. Meanwhile slice remaining tomato; thinly slice a few spinach leaves for garnish.
6. To serve, invert polenta loaf onto platter. Discard foil. Garnish top of loaf with tomatoes and spinach. Sprinkle with black pepper. Makes 6 servings.

Falafel With Spinach Salad

1 8-ounce container low-fat plain yogurt
1 6-ounce package falafel mix
3 ounces crumbled feta cheese (3/4 cup)
2 tablespoons low-fat milk (1%)
1 teaspoon lemon juice
1/8 teaspoon pepper
1 bunch spinach (about 3/4 pound)
3 tablespoons olive or salad oil
2 small tomatoes, cut into wedges

1. In medium bowl, mix 1/2 cup yogurt and 1 cup water until blended. Stir in falafel mix; let stand 15 minutes.
2. Meanwhile, in large bowl, with fork, mash 2 ounces feta cheese (1/2 cup) with remaining yogurt; reserve remaining feta cheese. Stir in milk, lemon juice, and pepper until blended. Remove tough stems from spinach; cut spinach leaves crosswise into thin strips; set aside.
3. Shape falafel mixture into 8 patties, each about 2 inches in diameter. In 12-inch skillet over medium-high heat, in hot olive or salad oil, cook patties 5 minutes or until crisp and brown on both sides, turning once.
4. To serve, add spinach to yogurt mixture in bowl; toss to coat. Arrange falafel patties on platter with spinach salad and tomato wedges. Sprinkle spinach salad with remaining crumbled feta. Makes 4 servings

Artichoke & Tomato Frittata

1 9-ounce package frozen artichoke hearts
salt
2 plum tomatoes
1 small onion
1 tablespoon olive or salad oil
2 8-ounce containers liquid whole eggs (reduced cholesterol)
1/2 teaspoon dried basil leaves

1. In 2-quart saucepan over high heat, heat frozen artichoke hearts, 1/4 teaspoon salt, and 1/4 cup water to boiling. Reduce heat to low; cover and slimmer 6 to 8 minutes until artichokes are tender; drain.
2. Meanwhile, dice tomatoes and onion. In nonstick 10-inch skillet with oven-safe handle, over medium heat, in hot olive or salad oil, cook onion until tender.
3. Preheat oven to 350°F. In bowl, with fork, mix liquid whole eggs, basil, 1 teaspoon salt, and 1/3 cup water. Pour egg mixture over onions in skillet; sprinkle with artichokes and tomatoes. Cook over medium heat until edge begins to set, about 3 to 4 minutes.
4. Place frittata in oven; bake 15 minutes or until set. Makes 4 servings.

Spinach & Cheese Tart

2 10-ounce bags spinach
2 large onions (about 8 ounces each)
2 tablespoons olive or salad oil
1/2 teaspoon salt
all-purpose flour
1 10-ounce package refrigerated pizza dough
2 ounces crumbled feta cheese (1/2 cup)
1 4-ounce package shredded part-skim mozzarella cheese (1 cup)
2 small tomatoes (about 4 ounces each)
3/4 teaspoon dried oregano leaves

1. Discard tough stems from spinach. Wash and drain spinach well; coarsely chop. Cut each onion lengthwise in half; cut each half crosswise into 1/4-inch-wide slices.
2. In 12-inch skillet over medium heat, in hot oil, cook onions 10 to 15 minutes until tender. Add spinach and salt; cook, stirring, just until spinach wilts. Remove from heat.
3. Grease 11-inch quiche dish or tart pan with removable bottom. On lightly floured surface, roll pizza dough into a 12-inch round. Ease pizza dough into quiche dish. Press dough against side of dish with floured fingers.
4. Preheat oven to 400°F. Spoon onion mixture over dough in quiche dish. Sprinkle onion mixture with crumbled feta cheese; top with shredded mozzarella cheese. Thinly slice tomatoes. Arrange tomato slices over cheese; sprinkle with oregano.
5. Bake tart 15 minutes or until crust is golden and cheese between tomato slices is lightly browned. Makes 4 servings.

Vegetable & Pasta Pie

2 cups all-purpose flour
salt
3/4 cup shortening
1/4 16-ounce package rotelli or rotini pasta (2 cups)
2 medium-size red peppers
2 medium-size yellow peppers
1 medium-size onion
2 tablespoons olive or salad oil
1 teaspoon dried basil leaves
1/4 teaspoon ground black pepper
1 large egg
1 15-ounce container part-skim ricotta cheese
1 10-ounce package frozen chopped spinach, thawed and squeezed dry
1 8-ounce package shredded part-skim mozzarella cheese (2 cups)
1 cup marinara or spaghetti sauce

1. In medium bowl, mix flour and 1/2 teaspoon salt. With pastry blender or two knives used scissors-fashion, cut in shortening until mixture resembles coarse crumbs. With fork, stir 5 to 6 teaspoons cold water into flour mixture until dough is just moist enough to hold together. Shape dough into a ball; cover with plastic wrap.
2. Prepare pasta as label directs, but do not use salt in water; drain.
3. Meanwhile, cut red and yellow peppers into 1-inch pieces. Chop onion. In 12-inch skillet over medium heat, in hot olive or salad oil, cook onion until tender-crisp; add red and yellow peppers, basil, black pepper, and 1/4 teaspoon salt, and cook, stirring occasionally, until vegetables are tender.
4. In cup, beat egg slightly. Reserve 1 tablespoon beaten egg; set aside. In another medium bowl, mix remaining egg with ricotta cheese, spinach, and 1/4 teaspoon salt.
5. Preheat oven to 400°F. Grease 9" by 2-1/2" springform pan. On lightly floured surface, with floured rolling pin, roll two-thirds of dough into a 15-inch round. Gently ease into springform pan, allowing dough to hang over side of pan slightly.
6. Sprinkle bottom of crust with half of mozzarella cheese; top with half of sautéed-pepper mixture. Spread half of ricotta-cheese mixture over pepper mixture; top with marinara sauce, then pasta. Sprinkle remaining mozzarella cheese over pasta; top with remaining sautéed-pepper mixture, then remaining ricotta-cheese mixture.
7. Roll out remaining dough to 11-inch round; lay dough over filling, allowing dough to hang over side of pan. Fold overhang

in toward center, pinching dough all around to make a stand-up edge; flute. Cut slits in top crust to allow steam to escape during baking. Brush top and edge with reserved egg. Bake pie 55 to 60 minutes until crust is golden and filling is hot.
8. Allow pie to cool 5 minutes for easier slicing. Remove side of springform pan. To serve, cut into wedges. Makes 8 servings.

Tuscan Rice Salad

1 cup parboiled rice
salt
3 large eggs
3 small carrots
1 small onion
1 small red pepper
1 small tomato
extra virgin olive oil or olive oil
1 15-1/2- to 19-ounce can garbanzo beans, drained
1 cup frozen peas, thawed
1/4 cup grated Parmesan cheese
2 tablespoons chopped parsley
2 medium-size lemons
1/2 teaspoon sugar
1/4 teaspoon pepper
lettuce leaves

1. Prepare rice as label directs, using 1/2 teaspoon salt in water. Meanwhile, hard-cook eggs.
2. While rice and eggs are cooking, dice carrots, onion, red pepper, and tomato. In 10-inch skillet over medium-high heat, in 1 tablespoon hot olive oil, cook carrots, onion, and 1/4 teaspoon salt, stirring, until tender-crisp. Add red pepper; cook, stirring, until vegetables are tender.
3. Remove shells from hard-cooked eggs and coarsely chop. In large bowl, mix hard-cooked eggs, cooked rice, vegetable mixture from skillet, diced tomato, garbanzo beans, peas, Parmesan cheese, and parsley.
4. Squeeze 1/2 cup juice from lemons. In cup, mix lemon juice with sugar, pepper, 3 tablespoons olive oil, and 1 teaspoon salt; gently stir into rice mixture in bowl to coat well. Arrange rice salad over lettuce leaves on platter. Cover and refrigerate if not serving right away. Makes 4 servings.

Asparagus Ragout With Wild Rice

1 4-ounce package wild rice (about 2/3 cup)
1 extra large vegetable bouillon cube or 2 envelopes instant vegetable broth and seasoning
1/2 cup parboiled rice
1 tablespoon chopped parsley
1 large onion, chopped
1 pound mushrooms
1 pound asparagus
3 tablespoons olive or salad oil
1/2 teaspoon salt
1 14-1/2- to 16-ounce can stewed tomatoes

1. In 3-quart saucepan over high heat, heat wild rice, bouillon cube, and 2-1/2 cups water to boiling. Reduce heat to low; cover and simmer 25 minutes. Stir in parboiled rice; over high heat, heat to boiling. Reduce heat to low; cover and simmer 20 minutes longer or until wild rice and white rice are tender and liquid is absorbed. Stir in chopped parsley.
2. Meanwhile, chop onion; slice mushrooms. Discard tough ends from asparagus; remove scales if stalks are gritty. Cut asparagus stalks into 2-inch pieces.
3. In 12-inch skillet over medium-high heat, in hot olive or salad oil, cook onion until almost tender. Add mushrooms, asparagus, and salt; cook, stirring occasionally, until vegetables are almost tender. Stir in stewed tomatoes; over high heat, heat to boiling. Reduce heat to low; simmer, covered, 5 minutes or until vegetables are tender. Arrange asparagus ragout and rice mixture on large platter. Makes 4 servings.

Corn Fritters With Cucumber & Radish Salad

Cucumber & Radish Salad (below)
1 cup all-purpose flour
1-1/2 teaspoons baking powder
1 teaspoon salt
1/2 teaspoon pepper
1 large egg
1 medium-size baking potato (about 8 ounces)
1 small zucchini (about 6 ounces)
3 green onions
1 cup frozen whole-kernel corn, thawed
salad oil

1. Prepare Cucumber & Radish Salad; set aside.
2. In large bowl, with wire whisk or fork, mix flour, baking powder, salt, pepper, egg, and 1 cup water; set batter aside. Peel potato; coarsely shred potato and zucchini; finely chop green onions.
3. Reserve 1 tablespoon chopped green onion for garnish. Stir potato, zucchini, corn, and remaining green onions into batter.
4. In nonstick 12-inch skillet over medium-high heat, in 1 tablespoon hot salad oil, drop mixture by 1/4 cups into 4 mounds, about 2 inches apart. With pancake turner, flatten each mound slightly to make a 4-inch round fritter. Cook fritters until golden brown on 1 side, about 3 minutes; reduce heat to medium and brown other side, about 3 to 5 minutes longer until potatoes are tender. Remove to platter; keep warm. Repeat with remaining mixture, adding 1 tablespoon salad oil each time.
5. To serve, place fritters on 4 dinner plates; sprinkle with

reserved chopped green onion. Arrange Cucumber & Radish Salad on plates with fritters. Makes 12 fritters or 4 servings.
Cucumber & Radish Salad: Cut each of 2 medium-size cucumbers lengthwise in half; remove seeds. Cut unpeeled cucumbers into bite-size chunks. Cut each radish from two 6-ounce bags radishes lengthwise in half. In medium bowl, mix cucumbers, radishes, 2 tablespoons olive oil, 2 tablespoons seasoned rice vinegar, 1/4 teaspoon salt, and 1/4 teaspoon pepper until blended.

Spanish Potato Omelet

1-1/4 pounds potatoes
1 medium-size red pepper
1 medium-size green pepper
1 medium-size onion
olive or salad oil
salt
5 large eggs
2 tablespoons grated Parmesan cheese
2 tablespoons chopped parsley
1/2 teaspoon coarsely ground black pepper
green salad (optional)

1. Peel and very thinly slice potatoes. Dice red and green peppers. Cut onion lengthwise in half, then cut each half crosswise into paper-thin slices.
2. In nonstick 10-inch skillet over medium heat, in 2 tablespoons hot olive or salad oil, cook potatoes, peppers, onion, and 1/2 teaspoon salt until vegetables are well coated with oil and begin to brown slightly.
3. Reduce heat to low; cover and cook, turning vegetables occasionally, until vegetables are fork-tender, about 15 minutes. Remove potato mixture to medium bowl to cool slightly. Wipe skillet clean.
4. In large bowl, with wire whisk or fork, beat eggs, grated Parmesan, parsley, pepper, and 1/2 teaspoon salt until blended. Stir in potato mixture.
5. In same skillet over medium-low heat, heat 1 tablespoon olive or salad oil, tilting skillet to grease side. Pour potato-egg mixture into skillet; cook until set around edge.
6. With spatula, gently lift edge as it sets, tilting skillet to allow uncooked portion to run under omelet. Shake skillet occasionally to keep omelet moving freely in pan. When omelet is set but still moist on top, increase heat slightly to brown bottom of omelet.
7. Turn omelet: Be sure mixture is loosened from bottom of skillet. Invert large plate over skillet; flip omelet onto plate; wipe skillet clean. Over medium heat, heat 1 tablespoon olive or salad oil in skillet. Slide omelet back into skillet, browned-side up. Cook, shaking pan occasionally to prevent sticking, until bottom of omelet is golden brown, about 5 minutes; invert omelet onto warm large platter.
8. To serve, cut omelet into wedges. Serve with green salad, if you like. Makes 4 servings.

Vegetable Strudel With Red-Pepper Sauce

1 small head green cabbage (about 1-1/2 pounds)
1 medium-size onion
1/4 cup olive or salad oil
1/4 teaspoon ground black pepper
salt
1/2 cup mixed peppers in oil, drained and minced
1 15- to 19-ounce can pinto beans, drained
10 sheets fresh or frozen (thawed) phyllo (about 1/3 16-ounce package)
nonstick cooking spray
1 tablespoon margarine or butter, melted
1 7-ounce jar roasted red peppers, drained
1 cup milk
1 teaspoon cornstarch
1/2 teaspoon sugar

1. Chop cabbage and onion. In 12-inch skillet over medium heat, in hot olive or salad oil, cook cabbage, onion, black pepper, and 3/4 teaspoon salt until cabbage and onion are very tender and lightly browned, about 20 minutes, stirring occasionally. Stir in mixed peppers and pinto beans. Remove skillet from heat.
2. Preheat oven to 375°F. On waxed paper on work surface, place 2 sheets of phyllo (each about 17" by 12"), one on top of the other; spray very lightly with nonstick cooking spray. Continue layering three more times; top with remaining 2 phyllo sheets.
3. Starting along long side of phyllo, spoon vegetable mixture to about 1/2 inch from edges to cover half of rectangle. From vegetable-mixture side, roll phyllo jelly-roll fashion.
4. Place roll, seam-side down, in jelly-roll pan. Brush with melted margarine or butter. Cut 6 slashes on top of strudel. Bake strudel 35 to 40 minutes until golden.
5. Meanwhile, make red-pepper sauce: In blender at medium speed or in food processor with knife blade attached, blend roasted red peppers, milk, cornstarch, sugar, and 3/4 teaspoon salt until smooth.
6. In 2-quart saucepan over medium heat, heat red-pepper sauce to boiling; boil 1 minute, stirring frequently. Keep sauce warm.
7. Cook strudel in pan on wire rack 5 minutes for easier slicing. Slice to serve. Pass red-pepper sauce to spoon over each serving. Makes 6 servings.

Spicy Thai Noodles (Pad Thai)

1 16-ounce package Oriental noodles or linguine
1/4 cup soy sauce
1 tablespoon sugar
2 tablespoons chili sauce
3 tablespoons salad oil
1 small red pepper, thinly sliced

1 tablespoon grated, peeled ginger root
1 garlic clove, minced
1 bunch green onions, chopped
2 large eggs, lightly beaten
1/2 pound bean sprouts (about 2 cups)
1 small tomato, cut into thin wedges
1/4 cup salted peanuts, coarsely chopped
1 tablespoon chopped fresh cilantro or parsley (optional)
1/4 teaspoon crushed red pepper
lime wedges for garnish

1. Prepare noodles as label directs; drain and keep warm.
2. Meanwhile, in cup, stir soy sauce, sugar, chili sauce, and 1/2 cup water; set aside. In 12-inch skillet over medium-high heat, in hot salad oil, cook red pepper, ginger, garlic, and all but 1/4 cup chopped green onions until tender and lightly browned, about 5 minutes. Push vegetables to one side of skillet.
3. To same skillet over medium-high heat, add eggs, stirring until set but still moist. Stir in bean sprouts and soy-sauce mixture; over high heat, heat to boiling. Add noodles and tomato wedges, tossing to coat with sauce; heat through.
4. Spoon noodle mixture onto large warm platter. Sprinkle with chopped peanuts, chopped cilantro, crushed red pepper, and remaining chopped green onions. Garnish with lime wedges. Makes 5 servings.

Farmer's Stew With Couscous

2 small zucchini (about 6 ounces each)
1/4 pound mushrooms
olive or salad oil
1 small butternut squash (about 1-1/2 pounds)
2 medium-size carrots
1 large onion
1 small bunch kale (about 1 pound)
1 15- to 19-ounce can garbanzo beans
1/3 cup dark seedless raisins
1 tablespoon lemon juice
2 teaspoons sugar
2 extra large vegetable bouillon cubes or 4 envelopes instant vegetable broth and seasoning
1 cup couscous (precooked semolina)

1. Cut zucchini and mushrooms into 1/4-inch-thick slices. In 8-quart Dutch oven over medium-high heat, in 1 tablespoon hot olive or salad oil, cook zucchini and mushrooms until lightly browned; with slotted spoon, remove to bowl.
2. While zucchini and mushrooms are cooking, with vegetable peeler, peel butternut squash; cut squash into 3/4-inch chunks. Cut carrots into 1/4-inch-thick slices. Cut onion lengthwise in half; cut each half crosswise into 1/4-inch-thick slices.
3. In same Dutch oven over medium-high heat, in 2 tablespoons hot olive or salad oil, cook squash, carrots, and onion until lightly browned. Meanwhile, remove tough stems from kale; coarsely chop.
4. To vegetables in Dutch oven, add kale, garbanzo beans with their liquid, raisins, lemon juice, sugar, 1 vegetable bouillon cube (or 2 envelopes) and 1/2 cup water. Over high heat, heat to boiling. Reduce heat to low; cover and simmer 5 minutes or until vegetables are almost tender.
5. While vegetables are simmering, prepare couscous as label directs without salt, adding remaining vegetable bouillon cube (or envelopes) to water.
6. Stir zucchini mixture into vegetable mixture; heat through. Spoon vegetable stew into center of warm deep platter; spoon couscous around stew. Makes 4 servings.

Stuffed Cabbage

1 cup regular long-grain rice
1 medium-size head green cabbage (about 2-1/2 pounds)
1 8-ounce package mushrooms
1 medium-size onion
1 small carrot
salad oil
1 10-ounce package frozen chopped spinach, thawed and squeezed dry
1 large egg
3/4 teaspoon salt
1/2 teaspoon pepper
2 14-1/2 to 16-ounce cans stewed tomatoes
1 teaspoon sugar

About 1-1/2 hours before serving:

1. Prepare rice as label directs.
2. Meanwhile, with knife, remove core from cabbage. Fill 8-quart saucepot three-fourths full of water; over high heat, heat to boiling. Place cabbage in water, cut-side up. Using 2 large spoons, gently separate leaves as outer leaves soften slightly; drain leaves in colander. Continue until 8 large leaves are removed from cabbage. (If leaves are not very large, remove several additional smaller leaves.) Trim tough ribs of leaves very thin. Coarsely slice remaining cabbage; set aside.
3. Chop mushrooms and onions; coarsely shred carrot. In 12-inch skillet over medium-high heat, in 2 tablespoons hot salad oil, cook mushrooms and onion until onion is tender; remove to large bowl. Stir in cooked rice, shredded carrot, spinach, egg, salt, and pepper until blended.
4. Onto center of each cabbage leaf, place one-eighth of rice mixture. Fold 2 sides of leaf toward center. Staring from an unfolded end, roll up cabbage jelly-roll fashion. Repeat to make 8 rolls in all.
5. In same skillet over medium-high heat, in 2 tablespoons hot salad oil, cook sliced cabbage 5 minutes. Stir in stewed tomatoes, sugar, and 2-1/2 cups water. Add cabbage rolls seam-side

down; over high heat, heat to boiling. Reduce heat to low; cover and simmer 40 minutes, occasionally spooning sauce over rolls. Makes 4 servings.

Lattice-Top Vegetable Pie

all purpose flour
salt
3/4 cup shortening
3/4 pound red potatoes
2 medium-size carrots
1 large celery stalk
1 medium-size onion
2 tablespoons olive or salad oil
1 extra large vegetable bouillon cube or 2 envelopes instant vegetable broth and seasoning
1 11-ounce can vacuum-packed whole-kernel corn, drained
1/2 10-ounce package frozen lima beans (1 cup)
milk
1 small bunch spinach (about 8 ounces), tough stems removed and coarsely chopped
1/4 pound Jarlsberg cheese, shredded (1 cup)

1. In medium bowl, mix 2 cups flour and 1/2 teaspoon salt. With pastry blender or two knives used scissors-fashion, cut in shortening until mixture resembles coarse crumbs. With fork, stir 5 to 6 tablespoons cold water into flour mixture, 1 tablespoon at a time, until dough is just moist enough to hold together. Shape dough into a ball.
2. On floured surface, with floured rolling pin, roll two-thirds of dough into a round 2 inches large all around than inverted 9-inch deep-dish pie plate. Gently ease dough into pie plate, allowing dough to hang over edge. Trim dough to 1-inch overhang; reserve trimmings. Cover pie plate and wrap remaining dough with plastic wrap; set aside.
3. Cut unpeeled potatoes into 3/4-inch pieces. In 3-quart saucepan over high heat, in 1 inch coiling water, heat potatoes to boiling. Reduce heat to low; cover and simmer 5 minutes or until potatoes are fork-tender. Drain.
4. Meanwhile, thinly slice carrots; chop celery and onion. In 12-inch skillet over medium-high heat, in hot olive or salad oil, cook carrots, celery, onion, and 1/2 teaspoon salt, stirring occasionally, until vegetables are tender-crisp. Add vegetable bouillon cube, stirring to break it up. Stir in 3 tablespoons flour; cook 1 minute, stirring constantly.
5. Stir in potatoes, corn, frozen lima beans, and 1-3/4 cups milk. Over high heat, heat to boiling; boil 1 minute. Remove skillet from heat; stir in spinach and Jarlsberg cheese. Spoon mixture into pie plate.
6. Preheat oven to 375°F. On floured surface, with floured rolling pin, roll remaining dough into 12-inch round; cut into 1/2-inch-wide strips. Moisten edge of bottom crust with water. Place half of strips about 1/4 inch apart across pie; do not seal ends. Fold every other strip back half-way from center. Place center across strip on pie and replace folded part of strips. Now fold back alternate strips; place second cross strip in place. Repeat to weave cross strips into lattice. Seal ends; fold overhang in toward center to make a stand-up edge; flute.
7. Brush crust with 1 tablespoon milk; bake 45 minutes or until rust is golden brown and filling is hot and bubbly. Makes 8 servings.

Green Bean & Mozzarella Salad

2 cups fresh green beans, cooked, drained
1 package (8 ounces) mozzarella cheese, cut into 1/2-inch cubes
1/2 cup prepared Good Seasons Zesty Italian Salad Dressing
6 fresh plum tomatoes, sliced
1/3 cup chopped fresh basil
1/8 teaspoon pepper

Mix all ingredients in large bowl. Cover. Refrigerate 1 hour. Makes 4 servings.

Oriental Noodles

1 8-ounce package linguine
1 6-ounce bag radishes
3 green onions, chopped
3 tablespoons salad oil
1/3 cup peanut butter
2 medium-size celery stalks, thinly sliced
2 tablespoons soy sauce
1 tablespoon cider vinegar
1-1/2 teaspoons sugar
1/4 teaspoon hot pepper sauce
1 hard-cooked egg, chopped

1. Prepare linguine as label directs; drain.
2. Meanwhile, cut each radish into quarters; chop green onions. Reserve 1 tablespoon green onion for garnish. In saucepan over medium heat, in hot salad oil, cook remaining green onions until tender.
3. In large bowl, with fork, heat peanut butter and 1/4 cup hot tap water until smooth. Stir in green-onion mixture, radishes, celery, and remaining ingredients except egg and reserved green onion. Spoon sauce on linguine. Sprinkle with chopped egg and reserved green onions. Toss to serve. Makes 4 main-dish servings.

Fiesta Pasta Salad

1 cup Real, Light or Cholesterol Free Reduced Calorie Mayonnaise
1/2 cup sour cream
1/4 cup chopped cilantro or parsley
2 tablespoons lime juice
1 to 2 pickled jalapeno peppers, seeded, minced
1 teaspoon salt
8-ounce twist macaroni (3 cups) cooked, rinsed, drained
2 large tomatoes, chopped
1 yellow or green pepper, chopped
1 medium zucchini, sliced
3 green onions, sliced

Combine mayonnaise, sour cream, cilantro, lime juice, jalapenos and salt. Stir in remaining ingredients. Cover; chill. Makes about 8 cups.

Dilled Potato Salad

1 cup Real, Light or Cholesterol Free Reduced Calorie Mayonnaise
1 tablespoon prepared mustard
2 tablespoons chopped fresh dill or 1-1/2 teaspoon dried dill
1/2 teaspoon salt
1/4 teaspoon pepper
1-1/2 pounds small red potatoes, cooked, quartered
1/3 cup sliced green onions

Combine mayonnaise, mustard, dill, salt and pepper. Stir in remaining ingredients. Cover, chill. Makes about 4 cups.

Citrus Slaw

1 cup Real, Light or Cholesterol Free Reduced Calorie Mayonnaise
1/3 cup frozen orange juice concentrate, thawed
2 teaspoons sugar
1/4 teaspoon salt
1/4 teaspoon pepper
6 cups shredded red or green cabbage
2 cups shredded carrots
1 green pepper, thinly sliced
1/3 cup golden raisins (optional)

Combine mayonnaise, orange juice concentrate, sugar, salt and pepper. Stir in remaining ingredients. Cover; chill. Makes about 5 cups.

Individual Mushroom & Onion Pizzas

1 12-ounce package mushrooms
1 large onion
2 tablespoons olive or salad oil
1 14-1/2 ounce can pizza-style chunky tomatoes
2 8-ounce packages Italian-bread shells (4 6-1/2-inch rounds)
1 8-ounce package shredded mozzarella cheese (2 cups)
1 teaspoon dried oregano leaves
1/2 teaspoon coarsely ground black pepper
1 tablespoon chopped parsley

1. Preheat oven to 450°F. Thinly slice mushrooms and onion.
2. In 12-inch skillet over medium-high heat, in hot olive or salad oil, cook mushrooms and onion until tender and golden. Stir in tomatoes; over high heat, heat to boiling. Reduce heat to medium-low; cover and simmer sauce 10 minutes to blend flavors.
3. Place bread shells on large cookie sheet. Top shells with mushroom sauce. Sprinkle with mozzarella cheese, oregano, and black pepper. Bake pizzas on bottom rack of oven 8 to 10 minutes until hot and bubbly. Sprinkle pizzas with chopped parsley. Makes 4 main-dish servings.

Minted Peaches & Pears With Ginger

1 16-ounce can pear halves in their own juice
1 16-ounce can sliced cling peaches in their own juice
1 tablespoon chopped crystallized ginger
1 tablespoon chopped fresh mint or 1/4 teaspoon peppermint extract mint sprigs for garnish

1. Drain pears, reserving 1/2 cup juice. Drain peaches.
2. In medium bowl, mix pears with their reserved juice, peaches, crystallized ginger, and chopped mint. Garnish with mint sprigs. Makes 4 servings.

Chunky Vegetable Salad

2 large tomatoes
1 large yellow pepper
1 medium-size cucumber
1/2 small red onion
1 tablespoon chopped fresh chervil or cilantro, or 1/2 teaspoon dried chervil or cilantro leaves
2 tablespoons olive or salad oil
2 tablespoons red wine vinegar
3/4 teaspoon salt
1/2 teaspoon sugar

1/4 teaspoon coarsely ground black pepper
fresh chervil or cilantro for garnish

1. Cut tomatoes into wedges. Cut yellow pepper and unpeeled cucumber into bite-size chunks. Finely chop red onion.
2. In medium bowl, mix tomatoes, yellow pepper, cucumber, red onion, and chervil with next 5 ingredients until blended. Garnish with chervil if you like. Makes 4 accompaniment servings.

Filet Mignon With Mushroom & Onion Gravy

4 beef tenderloin steaks (filet mignon), each about 6 ounces and 1-1/2 inches thick
1/2 teaspoon dried thyme leaves
1/4 teaspoon pepper
salt
olive or salad oil 1/4 pound shiitake mushrooms, stems removed and sliced 1/4 inch thick, or 1 8-ounce package regular mushrooms, sliced
1 small onion, finely chopped
2/3 cup milk
1/2 teaspoon cornstarch
parsley sprigs for garnish

1. Rub beef tenderloin steaks with thyme, pepper, and 1 teaspoon salt.
2. In 10-inch skillet over medium-high heat, in 1 tablespoon hot olive or salad oil, cook steaks 5 minutes; turn steaks and cook 4 to 5 minutes longer for rare or until of desired doneness. Remove steaks to 4 warm dinner plates; keep warm.
3. In drippings remaining in skillet and 1 tablespoon additional hot olive or salad oil, over medium-high heat, cook mushrooms, onion, and 1/4 teaspoon salt, stirring frequently, until mushrooms and onion are golden and tender.
4. Meanwhile, in cup, with wire whisk or fork, mix milk, cornstarch, and 1/4 cup water until blended; stir into mushroom mixture in skillet. Over medium-high heat, cook, stirring, until mixture boils and thickens; boil 1 minute.
5. To serve, spoon mushroom gravy over steaks. Garnish with parsley sprigs. Makes 4 main-dish servings.

Creamy Parmesan Sweet Corn Polenta

2-1/2 cups milk
3/4 teaspoon salt
2/3 cup cornmeal
1 11-ounce can whole-kernel corn
1 tablespoon margarine or butter

In 3-quart saucepan over high heat, heat milk and salt to boiling. Reduce heat to medium; gradually sprinkle in cornmeal, stirring with wire whisk. Cook over low heat, stirring frequently, until mixture is thick and creamy, about 10 minutes. Stir in corn with its liquid and margarine or butter; heat through. Makes 4 accompaniment servings.

Egg-White Frittata With Sautéed Vegetables

1 medium-size red pepper
1 medium-size onion
1/4 pound mushrooms
2 tablespoons olive or salad oil
1/4 teaspoon dried oregano leaves
1/8 teaspoon coarsely ground black pepper
salt
3 tablespoons grated Parmesan cheese
8 large egg whites

1. Preheat oven to 375°F. Dice red pepper, onion, and mushrooms.
2. In 10-inch skillet over high heat, in hot olive or salad oil, cook red pepper, onion, mushrooms, oregano, pepper, and 1/2 teaspoon salt until vegetables are tender and browned. Remove skillet from heat; stir in Parmesan cheese.
3. While vegetables are cooking, in large bowl, with mixer at high speed, beat egg whites until stiff peaks form.
4. Gently fold half of beaten egg whites into vegetable mixture in skillet. Then, fold mixture into remaining beaten egg whites in bowl. Do not overmix. Spoon mixture into two 2-cup shallow baking dishes or ramekins.
5. Bake frittata 15 minutes or until cooked through and golden brown on top. Serve immediately. Makes 2 main-dish servings.

Artichoke, Olive & Tomato Pasta

1 16-ounce package fusili or rotelle (corkscrew) macaroni
salt
2 6-ounce jars marinated artichoke hearts
2 tablespoons olive or salad oil
2 tablespoons red wine vinegar
1 tablespoon chopped parsley
1 teaspoon dried oregano leaves
1/2 teaspoon sugar
1/4 teaspoon coarsely ground black pepper
2 large tomatoes, cut into wedges
1/2 cup pitted ripe olives, coarsely chopped
1/4 pound Provolone cheese, shredded (1 cup)

1. Prepare fusilli as label directs, using 2 teaspoons salt in water; drain.

2. Into large bowl, drain marinade from 1 jar of marinated artichoke hearts; drain and discard marinade from second jar.
3. With fork or wire whisk, mix artichoke marinade with olive oil, red wine vinegar, chopped parsley, oregano, sugar, pepper, and 1/2 teaspoon salt until blended. Add fusilli, artichokes, tomatoes and olives; toss to coat well. Top with shredded Provolone; toss to serve. Makes 6 main-dish servings.

Vegetable Omelet

1 large green pepper
1 large onion
1 8-ounce package medium-size mushrooms
1-1/2 8-ounce containers liquid whole eggs (reduced cholesterol)
1/4 teaspoon ground black pepper
salt
olive or salad oil

1. Dice green pepper and onion; slice mushrooms.
2. In bowl, with fork, mix liquid whole eggs, ground black pepper, 1/2 teaspoon salt, and 1/3 cup water. Set aside.
3. In nonstick 12-inch skillet over medium heat, in 1 tablespoon hot olive or salad oil, cook green pepper, onion, and 1/4 teaspoon salt 5 minutes, stirring occasionally. Stir in mushrooms and cook until mushrooms are lightly browned and all liquid has evaporated, about 10 minutes longer. Remove vegetables to bowl; keep warm.
4. In same skillet over medium heat, in 2 tablespoons hot olive or salad oil, cook egg mixture until set around the edge. With metal spatula, gently lift edge as it sets, tilting skillet to allow uncooked portion to run under omelet. Shake skillet occasionally to keep omelet moving freely in pan. When omelet moving freely in pan. When omelet is set but still moist, spoon half of vegetable mixture over half the omelet. Tilt skillet and, with spatula, fold omelet in half; slide onto warm platter. Top with remaining vegetable mixture. Makes 4 main-dish servings.

Red & Yellow Pepper Sauté

2 large red peppers
2 large yellow peppers
2 tablespoons olive or salad oil
1/2 teaspoon dried oregano leaves
1/4 teaspoon sat

1. Cut red and yellow peppers into 1-inch-wide slices.
2. In 12-inch skillet over medium-high heat, in hot olive or salad oil, cook pepper strips, oregano, and salt, stirring frequently, until peppers are golden and tender-crisp. Makes 4 accompaniment servings.

Salmon-Avocado Open-Faced Sandwiches

1/2 cup mayonnaise
2 tablespoons minced dill pickle
2 tablespoons chili sauce
1/2 teaspoon lemon juice
1/8 teaspoon hot pepper sauce
2 slices pumpernickel bread
1 7-3/4-ounce can salmon, drained and flaked
6 pitted ripe olives, sliced
1 small avocado, sliced
1/2 16-ounce jar sliced pickled beets, drained
2 medium-size lettuce leaves

1. In small bowl, mix mayonnaise with next 4 ingredients.
2. For each serving, on dinner plate, place 1 slice bread; lightly spread bread with some mayonnaise mixture. On mayonnaise mixture, arrange half of salmon and top with half of olives.
3. On plate with sandwich, arrange half of avocado slices and beets. Spoon half of remaining mayonnaise mixture into a lettuce leaf; place on plate with sandwich. Makes 2 main-dish servings.

Chicken & Potato Stew

6 medium-size skinless, boneless chicken thighs (about 1-1/2 pounds)
2 tablespoons olive or salad oil
1 large onion, thinly sliced
salt
4 medium-size red potatoes (about 3/4 pound)
1 medium-size orange
1/4 cup chicken broth
1 tablespoon all-purpose flour
1 teaspoon chopped fresh rosemary or 1/4 teaspoon dried rosemary leaves

1. Cut each chicken thigh in half. In 12-inch skillet over medium-high heat, in hot olive or salad oil, cook chicken thighs, onion, and 1 teaspoon salt until onion is tender and thighs are browned and lose their pink color throughout, about 10 minutes. With fork, remove chicken to bowl, leaving onions in skillet.
2. Meanwhile, cut potatoes into 1-1/4-inch chunks. With vegetable peeler, cut two 2-1/2" by 3/4" strips of orange peel; reserve. Into 2-cup measuring cup, squeeze 1/4 cup juice from orange; stir in chick broth, flour, and 3/4 cup water.
3. To skillet with onion, add potatoes, orange-juice mixture, and 1/4 teaspoon salt; over high heat, heat to boiling. Reduce heat to low; cover and simmer 10 minutes or until potatoes are almost tender.
4. Return chicken thighs to skillet; stir in chopped rosemary and

cook until potatoes are tender and chicken is heated through. Cut reserved orange peel into thin strips. Garnish stew with orange peel. Makes 4 main-dish servings.

Beef & Pepper Fajitas With Tomato & Avocado Salad

1 large green pepper
1 large red pepper
1 large onion
1 garlic clove
olive or salad oil
salt
pepper
2 large tomatoes
1 large avocado
1 lime
1 teaspoon Dijon mustard
1 tablespoon chopped fresh cilantro or 1 teaspoon dried cilantro leaves
1 1-pound beef flank steak
1 teaspoon chili powder
1 teaspoon dried oregano leaves
8 7- to 8-inch flour tortillas
cilantro sprigs for garnish
1/2 cup sour cream

1. Thinly slice green and red peppers and onion; mince garlic. in 12-inch skillet over medium-high heat, in 1 tablespoon hot olive or salad oil, cook green and red peppers, onion, 3/4 teaspoon salt, and 1/4 teaspoon pepper until lightly browned. Stir in minced garlic and 1/2 cup water; over high heat, heat to boiling. Reduce heat to low; cover and simmer until vegetables are tender and liquid evaporates, about 10 minutes. Remove mixture to bowl.
2. While pepper mixture is simmering, cut tomatoes into wedges. Cut avocado lengthwise in half; remove seed and peel. Cut avocado into 1-inch chunks.
3. In medium bowl, squeeze juice from lime. With fork, stir in Dijon mustard, cilantro, 2 tablespoons olive or salad oil, 3/4 teaspoon salt, and 1/4 teaspoon pepper until blended. Stir in tomatoes and avocado, tossing gently to coat; set aside.
4. Cut flank steak lengthwise in half, then crosswise into 1/8-inch-thick strips. In same skillet, in 1 tablespoon hot oil, cook steak, stirring quickly and constantly, until meat loses its pink color. Stir in chili powder, oregano, and 1/2 teaspoon salt; cook 1 minute. Return pepper mixture to skillet; heat.
5. Meanwhile, heat flour tortillas as label directs.
6. To serve, arrange tortillas on platter with beef mixture and avocado salad. Garnish with cilantro sprigs. Let each person spoon some beef mixture and sour cream on a tortilla; then roll up to enclose filling. Makes 4 main-dish servings.

Warm Chicken-Breast, Potato & Arugula Salad

2 bunches arugula or watercress
1 pound small red potatoes, each cut in half
1 large red pepper
1 large yellow pepper
4 medium-size skinless, boneless chicken-breast halves (about 1-1/4 pounds)
olive or salad oil
salt
3 tablespoons red wine vinegar
1 teaspoon Dijon mustard
3/4 teaspoon sugar
1/4 teaspoon pepper

1. Use 1 bunch arugula to line platter; set remaining bunch aside.
2. In 3-quart saucepan over high heat, heat potatoes and enough water to cover to boiling. Reduce heat to low; cover and simmer 8 to 10 minutes, until potatoes are fork-tender; drain.
3. Meanwhile, cut red and yellow peppers into 1/2-inch-wide strips. Cut chicken-breast halves into 1/2-inch-wide strips.
4. In 12-inch skillet over high heat, in 2 tablespoons hot olive or salad oil, cook pepper strips and 1/4 teaspoon salt, stirring frequently, until tender-crisp. With slotted spoon, remove pepper strips to bowl.
5. In oil remaining in skillet and 1 tablespoon additional hot olive or salad oil over medium-high heat, cook chicken-breast strips and 1/4 teaspoon salt, stirring frequently, until chicken begins to brown and loses its pink color throughout.
6. In small bow, mix red wine vinegar, mustard, sugar, pepper, 1 tablespoon olive or salad oil, and 3/4 teaspoon salt until blended.
7. Return pepper strips to skillet with chicken. Add red-wine-vinegar mixture, potatoes, and reserved arugula or watercress, tossing to coat; heat through. To serve, spoon warm chicken salad over leaves on platter. Makes 4 main-dish servings.

Rice Almondine

1 medium onion, chopped
2 teaspoons margarine
1-1/4 cups chicken broth
1 tablespoon lemon juice
1/2 teaspoon garlic powder
1-1/2 cups Minute Instant Brown Rice
1 cup frozen cut green beans, thawed
2 tablespoons toasted sliced almonds
1/2 teaspoon dill weed

Cook and stir onion in hot margarine until tender. Add broth, lemon juice and garlic powder. Bring to boil. Stir in rice. Return to boil. Reduce heat to low; cover and simmer 5 minutes. Remove from heat. Stir in green beans, almonds and dill; cover. Let stand 5 minutes. Serves 6.

Cod & Vegetable Stew

1 large onion
1 tablespoon olive or salad oil
3/4 teaspoon salt
5 medium-size red potatoes (about 12 ounces)
1 1-1/4-pound piece cod fillet
1/2 medium-size bunch spinach (about 1/2 pound)
1 14-1/2-ounce can pasta-style stewed tomatoes
1 13-3/4- to 14-1/2-ounce can chicken broth

1. Cut onion lengthwise in half; cut each half crosswise into 1/4-inch-thick slices. In 4-quart saucepan over medium heat, in hot olive or salad oil, cook onion and salt until tender but not browned.
2. Meanwhile, cut unpeeled potatoes into 3/4-inch chunks. Cut cod fillet into 1-1/2-inch chunks. Discard tough stems from spinach; coarsely slice spinach.
3. When onion is tender, add stewed tomatoes, chicken broth, potatoes, and 1 cup water; over high heat, heat to boiling. Reduce heat to low; cover and simmer 10 minutes or until potatoes are almost tender. Gently stir in cod and spinach; cook 5 minutes longer or until cod is cooked through and potatoes are fork-tender. Serve stew in soup bowls. Makes 4 main-dish servings.

Rosemary Lamb Chops With Lemon-Garlic Sauce

8 lamb loin chops, each 3/4 inch thick (about 2 pounds)
1 teaspoon salt
1 teaspoon dried rosemary leaves, crushed
1/2 teaspoon coarsely ground black pepper
all-purpose flour
2 tablespoons olive or salad oil
1 tablespoon lemon juice
3/4 teaspoon chicken-flavor instant bouillon
1 garlic clove, crushed with garlic press or finely chopped

1. Trim excess fat from lamb chops. On sheet of waxed paper, mix salt, rosemary, pepper, and 1 tablespoon flour; use to coat lamb chops.
2. In 12-inch skillet over medium-high heat, in hot olive or salad oil, cook lamb chops 4 minutes on each side for medium-rare or until of desired doneness, turning chops once. Remove lamb chops to platter; keep warm.
3. While lamb chops are cooking, in cup, mix lemon juice, chicken bouillon, 2 teaspoons flour, and 3/4 cup water until blended.
4. Disregard all but 1 teaspoon fat from skillet. Over medium heat, cook garlic, stirring constantly, just until garlic begins to brown. Add lemon-juice mixture, stirring to loosen brown bits from bottom of skillet. Over high heat, heat to boiling; boil 1 minute. Spoon sauce over lamb chops on platter. Makes 4 main-dish servings.

Tomato & Feta Cheese Orzo

3/4 cup orzo (rice-shaped pasta)
salt
1 14-1/2- to 16-ounce can stewed tomatoes
2 tablespoons chopped parsley
2 ounces feta cheese, crumbled (1/2 cup)
About 20 minutes before serving:

1. In 3-quart saucepan, prepare orzo as label directs, using 1 teaspoon salt in water; drain. Return orzo to saucepan.
2. Stir stewed tomatoes and chopped parsley into orzo in saucepan, using spoon to break up tomatoes; heat through.
3. Serve orzo mixture sprinkled with crumbled feta cheese. Makes 4 accompaniment servings.

Panfried Pork Chops

1 large onion
2 tablespoons olive or salad oil
4 pork loin blade or loin chops, each 3/4 inch thick
3/4 teaspoon salt
1/2 teaspoon coarsely ground black pepper
2 tablespoons cider vinegar

1. Cut onion into thin slices, In 12-inch skillet over medium heat, in hot olive or salad oil, cook onion until tender and lightly browned, about 10 minutes. With slotted spoon, remove onion to small bowl.
2. Trim excess fat from pork chops. Sprinkle pork chops with crushed fennel seeds, salt, and black pepper. In oil remaining in skillet over medium-high heat, cook pork chops until pork is browned on both sides and just loses its pink color throughout, about 10 minutes, turning chops once. Remove pork chops to platter; keep warm.
3. To drippings in skillet, add cider vinegar and 1/3 cup water, stirring to loosen any brown bits on bottom of skillet. Stir in onion; heat through.
4. To serve, spoon onion mixture over pork chops on platter. Makes 4 main-dish servings.

Egg Noodles & Spinach

1/2 16-ounce package extra wide egg noodles
salt
1 large bunch spinach (about 1 pound)
3 tablespoons olive or salad oil
1/4 teaspoon pepper

1. Prepare egg noodles as label directs, using 1 teaspoon salt in water.
2. Meanwhile, rinse spinach leaves well and drain; remove and discard tough stems. Coarsely chop spinach.
3. Drain noodles; set aside. In same saucepot that noodles were cooked in, over high heat, in hot olive or salad oil, cook spinach, pepper, and 1 teaspoon salt, stirring, and until spinach just wilts.
4. Return noodles to saucepot, tossing to mix well; heat through. Makes 4 accompaniment servings

Apple-Cabbage Slaw

1/2 small head green cabbage (about 1/2 pound)
1/2 small head red cabbage (about 1/2 pound)
1 medium-size Red Delicious apple
1 tablespoon cider vinegar
1 tablespoon salad oil
2 teaspoons sugar
3/4 teaspoon salt
1/4 teaspoon celery seeds

1. Thinly slice green and red cabbage; discard any tough ribs. Cut apple into 1/2-inch chunks.
2. In large bowl, combine cabbage, apple, vinegar, and remaining ingredients; toss to coat. Makes 4 accompaniment servings.

Ravioli With Tomato & Eggplant Sauce

2 13-ounce packages frozen jumbo round cheese ravioli
2 medium-size zucchini (about 10 ounces each)
2 large tomatoes (about 8 ounces each)
1 medium-size eggplant (about 1-1/4 pounds)
1 large onion
olive or salad oil
salt
2 tablespoons red wine vinegar
1 tablespoon light brown sugar

1. Prepare ravioli as label directs; drain.
2. Meanwhile cut zucchini into 1-1/2 inch chunks. Chop 1 tomato; cut remaining tomato into wedges. Cut eggplant into 1-inch chunks. Chop onion.
3. In 12-inch skillet over high heat, in 1 tablespoon hot olive or salad oil, cook zucchini and 1/2 teaspoon salt until lightly browned. With slotted spoon, remove zucchini to bowl.
4. In same skillet over medium-high heat, in 2 tablespoons hot olive or salad oil, cook eggplant, onion, and 1 teaspoon salt until lightly browned. Stir in chopped tomato, vinegar, brown sugar, 1 cup water, and 1 teaspoon salt, stirring to break up tomatoes. Return zucchini to skillet; over high heat, heat to boiling. Reduce heat to low; cover and simmer until eggplant and zucchini are tender, about 10 minutes, stirring occasionally.
5. Add ravioli and tomato wedges to eggplant mixture; heat through. Makes 4 main-dish servings.

Sesame Chicken Sandwiches

1 tablespoon cornstarch
3/4 teaspoon salt
1 large egg white
1 2.6-ounce jar sesame seeds
4 medium-size boneless, skinless chick-breast halves (about 1-1/4 pounds)
olive or salad oil
1 bunch spinach
1 medium-size red pepper
1 small onion
1 17-inch-long loaf French bread (10 ounces)
2 tablespoons teriyaki sauce

1. Mix cornstarch and salt on sheet of waxed paper. In pie plate, with fork, beat egg white and 1 tablespoon water until blended. Place sesame seeds on another sheet of waxed paper. Dip each chicken-breast half in cornstarch mixture, then egg-white mixture, then sesame seeds to coat.
2. In 12-inch skillet over medium-high heat, in 2 tablespoons hot olive or salad oil, cook chicken-breast halves until sesame seeds are golden brown. Turn chicken; reduce heat to medium. Cook chicken until sesame seeds are golden and juices run clear when chicken is pierced with a knife, about 5 minutes longer. Remove chicken to plate; keep warm.
3. While chicken is cooking, trim tough stems from spinach; cut red pepper into 1/4-inch-wide strips; chop onion.
4. Preheat broiler if manufacturer directs. Cut French bread crosswise into 4 pieces. Cut each piece horizontally in half. Arrange bread, cutside up, on large cookie sheet. With oven rack at closest position to source of heat, broil bread about 30 seconds or until lightly toasted.
5. In same skillet over medium-high heat, in 1 tablespoon hot olive or salad oil, cook onion 5 minutes or until it begins to soften. Add red pepper strips and cook until onion and red pepper are tender. Add spinach and teriyaki sauce; cook just until spinach wilts.
6. Arrange half of vegetable mixture on bottom halves of bread. Top with chicken-breast halves, remaining vegetable mixture,

then top halves of bread. Makes 4 main-dish servings.

Stir-Fried Chicken Salad

1/2 pound fresh bean sprouts
1 piece peeled ginger root, about 2" by 1/2" by 1/2"
1 large green onion
1 large red pepper
1 bunch radishes
4 large skinless, boneless chicken thighs (about 1-1/2 pounds)
1 large head romaine lettuce
olive or salad oil
1/2 teaspoon salt
3 tablespoons seasoned rice vinegar
1 tablespoon soy sauce
1/4 teaspoon crushed red pepper

1. In 3-quart sauce pan over high heat, heat 1 quart water to boiling. Stir in bean sprouts and cook 1 minute; drain.
2. Meanwhile, slice ginger root and green onion into 2-inch-long match-stick-thin strips. Slice red pepper into 1/4-inch-thick strips; cut each strip diagonally in half. Cut each radish into quarters. Cut chicken thighs into 1-inch pieces. Into large serving bowl, tear romaine lettuce into bite-size pieces.
3. In 12-inch skillet over medium-high heat, in 2 tablespoons hot olive or salad oil, cook ginger root and green onion until lightly browned. With slotted spoon, remove green-onion mixture to bowl.
4. In oil remaining in skillet over medium-high heat, cook chicken and salt until the chicken loses its pink color throughout, stirring often.
5. While chicken is cooking, in small bowl, with fork or wire whisk, mix rice vinegar, soy sauce, crushed red pepper, and 1 tablespoon olive or salad oil. Set dressing aside.
6. When chicken is done, top lettuce with bean sprouts, red pepper, radishes, then chicken; sprinkle with green-onion mixture.
7. To serve, pour dressing over salad; toss to coat well. Makes 4 main-dish servings.

Sautéed Zucchini & Mushrooms

2 tablespoons olive or salad oil
2 medium-size zucchini (about 8 ounces each), sliced 1/2 inch thick
1 10-ounce package mushrooms, each cut in half
1/2 teaspoon salt
1/4 teaspoon pepper
1 tablespoon balsamic or red wine vinegar
1/2 teaspoon sugar

About 15 minutes before serving:
1. In 10-inch skillet over medium-high heat, in hot olive or salad oil, cook zucchini, mushrooms, salt, and pepper, stirring occasionally, until vegetables are golden brown and tender-crisp.
2. Stir in balsamic vinegar, sugar, and 1 tablespoon water. Remove skillet from heat. Makes 4 accompaniment servings.

Turkey Cutlets With Provolone, Basil & Roasted Peppers

4 6-ounce turkey cutlets, each 1/4 inch thick
1/4 pound provolone or mozzarella cheese, shredded (1 cup)
1/3 7-ounce jar roasted red peppers, chopped (1/4 cup)
2 teaspoons dried basil leaves
3 tablespoons dried bread crumbs
2 tablespoons grated Parmesan cheese
1 tablespoon dried parsley flakes
1/2 teaspoon salt
1/2 teaspoon pepper
2 tablespoons pepper
2 tablespoons milk
2 tablespoons olive or salad oil
basil sprigs for garnish

1. On half of each turkey, cutlet, arrange one-fourth each of shredded cheese, chopped roasted peppers, and basil. Fold other half of turkey cutlets over filling. Press edges of turkey cutlets together to seal slightly.
2. On waxed paper, combine bread crumbs, Parmesan cheese, parsley flakes, salt, and pepper. Pour milk into pie plate. Dip turkey cutlets, one at a time, into milk, then into bread-crumb mixture.
3. In 12-inch skillet over medium heat, in hot olive or salad oil, cook turkey cutlets about 10 minutes or until golden brown and fork-tender and cheese melts, turning once. Arrange turkey cutlets on platter; garnish with basil sprigs. Makes 4 main-dish servings.

Lamb Kabobs with Warm Lentil Salad

1 cup dry lentils
1 bay leaf
1-1/2 pounds lamb cubes for kabobs, cut into 1-1/2-inch chunks
1/2 pint cherry tomatoes
1-1/2 teaspoons dried oregano leaves
1 small garlic clove, minced
salt
olive or salad oil
pepper

1 small garlic clove, minced
salt
olive or salad oil
pepper
1 small carrot, shredded
1 tablespoon chopped fresh mint or 1 teaspoon dried mint leaves
2 tablespoons lemon juice

1. Prepare lentil salad: Rinse lentils with running cold water and discard any stones or shriveled lentils. In 2-quart saucepan over high heat, heat to boiling lentils, bay leaf, and enough water to cover by 2 inches. Reduce heat to medium-low; cover and simmer 20 minutes or until lentils are tender.
2. Meanwhile, prepare lamb kabobs: Preheat boiler if manufacturer directs. In large bowl, gently mix lamb cubes, cherry tomatoes, oregano, minced garlic, 1 teaspoon salt, 2 teaspoons olive or salad oil, and 3/4 teaspoon pepper. On four 12-inch-long all-metal skewers, alternately thread lamb and cherry tomatoes. Place skewers on rack in broiling pan. Place pan in broiler at closest position to source of heat; broil kabobs 8 to 10 minutes, turning skewers once, until lamb is medium-rare.
3. When lentils are done, drain well; discard bay leaf. In medium bowl, mix lentils, shredded carrot, chopped mint, lemon juice, 2 tablespoons olive or salad oil, 3/4 teaspoon salt, and 1/4 teaspoon pepper until blended.
4. To serve, arrange lentil salad on 4 dinner plates with kabobs. Makes 4 main-dish servings.

Seafood Fettucini

2 tablespoons butter or margarine
4 teaspoons flour
1-1/2 cup half-and-half
1/4 cup grated Parmesan cheese
1 package Louis Kemp Crab Delights
6 ounce cooked fettucini
1 tablespoon fresh parsley, chopped

Melt butter, stir in flour. Gradually add half-and-half, stir until thickened. Add Parmesan; cook and stir until smooth. Fold in Crab Delights, heat 3 minutes, stir occasionally. Toss fettucini with sauce, sprinkle with parsley. Serve immediately.
Serves 4.

Szechuan Pork & Broccoli Lo Mein

1 pork tenderloin (about 1 pound)
3 tablespoons soy sauce
1 tablespoon dry sherry
1/2 teaspoon crushed red pepper
1 large head broccoli (about 1-1/2 pounds)
1 large red pepper
1 medium-size onion
1 8-ounce package linguine
salt
olive or salad oil
1 6-ounce package frozen Chinese pea pods, thawed
2 teaspoons cornstarch
1/2 teaspoon chicken-flavor instant bouillon

1. Trim fat from pork tenderloin, if any. Cut the pork tenderloin crosswise into thin slices. In bowl, mix pork, soy sauce, sherry, and crushed red pepper.
2. Cut broccoli into 2-1/2" by 1" pieces. Slice red pepper into 1/2-inch-wide pieces; cut onion into thin wedges.
3. In saucepot, prepare linguine as label directs, using 2 teaspoons salt in water.
4. In 12-inch skillet over high heat, in 1 tablespoon hot olive or salad oil, cook broccoli, stirring quickly and frequently, until evenly coated with oil. Add 1/4 teaspoon salt and 1/2 cup water. Reduce heat to medium; cover and cook 2 minutes. Uncover and stir-fry broccoli 5 minutes or until tender-crisp. Remove broccoli to bowl.
5. In same skillet in 2 tablespoons additional hot olive or salad oil, cook red-pepper strips, onion wedges, and 1/4 teaspoon salt until red pepper and onion are tender-crisp, stirring frequently. Stir in pea pods and cook until pea pods are tender-crisp and red pepper and onion are golden brown; remove to bowl with broccoli.
6. In same skillet over high heat, in 2 tablespoons additional hot olive or salad oil, cook pork mixture, stirring quickly and constantly, just until pork loses it pink color and is tender, about 5 minutes. Remove the pork to bowl with vegetables.
7. In small bowl, mix cornstarch, chicken-flavor bouillon, and 1 cup water; pour mixture into skillet. Over high heat, heat to boiling, stirring to loosen any brown bits from bottom of skillet. Stir in the pork mixture; heat through.
8. Drain linguine; return to saucepot. Add pork mixture; toss to mix well. Makes 4 main-dish servings.

Open-Faced Roasted Eggplant & Mozzarella Sandwiches

1 medium-size eggplant (about 1-1/2 pounds)
olive or salad oil
1 8-inch-long loaf semolina or Italian bread
1 9-ounce package fresh large mozzarella cheese balls in water (boconccini), drained, or 1 8-ounce package mozzarella cheese
1 teaspoon dried oregano leaves

1/4 teaspoon crushed red pepper
1/4 teaspoon salt
8 oil-package dried tomatoes, drained
1 small bunch basil

1. Preheat broiler if manufacturer directs.
2. Slice egg-plant crosswise into 1/4-inch-thick slices. Place eggplant slices on rack in broiling pan; brush both sides of slices with 2 tablespoons olive or salad oil. Broil eggplant 10 to 12 minutes until browned, turning slices once halfway through broiling time.
3. Diagonally slice both ends from loaf of semolina bread; reserve for making bread crumbs another day. Slice remaining bread diagonally into 8 slices. Thinly slice mozzarella cheese.
4. In a small bowl, with fork, mix oregano, crushed red pepper, salt, and 2 tablespoons olive or salad oil. Brush each bread slice with herb mixture.
5. Arrange the bread slices on a large platter. Top with the broiled eggplant, mozzarella, and dried tomatoes; tuck basil leaves in between mozzarella slices. Makes 4 main-dish servings.

Asparagus, Garbanzo & Pasta Salad

3/4 16-ounce package penne or rotelle (corkscrew) macaroni
salt
2 pounds asparagus
3 medium-size plum tomatoes (about 8 ounces)
1 bunch fresh basil
1/3 cup lemon juice
1 teaspoon sugar
1/4 teaspoon pepper
olive or salad oil
1 9-ounce package fresh small mozzarella cheese balls in water (ciliegine), drained, or 18-ounce package mozzarella cheese, cut into bite-size chunks
1 15-to 19-ounce can garbanzo beans, drained

1. Prepare penne as label directs, using 2 teaspoons salt in water; drain.
2. Meanwhile, discard tough ends from asparagus; trim scales if stalks are gritty. Cut the asparagus into 2-inch pieces. Cut tomatoes into 2-inch pieces. Cut tomatoes into 1-inch chucks. Reserve 6 basil sprigs for garnish. Measure enough remaining basil leaves to equal 1/3 cup packed leaves. Slice basil leaves into thin strips.
3. Prepare salad dressing: In large bowl, with fork, mix lemon juice, sugar, pepper, 3 tablespoons olive or salad oil, and 1 teaspoon salt.
4. In 12-inch skillet over medium-high heat, in 1 tablespoon hot olive or salad oil, cook asparagus and 1/4 teaspoon salt until asparagus is tender-crisp.
5. To bowl with dressing, add penne, tomatoes, asparagus, sliced basil, mozzarella balls, and garbanzo beans. Toss to mix well. Spoon salad onto 6 dinner plates; garnish with fresh basil sprigs. Makes 6 main-dish servings.

Stir-Fried Bok Choy

2 medium-size heads bok choy (Chinese cabbage), about 1 pound each
2 tablespoons salad oil
1 teaspoon salt
1/2 teaspoon sugar

1. Cut stem end from both heads of bok choy. Trim any tough stems and discolored leaves. Rinse bok choy in running cold water; drain well. Cut stems and leaves crosswise into 1-1/2 inch pieces.
2. In 5-quart Dutch oven or saucepot over high heat, in very hot salad oil, cook bok choy, stirring quickly and frequently, until evenly coated with salad oil. Sprinkle with salt and sugar and continue stir-frying 2 to 3 minutes longer, until bok choy is tender-crisp. Makes 4 main-dish servings.

Quick Paella

1 medium-size red pepper
1 medium-size green pepper
1 large onion
3 tablespoons olive or salad oil
1 14-1/2- to 16-ounce can stewed tomatoes
1 13-3/4- to 14-1/2-ounce can chicken broth
1-1/2 cups parboiled rice
1 teaspoon turmeric
1 teaspoon paprika
1 pound mussels
1 10-ounce package frozen Fordhook lima beans
1 12-ounce or 1 8-ounce packages refrigerated, fully cooked spicy chicken wings
1/4 pound slice pepperoni

1. Cut peppers and onion lengthwise in half, then crosswise into 1/4-inch-wide strips. In 12-inch skillet over medium-high heat, in hot olive or salad oil, cook peppers and onion until lightly browned.
2. Meanwhile, in 2-quart saucepan over high heat, heat stewed tomatoes, chicken broth, and 1-1/2 cups water to boiling. Reduce heat to low; keep warm.
3. Into vegetables in skillet, stir rice, turmeric, and paprika; cook 1 minute. Stir in hot chicken-broth mixture; over high heat, heat to boiling. Reduce heat to low; cover and simmer 15

minutes or until rice is almost tender.
4. Into rice mixture, stir mussels, frozen lima beans, chicken wings, and pepperoni; over high heat, heat to boiling. Reduce heat to low; cover and simmer 5 minutes or until mussels open, lima beans are tender, and chicken is heated. Makes 6 main-dish servings.

OUTDOOR/INDOOR COOKING

FOR A PERFECT BARBECUE

Successful grilling depends on a good fire. It should be hot enough to maintain steady heat, but not so hot that it blackens the food. Follow these basic ground rules:
*Place your charcoal grill out in the open, not in an enclosed area. If the weather's bad and you're grilling in the garage, leave doors wide open, position the grill just inside the driveway entrance.
*Start with a bed of coals big enough to outlast the cooking. If you need to add more coals later, place them around the outer edge of the hot ones, so the hot coals ignite them.
*Let coals burn for 20 to 40 minutes before you start cooking. (In daylight, they are ready when they are covered with gray ash; at nighttime, they will glow red.)
*Never add starter fluid <u>after</u> you've started the fire. The fluid can catch fire as you pour it, which is extremely dangerous.
* If you use nonstick cooking spray on the grill rack to keep food from sticking, be sure to spray it on <u>before</u> you start the fire.
*To tell if coals are hot enough, hold your hand over the, palm down, <u>at cooking height</u>, and count the number of seconds you can keep it there comfortably. If 2 or 3 seconds, coals are hot (above 375°F.); if 4 seconds, temperature is moderate (above 200°F. Another way is to use a barbecue thermometer, available in hardware stores; you attach it to the grill.
*To lower the heat during grilling, raise the rack, close the vents, or push coals apart.
*To raise the heat during grilling, lower the rack, open the vents, or push the coals closer together.
*If fat spatters and flares up, take one of these four steps: Raise the cooking rack; quickly remove the food from the grill and push coals father apart; close the vents; or cover the grill, if it has a cover. <u>Do not</u> douse red—hot coals with water; the ashes will only fly onto the food and make an unappetizing mess.
*Extinguish coals completely when you have finished barbecuing. If the grill has a cover, close the vents and put the cover down to cut off the oxygen supply. If it doesn't have a cover, douse coals with water to put out the fire; save coals, and reuse them after they have thoroughly dried out.

10 FLAVOR SECRETS

1. Sprinkle some orange, lemon, or grapefruit peels over hot coals in the last few minutes of grilling to add zesty flavor to chicken, ham, fish, pork, or beef.
2. For convenience, marinate foods in zipperlock plastic storage bags; just turn the whole bag over a few times to distribute marinade. Otherwise, use a deep glass or stainless steel—<u>not</u> aluminum-container.
3. Try marinating food in store-bought Italian or oil/vinegar salad dressing-but don't get one with a thick consistency (it will char too quickly). Delicious on beef, fish, chicken!
4. Quick basting sauce: Brush beef or poultry with your favorite spaghetti sauce during the last few minutes of grilling.
5. Turn up the outdoor flavor in foods—even if you're broiling them inside—by lightly brushing them with liquid smoke during cooking. Look for this bottled seasoning wherever sauces or condiments are sold.
6. For good taste—and for safety's sake, to kill any bacteria from raw foods—be sure to heat leftover marinade to full boiling, then simmer for five minutes before serving as a sauce.
7. Brush on thick marinades—made with honey, sugar, jelly, preserves, pureed fruit, or other sticky ingredients-only during the last few minutes of grilling, to prevent burning. Light sauces made with oil and seasoned without sugar can be brushed on food earlier if desired.
8. Add aromatic wood chips to hot coals to produce smoke that seasons grilled food. (To bring out the flavor and prolong burning time, soak chips first. Place in water, press a small plate on top to hold chips down.) Choose from mesquite, apple, peach, pear, hickory, alderwood, and pecan; grapevine cuttings lend nice flavor too. Add large chips at the start of grilling, small chips near the end.
9. Sprinkle fresh rosemary sprigs over coals near the end of cooking to enhance lamb. Try fresh thyme for seafood, bay leaves for steak or burgers. When basting meats or poultry with barbecue sauce, scatter fresh basil, oregano, marjoram, or all three over the coals for tantalizing flavor.
10. Dampen a couple of whole, unpeeled garlic cloves and place on coals during the last few minutes of cooking to add a little something extra to meat, poultry, seafood. Barbecue doesn't get any better than this!

COOKING TIPS

Burgers: The best burger starts out thick, not too firmly packaged. Grill until desired doneness, turning occasionally.
Ribs: Pork ribs come out perfectly tender if you parboil them for an hour, finish them on the grill. It's not necessary to parboil beef ribs; grill until of desired doneness.
Steak/chops: Get steaks that are at least 1" thick so they don't dry out and turn leathery. Trim excess fat from steaks and chops; slash remaining fat at 1-inch intervals so edges don't curl. Grill until desired doneness. (Note: Cook pork chops until meat just losses its pink color inside.)
Chicken: Grill until juices run clear when thickest part is pierced with a knife.

Fish/shellfish: Use a grill topper. Cook fish until it flakes easily when tested with a fork. Cook shrimp and scallops until opaque in the center.

Grill toppers, flat grates made of perforated, porcelain-coated steel or expanded stainless-steel mesh, really simplify barbecuing. They are ideal for cooking small, unskewered foods-such as scallops, shrimp, vegetables, fruit, and franks—which can fall through grill slats. (Turn these foods easily using tongs or a pancake turner.) Grill toppers are also great for tender foods that fall apart easily, like fish fillets. Look for rust-resistant, easy-clean grill toppers in stores where barbecue equipment is sold.

Mushroom-Stuffed Chicken Breasts

olive or salad oil
1 12-ounce package mushrooms, finely chopped
soy sauce
6 large chicken breast halves, with skin and bones (about 3-1/2 pounds)
2 green onions, finely chopped
1/4 teaspoon coarsely ground black pepper
12 jumbo mushrooms
3/4 teaspoon salt

1. Prepare outdoor grill for barbecuing.
2. In 12-inch skillet over medium-high heat, in 1 tablespoon hot olive or salad oil, cook chopped mushrooms until golden and all liquid evaporates, stirring occasionally. Stir in 1 tablespoon soy sauce.
3. Loosen skin on each chicken breast half; spoon mushroom mixture between meat and skin.
4. In small bowl, mix chopped green onions, pepper, 3 tablespoons soy sauce, and 2 tablespoons oil. In large bowl, toss jumbo mushrooms with salt and 2 tablespoons oil.
5. Place chicken breast halves on grill over medium heat; cook until golden on both sides, about 10 minutes. Then, to avoid charring, stand chicken pieces upright, leaning one against the other. Rearrange pieces from time to time and cook 20 to 25 minutes longer until chicken is fork-tender and juices run clear when chicken is pierced with a knife.
6. During last 10 minutes of cooking, brush chicken frequently with soy sauce mixture. Place mushrooms on grill with chicken; cook mushrooms about 10 minutes, turning occasionally, until tender. Makes 6 main-dish servings.

TO BROIL IN OVEN: About 1 hour before serving, prepare mushroom stuffing, chicken breast halves, and soy sauce mixture as about in steps 2, 3, and 4. Preheat broiler if manufacturer directs. Place chicken, skin side down, on rack in broiling pan. Place pan in broiler, with chicken about 5 to 7 inches from source of heat (or with oven control set at 450°F.); broil chicken 20 minutes. Meanwhile, toss mushrooms with salt and olive oil as in step 4. Brush chicken with some soy sauce mixture; turn chicken skin side up. Arrange mushrooms on rack with chicken. Broil 15 to 20 minutes, brushing chicken occasionally with remaining soy sauce mixture, until chicken is fork tender and juices run clear when chicken is pierced with a knife and mushrooms are tender.

Tex-Mex Stuffed Burgers

1 pound ground beef or ground turkey
16 saltine crackers with unsalted tops, crushed (about 1/2 cup)
1 small green pepper, minced
1 small red pepper, minced
1 teaspoon grated onion
3/4 teaspoon salt
1/4 teaspoon coarsely ground black pepper
1/4 pound Monterey Jack cheese with jalapeño peppers or Monterey Jack cheese, shredded (1 cup)
4 hamburger buns with sesame seeds, split
4 lettuce leaves
1 small tomato, diced

1. Prepare outdoor grill for barbecuing.
2. Meanwhile, in medium bowl, mix ground beef, crackers, green and red peppers, onion, salt, and black pepper. Shape meat mixture into 4 balls. Make indentation in center of each ball; place 1 heaping tablespoon shredded cheese into each indentation. Shape beef mixture around cheese; flatten each into a 3/4-inch thick round patty.
3. Place burgers on grill over medium heat. Cook burgers 7 to 10 minutes for medium or until of desired doneness, turning burgers occasionally with pancake turner. During last few minutes of cooking time, top burgers with remaining cheese and arrange buns, cut side down, on grill; cook until cheese melts and buns are lightly browned and toasted.
4. To serve, arrange lettuce leaves on bottom halves of toasted buns; top with burgers. Spoon diced tomato on top of burgers. Replace tops of buns. Makes 4 main-dish servings.

TO BROIL IN OVEN: About 40 minutes before serving, preheat broiler if manufacturer directs. Prepare burgers as above in step 2. Place burgers on rack in broiling pan. Place pan in broiler at closest position to source of heat and broil burgers about 10 minutes for medium or until of desired doneness, turning burgers once. Top burgers with cheese, toast buns, and serve as above.

Grilled Catfish Fillets

1 tablespoon paprika
2 tablespoons salad oil

1 teaspoon salt
4 small catfish fillets (about 6 ounces each)

1. Prepare outdoor grill for barbecuing.
2. In pie plate, stir paprika, salad oil and salt. Dip catfish fillets in paprika mixture to coat.
3. Place catfish on grill topper on grill over medium heat. Cook catfish 5 to 10 minutes until fish flakes easily when tested with fork, turning fish once with pancake turner. Makes 4 main-dish servings.
TO BROIL IN OVEN: Preheat broiler if manufacturer directs. Prepare catfish as above in step 2. Place fish on rack in broiling pan. With broiling pan at closest position to source of heat, broil fish 5 to 10 minutes until fish flakes easily when tested with a fork, turning once.

Quick Barbecue Beans

1 medium-sized onion
2 tablespoons salad oil
4 teaspoons chili powder
4 15-1/4- to 19-ounce cans red kidney beans
1 10-ounce package frozen Fordhook lima beans
2/3 cup chili sauce
2/3 cup dark molasses
2 tablespoons Worcestershire
1 teaspoon salt

1. Chop onion. In 4-quart saucepan over medium heat, in hot salad oil, cook onion until tender and lightly browned, about 15 minutes, stirring occasionally. Stir in chili powder; cook 1 minute.
2. Drain kidney beans, reserving 1-1/3 cups liquid; discard remaining liquid.
3. Into onion mixture, stir kidney beans, reserved bean liquid, frozen beans, frozen lima leans, chili sauce, molasses, Worcestershire, and salt; over high heat, heat to boiling. Reduce heat to low; simmer, partially covered, 30 minutes, stirring occasionally. Makes 10 accompaniment servings.

Summer Macaroni Salad

salt
1 9-ounce package refrigerated cheese-filled spinach tortellini
1/2 16-ounce package elbow twist or elbow macaroni
3 large celery ribs
2 medium-sized carrots
3/4 cup mayonnaise or whipped salad dressing
1/3 cup milk
1/4 cup chopped parsley
3/4 teaspoon pepper

1. In 4-quart saucepan over high heat, in 3 quarts boiling water and 1 teaspoon salt, cook tortellini as label directs. With slotted spoon, remove tortellini to colander; drain. Add elbow twist macaroni to boiling water remaining in saucepan; cook as label directs; drain.
2. Meanwhile, thinly slice celery; coarsely grate carrots.
3. In large bowl, with wire whisk or fork, mix mayonnaise or whipped salad dressing, milk, parsley, pepper, and 1-1/2 teaspoons salt until blended. Add macaroni, celery, and carrots, tossing to coat well. Cover and refrigerate if not serving right away. (If salad becomes dry after refrigerating, stir in additional milk just until mixture is moist and creamy.) Makes 8 accompaniment servings.

Maple Corn on the Cob

8 medium-sized ears corn
1/4 cup maple or maple flavor syrup
2 tablespoons Dijon mustard
1 teaspoon salt

1. Remove husks and silk from corn. In 8-quart saucepot over high heat, in 2 to 3 inches boiling water, heat corn to boiling. Reduce heat to low; cover and simmer 5 minutes; drain.
2. In pie plate, stir maple syrup, mustard, and salt until blended. Dip corn in maple syrup mixture. Makes 8 accompaniment servings.

Potato Salad Piquante

3 pounds medium-sized red potatoes (about 16)
1 5- to 5-3/4-ounce jar pimento-stuffed olives
1/4 cup mayonnaise
2 tablespoons chopped parsley
2 tablespoons olive or salad oil
3/4 teaspoon cracked black pepper

1. In 5-quart saucepot over high heat, heat potatoes and enough water to cover to boiling. Reduce heat to low; cover and simmer 15 to 20 minutes until potatoes are tender; drain; when cool enough to handle, cut each into quarters.
2. Drain olives, reserving 3 tablespoons olive liquid. In blender at high speed or in food processor with knife blade attached, blend olives, reserved olive liquid, and remaining ingredients until finely chopped.
3. In large bowl, combine potatoes and olive mixture; toss to coat. Arrange potato salad on platter. Cover and refrigerate if not serving right away. Makes 10 accompaniment servings.

Barbecued Chicken with Creole Sauce

1 tablespoon olive or salad oil
1 medium-sized onion, chopped
1 medium-sized green pepper, chopped
1 garlic clove, minced
1 cup ketchup
2 tablespoons light brown sugar
3 tablespoons red wine vinegar
1-1/4 teaspoons salt
1/2 teaspoon hot pepper sauce
2 3-1/2-pound broiler-fryers, each cut into quarters
parsley sprigs for garnish

1. Prepare outdoor grill for barbecuing.
2. Meanwhile, in 2-quart saucepan over medium-high heat, in hot olive or salad oil, cook onion and green pepper until vegetables are tender; add garlic and cook, stirring, 1 minute. Stir in ketchup, brown sugar, red wine vinegar, salt, hot pepper sauce, and 2 tablespoons water; over high heat, heat to boiling. Reduce heat to low; cover and simmer 5 minutes to blend flavors. Remove half of sauce to bowl for brushing on chicken while grilling; keep remaining sauce warm.
3. Place chicken on grill over medium heat; cook until golden on both sides, about 10 minutes. Then, to avoid charring, stand pieces upright, leaning one against the other. Rearrange pieces from time to time and cook until fork-tender, about 25 minutes longer. During last 10 minutes of cooking, brush chicken pieces frequently with barbecue sauce. If you like, garnish chicken with parsley sprigs. Serve chicken with reserved barbecue sauce. Makes 8 main-dish servings.
TO BROIL IN OVEN: About 50 minutes before serving, preheat broiler if manufacturer directs. Prepare sauce as above in step 2. Place chicken, skin side down, on rack in broiling pan. About 5 to 7 inches from source of heat (or with oven control set at 450°F.), broil chicken 20 minutes or until golden. Brush generously with sauce; broil 1 to 2 minutes longer. Turn chicken pieces skin side up; broil 10 minutes. Brush generously with sauce; broil 5 minutes. Brush with remaining sauce and continue broiling about 5 minutes longer or until chicken is fork-tender and juices run clear when chicken is pierced with a knife. Serve as above.

Tomato & Cucumber Salad with Avocado Dressing

1 medium-sized avocado
1 tablespoon milk
1 tablespoon lemon juice
1-1/2 teaspoons salt
1 bunch watercress, tough stems removed
4 medium-sized tomatoes
3 medium-sized cucumbers (about 2 pounds)

1. Prepare avocado dressing: Cut avocado lengthwise in half; remove and discard seed. With spoon, scoop avocado from each half into food processor with knife blade attached or into blender; at medium speed, blend avocado, milk, lemon juice, salt, and 1/2 cup loosely packed watercress until smooth. Spoon into large bowl.
2. Cut each tomato into 8 wedges. Peel cucumbers; cut each cucumber lengthwise in half; with spoon, remove and discard seeds. Cut cucumbers into bite-sized chunks. Place tomato wedges and cucumber chunks in bowl with avocado dressing; gently toss to coat.
3. To serve, line platter with remaining watercress; top with tomato-cucumber salad. Makes 10 accompaniment servings.

BBQ Pork Ribs with Sweet Peaches

6 pounds pork spareribs, cut into 2-rib portions
3 tablespoons aromatic bitters
2 teaspoons salt
1 teaspoon crushed red pepper
1 teaspoon fennel seeds, crushed
1/4 teaspoon ground ginger
1 12-ounce jar peach preserves
6 medium-sized peaches

1. In 8-quart saucepot over high heat, heat spareribs and enough water to cover to boiling. Reduce heat to low; cover and simmer 1 hour or until spareribs are fork-tender. Remove ribs to platter. If not serving ribs right away, cover and refrigerate.
About 1 hour before serving:
2. Prepare outdoor grill for barbecuing.
3. Meanwhile, in small bowl, mix bitters, salt, crushed red pepper, fennel seeds, ginger, and 3/4 cup peach preserves (reserve remaining preserves for brushing on peaches during grilling).
4. Place ribs on grill over medium heat; cook 15 to 20 minutes until heated through, turning ribs often and brushing with peach sauce frequently during last 10 minutes of cooking.
5. Cut each peach in half; remove pits. Place peach halves on grill with ribs and cook, turning peaches occasionally and brushing with remaining peach preserves until peach halves are hot and browned, about 5 minutes. Makes 6 main-dish servings.
TO BROIL IN OVEN: About 1-1/2 hours before serving or day ahead, prepare spareribs as above in step 1. Prepare peach sauce as above in step 3. About 30 minutes before serving, preheat broiler if manufacturer directs. Arrange cooked ribs, overlapping slightly, on rack in broiling pan. Place pan in broiler, with ribs about 5 to 7 inches from source of heat (or with oven control set at 450°F.); broil ribs 10 minutes, turning them once. Brush ribs generously with peach sauce; broil 10 minutes longer or until heated through, turning ribs occasionally. Place ribs on platter; keep warm while broiling peaches. Cut each peach in half;

discard pits. Place peach halves, cut side up, on rack in broiling pan; brush with remaining peach preserves. Place pan in broiler at closest position to source of heat and broil about 5 minutes until hot and browned.

Sweet & Sour Chicken Wings

1/4 cup red wine vinegar
1/4 cup soy sauce
1/4 cup sugar
1 tablespoon cornstarch
2 tablespoons Oriental sesame oil
2 pounds chicken wings (about 12)
1/2 teaspoon salt
1/4 teaspoon pepper
1 green onion, chopped for garnish

1. Prepare outdoor grill for barbecuing.
2. Meanwhile, prepare sweet-and-sour sauce: In 1-quart saucepan, combine red wine vinegar, soy sauce, sugar, cornstarch, sesame oil, and 1/4 cup water. Over medium-high heat, heat until sauce boils and thickens; boil 1 minute. Remove saucepan from heat. Sprinkle chicken wings on grill over medium heat. Cook 25 to 30 minutes until wings are tender and golden, turning wings frequently and brushing with sweet-and-sour sauce during last 10 minutes of cooking.
4. Remove wings to platter; sprinkle with chopped green onion. Makes 4 main-dish servings.

TO BROIL IN OVEN: About 40 minutes before serving, preheat broiler if manufacturer directs. Prepare sweet-and-sour sauce and sprinkle wings with salt and pepper as above in step 2. Place wings on rack in broiling pan. Place pan in broiler, with wings about 5 to 7 inches from source of heat (or with oven control set at 450°F.); broil 25 to 30 minutes until wings are tender and golden, turning wings occasionally and brushing with sweet-and-sour sauce during last 10 minutes of broiling.

Salmon Teriyaki with Squash

1/2 cup grated fresh peeled horseradish root or 2 tablespoons grated peeled ginger root
1/4 cup teriyaki sauce
olive or salad oil
2 medium-sized zucchini (about 10 ounces each)
2 medium-sized yellow straight neck squash (about 10 ounces each)
1/2 teaspoon salt
1/4 teaspoon lemon-pepper seasoning salt
4 salmon steaks, each 1/2 inch thick (about 6 ounces each)
1/2 cup shredded fresh horseradish

1. Prepare outdoor grill for barbecuing.
2. Meanwhile, in cup, mix grated horseradish or ginger root, teriyaki sauce, and 1 tablespoon olive or salad oil; set aside.
3. Cut each zucchini and yellow squash lengthwise in half. Brush zucchini and yellow-squash halves with 1 tablespoon olive or salad oil; sprinkle with salt and lemon-pepper seasoning salt.
4. Place vegetables on grill. Cook vegetables over medium-low heat, turning them occasionally, about 10 minutes or until tender.
5. Arrange salmon steaks on grill topper; place grill topper on rack on grill. Over medium heat, cook salmon 4 to 5 minutes on each side until salmon flakes easily when tested with fork, brushing salmon occasionally with teriyaki sauce mixture.
6. Serve salmon steaks and vegetables with shredded horseradish. Makes 4 main-dish servings.

TO BROIL IN OVEN: About 30 minutes before serving, preheat broiler if manufacturer directs. Prepare zucchini and yellow squash as above in step 3. Place zucchini and yellow squash on rack in broiling pan. Place pan in broiler, with vegetables about 5 inches from source of heat (or with oven control set at 450°F.) and broil zucchini and yellow squash 10 minutes or until tender, turning them occasionally and removing vegetables to platter as they are done. Keep vegetables warm while preparing salmon. Meanwhile, prepare teriyaki sauce mixture as above in step 2. Spread half of teriyaki sauce mixture over salmon steaks. Place salmon on rack in broiling pan. Place pan in broiler at closest position to source of heat; broil salmon 8 to 10 minutes until fish flakes easily when tested with a fork, turning salmon once and brushing with remaining teriyaki sauce mixture. Serve as above.

Butterflied Leg of Lamb with Tabbouleh Salad

1 8-ounce container plain nonfat yogurt
2-1/2 teaspoons salt
2 teaspoons coarsely ground black pepper
2 garlic cloves, minced
1/2 cup chopped parsley
lemon juice
1 5-1/2-pound lamb leg shank half, butterflied
1 5.25-ounce package tabbouleh wheat salad mix
1 large tomato, chopped
1/4 cup olive or salad oil
1/2 cup pitted ripe olives, coarsely chopped

1. In 13" by 9" glass baking dish, mix yogurt, salt, pepper, garlic, 1/4 cup chopped parsley, and 1/4 cup lemon juice. Add lamb, turning to coat with marinade; cover and refrigerate at least 3 hours, turning lamb occasionally.
2. Meanwhile, prepare tabbouleh as label directs with tomato, olive or salad oil, and 1 to 2 tablespoons lemon juice, adding chopped olives and remaining 1/4 cup chopped parsley. Cover

and refrigerate until ready to serve.
About 1 hour before serving:
3. Prepare outdoor grill for barbecuing.
4. Place lamb on grill over medium heat, reserving marinade in dish. Cook 20 to 25 minutes for medium-rare or until of desired doneness, brushing with marinade and turning lamb occasionally.
5. Remove lamb to cutting board; cut into bite-sized chunks. Serve with tabbouleh. Makes 16 Main-dish servings.
TO BROIL IN OVEN: About 4 hours before serving or early in day, prepare marinade and marinate lamb as above in step 1. Meanwhile, prepare tabbouleh wheat salad as above in step 2. About 40 minutes before serving, preheat broiler if manufacturer directs. Place lamb on rack in broiling pan. Place pan in broiler, with meat 3 to 4 inches from source of heat; broil lamb 25 minutes for medium-rare or until of desired doneness, brushing occasionally with marinade and turning lamb once. Serve as above.

Maple-Glazed Baby Back Ribs

4 racks pork baby back ribs (about 1 pound each)
1/3 cup maple-flavor syrup
1/3 cup chili sauce
3/4 teaspoon salt
1/4 teaspoon maple extract

1. In 8-quart saucepot over high heat, heat ribs and enough water to cover to boiling. Reduce heat to low; cover and simmer 1 hour or until ribs are tender. Remove ribs to platter; cover and refrigerate if not using right away.
About 1 hour before serving:
2. Prepare outdoor grill for barbecuing.
3. Meanwhile, prepare maple glaze: In small bowl, with fork, mix maple syrup, chili sauce, salt, and maple extract.
4. Place cooked baby back ribs on grill over medium heat. Cook 15 minutes or until heated through, turning ribs frequently and brushing with maple glaze during last 5 minutes of cooking. Makes 4 main-dish servings.
TO BROIL IN OVEN: About 1-1/2 hours before serving or day ahead, prepare ribs as above in step 1. About 25 minutes before serving, preheat broiler if manufacturer directs. Prepare maple glaze as in step 3. Place ribs on rack in broiling pan. Place pan in broiler, with ribs about 5 to 7 inches from source of heat (or with oven control set at 450°F.); broil ribs 15 minutes or until heated through, turning ribs occasionally and brushing ribs with maple glaze during last 5 minutes of broiling.

BBQ Beef Short Ribs with "Baked" Potatoes

4 medium-sized baking potatoes (about 6 ounces each)
2 teaspoons unseasoned meat tenderizer
2 teaspoons oregano-flavor liquid spice or 1 teaspoon dried oregano leaves
coarsely ground black pepper
4 pounds beef chuck short ribs, cut into serving-sized pieces
1 4-ounce package crumbled feta cheese (1 cup)

1. Prepare outdoor covered grill for barbecuing.
2. Meanwhile, wash and dry potatoes. Wrap each potato in double thickness of heavy-duty foil. In cup, mix tenderizer, oregano liquid spice, and 1-1/2 teaspoons pepper (if using dried oregano, add 1 teaspoon olive oil to mixture in cup). Rub spice mixture on short ribs.
3. Place potatoes on grill over medium heat; cook, covered, 30 minutes, turning potatoes several times.
4. After potatoes have cooked 30 minutes, place short ribs on grill with potatoes; cook, uncovered, turning frequently, 30 minutes for medium-rare ribs or until of desired doneness and potatoes are tender.
5. To serve, cut an "X" in top of each potato and squeeze to partially open. Arrange potatoes and short ribs on large platter. Let each person spoon some crumbled feta cheese on their potato, then sprinkle with cracked black pepper. Makes 4 main-dish servings.
TO PREPARE INDOORS: About 1-1/2 hours before serving, preheat oven to 450°F. Arrange potatoes (do not wrap with foil) on rack in center of oven. Bake 45 minutes or until potatoes are tender when pierced with a fork. Keep potatoes warm while preparing short ribs.
Turn over control to broil. Prepare spice mixture as above in step 2. Arrange ribs on rack in broiling pan. Place pan in broiler, with short ribs 3 to 5 inches from source of heat; broil 30 minutes for medium-rare, turning ribs occasionally. Serve short ribs with potatoes as above in step 5.

Marinated Lamb Chops with Grilled Tomatoes

1/4 cup red wine vinegar
2 garlic cloves, minced
2 teaspoons dried rosemary leaves, crushed
1-1/4 teaspoons salt
coarsely ground black pepper
8 lamb rib chops, each about 1 inch thick
2 large tomatoes
1 tablespoon olive or salad oil
2 tablespoons grated Parmesan cheese
1 tablespoon chopped parsley

1. Prepare outdoor grill for barbecuing.
2. Meanwhile, in 13" by 9" glass baking dish, mix red wine vinegar, garlic, rosemary, salt, and 1/2 teaspoon coarsely ground black pepper. Arrange lamb chops in 1 layer in baking

dish, turning to coat lamb chops with mixture. Allow lamb chops to marinate in vinegar mixture 15 minutes or until grill is ready, turning chops occasionally. Cut each tomato horizontally in half.
3. Place lamb chops on grill over medium heat. Brush tomatoes with olive or salad oil; place tomatoes, cut side down, on grill with lamb chops. Cook 8 to 10 minutes for medium-rare lamb or until of desired doneness, turning chops occasionally and tomatoes once, and brushing chops with remaining marinade halfway through cooking time.
4. To serve, sprinkle tomato halves with Parmesan cheese, chopped parsley, and 1/4 teaspoon ground black pepper. Makes 4 main-dish servings.
TO BROIL IN OVEN: About 40 minutes before serving, prepare lamb chops and tomatoes as above in step 2. Preheat broiler if manufacturer directs. Place lamb chops on rack in broiling pan. Brush tomatoes with olive or salad oil; place tomatoes, cut side down, on rack with lamb chops. With broiling pan at closest position to source of heat, broil lamb chops and tomatoes 8 to 10 minutes for medium-rare lamb or until of desired doneness, turning chops and tomatoes once, and brushing chops with remaining marinade halfway through cooking time. Sprinkle tomatoes with grated Parmesan, chopped parsley, and 1/4 teaspoon coarsely ground black pepper to serve.

Cabbage & Potato Packets

1/2 small head green cabbage (about 1-1/2 pounds)
2 medium-sized red potatoes
2 tablespoons margarine or butter (1/4 stick), softened
2 tablespoons chopped parsley
1/2 teaspoon caraway seeds, crushed
1/2 teaspoon salt
1/4 teaspoon coarsely ground black pepper

1. Prepare outdoor grill for barbecuing.
2. Meanwhile, remove core from cabbage half; discard. Thinly slice cabbage; discard tough ribs. Cut potatoes into thin slices. In cup, mix margarine or butter, chopped parsley, caraway seeds, salt, and pepper until blended.
3. Tear off four 16-inch-long pieces of heavy duty foil. Fold each piece in half to form 4 double-thickness foil rectangles. Arrange one-fourth of sliced potatoes on half of each foil rectangle; dot with margarine mixture. Fold foil over cabbage mixture, folding seams of foil several times to seal in juices.
4. Place foil packets on grill over medium heat; cook 20 minutes or until vegetables are tender, turning packets occasionally with tongs. Makes 4 accompaniment servings.
TO BAKE IN OVEN: About 1 hour before serving, preheat oven to 425°F. Cut cabbage and potatoes as above in step 2; place in 13" by 9" glass baking dish. Toss cabbage and potatoes with parsley, caraway seeds, salt, and pepper; dot with margarine or butter. Cover baking dish tightly with foil. Bake 45 minutes or until vegetables are tender.

Chicken Breasts Italiano

6 large boneless chicken breast halves with skin left on (about 2-1/2 pounds)
3/4 teaspoon salt
1 7-ounce container refrigerated pesto sauce
1/2 7-ounce container refrigerated pesto sauce
1/2 7-ounce jar roasted red peppers, chopped (about 1/2 cup)
1/4 teaspoon coarsely ground black pepper
arugula and tomato wedges for garnish

1. Prepare outdoor grill for barbecuing.
2. With meat mallet or dull edge of French knife, pound each chicken breast half to 1/4-inch thickness. Arrange chicken breast halves, skin side down, on work surface; sprinkle with salt.
3. Reserve 2 tablespoons pesto sauce. Spread remaining pesto sauce over each chicken breast half to within 1/2 inch of edge; sprinkle with chopped roasted red peppers.
4. Fold chicken breasts crosswise in half to enclose filling; secure with toothpick. Brush chicken breast halves with reserved pesto sauce: sprinkle with black pepper.
5. Place chicken on grill over medium heat; cook 15 to 20 minutes, turning chicken occasionally, until chicken is fork-tender and juices run clear when chicken is pierced with a knife.
6. To serve, arrange chicken on warm large platter. Garnish with arugula and tomato wedges. Makes 6 main-dish servings.
TO BROIL IN OVEN: About 35 minutes before serving, preheat broiler if manufacturer directs. Prepare chicken as above in steps 2 through 4. Place chicken breast halves on rack in broiling pan. Place pan in broiler about 5 to 7 inches from source of heat (or with oven control set at 450°F.); broil chicken 15 to 20 minutes, turning chicken once, until chicken is fork-tender and juices run clear when chicken is pierced with a knife.

Mixed Sausage Grill

2 medium-sized green peppers
2 medium-sized red peppers
2 medium-sized yellow peppers
1/4 cup hot pepper rings, drained
1 1-pound fully cooked kielbasa (Polish sausage)
4 fully cooked weisswurst or bockwurst (veal sausage)
4 knackwurst
1/2 cup apple jelly
1 teaspoon grated lemon peel
2 tablespoons olive or salad oil
1/2 teaspoon salt

1. Prepare outdoor grill for barbecuing.
2. Meanwhile, slice green, red and yellow peppers into 1/2-inch-thick slices; dice pepper rings. Cut few slits in kielbasa, wiesswurst, and knackwurst to prevent them from bursting while cooking. In cup, mix jelly and lemon peel.
3. In 12-inch skillet with metal handle on grill, over medium-high heat, in hot olive or salad oil, cook pepper slices and salt, stirring frequently, until peppers are tender, about 20 minutes. Stir in diced pepper rings; heat through. Remove skillet from heat; keep warm.
4. Place kielbasa, weisswurst, and knackwurst on grill over medium heat; cook 10 minutes or until heated through and browned on all sides, turning sausages often. Brush sausages with jelly mixture; cook 5 minutes longer.
5. Serve sausages with peppers. Makes 6 main-dish servings.
TO COOK INDOORS: About 40 minutes before serving, preheat broiler if manufacturer directs. Meanwhile, prepare peppers, sausages, and apple-jelly mixture as above in step 2. Arrange sausages on rack in broiling pan. Place pan in broiler, with sausages about 3 to 5 inches from source of heat; broil 15 minutes, turning sausages occasionally and brushing with apple jelly mixture during last 5 minutes of broiling. While sausages are cooking, in 12-inch skillet over medium-high heat, cook peppers as above in step 3. Serve as above.

Lobster & Clam Bake

1 medium-sized ear corn
4 cherrystone clams on the half shell
2 medium-sized mussels
1 1-1/4-pound lobster*
2 green onions
2 tablespoons white wine
1/2 teaspoon fish-flavor instant bouillon
1 tablespoon margarine or butter

1. Prepare outdoor covered grill for barbecuing.
2. Meanwhile, remove husk and silk from corn; cut ear crosswise into 3 pieces. With stiff brush, scrub clams and mussels with running cold water to remove sand. Putt off beards from mussels.
3. Tear off two 22-inch sheets heavy-duty foil; place one on top of the other; bring up edges slightly. Place corn, mussels, clams, lobster, and green onions on foil.
4. In cup, mix wine, bouillon, and 1/3 cup water (if not using wine, Increase water to 1/2 cup). Pour bouillon mixture over seafood; dot with margarine. Wrap ingredients in foil, being careful that seam is folded several times to seal in liquid.
5. Place foil packet on grill over medium heat; cover and cook 30 minutes or until corn is tender and lobster meat turns opaque.
6. To serve, cut packet open with kitchen shears. Serve with lobster cracker and fork. Dip lobster meat in broth in packet. Makes 1 main-dish serving. (For additional servings, prepare more packets and cook as above.)
TO BAKE IN OVEN: About 1 hour before serving, preheat oven to 450°F. prepare packets as above in steps 2 through 4. Bake 30 to 40 minutes.
*Ask fishman to sever the nerve of the lobster.

Zesty Steak & Potato Kebabs

1-1/2 pounds medium-sized red potatoes
3/4 teaspoon salt
1/2 teaspoon dried thyme leaves
1/4 teaspoon pepper
salad oil
1 1-1/4-pound beef top round steak (about 1-1/4 inches thick)
4 large green onions
1 16-ounce jar sweet red pepper slices
1 8-ounce can tomato sauce
1/4 cup packed brown sugar
1 0.7-ounce envelope Italian salad dressing mix

1. Prepare outdoor grill for barbecuing.
2. Meanwhile, cut each potato into quarters. In medium bowl, toss potatoes with salt, thyme, pepper, and 1 tablespoon salad oil. On 2 long skewers, thread potatoes, reserving any oil mixture remaining in bowl. Set aside.
3. With knife held in slanting position, slice across width of steak into 1/4-inch-thick slices. Cut green onions into 2-inch pieces. Cut red pepper slices into 1-1/2-inch pieces.
4. In large bowl, with fork, mix tomato sauce, brown sugar, salad dressing mix, and 1 tablespoon salad oil. Stir in steak slices to coat well.
5. On 4 long skewers, thread steak slices, accordion style, alternately with green onions and red peppers, reserving any tomato sauce mixture.
6. Place potato skewers on grill over medium heat; cook 25 to 30 minutes until potatoes are tender, turning skewers occasionally and brushing with remaining oil mixture in bowl.
7. Place steak skewers on grill over medium heat; cook 5 to 8 minutes for rare or until of desired doneness, brushing steak slices, green onions, and red peppers with reserved tomato mixture frequently and turning skewers occasionally. Makes 4 main-dish servings.
TO BROIL IN OVEN: About 45 minutes before serving, preheat broiler if manufacturer directs. Meanwhile, prepare potato kebabs as above in step 2 but use all-metal skewers. Arrange potato skewers on rack in broiling pan. Place pan in broiler, with skewers about 5 to 7 inches from source of heat; broil potatoes 20 to 25 minutes until tender, turning skewers occasionally and brushing with oil mixture in bowl. Place potato kebabs on platter; keep warm. While potatoes are cooking, prepare steak kebabs as above in steps 3 through 5 but

use all-metal skewers. Arrange steak skewers on rack in broiling pan. Place pan in broiler at closest position to source of heat; broil 5 to 8 minutes for rare, brushing skewers with reserved tomato sauce mixture and turning skewers once.

Pork Chops with Pear & Raisin Compote

1 16-ounce can pear halves, drained
2 tablespoons chopped crystallized ginger
2 tablespoons brown sugar
2 tablespoons dark seedless raisins
2 tablespoons lemon or lime juice
6 port loin blade or sirloin chops, each 3/4-inch thick
2/3 cup white wine Worcestershire
lime slices and parsley sprigs for garnish

1. Prepare outdoor grill for barbecuing.
2. Prepare pear compote: Dice pears. In medium bowl, combine pears, ginger, sugar, raisins, and lemon juice.
3. Place pork chops on grill over low heat. Cook chops 30 minutes or until chops lose their pink color throughout, turning chops occasionally and brushing frequently with Worcestershire, until they lose their pink color throughout, turning chops once.

Four-Bean Salad

1 10-ounce package frozen Fordhook lima beans
1 9-ounce package frozen cut green beans
1/3 cup tarragon vinegar or white wine vinegar
1/4 cup sugar
3 tablespoons olive or salad oil
2 tablespoons Dijon mustard
2 tablespoons chopped parsley
1-1/4 teaspoons salt
2 15-1/4- to 19-ounce cans red kidney beans, rinsed and drained
1 16- to 19-ounce can white kidney beans (cannellini), rinsed and drained
lettuce leaves for garnish

Early in day or day ahead:
1. Prepare lima beans and green beans as labels direct, but do not add salt to either; drain.
2. In large bowl, with wire whisk or fork, mix vinegar, sugar, olive or salad oil, mustard, parsley, and salt until well blended. Add red kidney beans, white kidney beans, lima beans, and green beans, tossing gently to coat.
3. Cover and refrigerate at least 6 hours to blend flavors, occasionally stirring mixture gently.
4. To serve, tuck lettuce leaves around bean salad. Makes 10 accompaniment servings.

Surf 'N' Turf Grill

1 jumbo yellow onion (about 1-1/4 pounds)
2 large red onions (about 8 ounces each)
1/2 teaspoon coarsely ground black pepper
olive or salad oil
salt
1 pound large shrimp
4 teaspoons fennel seeds
1 teaspoon rubbed sage
1 teaspoon ground allspice
1 teaspoon ground ginger
1 beef top round steak, 1-1/2 inches thick (about 2-1/2 pounds)

1. Cut yellow onion lengthwise into quarters; cut each red onion lengthwise in half. In 3-quart saucepan over high heat, heat yellow and red onions and enough water to cover to boiling. Reduce heat to low; cover and simmer 15 minutes or until onions are tender; drain. In medium bowl, toss onions with coarsely ground black pepper, 2 tablespoons olive or salad oil, and 1/2 teaspoon salt.
2. While onions are cooking, prepare shrimp and steak: Insert tip of kitchen shears under shell of each shrimp and snip along back through to tail, cutting about 1/4 inch deep to expose dark vein. Leaving shell on, rinse shrimp with running cold water to remove vein.
3. With mortar and pestle, crush fennel seeds. In large bowl, combine crushed fennel, sage, allspice, ginger, and 1-1/2 teaspoons salt. Rub steak with some spice mixture. Add shrimp and 1 tablespoon olive or salad oil to spice mixture remaining in bowl; toss to coat well.
4. Prepare outdoor grill for barbecuing.
5. Place onions on grill over medium heat. Cook 10 minutes, turning onions occasionally and brushing frequently with seasoned oil remaining in bowl. Remove onions to platter.
6. Place steak on grill; cook 20 to 25 minutes for medium-rare or until of desired doneness. During last 10 minutes of cooking steak, place shrimp on grill topper on grill next to steak; cook 5 to 10 minutes until shrimp are opaque throughout, turning shrimp occasionally.
7. Remove shrimp to platter with onions. Remove steak to cutting board. Cut steak into slices; arrange on platter with onions and shrimp. Makes 6 main-dish servings.
TO BROIL IN OVEN: Prepare onions as above in step 1. Prepare shrimp and steak as above in steps 2 and 3. Preheat broiler if manufacturer directs. Place onions on rack in broiling pan; with broiling pan at closes position to source of heat, broil onions about 10 minutes, turning occasionally and brushing with seasoned oil remaining in bowl. Remove onions to platter. Place steak on rack in broiling pan. With broiling pan at closest position to source of heat, broil steak 20 to 25 minutes for medium-rare or until of desired doneness, turning steak once. During last 10 minutes of cooking time, add shrimp to rack in

broiling pan with steak; broil shrimp 5 to 10 minutes until shrimp are opaque throughout, turning once.

Baked Red Snapper with Olives

1 large tomato
2 medium-size shallots or 1 small onion
1 medium-size shallots or 1 small onion
1 medium-size lemon
1 small red pepper
2 tablespoons capers
1/3 cup Niçoise olives, pitted, or 1/2 cup pitted ripe olives, sliced
olive or salad oil
1 teaspoon salt
1/2 teaspoon pepper
2 whole red snappers (each about 1-3/4 pounds), dressed and with head and tail left on
1 cup chicken broth
2 tablespoons chopped parsley
parsley sprigs for garnish

1. Seed and dice tomato. Thinly slice shallots; separate into rings. From lemon, grate peel and squeeze 2 tablespoons juice. Cut red pepper into matchstick-thin 1-inch-long strips. Chop capers.
2. Preheat oven to 350°F. In small bowl, mix Niçoise olives with shallots, lemon peel, red-pepper strips, capers, and 1 tablespoon olive or salad oil.
3. Rinse fish with running cold water; pat dry with paper towels. Place fish in large roasting pan. Brush fish with olive oil mixture, then sprinkle tops of fish with Niçoise olive mixture. Pour chicken broth and lemon juice around fish in roasting pan; sprinkle diced tomato around fish.
4. Bake 30 minutes until fish flakes easily when tested with a fork.
5. To serve, remove fish with pancake turners from roasting pan to warm large platter. Stir 1 tablespoon chopped parsley into sauce in roasting pan; spoon sauce around fish on platter. Sprinkle fish with remaining chopped parsley. Garnish with parsley sprigs. Makes 4 servings.

Spicy Beef Ribs with Grilled Pineapple

1 garlic clove 1 tablespoon olive or salad oil
1-1/2 teaspoons coarsely ground black pepper
1-1/2 teaspoons dry mustard
1-1/2 teaspoons fennel seeds, crushed
1 teaspoon salt
1/2 teaspoon ground cloves
4 pounds beef back ribs, cut into 1-rib portions (6 to 8 ribs)
1 medium-size pineapple
2 tablespoons granulated brown sugar
parsley sprigs for garnish

1. Into small bowl, with garlic press, crush garlic. Stir in olive or salad oil, pepper, dry mustard, fennel seeds, salt and ground cloves. Rub spice mixture over beef back ribs. Cover and refrigerate if not cooking right away.
2. About 35 minutes before serving, preheat broiler if manufacturer directs. Arrange ribs on rack in broiling pan. Place broiling pan in oven with ribs 4 to 5 inches from source of heat; broil 15 to 20 minutes for medium-rare, turning ribs once.
3. Meanwhile, cut off rind from pineapple. Slice pineapple lengthwise in half, then cut each half crosswise into 3/4-inch-thick slices.
4. When ribs are done, remove to large board or warm platter; keep warm. Arrange pineapple slices on same rack in broiling pan; sprinkle with 1 tablespoon granulated brown sugar. With broiling pan at closest position to source of heat, broil pineapple slices 5 minutes. Turn pineapple slices; sprinkle with remaining 1 tablespoon sugar and broil 5 to 7 minutes longer until pineapple is browned.
5. To serve, arrange pineapple slices on board or platter with ribs. Garnish with parsley sprigs. Makes 4 servings.
TO GRILL OUTDOORS: About 1-3/4 hours before serving or early in day, prepare beef ribs as above in step 1. Prepare pineapple as above in step 3; cover and refrigerate if not grilling right away.
About 1-1/4 hours before serving, prepare outdoor grill for barbecuing. Place ribs on grill over medium heat; cook 15 to 20 minutes for medium-rare, turning ribs frequently. Remove ribs to board or platter. In large bowl, toss pineapple slices with brown sugar. Place pineapple slices on grill over medium heat; cook 10 minutes or until browned on both sides, turning frequently.

Steak & Shrimp Barbecue

1-1/2 pounds large shrimp
2 green onions
3 tablespoons soy sauce
1 tablespoon olive or salad oil
3/4 cup currant jelly
1/3 cup bottled steak sauce
1 tablespoon cornstarch
1/2 teaspoon salt
1 beef top round steak, 1 inch thick (about 2 pounds)
unseasoned meat tenderizer
2 8-inch flour tortillas
1 16-ounce loaf favorite bread
crisp green salad

1. Prepare shrimp: Cut off legs from shrimp. Hold shrimp with curved side up and with tail away from you; insert tip of kitchen shears under shell and snip along back through to tail, cutting about 1/4 inch deep to expose vein. Keeping shell in place, rinse shrimp with running cold water to remove vein; pat dry with paper towels.
2. Mince green onions. In 11″ by 7″ glass baking dish, mix green onions, soy sauce, and olive or salad oil; add shrimp and toss to coat well. Cover and refrigerate 2 hours.
About 40 minutes before serving:
3. Preheat broiler if manufacturer directs.
4. In small saucepan over medium-low heat, heat currant jelly, steak sauce, cornstarch, and salt until melted, stirring frequently. Over medium heat, heat to boiling. Reduce heat to low; cook 1 minute or until jelly mixture thickens slightly. Sprinkle round steak with meat tenderizer as label directs.
5. Place steak on rack in broiling pan. With broiling pan 5 inches from source of heat, broil steak 10 to 12 minutes for medium-rare or until of desired doneness, turning steak once. During last few minutes of cooking time, brush steak frequently with jelly mixture. Remove steak to cutting board to rest while shrimp are cooking.
6. Place shrimp on rack in broiling pan. Place rack at closest position to source of heat. Broil shrimp 5 minutes, turning them once and brushing with soy sauce mixture remaining in dish.
7. Cut each tortilla into 6 wedges. Place tortilla wedges on rack in broiling pan. Broil tortilla wedges until lightly browned.
8. To serve, cut steak into large chunks. Serve steak and shrimp with tortilla wedges, bread, and crisp green salad. Makes 8 servings.
TO GRILL OUTDOORS: About 3-1/2 hours before serving, prepare shrimp as in steps 1 and 2.
About 1 hour before serving, prepare outdoor grill for barbecuing. Prepare steak as in step 4. Place steak on grill over medium heat; cook 20 minutes for medium-rare or until of desired doneness, brushing steak with jelly mixture at end of cooking time. During last 10 minutes of cooking steak, place shrimp on grill topper on grill next to steak; cook 5 to 10 minutes until shrimp are opaque throughout, turning shrimp occasionally, and brushing with any remaining marinade. Remove steak and shrimp to platter. Place tortilla wedges on grill; cook until lightly toasted. Serve as above.

Blackened Catfish with Coleslaw

1/2 small head green cabbage (about 1 pound)
1 large carrot
3 tablespoons white wine vinegar
2 teaspoons sugar
olive or salad oil
salt
1 tablespoon dried parsley flakes
1/2 teaspoon paprika
1/4 teaspoon onion powder
1/4 teaspoon ground red pepper
4 catfish fillets (about 6 ounces each)
2 medium-size nectarines

1. Separate leaves from cabbage. Cut out and discard tough ribs from cabbage leaves. Thinly slice cabbage to make about 5 cups, packed. Shred carrot.
2. In large bowl, mix vinegar, sugar, 2 tablespoons olive or salad oil, and 3/4 teaspoon salt. Add cabbage and carrot; toss to coat well with dressing. Cover and refrigerate.
3. In cup, mix parsley, paprika, onion powder, ground red pepper, and 3/4 teaspoon salt. Place catfish on sheet of waxed paper. Rub spice mixture on one side only of each fillet.
4. In nonstick 12-inch skillet over medium-high heat, in 1 tablespoon hot olive or salad oil, cook 2 catfish fillets, turning once, until golden on both sides and fish flakes easily when tested with a fork, 5 to 7 minutes. Remove catfish to platter, seasoning side up; keep warm. Repeat with remaining 2 fillets.
TO GRILL OUTDOORS: About 1-1/4 hours before serving, prepare coleslaw as in steps 1 and 2. Cut nectarines into wedges; set aside.
Prepare outdoor grill for barbecuing. Prepare catfish fillets as in step 3. Place catfish on grill topper on grill over medium heat. Cook catfish 5 to 10 minutes until fish flakes easily with a fork, turning fish once with pancake turner. Serve as above.

Mussels & Pasta Marinara

1/4 16-ounce package small shell macaroni (2 cups)
16 small mussels
2 tablespoons olive or salad oil
1 medium-size onion, diced
1 garlic clove, minced
1 35-ounce can Italian plum tomatoes
1 teaspoon salt
1 teaspoon sugar
1/2 teaspoon coarsely ground black pepper
1/4 cup chopped parsley

1. Prepare macaroni as label directs, but do not add salt to water. Drain; keep warm.
2. Meanwhile, with stiff brush, scrub mussels with running cold water to remove any sand; remove beards.
3. In 5-quart Dutch oven or saucepot over medium heat, in hot olive or salad oil, cook onion and garlic until tender, stirring occasionally. Stir in tomatoes with their liquid, salt, sugar, and pepper; over high heat, heat to boiling, stirring to break up tomatoes. Add mussels; heat to boiling. Reduce heat to low; cover and simmer, stirring occasionally, until mussels open, about 5 minutes. Discard any mussels that do not open. Remove Dutch oven from heat; stir in chopped parsley.
4. To serve, spoon cooked pasta into 2 large soup bowls. Spoon

mussels with their sauce over pasta. Makes 2 servings.

Pork Chops with Fresh Plums

5 medium-size potatoes (1-1/2 pounds)
3/4 cup low-fat milk (1%)
1 tablespoon minced parsley
salt
4 boneless center cut pork loin chops, each 1 inch thick (America's Cut)
olive or salad oil
3 medium-size red or black plums
1/2 bunch green onions
1 cup cranberry-raspberry juice
1 tablespoon brown sugar
2 teaspoons cornstarch
1/2 teaspoon beef flavor instant bouillon

1. Peel potatoes and cut each into quarters. In 3-quart saucepan over high heat, heat potatoes and enough water to cover to boiling. Reduce heat to low; cover and simmer 20 minutes or until potatoes are tender.
Drain potatoes; return to saucepan. Over low heat, add milk, parsley, and 1 teaspoon salt to potatoes in sauce pan. With potato masher, mash potatoes until smooth; keep warm.
2. Trim fat from pork chops. In 10-inch skillet over medium-high heat, in 1 tablespoon hot olive or salad oil, cook pork chops 5 minutes, sprinkling with 1/2 teaspoon salt. Turn pork chops and cook 3 to 5 minutes longer until pork just loses its pink color throughout, sprinkling with another 1/2 teaspoon salt. Remove pork chops to warm platter; keep warm.
3. While port is cooking, cut each plum into quarters; cut green onions into 2-inch lengths. In 2-cup measuring cup, stir together cranberry-raspberry juice, brown sugar, cornstarch, and beef bouillon.
4. When pork is done, in drippings remaining in skillet and 1 tablespoon hot olive or salad oil, cook plum wedges and green onions 2 to 3 minutes until lightly browned. Stir mixture in measuring cup and add to skillet; over high heat, heat until sauce boils and thickens slightly. Reduce heat to low; simmer 1 minute. Arrange mashed potatoes on platter with pork chops; pour plum sauce over pork. Makes 4 servings.

Fresh Tuna with Caper-Dill Sauce

3/4 cup mayonnaise
3 tablespoons milk
2 tablespoons capers, minced
1 tablespoon minced fresh dill or 1/4 teaspoon dried dill weed
1/4 teaspoon dry mustard
1/4 teaspoon salt
4 thin slices white bread
olive or salad oil
1/4 teaspoon coarsely ground black pepper
4 tuna steaks, each 1/2 inch thick and about 4 ounces
2 medium-size tomatoes, thinly sliced
fresh dill sprigs for garnish

1. In small bowl, mix mayonnaise dressing, milk, capers, dill mustard, and salt until blended; set aside.
2. Preheat broiler if manufacturer directs. Trim crust from bread slices. Brush bread slices with 1 tablespoon olive or salad oil; sprinkle with coarsely ground pepper. Place bread slices on cookie sheet; broil until lightly toasted on both sides, turning once. Cut each toasted slice diagonally in half.
3. Meanwhile, in nonstick 12-inch skillet over medium-high heat, in 2 teaspoons hot olive or salad oil, cook tuna steaks until cooked through, about 5 minutes, turning tuna steaks once.
4. To serve, arrange toast, tuna, and tomato slices on 4 dinner plates. Spoon caper-dill sauce over tuna. Garnish with dill sprigs. Makes 4 servings.

Roast Beef with Two Sauces

2 teaspoons dried thyme leaves
1-1/4 teaspoons coarsely ground black pepper
1 teaspoon salt
1 teaspoon ground sage
1/2 teaspoon garlic powder
1 4-pound beef eye round roast
Caper Sauce (below)
Horseradish Sauce (below)
fresh sage or parsley for garnish

About 1-1/2 hours before serving or early in day:
1. In cup, mix thyme, pepper, salt, sage, and garlic powder. Trim fat, if any, from eye round roast. Rub roast all over with herb mixture. Place roast on rack in small roasting pan.
2. Insert meat thermometer into center of roast. Roast in 325°F. oven 1 hour and 20 minutes or until thermometer reaches 130°F. for rare or until of desired doneness.
3. Meanwhile, prepare Caper Sauce and Horseradish Sauce. If not serving right away, cover and refrigerate until ready to serve.
4. When roast is done, cut into 1/2-inch-thick slices. Serve with Caper Sauce and Horseradish Sauce. Garnish with fresh sage or parsley. If not serving right away, cover and refrigerate to serve cold later. Makes 8 servings.

CAPER SAUCE: In small bowl, with fork or wire whisk, mix 3/4 cup olive or salad oil, 1/2 cup capers, chopped, 1/3 cup Dijon mustard, 1/4 cup water, 1 tablespoon chopped fresh chives, and 3/4 teaspoon coarsely ground black pepper until

blended.
HORSERADISH SAUCE: In small bowl, with fork or wire whisk, mix 3/4 cup mayonnaise, 1/2 cup prepared white horseradish, 3 tablespoons Dijon mustard, 3/4 teaspoon coarsely ground black pepper, and 1/4 teaspoon salt until blended.

London Broil with Roasted Garlic

1 small onion, minced
1/4 cup Worcestershire
1/4 cup chili sauce
1 tablespoon red wine vinegar
1 tablespoon minced fresh oregano or 1/2 teaspoon dried oregano leaves
1 teaspoon salt
1 beef top round steak, 1-1/2 inches thick (about 2 pounds)
1 whole large head garlic
olive or salad oil
1 12-ounce loaf of Italian bread

1. In zipper-top plastic bag, mix onion, Worcestershire, chili sauce, red wine vinegar, minced oregano, and salt; add round steak. Press all air out and close bag tightly. Refrigerate steak at least 6 hours or overnight, turning bag once or twice.
About 1-1/4 hours before serving:
2. Remove any loose papery skin from head of garlic, leaving head intact. Place head in center of sheet of heavy duty foil; drizzle with 1 teaspoon olive or salad oil. Loosely wrap foil around garlic, being careful seam is folded to seal in oil.
3. In 425°F. oven roast garlic 40 minutes or until garlic is tender. Remove to plate; keep warm.
4. Preheat broiler if manufacturer directs. Place beef top round steak on rack in broiling pan. Place pan in broiler 4 to 5 inches from source of heat; broil steak 10 minutes, brushing steak once with marinade. Turn steak; brush with remaining marinade; broil 8 to 10 minutes for rare or until of desired doneness. Remove steak to cutting board; deep warm.
5. Slice Italian bread horizontally in half. Brush cut sides with 1 tablespoon olive or salad oil.
6. Place bread on cookie sheet, cut sides up; place cookie sheet in oven on rack at closest position to source of heat. Broil bread 2 to 3 minutes or until golden brown. Slice bread crosswise into 2-inch pieces.
7. Discard foil from garlic. Arrange garlic and toasted bread on cutting board with steak. Let each person cut through skin of each garlic clove and spread some soft, sweet-tasting garlic on bread. Makes 6 servings.
TO GRILL OUTDOORS: Early in day or day ahead, marinate round steak as in step 1. About 1-1/4 hours before serving, prepare outdoor grill for barbecuing. Wrap garlic with foil as in step 2 and cut bread as in step 5.
Place garlic and steak on grill; cook 20 to 25 minutes for medium-rare steak or until of desired doneness, turning steak occasionally. Turn garlic package over once or twice during cooking; check garlic after 25 minutes to see if garlic is soft. During last 10 minutes of cooking steak, brush steak with marinade. When steak is done, remove to cutting board. Place Italian bread on grill, cut sides down, and grill until golden brown. Serve as in step 7.

Mandarin Pork

1 pork tenderloin (about 1 pound)
3 tablespoons soy sauce
1 teaspoon cornstarch
1/2 teaspoon crushed red pepper
1 bunch green onions
1 pound bean sprouts
1/2 pound Chinese pea pods or snap peas
3 large oranges
salad oil
1/2 teaspoon salt
1/2 cup orange juice

1. Cut port tenderloin crosswise into thin slices. In bowl, mix pork, soy sauce, cornstarch, and red pepper.
2. Thinly slice green onions. Rinse bean sprouts with running cold water and drain well. Remove stem and string along both edges of each pea pod.
3. From 1 orange, grate enough peel to measure 1 tablespoon; with knife, peel and section orange for garnish. From remaining 2 oranges, squeeze enough juice to measure 1/2 cup.
4. In nonstick 12-inch skillet over high heat, in 1 tablespoon hot olive or salad oil, cook Chinese pea pods and salt until pea pods are tender-crisp, stirring frequently; remove to bowl.
5. In same skillet over high heat, in 1 tablespoon hot salad oil, cook bean sprouts, stirring frequently, until tender-crisp; remove to bowl with pea pods.
6. In same skillet over high heat in 1 tablespoon hot salad oil, cook green onions until light brown; add pork mixture and cook, stirring frequently, just until the pork loses its pink color and is tender, about 3 minutes.
7. Return pea pods and bean sprouts to skillet with port; stir in orange juice and continue cooking until mixture boils and thickens slightly. Spoon mixture onto platter; garnish with orange sections and grated orange peel. Makes 4 servings.

Captain's Stew with Rice

1 cup parboiled rice
1/4 teaspoon turmeric
1-1/2 pounds sea scallops
2 tablespoons olive or salad oil

1 teaspoon salt
1 large onion, diced
1/2 16-ounce bag carrots, dices
1 14-1/2- to 16-ounce can stewed tomatoes
1 tablespoon chopped parsley
1 teaspoon fresh thyme leaves or 1/4 teaspoon dried thyme leaves
fresh thyme sprigs for garnish

1. Prepare rice as label directs, adding turmeric.
2. Meanwhile, rinse scallops with running cold water to remove any sand from crevices, Pat dry with paper towels. In 12-inch skillet over medium-high heat, in hot olive or salad oil, cook scallops with salt until lightly browned. With slotted spoon, remove scallops to bowl.
3. In drippings remaining in skillet, cook onion and carrots until browned and tender, about 10 minutes. Stir in stewed tomatoes, parsley, thyme, scallops with any liquid in bowl, and 1/4 cup water; over high heat, heat to boiling. Reduce heat to low; simmer 2 minutes or until scallops turn opaque throughout.
4. To serve, arrange yellow rice and scallop stew on warm large platter. Garnish with fresh thyme sprigs. Makes 6 servings.

Beef Patties with Shrimp Sauce

1/2 pound medium-size shrimp
1 medium-size carrot
1/2 medium-size bunch spinach
1 8-ounce package mushrooms
1 small onion
olive or salad oil
1 teaspoon salt
1/4 teaspoon pepper
1 pound lean ground beef
1/4 cup plain dried bread crumbs
1 large egg white
3/4 cup beef broth
1/2 cup milk
1-1/4 teaspoons cornstarch
1/2 cup frozen peas
1 cup regular long-grain rice, cooked as label directs

1. Shell and devein shrimp. Rinse shrimp with running cold water; pat dry with paper towels. Set aside.
2. Cut carrot into 1-1/2-inch-long matchstick-thin strips. Wash spinach well, removing tough stems; chop spinach leaves. Finely chop mushrooms and onion.
3. In nonstick 12-inch skillet over high heat, in 1 tablespoon hot olive or salad oil, cook mushrooms, onion, salt, and pepper, stirring occasionally, until vegetables are tender and golden. Stir in chopped spinach; cook, stirring, until spinach wilts.
4. In medium bowl, mix ground beef with vegetable mixture from skillet, bread crumbs, and egg white just until blended. Form ground-beef mixture into 12 balls; flatten each ball into a 2-1/2-inch round patty.
5. In same skillet over medium-high heat, in 1 tablespoon hot olive or salad oil, cook ground beef patties until golden brown on both sides and cooked through, turning once, about 5 minutes. Remove patties to plate.
6. In drippings remaining in skillet over medium-high heat, cook shrimp and carrot strips, stirring constantly, until shrimp turn opaque throughout.
7. In 2-cup measuring cup, with fork, mix beef broth, milk, and cornstarch until blended. Stir beef broth mixture and frozen peas into shrimp mixture in skillet. Over medium-high heat, cook, stirring to loosen brown bits from bottom of skillet, until mixture boils and thickens slightly; boil 1 minute.
8. To serve, arrange beef patties on 4 warm dinner plates. Spoon shrimp sauce over. Serve with rice. Makes 4 servings.

Cod with Crispy Potato Crust

Tomato Green Beans (right)
1 16-ounce bag carrots
salt
1 medium-size onion
olive or salad oil
2 large egg whites
1/8 teaspoon ground white pepper
cornstarch
2 large potatoes (1 pound)
4 cod or scrod fillets (each 6 ounces, about 1 inch thick)
1 tablespoon sugar
2 tablespoons balsamic or red wine vinegar
1/2 extra large vegetable bouillon cube or 1 envelope instant vegetable broth and seasoning

1. Prepare Tomato Green Beans; keep warm.
2. Peel carrots. Cut carrots lengthwise in half, then crosswise into 2-1/2-inch pieces. In 2-quart saucepan over high heat, heat carrots and enough water to cover to boiling. Reduce heat to low; cover and simmer 10 minutes or until tender-crisp; drain. Return carrots to saucepan; sprinkle with 1/4 teaspoon salt and keep warm.
3. Mince onion. In small saucepan over medium-high heat, in 1 tablespoon hot olive or salad oil, cook onion until tender and lightly browned. With slotted spoon, remove onion to medium bowl. Into onion in bowl, stir egg whites, pepper, and 1 tablespoon cornstarch.
4. Peel potatoes; shred onto clean kitchen towel. Wrap shredded potatoes in towel; squeeze out as much liquid as possible from potatoes. Stir potatoes into egg-white mixture.
5. Sprinkle cod fillets with 1 teaspoon salt. Place 2 tablespoons cornstarch on sheet of waxed paper. Coat cod fillets with cornstarch. Spread scant 1/4 cup potato mixture on top of each

cod fillet, pressing firmly; turn fillets over and spread each with another scant 1/4 cup potato mixture, pressing firmly onto fish.
6. In nonstick 12-inch skillet over medium heat, in 2 tablespoons hot olive or salad oil, cook 2 potato-coated cod fillets 10 to 15 minutes until potato coating is well browned on both sides and fish is cooked through, turning cod over halfway through cooking time. Remove cod fillets to plate; keep warm. In same skillet in 1 more tablespoon hot olive or salad oil, cook remaining cod fillets.
7. While cod is cooking, in 1-quart saucepan, stir sugar, balsamic vinegar, vegetable bouillon cube, 1 teaspoon cornstarch, and 3/4 cup water; over high heat, heat to boiling. Reduce heat to low; simmer 1 minute or until sauce thickens slightly. Serve cod with green beans and carrots; pass the balsamic-vinegar sauce to spoon over cod. Makes 4 servings.
TOMATO GREEN BEANS: Trim ends from 1 pound green beans. Chop 1 medium-size onion and 1 medium-size tomato. In 10-inch skillet over high heat, in 1/2 inch boiling water, heat green beans to boiling. Reduce heat to low; cover; cover and simmer 5 to 10 minutes until green beans are tender-crisp; drain. Wipe skillet dry. In same skillet over medium-high heat, in 1 tablespoon hot olive or salad oil, cook onion 3 minutes; add green beans and 1/2 teaspoon salt and cook, stirring frequently, until green beans are browned and tender. Stir in tomato; cook 2 to 3 minutes longer until any liquid from tomatoes evaporates.

Shrimp & Potato Salad Mold

8 medium-size red potatoes (2 pounds)
1-1/2 pounds large shrimp
1 10-ounce package frozen peas and carrots
3/4 cup mayonnaise
1/3 cup milk
3 tablespoons Dijon mustard
1-1/4 teaspoons salt
parsley leaves for garnish

1. In 1-quart saucepan over high heat, heat unpeeled potatoes and enough water to cover to boiling. Reduce heat to low; cover and simmer 25 to 30 minutes until potatoes are fork-tender; drain. Cool potatoes slightly; peel and cut into 1/2-inch cubes.
2. Meanwhile, shell and devein shrimp. In 3-quart saucepan over high heat, heat 3 inches water to boiling. Add shrimp; heat to boiling. Reduce heat to low; simmer 1 minute or until shrimp turn opaque throughout; drain.
3. Cook frozen peas and carrots as label directs; drain.
4. In large bowl, mix mayonnaise, milk, Dijon mustard, and salt. Gently toss potatoes and peas and carrots with remaining mayonnaise mixture.
5. Line shallow 1-1/2 quart casserole with plastic wrap; then line bottom and side of casserole with cooked shrimp in one layer, fitting them as close as possible. Cut any remaining shrimp into small pieces and stir into potato mixture in bowl. Spoon potato mixture into casserole, packing down with back of spoon. Cover and refrigerate at least 1 hour or until chilled.
6. To serve, invert mold onto platter; discard plastic wrap. Tuck parsley leaves among shrimp for garnish. Makes 6 servings.

Shrimp-Stuffed Sole in Lettuce Bundles

1/4 pound medium-size shrimp
8 large romaine-lettuce leaves
1 tablespoon margarine or butter
1 medium-size shallot or 1/2 small onion, finely chopped
salt
1 tablespoon all purpose flour
1/2 cup milk
1 cup regular long grain rice
4 sole or flounder fillets (about 6 ounces each)
1 tablespoon olive or salad oil
1 8-ounce package mushrooms, sliced
1/4 cup dry white wine
1 medium-size tomato, seeded and diced
parsley sprigs for garnish

1. Shell and devein shrimp, reserving shells. Rinse shrimp with running cold water; pat dry with paper towels; coarsely chop.
2. In 1-quart saucepan over high heat, heat shrimp shells and 3/4 cup water to boiling. Reduce heat to medium-low; cover and simmer 10 minutes. Drain shells, reserving shrimp broth.
3. Meanwhile, trim rib on each lettuce leaf very thin. In 10-inch skillet over high heat, heat 1/2 inch water to boiling. Reduce heat to medium; place lettuce leaves, one at a time, into simmering water just until wilted, about 30 seconds. Remove lettuce leaves to paper towels to drain.
4. In same saucepan over medium heat, in hot margarine or butter, cook shallot and 1/4 teaspoon salt until shallot is tender; stir in shrimp. Cook, stirring, until shrimp turn opaque. Add flour; cook, stirring constantly, 1 minute. Stir in milk; cook, stirring until mixture boils and thickens. Boil 1 minute. Set mixture aside.
5. In 2-quart saucepan, prepare rice as label directs. Keep warm.
6. Arrange 2 lettuce leaves on work surface, slightly overlapping; place 1 sole fillet lengthwise along center of leaves. Spoon one-fourth shrimp mixture onto center of fillet; fold both ends of fillet over to enclose shrimp mixture. Fold sides of lettuce leaves over sole, then fold ends over to fully enclose sole fillets. Repeat with remaining lettuce leaves, sole fillets, and shrimp mixture to make 4 lettuce bundles in all.
7. In same 10-inch skillet over medium-high heat, in hot olive or salad oil, cook mushrooms and 1/2 teaspoon salt until mushrooms are golden and tender. Add shrimp broth, white wine, and diced tomato.
8. Arrange lettuce bundles, seam sides down, in sauce in skillet; over high heat, heat to boiling. Reduce heat to low; cover and simmer 12 to 15 minutes until fish flakes easily when tested with a fork (cut a small slit through lettuce leaf in one bundle

to test fish).
9. To serve, place lettuce bundles on each of 4 warm dinner plates; spoon sauce over. Serve with rice. Garnish with parsley sprigs. Makes 4 servings.

Lamb & Sausage Kabobs with White-Bean Puree

2 small red potatoes (about 1/2 pound)
extra virgin olive oil or olive oil
1/2 small onion, minced
1 16- to 19-ounce can white kidney beans, drained
salt
coarsely ground black pepper
1/4 8-ounce loaf French bread, thinly sliced
1 small garlic clove, minced
1 tablespoon Dijon mustard
1 tablespoon red wine vinegar
2 fully cooked weisswurst or bratwurst
2 lamb loin chops, each 3/4 inch thick
1/2 14-ounce can artichoke hearts, drained
1/2 7-ounce jar roasted red peppers, drained

1. In small saucepan over high heat, heat potatoes and enough water to cover to boiling. Reduce heat to low; cover and simmer potatoes 15 minutes or until tender. Drain potatoes; set aside.
2. Meanwhile, prepare white-bean puree: In 2-quart saucepan over medium-high heat, in 1 tablespoon olive oil, cook onion until tender but not browned. Remove saucepan from heat; stir in kidney beans and 1/4 teaspoon salt.
3. In food processor with knife blade attached, or in blender at medium speed and with center part of blender cover removed, puree bean mixture until smooth. Spoon puree into bowl; sprinkle with black pepper. Cover and set aside until ready to serve.
4. Preheat broiler if manufacturer directs. Toast bread slices in broiler; set aside.
5. In cup, with fork, mix garlic, Dijon mustard, red wine vinegar, 1 teaspoon olive oil, 1/2 teaspoon salt, and 1/4 teaspoon black pepper. Cut each sausage crosswise in half.
6. On two 14-inch all-metal skewers, thread lamb, sausage, potatoes, artichoke hearts, and roasted red peppers. Brush all over with mustard mixture. Place skewers on rack in broiling pan. Place pan in broiler about 4 to 5 inches from source of heat. Broil kabobs 8 to 10 minutes until lamb is medium-rare and sausage and vegetables are lightly browned, turning kabobs once.
7. Serve kabobs with white-bean puree and toast. Let each person spread white-bean puree on toast to enjoy instead of using butter. Makes 2 servings.
TO GRILL OUTDOORS: About 1 hour before serving, prepare outdoor grill for barbecuing. Meanwhile, prepare white-bean puree and kabobs as above. Place skewers on grill over medium heat; cook 6 minutes, turning occasionally, until lamb is medium-rare and sausage and vegetables are lightly browned. Serve as above.

Stuffed Pork Loin with Apple Succotash

1 3-pound boneless pork loin roast
salt
1/2 cup seasoned dried bread crumbs
1 4-ounce jar whole pimentos
1 cup loosely packed basil leaves
1 teaspoon coarsely ground black pepper
2 teaspoons olive or salad oil
1 10-ounce package frozen baby lima beans
2 17-ounce cans whole-kernel corn
1 large Red Delicious apple
basil sprigs for garnish

1. Preheat oven to 325°F. Cut pork loin roast horizontally in half, almost but not all the way through; spread pork loin open. Sprinkle inside of pork roast with 1 teaspoon salt.
2. Sprinkle bottom half of pork roast with 1/4 cup bread crumbs. Drain pimentos; arrange over bread crumbs. Top pimentos with single layer of basil leaves. Sprinkle with remaining bread crumbs. Fold pork roast closed over filling. With string, tie pork roast at 1-inch intervals.
3. Chop remaining basil. In cup, mix basil, pepper, 2 teaspoons salt, and the olive or salad oil. With hands, rub basil mixture over pork roast. Place roast on rack in broiling pan. Insert meat thermometer into center of roast. Roast 1 hour 10 minutes or until thermometer reaches 160°F. Remove pork from oven; let rest 10 minutes for easier slicing.
4. When pork roast is almost done, prepare lima beans as label directs. Drain corn; dice apple. When limas are tender, drain. Stir in corn, apple, and 1/4 teaspoon salt; over medium heat, heat through.
To serve, discard string from pork roast. Cut pork into 1-inch-thick slices. Arrange pork slices and bean mixture on warm large platter; garnish with basil sprigs. Makes 10 servings.

Grilled Steaks with Pasta Salad

Eggplant & Basil Pasta Salad
4 boneless beef top loin steaks, each 3/4 inch thick (about 2 pounds)
2 teaspoons salt
1 teaspoon coarsely ground black pepper
1 teaspoon curry powder
2 tablespoons red wine vinegar
basil sprigs for garnish

1. Prepare Eggplant & Basil Pasta Salad. Cover and refrigerate

if not serving right away.
2. About 20 minutes before serving, preheat broiler if manufacturer directs.
3. Trim fat, if any, from steaks, in cup, combine salt, pepper, and curry powder. Into 13" by 9" glass baking dish, measure red wine vinegar. Place steaks in vinegar, turning to coat both sides. Sprinkle steaks with half of curry mixture; turn and sprinkle with remaining curry mixture.
4. Place steaks on rack in broiling pan. With oven rack at closest position to source of heat, broil steaks 4 minutes. Turn steaks and continue broiling 5 minutes for medium-rare or until of desired doneness.
5. Serve steaks with pasta salad. Garnish with basil sprigs. Makes 4 servings.
EGGPLANT & BASIL PASTA SALAD: Preheat broiler if manufacturer directs. Cut 1 medium-size eggplant (about 1-1/2 pounds) crosswise into 1/2-inch thick slices. Cut the slices into 1/2-inch-thick strips. Cut 1 medium-size onion into 1/2-inch wedges. In large bowl, toss eggplant strips and onion wedges with 1 tablespoon olive or salad oil, 1 teaspoon salt, and 1/4 teaspoon pepper.
Place vegetable mixture on rack in large broiling pan; set bowl aside. With oven rack at closest position to source of heat, broil vegetables 15 to 20 minutes until browned on all sides and tender, stirring once or twice. Meanwhile, prepare one-half 16-ounce package bow-tie pasta as label directs; drain. Cut 2 medium-size plum tomatoes into thin wedges; cut 1/2 cup loosely packed basil leaves into thin strips.
When eggplant mixture is done, return to bowl. Add pasta tomatoes, basil and 1 tablespoon lemon juice; toss.
TO GRILL OUTDOORS: About 1-1/4 hours before serving or early in day, prepare Eggplant & Basil Pasta Salad as above
About 45 minutes before serving, prepare outdoor grill for barbecuing. Prepare steaks as in step 3. Place steaks on grill over medium heat. Grill steaks about 10 minutes for medium-rare or until of desired doneness, turning steaks occasionally. Serve as above in step 5.

Beef with Peanut Sauce & Rice

1 medium-size lemon
1 small garlic clove, minced
1 tablespoon Dijon mustard
1/4 teaspoon crushed red pepper
soy sauce
sugar
1 1-1/2-pound beef flank steak
1/4 pound Chinese pea pods
1 bunch radishes
1/2 bunch green onions
1 tablespoon salad oil
salt
1 cup parboiled rice
1/4 cup creamy peanut butter
1 tablespoon white wine vinegar
about 2-1/2 dozen 10- to 12-inch bamboo skewers

1. Grate peel from lemon. Into 13" by 9" glass baking dish, squeeze 1 tablespoon lemon juice; stir in lemon peel, garlic, mustard, crushed red pepper, 1/4 cup soy sauce, and 1 tablespoon sugar.
2. Trim fat from flank steak, Holding knife almost parallel to work surface, cut flank steak crosswise into 1/4-inch-thick slices. Add steak slices to soy sauce mixture in baking dish; toss to coat. Set aside.
3. Cut Chinese pea pods crosswise into 1/8-inch-thick slices. Coarsely chop radishes and green onions. In 2 quart saucepan over medium-high heat, in hot salad oil, cook pea pods, radishes, green onions, and 1/4 teaspoon salt until they are tender-crisp, about 3 minutes. With slotted spoon, remove pea pod mixture to bowl.
4. In same saucepan, prepare rice as label directs but use only 1/2 teaspoon salt and do not add margarine or butter. When rice is done, stir in pea pod mixture; keep warm.
5. Meanwhile, prepare peanut sauce: In small saucepan over medium-high heat, heat peanut butter, white wine vinegar, 3/4 cup water, 2 tablespoons soy sauce, and 1 teaspoon sugar to boiling, stirring constantly. Reduce heat to low; simmer, stirring until smooth. Keep warm.
6. Preheat broiler if manufacturer directs. Thread 1 slice flank steak lengthwise on each bamboo skewer; arrange skewers in 2 rows on rack in broiling pan with blunt ends at sides of pan; shield blunt ends with strips of foil to prevent burning. Place pan in broiler at closest position to source of heat; broil 7 minutes, turning skewers once halfway through cooking time.
7. To serve, discard foil. Arrange skewers on warm large platter with vegetable rice. Serve peanut sauce in bowl to spoon over steak. Makes 6 servings.

Veal Chops with Lentil & Black Bean Ragoût

3 tablespoons soy sauce
2 tablespoons minced peeled ginger root
4 veal rib chops, each 3/4 inch thick and about 8 ounces
1 large carrot
a small onion
olive or salad oil
1/2 cup dried lentils
1 envelope instant vegetable broth and seasoning
1 large bunch radishes
2 tablespoons distilled white vinegar
1/4 teaspoon sugar
1/4 teaspoon salt
1/4 teaspoon coarsely ground black pepper
1 15- to 16-ounce can black beans
1 small head Boston lettuce

1. In 13" by 9" metal baking pan, mix soy sauce and ginger root. Trim fat from veal chops. Add veal chops to soy sauce mixture, turning to coat. Set aside.
2. Dice carrot and onion. In 2-quart saucepan over medium heat, in 1 tablespoon hot olive or salad oil, cook carrot and onion until tender. Stir in lentils, instant vegetable broth, and 1-1/2 cups water; over high heat, heat to boiling. Reduce heat to low; cover and simmer, stirring occasionally, until lentils are tender and most of liquid is absorbed, about 25 to 30 minutes.
3. Meanwhile, slice radishes paper-thin. In small bowl, mix vinegar, sugar, salt, coarsely ground black pepper, and 1 tablespoon olive or salad oil. Stir in radishes.
4. Preheat broiler if manufacturer directs. Place pan with veal chops in broiler at closest position to source of heat; broil chops 8 to 10 minutes for medium-rare or until of desired doneness, turning chops once.
5. To serve, rinse and drain black beans. Stir black beans into lentil mixture; heat through. On 4 dinner plates, arrange Boston lettuce leaves; top with sliced radishes with their dressing. Spoon lentil mixture onto plates; top with veal chops. Spoon any drippings from pan over veal chops. Makes 4 servings.

Barbecued Beef Sandwiches with Carrot Salad

Carrot Salad
1 1-pound beef flank steak or round steak
2 medium-size red peppers
1 large onion
olive or salad oil
1 tablespoon chili powder
1 8-ounce can tomato sauce
2 tablespoons Worcestershire
2 tablespoons cider vinegar
1 tablespoon brown sugar
4 hamburger buns

1. Prepare Carrot Salad; cover and refrigerate until ready to serve.
2. With knife held in slanting position, almost parallel to the cutting surface, cut steak crosswise into paper-thin slices. Cut red peppers into 1/2-inch-thick strips; cut onion into 1/4-inch-thick slices.
3. In 12-inch skillet over high heat, in 1 tablespoon hot olive or salad oil, cook steak, stirring quickly and frequently, until steak loses its pink color throughout, about 2 to 3 minutes. Remove steak to bowl.
4. In same skillet over high heat, in 1 tablespoon hot olive or salad oil, cook peppers and onion until tender-crisp and lightly browned. Stir in chili powder; cook 1 minute.
5. Add tomato sauce, Worcestershire, vinegar, brown sugar, and 3/4 cup water; over high heat, heat to boiling. Reduce heat to low; cover and simmer 15 minutes, until vegetables are very tender. Return steak to skillet; heat through.
6. Serve barbecued beef mixture in hamburger buns. Serve with Carrot Salad. Makes 4 servings.

CARROT SALAD: Cut 1-1/2 16-ounce bags carrots and 1/2 European cucumber, peeled, into matchstick-thin strips. In large bowl, mix carrots and cucumber with 2 tablespoons olive or salad oil, 2 tablespoons cider vinegar, 1 tablespoon chopped fresh dill or 1 teaspoon dried dill weed, 1 tablespoon Dijon mustard, 1 teaspoon sugar, 3/4 teaspoon salt, and 1/2 teaspoon ground ginger.

Crab & Avocado Salad

4 large eggs
4 medium-size red potatoes (about 1 pound)
1 16-ounce container lump crabmeat
1 large celery stalk
2 tablespoons olive or salad oil
2 tablespoons cider vinegar
1 tablespoon minced peeled ginger root or 1 teaspoon ground ginger
1 tablespoon chopped parsley
1 teaspoon sugar
2 teaspoons soy sauce
1/2 teaspoon salt
1/4 teaspoon crushed red pepper
2 large avocados
radish roses for garnish

1. In small saucepan, hard-cook eggs.
2. Meanwhile, cut each unpeeled potato into 1/8-inch-thick slices. In 10-inch skillet over high heat, heat potatoes and enough water to cover to boiling. Reduce heat to low; cover and simmer 5 minutes or until potatoes are fork-tender; drain. Set aside.
3. While eggs and potatoes are cooking, pick over crabmeat to remove any pieces of shell or cartilage. Finely chop celery.
4. Remove shells from hard-cooked eggs and cut each egg in half; remove yolks (reserve yolks for use in sandwich fillings or salad another day). Cut egg whites into bite-size pieces. In medium bowl, gently mix egg whites, crabmeat, and celery; set aside.
5. In cup, mix olive or salad oil, cider vinegar, ginger, chopped parsley, sugar, soy sauce, salt, and red pepper until dressing is blended.
6. Remove seed and peel from each avocado. Cut avocados lengthwise into thin slices.
7. To serve, arrange potatoes, avocado slices, and crab salad on 6 dinner plates; drizzle with dressing. Garnish with radish roses. Makes 6 servings.

Baking Powder Biscuits

2 cups all-purpose flour
1 tablespoon baking powder
1 teaspoon salt
1/4 cup shortening
3/4 cup milk

1. Preheat oven to 450°F.
2. In large bowl, mix flour, baking powder, and salt. With pastry blender or two knives used scissors-fashion, cut in shortening until mixture resembles coarse crumbs. Stir in milk; quickly mix just until mixture forms soft dough that leaves side of bowl.
3. Turn dough onto lightly floured surface; knead 6 to 8 strokes to mix thoroughly. With floured hands, pat dough into a 8" by 6" rectangle. Cut lengthwise into 3 strips; cut each strip crosswise into 4 pieces.
4. With pancake turner, place biscuits on ungreased cookie sheet, 1 inch apart. Bake 15 minutes or until golden. Makes 12 biscuits.

Dinner Rolls

1/3 cup sugar
1-1/2 teaspoons salt
2 packages active dry yeast
About 5 cups all-purpose flour
1 cup milk
4 tablespoons margarine or butter (1/2 stick)
2 large eggs
Egg Glaze (optional)

1. In large bowl, combine sugar, salt, yeast, and 1-1/2 cups flour. In 1-quart saucepan, heat milk and margarine or butter until very warm (120° to 130°F.). Margarine or butter does not need to melt.
2. With mixer at low speed, gradually beat liquid into dry ingredients just until blended. Increase speed to medium; beat 2 minutes, occasionally scraping bowl with rubber spatula. Beat in eggs and 1/2 cup flour to make a thick batter; continue beating 2 minutes, scraping bowl often. With wooden spoon, stir in 2-1/4 cups flour to make a soft dough.
3. Turn dough onto lightly floured surface and knead until smooth and elastic, about 10 minutes, working in more flour (about 3/4 cup) while kneading. Shape dough into ball; place in greased large bowl, turning dough to grease top. Cover; let rise in warm place (80° to 85°F.) until doubled, about 1 hour.
4. Punch down dough. Turn dough onto lightly floured surface; cover and let rest 15 minutes.
5. Grease large cookie sheets or muffin-pan cups, depending on type of rolls desired. Shape dough into rolls as directed at right. Cover; let rise in warm place until doubled, about 30 minutes. Brush rolls with Egg Glaze if desired.
6. Preheat oven to 400°F. Bake rolls 10 to 15 minutes until golden. Remove from cookie sheets or pans. Serve rolls warm or cool on wire racks to serve later. Makes 24 rolls.

Egg Glaze: In small bowl, with fork, beat 1 large egg with 1 tablespoon milk until blended.
For Dinner Buns: Grease cookie sheets. Cut dough into 24 pieces. Shape each piece into 2-inch ball; with floured hands, roll each ball 4 inches long, tapering ends slightly. Place rolls, 2 inches apart, on cookie sheets; with knife, make a slash lengthwise through center of each roll. Let rise; brush with Egg Glaze if desired.
For Cloverleafs: Grease twenty-four 2-1/2- or 3-inch muffin-pan cups. Cut half of dough into 36 equal pieces: shape each piece into ball. Place 3 balls in each muffin-pan cup. Repeat. Let rise; brush with Egg Glaze if desired.
For Crescent Rolls: Roll half of dough into 9-inch round. With sharp knife, cut round into 12 wedges; starting at side opposite point, roll up each wedge toward point. Place rolls on cookie sheet; curve ends toward each other. Repeat, Let rise; brush with Egg Glaze if desired.

Herb & Garlic Bread

1 16-inch long Italian bread
1 garlic clove
1/4 cup olive oil
1 tablespoon chopped parsley
1/2 teaspoon salt
1/2 teaspoon dried oregano leaves
1/4 teaspoon coarsely ground black pepper

1. Prepare outdoor grill for barbecuing.
2. Meanwhile, cut Italian bread crosswise into 1-inch-thick slices, but do not cut all the way through.
3. Mince garlic, then, using flat side of French knife or mortar and pestle, crush garlic to form paste. In cup, mix garlic paste, olive oil, parsley, salt, oregano, and pepper.
4. With pastry brush, brush garlic mixture lightly on cut sides of bread slices, brushing any remaining garlic mixture on top of loaf.
5. Wrap loaf in double thickness of heavy-duty foil. Place loaf on grill over medium heat. Cook about 20 minutes, turning loaf occasionally, until bread is heated through and crisp. Makes 8 accompaniment servings.
TO BAKE IN OVEN: About 40 minutes before serving, preheat oven to 425°F. Prepare Italian bread and garlic mixture

as above. Wrap loaf loosely in foil, leaving top seam of foil slightly open. Bake loaf 20 minutes until bread is heated through and crisp.

Old-Fashioned Brownies

Here are Grandma's rich, fudgy brownies, luscious as ever but lower in fat. How did we do it? With cocoa powder instead of chocolate, no-cholesterol egg substitute, and light corn-oil spread.

3/4 cup light corn-oil spread (1-1/2 sticks)
2 cups sugar
1 cup all-purpose flour
1 cup unsweetened cocoa
3/4 cup thawed frozen no-cholesterol egg substitute
2 teaspoons vanilla extract 1/2 teaspoon salt
1/2 cup walnuts, coarsely broken

1. Preheat oven to 350°F. Line an 8" x 8" metal baking pan with foil.
2. In heavy 3-quart saucepan over low heat, melt corn-oil spread, stirring frequently. Remove from heat. With spoon, stir in sugar, flour, cocoa, egg substitute, vanilla, and salt. Spread batter evenly in pan. Sprinkle nuts on top.
3. Bake 45 to 50 minutes until toothpick inserted in center comes out clean. Cool brownies in pan on wire rack.
4. When cold, cut brownies crosswise into 3 strips, then cut each strip into 3 pieces. Store tightly covered. Makes 9 brownies.

Oatmeal Cookies

These chewy, jumbo cookies make a hearty snack that is full of wholesome ingredients like high-fiber whole oats, crunchy wheat germ, and honey.

2/3 cup packed light brown sugar
2/3 cup honey
6 tablespoons light corn-oil spread (3/4 stick)
1/4 cup thawed frozen no-cholesterol egg substitute
2 teaspoons vanilla extract
1 cup all-purpose flour
1 cup whole-wheat flour
1/2 cup wheat germ
1-1/2 teaspoons baking soda
3/4 teaspoon salt
2-1/2 cups quick-cooking or old-fashioned oats (uncooked)

1. Preheat oven to 375°F. In large bowl, with mixer at medium speed, beat brown sugar, honey, corn-oil spread, egg substitute, and vanilla extract until smooth. With mixer at low speed, beat in all-purpose flour, whole-wheat flour, wheat germ, baking soda, and salt until blended. With spoon, stir in oats.
2. Spray 2 large cookie sheets with nonstick cooking spray. Spoon dough by level 1/3-cup measures onto cookie sheets, about 3 inches apart. With floured hands, roll dough into balls.
3. Bake cookies 12 to 15 minutes until golden; remove to wire racks to cool. Store cookies in tightly covered container. Makes about 14 jumbo-size cookies.

Apple Crumble

For a change of pace, instead of baking your usual apple pie, whip up this delicious crumble in half the time.

1 cup low-fat granola cereal
2 tablespoons salad oil
brown sugar
all-purpose flour
8 medium-size Golden Delicious apples (about 3 pounds)
1/2 12-ounce package pitted prunes (1 cup)
2/3 cup apple cider or apple juice
1 tablespoon lemon juice

1. Prepare crumble topping: In small bowl, with fork, stir together granola, salad oil, 1/4 cup packed brown sugar, and 1/4 cup flour until blended; set aside.
2. Preheat oven to 400°F. Peel and core apples; cut into 1/4-inch slices. Coarsely chop prunes. In large bowl, toss apples, prunes, apple cider, lemon juice, 1/3 cup packed brown sugar, and 1/4 cup flour until the apple slices are evenly coated.
3. Spoon apple mixture into shallow 3-quart glass or ceramic baking dish; sprinkle granola mixture over apple mixture. Cover with foil and bake 40 minutes. Remove foil; bake 20 minutes longer or until apples are tender and crumble topping is browned. Cool slightly on wire rack to serve warm. Or, cool completely to serve later. Makes 12 servings.

Chocolate Cake

4 large egg whites
1-1/2 cups sugar
1 16-ounce container plain low-fat yogurt
1-1/2 cups all-purpose flour
1 cup unsweetened cocoa
1/2 cup light corn-oil spread (1 stick)
1-1/2 teaspoons baking soda
1/2 teaspoon baking powder

1/2 teaspoon salt
1 teaspoon vanilla extract
1 tablespoon seedless red raspberry preserves
1 cup thawed frozen light whipped topping
1 1-ounce square semisweet chocolate, grated

1. Grease 9" by 3" springform pan. Line bottom with waxed paper; grease paper. Wrap outside of pan with heavy-duty foil. Preheat oven to 350°F.
2. In small bowl, with mixer at high speed, beat egg whites until soft peaks form; gradually sprinkle in 1/2 cup sugar, 2 tablespoons at a time, beating until whites stand in stiff peaks; set aside.
3. In large bowl, with mixer at low speed, beat yogurt, next 7 ingredients, and remaining 1 cup sugar until blended. Increase speed to high; beat 5 minutes or until light and fluffy, occasionally scraping the bowl with rubber spatula. Gently fold egg-white mixture into batter.
4. Gently pour batter into springform pan. Set springform pan in large roasting pan. Fill roasting pan with boiling water to come halfway up side of pan. Bake 1 hour or until toothpick inserted in center of cake comes out almost clean. Top of cake may crack. Cool cake in pan on wire rack 15 minutes. Remove side of springform pan; cool cake completely on rack.
5. Invert cooled cake onto cake stand or plate; remove pan bottom. In cup, stir raspberry preserves until smooth; brush over top of cake. With metal spatula, spread 1/2 cup whipped topping on side of cake. (Overhandling whipped topping will cause it to deflate, so work as quickly and gently as possible.) Gently spoon remaining whipped topping into decorating bag with medium star tube. Working quickly, pipe whipped topping around top edge of cake in decorative pattern. Pipe any remaining whipped topping in center of cake. Press grated chocolate onto side of cake. Refrigerate cake, if not serving right away. Makes 12 servings.

Banana Cream Pie

1 cup all-purpose flour
salt
1/4 cup plus 2 tablespoons shortening
3 cups low-fat milk (1%)
1/2 cup cornstarch
1/2 cup sugar
1 8-ounce container liquid whole eggs (reduced cholesterol)
2 tablespoons light corn-oil spread (1/4 stick)
2 teaspoons vanilla extract
2 tablespoons lemon juice
4 medium-size bananas
1/2 8-ounce container thawed frozen light whipped topping
2 tablespoons apricot-flavor all-fruit spread, melted

1. In bowl, stir flour and 1/2 teaspoon salt. With pastry blender or two knives used scissor-fashion, cut in shortening until mixture resembles coarse crumbs.
2. Sprinkle 2 to 3 tablespoons cold water, 1 tablespoon at a time, into flour mixture, mixing lightly with a fork after each addition, until pastry is just moist enough to hold together. Shape pastry into a ball.
3. On lightly floured surface, with floured rolling pin, roll pastry into a round about 2 inches larger all around than 9-inch pie plate. Line pie plate with pastry. Trim pastry edge, leaving 1-inch overhang; fold overhang under to make stand-up edge; flute.
4. Preheat oven to 425°F. With fork, prick pie shell in many places to prevent puffing during baking. Bake 15 minutes or until pie shell is golden. Cool on wire rack.
5. Meanwhile, in 3-quart saucepan, mix milk, cornstarch, sugar, liquid whole eggs, and 1/4 teaspoon salt until well mixed. Cook over medium-low heat, stirring constantly, until mixture boils and thickens; boil 3 to 5 minutes. Remove saucepan from heat; stir in light corn-oil spread, vanilla extract, and 1 tablespoon lemon juice.
6. Pour custard filling into cooled pie shell; cover with plastic wrap and refrigerate about 4 hours or until custard is set.
7. To serve, slice 2 bananas into thin slices; sprinkle bananas with lemon juice. Arrange sliced bananas over custard filling in pie shell. Top with light whipped topping. Slice remaining 2 bananas into thin slices; arrange over whipped topping. Lightly brush bananas with melted apricot all-fruit spread. Refrigerate if not serving right away. Makes 12 servings.

Carrot Cake

About 3 to 4 large carrots
1 medium-size zucchini
3 cups all-purpose flour
1/2 cup sugar
2 teaspoons ground cinnamon
2 teaspoons baking soda
1 teaspoon baking powder
1 teaspoon salt
1/2 teaspoon ground ginger
1 20-ounce can crushed pineapple in unsweetened pineapple juice
1 cup packed light brown sugar
1 8-ounce container frozen no-cholesterol egg substitute, thawed
2/3 cup salad oil
1 tablespoon vanilla extract
1 cup dark seedless raisins
3/4 cup confectioners' sugar (optional)

1. Shred carrots to make 2 cups; shred zucchini to make 1 cup; set both aside.

2. Preheat oven to 350°F. Grease 10-inch Bundt pan. In large bowl, mix flour, sugar, cinnamon, baking soda, baking powder, salt, and ginger.
3. Drain pineapple well, reserving juice. In medium bowl, with wire whisk or fork, mix drained pineapple, brown sugar, egg substitute, salad oil, and vanilla extract until smooth. Stir pineapple mixture, shredded carrots and zucchini, and raisins into flour mixture just until flour is moistened.
4. Pour batter into Bundt pan. Bake 55 minutes or until toothpick inserted in center of cake comes out clean. Cool cake in pan on wire rack 10 minutes; remove cake from pan and cool completely on rack.
5. When cake is cool, if you like, make glaze: In small bowl, mix confectioners' sugar with 2-1/2 teaspoons reserved pineapple juice to make a spreadable glaze; save remaining pineapple juice for use another day. With spoon, drizzle glaze over top of cake, allowing some glaze to drip down side. Makes 16 servings.

Sour Cream Pound Cake

1 cup sugar
2 large egg whites
1 large egg
1 cup light sour cream
1/2 cup salad oil
1/3 cup low-fat milk (1%)
1 teaspoon vanilla extract
1 teaspoon lemon extract
2 cups all-purpose flour
1/2 cup cornmeal
1 1/2-ounce envelope natural butter-flavor granules
2 teaspoons baking powder
1/8 teaspoon salt
2 tablespoons light corn syrup
1 teaspoon lemon juice

1. Preheat oven to 325°F. Grease and flour 9″ x 5″ loaf pan.
2. In large bowl, with mixer at medium-high speed, beat sugar, egg whites, and whole egg until frothy. Beat in light sour cream, salad oil, low-fat milk, vanilla extract, and lemon extract until blended. Reduce speed to low; add flour, cornmeal, butter-flavor granules, baking powder, and salt; beat until well mixed, constantly scraping bowl with rubber spatula. Increase speed to high; beat 1 minute, occasionally scraping bowl.
3. Spoon batter into pan. Bake 1 hour and 10 minutes or until toothpick inserted in center of cake comes out clean. Cool cake in pan on wire rack 10 minutes; remove from pan; cool completely on rack.
4. Prepare glaze: In cup, mix corn syrup and lemon juice. Brush over top of cooled cake. Makes 16 servings.

Classic Cheesecake

2/3 cup graham-cracker crumbs
2 tablespoons light corn-oil spread (about 1/4 stick)
1/4 teaspoon ground cinnamon
3 8-ounce packages light cream cheese (Neufchâtel), softened
1 16-ounce container light sour cream
1-1/2 cups sugar
1/2 cup thawed frozen no-cholesterol egg substitute
2 teaspoons vanilla extract
1/2 teaspoon salt
1/2 teaspoon ground ginger
3 medium-size kiwifruit
1 pint strawberries
2 tablespoons orange marmalade-flavor all-fruit spread, melted

1. Preheat oven to 350°F. In 9" by 2-1/2" springform pan, with hand, mix graham-cracker crumbs, corn-oil spread, and cinnamon until well blended. Press mixture onto bottom of pan; set aside.
2. In large bowl, with mixer at medium speed, beat cream cheese until smooth. With mixer at low speed, slowly beat in light sour cream, sugar, egg substitute, vanilla extract, salt, and ginger until well blended. Pour cream-cheese mixture over graham-cracker crust.
3. Bake cheesecake 45 to 50 minutes. (Center of cheesecake may appear loose.) Cool cheesecake in pan on wire rack. Refrigerate cheesecake at least 6 hours.
4. To serve, carefully remove side of springform pan. Peel and slice kiwifruit. Slice each strawberry lengthwise in half; arrange fruit on top of cheesecake. Brush fruit with melted orange marmalade. Makes 12 servings.

Chocolate Soufflé

Heavenly

1 package chocolate-flavor pudding and pie filling for 4 servings
2 cups low-fat milk (1%)
1/4 teaspoon almond extract
sugar
6 large egg whites
1/2 teaspoon cream of tartar
confectioners' sugar

1. Prepare pudding and pie filling as label directs, but use low-fat milk. Stir in almond extract. Cover with plastic wrap; cool.
2. Spray eight 8-ounce soufflé dishes (or ramekins with straight sides) with nonstick cooking spray. Sprinkle inside of each

soufflé dish with 1 teaspoon sugar.
3. In large bowl, with mixer at high speed, beat egg whites and cream of tartar until soft peaks form; gradually sprinkle in 1/4 cup sugar, 2 tablespoons at a time, beating well after each addition, until sugar completely dissolves and whites stand in stiff glossy peaks. With rubber spatula, gently fold in pudding mixture.
4. Preheat oven to 350°F. Spoon soufflé mixture into soufflé dishes. With wet knife or small metal spatula, smooth top of each soufflé.
5. Carefully place filled soufflé dishes in large baking pan (17" by 11-1/2"); place pan on oven rack. Pour enough boiling water into pan to come halfway up sides of soufflé dishes. Bake soufflés 25 minutes or until puffy.
6. When the soufflés are done, lightly sprinkle with confectioners' sugar. Serve immediately. Makes 8 servings.

Berry-Berry Shortcake

1 10-ounce package frozen, quick-thaw raspberries in light syrup
1 teaspoon cornstarch
1-1/2 cups all-purpose flour
1 teaspoon baking powder
1/2 teaspoon baking soda
1/4 teaspoon salt
sugar
4 tablespoons light corn-oil spread (1/2 stick)
1/2 cup buttermilk*
1 pint vanilla-flavor light frozen dairy dessert (98% fat free)
1 cup strawberries

1. Thaw raspberries as label directs. Drain syrup from raspberries into 1-quart saucepan; stir in cornstarch. Reserve raspberries. Over medium heat, heat raspberry syrup mixture until it boils and thickens slightly, stirring occasionally; boil 1 minute. Refrigerate syrup until slightly cooled, about 30 minutes.
Meanwhile, prepare shortcakes: Preheat oven to 425°F. In medium bowl, mix flour, baking powder, baking soda, salt, and 2 tablespoons sugar. With pastry blender or two knives used scissor-fashion, cut in corn oil spread until mixture resembles coarse crumbs. With fork, stir in buttermilk; quickly mix must until mixture forms soft dough; knead in bowl 4 to 5 times to mix thoroughly.
3. Spray small cookie sheet with nonstick cooking spray. On floured work surface, with floured hands, press dough into 6" by 5" rectangle. With knife, cut rectangle lengthwise in half; cut each half crosswise into thirds to make 6 shortcakes. With pancake turner, place shortcakes on cookie sheet. Brush tops with 2 teaspoons water; sprinkle with 1 teaspoon sugar. Bake 12 to 15 minutes until golden brown.
4. To serve, remove light frozen dairy dessert from freezer to soften slightly. Hull strawberries and cut each lengthwise in half. Stir strawberry halves and reserved raspberries into raspberry syrup. With serrated knife, cut each shortcake horizontally in half.
5. Place bottom halves of shortcakes on 6 dessert plates; top with frozen dairy dessert, then berry sauce. Replace top halves of shortcakes. Makes 6 servings.
*Or, place 1-1/2 teaspoons lemon juice in 1-cup measuring cup and stir in enough milk to equal 1/2 cup. Let stand 5 minutes to thicken.

Marble Cake

1-3/4 cups sugar
1 cup light corn-oil spread (2 sticks)
3 cups cake flour (not self-rising)
1 cup low-fat milk (1%)
1 8-ounce container liquid whole eggs (reduced cholesterol)
1 tablespoon baking powder
2 teaspoons vanilla extract
1/2 teaspoon salt
1/2 cup unsweetened cocoa
confectioners' sugar

1. Preheat oven to 350°F. Spray 9-inch fluted tube pan (about 3 quarts) with nonstick cooking spray.
2. In large bowl, with mixer at low speed, beat sugar and light corn-oil spread just until blended. Increase speed to high; beat until light and fluffy, about 5 minutes. Reduce speed to low; add cake flour, milk, liquid whole eggs, baking powder, vanilla extract, and salt; beat until well mixed, constantly scraping bowl with rubber spatula. Increase speed to high; beat 2 minutes, occasionally scraping bowl.
3. Remove 3 cups batter to medium bowl. To batter in large bowl, add cocoa (if cocoa is lumpy, press through sieve into batter) and 2 tablespoons water. With mixer at low speed, beat until blended.
4. Spoon cocoa batter into tube pan. Top with vanilla batter. Bake 60 to 65 minutes until toothpick inserted in center of cake comes out clean. Cool cake in pan on wire rack 10 minutes. Remove from pan; cool completely on rack. Sprinkle top of cake lightly with confectioners' sugar to serve. Makes 16 servings.

Blueberry-Cornmeal Muffins

3/4 cup all-purpose flour
1/3 cup cornmeal
1 teaspoon grated lemon peel
1/2 teaspoon baking powder
1/4 teaspoon baking soda
1/4 teaspoon salt

sugar
3 tablespoons light corn-oil spread
1/2 8-ounce container plain nonfat yogurt (about 1/2 cup)
1/4 cup thawed frozen no-cholesterol egg substitute
1 cup fresh or frozen blueberries

1. Preheat oven to 350°F. Grease 24 mini muffin-pan cups.*
2. In large bowl, mix flour, corn-meal, lemon peel, baking powder, baking soda, salt, and 1/3 cup sugar. With pastry blender or two knives used scissor-fashion, cut in corn-oil spread to resemble coarse crumbs.
3. With fork, stir in yogurt and egg substitute just until flour is moistened. Stir in blueberries. Spoon batter into muffin-pan cups; sprinkle tops with 2 teaspoons sugar.
4. Bake muffins 15 to 20 minutes until tops are golden. Remove from muffin-pan cups to wire racks. Serve muffins warm, or cool on wire racks to serve later. Makes 24 mini muffins.
*Or, for larger muffins, use twelve 2-1/2″ by 1-1/4″ muffin-pan cups; bake about 20 to 25 minutes.

Country Wheat Bread

1-1/2 teaspoons salt
2 packages quick-rise yeast
3 cups whole-wheat flour
1/2 cup honey
1/4 cup salad oil
1 large egg
about 4 cups all-purpose flour

1. In large bowl, combine salt, yeast, and whole-wheat flour. In small saucepan over low heat, heat 1-2/3 cups water until very warm (125° to 130°F.)
2. With mixer at low speed, gradually beat water into dry ingredients just until blended. Increase speed to medium; beat 2 minutes, occasionally scraping bowl with rubber spatula.
3. Beat in honey, salad oil, egg, and 1 cup all-purpose flour to make a thick batter; continue beating 2 minutes, scraping bowl often. With wooden spoon, stir in 2-1/2 cups all-purpose flour to make a soft dough.
4. Turn dough onto floured surface and knead until smooth and elastic, about 10 minutes, working in more flour (about 1/2 cup) while kneading. Cover dough and let rest 10 minutes for easier shaping.
5. On large cookie sheet, shape dough into 10" by 5" oval loaf. Cover loaf loosely with plastic wrap; let rise in warm place (80° to 85°F.) until doubled, about 30 minutes.
6. Preheat oven to 375°F. Sprinkle loaf lightly with all-purpose flour. Bake 30 minutes or until loaf sounds hollow when lightly tapped with fingers. Remove loaf from cookie sheet; cool on wire rack. Makes 1 loaf or 12 servings.

Watermelon Ice

1 5-pound wedge watermelon
3/4 cup light corn syrup
2 tablespoons lemon juice
1/4 teaspoon salt
1/4 teaspoon almond extract (optional)
2 envelopes unflavored gelatin
watermelon for garnish

1. Remove and discard peel and seeds from watermelon. Cut enough watermelon into bite-sized chunks to equal 8 cups. In blender at low speed or in food processor with knife blade attached, blend one-third of watermelon chunks with corn syrup, lemon juice, salt, and almond extract until smooth. Pour pureed watermelon mixture into 13" by 9" glass baking dish until blended.
3. Cover dish with foil or plastic wrap and freeze, stirring occasionally, until partially frozen, about 2 hours.
4. Spoon watermelon mixture into chilled food-processor bowl with knife blade attached; blend until fluffy but still frozen, stopping processor occasionally to scrape down sides. (Or, spoon mixture into chilled large bowl; with mixer at medium speed, beat until fluffy.) Return mixture to baking dish; cover and freeze until firm, about 2 hours.
5. To serve, let ice stand at room temperature 15 minutes to soften slightly for easier scooping. Meanwhile, cut watermelon for garnish into tiny triangles. Garnish each serving with a triangle of watermelon. Makes about 8 cups or 16 servings.

Easy Cheesecake Recipe

Mix 2 (8-ounce) packages cream cheese, softened.
1/2 cup sugar
1/2 teaspoon vanilla (at medium speed until well blended)
Blend in 2 eggs
Stir in 1/2 cup mini semi-sweet chocolate chips
Pour batter into a Graham Cracker pie crust (6 ounces). Sprinkle with 1/4 cup mini semi-sweet chocolate chips. No springform pan needed.
Bake at 350°F. for 40 minutes, or until center is almost set. Cool. For best results refrigerate for 3 hours. 8 servings.

Peanut-Butter Muffins

1-3/4 cups all-purpose flour
1/2 cup sugar
1 tablespoon baking powder

1/2 teaspoon salt
3/4 cup milk
1/2 cup peanut butter
1/3 cup salad oil
1 large egg
1/2 cup raisins

1. Preheat oven to 400°F. Grease twelve 2-1/2" by 1-1/4" muffin-pan cups.
2. In large bowl, with fork, mix flour, sugar, baking powder, and salt. In medium bowl, with wire whisk, beat milk, peanut butter, salad oil, and egg until smooth. Stir peanut-butter mixture into flour mixture just until moistened (do not overmix, or muffins will be tough; batter should be lumpy). Stir in raisins.
3. Spoon batter into prepared muffin-pan cups. Bake muffins 20 minutes or until well risen and golden and toothpick inserted in center of a muffin comes out clean and dry. Makes 12 muffins.

Easy Freezer Sorbet

2 medium-sized cantaloupes (each about 2-1/2 pounds)
1 medium-sized honey dew melon (about 5 pounds)
2 envelopes unflavored gelatin
1 cup light corn syrup
1/4 cup lemon juice
1/2 teaspoon salt
mint sprigs for garnish

1. Remove and discard peel and seeds from cantaloupes; cut into large chunks. In blender at medium speed or in food processor with knife blade attached, blend cantaloupe chunks until smooth. Pour into 9" by 9" metal baking pan; set aside.
2. Repeat with honeydew; pour into another 9" by 9" baking pan.
3. In 1-quart saucepan, evenly sprinkle gelatin over 1/2 cup water; let stand 1 minute to soften. Cook over medium heat until gelatin completely dissolves, stirring frequently.
4. With wire whisk or fork, stir half of gelatin mixture, 1/2 cup corn syrup, 2 tablespoons lemon juice, and 1/4 teaspoon salt into each pan of pureed melon. Cover baking pan with foil or plastic wrap. Freeze until partially frozen, about 3 hours, stirring occasionally to prevent ice crystals from forming.
5. Spoon cantaloupe mixture into chilled food processor bowl with knife blade attached; blend until fluffy but still frozen. (Or, spoon mixture into chilled large bowl; with mixer at medium speed, beat until fluffy.) Return mixture to baking pan; cover and freeze until firm, about 2 hours.
6. Repeat with honey dew mixture.
7. To serve, let sorbets stand at room temperature 10 to 15 minutes to soften slightly for easier scooping. Scoop some of each sorbet into each dessert dish. Garnish with mint sprigs. Makes about 8 cups or 16 half-cup servings.

Hippity Hop Bunny Cake

2-1/4 cups flake Coconut
Red food coloring
2 (9-inch) round cake layers
8 ounces whipped topping
Assorted candies for garnish

Tint 1/4 cup coconut pink with red food coloring.
Cut 1 layer: arrange other layer as shown.
Frost with whipped topping, sprinkle with remaining coconut.
Decorate with assorted candies.
Makes 12 to 16 servings.
Store cake in refrigerator.

Chocolate Chunk Oatmeal Cookies

1-1/2 cups packed light brown sugar
1-1/4 cups salad oil
2 teaspoons vanilla extract
2 large eggs
2-1/2 cups all-purpose flour
2 teaspoons baking soda
1 teaspoon salt
3-1/2 cups quick-cooking oats (uncooked)
1 8-ounce package semisweet chocolate squares (8 1-ounce squares), coarsely chopped
1 4-ounce can walnuts (about 1 cup), chopped

1. Preheat oven to 375°F. In large bowl, with mixer at medium speed, beat brown sugar, salad oil, vanilla, and eggs until smooth. At low speed, beat in flour, soda, and salt until blended. With spoon, stir in oats, chocolate, and walnuts.
2. Shape level 1/4 cups of dough into balls and place on greased large cookie sheet, about 3 inches apart, flattening balls to about 3-inch rounds. Bake 10 to 12 minutes until cookies are golden; remove to wire racks to cool. Repeat with remaining dough. Store cookies tightly covered. Makes about 2 dozen.

Summer Fruit Basket with Orange Cream

2 large oranges
1 8-ounce container whipped cream cheese
1/3 cup confectioners' sugar
1/2 cup milk
1-1/2 teaspoons pure orange extract
1 oblong watermelon, about 20 pounds, chilled
1 medium-sized pineapple, chilled
1 pint strawberries
4 large kiwifruit

2 medium-sized nectarines
1/2 pound red seedless grapes
garnish: Herb sprigs, nontoxic flowers, green florist wire, clear thread or nylon fishing line

1. Prepare orange cream: Grate peel from oranges. Wrap half of orange peel with plastic wrap and refrigerate to use for garnishing orange cream. Reserve oranges for fruit mixture. In small bowl, with wire whisk or fork, beat cream cheese, confectioners' sugar, milk, and orange extract until smooth. Stir in remaining half of the grated orange peel. Cover and refrigerate until ready to serve.
2. Prepare watermelon basket: With sharp knife, cut lengthwise slice about 2 inches from top of watermelon. Scoop out pulp from both sections of watermelon and cut into bite-sized chunks. Place 10 cups watermelon chunks in large bowl; refrigerate remaining watermelon to eat another day. Cut a thin slice of rind from bottom of watermelon shell, if needed so it will stand level. Cut scalloped edge around rim of watermelon shell.
3. Peel and cut reserved oranges into sections; place in bowl with watermelon. Cut off crown and stem end from pineapple. Cut off rind and core, then cut pineapple into bite-sized chunks; place in bowl with watermelon. Hull strawberries and cut each in half if they are large; peel kiwifruit and cut into bite-sized chunks. Cut nectarines into wedges. Place fruit in same bowl; add grapes and toss to mix. Fill watermelon shell with fruit; cover with plastic wrap and refrigerate until ready to serve.
4. Meanwhile if you like, make a handle to garnish watermelon shell by using fresh herb sprigs and nontoxic flowers from your garden or local nursery. Use green florist wire, cut into 18-inch lengths for handle. Wrap herb sprigs completely around wire and secure with clear thread or nylon fishing line; tuck in flowers. Wrap with damp paper towels and plastic wrap and refrigerate until ready to serve fruit.
5. To serve, insert ends of herb handle into watermelon basket. Garnish orange cream with reserved grated orange peel. Pass the orange cream to be spooned over servings of fruit. Makes 16 servings.

Pistachio & Sherbet Cake

1 quart raspberry sherbet
1 quart rainbow sherbet
2/3 cup shelled pistachios (about 1 6-ounce jar pistachios in shell)
1 cup heavy or whipping cream
1 package pistachio-flavor instant pudding and pie filling for 4 servings. 1-1/2 cups milk

1. Place both containers of sherbet in refrigerator about 20 minutes to soften slightly. Chill 9″ by 3″ springform pan. Carefully spoon softened raspberry sherbet over pistachios, pressing with back of spoon to remove any air pockets. With medium-sized ice-cream scoop, scoop rainbow sherbet and place on top of raspberry layer, arranging scoops side by side in one layer. Place in freezer while preparing pudding.
3. In small bowl, with mixer at medium speed, beat heavy or whipping cream until stiff peaks form.
4. In medium bowl, with wire whisk or fork, prepare pudding mix as label directs, but use only 1-1/2 cups milk. Fold whipped cream into pudding. Spoon pudding mixture over balls of rainbow sherbet; spread to fill in any empty spaces between balls. Sprinkle top of cake with remaining chopped pistachios. Cover pan with plastic wrap; freeze 6 hours or overnight.
5. To serve, remove side of pan; let sherbet cake stand at room temperature about 15 minutes for easier slicing. Makes 16 servings.

Index

Apple
Butter, 152
Cake, 59
Cake, Upside Down, 105
Cider, Hot, 27
Crumble, 309
Dumplings, 157
Fritters, 69, 158
Gelatin Dessert, Baked, 177
Pie, 130, 131
Pie, Mother's Old-Fashioned, 250
Pudding, 157, 158
Roll, 58
Slaw, with Cabbage, 286
Snow, 177
Stuffing, 215, 233
Trifle, 167
Applesauce, 76, 210
Gelatin Dessert, 174
Red, 144
Apricot
Filling, with Pineapple, 152
Gems, 158
Icing, 74
& Pork Roast, 210
Puree, 75
Sauce, 122
Tartlets, with Pineapple, 152
Upside-Down Cake, 106
Artichoke
and Chicken Breasts with Mushrooms, 263
and Cracked-Wheat Salad, 270
Pasta with Olive & Tomato, 282
& Tomato Frittata, 276
Asparagus, 226
canned, 247
Quiche, 266
Ragout with Wild Rice, 277
Risotto, 272
Salad, with Pasta & Garbanzos, 289
Sauce, 226
Avocado
Salad, 184
Salad, with Crab, 307
Salad, with Tomato, 284
Soup, 190

Banana
Cake, 78
Cream Pie, 131, 132, 310
Custard Pie, 133
Dainty, with Pineapple, 170
Filling, 123
Fritters, 70
Puffs, 158
Sauce, 177
Whip, 124
Barbecue
Beans, Quick, 292
Beef Sandwiches with Carrot Salad, 307
Beef Short Ribs with "Baked" Potatoes, 295
Chicken with Creole Sauce, 293
Pork Ribs with Sweet Peaches, 293
Steak & Shrimp, 299
Barley
-Stuffed Peppers, 274
Water, 242
BEANS *See also* Lentil
Baked, 228
Baked, Boston, 236
Barbecued, Quick, 292
canned, 247
Curried, with Broccoli, 274
& Goat-Cheese Salad, 268
Green, & Mozzarella Salad, 280
Kidney, with Bacon, 237
Lentil & Black Bean Ragoût, 306
Lima, 230
Red, 228
Salad, Four-, 298
BEEF
Burgers, Tex-Mex Stuffed, 291
Chipped, Creamed, 206
Fajitas, with Tomato & Avocado Salad, 284
Filet, 251
Filet Mignon with Mushroom & Onion Gravy, 282
Filet Mignon with Mushroom Sauce and Crisp Potato Pancakes, 251
Loaf, 206, 211
Loaf with Braised Onions, 254
London Broil with Roasted Garlic, 302
Patties with Shrimp Sauce, 303

Pot Roast Gravy, 206
Pot Roast with Potatoes, 209
Pot Roast, Savory, 206
Pot Roast, Yankee, 253
Prime Rib Au Jus, 204
Ribs with Grilled Pineapple, Spicy, 299
Roast, 205
Roast, with Two Sauces, 301
Sandwiches, Barbecued, with Carrot Salad, 307
Scraped, 244
Short Ribs, BBQ, with "Baked" Potatoes, 295
Steak and Potatoes, 254
Steak, Black Pepper with Herbed Potatoes, 252, 262
Steak, Flank or Round, Stuffed & Rolled, 206
Steak, Grilled, with Pasta Salad, 305
Steak, Hamburger, 205
Steak, Pan-Broiled, 205
Steak & Potato Kebabs, Zesty, 297
Steak & Shrimp Barbecue, 299
Steak, Swiss, 206
Stew, 253
Surf 'N' Turf Grill, 255, 298
Tea, 244
Teriyaki and Rice, 251
Tortillas, 252

Beets, Pickled, 229

Berry
canned, 247
Frappe, 176
Pie, 131
Pudding, 159

BEVERAGES
Albumen, 243
Chocolate, 23-25
Coffee, 16-18
Dairy, 25-26
Hot Toddy, 15
Punches & Fruit Drinks, 26-28
Tea, 18-23

BISCUITS 52, 55, 252
about, 55
Baking Powder, 43, 56, 308
Baking Powder (Crescents), 45
Bran, 55
Butterscotch, 48
Cheese, 48, 55
Cheese, 20-Minute, 56
Emergency or Drop, 55
Old Fashioned Sausage, 47
Orange Blossom, 3
Orange Tea, 47
Soda, 55
Sour Milk or Buttermilk, 48
Tea, 48, 56
Whole Wheat or Health, 55

Bok Choy, Stir-Fried, 289

BREADS *See also* Rolls and Buns
about, 32-34
Baking Powder, 39
Brown, Boston, 39, 40
Brown, Steamed, 37
with Compressed Yeast, 35
Corn, 38, 39,
Corn, Plantation, 39
Corn and Rice Pone, 39
Corn, Spider, 39
Corn Spoon, Soft, 41
Date, 38
Gingerbread, 41
Gingerbread, Coconut, 42
Gingerbread, Hasty, 42
Gingerbread, Soft, 41
Graham, 37, 38
Health, 49
Herb & Garlic, 308
Nut, 37, 40, 41
Nut and Raisin, 40
Orange, 37
Peanut Butter, 38
Prune or Date, 38
Quick, 40
Quick, about, 44
Sponge, 34
Wheat, Country, 313
White (with Dry Yeast), 35
White (Quick, with Yeast), 34, 35
White (Quick, with Potato), 34
White (Sponge, with Compressed Yeast), 36
Whole Wheat "Health", 36
Whole Wheat (Quick, with Yeast), 36

Broccoli
Curried, with Beans, 274
Lasagna, 266

Brownies *See* Cookies

Brussels Sprouts, 230

Butterhorns, 44

Buttermilk
Biscuits, 48
Sweet Dough, Quick, 48

C

Cabbage
Boiled New, 230
& Potato Packets, 296
Scalloped, 226, 229
Stuffed, 226, 279

CAKE ICINGS
See also Fillings; Puffs; Sauce, Dessert
Apricot, 7-Minute, 74
Boiled, 82, 85, 99, 123
Boiled, Brown Sugar, 121
Broiled, 91
Brownie, 84
Butter, Ornamental, 88
Caramel, 9, 78, 85, 125
Caramel Nut, 75
Chocolate, 79, 87, 88, 125
Chocolate Butter, 73
Chocolate, Creamy, 85
Chocolate, Hungarian, 79
Chocolate, "My Favorite" Uncooked, 125
Chocolate Nut, 77
Chocolate Peppermint, 75

Chocolate Seven-Minute, 90
Coconut, 97, 112
Coconut Seven-Minute, 88
Comfort, 78
Cream Cheese, 84
Creole 7-Minute, 91
Ice Cream, 101
Lady Baltimore, 96
Lemon Ginger, 74
Maple, 126
Meringue, 86, 125, 139
Meringue, Pumpkin Mince, 145
Meringue, Unbaked Honey, 145
Mocha, 96, 126
Mocha, Fluffy, 126
Morocco, 89
Orange, 37, 99, 117, 126
Peppermint Glaze, 83
Pineapple, 83
Powdered Sugar, Uncooked, 111
Raisin Butterscotch, 95
Special, 77
Sweet, 50
Uncooked, Fluffy, 126
White, 87
CAKES, **CUP CAKES**, AND **SMALL CAKES** *See also* Rolls and Buns
about, 72
Angel, Caramel, 75
Angel, Chocolate, 82
Angel, Dark, 73
Angel Food, 73
Angel Food, Mock, 73
Angel Food, Simple, 74
Angel Fruit, 74
Angel, Peppermint and Chocolate, 75
Angel's Ginger, 74
Apple, 59
Apple Sauce, 76
Aristocratic, 3
Bachelor Bait, 76
Banana, 78
Birthday, 77
Bride's, 76
Brown-Eyed Susan, 77
Brown Stone Front, 79
Brownie, 84
Caramel, 79
Caramel or Burnt Sugar, 78
Carrot, 310
Cheese, 90
Cheese, Classic, 311
Cheese, Philly 3-Step, 313
Chocolate, 80, 309
Chocolate Cream, 80
Chocolate, Delicious, 86
Chocolate Layer, 87
Chocolate Layer, Old-Fashioned, 84
Chocolate Moderne, 81
Chocolate Nut, 81
Chocolate Potato, 81
Chocolate Prune, 83
Chocolate Ribbon, 80
Chocolate, Spanish, 103
Chocolate Tier, 81
Chocolateer, White Top, 82
Cinnamon Breakfast, 59
Cococake, Spiced, 85
Coconut Layer, Kate Smith's Favorite, 88
Coconut Marshmallow Layer, 97
Coconut, Southern, 83
Coffee, about, 55
Coffee, 60, 63
Coffee, Almond, 59
Coffee Cake Topping, 53
Coffee, Five-Minute, 53
Coffee, Individual, 61
Coffee, Nut Frosted, 60
Coffee, Quick, 59
Coffee, Top Mixture, 60
Country Pork, 88
Cream Layer, 87
Cup Cakes, Orange, 117
Cup Cakes, Spice, 100
Dark, 10
Date, 90
Delicate, 90
Delicious Nut, 8
Devil's Food, 88, 89
Devil's Food, Coconut, 90
Devil's Food, Deep South, 84
Devil's Food, New, 89
Drop, individual, 114
Easily-Made, 90, 91
Emergency, 91
Fancy Tea Rings, 46
Fig, 93
Fig, Ribbon, 92
Form (with Yeast), 92
Foundation, 92
Four-Egg Yolk, 83
Fruit Gingerbread with Whipped Cream, 94
Fruit, 93
Fruit, Black and White, 86
Fruit, Christmas, 93
Fruit, Economy, 93
Fruit, Star-of-England, 92
Frying Pan, 94
Gentlemen's Favorite, 94
Gingerbread, 94
Glacé, House of Orange, 86
Harvest (2 Egg Yolks), 94
Hippity Hop Bunny, 314
Jelly Roll, 95
Lady Baltimore, 95
Layer, 95
Layer, "Sunny," 104
Lemon Jelly, 96
Mahogany, 8, 96
Marble, 312
Marble, Old-Fashioned, 98
Milk Drop, Sweet, 119

Mint Chocolate Log, 82
Mocha, 97
Mocha Layer, 96
Molasses Cakes, Little, 95
Nougat Dream, 97
Nut, 9, 10
One Egg, 98
Orange, 98
Orange Cream (4 egg whites), 99
Orange Ice-Box, 98
Orange Layer, 99
Patty Cakes, 117
Peach, 60
Peppermint Candy, 101
Pistachio & Sherbet, 315
Potato, 102
Pound, 102
Pound, Sour Cream, 311
Pound, White, 107
Prune, 100, 102
Prune Confection, 100
Prune Cream, 101
Prune, Cup or Loaf, 100
Prune (Layer or Loaf), 101
Raisin and Currant, 102
Raisin Tea Ring, 61
Rhubarb, 72
Sally Lunn, 60
Short, 104, 135
Short, Berry-Berry, 312
Sour Cream Drop Cakes, 118
Sour Cream Sweet, 85
Spice Cakes, 118
Spice, East India, 91
Spice Nut, 97
Spice, Quick, 102
Sponge, 103
Sponge Drops, 119
Sponge, Inexpensive & Variations, 104
Sponge, Orange, 103
Sponge, Special, 73
Sunshine, 104
Upside-Down, Apple, 105
Upside-Down, Apricot Cobbler-Cake, 106
Upside-Down, Cherry Topsy-Turvies, 104
Upside-Down, Ginger-Apple, 105
Upside-Down, Peach Toffee, 106
Upside-Down, Prune, 100
Upside-Down, Prune Polka Dot, 105
Upside-Down, Spiced Humpty-Dumpty, 106
Variety, 107
Velvet Lunch, 107
White, Featherweight, 91
White Layer, 107
White Loaf or Tutti Fruiti, 107
CAKES, GRIDDLE
about, 65
Araby Pancakes, 67
Basic, 65
Buckwheat, 66
Corn, 65
Corn Meal, 66
Crumb, 67
with Eggs, 66
French Pancakes, 66
Hot, 66
Mexican Pancakes, 67
Rice, 66
Sour Milk, 65, 67
Sweet Milk, 65
Whole Wheat Hot Cakes, 66
CANNING *See also* individual names of fruits, vegetables
about, 246
Can-Cooked Method, 246, 248
jams, 247
Open-Kettle Method, 246
use of sugar, 246
Caper Sauce, 232
Carrot
Cake, 310
Creamed, 229
Pie (Mock Pumpkin), 134
Pudding (Mock Plum), 159
Salad, 307
CASSEROLES
Rice and Meat, 215
Tuna-Potato Chip, 193
Catfish
Blackened, with Coleslaw, 300
Fillets, Grilled, 291
Pan-Sautéed Cajun, 261
Cauliflower, 230
Baked, 229
Celery
Creole Style, 227
Soup, Cream of, 190
Stuffed, 183
CEREALS
about, 30
fireless cooking, 14
Hominy, Browned, 30
Steamed Rice, 30
Charlotte
Chocolate, 177
Custard with Sponge Cake, 169
Russe, 169, 174
CHEESE
Baked with Egg, 217
Baked with Rice, 220
Biscuits, 48, 55, 56
Cake, 90
Cake, Classic, 311
Cake, Philly 3-Step, 313
Cottage, 220
Diamonds, 50
Fondue, 220
Pastry, Cream, 148
Pastry, with Fruit, 154
Rarebit, 220
Rings, 134
Rolls, 45
Salad Combinations, 181

Salad, with Nuts, 181
Sandwiches, 238
Sandwiches, Sesame, 286
Sauce, 67, 202, 232, 236
Scallop Shells or Ramekins, 236
Soufflé, 170, 220, 237
Soufflé, with Corn, 272
& Spinach Tart, 276
Straws, 155, 236
Stew, with Potatoes, 283
Cherry
canned, 247
Cobbler, 159
Gelatin, 173
Gelatin, with Almonds, 177
Pie, 131
Pie, Mock, 137
Pudding, 159
Puffs, 160
Salad, 174
Surprises, 171
Upside-Down Topsy-Turvies, 104
CHICKEN
a la King, 212
a la Maryland, 212
Alabama, 1
Barbecued, with Creole Sauce, 293
Breasts, Italiano, 296
Breasts, Mushroom-Stuffed, 291
Breasts with Mushrooms & Artichokes, 263
and Broccoli, 214
Chili Broiled, 263
Creamed, 243
Creamy, with Vegetables and Savory Biscuits, 252
Crispy, with Asparagus Sauce, 214
Croquettes, 222
Fricassee, 212, 213
Fried, about, 212
Fried, 213
"Fried," 263
Fried, Caribbean, 214
Mousse, 2
Patty, 2
Patty, Supreme, 152
Pie, 212, 214
Pot Pie, 264
Roast, with Stuffing 212
Salad, 9, 180, 183, 264
Salad, with Potato & Arugula, 284
Salad, Stir-Fried, 287
Salad, Summertime, 263
Soup, 190
Wings, Sweet & Sour, 294
Chili
Con Carne, 228
with Tofu, 271
with Turkey, 265
Chinese "Pepper Steak", 267
CHOCOLATE
beverages, 23-25
Blanc Mange, 168
Cake, with Potato, 81
Cakes *See* Cakes
Charlotte, 177
Cinnamon Rolls, 51
Colombian, 24
cookies *See* Cookies
fillings *See* Fillings
French, 24
hot, 24
Icing *See* Cake Icing
Malted Milk, 25
Mexican, 24
Milk, Hot, 25
Pastry, 140
Pie, 135, 136
Pudding *See* Puddings
Sauce *See* Sauce, Dessert
Soufflé, 311
Chow Chow, 249
Clam
Bisque, 200
Chowder, 198
Croquettes, 200
Devils, 199
Fritters, 69, 198
Italienne, 200
Michele, 201
Molds, 199
Novelty, 199
Omelet, 198
Patties, 198
Pie, 135
Poulet, 199
Sauté on Toast, 199
Savory, 199
Scalloped, 200
Scramble, 201
Soufflé, 200
Cocoa, 23
Syrup, 23
Coconut
Cake *See* Cakes
Cakes, French, 115
Cookies, with Chocolate, 111
Couscous, 257
Filling, 97, 112
Gingerbread, 42
Gelatin, with Orange, 174
Pie *See* Pies
Soufflé, 169
Cod
Chilled with Peppers, 259
with Crispy Potato Crust, 303
Codfish Balls, 195
Scalloped Flaked, 195
COFFEE
about, 16
Breakfast, 17
Café au Lait, 17
Camp, Old, 16
Demitasse, 17

Dinner, Special, 18
Iced, 17
International, 17
Irish, 17
Mocha Dessert, 17
Spiced, 17
Cole Slaw, 181, 230
COOKIES, 111
Anise Seed, 109
Brownies, 112
Brownies, Old-Fashioned, 309
Caramel or Butterscotch, 112
Children's, 111
Chocolate Chunk Oatmeal, 314
Chocolate and Coconut Dream, 111
Chocolate Cream, 111
Chocolate Turtle, 119
Christmas, Almond, 109
Christmas, Rich, 118
Coconut Cakes, French, 115
Currant, 111
Date, 113
Date, Australian, 109
Date Bars, 113
Drop Cakes, 114
Fig Bars, 115
Fruit Nut Bars, 114
Ginger Drops, 115
Ginger Snaps, 115
Ginger Snaps or Molasses Cookies, Less Expensive, 115
Macaroons, 112
Molasses, Inexpensive, 116
Nut, 116
Nut, California, 109
Nut Sticks, 116
Oatmeal, 116, 117, 309
Oatmeal Fruit Filled, 117
Oatmeal Macaroons, 3
Our Hermits, 116
Peanut, 117
Peanut Butter, 118
Peanut Wafers, 9
Sour Cream, 4
Sugar, 119
Vanilla Wafers, 119
Washboard, 108
Corn
a la Southern, 227
Boiled, 230
Bread, 38, 39
Bread, Spoon, 41
Cakes, 65
Cakes, Corn Meal, 66
canned, 247
& Cheddar Soufflé, 272
Chowder, 188
Fritters, 69
Fritters, with Cucumber & Radish Salad, 277
Gems, Green, 62
On the Cob, Maple, 292
Pone, with Rice, 39
Pudding, 237
Soufflé, 229
Crab
Boiled, 197
Salad, with Avocado, 307
Cranberry
drinks *See* Punches
Gelatin, 176
Pie, 136
Sauce, 233
CROQUETTES
Chicken, 222
Clam, 200
Meat, 216
Nut and Potato, 221
Rice, 221
Salmon, 201, 221
Sauce for, White, 201
Crullers, Sour Cream, 2
Crumble, Apple, 309
Crumpets, Swedish, 58
Cucumber
& Radish Salad, 277
& Tomato Salad with Avocado Dressing, 293
Currant
Buns, 46
Cake, with Raisins, 102
Cookies, 111
Jelly Sauce, 233
Spiced, 248
Tea Cakes, 62
Curried Beans & Broccoli, 274
Custard *See* Puddings

DAIRY DRINKS
Chocolate Milk, Hot, 25
Eggnog, 26
Eggnog, Spoon-Up, 25
Flavored Milks, 25
Milk Shakes, 25
Mocha Cooler, 25
Sodas, Ice-Cream, 25
Date
Bread, 38
Cake, 90
Cookies, 109, 113
Filling, 113
Muffins, 57, 62
Pudding, 162
Tea Cakes, 114
Doughnuts, 53, 114
Drops, 53
Sour Milk, 114
Dressing *See* Stuffing
DUMPLINGS, 157
Apple, 157
Peach, 164
Potato Platter, 270
for Stew, 207, 209

Eggnog, 26, 243

Holiday, 27
Sparkling Orange, 27
Eggplant
Fried, 227
& Mozzarella Sandwiches, 288
Pasta Salad with Basil, 305
& Potato Moussaka, 273
Stuffed, 227
EGGS
Baked, 216
Baked with Cheese, 217
Boiled, 216
Coddled, 243
Curried (for Fifty), 2
Deviled, 180
Florentine, 217
Omelet, Creamy, 217
Omelet, French, 217
Omelet, Pepper & Tomato with Roast Potatoes, 275
Omelet, Plain, 217
Omelet, Puffy, 217
Omelet, Spanish Potato, 278
Omelet, Vegetable, 283
Omelets, Fancy, 217
Poached, 216
Poached in Cream, 217
Sandwiches, 238
Sauce, 232
Scalloped with Ham, 217
Scrambled, 216, 243
Stuffed, 218
with Tomatoes, 237

Falafel with Spinach Salad, 275
Farmer's Stew with Couscous, 279
FATS
Deep Fat Frying, 13
Lowfat Seasoning, 12
Shortening, about, 33
Fettuccine Alfredo, 265
Fig
Bars, 115
Blanc Mange, 162
Cake, 92, 93
Envelopes, 63
Pudding, 162, 174
FILLINGS
Apricot-Pineapple, 152
Banana, 123
Banana Whip, 124
Butterscotch, 125
Chicken, Supreme, 153
Chocolate, 87, 112
Chocolate Almond, 154
Chocolate Jelly, 125
Coconut, 97, 112
Cream, 87, 113, 122
Cream Puff, Economical, 111
Custard, 110
Custard for Queen Patties, 154
Date, 113
Lady Baltimore, 96
Lemon, 125
Lemon Butter, 153
Lemon Pie, 3
Macaroon, 153
Marseilles, 153
Marshmallow, 126
Marshmallow Divinity, 153
Mocha, 96
Nougat Cake, 97
Orange, 86, 99, 126
Orange Cream, 126
Peppermint Whipped Cream, 83
Strawberry, 126
Tart, Banbury, 152
Tart, Orange, 154
Tart, Supreme, 155
Whipped Cream, 110
Finnan-Haddie
Broiled, 194
Creamed, 195
Fireless Cookery, 13
FISH *See also* Clam, Crab, Oysters, Salmon, Shrimp
about, 194
Baked, 197
Baked, With Stuffing, 194
Broiled, 196
Catfish, Blackened, with Coleslaw, 300
Catfish Fillets, Grilled, 291
Catfish, Pan-Sautéed Cajun, 261
Chowder, 188, 197
Cod, Chilled with Peppers, 259
Cod, with Crispy Potato Crust, 303
Cod, Scalloped Flaked, 195
Cod & Vegetable Stew, 285
Codfish Balls, 195
Finnan-Haddie, Broiled, 194
Finnan-Haddie, Creamed, 195
Fried, 197
Fry, 261
Lobster & Clam Bake, 297
Lobsters or Crabs, Boiled, 197
Mackerel, Broiled Salt, 195
Mussels & Pasta Marinara, 300
Planked, 197
Salad, 184
Sandwiches, 238
Sauce, 196
Scrod with Lemon-Garlic Bread Crumbs, 258
Seafood Fettucini, 288
Shell Fish a la Newburg, 198
Shrimp-Stuffed Sole in Lettuce Bundles, 304
Smelts, Fried, 195
Snapper, Red, Baked with Olives, 299
Sole, Fillet, Rolled, with Rice, 260
Stew, Captain's, with Rice, 302
Stew, Hearty Seafood, 261
Surf 'N' Turf Grill, 255, 298
Swordfish with Warm Cabbage Slaw, 259
Tilefish with Browned-Butter Sauce, 260
Tuna, Fresh, with Caper-Dill Sauce, 301

Tuna Fish a la King, 201
Frittata
Artichoke & Tomato, 276
Egg-White with Sautéed Vegetables, 282
FRITTERS
Apple, 69, 158
Banana, 70
Banana, Quick, 70
Batter, 197
Clam, 69, 198
Corn, 69
Corn, with Cucumber & Radish Salad, 277
Corn with Sweet Milk, 69
Plain Batter, 68
Frosting *See* Cake Icing
FRUIT
Bread Pudding, 162
Cake, 93
Cake, Angel, 74
Cake, Black and White, 86
Cake, Christmas, 93
Cake, Economy, 93
Cake, Gingerbread with Whipped Cream, 94
Cake, Star-of-England, 92
Cocktail, 173
Cup, 175
drinks *See* Punches
Nut Bars, 114
Pastry, 154
Salad, 8, 181
Sandwiches, 238
Sauce, 124, 167
Summer Fruit Basket with Orange Cream, 314
Turnover, 131
Whip, 169
Frying, Deep Fat, 13
Fudge, 120

GELATIN DESSERTS
about, 173
Apple De Luxe, Baked, 177
Apple Sauce Molded, 174
Apple Snow, 177
Berry Frappe, 176
Cardinal Salad, 175
Charlotte Russe, 174
Cherry, 173
Cherry Almond, 177
Chocolate Charlotte, 177
Coconut Orange, 174
Coffee, 175
Cottage Cheese Salad, 175
Cranberry Mold, 176
Cream Fig Pudding, 174
Fruit Cocktail, 173
Fruit Cup, 175
with Fruit Juices, 176
Health Salad, 174
Horseradish Relish, 175
Imperial Salad, 174
Lemon, 174
Macaroni Salad, 174
Macaroon Dessert, 177
Macedoine, 176
Mint, 175
Neapolitan, 174
Nut Frappe, 176
Orange, 175
Oranges, Quartered in Gelatin, 177
Paradise Pudding, 175
Peach Whip, 176
Peaches, Spiced Jellied, 176
Pineapple Bavarian Cream, 174, 178
Plum Pudding, 176
Prune Cream, 178
Prune Dessert, New, 176
Raspberry, 175
Raspberry Bavarian Cream, 175
Salmon Salad, 176
Snow Pudding, 177
Spanish Salad, 175
Star-Spangled Snacks, 178
Strawberry, 173
Strawberry Loaf, 173
Gems *See also* Rolls and Buns
about, 55
Gingerbreads, 41-42
Goose, Roast, 214
Gravy, 233
Brown, 233
Giblet, 213
Pot Roast, 206
Gumbo, Vegetable, 271

HAM
Baked, 210
Fried, Plain, 210
Hormel 'n Cheddar Success, 257
Sandwiches, Deviled, 239
Helpful Hints, 12-14
Hominy, Browned, 30
Hummus, Open-Faced Sandwiches, 267

Ice Ring for Punch Bowl, 27
Ice-Cream Sodas, 25
Ices *See* Sorbet

Jam, Raspberry, 247
Jellies, 248
Juice
Egg and Orange, 244
Pineapple 244
Tomato, Mulled, 28

Kidney Stew, 208
Kohlrabi, 230

LAMB
Chops, Marinated, with Grilled Tomatoes, 295
Chops, Pan Broiled, 209
Chops, Rosemary with Lemon-Garlic Sauce, 285
Kabobs, with Sausage and White-Bean Puree, 305

Kabobs, with Warm Lentil Salad, 287
Leg, Butterflied with Tabbouleh Salad, 294
Leg with Toasted Coconut Couscous, 257
Mutton Leg, Braised, 209
Roast Leg with Scallions and Potatoes, 208
Roast, 209
Shoulder, Roast Stuffed with Potatoes, 209
Stew, 209
Lasagna, 219
with Broccoli, 266
Primavera, 221
Lemon
Bread Crumbs, 258
Bread Pudding, 163
Filling *See* Fillings
Gelatin, 174
Icing, with Ginger, 74
Jelly Cake, 96
Pie *See* Pies
Potato Salad, 267
Sauce, 124, 166
Tarts, 153
Lemonade, 27
Lentil
& Black Bean Ragoût, 306
Salad, 287
Limeade, 27
Linguine with Shrimp & Fresh Tomato Sauce, 258
Liver
and Bacon, 208
Braised, 208
Lobster
a la Newburg, 7
Boiled, 197
Salad, 184
LUNCHES
Box, about, 237
Cold, 238
Luncheon or Sandwich Rolls, 49
Quick Luncheon Rolls, 52
for School Children, 239

Macaroni, 220
and Cheese, 221, 236, 266
and Oysters, 7
Salad, 174
Salad, Summer, 292
Macaroons *See* Cookies
Mackerel, Broiled Salt, 195
MEAT *See also* Beef, Ham, Pork, Poultry, Veal, etc.
about, 205
Baked, with Rice, 216
Casserole, with Rice, 215
Croquettes, 216
fireless cooking, 14
Hash, 215
Left-over, 215
Loaf, 206
Meat Substitutes, 216
Minced, on Toast, 215
Roasting Time Table, 205
Sandwiches, 238
Shepherd's Pie or Scalloped Meat, 215
Stew, 216
Turnovers, 45
Meatballs & Spaghetti, 255
Meatless Dishes, 265
Meringue *See* Pies; Cake Icings
Pudding, with Pineapple, 164
Milk *See also* Dairy Drinks
Flavored, 25
heating, 13
Peptonized, 243
Shakes, 25
Mocha
Cake, 96, 97
Coffee, 17
Cooler, 25
Icing, 96, 126
Sauce, 123
Mountain View Special, 2
Moussaka, Eggplant & Potato, 273
MUFFINS, 52, 61 *See also* Rolls and Buns
about, 55
Blueberry, 61
Blueberry-Cornmeal, 312
Bran, 56
Caramel, 51
Cereal, 61
Cornmeal, 53, 56
Crumb, 61
Date, 57, 62
Gluten, 244
Huckleberry, 61
Peanut Butter, 313
Potato Flour, 2
Prune Filled, 57
Rice, 57, 62
Sweet Milk, 56
Mushroom
Chicken Breasts with Artichokes, 263
Chicken Breasts, Stuffed, 291
Creamed, 227
Dream, 1
& Rice Mold, 266
Sauce, 251
Soup, Cream of, 191

Noodles
Egg, with Spinach, 286
Oriental, 280
Spicy Thai, 278

Oatmeal
Cookies, 116, 117
Gruel, 242
Macaroons, 3
Water, 242
Okra, Rice and Tomatoes, 227
Olive Sandwiches with Cheese, 239
Omelet *See* Eggs
Onion

Boiled in White Sauce, 227
Soup, 189
Soup, French, 270
Orange
Bread, 37
Biscuits, 3, 47
Cake, 86, 98, 99
Cake, Sponge, 103
Cookies, 116, 117
Cup Cakes, 117
Eggnog Punch, 27
Fillings, 86, 99, 126
Gelatin, 175, 177
Gelatin with Coconut, 174
Icing, 37, 99, 117, 126
Juice, 244
Pie, 142
Pie, Meringue, 142
Pudding, Cream, 170
Pudding, Individual, 163
Rolls, 49
Sauce, 124, 164, 166
Swizzle, 27
Tarts, 154
Oriental Noodles, 280
Orzo, Tomato & Feta Cheese, 285
Outdoor/Indoor Cooking, 290
Oven Temperatures, 14
Oyster Plant, 231
OYSTERS
Creamed, 197
Dressing, 213
Fried, 196, 198
and Macaroni, 7
Puree, 1
Salad, 7
Scalloped, 196
Stew, 189, 196

Pad Thai, 278
Paella, Quick, 289
Pancakes *See* Cakes, Griddle
Parsnips
Browned, 231
Glazed, 223
Pasta *See also* Macaroni, Ravioli
Artichoke, Olive & Tomato, 282
Orzo, Tomato & Feta Cheese, 285
Salad, with Asparagus & Garbanzos, 289
Salad, with Eggplant & Basil, 305
Salad, Fiesta, 281
Seafood Fettucini, 288
PASTRIES, 129, 214
about, 151
Cheese Straws, 155
Chocolate, 140
Circlets, Marseilles, 153
Cream Cheese, 148
Flaky, 148
Fruit, with Cheese, 154
Hearts, Reception, 154
Paste, Plain, 151
Paste, Puff, 152
Patties, Macaroon, 153
Patties (Paté), Queen, 154
Patty, Apple Butter, 152
Plain, 141
Tart, Spinach & Cheese, 276
Tartlets, Apricot-Pineapple, 152
Tarts, Banbury, 152
Tarts, Lemon Butter, 153
Tarts, Marshmallow Divinity, 153
Tarts, Orange, 154
PATTIES *See also* Pastries
Chicken, 2, 236
Chicken, Supreme, 152
Shells, 155
Shells, Royal, 236
Pea
Salad, 8
Soup, Cream of, 191
Soup, Split, 188
Peach
Cake, 60
Cake, Upside Down, 106
canned 247
Dumplings, 164
Gems, 158
Jellied, Spiced, 176
Minted, with Pears & Ginger, 281
Pie, Deep Dish, 147
Pudding, Sandwich, 164
Puffs, 164
Salad, 182
Sauce, 122
Soufflé, 170
Whip, 176
Peanut Butter
Bread, 38
Cookies, 118
Muffins, 313
Pear
canned, 247
Salad, 184
Pepper
Fajitas with Beef, and Tomato & Avocado Salad, 284
Pimiento Sauce, 232
Red & Yellow Sauté, 283
Stuffed, 228
Stuffed, with Barley, 274
& Tomato Omelet with Roast Potatoes, 275
Pickles, 248
Sweet Tomato, 249
PIES *See also* Pastry
about, 128-129
Angel, Tennessee, 148
Apple , 130
Apple Cream, 131
Apple, Fried, 130
Apple, Mother's Old-Fashioned, 250
Apple, Old-Fashioned, 130
Banana Cream, 131, 310

Banana Cream, New, 132
Banana Custard, 133
Berry, 131
"Bridge", 133
Butterscotch, 132
Caramel, 134
Carrot (Mock Pumpkin), 134
Cheese Rings, 134
Cherry, 131
Cherry, Mock, 137
Chicken, 213, 214
Chicken Pot, 264
Chiffon, 4
Chocolate, 135, 136
Chocolate Cream, 133, 134
Cinderella Coach-and-Six, 145
Clam or Oyster, 135
Coconut, 136
Coconut Cream, 136
Coconut Custard, 134
Cranberry, 136
Cream, 136
crust, 129
crust, Graham Cracker, 130
Custard, 136
Grape, 137
Lemon, 3
Lemon 3-Decker, 139
Lemon Chiffon, 138
Lemon Cream, 137
Lemon Fluff, 138
Lemon Meringue, 138, 139
Lemon Pie-Cake, 139
Lemonaire, Black Bottom, 139
Meat, 142
Meringue, Old-Fashioned, 141
Mince Meat, 140, 141
Mince, Mock, 141
Minced, Fruited, 141
Molasses Pecan, 127
O-So-Good, 142
Orange, 142
Orange Juice, Frosted, 142
Orange Meringue, 142
Peach, Deep Dish, 147
Pineapple, 146
Pineapple Cream, 143, 146
Pineapple Icebox, 146
Prune, 143
Prune Whip, 142
Pumpkin, 143, 144
Pumpkin Parfait, Thanksgiving, 144
Pumpkin, Peter, 145
Pumpkin, Pilgrim, 146
Pumpkin Pudding, 145
Raisin, 147
Rhubarb, 147
Rhubarb and Raisin, 147
Shepherd's or Scalloped Meat, 215
Sour Cream, 148
Squash, 148
Strawberry, 148
Tomato-Pesto Custard, 272
Turnovers, Fruit, 131
Veal and Ham, 208
Vegetable, Lattice-Top, 280
Vegetable & Pasta, 276
Vinegar, 149
Whip Cream, 149

Pineapple
Bavarian Cream, 174, 178
Dainty, with Banana, 170
Filling, with Apricot, 152
Icing, 84
Juice, 244
Meringue, 164
Pie, 143, 146
Rice Cream (for Forty), 4
Rolls, 47
Tartlets, with Apricot, 152

Pizza
Individual Mushroom & Onion, 281
Stuffed, 269

Plum
Conserve, 248
Gelatin Pudding, 176
Pudding *See* Puddings

Polenta
Creamy Parmesan Sweet Corn, 282
Creamy with Ratatouille, 271
Layered, 275

Pone, Corn and Rice, 39

PORK
Chop, Schnitzel, 256
Chop Supper, 256
Chops with Fresh Plums, 301
Chops, Panfried, 285
Chops, with Pear & Raisin Compote, 298
Chops and Potatoes with Condensed Milk, 211
Cutlets with Vegetables Italienne, 257
Loin, Roast, 210
Loin, Stuffed, with Apple Succotash, 305
Lo Mein, Szechuan with Broccoli, 288
Mandarin, 302
Ribs, Baby Back, Maple-Glazed, 295
Ribs, BBQ with Sweet Peaches, 293
Roast with Apricots, 210

Potato
Bread, 34
Bread, Quick, 34
Cake, 102
Cake, with Chocolate, 81
Cakes, 230
Croquettes, with Nuts, 221
Dumpling Platter, 270
flour, Muffins, 2
French Fried, 230
Moussaka, with Eggplant, 273
Omelet, Spanish, 278
Pancakes, 251
Rolls, 50, 59
Salad, 7, 180

Salad, Dilled, 281
Salad, German, 179
Salad, Lemon-Flavored, 267
Salad, Old-Fashioned, 10
Salad, Piquante, 292
Salad, with Shrimp (Mold), 304
Scotch, 237
Slices, Cheddar Baked, 226
Soup, Cream of, 191
Stuffed Baked, 229 , 231
Sweet, Candied, 230
Sweet, Soufflé, 226
Veggie-Topped, 273
Poultry *See also* Chicken, Goose, Turkey
Dressing, 213
how to clean, 211
Prune
Pudding, Spiced, 164
Stuffing, with Apple, 213
Bread, 38
Cake *See* Cakes
Gelatin, 176, 178
Muffins, 57
Pie, 142, 143
PUDDINGS
about, 157
Apple, Favorite, 158
Apple Flop, 157
Apple Trifle, 167
Bavarian Cream, Pineapple, 174
Bavarian Cream, Raspberry, 175
Berry, Steamed, 159
Blanc Mange, 158, 168
Blanc Mange, Chocolate, 168
Bread, Chocolate, 160
Bread, Delicious Lemon, 163
Bread, Fruit, 162
Bread, Nut and Raisin, 163
Carrot, Baked (or Mock Plum), 159
Charlotte Russe, 169
Cheese Soufflé, 170
Cherry, 159
Cherry Surprises, 171
Chocolate, 160
Chocolate (Cheap), 160
Chocolate Dessert, Dainty, 168
Chocolate Nut, 161
Chocolate, Steamed, 160
Cobbler, Cherry, 159
Coconut Cream Soufflé, 169
Corn, 237
Cottage, 161
Custard, Almond, 168
Custard, Baked, 159, 167, 243
Custard, Boiled, 167
Custard, Butterscotch, 168
Custard, Caramel, 167
Custard Charlotte with Sponge Cake, 169
Custard, Coffee, 169
Custard, Soft, 158, 243
Date, 162
Fig, 162
Fig Blanc Mange, 162
Fig, Cream, 174
Fig, Steamed, 162
Fruit Whip, 169
Graham, 162
Graham Delight, 163
Huckleberry, 163
Junket, 243
Orange Cream, 170
Orange Cream with Sliced Oranges, 170
Orange, Individual, 163
Peach Sandwich, 164
Peach Soufflé, 170
Pineapple and Banana Dainty, 170
Pineapple Meringue, 164
Plum, 176
Plum, Christmas, 165
Plum, Mock, 165
Poor Man's, 165
Prune, Spiced, 164
Puzzle, 165
Salmon, 9
Snow, 177
Snowballs, 166
Spanish Cream, 244
Tapioca, 166
Yorkshire, 161
Puffs
Banana, 158
Cherry, 160
Cream, 54, 110
Economical, 110
Paste, 152
Peach, 164
Pumpkin
Meringue, 145
Pie, Mock, 134
Pies, 143-146
PUNCHES & FRUIT DRINKS
Apple Cider Punch, Hot, 27
Cranberry-Apple Punch, 26
Cranberry Cider, Spiced, 28
Cranberry Punch, Sparkling, 26
Daiquiri Punch, 26
Eggnog, Holiday, 27
Eggnog, Sparkling Orange, 27
Fruit Glow Punch, 26
Ice Ring for Punch Bowl, 27
Lemonade, 27
Limeade, 27
Orange Swizzle, 27
Raspberry Shrub, 27
Rosé Punch, 26
Tahitian Punch, 26
Tomato Juice, Mulled, 28

Quick Breads *See* Breads; Rolls and Buns

Ragoût
Asparagus, with Wild Rice, 277

Lentil & Black Bean, 306
Raisin
Bread, with Nuts, 40
Cake, 102
Icing, with Butterscotch, 95
Pie, 147
Pudding, Bread, 163
Rolls, with Nuts, 50
Tea Ring, 61
Rarebit, 220
Raspberry
Bavarian Cream, 175
Gelatin, 175
Jam, 247
Shrub, 27
Ravioli
in Broth with Vegetables, 266
with Tomato & Eggplant Sauce, 286
RELISHES *See also* Pickles
Chili Sauce, 234
Gelatin Horseradish, 175
Mustard Pickle, 234
Tomato Catsup, 249
Rhubarb
Cake, 72
Pie, 147
RICE
Almondine, 284
Baked, with Cheese, 220
Baked, with Meat, 216
Cakes, 66
Casserole, with Meat, 215
Cream, Pineapple (for Forty), 4
Croquettes, 221
Muffins, 57, 62
& Mushroom Mold, 269
Pone, with Corn, 39
Salad, Tuscan, 277
Steamed, 30
& Vegetable Bundles, 268
Water, 242
Wild, with Asparagus Ragout, 277
Risotto, Asparagus, 272
ROLLS AND BUNS *See also* Biscuits; Muffins; Scones
Apple Roll, 58
Apricot or Peach Gems, 158
Breakfast Gems, 62
Butterfly Rolls, 50
Butterhorns, 44
Buttermilk Sweet Dough, Quick, 48
Butterscotch-Pecan Rolls, 51
Cheese Diamonds, 50
Cheese Rolls, 45
Cinnamon Buns, 49, 51
Cinnamon Rolls, 51, 58
Cinnamon Rolls, Chocolate, 51
Cinnamon Rolls, Quick, 63
Corn Gems, Green, 62
Currant Buns, 46
Date Tea Cakes, 114
Dinner Rolls, 308
Egg Rolls, 46
Fig Envelopes, 63
Frosted Orange Rolls, 49
Graham Gems, 50, 62
Hot Cross Buns, 45
Hot Cross Buns with Mashed Potato, 46
Luncheon or Sandwich Rolls, 49
Luncheon Rolls, Quick, 52
Meat Turnovers, 45
Molasses Gems from Grandma Broman, 53
Nut and Raisin Rolls, 50
Parker House Rolls, 46, 52
Philadelphia Cinnamon Buns, 49
Pineapple Rolls, 47
Popovers, 52, 57
Potato Rolls, 59
Refrigerator Rolls, 47
Rusks, 49
Rye Rolls, 49
Salad Rolls, 56
Snowballs, 58
Swedish Crumpets, 58
Sweet Roll Dough, Traditional, 48
Sweet Tea Rolls (Finger Rolls), 58
Tea Cakes, Currant, 62
Tea Rolls, 4
Whipped Cream Gems, 3
Rusks, 49

SALAD DRESSINGS
Boiled, 183
Cooked, 182, 183
French, 185
Fruit Salad, 181
Mayonnaise, 182
Mayonnaise, No Egg, 182
Roquefort, 185
Russian, 185
Thousand Island, 185
SALADS
about, 180
Apple-Cabbage Slaw, 286
Artichoke with Cracked-Wheat, 270
Avocado (Alligator Pear), 184
Avocado and Grapefruit, 184
Bean, Four, 298
Bean & Goat-Cheese, 268
Cardinal, 175
Carrot, 307
Celery, Stuffed, 183
Cheese and Nut, 181
Cheese Combinations, 181
Cherry, 174
Chicken, 9, 180, 183, 264
Chicken-Breast, Potato & Arugula, 284
Chicken, Stir-Fried, 287
Chicken Summertime, 263
Citrus Slaw, 281
Cole Slaw, 181, 230
Cottage Cheese, 175
Crab & Avocado, 307

Cucumber & Radish, 277
Egg, 180
Eggs, Deviled, 180
Fish, 184
Fruit, 181
Fruit, for Dessert, 8
Green Bean & Mozzarella, 280
Health, 174
Imperial, 174
Lentil, Warm, 287
Lobster, 184
Macaroni, 174
Macaroni, Summer, 292
Macedoine, 181
Marquise, 184
Oyster, 7
Pasta, with Asparagus & Garbanzos, 289
Pasta, with Eggplant & Basil, 305
Pasta, Fiesta, 281
Pea, 8
Peach, 182
Pear and Cream Cheese, 184
Potato, 7, 180
Potato, Dilled, 281
Potato, German, 179
Potato, Lemon-Flavored, 267
Potato, Old Fashioned, 10
Potato, Piquante, 292
Potato, with Shrimp, 304
Salmon, 176
Spanish Gelatin, 175
Spinach, with Falafel, 275
Spinach Supper, 257
Squid, 259
Tabbouleh, 294
Tomato, 183
Tomato & Avocado, 284
Tomato & Cucumber, with Avocado Dressing, 293
Tuscan Rice, 277
Vegetable, 184
Vegetable, Chunky, 281
Waldorf, 181
Salmon
Broiled with Corn & Tomato Salsa, 258
Croquettes, 201, 221
Loaf, 196
Pudding, 9
Salad, 176
Sandwiches, with Avocado, 283
Scalloped, 10
Teriyaki with Squash, 294
SANDWICHES
about, 237, 238
Almond, Salted, 239
Beef, Barbecued, with Carrot Salad, 307
Chicken, Sesame, 286
Club, 239
Dream, 239
Eggplant (Roasted) & Mozzarella, Open-Faced, 288
Ham, Deviled, 239
Hummus, Open-Faced, 267
Luncheon or Sandwich Rolls, 49
Olive and Cheese, Stuffed, 239
Quick Luncheon Rolls, 52
Rochester, 240
Salmon-Avocado Open-Faced, 283
Sardine and Egg, 239
Tomato Club, 3
Tongue, 239
Sardine and Egg Sandwiches, 239
SAUCE *See also* Gravy
Brown, 233
Butter, Maitre d'Hotel, 203, 233
Caper, 202, 232
Caper-Dill, 301
Cheese, 67, 202, 232
Chili, 234
Cocktail, 232
Cream or White, 231
Cream, Thick, 202
Cream, Thin, 202
Currant Jelly, 233
Egg, 202, 232
Egg (for Fish), 203, 232
for Fish, 196
Fish and Vegetable, about, 202
Golden, 231
Hollandaise, 203, 231
Hollandaise, Mock, 202, 232
Horse-Radish, 203, 233
Mint, 231, 233
Peanut, 306
Pimento, 202, 232
Tartare, 203, 232, 233
Tomato, 202
White, 202
White, for Creamed Vegetables, 229
White, for Croquettes, 201
SAUCE, DESSERT *See also* Cake Icing
Apple, 210
Apricot and Peach, 122
Banana, 177
Butterscotch, 122
Caramel, 122, 167, 232
Caramel Syrup, 76, 78
Chocolate, 89, 122, 166
Chocolate Candy, 89
Chocolate Mint, 89
Cottage Pudding, 161
Cranberry, 233
Cream, 122
Custard, 124
Foamy, 124, 166
Fruit, 124, 167
Hard, 124, 165, 166
Lemon or Orange, 166
Lemon, 124
Maple, 123
Mocha, 123
Nut, 123
Orange, 124, 164
Pudding, Plain, 124

Sausage
Biscuits, Old Fashioned, 47
Grill, Mixed, 296
Kabobs, with Lamb and White-Bean Puree, 305
Scones, 62
Cream, 58
Exposition, 58
Scrod with Lemon-Garlic Bread Crumbs, 258
Seasoning, Lowfat, 12
Shakes, Milk, 25
Shrimp
Barbecue, with Steak, 299
Linguine with Fresh Tomato Sauce, 258
& Potato Salad Mold, 304
Scampi, 261
Spicy Stir-Fried, 258
-Stuffed Sole in Lettuce Bundles, 304
Wiggle, 201
Smelts, Fried, 195
Sodas, Ice-Cream, 25
Sole, Fillet, Rolled, with Rice, 260
Sorbets and Ices
Easy Freezer Sorbet, 314
Pistachio & Sherbet Cake, 315
Watermelon Ice, 313
SOUP
about, 187
Avocado, 190
Bean, 188
Bean, Black, 188
Bean, Italian, 192
Celery, Cream of, 190
Chicken, 190
Clam Chowder, 198
Corn Chowder, 188
Cream, 189
Creole, 189
fireless cooking, 14
Fish Chowder, 188
Garnishes for Cream Soups, 189
Minestrone, 267
Mushroom, Cream of, 191
Onion, 189
Onion, French with Cabbage, 270
Pea, Cream of, 191
Pea, Split, 188
Potato, Cream of, 191
Scotch Broth, 187
Stock, 187
Tomato, Cream of, 189, 190
Sour Cream
Cake, 85
Cake, Pound, 311
Cakes, drop, 118
Cookies, 4
Crullers, 2
Pie, 148
Spaghetti, 220
and Meatballs, 255
and Tomatoes, 221
Spanish Potato Omelet, 278
Spinach, 230
Au Gratin, 228
with Egg Noodles, 286
Salad, with Falafel, 275
Supper Salad, 257
Tart, with Cheese, 276
Squash
Kabobs with Toasted-Walnut Orzo, 269
Pie, 148
Squid Salad, 259
Steaming, fireless cooking, 14
STEW, 207
Beef, 253
Captain's, with Rice, 302
Cheese & Potato, 283
Cod & Vegetable, 285
Farmer's, with Couscous, 279
Kidney, 208
Lamb or Mutton, 209
Meat, 216
Oyster, 189, 196
Seafood, 261
Veal with Dumplings, 207
Storage Tips, 12
Strawberry
Filling, 126
Gelatin, 173
Gelatin Loaf, 173
Pie, 148
Strudel, Vegetable, with Red-Pepper Sauce, 278
STUFFING
Apple, 215, 233
Oyster, 213
Potato, Mashed, 213
Poultry, 213
Prune and Apple, 213
for Roast Chicken, 212
Succotash, 227
Sweet & Sour Chicken Wings, 294
Sweetbreads
Broiled, 243
Creamed, 211
Swordfish with Warm Cabbage Slaw, 259
Syrups *See* Sauces, Dessert

Table of Measures and Weights, 14
Tarts *See* Pastries
Tea
about, 18
Beef, 244
Iced, 18
reading tea leaves, 19-23
Spiced, 19
Tea Cakes *See* Rolls and Buns
Tex-Mex Stuffed Burgers, 291
Tilefish with Browned-Butter Sauce, 260
Toast
Buttered, 70
Cinnamon, 70
Cream, 70
French, 70, 237

Water, 242
Tofu Chili, 271
Tomato
Baked, 230
Broiled, 227
Catsup, 249
with Eggs, 237
Fried, 228
Frittata, with Artichoke, 276
Juice, Mulled, 28
Pesto Custard Pie, 272
Pickles, Sweet, 249
Salad, 183
Salad with Cucumber, & Avocado Dressing, 293
Sandwich, Club, 3
Sauce, 202
Soup, Cream of, 189, 190
Tongue Sandwiches, 239
Tortillas, Beef, 252
Tuna
Casserole with Potato Chips, 193
Fish a la King, 201
Turkey
and Chili, 265
Cutlets, with Provolone, Basil & Roasted Peppers, 287
Meat Loaf, 265
Piccata, 264
Turnips, Hashed, 228
Tuscan Rice Salad, 277

VEAL
Baked with Tomato Sauce, 210
Birds, 207, 211
Chops with Lentil & Black Bean Ragoût, 306
Cutlets, 207, 210
Loaf, 207
Pie with Ham, 208
Roast, 207
Stew with Dumplings, 207
Stuffed with Roasted Potatoes, 255
VEGETABLES *See also* individual names
about, 224
Buttered, 226
Creamed, 229
fireless cooking, 14
General Rules for Cooking, 224
Gumbo, 271
Omelet, 283
& Pasta Pie, 276
Pie, Lattice-Top, 280
Salad, Chunky, 281
Sandwiches, 238
Sautéed with Egg-White Frittata, 282
Stew, with Cod, 285
Strudel with Red-Pepper Sauce, 278
Veggie-Topped Potatoes, 273

Waffles, 68
Gold Medal, 68
Watermelon Ice, 313

Zucchini, Sautéed with Mushrooms, 287

"Everyone's here. Time to eat!"
– Ida Franks